Competitive marketing

Since its first publication in 1984, *Competitive Marketing* has firmly established itself as the most rigorous, analytical, and informed introduction to marketing strategy available. This third edition extensively expands on and revises previous editions by building on key topics, using far more illustrations and case studies, and extending the coverage to include such areas as service marketing, business-to-business, nonbusiness, and international marketing, as well as issues of marketing ethics. Written for advanced students, it combines analytic depth and width of coverage in presenting marketing as a discipline and as an area of management expertise.

John O'Shaughnessy covers all the major areas of marketing from a variety of perspectives: he explains the basic concepts, discusses business applications and evaluates current theory and practice—*Competitive Marketing* is a truly comprehensive guide to marketing theory. Readers will not only gain an understanding of the key ideas, but also a sense of the limitations and the challenges of marketing; they will not only learn what we know, but also what we don't know about the discipline.

Competitive Marketing does not aim simply to put across rules or principles, though these have their place. More importantly, it aims to develop the reader's ability to make good decisions when it comes to marketing. This is a book for serious students of marketing, designed to provide them with the fundamentals without dodging the complexities.

John O'Shaughnessy is Professor Emeritus at the Graduate School of Business, Columbia University, New York and a Senior Associate of the Judge Institute, Cambridge University. He has published widely, most recently *Explaining Buyer Behavior*, and has extensive international consultancy experience.

Competitive marketing

A strategic approach
Third edition

John O'Shaughnessy

London and New York

Coventry University

First published 1984
by the Academic Division of
Unwin Hyman Ltd

Second revised edition 1988
Reprinted 1990

Reprinted 1992
by Routledge
11 New Fetter Lane, London EC4P 4EE
29 West 35th Street, New York, NY 10001

Third revised and enlarged edition 1995

© 1984, 1992, 1995 John O'Shaughnessy

Typeset in Times by Florencetype Limited, Stoodleigh, Nr
Tiverton, Devon

Printed and bound in Great Britain by Clays Ltd, St Ives plc

British Library Cataloguing in Publication Data
A catalogue record for this book is available from the British
Library.

Library of Congress Cataloguing in Publication Data
O'Shaughnessy, John.
   Competitive marketing/John O'Shaughnessy.—[3rd ed.]
      p.   cm.
   Includes bibliographical references and index.
   ISBN 0-415-09317-1
   1. Marketing—Management. I. Title.
HF5415.13.078   1995
658.8—dc20
                                        94-39927
                                           CIP

ISBN 0-415-12786-6 (hbk)
ISBN 0-415-09317-1 (pbk)

Contents

Figures

Tables

Preface to the third edition

This edition is a major revision and expansion of the last edition of *Competitive Marketing*. The revision makes the text more accessible by its fuller treatment of topics and by a richness of marketing illustrations. The text has also been expanded to include much more on service marketing; business-to-business marketing; nonbusiness marketing; international marketing and ethical issues in marketing.

The revision focuses on providing more conceptual and explanatory depth than that provided by other basic texts. On this basis, it can be regarded as an advanced text or a second level text in marketing. The book aims at nurturing the reader into clarity of thought and argument on marketing issues so he or she is able to see through the verbal fog and ill-grounded faith in much that passes for healthy marketing thinking. The book is less concerned with defending the orthodoxies of marketing than in showing where progress still needs to be made. Our knowledge of a subject area progresses in depth from grasping what is said or written to appreciating applications and then onto the limitations of what is known. We learn most when at the boundaries of what is known and are aware of the weaknesses of current claims. It is for this reason the book seeks to critically appraise the body of knowledge we already have.

But marketing has progressed a good deal since the last edition of this book was written eight years ago. There has been consolidation, and less obscurity about concepts, problems and issues. The greatest advance has been in demonstrating the application of social science concepts and findings to marketing and this has had a major impact on this revision. However, it should not be a one-way traffic. Behavioral concepts and findings need to be questioned in the light of actual behavior by real consumers and buyers in real markets. In this way we get a better estimate of the range of behavior to which the concepts and findings can be reliably applied and their power to provide explanatory depth. The same is true of mathematical models. Without a background of substantive knowledge of markets and marketing, there is always a danger of sacrificing reality for intellectual rigor: of arguing from a too simplistic conceptual base or seeking precision at the cost of misrepresenting the complexity of market behavior.

Every author of a textbook is indebted to colleagues. Insights may arise from individual reflection on concepts and experience but ideas are matured in discussion with others. Particular thanks are due to Morris Holbrook and Roger Dickinson for reading the initial draft of the book and making extensive comments which proved invaluable in preparing the final revision. I am indebted to them.

Part I

Marketing and marketing planning

Chapter 1

The nature of marketing

Success in business is success in a market. Firms go out of business not by closing factories but by unprofitable marketing. Entrepreneurs usually enter a business by developing products (that is, goods and services) but stay in business only by creating and retaining customers at a profit. It is the task of marketing to guide the firm into generating only those products for which customers can be attracted; to position the product in a market and support it with the right promotion, servicing, pricing, and distribution, that is, right from the customer's point of view. This book deals with that task.

DEFINITION OF MARKETING

There are a number of ways to define a subject. An *analytic* definition seeks to capture its essence by showing in exactly what way marketing differs from other activities of the firm. For example:

> Marketing covers those activities that relate the organization to those parts of the outside world that use, buy, sell or influence the outputs it produces and the benefits and services it offers.

Analytic definitions of marketing tend to be somewhat abstract and meaningful only to those already familiar with the subject. In any case, they are usually controversial. This is because, when we accept a particular definition of a subject, we endorse a particular perspective or way of looking at the topic. In fact, analytic definitions often preface an argument just to induce a certain perspective to facilitate persuasion. Thus the debates over whether law is to be defined in terms of principles certified by reason, or the decree of those with the power to enforce their will, or in the nature of reciprocal agreements among the citizen population, are not just academic debates. When one definition is accepted rather than another, then one set of attributes of the subject is accepted as being more fundamental than another. This is a key issue since the consequences deduced from a definition relate to what attributes are stressed. Thus the above analytic definition of marketing views marketing as an activity that spans the boundary between the company and the business world, from which it might be deduced that marketing undertakes activities that facilitate the development of favorable relationships with those whose decisions affect the commercial success of the company. This deviates somewhat from a view of marketing as the art of creating and maintaining customers; a definition that sees marketing as the skill of finding and securing customers. Another analytic definition defines marketing as the "performance of business activities directed toward, and incident to, the flow of goods and services from producer to consumer to user." This definition views marketing as a business activity (not for nonbusinesses) and directs attention more toward promotion and distribution than anything else. In practice, none of these definitions receives universal endorsement. This is because there are widely differing views over what constitutes the "essence" of marketing.

Less in dispute are the activities embraced by the term "marketing": activities that are often implicit in any analytic definition of marketing. This is fortunate since it allows us to define marketing in more concrete terms using the *operational* definition. This definition relates the subject to be defined to our experience. It takes the form, "as you do this or observe that, you will understand the meaning of the concept." When we define an "excellent" salesperson as one who achieves 30 percent more sales than the standard set, we are defining operationally. Andrew Jackson, a past president of the United States, was operationally defining democracy when he said, "if a citizen has the right to cuss the Government and all the Government can do is cuss back or go fishing, that's a democracy." Similarly, whenever those in an organization are debating what to offer; to whom; when; where; how and for how much; or are undertaking activities associated with these questions, they are engaging in marketing, since the fundamental activities of marketing are:

- defining markets that fall within the firm's business;
- finding out what those in the market want (or potentially might want);
- if those in the market want different things, to group them into categories according to what they seek;
- selecting those customer categories whose wants and needs can be better met by the firm than by rival organizations;
- determining the offering (product, price, promotion and distribution) that meets the want;
- making the offering available;
- informing prospective or actual customers about the offering and where it might be obtained;
- deciding on a continuous basis what offerings to add, subtract, modify and upgrade to meet changing wants and circumstances; and
- cooperating with other functions of the business and external organizations to secure the resources and help needed to implement marketing plans.

The above are the activities involved in marketing and which are typically carried out by a marketing department. However, some marketing departments do not have responsibility for all these activities or have even wider responsibilities including dealing with an organization's suppliers. In any case, marketing as a subject area is involved with the total configuration of features/benefits (that is, the *offering*) sought by customers and provided by the producer. An offering consists not just of the product itself (including its packaging and other tangible and nontangible benefits that add value for the customer) but its price, promotion, and distribution. The focus here is on "benefits." Marketers speak of the marketing of benefits not just of the marketing of products. There are several reasons for this:

- customers are interested in what a product can do for them and/or the organizations for whom they are buying; appeals on the basis of benefits are the persuaders since they tell customers what beneficial effects buying, possessing, using, or consuming the product will bring;
- the product can be given different meanings in terms of benefits for different audiences since not everyone buys the same product for the same reasons;
- talking about benefits focuses the attention of marketers to what it is about the

product that customers really want since the product may contain elements that are positively not wanted (e.g. fattening calories).

The general public associates marketing exclusively with business. But the marketing activities listed above are not restricted to commercial organizations. Whether an organization has patrons and clients or creditors and customers is irrelevant to the need to carry out, implicitly or explicitly, activities that are essentially of a marketing nature.

Kotler[1] speaks of three stages of marketing consciousness:

1 consciousness one: where marketing is restricted to business and the market transaction;
2 consciousness two: where marketing is expanded to embrace all organizations that undertake customer or client transactions; and
3 consciousness three: which extends the scope of marketing still further. Thus museums, universities, libraries, and charities need to market their *cause*, as well as their product, to gain political and social support as well as financial.

In extending the scope of marketing, marketers are claiming that there are marketing problems in nonbusiness organizations and (if we accept Kotler's consciousness three stage) that there are marketing problems in dealing with all of an organization's "stakeholders," such as the government, environmentalists, unions, etc., and not just customers and competitors. But a practical problem is only a marketing problem to the extent that marketing approaches and techniques are better able to solve the problem than rival approaches. In the final analysis it is a matter of empirical inquiry to demonstrate marketing's distinct contribution in all these areas of suggested application. Marketers are doing this. In the case of some of the applications quoted, however, it may be that solutions, whose theoretical basis and basic approach reside purely in psychology, are being claimed for marketing. Other applications appear merely to redescribe existing approaches (for example to fund-raising) in marketing terms without demonstrating the advantages gained by mere redescription.

MARKETING'S FOCUS AND MODE OF THINKING

Marketing's focus

Just as the physicist studies the atom as the basic unit of analysis, so marketing, as a discipline, seeks some basic focus. Academics have suggested the focus should be the concept of exchange[2,3] or the transaction.[4] There are problems with making either exchange or the transaction the focus for marketing. There is already a well-established branch of sociology, known as "exchange theory," while transactions are simply individual exchanges where something concrete passes. The question therefore arises of the distinctiveness of marketing exchange problems as contrasted with those dealt with in sociological exchange theory and economics. It is significant that exchange as marketing's basic unit of analysis has been more talked about than applied though there have been exceptions.[5] The concept of exchange to some marketers seems sterile, that is, does not have the seed for development. This is because exchange theory views customers as simply seeking to maximize rewards and minimize costs which seems an inadequate basis for explaining all we would wish to explain about buying behavior. Others claim that making either exchange or the transaction the focus of marketing completely misses the importance of the social processes that bind buyers to sellers in ongoing relationships that lead to exchanges.[6] Such social processes are an important research area given a marketing mission of creating trust and loyalty.

Marketing's mode of thinking

Although some attention has been paid to the focus of *marketing as a discipline*, there has been less discussion of the key mode of thinking in *marketing management*. If the key mode of thinking in surveying is accuracy of measurement, in construction, durability, and in mechanical engineering, efficiency, what is the mode of thinking most relevant to marketing *as an activity*? One way of answering this question is to think about the unifying features of the problems encountered in marketing. They revolve around the design of offerings (product, price, promotions, and distribution systems) to secure and retain customers at a profit.

THE MARKETING CONCEPT AND ITS LIMITATIONS

Modes of influence

The *marketing concept* is in line with the idea that marketing's mode of thinking revolves around the design of offerings that are innovative, constantly updated, ahead of competition in some way and, last but not least, profitable. The marketing concept defines the market-oriented organization as being one where there is:

- a stress on product innovation;
- long-term and not just short-term planning;
- an emphasis on profitability and not just on sales volume;
- a marketing function that embraces all those activities dealing directly with customers or at least a strong system for inter functional coordination;
- knowledge of competition and competitive offerings; and
- customer orientation throughout the organization.

A core component of the marketing concept is *customer orientation* throughout the organization. Customer orientation means the organization understands its target customers (final customers *and* channel intermediaries) as a basis for designing its offerings. Customers are those actual or potential buyers of the organization's product (goods and services). They are not always those who are the consumers or users of the product since buyers may buy for others. Customer orientation contrasts with what has been labeled production orientation, whereby it is claimed that the production or engineering side of the business determines what is a "good" product and Sales are instructed to go out and sell it. The essential difference between production and customer orientation is the degree to which the firm bases its decisions on knowledge about the wants of its customers *and* takes these wants into consideration in all major company decisions.

Beyond this, interpretations of customer orientation, while often precise, tend to vary. A "soft" or weak interpretation of customer orientation simply argues that all decisions about the offering (product, price, promotion and distribution) must be based on an understanding of the wants of the consumer.[7] On the other hand, a "hard" interpretation of customer orientation claims that the firm must not only consult buyers/consumers about their wants but, if it is to succeed, must *go all out to provide the customer with what she or he wants.* If taken literally, it could lead to unprofitable marketing in that customers will want more than can be provided at the price they would be willing to pay.

Although the General Electric Co. (USA) is regarded as the first company that explicitly formulated the marketing concept, this has a certain irony, given that critics of GE called it a company "with its face to the chief executive and its 'ass' to the customer," at least before the advent of Jack Welch as CEO.[8] In any case, the recognition of the need to focus on what the customer wants has long been recognized. In the late 1800s it was said that Britain was losing out to Germany because the Germans gave customers what they wanted. One book that popularized this viewpoint in the 1880s was by Ernest Williams,[9] who wrote:

> As I have stated more than once, the last thing an English firm usually considers when soliciting orders is the tastes of its customers. These are our goods: "take them or leave them," is in effect the general message which our emissaries of commerce carry.

Marchand[10] points out that between World War I and World War II, trade journals and magazines constantly exhorted marketers to find out what consumers wanted and to give it to them. The problem lies in putting the concept into practice.

Although firms are often described as being either production or customer oriented, a number of other positions can be identified. Figure 1.1 illustrates these. Where an organization is positioned along the continuum of Figure 1.1 depends on the balance of

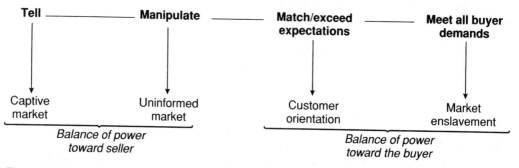

Figure 1.1 Orientation toward the customer as reflecting relative power balance

power between the firm (as the seller) and buyers. The more the dependency of the customer on the firm's product, the greater the relative power of the firm. We will discuss each of the positions shown along Figure 1.1.

Tell

Where the customer is very dependent on the firm's product (because, say, only the firm provides it and it is of central importance to the customer) the firm is in a position to dictate its terms, that is, to "tell" rather than to meet buyer demands. Some organizations, like a public transport authority, may, at least in the short period, have a monopoly because of the absence of acceptable substitutes. They may in effect, though still within limits, tell the consumer what she or he can have. The classic example here is the saying of Henry Ford: "You can have any color you want as long as it's black." He was able to say this (if indeed he did) because his Model T was the only feasible alternative for most in the market, given its price. However, the relative power of a firm vis-à-vis its customers is apt to be unstable and, as competition increases, power positions can be reversed as buyers seek to be less dependent on the seller's particular product or brand. A firm may not be a monopolist but its product may in fact be so superior to rival offerings that the seller can more or less dictate terms. What firms with an engineering, rather than a marketing, orientation may produce can coincide with what substantial numbers of people in the market actually want to buy. But it is foolish to rely on a coincidence of views between, say, engineering's creations and market wants. An interesting example here is Pilkington, the British glass company. In the 1970s, Alastair Pilkington's technological brilliance led to the development of the float glass process, allowing Pilkington in the 1970s to dominate the world glass industry. Yet, at that time, Pilkington had a purely technological rather than a market orientation. But this purely technological orientation later led it to the development of technically advanced products for which there were no markets. Thus the 10/20 windshield glass developed in the 1970s removed 98 percent of the risk of lacerations or head injuries from automobile windshield accidents. But Pilkington failed in marketing the product: automobile manufacturers refused to pay the 15 percent premium price over ordinary safety glass, which reflects on the ethics of the automobile manufacturers at the time as well as consumer priorities.

There is frequently a wide gulf between the engineer's concept of a "good" product and what constitutes a viable, commercial product. If offerings are developed in an observational vacuum as to the buyer's wants, a firm is likely to find itself trying to sell what too few people seek and competing against products having far greater appeal. Hewlett-Packard tended at one time to base their marketing decisions on what their engineers said they needed, or they would design a product for one customer and then try to market it to others. Such a policy did have early successes but later led to market failures and a change in Hewlett-Packard's orientation (*Fortune*, October 1, 1984).

Manipulate

Some firms seek to manipulate the consumer by distorting reality. Marketing is no more honest than those who practice it, and promotion in particular lends itself to duplicity. In fact, several eminent economists, such as Joseph Schumpeter, Frank Knight and Kenneth Galbraith, have claimed that firms are less preoccupied with want-satisfying than with want-creating, which can involve some element of manipulation. Galbraith[11] in particular sees larger corporations as a powerful force in shaping wants: "the myth that holds that the great corporation is the puppet of the market, the powerless servant of the consumer is, in fact, one of the devices by which power is perpetuated."

The controversy over whether wants (market demand) can be created or molded at will is of importance. A firm that believes that wants can be created, or demand can be molded, will be less concerned with discovering wants and will adopt something close to a promotion-cum-manipulation orientation. If the orientation is wrong, resources will be misdirected.

Vagueness of terminology makes it difficult to prove or disprove that a particular want has been "created" rather than discovered and aroused. What does it mean to say that a "want" has been created? If it means we can always get sufficient numbers of people to buy any product we care to produce, then there are reasons for being skeptical of this claim. It is true that many successful products were not suggested by the buying public. Railroads, telephones, television, and even zippers were not being demanded before they were invented. However, there is always a desire for better means of fulfilling the functions performed by these products. In other words, there was an underlying appetite for such innovation. The assertion that wants can be created assumes that consumers are motivationally empty until injected by marketers with wants created by advertising.[12] It seems truer to say that there are wants that are latent until activated by promotion. In fact, all persuasion to be effective must tap into the target audience's motives. As Walter Reuther, the United States automobile union leader, once said: "You can automate the production of cars but you cannot automate the production of customers."

There is no question, however, that some firms rely on extensive distortions of reality, exploiting the ignorance of consumers, to promote their products and continue to be a success without giving much serious thought to providing what is wanted. If uninformed, consumers can be deceived and continue to be deceived as to the benefits of certain products, particularly products like patent medicines for which hidden "miracle" qualities are often claimed. In China it is reported there is a brisk trade in "Shenglu spray" which claims to kill the AIDS virus in 30 seconds. Although this example is quoted because it is so dramatic, there are similar absurd claims made in Western countries. It may be that consumers learn as a result of experience, but such trial and error learning can be costly and not always effective. Deceit, however, has limits. Many products can be evaluated accurately, while there is always a danger of the deception becoming public knowledge and the seller acquiring a reputation for untrustworthiness. But in the absence of consumer vigilance and effective public policing, such limits may still offer too much temptation to the unscrupulous. The cosmetics industry is a case in point. There are creams being advertised as being capable of altering the cellular structure of the skin to erase wrinkles and hold back the aging of the skin.[13] Where there is uncertainty (and much buying occurs in conditions of buyer uncertainty), there is always scope for manipulation.

Match/exceed expectations

Customer orientation relates to the concept of consumer sovereignty in economics, defined as "the principle that what is produced, how it is produced, and how it is distributed is determined by consumer preferences expressed through individual choices in a free market."[14] Customer orientation is essentially a rule of conduct appropriate for firms in competitive markets composed of knowledgeable buyers. There is a need to keep close to the customer in competitive markets because competition has the effect of shifting the battleground. Thus while at one time the production of a low-cost, high-quality car was a guarantee of market success, this is no longer the case with manufacturers having to be flexible enough to respond at speed to frequent changes in consumer tastes. Customer orientation means not only keeping abreast of customer wants but galvanizing all functions of the business, whether marketing, manufacturing, research and development (R&D), purchasing and motivational systems, to cater to the customer. As one top car executive worded it, "If we aren't customer-driven, our cars won't be, either." IBM, in trying to overcome past misfortunes, now views each of its business processes—whether billing, order entry, or even public relations—as products in their own right because they have an impact on the customer.

Some writers speak of consumer orientation in terms of "satisfying" customers, but the term "satisfying" is much too vague when undefined. To what extent must the consumer be satisfied? A firm that merely satisfies loses out to the firm that pleases. As an advertisement for Federal Express says: "If you've been fairly satisfied with Emery Air Freight, you'll be completely satisfied with Federal Express." Another objection to just speaking of satisfying customers is that satisfaction suggests a feeling that is experienced only after buying goals have been achieved. But not all post-purchase can be associated with this type of feeling, for example, taking out a life insurance policy. In any case, a prospective buyer does not perceive the firm's product or brand in isolation but against real or imagined makes that can be substituted for it. This recognition, that everything depends on the alternatives displaced, has led a number of writers to claim that customer orientation should be replaced by a strategic orientation focusing first and foremost on competition. While it is necessary to take direct account of competition, this does not mean customers should no longer be the major focus since "beating competition" in practice means understanding customers better than competitors do. As one company executive worded it, "Our main goal is to put ourselves in the consumers' shoes. We have to understand what their needs are. If we start worrying about competition, then we're not putting our customers first." Perhaps an even more relevant quote is that from the executive who introduced Genuine Draft, a beer that sold 4.5 million barrels in 1989 to become, in the United States, the industry's most successful new product since Bud Light came out in 1981: "If we had focused on other brewers' products instead of on consumer trends we might never have come out with Genuine Draft."

The concept of customer orientation can be viewed as matching or exceeding buyer expectations since expectations depend on the alternatives open to the buyer. As Sam Walton of Wal-Mart once said, "Exceed your customers' expectations on both price and quality and they'll come back over and over." To speak of matching/exceeding customer *expectations* (see Figure 1.1) can be contrasted with meeting customer *aspirations*. The level of customer expectations is the level the customer believes is realizable, while the level of customer aspirations is the level the customer perceives as perfect, that is, the customer's ideal point. Since a buyer's preferences are based on what are considered to be relevant differences between competitive offerings, customer expectations are intimately related to

- what competition (known or anticipated) is offering
- what has been promised
- what appears reasonable given past or analogous experience, and
- the sacrifice paid in terms of price and mental and physical effort.

Thus, Ford captured 75 percent of the tractor market in 1925. This was not because the product met the farmer's aspirations level; on the contrary, the tractor had a marked tendency to overturn when towing on rough ground. Nevertheless, it was considered the "best buy" at the time. In 1928, International Harvester dominated the market by additional technological advances. Still later, Harry Ferguson stole the lead, and so on. Similarly, in 1956 IBM dominated the computer with the 650 computer. The 650 computer was far from perfect when compared with today's machines but, at the time, it was far ahead of competition in meeting the need for commercial data processing.

The more competitive the market (that is, where there is wide promotion of competitive brands and buyers are knowledgeable about rival makes), the more a firm must meet or exceed customer expectations if it is to stay in business. Customer orientation in the sense of trying to meet or exceed customer expectations so as to beat competition is a key posture for any firm in a competitive economy. This has always been so, though it is sometimes claimed that, in the past, there was such a scarcity of goods that customer orientation was unnecessary. A modest acquaintance with industrial history suggests otherwise; many firms became bankrupt because they failed to keep abreast of the changing expectations of their customers. It is, of course, true that for certain wants there were few alternative choices in the market so the gap in the chain of substitutes could be wide. Although there are fewer such gaps today, the difference is one of degree.

Meet all buyer demands

If a firm sets out to discover and cater to market wants, it is *adapting* to the market. To adapt to a market is to come to terms with the realities of the market and accept that there are strict limits on the extent to which customer wants can be influenced by persuasion. If a seller wishes to establish a continuing relationship with a buyer (to secure a customer and not just a sale), the seller must attend to the buyer's wants. In this way the seller strives to make changes in the firm's offering of smaller cost to the firm than the value to the buyer. But market adaptation is not *market enslavement*; a seller will try to influence perceptions and beliefs to induce acceptance of the seller's terms. Not to acknowledge this is failing to face marketing reality.

Customer orientation does not therefore mean customer domination. Firms that pay too little attention to the customer become noncompetitive, but for a firm to meet every whim is to play too subservient a role in influencing demand; a role that may be too costly for profitability, too restrictive to action, and unnecessary for competitive advantage. There are interpretations of customer orientation that sound dangerously like advocating market enslavement. High customer satisfaction and corresponding large sales do not necessarily spell profitability. It is for this reason that market orientation talks also about seeking profitability and not just sales.

For those in not-for-profit marketing, it may still not be acceptable to agree to "customer" demands even if such agreement considerably advances financial success and "market" expansion. For example, every established religion is concerned with getting its adherents to follow a certain (holy) way of life. A religion that adopts a posture (which some do) of changing doctrines and diluting calls for sacrifice simply to achieve wider acceptance, or maintain existing church membership, may, it might be claimed, increase "market share" or hang on to "market share" but at the expense of betraying its raison d'être.

Limitations of the marketing concept as the philosophy of business

The marketing concept is often advocated as *the* philosophy for business success in a free enterprise economy. As an overall philosophy of business, however, the marketing concept has a number of limitations

- evidence favoring the concept;
- operational problems;
- neglect of the firm's competitive strengths;
- balancing the demands of competing stakeholders;
- understates the power of persuasion; and
- conflict on occasion with consumer well-being.

Evidence

While there can never be any antecedent guarantee that principles like the marketing concept will, if adopted, lead to success, we would expect that those following the marketing concept would in general be the more profitable firms. But, however inherently sensible the marketing concept appears, we need to collect more "hard" evidence. At the most general level, it seems almost a truism to say, "he who serves best profits most." The debate is over approaches, applicability, feasibility, and the universal validity of the concept for different situations. As market orientation, and customer orientation in particular, involve a commitment of resources, it has been argued that it is not *always* the right policy to adopt; there may be situations where competition is mild, brand preferences stable, and the economy booming so there is little pressure to push customer orientation.[15] But at least one study claims a positive relationship between degrees of market orientation and profitability while at the same time claiming that market orientation is relevant to every market situation.[16] The prevailing view is that market orientation is becoming more important because of global competition, mature markets and constant changes in consumer tastes.

Operational problems

There are often serious operational problems in identifying market wants. People are not always conscious of their wants, just as someone may not be conscious of being cold and so is not actively trying to keep warm. On being told s/he looks cold, s/he may well reply, "Now that you mention it, I am . . . ." In other words, many wants are latent and are activated only on being presented with the product and informed of its potential. Consumers may not know what they want until they actually use the product or its full potential is demonstrated to them. Consumers, too, may get what they think they want but not want it when they get it. Wants are not like botany specimens waiting to be labeled but more like scenes of nature that have appeal; scenes we can always mix together to form still better scenes. The idea of consumers knowing what they want requires they be able to give some account of what would satisfy them, that is, give a description of what would count as a satisfactory product. Sometimes they can do this, but sometimes they cannot.

Even when consumers can and do articulate their wants, a marketer may not always respond since it is hard for someone who does not share some desire or some specific aspect of a want, to experience that want as valid.

Some interpretations of customer orientation view the consumer as a bundle of wants which act as a filter determining what products consumers will want and buy. But a person's motivational capacities are not made up of just a set of wants or needs but also the capacity of imagination, sensitivity and so on. If people can be motivated by appeals to the imagination ("What it really would be like to have an MBA") and sensitivity to (say) the plight of others then there can be changes in what they seek. If consumers are not just a bundle of wants already formed, we need not think of the job of marketing as confined to identifying wants already formed. Consumers in fact are open to persuasion by appeals to their imagination so they come to recognize that something they had never thought about is something whose possession could do much to enrich their lives.

Some writers claim that customer orientation leads firms into focusing on low risk products or style modifications instead of truly innovative products as customers have difficulty in visualizing and suggesting the truly innovative, as opposed to minor product modifications.[17] But this is to assume that customer orientation means developing only those products which emerge from asking customers what they want. But there are many other ways of identifying wants other than by direct interrogation (see Chapter 9).

There are, however, other operational problems. Thus, even if wants can be identified, there is no guarantee that such wants can be met technically. There is as yet no cure for AIDS though the need is there. Less obvious is the difficulty of identifying and creating the right image for a product. Thus we know that brand image is important as many buying decisions are made on image as a way to save deliberating the pros and cons of buying. As one grocery manufacturer discovered, the highest-quality food product at the lowest possible price may still get soundly beaten by competitors with a less old-fashioned image. Satisfaction depends not just on what a product is objectively but on what it is taken to be. In any case, several people may be involved in the purchase decision. Where each demands different attributes there is a problem in identifying the best compromise offering.

Neglect of competitive strengths and weaknesses

In its rejection of production orientation in favor of customer orientation, the marketing concept places the emphasis where it belongs, but neglects to consider the *fitness* of the firm to cater profitably to the wants it identifies. As a guide to strategy formulation, the marketing concept is thus incomplete and one commentator refers to the need for what he calls "imbricative" marketing:[18]

> It is in the imbrication, i.e., the overlap of this uniqueness and the market's that a firm finds its mission and asserts its individuality. . . . Therefore, the greater the degree of overlap between market requirements and firm skills, the greater the potential profitability.

However, the marketing concept was intended to be a precept for *marketing*, to act as a criterion in judging the validity of a firm's basic posture in a competitive economy. It should not be criticized for failing to go beyond its purpose. In any case, the goal of meeting/exceeding customer expectations presupposes the requisite business system for achieving this end.

Balancing demands of competing stakeholders

No firm is entirely autonomous. Though free to plan, a company has a number of stakeholders or constituents whose support it must win if it is to survive and prosper. One group is its customers, but other groups such as environmentalists, unions, government, suppliers, shareholders, and so on, also need to be considered. The demands made on the firm by these many self-willed groups may conflict, or at least blunt the edge of a full customer orientation. Thus for many years the domestic automobile firms in the United States could afford high wage settlements because they were essentially the only suppliers. With the Japanese entry, the market pressured for lower domestic car prices. Unionized labor did not exactly rush to oblige by higher productivity or lower wages. It is the recognition that a firm has many stakeholders or constituents that leads some writers to argue for the marketing concept to be grounded in the more relevant "constituency-based theory of the firm."[19] Certain firms do take account of all stakeholders and have a stakeholder hierarchy. Thus the so-called Vanguard companies in the United States adopt the following hierarchy:

- customers first: The social function of a business is to help customers solve their problems. Without their support nothing else is possible.
- workers second: Organizations are never any better at solving customer problems than represented by the skills and motivation of the people who work for the company.
- society is the third. It is society that gives the corporation the freedom to serve markets: in what it produces, how, where and at what price. In return for such freedom, there is an obligation on the firm to be a good citizen.
- investors come last on the ground that the extent to which the corporation has done a good job with its other constituents, there will be no need to worry about investors.

While seeking to harmonize the conflicting demands of stakeholders, management must generally lean toward the interests of its customers. The calculation of how much to concede, given the importance of meeting customer expectations, is a measure of the skill of management.

The problem of reconciling competing demands has led some writers to speak of need for a *human orientation* rather than a customer orientation and to talk as if the opposing demands of various groups could always be simultaneously satisfied with a little ingenuity. This is not possible. Top management more than ever before is obliged to balance off the interests of various groups.

Understates the power of persuasion

Earlier it was argued that consumers have latent wants and do not always know exactly what they want and so are open to persuasion. Buyers are not all knowledgeable about the products they buy; do not know all competing brands; often do not know what they want and possess not perfect but flawed rationality. Advertising and other forms of promotion can and do, within limits, influence buyer perceptions, goal priorities and the relative weight given to the various components of the seller's offering. If Galbraith and others exaggerate the power of promotion, there is a danger in the marketing concept of underemphasizing its potential. Advertising can indeed imbue a brand with symbolic meanings and such symbolic meanings are just as much a real part of the brand as its substantive properties: consumer satisfaction does not separate the tangible from the symbolic images with which the product is indelibly linked.

Conflict on occasion with consumer well-being

What if the consumer *wants* things which, though legal, are dangerous to health like cigarettes? What if the consumer *needs* something like car safety features which are not on his list of wants? What if students argue that they should determine the course syllabus on the ground that they are the customers? It is difficult, under the marketing concept, to argue that the marketer knows best what customers' "real" interests are. Furthermore, it may be against the firm's commercial interest to consider anything other than what the customer is willing to pay for.

All the above questions raise ethical issues. Even the one concerning the students' desire to determine the course syllabus since it is easy in statistics, say, to teach only the less demanding aspects; making it easy for the students but abrogating a responsibility to teach a course at the right level and content. In any case, all this leads to a consideration of ethical issues in marketing (see below).

Marketing's mission

The adoption of customer orientation is tied to the concept of marketing's mission. It is claimed here that the mission of marketing is to help the organization to build up customer *trust* as trust is the basis of customer *loyalty*. Customer trust implies a set of favorable beliefs that helps customers to accept or tolerate occasional lapses in product or company performance. Yet trust gives rise to certain customer expectations so that when there is a loss of buyer trust in a company or its product, the company experiences a loss of market power and a loss of power means the firm will find it harder to make amends with customers. Loyalty implies trust. Where trust exists there is a partial relinquishment of the demand for equal reciprocity in the exchange relationship, at least in the short run, in the expectation that things will even out over time. The trusting party believes that those trusted will make up for any negative experiences associated with past exchanges. Trust is earned through actions that build relationships and reputation while facilitated by a commonality of values. If a customer's trust seems justified, customer loyalty follows. While the object of loyalty is ordinarily taken to be a person or group of persons, we can also speak of loyalty to a brand or supplier. Loyalty suggests that customers will purchase a brand even when it is at a temporary disadvantage as trust operates through an emotional bonding. When buyers have bought a product for years and been satisfied with it, the buyer tends to become less calculative as sentiment intervenes. In general terms, when an organization constantly meets the expectations of its customers, trust and loyalty develop. A brand with a loyal following has a credible and attractive image and a high attractive image attracts new customers.

Customer loyalty means attachment to an organization, individual or brand whose performance objectively considered would not seem to warrant such attachment. At its most "irrational" loyalty is most commonly encountered in services and with football teams and political parties. A loyal customer is more likely to complain about a lapse in service or product performance than to switch brands. In the absence of feelings of loyalty, brand switching is emotionally costless.[20]

Loyalty cannot just be measured by habitual purchase or the consumer having a positive attitude toward the brand. This would be equivalent to regarding devotion as a synonym for loyalty. Loyalty is something more than devotion: it is devotion under conditions where rational self-calculation suggests withdrawing support. Loyalty is demonstrated when the object of that loyalty is under attack and at a disadvantage (e.g.

price disadvantage). It is because customer trust is basic to loyalty and a loyal following so basic to long-term marketing success, that anything that diminishes that trust is to be avoided. It is with this in mind that we turn to the next section on ethics and social responsibility.

MARKETING AND ETHICAL RESPONSIBILITY

Unethical conduct in business is a violation of community and customer trust. Questions of ethical responsibility arise over the actions of the firm in respect of:

- individual and public well-being;
- truthfulness in dealing with others; and
- justice, say, for injuries arising from faulty goods and services.

Individual and public well-being.   Criticism is leveled at health-undermining products like cigarettes, and the social consequences of, say, polluting the environment.

Truthfulness.   Truthfulness in advertising is a major public concern, with the demand that firms substantiate all claims about a product's safety and performance. More government regulation is urged to prevent deceptive advertising, unsolicited merchandise, engineered contests and misleading packaging.

Justice.   Justice is demanded to compensate customers who have suffered as a result of using a firm's products or when products fail to perform, or (to quote one commentator) "roofs leak, shirts shrink, toys maim, mowers do not mow, kites do not fly, television sets burn up, service is unobtainable and warranties are not honored."

It is the term "ethical" rather than "moral" that is generally used. While historically the difference between the two terms is simply that of origin in that the term "moral" is Latin and the term "ethical" is Greek, some philosophers have come to distinguish the two terms with the term "moral" being strongly evaluative and associated with the notion of obligation while the term "ethical" carries less such overtones. Nonetheless, we can use the two terms more or less interchangeably. However, those in top management should not simply ask: "What are our obligations?" but "How should we conduct our business to induce trust and loyalty"? The most basic question of ethics in business is whether business people should go beyond what the law demands if that leads to a sacrifice of profit. Thus Milton Friedman, the economist, claims that managers of public companies should not sacrifice profit to promote public well-being as this taxes stockholders without their consent.[21] Thus while Friedman argues that corporations should not deceive or engage in any fraudulent activity, they are not expected to go beyond self-interest. Critics of the Friedman position contend that the law can lag behind in matters of public interest and that stockholders have no right to demand the maximization of profit at the expense of public well-being.

For many business executives, social responsibility is a matter of enlightened self-interest; a way of warding off government regulation. It is accepted that extensive failure in the areas of social responsibility undermine confidence in the free enterprise system and encourage government regulation. If companies are not to undermine the free market system, they should, it is argued, as a minimum, not deceive but accurately portray their product and always keep their promises. Of course, a firm is acting neither ethically nor unethically if it finds it profitable to do the right thing. Thus the Whirlpool Corporation would regard its "cool line" (enabling customers to call the service director at all times) as a matter of good business. When firms in the public eye invest in public well-being, insist on honesty in their dealings and seek the just solution because these things pay, there is no problem. The problem arises when the firm's interests are not enhanced but may actually be undermined by putting public well-being first as would very much be the case if the tobacco giants ceased to market cigarettes!

Few firms go beyond enlightened self-interest. If a firm does go beyond, such behavior is termed *supererogatory*. Supererogatory behavior consists of actions that are praiseworthy if undertaken but whose omission is not considered blameworthy. However, actions regarded as supererogatory today may be demanded tomorrow as views change about what constitutes socially or ethically responsible behavior. Thus the public is much less tolerant of firms that pollute the environment or sell cosmetic products which involve testing on animals.

The fact that ethical standards seem tied to cultural norms has led to claims for cultural relativism. Thus some multinational firms bribe and indulge in other unethical conduct in foreign countries: actions they would never dream of doing at home. Such behavior, justified on the ground of cultural relativism, undermines a total commitment to ethical conduct. Cultural relativism resolves ethical conflicts between one culture and another by accepting that ethical standards are relative to the culture ("they have their ethics and we have ours"). If cultural (ethical) relativism is accepted, it makes no ethical sense to abstain from extensive bribery in countries where this is seemingly an acceptable way of doing business ("Just do in Rome what the Romans do") or to condemn abuses, for example, of child labor or the subjugation of women. However, to suppose that ethical conceptions of what is right and wrong have a "logically inherent relativity" to a given society is mistaken, though there must at the same time be the recognition that others are at varying distances from us.[22] There is evidence from both anthropology and history demonstrating the essential ethical similarities among different cultures. In accepting ethical relativism, we put up a rival standard, namely, universal ethical tolerance as the absolute virtue. To make ethical tolerance the absolute virtue means treating public well-being, honesty and justice as of secondary concern. This cannot be acceptable.

Books and articles on business ethics usually start by some survey of ethical theory. Although many writers doubt the utility of studying ethical theory, it does offer some insights. The most commonly discussed ethical theories in the marketing literature are "deontological" ethics and "consequentialism" but there are other positions which, even if related to these two, are sufficiently distinct to require separate treatment. The two additional positions considered here are "contractualism" and "communitarianism."

The deontological approach

The word "deontological" comes from the Greek for what one *must* do (there is no actual word for duty in ancient Greek). The adjective "deontic" in English, however, means being connected to duty. The deontological approach is associated with Kant (1724–1804), who argued that a person acts morally in doing "D" only if there is a principle "P" such that:

1   the person does "D" and the ultimate principle in doing "D" is the principle expressed in "P."
2   the person would choose "P" as an ultimate principle on which everyone should act.

Kant thus supports moral absolutism: all moral issues are judged against a rigid universal yardstick. For Kant, moral action is that which is done for duty and he bids us to act only on a rule which we would want to become a universal law to which all rational people conform. In other words, I would act ethically only on a rule which I can at the same time "will" that it should become a universal law. For Kant, acting from moral principle was the only way to escape from being driven by the desire for pleasure. Kantian ethics finds an echo in those who believe there are "oughts" that must never be violated, for example, in respect to lying or killing.

Kant failed to give an adequate account of how we come to know what is right and what is wrong but believed we arrived at universal principles or rules through reason. Few today would accept ethical rules that tolerate no exceptions as hard cases seem irresolvable by appeal to principle. There are also problems in application since whether an action exemplifies morally blameworthy or morally praiseworthy action depends somewhat on how the situation is defined (as witness the abortion controversy).

The consequentialist tradition

The consequentialist tradition focuses on the outcomes or consequences of the action as the basis for judging the ethics of the action. *Utilitarianism* comes under consequentialism and is the most well known form of consequentialism. Utilitarianism claims that ethical or moral judgments possess objective truth or falsity and there is a rational means for establishing this. John Stuart Mill (1806–1873) interpreted utilitarianism (founded by Jeremy Bentham) as the doctrine that the right action is that which, "conduces to the greatest good of the greatest number." Welfare economics, the use of cost/benefit analysis in the public domain and the acceptance that trade-offs are always possible among values, are all utilitarian thinking. There are variants of utilitarianism. There is, for example, "rule" as opposed to "act" utilitarianism. Act utilitarianism claims that acts are right when they increase welfare. Thus if public well-being is increased by a firm acting to clean up the environment then that action is regarded as ethically the right thing to do. In contrast, rule utilitarianism seeks morally binding rules for maximizing welfare, considering individual acts right or wrong depending on their conformity to such rules. Thus according to rule utilitarianism, the question is not whether an organization's specific advertising, say, is deceptive but rather whether social utility is enhanced if advertisers are, in general, free to deceive or not.

There is also "motive utilitarianism" where the rightness of the motive is considered. Sometimes motive utilitarianism is distinguished as a separate theory of ethics when it is grouped under the label of *teleological* ethics which takes account of the goodness or otherwise of the person's or organization's motives or intentions. It is argued that there is an important ethical or moral difference between intentionally causing something harmful to happen and unintentionally bringing about certain harmful consequences as a side-effect of pursuing some goal. However, good intentions may not excuse harmful actions if such actions arose from negligence.

Criticisms of utilitarianism are many. There is first the difficulty of weighing up the different pluses and minuses to measure additions to welfare over losses. But for John Rawls, a philosopher, utilitarianism runs into the more serious objection that we could increase the total welfare of society if on occasion we were prepared to sacrifice one person for the benefit of all, but most people would consider this unjust.[23] Utilitarianism and the deontological approach are usually regarded as the two extremes of ethical theory. Yet both share the characteristic of being normative rather than being descriptive of what actually happens. Additionally, both seek rules for people to follow. There have been attempts to combine the two on the grounds that

1 we are not in the arena of moral debate at all unless our ethics are based on considerations we are prepared to universalize about (Kant's position here), and
2 we cannot universalize judgments coherently without developing a universal sympathy with the desires of all affected by our actions so each of us must take account of the effects of our actions on the desires of all those affected (utilitarianism here).[24]

Here ethical judgments are both universal and prescriptive. They are prescriptive in that their role is to recommend some sort of conduct yet they are universal in that they should only be applied for reasons which would always lead to their application in similar circumstances. In terms of business ethics, what is being claimed here is that any business decision that has an ethical dimension should take account of those likely to be affected by the decision and that any action taken must be the action that would again be taken in like circumstances.

The contract view of ethics

Critics of utilitarianism claim that it conflicts with our common-sense intuition that we, as individuals, have "rights," perhaps unalienable rights as per the American Declaration of Independence. The idea of there being unalienable human rights is based on the belief that establishing freedom, justice and so on for everyone is in the interests of all human beings. Rights are put forward as representing a kind of moat put around us to protect our autonomy: with the violation of individual autonomy needing special justification. John Rawls, influenced by contract theories and Kantian liberalism, is credited with developing the most sophisticated rights theory. He regards the right to equal liberty as the most fundamental of all rights, from which all other legitimate rights can be derived. Every ethical rule he views as generating both a right *and* a duty just as the right of consumers not to be deceived generates the duty on advertisers not to deceive. Rawls, like other rights theorists, justifies autonomy by viewing morality as if it were based on a societal contract or agreement. Rawls is a contractarian. The rules we should live by represent something analogous to a bargain we strike with others in society; a social contract for the benefit of all. We get benefits from participation in society and it is "as if" we have agreed to cede certain limited elements of our autonomy to get these benefits. On this view people behave ethically if they follow the rules in respect to other people's rights. The identification of these rights is based on the simple idea that a fair system of rights is one which the parties agree to when they are unaware of how it will benefit them personally.

Some writers on business ethics regard each business like an individual who, in return for benefits from society, enter "as if" into a contract with society to limit the firm's freedom of action so as to respect the rights of others. The so-called Vanguard companies mentioned earlier talk in these terms: as if a tacit understanding, a social contract is in force. In return for its freedom in decision-making and the use of its wealth, a business organization is expected by society to organize activities to improve the material conditions within society.

What is missing in this account is justification: why should businesses feel bound by some hypothetical contract? Also, there is the problem of dealing with conflicting rights since the "rights" of one group (e.g. environmentalists) may conflict with the rights of another group (those with "rights" over their private property). Finally, it is not easy to anticipate a comprehensive system of rights that takes account of all individual circumstances.

Communitarianism and virtue ethics

Communitarianism is based on the premise that human behavior can only be understood by taking account of individuals in their social, cultural and historical settings. As an ethical approach, communitarianism focuses on the notion of "virtue" and the way "virtue" is understood in particular communities. Virtues are deeply internalized character traits formed by a long process of "habituation," backed by convictions and cemented through emotional attachment. Some philosophers claim that moral justification is always rooted in some community tradition and ethical judgments are always context-sensitive.[25]

Virtue ethics has links to Greek ethical thought. Aristotle, whose ethics were based on considerations of well-being and a life worth living, pointed out that all virtuous action is action for and to others and claimed that doing the right thing, that is, the virtuous thing, is not something that can be taught because being virtuous is a skill in judging and acting correctly in the changing circumstances of the world. Many managers would agree that ethical judgment, like judgment generally, is a skill (not simply a deduction from a rule) as individual circumstances always need to be considered.

Not all philosophers advocating virtue ethics put all their emphasis on community tradition, believing this makes for conservatism and takes too much for granted about communal consensus. These philosophers view the corporation as the relevant community with the different role relationships among employees constituting the relevant context that must be considered as these different role relationships generate different obligations. There is a rejection of the idea of a set of rules from which answers to ethical problems can always be deduced. What is needed is the skill to weigh competing concerns.[26] Individuals within the corporation make ethical decisions guided by the corporate values they have absorbed. However, since corporate values are part of the corporate culture, the focus should be on creating the right cultural climate that fosters the right virtues. Corporate culture consists of the set of values, beliefs, stories, and myths that permeate the organization and provide guidance on what would be considered the right thing to do, ethical or otherwise. If the cultural climate is not openly supportive of ethical behavior, the motivational climate for ethical conduct will be missing.

Motivation to comply.   Benedict Spinoza (1632–1677) pointed out long ago that it is empty verbiage to recommend any system of ethics unless it engages people's real motivations. The deontological position and utilitarianism see that motivation as coming from the desire to be rational and do the right thing. Those in the contract tradition of rights see it as a matter of enlightened self-interest while the virtue theorists see the motivation stemming from the emotional commitment to an habitual way of life and the social norms and values of the community. But David Hume (1711–1776) insisted on the emotional basis of ethical conduct. Along the same lines, Frank, an economist, claims that the motivation to ethical conduct is usually lacking when there is no emotional commitment to ethical behavior since emotions signal situations demanding a response. In the case of ethical issues this means a response to the feelings of anticipated shame and guilt when ethical values are violated.[27] He argues that people will always be tempted to grab short-term easily obtained (unethical) gains unless they have this emotional commitment. He claims that, in the long run, ethical conduct, by building up trust, is tied to business success.

If companies made breaches of ethics a traumatic experience, this would do much to introduce the emotional ingredient. As Aristotle said long ago, you get a good adult by habituating the child to do the right thing. Ethical behavior is very much a function of indoctrination and social conditioning and it is doubtful whether abstract knowledge of right and wrong has very much influence.

Ethics in business.   When business actions are manifestly at variance with public well-being, the law usually intervenes. There are also situations when the firm should do the right thing regardless of legal requirements. Unfortunately, there are occasions when it is difficult to determine the "right" thing to do. Business executives cannot just ignore primary company interests when these are endangered and threatening the firm's viability. It is simplistic to claim that the higher moral ground is always the common good, as businessmen also have a duty to the firm's employees and stockholders.

Are there guidelines to developing a system of business ethics? *Objective relativism* is of interest here.[28] This position claims that the right ethical decision is *relative* to circumstances and, though relative to circumstances, decisions or actions can be ethically *objectively* right or *objectively* wrong. It is somewhat the same with proverbs. Thus we have the conflict between the proverbs "too many cooks spoil the broth" and "many hands make light work." Their appropriate application is relative to the circumstances but it would be an objective rather than a subjective matter in saying which proverb applies to which set of circumstances. The concept of objective relativism is not unlike Aristotle's point about principle and circumstances coming together in the particular situation. What are the criteria, though, for testing whether some proposed ethical decision is appropriate to the circumstances? One set of criteria that seems appropriate for ethical decision-making in business is the following:

- The proposed decision should be able to withstand rational criticism, that is, be defensible: the sort of decision that would be taken by most reasonable people given the circumstances. There is a link here with Kantian ethics.
- The basic assumptions behind the decision should have wide appeal. In any society or corporate culture there are social norms or standards for judging ethical behavior. Employees must be directed to carry out their job in a way that avoids any actions which, if revealed, the firm would be ashamed to acknowledge. In stressing corporate culture and social norms there is a link here to virtue ethics.
- The decision should be one the organization can live with. In business life, right and wrong are by no means clear-cut. As one critic says, much advice offered on business ethics leans toward moral absolutism.[29] Right conduct is somewhere between the pursuit of profit regardless and the imaginary state of complete business altruism.

Although there is still the need for skill in applying these criteria, the criteria do represent fairly concrete guidance while still being linked to the various theoretical positions sketched earlier. There has been a growth in codes of ethics, covering such topics as bribes, misappropriation of company assets, decisions affecting the various interests of stakeholders and so on. Many such codes are designed merely to protect the company or are mere window dressing, unmonitored except as they affect company profits. They frequently assume that everything is within the control of the employee without recognizing the influence of corporate culture which may not be conducive to ethical conduct. An organization needs to create a motivational climate that reinforces the "will" to take the right ethical decision. Nonetheless codes can be useful providing they contain not just specific "do nots" but a narrative that suggests the ethical system lying behind the specific rules. When management draw up a code of ethics, it is at least a public declaration that lends support to the "will to do the right thing" and provides others with some basis for objecting to proposed unethical action.

The decisions and actions of an ethical corporation symbolize a set of values with which buyers can identify. On the other hand, an unethical corporation symbolizes an entity it would be foolish to trust. When corporations in their dealings with customers seek the small legal but unethical gain (common in services like banking), it does not pass unnoticed even if it is not actually questioned. Ethical conduct cannot be reserved for just the big challenges if a firm is to build up trust with customers: it must manifest itself in every decision and action since it is the unflawed image of integrity that is so attractive.

MARKETING TECHNOLOGY

There are many debates in the literature over whether marketing is an art or a science; but it is perhaps more useful to regard marketing in practice as a technology. Technology relates to the distinction made between "knowing that" and "knowing how": technology is knowing how. Technology can be defined as the design of systems (e.g. planning systems) that succeed or fail.[30] Technology is concerned with finding out what should be done to reach some goal, so technological knowledge is knowledge of what is effective in producing the results that are sought. Every technology is composed of rules of action and rule-governed techniques. A rule of action takes the form: "In order to do X, we must do Y" for instance, "in order to continue to grow or hold and defend a market position in a mature market, we must think in terms of catering to some market segment better, or entering new segments, or simply seeking to lower costs." Rules are not "true" or "false" but effective or ineffective in achieving whatever is viewed as success. But the application of the rules themselves involves skills that are acquired through practice since rules can often be vague and ambiguous when we are seeking to apply them. As far as science enters into technology, it is to give grounding to the rules governing the technology. Thus we can export the objective fruits of science throughout the world, but we have difficulty exporting how to do good research, since doing research is a technology governed by rules of loose texture: rules that the researcher learns to apply from a master researcher.

Just as printed music sets the framework for a musician's performance rather than complete instructions for performing the music, the rules implicit in textbooks on marketing set only the framework. Hence the rules of marketing are more like "heuristics" ("rules of thumb") or maxims (rules with exceptions). Both heuristics and maxims differ from algorithms (like the rules of the differential calculus), which are guaranteed to produce a solution in a finite number of steps: with heuristics and maxims there may be no such guarantee. The rules of a technology do not necessarily explain (though the rules will have some underlying rationale) but simply say what needs to be done to achieve whatever is sought. This is why we speak of rules being "right" or "wrong" rather than true or false, though technological rules do involve claims to truth as they implicitly assert certain results are possible by saying how the results can be achieved.

Any textbook on marketing management will set out rules on how to do something, for example, the rules to follow in drawing up a marketing plan; to segment a market; to develop and launch a new product; to set out a promotional campaign and so on. Each rule must be assessed by the manager in terms of its seeming contribution to producing the end results that are sought.

Marketing management is never a mechanical application of rules whether the rules are called rules, principles, heuristics, maxims, or whatever. The trouble with all rules is that, when very general, they seem to have little applicability to the individual case. On the other hand, the more specific the rule, the more it becomes like a recipe, with no room left for marketing creativity. The creative manager will rise above conventional rules with an element of invention. Rules need to be blended with creativity and applied with skill if performance is to rise above the mediocre.

The concept of objective relativism discussed earlier applies here also: rules are relative to circumstances yet a rule can often be shown to be objectively appropriate for the circumstances. There is a need to recognize which rules are relative to what circumstances with creative managers plucking one rule from here and another from there to form some unique combination appropriate for the circumstances. Interpreting a rule's appropriateness is less a matter of paying attention to the rule so much as paying attention to the situation or circumstances to which it is to be applied. Rules are usually guidelines not formulas since there is often uncertainty as to the precise population of markets to which they can be applied. It is all too common an error to generalize illicitly from what has been successful in the past or in one market and apply it to a changed market situation. Thus the rule implicitly followed in the past by the Japanese in selling their cars and electronic products ("For success in these markets build a more reliable product and sell it for a lower price than competition") was not a success in all markets entered by the Japanese and may no longer be in the future. The rules of one game are not those of another and few in marketing can play all games successfully. The truth is that memorizing rules is far less useful to the practical manager than is the development of good judgment. This is not surprising since those who depend on rules will be slow to act in coming to grips with the reality of an unfamiliar marketing situation. If marketing, as a practical activity, is a technology, what are the implications? First, it means that progress in the study of marketing management is progress in the discovery of rules and techniques for coping with marketing management problems. Second, marketing management involves skill in using the rules and, like all skills, is learnt from practice under the guidance of experts. Books can never be a substitute for such experience. A master chef may write a cookery book, but no one expects to equal the master by following the recipes, any more than knowing the rules of grammar makes the student a master of the language. The application of rules always involves subtleties that are discovered by doing. In marketing, as in other areas of management, there is a need for practical wisdom, what is sometimes called "phronesis" which is wisdom that fits the situation. Phronesis does not just arise from learning formulas from a textbook. In fact, the rules have not always been articulated so phronesis must arise to some extent from experience in doing the actual job.

Although science is associated with prediction and control, the older conception of the purpose of science was science as explanation and understanding. Whenever a technology is not scientifically well grounded in explanation, there is a tendency to be conservative and apply conventional rules slavishly. This is because there is so much uncertainty about the consequences of not doing the orthodox when explanations are inadequate. Hence marketing academics see the need to be concerned with providing a better explanatory basis for marketing, particularly by providing a deeper understanding of buyer behavior.

DOMAINS OF MARKETING OTHER THAN CONSUMER GOODS

We have said that the rules of one game are not those for another and it could be claimed that, because of this, there are no experts in marketing but only experts in markets. In particular, expertise varies with whether the marketing is consumer or industrial, nonbusiness (not-for-profit) or service and further refinement is often put forward. But most marketers would claim that the content of a book like this has applicability to all areas of marketing though each area will have its own distinct problems, requiring specific knowledge of the area to guide application. As Montaigne once said: "If we were not alike, we could not be distinguished from the beasts but if we were not different we could not be distinguished from each other." This final section of this chapter describes some of the peculiarities of business-to-business (industrial) marketing, service marketing, and nonbusiness (not-for-profit) marketing.

Business to business marketing

Business to business or industrial marketing is the marketing of products (technical services, equipment, components, consumable supplies, raw or processed materials) to:

1 commercial enterprises (users, industrial distributors, original equipment manufacturers (OEM), other manufacturers, service companies such as banking, accounting firms, and advertising agencies);
2 institutions (schools, hospitals, hotels, etc.); or
3 the government (central, state/county, local). (Business to business marketing, strictly speaking, should also include selling to channel intermediaries like retailers and wholesalers but this is left to Chapter 15 on distribution.)

Although the marketing of some industrial products has more in common with the marketing of consumer products than with mainstream industrial marketing, the marketing mix of elements in the typical industrial marketing strategy is markedly different from the mix in the typical consumer strategy. In particular, face-to-face selling plays a more dominant role and more attention is paid to individual customer wants and to the factors lying behind the buyer's demand for the product. Hence in the chapter on sales management (Chapter 13), particular attention is given to industrial marketing since sales representation is typically so vital. More specifically, industrial markets tend to be distinguished from consumer marketing in the following respects:

Larger unit of purchase

While the individual consumer seldom makes a single large money purchase, buyers of industrial products typically do. Such large orders may justify a direct sales call with negotiation and competitive bidding being used to get the best terms. This can also be a distinguishing characteristic of large supermarket chains with central buying.

Infrequent purchase

Many of the items sold by industrial marketers, like capital equipment or mainframe computers, are infrequently bought. The seller may be uncertain when buyers will return to the market to ensure the seller's product is again considered next time around. The seller may have to deal with this problem by having sales people keep in contact or the seller must rely on being listed in various catalogues used by buyers or the seller must send out brochures on a regular basis.

Fewer buyers

The number of potential buyers tends to be relatively small so that each buyer assumes greater importance for the seller. This characteristic also distinguishes a high percentage of grocery purchases that are bought by just a few central buyers in the big supermarket chains.

Derived demand

The demand for industrial products tends to be derived from the demand for the outputs the seller's products help to produce. As a consequence, it is not unusual for sellers to promote sales of their customers' products, just as a rayon producer might advertise the virtues of rayon dresses. However, the relationship between the demand for the seller's product and the industrial customer's product may be very indirect, as in the case of capital equipment, where the demand for the seller's product can fluctuate much more widely than the demand for the customer's product. This is called the "acceleration principle" whereby the demand for capital equipment tends to decline much more rapidly during a slump in sales of the customer's product and recover more slowly during boom periods.

Buying characteristics

Industrial buyers are likely to use more objective criteria in buying than is the typical consumer. This is not to suggest that personal prejudices, emotions, likes and dislikes have no part in industrial buying. Industrial buyers, too, have egos to which sales people appeal and there is much that is subjective when making trade-offs between conflicting goals or seeking to judge the relative importance of various attributes. Nonetheless, objective criteria relating to technical, and economic criteria and the reliability/dependability of supply will tend to predominate since choices have to be justified to others. This tendency to emphasize objective factors is reinforced by those in buying having expertise in the technical aspects of the product and commercial aspects of buying.

Except for the purchase of standardized products and rebuys, much industrial buying is apt to involve long periods of deliberation and negotiation because of the sums of money involved and/or the complexity of the product. Thus a piece of equipment may have to be specially adapted to the buyer's needs while transportation and delivery conditions may involve special arrangements. Reciprocal buying in industrial markets is also common whereby a firm buys from supplier "X" because supplier "X" buys from it. Such practices, when extensive, can seriously complicate measuring *available* market potential.

Product characteristics

Industrial products are often highly technical with multiple possible uses. This means multiple markets or industries may want the product. As a result, direct selling by technical sales people is often required. Even for such a humble product as lubricating oil, industrial buyers require competent technical advice since there are more than 1,000 types and grades of lubricants, each one of which is designed for a specific job. Also, with multiple potential applications, a major problem lies in identifying the applications. Additionally, sales people may need to have appropriate problem-solving skills to demonstrate the relevance ("the benefits for the buyer") of the product to the application.

Industrial products usually require pre- and post-sales service. Presale service may have to be undertaken to conduct, say, trials, to solve application problems or demonstrate cost savings. A supplier may even go further. For example, a company interested in selling packaging machines to a candy manufacturer may analyze the candy maker's markets and show how some important market segment is being overlooked because of deficiencies in packaging. Post-sale service, on the other hand, may be essential to install equipment, train employees in the use of the product, undertake repairs, or make periodic inspections as well as just making calls to confirm all is well and signal to the buying company that the seller will support his promises.

Services

In the last paragraph services were adjunct to the selling of some physical product, that is, the service element of the offering was not the basic product being sold. But frequently service is the product as in banking, educational services, advertising, insurance, consulting, security services, hospital care, and professional services such as those given by lawyers, accountants, doctors, and financial advisers. These are the pure services which most approximate the definition of a service as something intangible that does not result in the ownership of anything. But this all depends on what is meant by "owning something" since insurance companies issue policies, and banks provide not just advice but money interest and money loans. The labeling of certain industries as service industries did not arise because those doing the labeling were concerned with differences in marketing. The distinction served the purpose of distinguishing services from manufacturing, with the suggestion that manufacturing was something more basic since services do not contribute to the physical stock of goods. Thus we classify under "services industries" restaurants, transportation, gasoline stations, retail stores, the recreation industries, and the wholesale trade where concern with the physical product may be more important than the service aspect. What all this means is that service industries vary widely and it is difficult, if not impossible, to provide a satisfactory analytic definition of services as traditionally listed. However, what can be said is that the service industries have been growing relatively to manufacturing in all the industrialized countries of the world. Services are now estimated to be around 60 percent of the Western democracies' gross national product. Service marketing is thus of paramount importance.

Once we acknowledge that the category labeled "service industries" did not arise because of marketing distinctions, it would be surprising if the various service industries had a common core of characteristics to distinguish them from the marketing of manufactured goods. Nonetheless, many of the pure services like financial services and professional services do have some elements in common that have implications for marketing:

Customization and personalized execution

Most pure services and many others are distinguished by the need to customize the offering and to personalize the carrying out of the service. Thus hotels, legal services, travel services, educational services, financial services, advertising, and restaurants must first identify the customer's requirements to determine what service is appropriate. This is not to suggest that all prospective service customers want customization if this raises costs (mental, physical or price) but most probably will.[31] In any case, it may be possible to suggest customization simply by offering a range of standard offerings as when an airline offers various types of meals, seats, and so on.

Once the service need is identified, how it is carried out becomes important. If, as is typical, service people are interacting with the customer, there is a need for courtesy and warmth to be projected. There will also be individual problems that need attention so a nurse, say, needs not only to be polite but to cater to individual needs in administering the recommended treatment. There is often a threshold level of service needed just to stay in business, that provides minimal customization and personalized execution. In general, the extent of customization will be the performance on which the service provider will be judged but, if customization is generally high, the extent to which the service is personalized in execution is what adds most to enhancing goodwill and loyalty.

Because services have to be customized, it is claimed the user is typically involved in the production of the service but this may only be in the most superficial sense. Thus, while I actively participate in providing information for an insurance policy, I do no more than buy a ticket for the theater or take my groceries to the checkout.

Buyer uncertainties

There are a number of buyer uncertainties associated with services that need to be taken into account.

Intangibility.   A service is intangible in the sense that it cannot be seen, touched, smelt or tasted in advance of being ordered since it is the actual ordering that sets off the process of producing and delivering the service. This means consumers, buying from the service supplier for the first time, must take plumbers, electricians, financial advisers, motor mechanics, TV repair engineers, on trust. Unless the customer is a habitual user of the service, mistrust is common with the buyer being fearful of future regret or being cheated. Thus while we typically pay for a physical product at the time of purchase, we typically pay for a service at the time it is completed, not only because there may be uncertainty about costs for the service provider but also as a way to ensure the service is satisfactory. However, once trust is established, loyalty to the person providing the service is apt to be greater than it is to a branded product.

If the product is intangible, prospective buyers must use surrogate indicators to evaluate the service such as the appearance of the premises, the looks of the staff, and word-of-mouth recommendation. It is no surprise that purchasers of major services tend to do more information search, and seek independent opinion about the service before patronizing it.[32] There are other claims, however, made under this heading of intangibility that are more controversial.

It is claimed that the intangibility of services leads to different evaluation processes. Given there are three evaluation processes:

1 search qualities which are the ones that can be determined prior to purchase;
2 experience qualities which arise with user experience; and
3 credence qualities which cannot be checked even after using the product

It is claimed that services possess few search qualities, many experience qualities and are particularly high in credence qualities.[33] Thus automobiles are regarded as easy to evaluate because they are high in search qualities whereas the accompanying services like insurance are difficult to evaluate as they are high in experience and credence qualities. There is the naive assumption here that physical presence always makes evaluation easier. This is so only if I am an expert on the product class, which the consumer seldom is. In fact the surrogate indicators I may use to judge whether the car is a good one, such as its brand-name and appearance, may not be all that different in kind from evaluating an educational program which I can often sample. It could be argued in fact that being high in experience qualities helps evaluation, for example, of a restaurant or a hairdresser. Under services with high credence qualities are put TV repair, legal services, root canal work, auto repair, and medical diagnosis. These services are meant to be particularly difficult to evaluate relative to physical products (goods) because of these credence qualities. It is not clear why this is so, given that many packaged goods such as drugs and beauty products are surely high in credence qualities in the sense the consumer is often not sure how good the product really is even after purchase. Why should auto repair be so high in credence qualities and houses none at all when both may only reveal their poor quality well after purchase?

It is claimed consumers use more personal sources in choosing services, but is this always so, for example, are more personal sources used in choosing a hotel, a travel agent, a TV repair person than in choosing a car? It is also claimed that few options come to mind for services. But does this follow from the absence of search qualities or from the fact that fewer services are apt to be conveniently available? Another claim is that the consumer is slower to adopt innovations in services, but was the consumer slower to adopt the ATM innovation in banking than the banks were to buy or lease the equipment? Would the consumer be slower to adopt a service innovation than, say, some innovative shampoo if both were equally promoted? Another claim is that brand switching is less likely with services. This may be so, but it may have more to do with the attachment that develops to the people who render the service. Finally, it is argued people are less likely to complain about services because they are more likely to attribute failure to themselves. This is still another claim requiring more empirical verification than the mere quoting of examples. It is not clear that people generally feel they are at fault when the hotel, the teacher, the waiter, the doctor, or the repair seem inadequate.

Although there is an element of truth in the claim about the intangibility of services that allows us to discuss a source of buyer uncertainty, it is easy to exaggerate the extent to which intangibility is important in distinguishing the marketing of services. Thus some physical products like a house may not have been built at the time of ordering and even if consumers are able to see and touch some physical product, this is no guarantee of certainty about the benefits offered. Consumers, too, must take the word of experts that the common aspirin tablet will reduce the risk of heart attack while, for the buying of many products, consumers also use surrogate indicators to judge likely effectiveness such as checking how the car doors shut to judge the quality of a car.

Nonstandardization. The execution of a service typically depends on people and the performance of people is nonstandardized while branded mass produced products are more or less standard. Although some services do not involve people (e.g. coin-operated washing machines), this factor of the nonstandardized human performance generally discriminates services. It means training staff to minimize the problem. Also the direct measurement of service is often difficult so resort is typically made to customer opinion surveys or random observation of job samples. Nonetheless it is extremely important to measure the level of service in that dissatisfied customers typically do not have a product to return and so are apt not to complain direct but prefer to "badmouth" the service to others.

Information gap. Many pure service providers are providers of information. This is particularly so with professional services such as lawyers, consultants, and doctors, but is also true of providers of mortgages, which can be technically very complex. This superiority of expertise (information) is power to the service provider and may be resented by customers/clients who may have suspicions they are being manipulated. This is why openness, friendliness, putting the client fully in the picture, and explaining in detail about what is going on is so very important. Management may reject consultants' reports, patients may reject doctors' advice, and students reject what is being taught, more because of the expert's manner than through the expert's demonstrated lack of expertise. Every consultancy firm knows that the most knowledgeable, the most brilliant consultants on the payroll are not necessarily the most successful with clients.

Simultaneous production and consumption

If we consider the services of a retail outlet, a dentist, fast food outlets, and a place of entertainment, the service is consumed as it is rendered. But for many services this is not so in that when the service is rendered (e.g. by consultants, R&D, design and architect services) it is not simultaneously consumed. Where it is a distinguishing characteristic, it means that it is easier to test market new products while the products seldom require a long process of development.

No storing of labor services

When hairdressers, waiters, doctors, accountants, hotel staff, teachers, and so on have no customers, they cannot store their labor. And this is a frequent problem since the demand for services can fluctuate wildly. But the demand for manufacturing products, too, can fluctuate wildly with labor time being wasted as a result. However, in the case of manufacturing, the fluctuations do not tend to be from day to day or month to month as in the case of pure services. Hence the problem of evening out the demand fluctuations tends to be more pressing for services while there is the problem of determining the maximum capacity level and what "slack" resources would be needed to cater to for the peak.

Guarantees

Many service providers such as doctors and stockbrokers cannot guarantee success. This is common for professional services. However, while it is true that standard products designed for standard applications can offer a guarantee, it is also true that many nonstandard industrial products for industrial applications cannot.

Nonbusiness marketing

Nonbusiness marketing is marketing by nonprofit organizations such as charities, hospitals, educational establishments, museums, private libraries, symphony orchestras, religious institutions, political organizations, labor unions, and government agencies. In looking through this list, it will be apparent that nonprofit organizations are not just concerned with fund-raising but may be marketing products such as tickets to the orchestra, articles in the museum, or social causes like a government anti-drink and driving campaign. Sometimes, in talking about nonbusiness marketing, writers speak of "person" marketing if it is the marketing, say, of a political candidate; or "place" marketing if the product is some tourist area; or "ideas" marketing if the product is some cause. This is to emphasize where the focus lies. One attempt to distinguish the characteristics of nonbusiness marketing points to the following.[34]

Multiple publics

There are at least two publics: the donors or patrons and those who use the service. The implication here is that nonprofit organizations need two marketing strategies: a resources attraction strategy and a resource allocation strategy. But so do some profit firms like a bank that has an attract strategy to get savings (resources) from depositors and a resource allocation strategy for the loan side of the business. Nonetheless the two strategies are more accentuated in nonbusiness marketing.

Nonprofit objectives

It is claimed that as nonprofit organizations do not have the goal of profit, options cannot be evaluated in money terms. But commercial organizations have multiple objectives not just profit and it is simplistic to think that all trade-offs in business can be evaluated in money terms in any meaningful way.

Services rather than physical goods

Most nonprofit organizations are involved with services, for example, a symphony orchestra. But some do market physical goods as do museums, stately homes, and even hospitals.

Language differences

As with professional services, nonprofit organizations have sought to avoid the language of the marketplace with its overtones of commerce though differences in language may capture real differences. In any case, customers may be called patients or students or benefactors or patrons or clients. Instead of speaking of products there are course offerings, treatment, enlightenment, education, or representation while price becomes a fee, tuition, or an honorarium and distribution may be adding new locations or touring.

The marketing of services, business to business marketing and nonbusiness marketing throw up special problems stemming from their distinct characteristics but all markets differ somewhat and there is always the danger of applying standard solutions when standard conditions do not exist.

CONCLUSION

This brief review of the nature of marketing is intended to give a flavor of the subject matter, the problems, status as a discipline, and application areas. The rest of the book is concerned with marketing management in a competitive environment with a stress on the concepts, techniques, findings, and approaches that have been developed to cope with marketing problems and issues. While typical problems can be identified and labeled, solutions vary with circumstances. Marketing is not a matter of following formulas. While learning rules can be important, it is not as important as developing good judgment and exhibiting creativity. The emphasis in this book is thus less on rules and more on concepts since concepts determine how we look at an issue while good marketing judgment is the application of the most relevant concepts to the problem.

NOTES

1 Kotler, Philip (1972) "A Generic Concept of Marketing," *Journal of Marketing*, 36 (April): 46–54.
2 Kotler, Philip and Levy, Sydney J. (1969) "A New Form of Marketing Myopia: Rejoinder to Prof. Luck," *Journal of Marketing*, 33 (July).
3 Bagozzi, Richard (1975) "Marketing as Exchange," *Journal of Marketing*, 39 (October).
4 Kotler, Philip (1972) "A Generic Concept of Marketing," *Journal of Marketing*, 36 (April).
5 Dwyer, F. Robert, Schurr, Paul H., and Oh, Sejo (1987) "Developing Buyer–Seller Relationships," *Journal of Marketing*, 51 (April).
6 Webster, Frederick E. (1992) "The Changing Role of Marketing in the Corporation," *Journal of Marketing*, 56 (October).
7 Houston, Franklin S. (1986) "The Marketing Concept: What it is and What it is not," *Journal of Marketing*, 50 (2) (April).
8 Tichy, Noel and Sherman, Stratford (1992) *Control Your Own Destiny or Someone Else will*, New York: Doubleday.
9 Williams, Ernest (1896) *Made in Germany*, London: Heinemann.
10 Marchand, Roland (1985) *Advertising the American Dream*, Berkeley: University of California Press.
11 Galbraith, John Kenneth (1977) "UGE: The Inside Story," *Horizon* (March).
12 Campbell, Colin (1987) *The Romantic Ethic and the Spirit of Modern Consumerism*, Oxford: Basil Blackwell.
13 McKnight, Gerald (1989) *The Skin Game*, London: Sidgwick and Jackson.
14 Penz, Peter G. (1986) *Consumer Sovereignty and Human Interests*, Cambridge: Cambridge University Press.
15 Kohli, Ajay K. and Jaworski, Barnard J. (1990) "Market Orientation: The Construct, Research Propositions, and Managerial Implications," *Journal of Marketing*, 54 (April).
16 Slater, Stanley F. (1990) "The Effect of a Market Orientation on Business Profitability," *Journal of Marketing*, 54 (October).
17 Bennett, Roger C. and Cooper, Robert G. (1981) "The Misuse of Marketing: An American Tragedy," *Business Horizons*, 24 (November).
18 Kaldor, A. G. (1971) "Imbricative Marketing," *Journal of Marketing*, 35 (April).
19 Day, George S. and Wensley, Robin (1983) "Marketing Theory with a Strategic Orientation," *Journal of Marketing*, 47 (Fall).
20 Hirschman, Albert, O. (1970) *Exit, Voice and Loyalty*, Cambridge MA: Harvard University Press.
21 Friedman, Milton (1962) *Capitalism and Freedom*, Chicago: Chicago University Press.
22 Midgley, Mary (1991) *Can't We make Moral Judgments?*, New York: St. Martin's Press.
23 Rawls, John (1972) *A Theory of Justice*, Oxford: Oxford University Press.
24 Hare, R. M. (1981) *Moral Thinking*, Oxford: Clarendon Press.
25 MacIntyre, Alasdair (1981) *After Virtue*, London: Duckworth.
26 Solomon, Robert C. (1993) "Corporate Roles, Personal Virtues: An Aristotelian Approach to Business Ethics" in Earl R. Winkler and Jerrold R. Coombs (eds.) *Applied Ethics: A Reader*, Oxford UK: Blackwell.
27 Frank, Robert (1988) *Passions within Reasons*, New York: W. W. Norton.

28 Putnam, Hilary (1981) *Reason, Truth and History*, Cambridge: Cambridge University Press.
29 Stark, Andrew (1993) "What's the Matter with Business Ethics?," *Harvard Business Review* (May–June).
30 Polanyi, Michael (1964) *Personal Knowledge*, Chicago: Chicago University Press.
31 Surprenant, Carol F. and Solomon, Michael R. (1987) "Predictability and Personalization in the Service Encounter," *Journal of Marketing*, 51 (April).
32 Murray, Keith B. (1991) "A Test of Services Marketing Theory: Consumer Information Acquisition Activity," *Journal of Marketing*, 55 (January).
33 Zeithaml, Valerie A. (1991) "How Consumer Evaluation Processes differ between Goods and Services" in Christopher H. Lovelock (ed.) *Services Marketing*, Englewood Cliffs, NJ: Prentice Hall.
34 Lovelock, Christopher and Weinberg, Charles (1978) "Public and Nonprofit Marketing comes of Age" in G. Zaltman and T. Bonoma (eds.) *Review of Marketing*, Chicago: American Marketing Association.

Chapter 2

Corporate strategy and marketing

INTRODUCTION

- What business should the firm be in?
- What strengths does the firm possess that should be exploited in marketing?
- What should be the investment objectives for each of the firm's product groups?

These questions are addressed in corporate level strategic planning. They involve top management since decisions about them bind the whole organization. But marketing also has a say since, though strategic planning at the corporate level limits the marketing department's room for maneuver, marketing considerations restrict the options open to top management. Thus, in considering what new businesses to enter, much will depend on marketing's assessments of the markets. Similarly, allocating funds for growth is wasteful unless marketing has reasonable grounds for believing such growth is possible. When plans are imposed top-down, they may be nothing more than utopian dreams while plans drawn up by marketing, without the input from the top, may be too ill-directed or conceived in ignorance of the firm's total business system.

THE INEVITABILITY OF PLANNING

Planning as a process looks ahead to decide what to do. Planning will always be poorly done unless its importance is recognized and a procedure instituted for going about it. However, the success of a plan can never be guaranteed and there must be a readiness to change plans if assumptions no longer hold. There is no way to avoid planning either in personal life or in business. Human beings can be defined as planning agents. We, as individuals, must plan because we must make choices about how to allocate our limited time and resources in the future. Organizations, too, cannot confine their decisions to present action but must deliberate, form intentions, and make future commitments. All such commitments are in the nature of plans with further planning needed to avoid conflicts among them. Managers are obliged to coordinate their present and future activities and coordinate their plans with the plans of others. This needs to be said since planning is so frequently attacked as if it were avoidable. It is not. However, there will always be controversies over exactly what planning should be done, in what detail and how far into the future it should be carried.

Businesses plan because they have the problem of adapting to the world outside. Every organization has two environments: the external environment and the environment inside the firm itself and a company is constantly seeking to *adapt* the internal (inside) environment to the world outside. To "adapt" is to "come to terms with": to get the best terms possible. This is something very different from surrendering to every demand of "stakeholders" in the external environment, whether these are shareholders, customers, unions, suppliers, or whoever. Thus customer orientation cannot be equated with complete acceptance of all market demands. It is this that distinguishes customer orientation from market enslavement. Customer orientation is a form of adaptation to the external environment that requires the firm to know what constitutes an offering that is sufficient for achieving the objectives that are sought. For instance, any automobile manufacturer can better satisfy customers by reducing price, giving a lifetime guarantee, increasing the numbers of dealers and the level of service, providing a free car whenever the customer's own car is in for service, and so on. There is never any problem in conceiving of better ways to satisfy wants. The problem lies in adding additional benefits in a profitable way. To dramatize this point one book makes the seeming paradoxical claim that: "The most appealing product is always the least profitable."

Since there is a preference for immediate over larger but delayed rewards, there is always pressure to simply plan for the immediate future and to dismiss long-term planning as futile. Thus serious planning is abandoned in favor of improvisation and reacting to competitive moves.

Although there is no certainty about the future, any organization will sensibly lean more toward planning than improvisation. In other words, an organization should lean toward being *proactive*. A proactive stance is one where the firm tries to forecast the future to influence it, that is, plan to adapt or come to terms with it in the best way possible. This contrasts with a *reactive* stance where action takes place only in response to events: there is no plan to try and get control over events, to adapt rather than surrender. There are many types of plans in any business or not-for-profit organization. There are the various financial planning systems, like the annual budgets. There are the very long-term plans and the more immediate strategic plans. In any case, organizations that undertake formal planning operate with a hierarchy of plans. There is first the planning that occurs at the corporate level to guide the whole organization. Planning at the marketing level will get direction from these higher level plans and in this sense marketing plans can be regarded as a way to implement or flesh out the higher level corporate plans in operational terms. In any case, whatever plans are drawn up by marketing they must cohere, support and be a means for achieving higher level plans.

We will now discuss the usefulness of a number of terms and concepts commonly employed in marketing planning. But a word of warning. Not all the terms have agreed definitions. They are used very loosely in the management literature which is a constant source of irritation to the student who equates loose terminology with loose thinking and an obstacle to reasoned debate.

PLANNING AT THE CORPORATE LEVEL

Planning at the corporate or top management level should embrace, as a minimum, a statement of overall objectives and a corresponding statement of corporate strategy.

Objectives

Objectives are the future results sought or the aims and expectations as to the future state desired. At the corporate level objectives can be split into vision and mission statements, and a statement of goals, each reflecting different levels of abstraction and precision.

Vision statement

The vision statement provides the vision of what top management sees as the reason for the firm's existence. It is a description of the ideal and, as such, is a picture of the potential future which it is hoped employees, perhaps scattered around the world, can rally round, understand, be committed to, and be motivated to help attain. Thus Steve Jobs, who built up Apple computers, put forward in 1980 a vision of the firm as making a contribution to the world "by making tools for the mind that advance humankind"; Disney's is a little bit more down to earth in simply being "to make people happy."

Mission statement

The mission statement states the long-term concrete ends to be achieved. It emphasizes a resolve to pursue ultimate ends through any sequence of moves that might be required. Just as Christianity, with its missionaries, adopted the mission of converting the whole world, so an organization should have some challenging long-term, operational goal that it is hoped to achieve within some time frame (though PepsiCo's stated mission to "Beat Coke" does not say before what date!). In any case, the mission statement represents an aspiration level. As a mission nears success, top management is apt to become more ambitious "since the moment you believe you have arrived, you limit the distance you might have traveled." Thus, one company defines its mission as "to develop leading edge businesses across a myriad of total systems fronts, from industrial automation to aerospace to medical systems." But sometimes vision and mission statements get combined as in the following statement made by Jack Welch of General Electric:

> A decade from now we would like General Electric to be perceived as a unique, high spirited, entrepreneurial enterprise . . . a company known around the world for its unmatched level of excellence. We want General Electric to be the most profitable highly diversified company on earth, with world quality leadership in every one of its product lines.[1]

Mission statements are often simply utopian; a tactic for self-aggrandizement that may not be costless in that mission statements do build expectations, and the extent to which people feel let down is the extent to which their expectations are not realized. But mission statements can be defended as stating what the organization sees as its long-term realizable objectives.

Goals

Goals are the specific concrete targets. As short-term objectives they are steps toward accomplishing the mission. A firm works back from mission to goals. In commercial firms, where financial objectives dominate, goals are in terms of return on investment

(ROI) or return on equity (ROE), earnings per share (EPS), and so on. But, even if left unsaid, such goals operate within certain value constraints while profit goals in themselves give too little direction to the company, operating more as a way of "keeping score" with the recognition that future plans assume profitable operations. In any case, all objectives, whether financial or otherwise are sought within constraints. Objectives differ from constraints in that objectives can happily be overfulfilled, while constraints, strictly speaking, must not be violated but there is no point in overfulfillment. The values of top management operate as one form of constraint. Thus implicit in one company's statement of goals are values such as the following:

- Ownership must remain in the family.
- Company headquarters must never be a mere holding company.
- The firm should aim to make a definite contribution to the economy.
- Small is beautiful: a division must have fewer than 1,000 employees.

Marketing sets goals such as market share that promote overall corporate goals. But whether at the corporate or the marketing level, they will be influenced by what managers believe is attainable. Thus goals are not set in a vacuum but are influenced by what resources are available and the chances of achieving the goals given the competition. Setting the right objectives at every level in the business is of fundamental importance. This is because to set the wrong objectives is to solve the wrong problem and this can be far more wasteful of resources than solving the right problem in an inefficient manner.

Corporate strategy

In the most general terms, strategy is a broad conception of how resources are to be deployed to overcome resistance to the achievement of objectives. On this definition, strategies presuppose having some set of objectives. Strategy can be distinguished from "policy." Where the implications of objectives and strategies are stated as rules to guide decision-making on a recurring class of problem, they form a "policy statement." Typical marketing policies govern warranties, return of goods, trade and quantity discounts, minimum order size, and distribution practices. Whereas a policy implies subordinates susceptible to direction, a strategy implies a system or organization to be guided. A policy also implies the need for procedures to carry out the policy, while a strategy implies a consideration of resource allocation. Finally, we talk of obeying a policy, but of following a strategy. Strategy is also distinguished from "tactics." Tactics consist of choosing and maneuvering short-term (fixed) means into positions of advantage for implementing a strategy. However, what at one level is called a strategy (because resources are being allocated to different tasks), at the higher level is just tactics since the lower level operates within the fixed constraints imposed by the higher level.

Corporate strategy defines the *business* into which the firm's resources are to be deployed and the *investment* objectives for each business or product group. More recently, it has been argued that corporate strategy, in a multidivisional firm, should also take account *of horizontal strategy* concerned with conserving resources and exploiting the synergy that might exist from coordinating the goals and strategies of related divisions or business units. We will consider each of these in turn.

Defining the business of the firm

A definition of the organization's business defines the business or portfolio of businesses into which the firm will channel funds, seek sales and do battle with its rivals. The definition of the firm's business tells marketing where to look for markets as these markets will fall within the boundaries of that definition. However, businesses can be defined in various ways, so what definition is most suitable for giving direction to the organization?

How we define a firm's business depends on our purposes. For many purposes it is perfectly satisfactory to describe an organization as being in the textile business, or in banking or the museum business. However, defining a firm's business in terms of its product, service or activity would not give enough direction to the firm. The definition of a firm's business that seems best for this purpose is the so-called product/market scope definition which defines in terms of:

- Customer target(s);
- Function(s) served; and
- Technology employed.

This definition is useful to marketing since it tells marketing where it is to operate by describing the target customer groups, their functional needs/wants while at the same time reminding marketing of the technology to be exploited so that the market opportunities that are seized are those that fit the firm's technology. When the definition of the firm's business is confined to describing just the firm's technology ("We are in electronics") or just the "need" being met ("We bring people the news") or just the customer group ("Our business is catering to the needs of young adults"), the definition would be too wide to give focus to the firm and direction for growth. Thus, to say a firm's business is in electronic instruments gives little direction when looking for additional markets, in contrast to a definition that describes the business of the firm as "serving the needs of laboratory technicians for electronic measuring devices so they can undertake chemical analysis."

This product/market scope definition of a business is not without its limitations, however, since much judgment is required to determine how widely to define customer targets, functions served, and technology or process employed. A small firm would be wise *not* to define these three elements of the definition too broadly as it would be too wide a definition to give direction to the firm. It may be wise to start narrowly and expand. As firms grow, though, they will need to broaden one or more elements of the definition, depending on what paths to growth offer most opportunities.

The product market/scope definition is drawn up for each individual business. It may also be applied to a set of product groups that have an underlying rationale in terms of function served, customer group and underlying technology. But the definition seems more difficult to apply when the organization is a holding company or conglomerate. Here the function would appear to be creating new businesses, with the customer group being the conglomerate itself and the technology being the technical process of acquisition. But the application seems somewhat forced and less useful.

What can be said is that the product/market scope definition of a business is helpful to marketers since all paths to growth are in terms of widening the customer group, function or technology while the definition, at any one time, sets the boundaries for marketing. As such, choosing a business to go into is not something to be taken lightly. There is a need to ask: "What are the requirements of success? Has the firm got what it takes to be a success?"

Investment objectives

A major criticism of top management in the past has been its demand that the investment objective for every business, for every product line, should be growth. This would suggest the firm had abundant resources; that each business and product line had equal chances of being equally profitable so that there was no need to establish priorities. These assumptions were and are unjustified and priorities in allocating resources were and are inevitable. What management often may not want to acknowledge is that a business or product group is at the stage of decline and no amount of pressure on marketing to do better will be of much help.

A key decision by top management, in conjunction with marketing, is to determine the investment objectives for each business. Investment objectives tell marketing what type and level of effort/expenditure to put into some business or offering. These objectives can be any of the following:

1 Growth in the business;
2 Hold/defend existing market position;
3 Turnaround/turnabout/rebuild the business;
4 Harvest/wind down the business;
5 Divest/sell the business; and
6 Liquidate the business.

As there are many ways to grow, to hold/defend a market position etc., each of these objectives can be sought by many different strategies. Nonetheless every marketing plan depends on a business's investment objective. A company may thus decide it can ill afford to push for growth on all fronts and that additional investment in some market is not warranted. The problem of choosing among investment objectives revolves around knowing the most profitable areas for the firm to channel resources into and the areas from which to withdraw. Differences in growth potential, cash flow potential, company capabilities in relation to market requirements, and the relative competitive strengths of the firm are the factors traditionally considered. What has been added since the 1970s has been the development of a number of analytical frameworks that allow a more systematic approach to determining the investment objective for each business. These are discussed later in this chapter.

Horizontal strategy

A horizontal strategy coordinates the goals and strategies of related business units and exploits any synergies there might be among the businesses. When synergy occurs between two businesses, the combined strength is something more than the sum of the parts. Michael Porter argues that multipoint competition, where two competitors, like Gillette and BIC, compete with each other in several businesses (ball point pens and disposable razors), makes horizontal strategy more important than ever.[2] This is because any firm taking action against a multipoint competitor must consider the entire range of jointly contested businesses since retaliation may come not just from the business being attacked. The interrelationships in need of coordination are listed below.

Tangible interrelationships.　These are the potential opportunities for sharing activities to reap economies resulting from having similar technologies, etc. Savings here can be far greater than the increased costs arising from increased coordination costs, and the losses arising from compromising on the uniqueness of each business's needs.

Intangible interrelationships.　These refer to the transference of skills and know-how from one business to another. Porter acknowledges that these may not materialize. Certainly, many successful marketing organizations have supported the takeover of another company on the ground that their marketing expertise will transfer, only to find such skills do not easily carry over into other businesses.

Competitor interrelationships.　With multipoint competition, attacking one competitor in one type of business may have implications for other businesses of the firm since the competitor may respond by attacking the firm's other businesses instead of the one doing the attacking. Porter lays great stress on the development of a horizontal strategy as if this should be the chief preoccupation of those running the company. For many small companies it would not have much significance in their planning while, even for the large corporations, it is not clear why it should have absolute priority since it is just one facet of relating the internal to the external environment whose importance will depend on actual circumstance.

PLANNING AT THE BUSINESS LEVEL

In recognition of the fact that a company can consist of several businesses, a distinction is sometimes made between planning at the corporate level and the top management planning that occurs for each business unit. This distinction can also be used to illustrate the hierarchical nature of company planning.

Business strategy: thrust and core competencies

When a firm successfully exploits R&D, its strategy is likely to be built on distinctive knowledge and know-how which constitutes its thrust. Sometimes this thrust is called the firm's "business strategy," suggesting resources should be deployed to exploit such strengths.[3] Certainly, a firm should seek to build on its distinctive knowledge and know-how so that any new products introduced by marketing should exploit the organization's thrust.

Recognition of the organization's thrust adds for marketing an additional restriction to that of business boundaries in that offerings should build on the organization's thrusts. The sort of knowledge and know-how that might be a firm's thrust might lie in R&D; marketing expertise; efficiency in manufacture; or financial expertise or excellence in management. Thus the thrust of the Intel company is innovation; that of Procter and Gamble is marketing; that of BIC is efficiency in manufacture while the consultancy firm of McKinsey would identify its thrust as expertise in management solutions. The decline of many a firm is due to moving away from its thrust. Often this movement away from thrust manifests itself in a proliferation of unprofitable products. Marketing management, not infrequently, encourage this error by being tempted to exploit some market opportunity that, while an opportunity for some company, is not an opportunity for them in that it does not exploit what the firm has to offer.

The management literature also speaks of the need to identify the "core competencies" of the business. These are defined as the collective learning of the organization that gives rise to certain capabilities like Sony's capability in miniaturization or Cannon's in optics.[4] The concept of core competencies was developed without reference to the related concept of thrust or business strategy though this had received wide publicity, being a term used by GE in their planning. Whereas the firm's thrust usually resides in some functional area like R&D or marketing and consists in the knowledge and know-how of the particular functional area, core competencies describe what distinctive, *demonstrated* capabilities the whole organization has as demonstrated in its outputs. Of course, core competencies are likely to draw on the firm's thrust if this distinctive knowledge and know-how is still of marketable value. Core competencies may be so adaptable as to allow the firm a wide set of advantages in many products. The concept of core competencies can be combined with the concept of thrust to give a broader concept of business strategy, so that business strategy becomes a plan for using the firm's distinctive know-how (thrust) and distinctive overall capabilities (core competencies) to win market success.

Competitive advantage versus critical advantage

A firm's thrust and core competencies are nothing but an illusion of strength unless they result in enhancing performance in the market. A firm's thrust and core competencies should give rise to some advantage over rivals in the market. In other words, they should give rise to a *competitive advantage*. Whereas the thrust and core competencies (the business strategy as now defined) tell us about the organization's distinctive know-how and competencies, a competitive advantage provides the logic of particular market success. Whereas the business strategy has reference to the company, the term competitive advantage refers to an offering's advantage in a market. A competitive advantage is always relative to that of rivals. This means that a successful firm could be simply the "best of a bad lot." Many a market entrant has been a success just by realizing that those at present in the market lack the expertise or whatever which competitors in more sophisticated industries just take for granted. A competitive advantage can reside in any component of the firm's offering and not just in its cost and quality. In fact, in many markets today, world class quality and costs may simply be the price of "being in the game" so firms are obliged to provide some other reason for preference.

A firm's competitive advantage is not always transparent. One study points out that, in practice, the differences between the firm and its competitors that are selected as advantages or disadvantages can be very subjective depending on what managers view as significant in the simplified representations (model) they have of the firm, its customers and competitors.[5] At least four distinct representations were found, differing in the amount of attention paid to competition and customers. The first representation was labeled the *self-centered* perspective in that it is "inner-directed," with little regard to either what competitors are doing or what customers believe. There are likely to be few customer or competitor pressures for such a representation to develop. The second perspective is *competitor-centered* in that it is based on comparisons of the firm with its major competitors. The market environment here is characterized by the high salience of competition. The third representation or perspective is *customer-oriented*, which focuses on customer benefits and customer satisfaction. Managers here rely mainly on customers to inform them of how they compare with the competition. The fourth representation is a *market-driven* perspective, which pays balanced attention to both customers and competition so the business is apt to collect a wide variety of information on customers and competitors. The market-driven perspective is important where there is extensive competition and complex customer behavior.

For something to be a critical as opposed to just a competitive advantage, it must be both central to the function for which the product is being bought and unique to the business. Both centrality and uniqueness are involved. Thus air safety is central to the airline traveler, but it is not critical if all airlines are deemed to have the same level of safety as no airline will be perceived as unique in air safety. In fact, unless air safety were unique, it would not even qualify as a competitive advantage. On the other hand, only one airline may offer a steak dinner on the flight to Florida (which happens), but such a unique service may not be critical as it is unlikely to be central for passengers. In sum, a competitive advantage must be unique to the firm possessing it if it is to be categorized as a competitive advantage but that advantage may or may not be of central importance to the buyer. If it is central, then the advantage is a critical advantage. The concept of a *critical advantage* is a sharper concept than that of a competitive advantage since there is a danger of claiming any unique difference is a competitive advantage. Of course, not all customer choices will be based on perceptions of criticalness. Just having a marginal advantage may on occasions be enough to swing the sale, but in such cases the firm's offering is highly vulnerable to competitive attack. Having a critical

global industry has been used to define an industry which is composed of firms whose success in one country is tied to their position in other countries so that it is important to coordinate their activities worldwide.

International marketing is never easy and can often be frustrated by protectionism as well as the increasing fragmentation of the world into trading blocks. All tendencies toward protectionism undermine the spirit of the General Agreement on Tariffs and Trade (GATT), and multilateral trade that, for many people, has contributed so much to postwar economic growth and the success of the free market economies. A current question relates to how well the World Trade Organization (WTO) which succeeds GATT in 1995 will manage to deliver on the GATT promise to create a much more open international trade order. The problem about world free trade is that the benefits of free trade are widely dispersed and difficult to pin down while the effect of it on domestic manufacturers is all too visible in (temporary?) loss of jobs. But the appeal of trade blocks is spreading: e.g. South Korea, Taiwan, Singapore, and Hong Kong; United States, Canada, and Mexico; and the European Union (EU). But common markets do not necessarily remove all barriers to trade within the community. Agreed rules can be reinterpreted toward protectionism. Thus at the time of writing Britain seeks to ban steel imports from Spain and Italy, Germany seeks to ban British beef, and the French try to ban British airlines from Orly airport.

There are real problems in being a global competitor, given the differences in cultures, and in legal, political and economic systems plus the added difficulties arising from the frequent absence of marketing support services, like market research and national economic data not being readily available. A company operating throughout the world has some major decisions to make when undertaking corporate-level planning. There is the question of

1 choice of products and markets;
2 decision on mode of entry;
3 the marketing plan to enter the market; and
4 the control system to check on performance.[15]

The decision as to which countries to sell to or operate in, is a major issue as it is not just a question of market potential but the political, and economic climate of the countries. The markets attracting attention today are

a) Central and Eastern Europe;
b) China and Southeast Asia; and
c) Latin America

Central and Eastern Europe are likely to retain significant state ownership or cooperatives with problems about how to cope in free markets. It is perhaps for this reason that GE's Jack Welch talks about its future being in China, India and Mexico (*Business Week*, November 8, 1993). Although, in Asia, much of the interest lies in trade with China, there is increasing interest in India where the middle class is now estimated to be around 200 million people. As one writer points out, India has a stable democracy, a strong legal system, English as the language of business, a managerial and technical work force, evolved financial markets, a clean record of dividend repatriation, and a vibrant private sector.[16]

The other major decision besides choice of markets abroad is whether to have the same offering everywhere. While the adoption of a global strategy has proved fairly easy for many industrial firms, drug companies, Coca-Cola and McDonald's and for some designer label goods, there is usually a need for some modification of the offering to allow for local conditions, tastes or differences in values and beliefs. Sometimes the decision is to go with a national strategy where offerings are simply adapted to local conditions. Thus all Ford vehicles sold in Europe are designed, developed, and produced in Europe. But such decentralization does not necessarily mean that investment objectives do not have to be approved at the corporate level. Usually they are as no subsidiary will have complete autonomy when there is the problem of determining global priorities.

NOTES

1 Case study on General Electric, Graduate School of Business, Columbia University.
2 Porter, Michael (1985) *Competitive Advantage: Techniques for Analyzing your Business and Competitor*, New York: The Free Press.
3 Rothschild, W. E. (1979) *Strategic Alternatives: Selection, Development and Implementation*, New York: Amacom.
4 Prahalad, C. K. and Hamel, Gary (1990) "The Core Competence of the Corporation," *Harvard Business Review* (May–June).
5 Day, George S. and Nedungadi, Prakash (1994) "Managerial Representations of Competitive Advantage," *Journal of Marketing*, 58 (April).
6 Buzzell, R. D., Gale, B. T., and Sultan, R. G. M. (1975) "Market Share: A Key to Profitability," *Harvard Business Review*, 53 (January).
7 Jacobson, Robert and Aaker, David A. (1985) "Is Market Share All that it's Cracked up to Be?" *Journal of Marketing*, 49 (Fall).
8 Jacobson, Robert (1988) "Distinguishing among Competing Theories of Market Share Effect," *Journal of Marketing*, 52 (Oct).
9 Alberts, William W. (1989) "The Experience Curve Doctrine Reconsidered," *Journal of Marketing*, 53 (July).
10 Woo, Carolyn Y. and Cooper, Arnold C. (1982) "The Surprising Case for Low Market Share," *Harvard Business Review*, 60 (November–December).
11 Hambrick, D. C. and MacMillan, I. C. (1982) "On the Product Portfolio and Man's Best Friend," *California Management Review*, 25 (1) (December).
12 Chandler, Alfred D. (1990) "The Enduring Logic of Industrial Success," *Harvard Business Review*, (March–April).
13 Wensley, Robin (1994) "Making Better Decisions: The Challenge of Marketing Strategy Techniques," *International Journal of Research in Marketing*, 11.
14 Armstrong, J. Scott and Brodie, Roderick J. (1994) "Porfolio Planning Methods: Faulty Approach or Faulty Research?" *International Journal of Research in Marketing*, 11.
15 Root, Franklin R. (1987) *Entry Strategies for International Markets*, Boston, Mass: Lexington Books.
16 Jain, Subhash C. (1993) *Market Evolution in Developing Countries: The Unfolding of the Indian Market*, New York: Haworth Press.

Chapter 3

The planning process and strategy formulation

RATIONALITY IN PLANNING

Formal planning stages

The last chapter dealt with the plans needed at the corporate and business unit level to give direction to marketing. This chapter centers on the planning process itself which is a systematic way of approaching the following questions:

- Where are we now and how did we get here?
- What is the future?
- Where do we want to go?
- How do we get there?
- How much will it cost?
- How can progress be measured?

Although the process of planning is traditionally associated with the sequence of steps that make planning a systematic and logical procedure, this is not sufficient. There is a need to consider the biases in decision-making that undermine strategic thinking and to recognize the political nature of the strategic planning process and last, but not least, there is the content of the strategy itself over and above the way we go about planning.[1] All these things are considered in this chapter as each of the following stages in planning is discussed:

- setting tentative objectives for the market;
- historical review and situation analysis;
- interpretation of the data collected;
- calculation of the planning gap (if any);
- problem diagnosis;
- search for strategies;
- evaluation of strategies and choice of strategy; and
- contingency planning.

Every organization that adopts a formal approach to planning will follow stages somewhat similar to these. This is not surprising as they mimic the typical steps in problem solving. Thus early in the century, John Dewey, the philosopher and educationalist, set out the six general steps in rational problem solving: the setting of goals; a feeling of difficulty in respect to achieving those goals; defining and exploring the problem; envisaging solutions; possible solutions evaluated; and finally a decision made. The only steps added to Dewey's list are the historical review/situation analysis and interpretation of data collected; Dewey assumed the problem solver had the requisite information at hand.

Formal planning is not just the domain of large companies. All organizations benefit from it. In fact formal planning can be much easier, while equally worthwhile, in small organizations because the problem of achieving an integrated and well-supported plan tends to be accompanied by less political strife. The major problem encountered in doing work in small organizations is that of having the requisite information, in that there is not usually any tradition of systematically collecting information for planning purposes.

In the last chapter, formal planning was defended on the ground of its being the rational thing to do; that thinking systematically about what course of action to adopt is better than just reacting and improvising as events occur. Systematic planning is likely to be more effective in achieving goals because built into the procedure are the rational checks that goals be specified and relevant options evaluated against the evidence.

Lack of thought on goals; insufficient information search about the problems and options and biased evaluation of proposed solutions are what undermine the problem-solving process. Formal planning imposes a discipline favoring reflection on goals, extensive search for solutions and an unbiased evaluation of the evidence for each option considered. This is not to suggest that planning cannot degenerate into a mere symbolic strategy (the symbol without the substance); feed the fantasy of being in absolute control of events and be on occasions destructive of creativity.[2] But none of these dangers need occur if management is aware of them. However, it is true that no one can be the most careful detailed planner and at the same time be wholly spontaneous.

There is still much debate over the concept of rationality as applied to planning. Thus rationality in economics is typically confined to the efficiency of means for attaining goals. Confining rationality to the study of appropriate means is too restricting since goals can be rationally evaluated on the basis of:

- *desirability* in that certain goals may be incompatible with corporate values such as, say, wanting to preserve the firm's family atmosphere that growth might destroy or it may be that other goals are more attractive;
- *feasibility* in that there is no point in setting goals that are just utopian;
- *operationality* in that, unless goals have some degree of clarity and precision, they cannot provide guidance; and
- *support* in that, unless the goals generate a winning coalition of support, they will be distorted when implemented.

Political dimensions of planning and planning content

No formal planning procedure can guarantee support and forcing a procedure, and the solutions it generates, onto an organization can be destructive. Planning is not just an intellectual exercise and focusing exclusively on the logic of planning has two weaknesses: ignoring the political aspects of planning and neglecting the content of plans.

Planning is political. Those who believe that planning in a rational way amounts to nothing more than ensuring that planning follows a systematic procedure are adopting a *procedural* planning model of rationality which fails to recognize that the planning process must receive the support of those concerned with its implementation. Formal rationality is not enough. Where action is taken to generate understanding and support of plans this is *practical* rationality if not formal rationality. There can be no practical rationality unless the planning system encourages free discourse and unhampered debate as the basis for generating support.

Those doing the planning must start by recognizing there is a need to generate commitment every step of the way. This in itself requires planning since too much openness and lack of direction at the start can bog down planning through polarization and delay. Planning is always political. The planning process that aims to produce plans, based purely on cold logic, is not a realistic one. Rationality in planning does not mean that planning must be cold. Values, and the emotions that accompany them at each stage in planning are, in fact, one type of evidence that needs to be considered. No planner's thinking is value-free but is grounded in a value system.

The second defect of viewing rationality in planning as being confined to procedural rationality is that it seems to suggest that following rationally defensible procedures is all that is required. This is like suggesting the right computer program is all that is needed to get the right answers, ignoring the need to have the right data. In other words, it is the *content* of the programs that is key. This is why theoretical contributions to planning, like those discussed in the last chapter and Porter's work included in this chapter, are so welcome.

Taken literally, a focus purely on *procedural* rationality would suggest that rationality is localized in the performance of a fixed sequence of actions. It is this belief that procedural rationality is what planning is all about that leads to the mechanical following of planning procedures and later claims that "planning does not work." Learning rules, though important, is not as important as having the right information and exercising good judgment. Rules at best provide merely the program or framework. But there is also the need to understand the material conditions of the world to which the rules are to be applied.

Plans in marketing are typically yearly plans with some firms tying the annual plan into some, say, five-year plan. Today's annual plan is the detailed plan for the immediate financial year which, if successful, is the first step to achieving the five-year plan that is reviewed and updated to reflect needed changes. This chapter considers the process of planning and strategy formulation on the assumption that the firm has set its objectives, defined its business or businesses, and determined investment objectives. Each of the planning stages will now be discussed.

SETTING TENTATIVE OBJECTIVES

No organization can set realistic, realizable objectives until it has the requisite information about the market and other factors happening in the external environment. But, on the basis of experience, marketing management will nonetheless set *tentative* goals on sales volume, market share, or whatever indicators represent progress toward accomplishing the firm's objectives.

For a manager to direct activity toward the achievement of the goal, it must be possible to imagine the goal in a way that is meaningful for guiding the activity. This is why goals purely in terms of profit are inadequate; they offer too little guidance.

HISTORICAL REVIEW AND SITUATION ANALYSIS

To develop a strategy requires information. This is the purpose of doing a historical review and situation analysis. *A historical review* records and orders historical facts about the company, or its products. But understanding how the current position has come about is not the same as understanding the situation as is. There is also a need for a *situational analysis*. Whereas a historical review is a sort of developmental analysis, a situation analysis is cross sectional in that it focuses on the current situation, ignoring processes through time. In practice, the historical review and the situation analysis are closely interwoven, the aim of both being to:

- develop a "reference projection" or a forecast of the future (e.g. in respect to earnings, market share and so on) on the assumption that current plans and practices remain unchanged.
- identify strengths, weaknesses, opportunities, and threats.
- determine the historical thrust and core competencies and corresponding competitive advantage(s).

A strategy is formulated for some business unit or program and the manager is guided in collecting background information by what is considered relevant to the success of that business, unit, or program. Table 3.1 is a typical checklist of the type of information collected. What information is *actually* collected will depend on what is believed by management to be relevant and this in turn depends on their understanding (model) of their business. But nothing is really relevant that does not relate to some definite question. New techniques for analyzing data or new theories are in effect new questions or new ways of asking questions and until these techniques and theories were introduced, certain facts were not considered relevant. As our understanding of marketing grows, there are changes in what we regard as relevant information. Some of the information suggested in Table 3.1, is fairly new to the marketing literature, being based on the portfolio analysis techniques discussed in the last chapter or Porter's work discussed later or insights from the buyer behavior literature. How much information to collect is a constant problem. There is a need for a "stopping rule" relating the cost and benefits of collecting more information. However, no such rule is at present sufficiently operational to be in general use.

Marketing is interested in changes that affect relevant markets. Hence trends or market changes need to be identified. Some of those currently worrying consumer marketing are:

- In consumer package goods like detergents, it has become harder than ever to obtain a technological lead.
- The erosion of trust in advertising, making persuasion appeals more difficult to visualize and develop.
- The big retailer chains which have become more powerful and concentrated.
- Competition becoming more and more global with the result that even well-entrenched companies like Unilever and P&G are under constant attack.

Table 3.1 Checklist for business planning

1. External environment
Social environment
- social movements e.g. the consumer movement
- sociocultural drift e.g. working wives, lifestyles
- agents for change e.g. rising educational levels
- demographic changes

Add for international markets:
- culture (values, beliefs e.g. religious, social institutions)
- language
- form of government, its ideology and stability
- foreign policy

Economic environment
- trends in GNP
- interest rates
- levels of discretionary income
- currency fluctuations
- inflation rates
- unemployment levels
- fiscal policies

Add for international markets:
- balance of payments
- wage/price controls

Technical environment
- government and industry spending on R&D
- technological forecasts
- patent protection

Legal environment
- government regulation and deregulation
- tax legislation
- trademark legislation
- international trade regulations
- employment laws.

2. Market
- barriers to entry
- rivalry
- substitutes from other industries
- power of buyers
- power of suppliers
- evolutionary stage
- growth rate
- demand fluctuations
- industry profitability

3. Customer
- different choice criteria
- shopping habits
- attitudes
- decision processes
- influences

4. Competition
- number of immediate rivals in served markets
- identity of and market shares of rivals
- strategies of competitors

- innovativeness and resourcefulness of competitors
- leadership in marketing, manufacture, and technology
- relative costs
- erosion of patent protection/proprietary knowledge

5. Company
- trends in sales, net income and net cash flow
- thrust/core competencies
- share of served markets
- growth path
- innovativeness
- capacity utilization
- cost trends

- With the growing heterogeneity of subcultures within the developed countries of the world has come an increasing emphasis on market segmentation based on subculture wants.
- With the proliferation of media reaching the consumer, the problem of reaching the consumer has increased since there is more uncertainty as to what media are relevant to the target audience or whether no specific medium reaches all.

Whatever major changes are occurring, they will be seen by one firm as a disaster and by another firm as presenting an opportunity. We refer now to Table 3.1.

Social environment.   The external environment can affect company performance via changes in the gross national product (GNP), government legislation, taxes, changes in interest rates, new technologies and demographics. A growth in national income brings with it a readiness to spend in new directions; an improved level of general education affects consumer tastes and responsiveness to different types of advertising; shifts in the age distribution of the population make different aggregate demands on industry and so on. All such trends affect markets. Thus the size of the liquor market varies directly with the level of economic activity and changes in the age composition of the population, while a drop in newspaper readership can be traced to such trends as increasing TV viewing and declining readership skills. Keeping abreast of all relevant factors can be complex when a company is obliged to do it in every country in which it has subsidiaries. Environmental changes in particular can mean that assumptions long taken for granted may no longer be valid. In any case, key environmental issues and events need to be identified and their likely impact evaluated. A common occurrence, for example, is exchange rate fluctuations. Currency fluctuations are worrying to a firm that makes most of its money from export. What firm would want to rely on a foreign source of supply when the cost of these supplies is apt to fluctuate by 30 percent within the year? If a recession is on the horizon, the problem will be to stay afloat by generating enough cash flow. If there is inflation, there will be a need to keep prices in parallel, if possible, to insure that they cover capital replacement costs.

Trends need to be identified *and* their likely turning points. Neither is easy. For example, the turn of the century concept of the airplane was as an elaborate and expensive toy with little commercial future. When the organization faces a volatile environment, there comes the need for flexibility and avoiding being too bound by self-imposed bureaucratic rules.

Market. Information on market structure reflects Porter's five factors (discussed below) of threat of entry; degree of rivalry; substitute inroads from other industries; and the bargaining power of buyers and suppliers. Additionally, information is needed on market growth, seasonality of sales and market share trends.

Customer. Although the "customer" could be considered under the category of "market," it deserves more visibility as the customer is the major player of interest. A marketing manager would like to know all about buying: who, what, where, when and how; perceptions and attitudes and trends among these. Just as the sculptor in clay, if she is to be successful, must know the behavior of clay under different conditions, marketing managers must know the behavior of their buyers in different situations.

Competition. The firm is seldom in the position where competition can be ignored; there are usually other companies out there with whom the firm must do battle. A firm must evaluate threats from competitors by knowing something about their performance in the market, their capabilities and their likely intentions. Although marketers often talk about their task being to beat competition, they will not do this by just looking at what competition is doing (although this is important) but by understanding the customer better than competition.

Company. To know about one's own company is to know about its strengths, and weaknesses, as a basis for considering a vulnerability analysis (identifying where the firm is vulnerable to being undermined) and in order to develop a competitive advantage based on the firm's thrust and core competencies.

INTERPRETATION OF DATA COLLECTED

"Facts" do not speak for themselves; the data collected have to be interpreted. Understanding presupposes interpretation. Every time we deliberate on data or even on our own experience, we are interpreting. The interpretation is key since how things are interpreted determines what strategies will appear most logical to consider. All strategies are based on some interpretation of the current situation.

The interpretation of a historical review is essentially a reconstruction of the past while a situation analysis is a description of the most relevant features of the present. No final, absolutely true interpretation can ever be proven as some conjecture is inevitable when facts are selected, connected and put into a plausible pattern. But interpretations are far from being arbitrary since any interpretation must square with the evidence. The better interpretations will be consistent with the agreed facts and account for the facts in a more coherent way: bringing the maximum number of facts into a meaningful relationship with the minimum of conjecture. Nonetheless, disagreements over interpretation will occur because facts are selected, ordered and weighted according to some "theoretical" perspective and set of values. Thus interpretation of events will be influenced by what is consistent with current thinking about future strategies. Just as someone, who believes that all dreams reflect secret fears and wishes, will be able to interpret dreams that way, managers are likely to select data to suit their case. But distortion in interpretation can be reduced by making clear:

- what really is known? e.g. actual sales;
- what is unclear? e.g. competitor intentions; and
- what is being presupposed that might be questioned? e.g. that certain trends will persist.

We all react to the situation as perceived and perceptions are influenced not only by our mental representations (model) of the market but by fears and wishful thinking. What is needed is "tolerance for ambiguity." A marketing manager with tolerance for ambiguity has a willingness to suspend judgment and to recognize that a developing situation is at variance with preconceptions.

What should be sought at this stage is an interpretation that includes an assessment of **strengths** and **weaknesses**, **opportunities**, and **threats**. This is the so-called SWOT analysis. This then can be followed by matching strengths against opportunities, weaknesses against opportunities, weaknesses against strengths and strengths against threats. Part of this analysis should include a *vulnerability analysis*, which aims to identify where the organization is vulnerable such as an overdependence on a few big customers or just one industry. The *critical success factors* should also be listed. These are those things which, unless done well, could lead to failure such as the importance of distribution in the marketing of gasoline. In identifying these critical success factors, it is helpful to work back from thinking about the total business system needed and in particular the necessary conditions for being a success. It is also useful to look for the following defects in past strategic decision-making:[3]

1 failure to *anticipate* what should have been anticipated;
2 failure to *learn* when the facts "were staring the organization in the face";
3 failure to *adapt* to known changes in the external environment when such adaptation was necessary.

For example, business commentators claim that IBM in the 1980s failed to anticipate that when it gave up leasing its computers to customers, it would lose that continuous relationship with its customers which had previously kept IBM close to its market. Similarly, IBM failed to learn that phasing out old technology slowly so as not to disrupt sales of its oldest machines, led to a loss in leadership as rivals rushed to fill the gap. Finally, IBM failed to adapt to changes in the market when mainframe computers (the specialty of IBM) were losing their dominance.

We can also look at the organization a little more broadly to try to identify systemic defects as reflected in:

- errors persisting,
- solutions continuing to fail, and
- solutions coming too late.

Where errors persist in an organization, it suggests an absence of learning and too little self-criticism in the organization. When solutions continue to fail, it suggests either a failure in creativity or to correctly anticipate conditions in the real world. Finally, if solutions come too late, it suggests indecisiveness and a failure in knowing when or how to adapt to the external environment. This failure to adapt is often the most serious because it indicates that the firm is not monitoring the market.

Past decisions will not all turn out right and it is fallacious to assume that a bad outcome implies the decision was badly made since it may have been the most rationally defensible answer at the time. In any case, past strategies are seldom absolutely wrong or right but possess different degrees of imperfections. The various techniques, like BCG's, GE's business screen, and Porter's analysis (discussed below), plus various quantitative techniques, all help to order and bring out the implications of the data collected. But the role of formal techniques in planning like mathematical modeling, computer simulation, and decision analysis will always be debated. The criticisms revolve not around the complexity of the techniques but whether they are complex enough to cope with the real world. But this is to ask too much. These techniques are useful in offering frameworks, analogies and models that help structure a problem situation and reduce mental overload as well as being a protection from a complete degeneration into ad hoc responses.

CALCULATION OF THE PLANNING GAP

Target projections and reference projections

What do the "facts" suggest will be the future if the firm takes no action to change current strategies? Such a prediction is known as a "reference projection." A reference projection is the future that can be expected in the absence of planned change. A reference projection is compared with some "target projection" or the set of tentative goals. Realistic goals depend on what strategies are finally adopted and so must await the development of strategy.

The planning gap (performance gap) is the difference between the target and the reference projections:

Planning Gap (Performance Gap) = Target projection less reference projection.

The planning gaps identified will depend on which performances are of interest. At the highest level, it could be earnings per share, sales and market share or various financial indices like ROI. At the marketing level, it would be in terms of sales, market share, costs, market penetration, or various behavioral indices like buyer attitudes.

PIMS database

One source of information that has been useful to setting both target and reference projections is the PIMS database. The aim of PIMS is to assess the **P**rofit **I**mpact of **M**arket **S**trategies (PIMS): to relate the strategic characteristics of the business and its environment to operating results. The program originated as an internal planning study of the General Electric Co. in 1960. In the early 1970s it was extended to other companies, and in 1975 was set up as part of the Strategic Planning Institute. This is an independent, nonprofit organization concentrating on cross-sectional studies of many markets and industries in the United States and Europe. Participating firms complete a questionnaire covering a description of the business, operating results, markets, competition, industry data, and forecasts about market size, prices, and costs. The study claims that thirty-seven variables "explain" 80 percent of the variance in return on investment (ROI).

PIMS defines a business as embracing a specific product line that is reasonably homogeneous in terms of technology employed and market served. This is similar to the product market scope definition of business introduced in the last chapter and used throughout this book.

PIMS defines *served* market as being that segment of the market the firm elects to serve. Where a business serves several markets, participating firms complete a separate questionnaire for each market. PIMS, in analyzing these questionnaires seeks to answer the following questions:

- What is the typical profit rate for each type of business?
- What are the firm's likely operating results in the future, given certain strategic characteristics?
- What strategic changes are likely to help improve future operating results?
- What are the profit and cash flow implications of contemplated and future strategies?

In providing answers to such questions, PIMS helps management establish both target and reference projections. PIMS claims an impressive body of findings. The findings are paraded as important conclusions from empirical research but many are little more than truisms. Other findings are based on correlations and so do not distinguish between causal factors and those in a state of mere coexistence. Without supporting explanations and appropriate tests, the findings could tempt management to deal with symptoms rather than causes. Take as an example, the finding that a narrow breadth of product line in the early or middle stage of the product life cycle is less profitable than at the late stage. Would simply broadening the product line at the early or middle stage in itself lead to higher profitability? Another finding claims that relative market share and quality are partial substitutes for each other as far as determining ROI is concerned. Yet quality is measured in terms of the respondent's own opinion as to the perceptions of customers!

The second major component of PIMS is an individualized service to each participating company:

- Par reports show the ROI and cash flows that are typical for each business given its market, competition, technology, and cost structure. These par values help management in establishing target projections. Also identified are the major strengths and weaknesses that are regarded as accounting for a high or low par value relative to all businesses in the PIMS database.
- Sensitivity reports deal with the likely effects on ROI and cash flow of strategic moves, based on the experiences of other businesses making "similar" strategic moves from a "similar" point in a "similar" environment.
- Optimum strategy reports purport to predict the best combination of strategic moves for the firm. Such predictions are based again on the experiences of other businesses in "like circumstances."

Both the sensitivity reports and the optimum strategy reports suggest that PIMS has developed causal models. In fact the relationships are simply correlational. While strong correlational data can be suggestive of a causal link, any set of correlations that relates to the past may be a poor guide to the future when the environment is dynamic, with industry trends uncertain and competitor reactions unpredictable. There is also the problem of using ROI as the major investment criterion and the operational problems of insuring consistency in market definition. Nonetheless, the PIMS database has been found useful by management in performance analysis while the sensitivity and optimum strategy reports might be at least suggestive.

The V-curve

The so-called V-curve emanates from PIMS findings. As Figure 3.1 shows, many industries are characterized by just a few highly profitable firms. The very large firms in an industry tend to be profitable through scale and scope effects and wide market coverage. The small firms in an industry tend to be profitable by focusing on some particular market niche (small segment of the market) and developing specialized approaches to exploiting that niche. This is welcome news since small firms (those employing fewer than 100 employees) usually constitute the highest proportion of firms in every country. In Italy, for example, small firms provide two thirds of private-sector industrial employment. But the medium-size firms at the trough of the V-curve tend to exhibit no competitive advantage and so tend to have the poorest performance. Alan J. Zakon of BCG, once summed up the V-curve (*Business Week*, June 1, 1981) as follows: "Almost every industry is beginning to form what we call a V-Curve. You can live well as a small company or as a big company. And you can be successful with a low-cost product or a high value-added product," but he says, "It's getting tougher and tougher to live anywhere in between." This has led to the folk wisdom that a firm must choose between being a global operator or a niche player. In fact, of course, there are many successful companies in the middle as it is an inevitable stage in growth. It would be surprising anyway (given the entrance fees) if other than successful small companies were represented in the PIMS database.

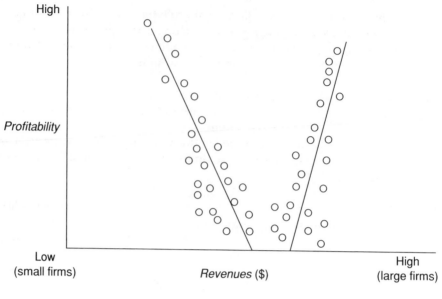

○ individual firms in the industry

Figure 3.1 The V-curve representation of an industry

PROBLEM DIAGNOSIS

If a firm has a large planning gap, we speak loosely of its having a problem. But more accurately, the planning gap is not the problem but the symptom of one; the recognition of a problem situation is not in itself the identification of a problem. We do not in fact discover a problem. We *diagnose* a problem which is to make a choice about how we are to formulate the problem. This, in turn, depends on what we believe would count as a solution to the difficulty encountered. Companies may, for example, define the problem as a problem of persuading the government to increase tariffs on their foreign competitor's products. Here the solution is viewed as increasing the firm's political muscle! The ability to solve a problem is not much help when the wrong problem has been diagnosed: problem diagnosis is what can distinguish the true professional from the mediocre.

We cannot even understand a problem without understanding what would count as a solution just as we cannot understand an objective without understanding what would count as the achievement of it. When faced with declining sales, the sales manager is apt to see the problem differently from the advertising manager, just as a failure to deliver to time and specification will be diagnosed differently depending on the professional asked. The operations researcher will look for poor inventory control; the systems and procedures expert will talk about complex procedures; the human resources manager may talk about a poor motivational climate and so on.

What all this means is that the problem that is addressed depends somewhat on which individual or group can make the problem, as they see it, count. But all management

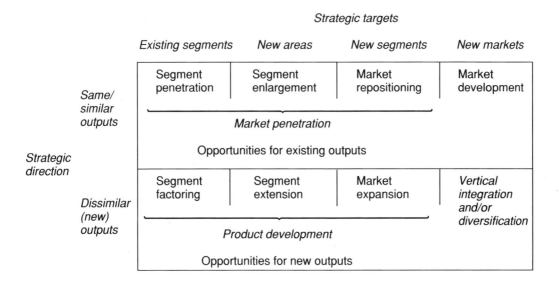

Figure 3.2 Growth options

Earlier it was said that a firm grows through changing the scope of its business; going into another business or broadening its technology, customer group or function served. But we can look at growth options in a more concrete way as in Figure 3.2.

- market penetration: same products/same markets;
- market development: same products/new markets;
- product development: new products/same markets; and
- diversification and vertical integration: new products/ and new markets.

Every major growth option comes down to changing the definition of the firm's business in that growth results in changes in the firm's technology or customer group or the function to which the firm caters.

Market penetration

A strategy may be chosen that simply seeks market penetration, that is, to sell to a higher percentage of buyers in the target market. A firm can have a high market penetration and a low market share and vice versa. Thus a firm may only sell to 20 percent of those in the market but its share is high because that 20 percent represents 80 percent of the demand. (This 80/20 rule is common in many markets.) By definition, with market penetration, the firm confines itself to the same product and the same market; only its customer size base has changed.

Market penetration can occur in three ways:

- segment penetration: same product and same segments;
- segment enlargement: same product but new areas; and
- market repositioning: same product but new segment.

The term segment refers to a market segment which is simply some subgroup of the market embracing a set of customers with a distinct subclass of want. A growth strategy that falls into the category of "segment penetration" seeks to sell more to the segment it already serves by catering to the segment better. It may do this by extending its distribution to attract more buyers, or using more promotion to convert from rivals or increase the level of usage with its existing customers. Segment penetration is usually the first strategy considered since it generally involves least risk.

If segment penetration seems to offer little promise, the firm might consider moving into new geographical areas. This is the "segment enlargement" strategy. Perhaps most companies first establish themselves in one part of the country and move out gradually to national coverage. If a market is defined in global terms then segment enlargement can be taken to cover expansion to other countries. One definition of the *global corporation* is one presenting roughly the same offering throughout the world. This contrasts with the *multinational* corporation which modifies its offering to local conditions. As the Japanese showed, there are many products that can be sold throughout the world, catering to the same segment (the "value for money" segment) by roughly the same offering.

Both segment penetration and segment enlargement can be achieved by the acquisition of competitors. Such *horizontal integration* is common in retailing, though elsewhere, as in the motor industry, chemicals and engineering, it has been undertaken more to take excess supply out of the market than to achieve segment penetration.

"Market repositioning" occurs when the product is promoted to appeal to a new segment of the market. Thus a brand of detergent that experienced declining sales, when promoted as a low suds detergent, had the decline reversed when it was repositioned as a powerful stain remover. The new segment, on occasions, may involve an entirely new group of consumers. For example, powdered soft drinks prior to the 1960s were just a children's drink. However, at least one company has successfully promoted the product to appeal to adults.

Market repositioning is frequently adopted to halt a decline in sales resulting from inroads by substitutes. Thus when sales of Bissell carpet sweepers were threatened by the newly introduced vacuum cleaner, the sweeper was repositioned in the market as a "handy, cordless, general picker-upper for use in between heavy use of the vacuum cleaner." The product still sells well.

Successfully repositioning a brand in the market is difficult and the success rate low. There are several reasons for this but the dominant one has to do with those in the market having already categorized the brand as catering to the original segment. If the brand was at one time well established in that segment, it will have acquired certain strong associations that are difficult to dispel when unwanted in the new segment. Yet there have been dramatic successes such as the Marlboro brand of cigarette which, at first, was unsuccessfully positioned as a woman's cigarette but repositioned to be given all the values associated with the cowboy of the West.

The problem of repositioning a brand becomes most acute when the brand has many loyal customers which the firm would like to retain. There is a danger in repositioning the brand of alienating the current set of customers. This commonly happens when magazines or newspapers try to reposition themselves to appeal to some different demographic group or readership group.

Market development

Market development occurs when a firm seeks new markets (new uses often for new users) for its product. In industrial marketing, finding new markets (applications) for products is commonly the major path to growth. But here are some examples in consumer marketing. Heinz not only sells its vinegar for flavoring food but sells Cleaning Vinegar as a floor, window, and carpet cleaning agent. Clorox used to sell its bleach purely as a laundry additive, now sells it to shine floors and windows. Arm & Hammer's baking soda, sold initially as a baking soda, is also sold as a refrigerator deodorizer, toothpaste, laundry detergent, and as a carpet and litter freshener. Procter & Gamble has repackaged diapers to sell to incontinent adults under the brand-name Attends. Mars sells its M&Ms not just as a candy but as a baking ingredient while Ralston Purina sells its Chex cereal as a party mix and Campbell's also sells its soups as sauces. Similarly, Dannon sells its yogurt as a substitute for eggs and oil in muffins while many car-wash products are repackaged dish-washing liquids. Many of these additional uses for the product had in fact been discovered by the consumer and the manufacturer was merely cashing in.

Market development in industrial markets generally presents no problems except for identifying the new applications. But in the case of consumer marketing, if the brand-name is used, there is always the danger of weakening the brand image in the sense that the benefits with which the brand is associated in the buyer's mind become hazy, vague and ambiguous. In any case, market development may fail if the approach is to make the one *identical* offering in all markets. Some modification of the offering is usually called for. Also there is a need for uniform quality standards since consumers will generalize from poor experience in one use of the brand to other uses.

"Jack of all trades, master of none" goes the old adage and the sentiment can also be expressed of a product since there is a tendency (unless the brand is bought for its versatility) on the part of consumers to view a multiuse brand as inferior to the brand that specializes in one application. It may even be that the additional uses are perceived as vulgarizing the original brand or consumers may have difficulty associating the brand with the additional uses. There is what psychologists call *functional fixedness* at work, in that when consumers get used to associating a brand with a particular function, this inhibits them from perceiving it as able to perform in some other function.

Sometimes taking the product into markets abroad is categorized as market development on the ground that the markets abroad are new areas with entirely new customers. While this is true, it seems more logical to reserve the term market development for developing new uses/functions for the product.

Product development

In the case of product development, the markets remain the same but entirely new products are developed to cater to them. Three forms of product development can be distinguished: segment factoring, segment extension, and market expansion.

1 *Segment factoring* occurs if the firm brings out a new product to compete side by side with its existing products in the same market segments. It is one way of meeting competition from possible substitutes. For example, it was an established soap manufacturer (P&G) that introduced detergents for washing clothes though it inevitably competed with its own sales of soap for that purpose. It could be argued that the new product developed a separate market or at least a distinct new segment of that market. This is true but not something necessarily recognized at the time.
2 *Segment extension* occurs if new product forms are developed for new geographical areas to suit local conditions just as nonalcoholic beers have been developed for certain Muslim countries.
3 *Market expansion* occurs if a new product is introduced for a segment that was previously ignored. For example, when the traditional Swiss watch manufacturers introduced a quartz watch, such a strategy was market expansion.

Vertical integration

New products/services for new markets may stem from vertical integration and/or diversification. Vertical integration occurs when a business acquires succeeding or preceding stages in the production and/or distribution of a product. The acquisition of preceding stages is backward integration (toward source of supply), while the acquisition of succeeding stages is forward integration (toward the final customer). In vertical integration the firm produces new outputs corresponding to the stages taken over. These new outputs can drastically change the nature of a business, as when a rubber manufacturer started to market products as diverse as footwear, upholstery, flooring, ebonite goods, and adhesives. Backward integration can improve coordination between supply and manufacture, guarantee sources of supply and achieve economies of scale and other cost savings. On the other hand, backward integration can impair flexibility, require large capital expenditure, lead to the underutilization of plant, place a heavy workload on top management and result in failure through lack of general management expertise.

Forward integration offers more control over the market and the possibility of reducing inventory costs while smoothing out sales and improving customer service. The disadvantages are similar to those of backward integration, with the added possibility of the firm competing directly with its own customers. Both backward and forward integration may leave the firm exposed to the fortunes of the one industry. In whatever way integration is effected, however, it constitutes a decision to substitute internal transactions (e.g. transfer pricing) for market transactions. It is also a common way of achieving technological and marketing convergence to produce a differentiated product.

Diversification

Although vertical integration is commonly regarded as a form of diversification, the two can be distinguished. In diversification the outputs (products) result from activities that are not vertically related to producing the original set of outputs. Vertical integration and diversification are also distinguished by the motives that lie behind their adoption. The motive for vertical integration is usually the desire to reduce costs and/or to gain greater control over production and/or distribution. It is a move toward greater self-sufficiency since vertical integration means fewer external dependencies. Diversification, on the other hand, is usually sought to exploit profitable market opportunities and to reduce the risk associated with the investment of a given sum.

There are several ways in which diversification can be brought about:

- Concentric diversification is the situation where the old and the new products are related in terms of both technology and markets. We can take as examples the radio manufacturer diversifying into tape recorders, or Elizabeth Arden into age-combating creams.
- Contiguous diversification is the situation where products are technologically dissimilar but markets related (e.g. skis and ski-wear) or alternatively products are technologically similar but markets dissimilar (e.g. pharmaceutical products and cosmetics).
- Conglomerate diversification is the situation where both technology and markets are radically different (e.g. detergents and automobiles). However, many conglomerates do have an underlying rationale. Thus General Electric would argue that its underlying rationale is high technology with supportive services. Sometimes though there can be doubt about the underlying rationale. Thus BIC's pens, razors, and lighters were all disposable and had marketing and production elements in common but its expansion into cheap perfumes, sold in supermarkets and drugstores in spray bottles, seems not to have much in common with its other products; the belief that there was a similar marketing rationale seems to stem from a lack of understanding of the market for perfume.

Both in the case of contiguous and conglomerate diversification, the use of the company name can weaken the company image as it weakens what product category the company stands for. Thus AT&T in the United States is strongly perceived as a phone company and the general public finds difficulty in regarding it as an expert in computers. Perhaps, Unilever is wise, in buying Fabergé and Elizabeth Arden, not to impose the Unilever name.

Whether new products are the result of integration or diversification, they can be added to the portfolio through a merger with another firm, the acquisition of another firm or through internal development. If the path chosen is internal development then extra capacity (supply) is added to the market. A merger occurs when the firms combine to form a single company (e.g. Burroughs and Sperry to form Unisys) and acquisition occurs when one firm purchases another. These two paths can be contrasted with the "joint venture" where one firm does not combine or buy the other but enters into some agreement to accomplish something together.

Joint ventures or alliances of various sorts are common in international marketing as a way of overcoming political and cultural barriers. Not only can these joint ventures bring together different competencies but they spread the risk and the cost of attempts to reach some market niche. Every American automobile manufacturer is engaged in a range of joint ventures with Japanese companies. Joint ventures like those in the car industry have resulted in making it impossible to categorize many products by country of origin.

Most acquisitions do not work out. Too much money is often paid for them while neither the buyer nor the acquired gain as a result. Perhaps Porter is right in arguing that the key to making successful acquisitions is to establish if there are synergies to be had. It is frequently claimed that, when a firm is in mature markets, it has no alternative but to diversify in a conglomerate way. This is a dubious claim. Both the Heinz company and Sara Lee are in mature food businesses but have managed to grow while nonetheless sticking to their core competencies.

Diversification has often led to disappointing results. Even with concentric diversification there is the problem of managing the new business particularly since what appears concentric may not be concentric enough to avoid serious problems, as occurred with Westinghouse's move into aircraft turbines from power-generation turbines. With respect to contiguous diversification, divergent marketing (particularly in the case of an industrial marketing firm embracing for the first time consumer marketing) can lead to a loss of customer understanding by top management while divergent production can mean the company has to think in terms of radically different frames of reference (e.g. in respect to quality) for the different businesses. Finally, conglomerate diversification can be a move away from the senior partner's thrust and core competencies and top management's field of expertise. In general, acquisitions can take an inordinate amount of time of top management particularly when there is a clash of corporate cultures as, say, between General Motors and Electronic Data Systems (EDS) run by Ross Perot. A common error is to believe that the acquired business is essentially like the existing business so that expertise is easily transferable.

Hold/defend

There are other investment objectives besides growth. There is the hold/defend objective as well as turnaround, harvesting, and divesting. The hold/defend is common when firms see no possibility of growth or are satisfied with their current position in the market. Thus General Motors, before the advent of Japanese competition, had been happy to hold onto its dominant market share: a much higher market share might have invited government interest! The aim is to retain existing customers while attracting enough of the new entrants into the market to replace those that leave. A hold/defend strategy may be adopted even if the market is growing since a firm may be happy with its market share or even with its sales level given the absence of resources to improve its relative position. In the most general terms, hold/defend strategies require the firm to keep abreast of competition by upgrading the firm's offering and matching whatever competition has to offer.

Turnabout/turnaround

The turnabout or turnaround objective is, as the name suggests, concerned with restructuring the organization or, more simply, "putting it on its feet" again. A firm in a situation that is ripe for a turnaround strategy typically faces persistent declines in market share, declining profit margins and working capital, increasing debt and probably high voluntary management turnover as it becomes clear that the firm is in trouble.

There are many reasons for a firm's decline. There are environmental factors like an economic slowdown; increasing competition; increased bargaining power of buyers; and sociocultural factors that affect demand. Any of these factors can reduce the appropriateness of a firm's strategies. There can also be just a general decline in management efficiency and concern. But, from a marketing point of view, a major reason for decline lies in moving away from the firm's thrust and core competencies with a proliferation of products that do not exploit what the firm has to offer. Alternatively, the business strategy itself becomes obsolete in that it no longer provides a basis for a competitive advantage.

In general, there are three general types of strategies that are undertaken to support a turnabout objective:

- the operational strategy of cost cutting and improving efficiency all round;
- the asset reduction strategy of getting rid of low-return, undervalued assets or units of the firm that are unrelated to the future strategy of the firm; and
- changing the direction of the firm to develop more revenue generating strategies.

Firms fairly close to breaking even (around 80 percent) can typically be turned around by cost cutting and this tends to be the most favored strategy. The danger with this strategy, though, is not just the effect on employee morale (and this can be serious) but that employees can be let go whose skills will be needed for future success. The fact is that all thrusts or core competencies in a final analysis reside in management and workers. It is easy not only to dilute thrusts and core competencies but sometimes even to destroy them through shortsighted redundancies. In any case, a firm that is, say, below 40 percent of breakeven usually has to consider some sort of asset reduction and revenue generating strategies through better marketing strategies.

Harvesting, divesting, and liquidating

"Harvesting" is a way of winding down a business by accepting a continuing decline in market share in exchange for an increase in net cash flow. Many a product that throws off no cash may in fact do so if all promotional support is withdrawn but only for so long since competitors rush in to exploit that absence of support. Thus GE pulled out of electron tubes by reducing promotional expenditure, raising prices, and so on to "squeeze" the business for all it was worth before finally getting rid of the business altogether. It is not always possible to harvest a business. Some products or businesses would continue to be a cash drain regardless of what support expenditure is withdrawn.

In such a situation, a firm will try to divest the business. Divestment carries the notion of an orderly approach to leaving the business:

- selling off the business, often to competitors;
- spinning off the business as an independent company with the firm perhaps still maintaining an interest; and
- partial divestment, for example, producing but no longer marketing the product.

But, of course, none of these may be viable options so the firm merely liquidates the business, selling off the firm's assets for whatever can be obtained.

An industry's competitive structure

Porter claims an industry's competitive structure, as reflected in the strength of just five forces, determines the state of competition (both the rules of competition and the strategies available for competing) and ultimately the profit potential of the industry.[4] The five forces that give rise to industry profitability are:

1   threat of entry;
2   degree of rivalry;
3   pressure from substitutes;
4   bargaining power of buyers; and
5   bargaining power of suppliers.

The five competitive forces together constitute the concept of "extended rivalry" in that all these forces offer competitive threats to the firm's level of profitability.

Threat of entry

The threat of entry into a business depends on the barriers to entry which are the drawbacks that new entrants face relative to incumbent firms. Barriers can be: economies of scale; proprietary product differences; brand identity; supplier/brand switching costs; capital investment in plant; access to distribution; the product differentiation advantages of incumbents; government policy; expected retaliation. Such barriers to entry should be distinguished from barriers to obtaining market share which is more related to rivalry.

Rivalry

Factors that make for high rivalry are: high exit barriers; high fixed costs; intermittent overcapacity; product differentiation; strong brand identities; high brand switching costs; high industry growth rate; industry concentration; informational complexity; diversity of competitors.

Pressure of substitutes

The threat of substituting some other product from another industry is increased by: the high performance of substitutes relative to their price; low switching costs and buyer propensity to substitute.

Bargaining power of suppliers

The factors that enter into the level of supplier power are: the absence or presence of substitutes; degree of concentration of suppliers; the cost of the supplier's product relative to the total purchases of the industry; the threat of forward integration by suppliers relative to the threat of backward integration by firms in the industry.

Bargaining power of buyers

The bargaining power of buyers increases with such factors as: volume bought; low costs in switching to substitutes; ability to integrate backward; buyer information about supplier costs; low buyer profits; price high in relation to total purchases.

Though Porter does not discuss the concept of power it is basic to his whole discussion of buyer and supplier power. Traditionally, power has been treated as the basis of influence with influence itself being regarded as the exercise of power. On this view, power in a relationship refers to the capacity that, say, "A" has to influence the behavior of "B", so that B does something he or she would not otherwise do. In a relationship between the firm and the buyer or the firm and the supplier, the firm is said to have most power when the supplier or the buyer are more dependent on the firm than the firm is on them. The firm will be less powerful vis-à-vis, say, the buyer when the seller's product fulfills no key function but is merely perceived as "icing on the cake" as was the original position in selling automatic teller machines (ATMs) to banks. Where there is an imbalance of power in a relationship, the more powerful may not exploit the situation (no more than a supplier may exploit a scarcity of his product in terms of extracting a higher price), since the exploited may go to great lengths to remedy the power imbalance.

When Porter argues that the five forces together form the *extended rivalry* facing the firm, it is an acknowledgment that each of these forces affects the industry's profit position. Thus a high threat of entry deters high prices and so reduces potential profits. High rivalry will decrease profits by obliging competitors to spend more on promotion and to be more cautious in increasing prices. The pressure of substitutes from other industries also affects profits by keeping prices down. Finally, powerful buyers can bargain more on prices as can more powerful suppliers.

Porter argues that the profit potential of the *individual* firm (as opposed to the industry) is a function of:

1 The profit potential of the industry which depends on the five forces already discussed.

2 The profit potential of the strategic group (within the industry) to which the firm belongs. This assumes an industry can be divided into strategic groups based on the similarity of their strategies. The profit potential of each strategic group will also depend on the same five competitive forces as specifically applied to each strategic group. There could be differences: for example, barriers to entry may be low generally in the industry (market as a whole) but high for some strategic group.

3 The firm's position within the strategic group since this could be advantageous to having higher than average profit. Therefore, low industry profitability does not mean that an individual firm in the industry cannot be highly profitable.

Generic strategies

Porter identifies just three generic strategies for coping with the five forces. The first strategy aims at overall cost leadership to produce a cost advantage. The danger of this strategy is that some technological innovation could wipe out the cost advantage, while an obsessive fixation with cost could result in an insensitivity to changing market wants.

The second strategy is that of differentiation whereby something unique is offered to the market. Given some market value in that uniqueness, it is a barrier to entry, shields the firm from rivals and substitutes, increases the dependency of customers and provides the possibility of muting supplier power through the size of its purchases. The risks associated with the strategy are either that the differentiation may be imitated (the advantage is not sustainable) or that a rival's cost (price advantage) is too great to be overcome by the benefits of the differentiation.

The third strategy is segmentation where cost leadership or a differentiated offering applies only to a part or segment of the market.

Critique. Porter's framework draws from industrial economics and is valuable to creating awareness of the possible forces of resistance to be overcome in developing an overall competitive stance. But several questions might be raised. Why only five forces? Porter believes that other forces that might come to mind are in fact reflected in the five forces. Thus he even views government action as manifesting itself through these five forces. But could not such an argument be used to justify having fewer than five forces? Some marketers already claim that they take account of supplier power when fixing profit margins, while inroads by substitutes are acknowledged in determining market potential and likely market growth. Porter would rightly argue that there should be explicit recognition of each of the five forces if management is to judge profit potential, and that these five factors form a set of mutually exhaustive and exclusive categories for management's purposes.

Are the generic strategies of overall cost leadership, differentiation and segmentation also exhaustive and mutually exclusive? If a firm seeks a competitive advantage by introducing a new-to-the-world product, or seeks to preempt competition by, say, monopolizing supplies or makes alliances with other firms to shut out competition, into which of the three categories do we place these moves? It is also not clear that there are three distinct strategies in that it is difficult to think of product differentiation that does not appeal to just a segment of the market or, if it appeals to the whole market, it is likely to come with a price tag that many in the market are just not willing to pay. In either case differentiation implies segmentation. Porter now refers to just two generic strategies: cost leadership and differentiation. Marketers would be tempted to say that both are paths to segmentation in that there can be price segments and there can be segments based on nonprice differentiation.

Porter suggests a choice must be made between seeking overall cost leadership and differentiation because the pursuit of differentiation is usually incompatible with cost leadership in that differentiation is apt to raise costs. However, there are many cases where a firm has gained differentiation through being the technological leader yet has gained overall cost leadership through economies of scale and experience curve effects.

A more vexing issue is the extent to which Porter's system is operational. Although he speaks of the need to assess the relative power of the five forces at work, he has no operational measure of power. The relative power of the firm vis-à-vis each of the five forces depends presumably on which side has most control over the means that are critical for the attainment of the other's goals. This type of discussion is absent from Porter's work and measurement problems are ignored. There is a conceptual vagueness about many of his ideas, while some soft theories are paraded as hard facts. Yet there are few who would deny the usefulness of what he has to say.

Porter's evolutionary stages

Porter identifies three stages in an industry's evolution:

1 emerging industries
2 transition to industry maturity
3 declining industries.

These stages have much in common with the product life cycle stages discussed later in product management (Chapter 9). But here we focus purely on the Porter analysis for the insights it provides to marketing management.

Emerging industries

Porter follows the economist's practice of using the term industry rather than "market" though he defines an industry as "a market in which similar or closely related products are sold to buyers." When an industry is emerging, there is high uncertainty in the market. *Sellers* worry over likely technological developments, what the market really wants, possible applications, while there is uncertainty over experience curve effects, distribution, standardization possibilities, what markets to enter and the difficulties in establishing the requirements for success. On the other hand, *buyers* are uncertain over product performance, potential applications, comparative brand advantages, and the likelihood of technological obsolescence.

Porter claims that a firm in an emerging industry must judge the extent to which it can shape the five forces to its advantage. Thus a firm may erect barriers to entry through cost leadership; hasten the rate of conversion from substitutes by reducing the fear and cost of switching products; try to reduce rivalry by encouraging acceptance of the "rules of the competitive game"; and decrease buyer power by reducing buyer uncertainties and supplier power by securing long-term sources of supply.

Transition to maturity

In the transition to industry maturity there is slowing growth, falling profit margins, excess capacity, intense competition and less product innovation, with a shift in focus to nonproduct aspects or benefits of the offering (for example, product image and service). Customers themselves become more knowledgeable about the product and this tends to increase their power vis-à-vis the individual seller.

Porter lists errors commonly made in the transition to industry maturity. One error lies in sacrificing market share for short-run profits by not reacting to aggressive promotions by rivals. Another error lies in neglecting market penetration and market development to focus exclusively on product development. Finally, intense competition tempts firms into adopting ill-focused strategies that lack the resources necessary for success.

The transition to industry maturity should be a transition to a more efficient, better coordinated, tighter controlled organization where market share is increased not so much by converting from rivals but by retaining current customers, increasing their level of business and attracting new entrants to the market. More specifically, market share is likely to be enhanced either by catering more closely to segment wants (for example, the focus on the low-tar segment of the cigarette market by Philip Morris with its Merit brand) or by developing new segments (for example, the light beer segment that was developed by Miller in the United States).

Declining industries

Industries decline as wants change, better substitutes come along or demographic trends (for example, in the birth rate) depress certain markets (for example, the market for baby products). Porter claims that there is a danger of not anticipating the onset of the decline and instead undertaking a war of attrition with rival firms.

If a firm decides not to divest, it must check that it has the competitive strengths to remain in those segments where demand is least affected: there are usually pockets (niches or small segments) of steady demand in most declining markets. Porter suggests that a firm should, depending on its strengths vis-à-vis competition, seek market share dominance or the dominance of some particular niche. If neither of these is desirable, feasible or commercially viable, the firm may find it wise to divest.

Fragmented industries

A fragmented industry is defined as an industry where there are no dominant firms either in market share or in technology: there is no market or technological leader. At any stage in evolution an industry can be fragmented. Thus, fragmentation is not a stage in industry evolution but Porter considers it an important subcategory from the point of view of developing a competitive position. Porter points out that there are two strategic options open to a firm in a fragmented industry: either it can seek partial consolidation of the industry or it must learn to cope with fragmentation. Partial consolidation can be brought about by:

- low-cost leadership: for example, BIC in ball-point pens;
- technological breakthrough: for example, the Charles River Breeding Laboratories with their process of developing disease-free laboratory animals;
- making enough acquisitions in the industry to develop enough critical mass to bring about a de facto partial consolidation; and
- differentiation sufficiently distinctive for others in the industry to standardize on it: for example, IBM in personal computers.

Porter acknowledges that partial consolidation is not always possible. Sometimes a firm must learn to cope with fragmentation either through low-cost efficiency or by increasing value-added. Efficiency seeks a "no frills" operation and close control over performance and cost while increased value-added may be accomplished by providing additional services.

Critique. In relating evolutionary stage to strategy recommendations, Porter views evolutionary stage as considerably restricting the options open to the planner. Yet the evidence in support of the relationship between evolutionary stage and the restricted set of strategic options is not set out, as if the relationship is self-evident. There is in any case the question of whether the strategic options discussed are exhaustive and mutually exclusive.

In respect to the emerging stage, Porter does not pretend to provide exhaustive, mutually exclusive strategies for shaping the five forces but the five forces can be related to his three generic strategies, for example:

- ease of entry: cost leadership could be a barrier here;
- substitution: a firm could reduce the cost of switching;
- rivalry: a firm could provide leadership so others follow;
- buyer power: a firm could reduce buyer power by seeking a critical advantage; and
- supplier power: a firm could reduce supplier power by having multiple suppliers or long-term contracts.

The strategies recommended for the *evolutionary* stage of transition to maturity are not exhaustive. For example, Porter does not consider the possibility of market development, that is, finding new uses/applications for the product nor does he appear to consider the possibility of repositioning in the market or marketing in some new area. Nor are Porter's strategies, of opening up new segments or catering to segments better, mutually exclusive in that both new segments and catering to a segment better could be via lower prices. The strategies for the decline stage are also not exhaustive in that products can be revitalized, for example, by providing new reasons for buying (e.g. bicycles and health) or innovation (e.g. thin steel revitalized the market for steel in packaging).

Porter deals only with strategies corresponding to evolutionary stage or fragmentation. He does not define the business systems required to exploit the strategies. This needs to be said since all strategies are not available to the individual firm; only those firms that have the thrust and core competencies plus the business system suited to exploiting the strategy.

EVALUATION OF STRATEGIES

Management evaluates strategies before and after implementation. In either case strategies are evaluated against criteria. In general terms, the evaluative criteria *after* implementation revolve around the strategy's effectiveness and reliability. Thus a strategy is effective if it achieves its goals and it is reliable if it is able to do so consistently.

In evaluating strategies as a basis for selecting one, the criteria should help predict a strategy's likely effectiveness and reliability after implementation. This is seldom a straightforward process since facts are often uncertain, values and priorities often in dispute, while the stakes can be high with the decision urgent and under time pressure. A further complication arises from the fact that the key marketing decisions (the sort being discussed in this chapter) are taken by top management with the involvement of marketing management.

Given the many uncertainties, strategy choice is not just a matter of logic alone: proposed strategies are not ruled out by logic alone. If the marketing view is to have any influence, a persuasive case has to be made by marketing management. In other words, top management must "buy" marketing's solution and this means persuasion. This does not mean that good rational arguments are not important but simply that the result of any debate over alternative courses of action is a decision but reaching a decision is not the same as reaching a conclusion to a deductive argument. The fact is that, regardless of effort, the final choice does not rule out the possibility of one of the rejected alternatives being much better: certainty cannot be achieved by just method. There is also the possibility of biases in evaluation such as seeking only confirmatory evidence for some favored strategy, or interpreting ambiguous evidence to fit presuppositions. If early information supports a favored position, information search is likely to cease, while if it does not, then search is likely to continue.

If difficulties are not immediately anticipated and current strategies are not in crisis, it is hard to suggest anything innovative as it would seem to be "rocking the boat." Yet planned change during "good times" is less pressure-driven and less starved of resources than when the firm is reacting to adverse events. A firm that stands still in changing times is a firm that becomes less and less adapted to its environment. In any case, every proposed strategy should be evaluated for desirability, practical feasibility and commercial viability.

Desirability

The first step in evaluation is to think about goals. What would count as success? A common error is not to think sufficiently broadly about goals. A common reason for irreconcilable conflicts among parties to any decision lies in one party having an extremely narrow set of goals. Goals are typically multiple and conflicting so there is a need to establish priorities or, alternatively, set some of the goals as constraints or semi-constraints. Debate is to be encouraged to avoid "groupthink." With groupthink there is a collective sense of not needing outside opinions or ideas; a sense of collective certainty, invulnerability and an illusion of unanimity. These are just the conditions leading to an inadequate consideration of goals and of alternatives.

Under the heading of desirability we might ask the following:

- Does the proposed strategy promote objectives? Any proposed strategy must contribute to the company's mission and goals, cohere with investment objectives and, in the case of the marketing strategy, exploit the firm's thrust. But there will be other goals and values that need to be considered, since the single-minded pursuit of just these goals may give rise to undesirable side effects. This is where the values of management enter into the evaluative process. Thus sometimes management wish to avoid certain involvements (e.g. like businesses where there are strong unions) or have no taste for reconciling the interests of diverse groups like the government, customers and unions.
- Is the degree of risk acceptable? Risk here is the probability of earning less than what is sought and the magnitude of possible losses. Measuring the degree of risk associated with the various proposed strategies is still largely a matter of judgment. There can never be certainty, since the relationship between options (strategies) and outcomes (results) is never entirely clear when long-term consequences are influenced by competitive reactions and changing buyer tastes. In general, the more the firm moves away from its existing markets and expertise, the more risky the strategy.
- Does the strategy promote portfolio balance? There is a need for a balance in a firm's product portfolio. BCG was right to draw attention to the dangers of having a portfolio of just cash cows, just stars, or dogs.
- Is the investment that will be required acceptable? The investment requirement has to be estimated. There are the initial entry-level costs and the costs of securing market share. Start-up or entry costs can usually be estimated but more problematic is the money needed to achieve some degree of success. Even a firm such as the tobacco giant R. J. Reynolds, in diversifying into food, transportation, and packaging, frequently underestimated the cash needs of its acquisitions to allow them to grow. If a strategy is desirable, there must be a *strategic fit* between the strategy and behavior in the market; between strategy and internal capabilities and resources and, finally, a fit between the strategy and the higher level plans since any strategy is part of

some hierarchy of plans. But even if all these "fits" were in place, it would merely show that means suit ends. This is not enough in itself since it does not take account of possible undesirable side effects (dysfunctional consequences). Unintended side effects should be considered though they are typically difficult to predict. Managers tend to be overconfident when confidence in a strategy is high and so seek evidence for the strategy rather than against.

Practical feasibility

The problem of feasibility receives too little attention in discussions on strategy formulation. Although it is accepted that judging feasibility involves judgment and an imaginative recreation of the likely problems encountered in implementing the strategy, it is seldom emphasized enough how important is experience in judging feasibility. Think about an area in which you are *not* likely to be an expert, namely military strategy. In the Gulf War strategies had to be evaluated. But this required intimate knowledge as to the capabilities and consequently the role of the air force, the navy, the tanks, and the ground troops. In addition, we would need to know about the likely behavior of troops and the enemy under various assumed conditions as well as about specific problems like the logistics involved in getting food and equipment to the front. Similarly the feasibility of a marketing strategy necessitates knowing about the role of product, price, promotion and distribution in the design of an offering; knowing about the likely behavior of customers, and competitors if the strategy is adopted and knowing a good deal about the specifics of marketing like distribution possibilities.

Commercial viability

Success in a market can never be guaranteed if success involves challenging goals. There is always, too, the question of trade-offs since trade-offs are tied to values. Thus in a turnabout strategy the effect on profit might be good but the effect on morale might be disastrous while a willingness to do such trade-offs reflects top management's values. Under the heading of commercial viability, we ask the following:

- Will the strategy yield the profit/cash flow sought? Estimates of potential payoffs can range all the way from what is little more than prophecy to predictions of sales, and costs and profits based on hard evidence.
- Does the strategy contribute to minimizing likely competitive retaliation? The selection of any strategy is accompanied by the selection of rivals with whom the firm will do battle. The question arises whether the strategy minimizes the potential for competitive retaliation by, say, preempting competition or by avoiding provocation by seeking market niches that do not challenge the giants.
- What are the impediments to achieving commercial goals? This requires us to think about obstacles that may be in the way of success and to plan to get round them.

We make decisions about strategy on the basis of beliefs about the outcomes of each option in relation to goals. Errors occur when we do not consider all the goals of interest or we do not examine enough options or objectively weigh up the evidence. Weighing up the evidence is difficult since the process can be so distorted by wishful thinking; which particular bit of evidence is examined first and by stress. When every option considered seems inadequate, the quality of decision-making deteriorates as anxiety leads to diminished search. In any case, evidence cannot be measured as we would a piece of string so subjective judgment is involved. Although we aim to select optimum strategies (where any alternative would be less good) or at least to select optimal strategies (where those selected cannot be bettered but might be equaled) such is usually beyond us. In fact, no adequate strategy might be forthcoming, in which case it is "back to the drawing board" to redefine the firm's business or rethink the reasonableness of our goals.

When no particular strategy ranks higher than the others on each and every criterion, some system is needed for ranking them. Table 3.2 illustrates how this might be done in the same way as in assessing attractiveness and industry position in Chapter 2. Column 1 lists the evaluative criteria used to choose one of four paths to growth. Column 2 weights each criterion on its relative contribution to objectives. Column 3 rates each of the four options on a scale of 1–3 reflecting the importance of each option relative to the criterion. Column 4 gives column 2 multiplied by column 3. The sums or overall

Table 3.2 Choosing a path to growth

Evaluative criteria	Criterion weight	Rating of growth options[a]				Points awarded			
		A	B	C	D	A	B	C	D
(1)	(2)	(3)				(4)			
Objectives	1	1	1	2	3	1	1	2	3
Risk	1	3	2	1	1	3	2	1	1
Values	necessary condition	✔	✔	✔	✔				
Balanced portfolio	1	1	3	1	1	1	3	1	1
Financial investment	1	2	1	1	1	2	1	1	1
Practical possibility	necessary condition	✔	✔	✔	✔				
Potential payout	1	2	2	1	1	2	2	1	1
Compatibility between firm's business system and requirements for success	4	3	2	1	1	12	8	4	4
Minimize likely competitive retaliation	1	1	2	2	1	1	2	2	1
	10					22	19	12	12

[a] A = Market penetration
   B = Market development
   C = Product development
   D = Diversification

scores of each of the growth options show option "A" (market penetration) as receiving the highest score.

Such an evaluation system is subject to criticism. In the first place, different evaluators weight and rate differently so the reliability of the procedure can be questioned. Also each criterion in column 1 is not necessarily completely independent of the others as assumed in the process. Where a particular criterion (for example, risk) manifests itself in several criteria, this leads to its being overrepresented in the overall score. There is finally the assumption that the numbers are just additive in a linear way. But nonetheless it provides a useful basis for discussion. The approach, known as the *multiattribute model* of decision-making, is also taken into account in consumer decision-making; we will comment on it further in the next two chapters.

CONTINGENCY PLANNING

Behind every plan are assumptions that need to be realized if the plan is to succeed. Certain things are assumed to remain constant like government policy or certain trends are assumed to persist like the increasing cost of healthcare. A good number of these assumptions are constantly being invalidated by a rapidly changing environment. Where different sets of assumptions are equally tenable, contingency plans are needed. More typically, firms allow for certain of the major assumptions being invalid and so have contingency plans in reserve. More and more firms see the need to develop contingency plans, just as the military do because the need there is so much more obvious.

Monitoring the plan's assumptions as it is put into effect is a major check on the plan's continuing validity. When assumptions are no longer valid, plans need to be revised or previously devised contingency plans put into effect. But plans in practice need to be modified all the time while planning must relate to today's decisions if it is to be treated seriously by operational managers: long-term planning should be tied to guiding today's decisions.

THE MARKETING PLAN AND MARKETING STRATEGY

Any firm that has adopted a systematic approach to planning will have followed something like the sequence of stages discussed in this chapter. But, to repeat, following a sequence of stages is like following some computer program; it does not bring forth a successful strategy in itself as this depends on the data entering the program. The key lies in effectively answering the following questions:

1 What should be the content of the objectives?
2 What is the most relevant information to collect?
3 What is the correct problem diagnosis?
4 What strategies should be considered given our objectives?
5 What evidence is relevant to the evaluation of proposed strategies?

The typical annual marketing plan includes: a historical review/situation analysis; company objectives and marketing goals; the marketing budget and the core of the plan which is the marketing strategy itself. We focus now on that strategy since filling in the content of that strategy is what most of this book is about. An outline marketing strategy is shown as Appendix 3.1.

Marketing strategy is the broad conception of how product, price, promotion and distribution are to function in a coordinated way to overcome resistances to meeting marketing goals. In other words, the content of a marketing strategy shows how the proposed key features of the firm's offering (product/service, price, promotion and distribution) are intended to achieve marketing and company objectives. In particular any marketing strategy should be directed by the mission of creating customer good-will since such goodwill leads to trust and trust to loyalty and so on along the lines shown in Figure 3.3.

Although there is no general agreement as to what exactly goes into a marketing strategy, the following can be offered as a guide: statement of objectives; the investment objective for the brand; the competitive strategy; the core (segmentation) strategy; the brand support strategies; the strategic rationale.

1 Statement of objectives. Objectives preface the strategy as a reminder of the end results to be achieved. Marketing objectives typically reflect expectations in terms of sales, market share and other performance measures.
2 Investment objectives for the brand and path to growth (if appropriate). Investment objectives need to be given as this is the basic guide for the allocation of resources. Where the investment objective is growth, a statement of the growth path signals likely problems ahead. Thus "market repositioning" suggests there may be a problem in getting the product viewed in the new way.
3 Competitive strategy. Market success requires that sufficient demand exists at the prices envisaged; that the firm has what it takes to meet consumer demands; and, last but not least, that the firm has an edge over competition for sufficient numbers in the market. The marketing strategy needs to state what edge it has over competition and how competition will be beaten.
4 Core (segmentation) strategy. The segmentation strategy is regarded as the core strategy for all the other strategies that comprise the marketing strategy. This is because all other strategies build on it as it both defines the target group of customers and the buying inducement. Here target customers are identified so the firm can choose appropriate channels to reach them and choose appropriate promotions to persuade them. The buying inducement is what positions the product/service advantageously vis-à-vis its competitors. This buying inducement stems ideally from the firm's thrust and competencies and reflects the brand's competitive advantage. The buying inducement should preferably have criticalness, that is, be both of central importance yet unique to the firm. If a firm is to fit the marketing environment better than its rivals, the firm must have something which sufficient numbers of buyers prefer; sufficient to result in superior market performance.
5 (Brand) support strategies. The segmentation strategy must be supported by appropriate product design, promotion, pricing and distribution. The key elements in the

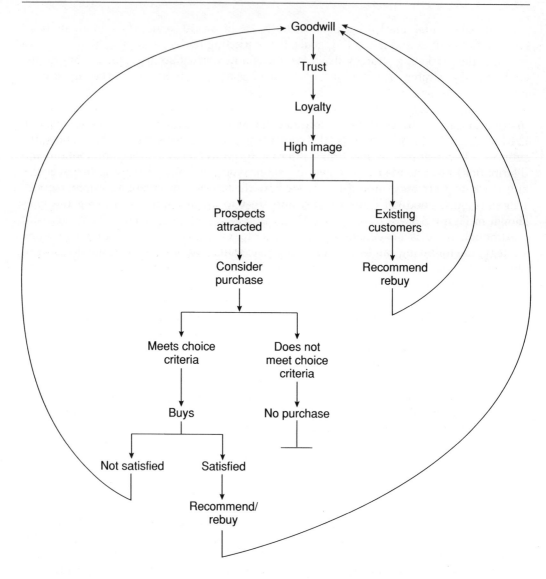

Figure 3.3 Marketing strategy mission

strategies of promotion, pricing and distribution form the (brand) support strategies. However, the term "support" can be misleading if it conveys the notion of being merely contributory rather than necessary to market success. On the contrary, promotion, pricing and distribution are each capable of being the basis of the brand's buying inducement.

6 Strategic rationale. It is most important to justify what is being proposed. This is the strategic rationale statement that provides the empirical evidence or the theoretical

support for each element of the strategy and its overall stance. This rationale should show, too, that the strategy is both coherent and comprehensive. By coherence is meant not just logical consistency but how the individual elements of the strategy interrelate so as to provide each other with mutual support.

A marketing strategy is composed of a set of substrategies concerned with competition, segmentation, promotion, pricing and distribution. An older view is to focus on the "marketing mix" of product, price, promotion, and distribution. Every market has its own logic whereby excellence on one element of the mix, whether product, price, promotion, or distribution, is often a necessary condition for success. Key elements might be advertising in the case of analgesics, distribution in the case of gasoline, pricing in the case of basic commodity products and product performance in the case of machine tools. Knowing the key factor in the marketing mix can be crucial in thinking about marketing strategy since it means knowing what to emphasize. Thus Volkswagen's initial success in the United States was based on the recognition that the provision of service facilities was the key. But though the concept of the marketing mix is thus a useful one, it cannot be a substitute for strategic thinking as it would suggest that the only problem in marketing was getting the right balance among the mix of factors. One study argues that the four mix factors are not mutually exclusive as traditionally defined and proposes a tighter classification on the ground that what is being classified are essentially four marketing functions, namely:[5]

- configuration: developing something valued by the buyer;
- valuation: determining the compensation and sacrifice demanded;
- facilitation: making the offer available; and
- symbolization: bringing the offer to the attention of the prospect and influencing purchase.

INTERNATIONAL MARKETING STRATEGIES

Global markets

More and more companies are trying to compete worldwide rather than confining themselves to just the domestic market. The reasons have to do with more homogeneity of wants worldwide as a result of exposure through the media to a cosmopolitan culture; the lowering of barriers against trade and foreign investment; cheap computing; travel access and other factors that make the world seem smaller and more homogeneous. Also more parts of the world look inviting because of economic growth. Thus Indonesia may only have an income per head of under $600 per annum but it is increasing while the top 10 percent spend as much as the average consumer in Portugal.

One of the sharpest debates in recent years has been over the extent to which a global marketing strategy is possible or desirable. In other words can the world be regarded as just the domestic market writ large, with similar segments as the domestic market? Certainly, there are standardized products that sell all over the world. The most prominent example is Coca-Cola, which is truly a global brand. But also with products like drugs and technical products, whether radios, airplanes, tanks, or dyes, the needs are much the same across the globe. The photocopying need is the same in Europe as it is in Africa and the Far East. In the case of certain high-class luxury products (e.g. Rolex watch) there is no need even to change the advertising. Consumers everywhere buy images of wealth and status. It is also true, as the Japanese showed, there is a world market for standardized, engineered or electronic products that perform well on the basic functions and sell at a relatively low price. The Gillette Co. sells the same Sensor razor in seventeen countries of the world in virtually the same way.

While there are many examples of the same product being sold throughout the world, it is also true that products often have to be modified to suit the local market. Thus even in Europe, the French prefer a top-loading washing machine while the British prefer front loaders; the Germans prefer their machines to have high spin speeds while the Italians have a preference for lower spinners. But it could be claimed here that such differences amount to nothing more than different countries falling more heavily into one market segment rather than another. After all there are strong regional and sub-cultural differences within every country.

There remain differences in food tastes throughout the world. Britain's most popular cookie, McVitie's Digestive, is not a success in the United States, no more than America's soft cookie is a success in Britain. While canned soups sell well in the United States, they do not do so in Brazil. Companies selling food products typically allow for local tastes. Thus Nestlé has over 200 blends of Nescafé to cater to different tastes throughout the world. Even McDonald's uses a less sugary sauce in Paris for putting on its Big Mac. Established food habits are fairly cultural and not easy to change. Where success has come about, it has not been "you change to my coffee from yours" but by pushing an entirely new concept like Coca-Cola.

Although one strategy is to manufacture where it is cheapest and sell the same standard offering throughout the world, an alternative strategy, much more congenial to most firms, is to tailor their offering to specific segments: to exploit, rather than seek to overcome, national differences. Many of the most successful companies in international markets set up overseas operations not to achieve low cost but to get closer to the customer and their success is not based on low prices but by selling innovative new products or services.

If product standardization throughout the world is often an impossible goal, there is an even greater problem with the rest of the marketing mix. Pricing is difficult to standardize because of fluctuating exchange rates, local duties and differences in competition. Advertising is particularly difficult to standardize though there are notable exceptions like the Marlboro cigarette advertisement. Advertising that goes down well in the United States does not do so in Japan. There are indeed different national types of advertising. The British favor humor and word play to persuade; Germans favor putting across cold facts; the French use sex or style; the Spanish melodrama and the Italians like to shout and sing in praise of the brand. In any case, the buying inducement can vary. P&G's buying inducement for its "All Cheer" detergent in the United States is that one can use it in all temperatures. But in Japan, they are only interested in its being used in cold water. Similarly, its Pampers, disposable diapers, were initially marketed in Thailand on the basis of convenience but in Thailand this was not a socially appropriate motive (suggesting mothers were more interested in their comfort or leisure than their babies) so the advertising was changed to a "nighttime-use" theme suggesting the diaper kept babies more comfortable at night. The new theme has been a success.

Strategies in international markets and the home base

There are a number of generic strategies that might be adopted for international markets. A firm could have a narrow product line catering to just one or two markets throughout the world. P&G did this in Japan with detergents and diapers but this proved too narrow to sustain their operation there. This was because other competitors lowered their prices and increased their advertising. They were willing to lose money on these items to drive P&G out of the markets as they had other products in the markets on which to make their profits.

A contrasting strategy is to have a broad product line to sell globally or sell to just a few countries or to produce and market only in those countries which protect local industries. There are other combinations and a great deal of judgment is involved in deciding which is most appropriate. But the problem in international strategy that has attracted the most interest is the choice between two models of how the home company and its subsidiaries are related.

One model throws up the image of the dominant home company with its satellites tightly controlled around the world. The other model is of the truly global firm, manufacturing where costs are lowest and operating with more or less equal partners throughout the world; described by one writer as like "stateless world citizens independent of their original nationalities." The aim here is to free each national market from central bureaucracy, with authority dispersed so that local needs become paramount.

Porter opts for something roughly approaching the first model rather than the second since he stresses the importance of the home base as crucial to a firm's competitiveness abroad. This view contrasts with the claim that the globalization of markets is making nations less important. Porter is asserting that the opposite is more likely to be true as he claims that national conditions play a key role in global market access. To Porter, the advantages of the home market are what makes a firm successful abroad. While expanding abroad will help make a company more competitive, the key to its success still comes from its national base. In his most recent book, Porter argues that four broad attributes are the attributes of the nation that is home to an internationally successful industry.[6] These four factors relate to the question of why particular industries in particular nations obtain and sustain a competitive advantage against competitors in the rest of the world. They are described as follows by Porter as:

1 *Factor Conditions*: the nation's position in factors of production, such as having the skilled labor or infrastructure, necessary to compete in a given industry.
2 *Demand conditions*: the nature of the home market demand for the industry's product or service.

3 *Related and supporting industries*: the presence or absence in the nation of supplier industries and other related industries that are internationally competitive.
4 *Company strategy, its structure and industry rivalry*: the conditions in the nation governing how companies are created, organized, and managed, as well as the nature of domestic rivalry.

If Porter is right, and a company aspires to be dominant internationally, it should belong to the nation where that industry is dominant so the four factors are in alignment. However, these four factors are simply an orienting model, in that they orient the reader to a useful classification of success factors. There have been companies that rose above the deficiencies of the home nation as Japan did after World War II. Porter's research simply illustrates his thesis rather than test it. In fact, the four factors can be shown to be Porter's five factors discussed earlier but reinterpreted to fit in with the goal of explaining why particular industries in particular nations obtain and sustain a competitive advantage against competitors in the rest of the world.

NOTES

1 Hutt, Michael D., Reingen, Peter H., and Ronchetto, John R. (1988) "Tracing Emergent Processes in Marketing Strategy Formation," *Journal of Marketing*, 52 (January).
2 Mintzberg, Henry (1993) *The Rise and Fall of Strategic Planning*, New York: The Free Press.
3 Cohen, Eliot A. and Gooch, John (1990) *Military Misfortunes: The Anatomy of Failure in War*, New York: The Free Press.
4 Porter, Michael E. (1980) *Competitive Strategy: Techniques for Analyzing your Business and Competitors*, New York: Free Press; (1985) *Competitive advantage*, New York: Free Press.
5 Van Waterschoot, Walter and Van den Bulte, Christophe (1992) "The 4P Classification of the Marketing Mix Revisited," *Journal of Marketing*, 56 (October).
6 Porter, Michael E. (1990) *The Competitive Advantage of Nations*, New York: Free Press.

APPENDIX 3.1   SPECIMEN (HYPOTHETICAL) MARKETING STRATEGY

Relating to Benson's corporate objective of seeking growth via contiguous diversification to meet unfilled consumer wants (in this case for a higher quality nut).

Benson's Mixed Nuts
Overall Marketing Objectives and Strategy

A. Marketing objectives
1 *Directional mission*. Diversification to achieve a more balanced product portfolio and an increase in earnings per share from — to — in the next three years.
2 Specific goals in the next three years for Benson's Mixed Nuts are:
   (a) volume sales of 3 million cases on completion of national expansion (1994–1995);
   (b) sustained growth in volume of 5 percent per annum.

B. Product strategy
Future growth in earnings via a policy of new product development and diversification into the snack food market.

C. Competitive strategy
Leapfrog via technological differential advantage of crisp-dryness of Benson's mixed nuts. We anticipate Benson's will take away volume

12 percent from "A" brand
8 percent from "B" brand
6 percent from "C" brand

Each of the brands A, B, and C is expected to respond by an imitative competitive strategy. We believe we need to anticipate such action by maintaining "taste" leadership in the segment.

D. Core (segmentation) strategy
(i) *Customer targets.*
    (a) Marketing effort will be directed at the upper income segment of the snack food market who are buyers of nuts and seek a higher quality product.
    (b) Within the quality segment, Benson's will be marketed as suitable for all established uses in food preparation and special occasions like dinner parties.
(ii) *The buying inducement.* Benson's will be positioned in the market as the brand with a revolutionary new crisp-dry flavor suitable for all occasions. This will be the use function or end result benefit stressed.

E. (Brand) support strategies
The key elements in Benson's marketing support program are as follows:

(i)   *Promotional strategies* will mainly develop consumer insistence for Benson's via national advertising to support the claim that Benson's has the revolutionary new flavor. The dollar weight of promotions expenditure will be directed at the high income/heavy multiple user category. Advertising will occur all year round, though it will be heavier in peak buying months during May–September.
(ii) Temporary *price* reductions will be used to stimulate trial and purchase continuity.
(iii) *Distribution and service.* Distribution will be direct to 6,000 major wholesalers. A support system for the wholesalers will seek to train their salespeople, offer incentives for outstanding sales performance, and distribute and set up points-of-sale aids in the major retailing accounts.

Benson's Nuts
Strategic Rationale

A. Marketing objectives
(i)   The goal of 3 million users per annum will contribute to the mission of increasing earnings.

(ii)   The 3 million users represent a 10 percent market (segment) share. It is the market (segment) share identified during the test market. The 10 percent market share is below the six major brands but higher than other brands (in the competitive fringe).

(iii) The growth in volume of 5 percent per annum in the next five years is feasible given that

(a) the growth in the segment is estimated at 2 percent per annum;

(b) an additional growth rate of 3 percent is consistent with our experience of— brands in the same position of entering mature markets.

B. Product strategy

This path to growth was discussed and adopted at the series of Board Meetings.

C. Competitive strategies

The strategic path chosen is a "leapfrog" in that the crisp-dryness of Benson's flavor:

(i)   is perceived by 80 percent of respondents (see Benson's Marketing Research exhibits) to give the product a critical advantage;

(ii)   gives Benson's a preemptive strategic posture since competitors will be unable to copy and launch their competitive entry for at least two years given the technological and logistical problems involved.

D. Core (segmentation) strategy

(i)   *Customer targets.* Although all snack foods are indirect competitors of Benson's nuts, its chief rivals are in the nut segment of the market. Of this nut segment, Benson's will focus on the high income/heavy user because:

(a) product blind tests show Benson's to be particularly preferred by this subsegment;

(b) this subsegment, while making up only 12 percent of households, consumed 35 percent of nuts. Price sensitivity is low within the range X to $X + 1$. (See Benson's Marketing Research file.)

(ii)   *Buying inducement.* Benson's will be positioned as the "nut" with the revolutionary new flavor that makes the flavor of all other nuts less acceptable.

All market tests indicate that Benson's is perceived by the majority in the segment as having a superior, quality taste. This suggests promoting the product as suited to all "special" uses and occasions. We will seek to develop new use occasions in food preparation.

The "crisp-dry" benefit promise is viewed as the best way to position Benson's, as taste is the dominant product attribute determining consumer preference; nutritional value seems irrelevant. (See Benson's Marketing Research file.) Blind tests research indicates that Benson's taste readily distinguishes it from other brands and is the major basis for preferring Benson's. Only 10 percent of consumers in the segment expressed preference for rival brands.

E. Brand (support) strategies

(i)   *Advertising* is needed to activate the latent want, to convert from rivals and to maintain purchase continuity. The copy strategy and copy platform will promise a distinctive (revolutionary) new flavor and invite trial purchase.

There are no data, as yet, to Benson's relative regional appeal but tentatively it is proposed to allocate media funds in line with the purchase levels for the product category in various parts of the country via:

Total	*Relative Purchase Index*			
US	East	West	Central	South
100	140	80	120	60

With experience of the brand's regional acceptance, promotional support will be adjusted to incremental returns.

The year-round promotional support for Benson's is consistent with year-round sales, while giving more weight to the June–September period is consistent with the fact that these are peak months for sales.

(ii)   The general strategy in *pricing* is to price at a level consistent with the superior quality product. However, since the immediate aim is to stimulate trial purchase, temporary price offers have been recommended.

Part II

Buyers, markets, and competition

Chapter 4

Images of buyers/consumers and what influences them

ASSUMPTIONS ABOUT BEHAVIOR IN MARKETING STRATEGY

Major problems in marketing relate to understanding, reinforcing, or changing behavior so this chapter and the next are important even if they do no more than offer insights. Marketing strategy makes myriad assumptions about human behavior, whether that behavior is buyer behavior, the behavior of channel intermediaries, or the behavior of competitors. Many of these assumptions (e.g. about the demand for the product) will be factually based, either through marketing research or recent direct experience. Other assumptions are that certain trends will persist (e.g. working wives) and certain habits (e.g. watching TV) will continue. But there are other assumptions that rest on our understanding human behavior. This chapter and the next help us in that understanding. The chapter describes several perspectives which the social sciences adopt to study people as well as discussing some of the more common behavioral concepts and ideas on how behavior is influenced. The discussion of behavioral concepts is vital for explaining many actions. Without knowledge of such concepts, discussion of buyer behavior is likely to be impoverished, resulting from

a) not knowing what might be important, and
b) not having a precise vocabulary with which to comment on buyer behavior.

But in reading about buyer behavior or in reading research reports that include sections on buyer behavior, managers should also understand the author's basic stance on studying behavior so as to intelligently evaluate what is said. This is the purpose of the first part of this chapter. The next chapter brings together into an overall framework that can be used to identify and describe different buying states, different buying situations and the reasons for buying. Reading both these chapters at this stage provides a background to the rest of the book, making other chapters more meaningful.

Marketing managers are interested in buyer influences, motivations, motivational processes, in fact anything that is relevant to buying. In the design of the offering (product, price, promotion, and distribution), there are many concepts and findings in the social sciences that can help. In particular, every marketing manager has an interest in the following questions and the social sciences offer at least partial answers:

1 How can we best view people?
2 What types of influences affect behavior?
3 What characteristics, dispositional states of the buyer, affect the impact of those influences?
4 What mental processes occur in intentional actions like buying?
5 How rational is the buyer?

The rest of this chapter is concerned with these questions.

HOW CAN WE BEST VIEW PEOPLE? THE CONTRIBUTION OF THE SOCIAL SCIENCES

We look to the social sciences for a better understanding of behavior. The social sciences, like science generally, look for theories that are general rather than tied to concrete cases as theory aims at having as wide an application as possible. All theories of human behavior are abstractions from real life that are intended to highlight, describe, and explain the salient features of some specific aspect of human behavior. Valid social science theories can enrich our understanding of buyers, buying and post-purchase consumption by providing a way to interpret behavior that is otherwise puzzling and seemingly incoherent. However, social science theories are neither comprehensive nor refined enough to entirely displace commonsensical understanding of the concrete situation. What must be recognized is that there are no universal laws of a nontrivial nature that can be used to explain human action (voluntary behavior). It is not even clear there are timeless truths about human beings of a nontrivial nature. It is a fantasy to suppose there are eternal, immutable laws covering the intentional actions of all people in all cultures in all times. Those who seek such laws end up putting their stamp on the ephemeral as revealed truth. However, the attraction of searching for laws is obvious since a law can be applied with confidence as opposed to using some statistical or other generalization where we have to worry about whether the particular case is representative. Although throughout this chapter, statements are made about behavior, it should always be understood we are talking about tendencies rather than universal laws.

There are no universal laws for predicting how buyers, competitors or distributors, or other groups of people will behave under different circumstances. Accurate prediction of an individual's action would require not only complete knowledge of the individual's cognitive processes and biology but also all environmental and nutritional influences. What the behavioral sciences do provide is a number of mechanisms, dispositional tendencies or types of influences, that come into play. It is generally easier to explain after the action which factors were at work; predicting behavior is more hazardous. Judgment is required. Judgment and common-sense knowledge are necessary to supplement social science knowledge as social science, without universal laws, cannot be expected to provide certainty in the individual case or be that comprehensive.[1] Explaining any interesting action is likely to depend on applying a variety of forms of human understanding to the unique situation as such action is likely to be prompted by many factors within a context of conditions that are unlikely to recur in precisely that form. As observers we make sense of such cases through our general understanding of people and situations, aided by social science concepts. We can, on occasions, listen to the consumer, note the choices made, and understand the reasons behind choices better than the individual making them. Unfortunately, in promoting social science, advocates often promote contempt for common sense (e.g. "common sense says the world is flat"). While it is true that common sense intuitions about behavior can be wrong, it is also true that social science can be overconfident and also wrong, though we hope its methods incorporate more self-correction than is the case with common-sense errors. But no methods guarantee to throw up fruitful hypotheses. In fact Ludwig Wittgenstein, the philosopher, was adamant in claiming that psychological insight stems not from any general principles but from actual experience. And marketing managers do have experience which should not just be dismissed. We all know a good deal simply from our experience as human beings, for instance, that music associated with past events can affect us emotionally. We all have insight into what people are likely to want and why they would want it. This is because we have understanding about human purposes, human feelings, hopes and fears.

There are no universal laws when it comes to predicting action. However, if behavior includes not only (intentional) action but involuntary behavior there can be prediction e.g. tapping the knees causes a reflex response. This is because there are two classes of human behavior:

1   intentional action e.g. an eye wink, and
2   involuntary behavior e.g. the eye blink

Human action is voluntary behavior and assumed to be intentional in that all voluntary action is purposive. It could be argued that *intentionality* is the most distinctive feature of human action in that lying behind action is some intention or purpose. Every decision-maker acts as an agent forming action–consequence sequences (that is, thinking about what actions to take and their likely consequences) and choosing that action–consequence sequence that most meets his or her goals or wants. Unless we can imagine the consequences of action and deal with possible scenarios, we cannot take a rational approach to the future. Thought experiments are thus a vital part of rational thinking. Action is guided by beliefs as to the action to take. Explanation in terms of wants (or cognates of the term like goal or desire) and beliefs make action intelligible, meaningful and understandable to us as human beings. If we look at the triad of "wants-beliefs-action," we need two of the three to try and predict the third. Hence we need to know about relevant wants and beliefs to try and predict action. Thus knowledge of motives cannot predict specific action unless we know a person's beliefs. Similarly, attitudes, built up from statements on beliefs, will not be predictive of buying action unless we assume something about wants. Thus we can have a very favorable attitude to a product (e.g. disposable diapers) without necessarily buying it. However, motives and attitudes do have *a directional* tendency (e.g. a status motive or an unfavorable attitude toward a brand) that *proscribe* certain actions but do not *prescribe* action with any degree of precision.

Involuntary behavior is caused behavior; caused by forces over which we have no control like the hiccup and the sneeze. The distinction between voluntary and involuntary behavior is considered basic to talk of ethical behavior. This is because, if all behavior was involuntary and so inevitable (given some context and stimulus), then any talk about what people ought to do or holding people responsible for their actions would seem somewhat pointless. Yet, in practice, the distinction between involuntary behavior and intentional action is not clear cut in marginal cases. There are also those who argue the distinction is misleading if it suggests that some behavior is not caused since the "reasons" that move us to action can be regarded as causes. For some philosophers and psychologists the very notion of cause is basic to what it means to act for a reason, to have an intention, to act freely or to act against one's immediate desires or best judgment. But those accepting this view agree there are no strict laws of the form: If a person has such and such a want plus certain beliefs in such and such conditions, he or she will act in such and such a way. Where causal laws are sought they are not of this form.

Images of Man

Various social sciences focus on different factors in explaining behavior. Psychology seeks explanations in terms of biological, developmental, and cognitive processes; sociology focuses on societal and social group influences while social psychology focuses on the individual within the social group, not on the groups themselves. But the big split in the social sciences is between those who search for causal laws ("scientific" explanation) and those who claim such laws can apply only to involuntary *movements* and not intentional action (voluntary behavior). Somewhat reflecting this debate are the various positions on how to view the consumer:

1 As simply responding to the push and pull of past impressed events and immediate stimuli. This covers:
   a) *Classical* (Pavlovian) conditioning and operant conditioning in behaviorist psychology.
   b) Sociological or anthropological studies that focus exclusively (most do not) on the search for external causes of behavior like culture, or other social, environmental factors.
2 As rationally reflective, as in the following examples:
   a) Economics which assumes that people will act according to rational self-interest.
   b) Cognitive psychology which focuses on how information is processed to (say) form attitudes.
3 As a social being guided by social norms. This is one viewpoint in social psychology and sociology.
4 As acting in response to unconscious desires and beliefs. This is the traditional psycho-analytic approach.
5 Behavior as *largely* genetically determined as assumed in sociobiology and psychometrics. *Sociobiology* deals with the social behavior of organisms in the light of evolution. It seeks to establish relationships between our genetic makeup, cognitive processing, and culture. Sociobiology has yet to influence researchers in marketing perhaps because the strong claims made by its advocates seem highly implausible and the hard evidence is missing. *Psychometrics* covers those branches of psychology concerned with measurement, for example, the measurement of intelligence and personality and will be discussed later in the book.
6 As a free agent acting for reasons (wants and beliefs) that can go beyond mere self-interest. This is the common-sense view called *ethnopsychology* in psychology and *folkpsychology* in philosophy in that it is the psychology of the culture and not confined to a small class of experts.[2]

The above is one listing of social science perspectives. It draws attention to different images of Man that affect research methodologies. We now consider some of these images in more detail.

Ethnopsychology or folkpsychology

People react to one another in terms of their own psychology (folkpsychology) rather than the psychologists' psychology. In daily life we seek *reasons* for people's actions. The *reason-giving explanation* is the natural starting place for explaining action not only in courts of law but in social science and history. Reasons lead to intentions or a commitment to action. It is argued that, if we are to capture the salient features of mental life, then those investigating human action must frame their explanations in terms of reasons using the concepts of beliefs and wants (or cognates of these terms). Marketing managers can be very skilled at answering questions about consumer or buyer behavior because they have a certain context sensitivity to likely reasons for action and come to recognize certain patterns of behavior as related to future actions. But many psychologists eschew the reason-giving type of explanation on the grounds:

1 It does not lend itself to theory development as per the natural sciences. They argue that such teleological explanations (those based on the goals and wants that are sought) were abandoned with Newton when the focus shifted to causal explanation. But the question arises whether the natural sciences are always the most suitable model for understanding human action. Those who confine their methods to the methods of the natural sciences inevitably restrict what questions are asked and what behavior to explain.
2 The reason-giving explanation is not one that is falsifiable and the possibility of falsification is the mark of scientific explanation. This view is questionable since reason-giving explanations can be tested against different types of evidence.
3 Reason-giving explanation inhibits the search for causal laws, that is, the factors causing the action (e.g. poverty causes crime). In reply, it is argued that external causes like poverty do enter into reason-giving explanations, but to restrict explanations to just push forces like poverty will always result in the explanation being inadequate unless the findings can be related to wants and beliefs. Thus we can still ask "why?" poverty causes crime to try and identify the motives and beliefs at work.
4 Reasons would not capture unconscious influences or all the other influences at work. This is so. Unconscious influences can be at work and not all the influences affecting behavior are likely to be captured in the reasons given for undertaking some action.

However, in spite of the limitations of the reason-giving explanation it is still true that for buyer action to be intelligible to us, explanations must directly or indirectly be tied to wants and beliefs as knowledge of the wants and beliefs lying behind action gives *meaning* to the action. Reasons give meaning to action because wants and beliefs are tied to the rationality principle viz.: "If any person wants to achieve goal 'A' and believes that action 'B' is a way to achieve goal 'A' in the circumstances, then that person will be predisposed to take action 'B', other things remaining equal." If consumers were completely illogical and there were no reasons for their action, marketers would simply have no idea where to start to discover what they wanted or why they wanted it. One of the problems in devising a competitive strategy is the problem of anticipating how rational managers, intent on not revealing their hand, will act and react.

The prediction of buying action rests on the assumption of fairly rational buyers, by assuming that buyers will buy the offering that comes closest to what they want. Predicting buying action also presupposes *some* intersubjective understanding. Thus we have no problem predicting consumers will not want to eat mud pies, or want to return to sundials for telling the time but would like to have cheaper air fares and cars that can slide sideways from awkward parking slots.

Unlike the economist, ethnomethodology (folkpsychology) does not assume that the reasons for choosing action "A" rather than "B" will always be self-interested reasons since reasons can be more tied to social appropriateness and personal integrity than tied to what is most efficient for achieving narrow (material) self-interest. Reflection allows us to put desires at a distance to evaluate them. Intentional action is not just a dependent variable to be predicted simply from knowledge of a ranking of the relative strength of wants. Consumers do not always act on the strongest desires but may, for example, exercise self-control and "savor" the long term payoff.

Ethnopsychology comes under *hermeneutics* or interpretative psychology (discussed later) since the focus is on understanding actions through interpreting them.

Behaviorism

Behaviorism, as a branch of psychology, assumes that actions are the result of conditioning or the establishment of a connection between a stimulus and a response. Behaviorism in the form of *operant conditioning* claims that we emit behavior all the time and those emitted behaviors that are reinforced recur while those that are not reinforced die away. Thus according to operant conditioning, all behavior is contingent on being reinforced.

Reinforcement is simply anything in the environment which increases the probability of response of some emitted behavior and a reinforcer is anything that increases the probability of occurrence of a given *class* of responses. The term "reinforcer" is distinguished from "reward" in that what might be considered a reward subjectively may not in fact work to strengthen the emitted behavior. Thus if a pigeon pecks a key and receives food and key pecking thus increases, then food is termed the reinforcer. If pecking does not increase then food (normally viewed as a reward) is not a reinforcer in this instance. Behaviorism focuses on reinforcement of behavior and eschews punishment. In fact what is termed *negative reinforcement* is simply the withdrawal of a punisher and is thus still reinforcement. Behaviorism is essentially a psychology of learning, claiming that we learn what we have been reinforced to learn. Learning occurs most quickly when reinforcement is continued in that every response is rewarded. An obvious example is the way receiving good grades encourages further learning to continue the reinforcement. However, there is quick cessation of the behavior when reinforcement stops. Learning via conditioning, though, is not the only way of learning. In fact, many psychologists regard this as the most trivial type of learning. There can also be *incidental learning* or learning that occurs without reward, effort or purpose which can happen through, say, watching television. There is the learning that arises from *imitation*; observing and "imitating" others as when consumers copy some celebrity in buying the same brand of perfume. *Extinction* is the process of eliminating the occurrence of a conditioned response, typically by withholding the reinforcer (e.g. a discounted price) that was involved in its acquisition.

The behaviorism of B. F. Skinner is not concerned with mental concepts such as beliefs, attitudes, motives etc. (A "motive" to Skinner is some property of the stimulus by which it gains control over the behavior.) While initially denying the existence of subjective entities, Skinner later spoke of behavior being both overt (public) and covert (private) with all thoughts being regarded as covert (private) events. However, Skinner always eschewed looking at mental events as a stage in some causal chain of $S \Rightarrow O \Rightarrow R$ (stimulus $\Rightarrow$ organism [mental event] $\Rightarrow$ response) on the ground if the "mental way station" itself fails to divert attention from the first stage (the stimulus), it would surely divert attention from the last stage (the response). Skinner was right to emphasize the dangers in the use of mental constructs like motive and attitude but ignoring cognitive processes altogether reduces psychology to ignoring too many basic questions about human behavior. Today most psychologists would wish to link the environment (the external stimulus) to behavior (response) through mental constructs like attitude, beliefs, emotion and motives. Like Freud and today's cognitive psychologists, Skinner is of the opinion that there are limits to self-knowledge. But for Skinner the reason for this has to do with language in that a necessary condition for knowledge of one's thinking (private events) is to have competence in a language of private events. This is now controversial in that some psychologists argue that people are born knowing a preverbal language and thought is couched in this before being clothed in words whether English, Chinese, or Apache.[3]

The only explanatory basis for behaviorism can be found in the so-called Law of Effect that claims we tend to repeat acts that are followed by positive consequences and avoid acts followed by negative consequences. What makes behaviorism meaningful to marketers is that common-sense (ethnomethodology) endorses the Law of Effect and such behaviorist propositions as the following:

- The greater the number of rival brands, the less dependent is the consumer on any one brand.
- The more brand "B" provides additional sources of reinforcement for consumer "A", the more dependent is consumer "A" on brand "B."
- The less satisfied consumer "A" is with brand "B," the less the likelihood of "A" continuing to buy brand "B" as more brands become available.
- The more the advantages in terms of reinforcement of brand "B" over its rivals, the more consumer "A" will try to get it.
- Consumers buy whatever brands yield most for least cost.
- Consumers repeat buy whatever has proved a reinforcer in the past, other things remaining equal.
- Present stimuli (e.g. shopping at a particular store) associated with past reinforcement, will evoke buying similar to that in the past.

- Repeat buying occurs only as long as the practice continues to be reinforced.
- Consumers display what we describe as emotional behavior if their actions (e.g. looking for a favorite brand) previously rewarded in a similar situation suddenly go unrewarded (e.g. store being out of stock).

While the above propositions seem trivially true, reinforcement theories in general have typically proved to be unfalsifiable as it is not so easy to specify in advance what will be a reinforcer.

There are variations of behaviorism. The earliest was Pavlovian or *classical* conditioning. In Pavlov's classic experiment, a sounding of a bell was paired with food that reliably produced salivation in dogs as a reflex response. After some trials, the bell itself was sufficient to produce salivation. This was the *conditioned* response. Pavlovian conditioning is a S⇒R (stimulus⇒response) psychology. Skinner's operant conditioning is not since, in operant conditioning, behavior is viewed as being acquired, shaped and maintained by stimuli *following* responses not by stimuli preceding responses. Skinner viewed operant conditioning as not only subsuming classical conditioning but as an advance over classical (Pavlovian) conditioning because it came to grips with the two problems to be overcome for any psychology to be considered successful. The first problem is to account for human creativity (novelty in behavior) and the second problem is to account for the fact that people are motivated by future goals. Skinner felt operant conditioning got over both these problems.

Under behaviorism also come *drive-reduction* theories. Here being motivated is taken to be a state of physiological disequilibrium with behavior seeking to restore equilibrium. While this makes sense when applied to the biological needs of hunger and thirst, no other wants can be traced to any physiological disequilibrium. Satiety is usually equated with the concept of equilibrium but some of our most important motives like wanting respect, power etc. seem insatiable while other motives seem connected more with deliberation and choice than any physiological disequilibrium.

One behaviorist concept is that of *partial reinforcement* and its effect on extinguishing a response. If behavior is reinforced every time it is emitted, the behavior is likely to cease when the reinforcement is withdrawn. But if reinforcement is partial, only occurring sometimes when the behavior is emitted (e.g. finding periodically a bargain in a certain store), the behavior may persist longer (e.g. still visit the shop in hope of a bargain). Thus with the intermittent schedule, learning takes longer but learning lasts longer. But when it comes to people as opposed to pigeons (the typical subject used by Skinner), much will depend on the information possessed (beliefs) in that I may know there are going to be no more bargains.

Behaviorism does offer insights for marketing and some marketing academics have made serious attempts to expand it and tie it less to its dogmatic rejection of all reference to mental happenings.[4] But for many marketers, operant conditioning has serious defects in assuming people like buyers do not adopt new and appropriate behaviors in new situations, or the extinction of nonrewarding behavior is as slow as that suggested, while it seems crass to believe that new behavior in new environments does not occur unless present behavior is linked to it by a continuous chain of reinforcement. It could also be argued that in classical conditioning, subjects, whether dogs or people, are simply demonstrating their capacity to recognize signals while so-called "extinction" is not a cessation of learning as suggested but an instance of new learning.

Psychoanalytic psychology

Psychoanalytic psychology stems from the work of Sigmund Freud. Freud questioned the degree to which we know what motives lie behind our actions and argued that people hide their real motives and intentions. For Freud, our unconscious motivated dispositions are the most basic motivators and Freud denied that these could be manipulated by rewards and punishments.

Psychoanalytic psychology is no longer regarded as a general psychology but as a psychology that focuses on unconscious inner conflicts as people strive toward achieving their goals. Freudian psychology claims that the interplay of three systems of the mind cause behavior namely, the id (the primitive urges of the flesh), the superego (society's social constraints/conscience), and the ego (the public and consciously known self). Psychoanalytic psychology can be interpreted as being concerned with the effects of repressed desires (wants) and neurotic beliefs. The id could be viewed as pressing desires; the superego as beliefs about social appropriateness and what constitutes moral behavior, while the ego might be regarded as the decision processing center that checks and screens desires to ensure they fit some acceptable self-image. It is the job of the ego to reconcile the competing demands of the id and the superego.

Freudian psychology claims we can access the unconscious via slips of the tongue, depth interviewing and most important, the analysis of dreams. In these ways, the relevant beliefs and desires can be discovered so that these can be confronted and exposed through rational argument, with the result that they lose their power over us. Dreams were considered the most important because they are places where socially unacceptable thoughts are most likely to occur, often in coded form. Freudian therapy thus does assume self-knowledge is possible since knowing about one's desires and feelings is essential to the cure of neurosis. However, Freud undermines our *trust* in self-knowledge since what we think to be our real motives are not likely to be our real ones. This is because the mind's eye does not have access to the unconscious, irrational part of self.

Defense mechanisms are the unconscious strategies of self-deception. For example, *rationalizations* protect the ego against the harsher aspects of reality. Such rationalization is common in buying and can be a problem when asking buyers directly about their reasons for buying.

An *unconscious motive* in Freudian theory is one forbidden by the superego and not acknowledged by the conscious self. The unconscious is distinguished from the *subconscious* or what Freud called the "preconscious" level which is the level of mental life assumed to exist just below the threshold of consciousness. *Subliminal perception* (discussed later in advertising) is associated with this subconscious level.

There have been many deviations from Freud by psychotherapists. Thus Alfred Adler was convinced that the will to power was as important as the sex drive in human motivation and believed that the frustration of the "will to power" gives rise to feelings of inadequacy and neurotic behavior. Carl Jung formulated the concept of an *archetype* or inborn images held in common by all people, like the Hero, the Evil One, the Wise Old Man, and so on. (Advertising sometimes seeks to link brands to such archetypes.)

A number of techniques such as motivation research and focus groups (discussed later in the book), stem from the psychoanalytic movement. But psychoanalytic psychology has not fared well, being generally dismissed by mainstream psychology because, in general, it cannot be validated by experiment. However, many Freudian concepts have been adopted by the mainstream, like the concept of the unconscious or the importance of early experiences in determining values and emotional makeup. In psychiatry itself there has been the steep ascendance of biological psychiatry which views mental illness as typically arising from chemical imbalances in the brain. In applying psychoanalytic psychology to marketing the focus has been on identifying the *unconscious meaning* of the product or whatever so that the seller can develop advertising and sales appeals that tap the buyer's deepest motivations. Freudian psychology holds that actions and things like goods and services can symbolize ("stand for") other things and, as a consequence, attract to themselves the emotions attached to what they symbolize. As we will see later in Chapter 8, projective techniques are used to uncover these unconscious motivations and meanings.

Cognitive psychology

By the 1970s, psychologists, using the computer as an analogy, returned to mental processes. Although behaviorism is correct in asserting that it is impossible to know what goes on in the mind as opposed to

a) knowing what information is fed to the mind, and
b) observing subsequent behavior,

psychology claims it should not rule out attempts to model the inner workings of the mind since the physical world is represented in consciousness by *mental representations*.

The fact that we can think about and imagine nonexistent things like pink elephants supports the view that the contents of the mind are mental representations, a view promoted by the psychologist William James at the end of the nineteenth century.

What makes a psychology cognitive in the most general sense is a focus on mental processes. "Cognition" is the faculty of knowing and perceiving. Cognitive psychology studies perceiving and knowing and the related processes of remembering, paying attention, language use, problem solving and manipulating things around us with, say, our hands. Cognition contrasts with conation (the exercise of the will to action) and affective experiences (feelings/emotions) but these cannot be easily separated.

There are two types of explanation favored by the cognitive psychologist. One is the *design-stance*, focusing on how information is processed. Here the metaphor of the mind as a computer helps to direct research in cognitive psychology. One strategy is to identify an analogous computer program and experiment to choose which best describes the mental capacity of interest. In the early days of computers, the terms we use to describe the elements of the brain, like "memory" were used to describe the computer. Now computer terminology is used to talk about the brain, with the use of terms like inputs, accessing, or retrieval systems. But at some point the metaphor of the mind as a computer breaks down. For example, brains do not have the same flexibility as computers so that "circuits" that deal with vision cannot just be switched over to deal with, say, hearing. Also with humans (unlike computers) there are two types of learning: *declarative* learning which is the explicit learning to remember objects and events and *procedural* learning which is the learning that unconsciously occurs in learning how to perform some skill. The second type of explanation could be called the *intentional-stance* since explanation here is in terms of wants, intentions and beliefs (or cognates of these terms) but this type of explanation is not where the major interest of cognitive psychologists lies.

The focus in cognitive psychology is on the "software" lying behind mental processes. It is not altogether clear what a mental process is like except it is somehow like the processes occurring within a computer or telephone switchboard. Some of these processes are assumed to form some logical sequence; others are assumed to be unconscious and to pass through discrete stages of cognitive development. Because cognitive psychology mostly focuses on how we process information, it is referred to as the *information processing approach*. It views the mind as a machine so that the mind is simply the brain in action. It sees people as constructing mental models of, say, the buying situation, and manipulating these models to try to find solutions to their problems. The whole approach has a rational orientation by its appeal to processes that seem logical.

Traditionally, the focus in cognitive psychology has been on understanding the mind's programs and not on the hardware. This means that "design-stance-explanations" do not involve coming to grips with physiology and the actual physical and chemical properties of the nervous system. But this may change with the new "connectionist" models in computer science which question the sharp distinction between software and hardware. The connectionist models learn to perform tasks rather than just being programmed to carry out tasks. It is argued that humans do things like recognizing faces faster than the standard computer because humans do many computations in parallel.

The connectionist model dominates in parallel distributed processing which is a new computer architecture. Here there is no one place labeled "long-term memory" or domain specific long-term memory stores. In fact there are no stores stocked with memory at all. Cognitive psychologists are like Sherlock Holmes when it comes to inferring mental processes from information inputs and behavioral outputs. There are always alternative explanations of experimental data. What is discovered should not be regarded as ultimate truth but "rather well-constructed Sherlock Holmes stories."

A major claim of cognitive psychologists is that much behavior is governed by implicit, nonconscious knowledge rather than conscious knowledge. Thus the consumer may not be aware of how packaging or brand image influences his or her choice of brand. People do not necessarily know what causes their behavior or mental state and conscious knowledge alone does not initiate all mental activity. We often "know more than we can tell." Accurate self-knowledge cannot be guaranteed by just introspection of happenings in the mind since these can be misinterpreted. Psychological knowledge, history, culture, and so on can in fact help in such interpretation.

If perfect rationality in buying is purchasing only what serves long-term interests, then, in general, buying does not reflect perfect rationality. For one thing buyers are not always aware of what their long-term interests are. Buyers also do not have complete information about options and their likely consequences for future satisfaction but have to cope with messy data that are incomplete, ambiguous, inconsistent or based on second-hand opinions that lead to suboptimum purchases. On the other hand, just to say that irrationality is anything less than perfect rationality would be silly. Irrationality can be viewed as deliberately harming one's interests without compensating reason (like cutting off one's leg without medical reason). On this definition, buyers are not irrational. They can best be described as having *flawed rationality* in that they frequently reach "sensible" conclusions from what turn out to be erroneous beliefs. This flawed rationality should not be treated as just an occasional aberration but as something that is characteristic of human beings.

Gilovich argues (like other psychologists) that our judgments become distorted through cognitive processes that normally help us accurately perceive and understand the world.[5] Here are some examples translated into marketing:

- Consumers expect every brand in a product category to have the attributes commonly associated with that category so that we expect, say, every germ-killing mouthwash to taste unpleasant.
- Buyers tend to overextend some belief about how an attribute should manifest itself and expect, say, a durable product to look robust so that a light computer or vacuum cleaner might be rejected because it is not perceived as durable enough.
- Buyers tend to seek just confirmatory evidence. This may arise from wishful thinking but may also occur because confirmatory evidence is cognitively simpler to deal with. Thus advice against buying some brand may direct attention only to evidence against buying.
- Buyers tend to manipulate ambiguous evidence to fit expectations, for example, that all American cars are of poor quality.
- Buyers tend to estimate the likelihood of something by how readily examples of it come to mind. This *availability rule* is very tied to how dramatic the event was when it happened. Thus when a particular make of car is associated with some well-publicized accident due to a defect, this can do untold damage to future sales.

Still other generalizations from cognitive psychology are:

- When post-purchase experience, whether bad or good, stands out it is known as a *two-sided event*. In such a case, both a very poor experience or a very good experience is likely to be well remembered.
- When brands are similar on some characteristic dimension (e.g. the tube in which the toothpaste is packaged), it is the similarities among the brands that are noticed which can make them appear undifferentiated. It is thus important for the seller to emphasize differences.
- When consumers have a prior tentative preference for a brand, it is apt to influence not only the kind of information considered but also the amount of information

collected. If the early information supports this prior preference, information search ceases while, if it does not, the search is likely to continue, seeking largely confirmatory evidence including the approaching of "advisers" most likely to give it.

- Consumers tend to be overconfident in buying when their confidence is high and underconfident when their confidence is low. Overconfidence leads to less scrutiny of buying options while underconfidence can lead to indecision.
- Strong desires influence beliefs leading to self-deception or wishful thinking.
- Consumers seek to conserve their "cognitive energy" by using rules of thumb or mental shortcuts and subsequently rationalize about their behavior to make it appear more rational than it was. A good deal of deceptive advertising seeks to exploit such tendencies.
- Buyers dislike losses more than equivalent gains so that it is more painful to discover one has paid an excess of $10 than it is pleasurable to be given an unexpected rebate of $10.

Studying mental processing is not like studying some observable process and there can be many assumed mental processes to account for experimental findings. Terms like "cognition" are not in the same world of discourse as words like "trees" and "house" but are "hypothetical constructs," that is, invented, hypothetical man-made concepts to account for what is observable. Thus it is "as if" people have attitudes, etc.

The chief limitation of cognitive psychology for marketing is its neglect of emotion and motivation though things may be changing in respect to emotion.[6] Emotion is important for marketing. Emotions are aroused when some happening is evaluated as so highly desirable or undesirable that some autonomic, physiological reaction occurs. Emotions are tied to values so that threats to values like the value we put on maintaining our self-esteem, can be emotionally arousing.

Motivation is the other neglected topic in cognitive psychology as it is just usually assumed to exist rather than explained. The psychological study of motivation presupposes there are general things that can be said about the motives of people in that people are disposed to be stimulated by certain categories of needs or wants, such as the need for others and the need to enhance self-esteem.

Microeconomics

Classical microeconomics is based squarely on wants and beliefs. The assumption is that beliefs are true in that the decision makers possess perfect information about alternatives and their consequences and also that wants can be ranked according to their contribution to (subjective) utility. The consumer thus arrives at a unique optimum choice via the rationality principle where the rationality principle becomes the maximization of utility or subjective value. Rationality is equated with pure self-interest while high rationality is assumed because this makes predicting behavior more manageable. But in real life, perfect information is not available and wants can be fickle while rationality is flawed. There is also the assumption that, if the consumer prefers brand X to brand Y in one context, then Y will not be preferred to X in another context. But this assumption can be shown to be violated when other brands are introduced into the market leading to a reevaluation of the relative importance of attributes while preferences themselves can depend strongly on how information about the alternatives is presented. Other approaches in economics allow for variation in belief by relaxing the assumption about the possession of perfect information. This is done by the introduction of the concept of expectations or *expectancies*. Thus the consumer may believe that brand X has more appeal (i.e. has the highest subjective utility) than brand Y but suspects there is a higher probability of getting the benefits associated with brand Y and that this should be taken into account. In deciding what to do, she analyzes her choices into the outcomes (consequences) that can occur under different conditions. To compute the utility of each choice, she multiplies the utility of the outcome by the probability of getting the conditions that give rise to it. She then adds up these expected utilities for each of the different outcomes, repeating the procedure for each alternative choice to choose the alternative that yields the highest expected utility, following the rule of maximizing subjective expected utility (SEU). With regard to expectancies, those subscribing to the model of *adaptive expectations* view the decision-maker as constantly updating expectations on the basis of experience while those subscribing to the model of *rational expectations* claim that decision-makers have expectations which they perceive as being borne out on average and so treat any deviations from expectations as random.

Critics argue that the above model of rationality imposes impossible demands on decision-makers while empirical evidence suggests consumers do not have comprehensive, consistent utility functions that would enable them to rank alternatives on the basis of relative utility. In practice, economists recognize that information is often uncertain, incomplete and costly to obtain. But they typically assume people pursue only self-interest (altruism out) and that payoffs to actions are easy to calculate. Though useful for the economists' purposes, they are not assumptions that can be taken for granted by marketers.

The most recent approach in economics focuses on *revealed preference*. But to focus on revealed choice as revealed in market choices, is to focus just on the action itself. But since we cannot predict wants and beliefs from action alone this approach abandons any claim to explain individual action.

Social psychology, sociology, and cultural anthropology

Marketing draws not only from individual psychology and economics but also from social psychology, sociology and anthropology. Social psychology studies "how behavior, thought and the feelings of individuals are influenced by the actual, imagined or implied presence of others." Sociology studies human social relationships, social groups, and social interaction patterns as well as social institutions. Cultural anthropology is the study of the whole culture and the complex structures that make up societies. There is a good deal of overlap among these disciplines particularly between sociology and social psychology.

One of the earliest theories to be applied to buyer behavior is the theory of *cognitive dissonance* developed in the 1950s by Leon Festinger, a social psychologist. It is one view of how people rationalize about their behavior. Cognitive dissonance arises whenever someone simultaneously holds two inconsistent beliefs (cognitions, attitudes, or opinions). Such inconsistency is uncomfortable and people strive to reduce the conflict in the most convenient way, for example, by changing one or both cognitions so that they cohere. Resolution of the conflict can be a basis for attitude change. Every choice made by a buyer is a potential source of dissonance as the loss of the (believed to be attractive) displaced alternative can be dissonant with the belief that another product has already been chosen. Typically consumers seek confirmatory evidence that they did indeed buy the best and sellers help by offering reassurance (e.g. after buying a car, telling the customer he got the best deal possible).

Festinger claimed that when people are confident about their proposed action (e.g. buying), they believe their action to be desirable, rationally defensible, and socially appropriate so the proposed action possesses *subjective validity* for them. On this basis, the central problem for Festinger in seeking to influence buyers is to uncover their bases of subjective validity. In other words, we want to know what our target customers think is desirable, can be rationally defended, and is socially appropriate, *and* what is not.

Exchange theory in sociology is frequently quoted as basic to an exchange theory for marketing. In exchange theory, the focus is on social interactions, viewed as economic transactions, with all parties to the exchange seeking to maximize their "net profit," profit being interpreted broadly as embracing both material and psychological benefits. There are several variations of exchange theory: exchange behaviorism; exchange structuralism; power exchange theory and exchange decision theory. *Exchange behaviorism* has had most attention in marketing. As it is tied to behaviorism in psychology, it is not surprising that the two are fairly similar in their implications for marketing. Exchange theory, in the form of *exchange decision theory*, offers support for the common-sense view that the alternatives open to two parties in an exchange determine the limits within which the exchange will fall.[7] Thus the consumer may believe she or he has no alternative to paying a high price or, on another occasion, buying something which she or he considers substandard. For example, if the buyer:

- perceives there is no adequate substitute for the seller's offering;
- cannot coerce the seller into changing the offering (for instance, getting the government to legislate on pricing), and
- is not prepared to forgo the product and has the money to pay for it

then the buyer will buy the product even if it falls below what might be reasonably expected.

Hermeneutics

For some social scientists, it is the "meaning" of things (what they mean *for* us and mean *to* us) that defines, directs, delimits and governs action. This is typically the claim of "hermeneutics" or interpretive social science. Whereas "perception" is the apprehension of ordinary sense-objects such as houses, horses and chairs etc. and "sensation" is the apprehension of isolated sense qualities like the smell of something, "meaning" is of a higher order than either sensation or perception since it is the interpretation of the significance of things for the individual. We all have a strong need to make sense of the world around and the search for such meaning is influential in the way data is interpreted.

The interpretative social sciences generally view the consumer as rule-following as opposed to being compelled along by causal laws. Rules, unlike the laws in natural science, can be broken and changed. Rules emanate from social living and many are implicit like the rule that the person who answers the telephone should be the first to speak. Ethnopsychology, the psychology of the lay person mentioned earlier, interprets the meaning of action by seeking the reasons for it. Hermeneutics is rooted in ethnopsychology and its cultural background.

This focus on "meaning" is a focus shared by several "schools" drawn from psychology, social psychology, sociology and anthropology. *Ethogeny*, (a fairly new sub-branch of hermeneutics) for example, focuses on how action is made meaningful by those who carry out the action and those who observe the action being carried out.[8] *Ethnomethodology* (not to be confused with ethnopsychology) studies the "folk methods" used by people in everyday life to give meaning to the roles they and others play in life and to the nature of the institutions that surround them.[9] *Symbolic interactionism*, while viewing interaction between people as symbolic exchanges, aims at discovering the ways by which such exchanges are rendered meaningful.[10] Finally, anthropologists such as Geertz in cultural anthropology focus on symbols and how they function to mediate meanings.[11] Although all these approaches may differ somewhat in what they look for, they would seem to share the notion that the meaning of action involves understanding the point of the action (intentions), its significance, and the wants and beliefs that guide and shape it.

How does this view of "meaning" as directing action relate to talk about "motives" and reasons? A "motive," as commonly conceived, is a disposition to seek certain goals and/or relieve certain inner tensions. In terms of the reason-giving explanation, a "motive" is simply a psychological term for a general category of "want." On this basis, a motive, as a want, cannot predict action since there is a need to know relevant beliefs. If we accept that this is so then "meaning" is more than a motive since it implies a set of beliefs. *When we say that meaning directs behavior, we are saying that it is beliefs about what something signifies for a person's wants that determines his or her actions.* On this basis, "meaning" is not something distinct from wants and beliefs but a convenient way of capturing in one construct the idea of wants, beliefs and the intentions directing action. This concept of meaning relates to the concept of *involvement*. In marketing we speak of someone having high or low involvement with a purchase. When we speak of a purchase having high involvement, this is equivalent to saying the purchase has high meaning for them. But this begs the question as to what gives rise to this high involvement or makes the purchase so meaningful?

It is not just a matter of the purchase being important in the life of the consumer: centrality to the function for which the product is bought is necessary but not sufficient. There must also be a risk (e.g. because of the product's high price) attached to the purchase. High centrality plus perceived high risk attached to the purchase makes it highly meaningful for the buyer and implies high involvement by the consumer in the purchase. The concept of involvement is commonly quoted to explain behavior. For instance, it is claimed that, in a low involvement situation, the status of the celebrity endorsing the brand has more effect on consumer attitudes toward the brand than in a high involvement situation where celebrity endorsement has little or no effect. Although marketing texts also talk of high and low involvement *products*, strictly speaking, involvement is not a function of the type of product bought but a function of the consumer in that what purchases a particular buyer finds centrally important and risky may not be the same as for others.

SOCIAL ATTACHMENTS THAT AFFECT BEHAVIOR

Consumers are not isolated units but are members of a society, interacting with others and being influenced by them. In Figure 4.1, these social attachments include culture, reference groups, and social class.

Culture

There have been many views on culture. Traditionally, there is the concept of high culture as representing the best that has been created and written in the world. But anthropology had another view; culture as a way of life in a society. But even anthropologists can differ when it comes to operationalizing the concept. One view defines culture as the total accumulated stock among members of a society of internalized values, standards of behavior (norms), beliefs, including the style of thinking and feeling, that are unique to that society and learnt and passed on from generation to generation. Another view of culture focuses purely on what is observable like buildings, clothing, as well as the stories, myths and heroes of that society. Other definitions try to capture both the mental and the material, with culture being defined as the total way of life, embracing the values, norms, institutions, records, and other artifacts that distinguish a particular society. What is agreed is that culture is something that is learnt; that the various elements of culture are interrelated and, finally, a people's sense of their separate culture is what defines them as a separate culture.

Human beings perceive the world and the happenings within it from the perspective of culturally induced biases. To live in a culture is to absorb certain concepts, ways of looking at the world, and certain standards or norms of behaving with the prevailing

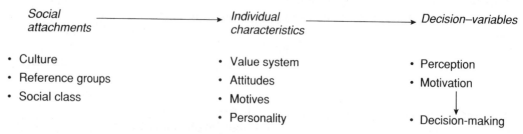

Figure 4.1 Social attachments affecting behavior

norms reflecting the society's social values. Norms and values provide standards for judging what is socially appropriate and, as such, influence attitudes. Cultures change but slowly through *cultural drift*, that is the cultural changes arising from an accumulation of small, unplanned, unnoticed or undetected modifications.

Cultures in the world vary in many ways, for example, in the extent to which individualism is encouraged; the extent to which people seek to avoid uncertainty and the extent to which the society is masculine or male-dominated. The United States in particular is regarded as a very individualistic culture with its emphasis on freedom from all traditional and hierarchical bonds. Edward Hall, the anthropologist, identifies two broad cultural differences of interest to marketers: what he calls "monochronic time" cultures and "polychronic time" cultures.[12] The monochronic time cultures such as the United States emphasize schedules and promptness while polychronic time cultures like the Arab cultures are characterized by people doing many things at the same time; including dealing with several people at once which can make scheduling and time coordination very difficult.

By virtue of people's participation in a culture, there is a sharing of symbols, and values. A symbol is something meaningful through its signifying something else like the country's flag symbolizes the country itself, while cultural values are the preferences for the type of life sought or the things esteemed in the society. The lifestyles of those within the culture depend upon the shared meanings of symbols and events and it is these that influence modes of discourse and the possibility of negotiating differences. A background of shared social norms and values is necessary for any society to function so such norms and values have high symbolic meaning for the nation. This can also be true of subcultural norms. Thus a group that dresses in a distinct way sees clothing as symbolizing the values of the group.

Cultural changes in society are heralded by seeming changes in what receives attention. Thus the animal rights movement suggests a change in values: a wish to symbolize a commitment to promoting a less cruel society. For some social scientists, culture and people's search for the meaning of things within that culture are what determines behavior. Culture affects consumer goals and what are considered to be socially appropriate means for meeting those goals which, in turn, affects attitudes and the perceptions of products and promotions.

Within a culture, there are subcultures based say, on age, social class, religion, ethnicity, or geographical location. Although these are affected by the broader culture, they may be sufficiently distinct to be segments of a market. In thinking about marketing to another culture or subculture, questions arise as to the functions served by the product; the values and beliefs relevant to the purchase and the communication problems that are likely to occur. These questions must be asked also for the domestic market but they are more difficult to answer for an unfamiliar culture.

The clothing styles adopted by subcultures are often perceived by the majority culture as a threat to unity and cohesion.[13] The idea of the subculture's dress style as a coded response to changes within the whole society has become a key concept in the study of style. Subcultures like the "punks" set out to challenge the main culture by flaunting their hair style and dress and generally showing their contempt for the main culture's values.

Understanding a culture is not a matter of logic since an unfamiliar culture is often idiosyncratic to foreigners since they see the culture through the concepts or conceptual lens employed in their own culture. Misunderstandings occur in cross-cultural communications if the relevant signaling conventions differ. Hence there will inevitably be some dependence on the nationals of the foreign country for an understanding of the nuances of the culture. It is only in this way that the embarrassing errors reported in textbooks on international marketing can be avoided. The world as a "global village" is a long way off even though television has changed society and societies by giving rise to more commonality of attitudes while people throughout the world are becoming more cosmopolitan and less parochial. There are few cultures today that have not been influenced by other cultures. Today there is such a large cultural interchange that to talk of completely separate cultures is misleading.

In the late nineteenth century, Veblen, an economist, claimed that, as individual income rises above what is necessary to survive, more and more of the "discretionary income" will be spent on products that stimulate "the esteem and envy of fellow men." Much discretionary income throughout the world is spent on signaling social standing and enhancing social recognition. But it is the culture that determines what possessions make rank visible. This is so even though there are commonalities in what constitutes luxury goods like: fashion goods; cars; perfumes; cosmetics; watches; leather goods etc. Luxury goods are what are termed *positional goods* in that they are valued not despite their high price but because they are known to be expensive. But what signals snob appeal can wax and wane. Thus in a depression it is less socially appropriate to openly indulge in conspicuous consumption.

Even in foreign markets where there is no need to modify the product, the advertising may have to be changed. This is because the job to be done can vary with the beliefs of the culture while various advertising themes vary in cultural appropriateness. Advertising is always to some extent a mirror of the culture even if that mirror is sometimes a fun-house mirror of distortion. Thus, even the famous Marlboro cigarette advertisement (shown throughout the world) was changed for Chinese culture. The cowboy was shown riding a white horse in Hong Kong because a white horse is a symbol of esteem and counterbalances the cowboy association with low class manual labor!

The concept of culture is also applied in speaking of corporate culture and this will be discussed in the last two chapters in the book.

Reference groups and group behavior

Consumers do not behave as isolated individuals. They belong to various groups. Traditionally, in the organizational behavior literature, a "group" is a set of two or more individuals who are in reciprocal communication or associate with each other for some purpose. There are the primary groups like work groups, family groups and social groups that have direct contact with each other but also the more remote (secondary) groups like trade unions whose members associate with each other to further their common interests. In marketing, the groups of interest are buyer groups and reference groups.

A *reference group* consists of those whose standards, as perceived by the individual consumer, are the standards that the individual uses to guide his or her own behavior. The consumer need not be a member of the group since some groups are those to which the consumer aspires to join. Reference groups serve a *comparative* and a *normative* function. A group is a "normative reference group" if the individual consumer uses the group to establish behavioral standards, for example, in dress. A group is a "comparative reference group" if it is used by the consumer as a basis of comparison to evaluate personal qualities and buying actions. There are "positive" and "negative" reference groups for every consumer: *positive reference groups* are those with which the individual identifies, accepts, and wants to join or maintain membership, while *negative reference groups* are those privately rejected and used to define what we do not want to be. When the term reference group is used, however, without any qualification, it is interpreted to mean some positive reference group.

The more attractive the reference group, the more the motivation to adhere to the group's norms. "Group norms" are the accepted standard ways of thinking, feeling or behaving that are shared by members of the group. They result from social interaction: the behavior of people within the social group determines social norms and, for example, what is fashionable or popular with the group. The norms are both *descriptive* of behavior (i.e. reflect similarities in behavior among members of the group) and *prescriptive* of behavior (i.e. they reflect shared beliefs about what constitute appropriate opinions and behavior). One way to change people is to show that what they believe or the way they act is not in line with the social norms of their positive reference groups. A person who arrives at some conclusion, which no one else in their social milieu believes, will have little confidence in the validity of that conclusion and anyone who acts in a socially inappropriate way invites social disapproval. It is difficult to change behavior if that change conflicts with reference group norms.

Reference groups can on occasions influence what product is bought but not the brand while, on other occasions, they can influence the brand bought but not the decision to buy the particular product. *Conformity* to group norms is motivated both by *social conformity* and *informational conformity*. Social conformity arises from the desire for acceptance. People want to harmonize their relations with others and social conformity is the result. When beliefs are not built on tangible, physical reality but relate to social reality (e.g. status symbols) where things are ambiguous, social conformity offers a safe anchor for beliefs. Social conformity is more common if the purchase is socially visible like a car or the product is for a social occasion like wine, or the purchase has relevance for the buyer's social group such as clothing. *Informational conformity*, on the other hand, stems from the desire to make sense of the world around. In other words, while social (normative) conformity to group norms emanates from the desire to be accepted, informational conformity is a way of seeking a more accurate view of reality. Much conformity, however, involves both informational and normative influence. Group influence can be powerful since the attachment to various groups is one aspect of a person's social identity.

Sometimes certain norms or expectations attach to the "roles" played within groups. Those sociologists who distinguish between role and status (relative rank) in a group, define *role* as the behavior expected of a person with a given status in the group. Within the family there can be reciprocal or complementary roles as, say, between husband and wife. There can be an array of roles associated with a given position as occurs with the traditional housewife in her role of mother and household manager. There can thus be role conflict if divergent role expectations occur as when, say, purchasing managers see a conflict between their role as advisors and their role of questioning whether the proposed purchase should be made, given that there are equal substitutes available that cost less. When responsibilities are ambiguous or unstable, a person suffers from such *role ambiguity*. In any case, the roles people play within some group affect their purchasing decisions. This is particularly so in organizational buying.

Social groups are social communication networks. The informal *word-of-mouth* communication that occurs within groups may on occasions be far more influential than mass advertising in determining what brand of product is bought, because such communication carries more credibility and perhaps more pressure to conform. Members of a family group influence each other while certain purchases are jointly decided or dominated by one or other family member. Most commonly the wife takes on the role of *gatekeeper* who can screen what products or brands are bought.

Immersion in a group, that is, identifying strongly with some group, tends to reduce an individual's self-awareness so less attention is focused on an individual's own feelings, beliefs and wants. This reduces an individual's own deliberation and encourages action in accordance with group pressures. This is one explanation of the mass panic that periodically occurs in the stock market. When people are made self-aware by, say, using their name and addressing them directly, they are more likely to act in accordance with their standards, say, of personal integrity.

Social class

A social class is a social category, usually defined by its members having roughly equivalent socioeconomic status relative to other strata of society. Occupation and income are the typical criteria for distinguishing social classes in marketing but some researchers stress other factors such as education, lifestyle, prestige, or values as better descriptive measures. A consumer who is very conscious of social class will use it as a reference group but social class is so pervasive a concept in marketing that it is usually treated on its own.

Different social classes have different backgrounds and such differences complicate communications and provide a basis for misunderstanding. Thus a strategy of persuasion that is successful with one social class may not be successful with another. This is so well accepted in advertising that knowledge of social class is essential information for any campaign. Apart from problems of communication, social class is a guide to values in many countries of the world since values relate to patterns of buying or can even be a discriminator in buying such products as clothing, food and automobiles.

INDIVIDUAL CHARACTERISTICS THAT AFFECT BEHAVIOR

When we think of individual characteristics we generally think in terms of gender, age, marital status and so on. While these are factors that do influence what products are bought and will be considered later in the book, this section is concerned with theoretical abstractions such as values, attitudes, motives and personality that describe *dispositional tendencies*. These abstractions are essentially *hypothetical constructs* as they are not observable, but seem "as if" they exist. Thus it is "as if" attitudes, motives, values, and personality exist. If we opened up the brain we would not find anything that could be labeled "attitudes." The concept of attitude may no more mirror what happens in the head than a tune mirrors a musical score. But just as researchers are interested in relating culture to buying practices, they are interested in relating measures of entities like attitude to brand choice and intention to buy or in relating these entities to each other such as "values" to "attitudes."

Values and value systems

People's values are reflected in what they esteem as shown in their preferred lifestyle. If we know a person's values, we know what will be significant for him or her. But values have an intensity as well as content. If we rank a person's values on the basis of their intensity, the result forms that person's *value system*. Hence a person's value system is his or her hierarchy of values. In the next chapter, we view the consumer's value system as being reflected in his or her preferred life vision.

Most of our deepest values seem to be formed in early childhood, being grounded in early emotional experiences. Values are tied to the emotions so that threats to values can be emotionally arousing and what people get emotional about is a guide to those values. Whenever we make major trade-offs in decision-making, such trade-offs connect to values and this in itself can be emotional, leading to cognitive dissonance.

Since values are linked to a preferred life vision, they relate to lifestyle, and products bought are likely to cohere with that lifestyle. Although values and value systems tend to be stable and enduring, being grounded in early and later significant life experiences, values and value systems do change. Thus values are changing in Western societies in respect to marriage, community, piety and so on, with people becoming more individualistic and self-centered though (surprisingly) this has not meant that people are less inclined to help others through charities. Most advertising, explicitly or implicitly, appeals to values. Thus there are appeals to the values of being healthy, beautiful, or slim. But perhaps the most obvious appeals to values are by not-for-profit organizations doing fund-raising. It is such organizations that can arouse the most intense emotions like anger at injustice.

Attitudes

An *attitude* is a disposition to respond positively or negatively to some person, event or other phenomena. Measures of attitudes and measures of values are related which is not surprising since they are related in meaning. However, values are regarded as more stable than attitudes.

The term "attitude" is one of the most frequently used terms in marketing, but it is often used vaguely. Its chief use is to compare consumers' evaluations of a product or brand along a favorable/unfavorable continuum as a basis for predicting behavior and influencing attitudes on the assumption that attitudes relate to buying action. But the fact is that there are many possible properties of an item to which the consumer might have an attitude which makes it difficult to get out a valid summary statement or valid attitude measure. Attitude measures can vary, not only with the method used to do the measuring, but depending on what aspects of an offering or situation is focused on. Thus I may have a highly favorable attitude toward my computer but possess a negative attitude toward its simplicity in use.

There are several theoretical positions on attitudes. There are those who propose a *tripartite* view where attitude has three components, namely,

a) a cognitive component or the consciously held beliefs about the object of the attitude,
b) an affective (evaluative) component or the negative, neutral or positive feeling toward the object of the attitude, and
c) a conative component or the disposition to action.

On this view, my negative attitude toward buying a house in the country will have developed from three types of information

a) beliefs about the country and living there,
b) feelings about living in the country, and
c) choices and actions taken or disposed to take.

Other theoretical positions take a unidimensional view of attitude, taking just one of the three. Thus behaviorally oriented theorists focus on the conative component, some cognitive psychologists focus on the cognitive component and, in marketing (less commonly in the consumer behavior literature), attitude measures typically only measure the affective (evaluative) component. Those interested in the so-called hierarchy of effects models (to be discussed at length in the chapters on advertising used to describe attitude change), find it useful to adopt the tripartite view. The tripartite view suggests attitudes can come about through changes in cognition or in evaluation or in behavior.

Where there is high involvement with a purchase, attitudes develop before actual purchase. On the other hand, where there is low involvement with a product, buying can occur before attitudes are formed. This at least is the current orthodoxy though it seems difficult to imagine buying without some attitude being in place since there is likely to be a like/dislike reaction when faced with any brand option.

One claim is that attitudes perform four functions for an individual:

1 a utilitarian function with favorable attitudes toward products that best meet the function;
2 a value-expressive function with favorable attitudes toward whatever enhances self-image;
3 an ego-defensive function with favorable attitudes toward products that seem to protect the buyer from negative effects; and

4 a knowledge function with a favorable attitude toward products that give order and meaning to the world around.[14]

These four functions are an attempt to identify the implicit motivations in buying. It is not clear that they do cover all the reasons for buying (see next chapter).

There are many different measures of attitude which are discussed in Chapter 8. But these measures have not, in general, been highly predictive of behavior. There are several reasons for this. Attitudes may be in conflict, or a host of other influences may be at work that counteract the influence of any particular attitude. After all, an attitude is a dispositional term suggesting that attitudes manifest themselves in behavior only under certain conditions. In fact, knowing a person's attitude (for example, toward some product) without knowing that person's goals (wants) is not likely to be highly predictive of behavior. Thus we may have a very favorable attitude toward bicycles (environmentally clean, etc.) but do not buy them.

In marketing, attitudes tend to be more predictive of behavior (or at least, buying intentions) than in social science generally. This is because relevant goals can be assumed of those in the market. But specific attitude measures are better predictors than general attitude measures. Thus an attitude toward purchasing product "X" is likely to be more predictive of purchase than a simple measure of attitude toward "X".

In the organizational behavior literature, interest has lain in "self-perception theory," with the focus not being on how attitudes influence behavior but how behavior influences attitudes. The behavior⇒attitude relationship, as would be expected, can be quite strong. *Self-perception theory* asserts that people learn about their own attitudes, motives and other dispositions by considering their actions. The essence of self-perception theory is that we make inferences about ourselves from observing our own behavior. Thus if asked what type of shirts I like, I might mentally review my past purchase of shirts to determine what seems to be my preferences. The process of self-perception involves learning about ourselves in the same way as we try to understand others.

Self-perception theory seems most suited to explaining newly forming connections between attitudes and behavior. But sometimes it is quoted to suggest we are no more expert about our own actions and intentions than we are about others'. Introspection on this view provides no advantage. In reply it would be claimed that the observation of another's actions provides no definite guidance to the beliefs and wants lying behind the action. Thus I may see someone take an aspirin and assume she wanted to cure a headache and believed an aspirin would help. In fact, she herself would surely know whether this was true or whether aspirin was being taken because she wanted to decrease the risk of heart attack and believed that taking aspirin regularly would help. Only she, too, would know how confident she was in her beliefs about aspirin. Similarly, seeing someone go to church would suggest a belief in God but this might not be true. Many people apparently go to church who claim not to believe in God which suggests their beliefs are not determined by their behavior.

Attitude formation and change are major topics in marketing. There is interest in reinforcing or changing attitudes on the assumption attitude denotes some "mediating variable" between stimuli and responses that accounts for the nature of the response. One view is that attitudes enter into forming intentions and people generally seek to act in accordance with such intentions. But the term attitude change covers a vast number of theories concerning the processes by which individuals are persuaded. These processes are discussed later in Chapters 11 and 12 on advertising. Changing or intensifying attitudes may not be needed to change behavior. Where there is low involvement with the product, there are no major attitudinal barriers to be overcome while advertising may shape perceptions of the product to be in line with existing attitudes.

Motives

While to have an attitude is to have a disposition to react in some way to some event, person or item, to have a motive is to be disposed to act to satisfy a certain category of want. But there is no one-to-one relationship between motive and specific behavior. Thus the hunger motive does not lead to the same food being always purchased. This is because motives give only a directional tendency: we need to know relevant beliefs to predict how the individual is likely to act to satisfy the motive. In any case, many motives, rather than one single motive, are apt to operate at the time of buying. Also it cannot be assumed that all motives operate at the same level of intensity and salience in every culture or substrata of society or that the strengths of various motives remain constant through time. Nonetheless, social motives like wanting community with others, making sense of the world around and wanting recognition and status, are highly visible and stable motives.

There have been attempts to list categories of motives but none of these lists have had much impact in marketing. To say consumers have certain physiological needs, safety needs, affiliation needs (associated with seeking loving relationships with others), esteem needs and self-actualization (i.e. need to realize one's full potential) needs has not proved very helpful since these categories of motives (known as Maslow's hierarchy of needs) are neither exhaustive nor particularly operational in practice. The next chapter tries to get around this problem by focusing on categories of choice criteria.

Behavior is generally motivated in that people rarely behave in just a random way but act with a purpose. Emotions are important determinants of motives both in arousing them and giving them some directional tendency. Emotions arise as a reaction to the perceived negative or positive aspects of some object, person or happening in the world or in our imagination. Emotions will be considered in more detail in the chapters on advertising. There have also been attempts to list universal, inner dispositional compulsions like the desire to be consistent; to know what causes what; to categorize; to search for novelty and seek some degree of autonomy. Each of these has intuitive appeal and can be helpful to marketing. However, one concept that is most useful is the concept of "possible selves" which represents what we would like to become, what we are afraid of becoming and what we might become. Tied to the concept of "possible selves" are the following:

Self-concept/self-image.   This consists of the properties a person believes apply to him or her. Thus typical properties are gender, ethnicity and social class. These properties can be intrinsic ("I am blond") or comparative ("I am more slim than any of my friends").

Consumers seek to buy an image. An individual's self-concept arises both from within himself and from external influences such as feedback from others. Comparisons with others are not objective since we compare ourselves with others but bias the comparison for purposes of self-enhancement.

Self-esteem/self-worth/self-respect/self-regard.   These are the subjective counterpart of the ego and depend on the private valuations we put on the properties constituting our self-image. These valuations are tied to societal values, acquired through socializing with others. But self-esteem is not a constant but can vary with the type of people we are with and the situation, since different people will be perceived as judging our "assets" differently. In any case, low self-esteem tends to be tied to being more susceptible to external influence. There is a disposition to buy that which supports self-esteem.

Self-confidence.   This is the feeling of confidence and the feeling of being able to have an impact on others. A good deal of advertising of personal toiletries and cosmetics is tied to enhancing self-confidence.

Ideal-self/symbolic self.   This is the self we wish others to take us to be. One part of this ideal is an image of ourselves as moral agents. Typically much fund-raising for charities seeks to tap this aspect of "what people would like to become morally."

Personality

There is interest in "personality" theory since so many marketers believe that brands purchased (e.g. makes of car) often match the consumer's personality or are bought to cover personality defects. Advertising commonly tries to create personalities for products that fit some personality type. But this begs the question of what is covered by the term personality.

Strictly speaking, personality covers the whole field of individual differences that stem from hereditary and upbringing. Not surprisingly, psychologists have sought something more manageable but the result has been a proliferation of theories. The oldest are "type theories" which assert each individual is a representation of some sort of balance of temperaments, for example, extrovert versus introvert. There are, too, the "multitrait theories" that assume a person's personality is a compendium of traits like being venturesome, sensitive, timid and so on. There are also "single-trait" theories like the concept just discussed of "possible selves" or the "authoritarian personality" or the so-called "locus of control" which refers to whether individuals feel their lives are controlled by themselves or by external forces over which they have no control. There are many "psychoanalytic theories" that revolve around the notion of an integrated personality: the idea that the adult personality evolves gradually over time, depending on the manner in which the integration of development factors occurs. There are also the "social learning theories" based on the notion of personality being those aspects of behavior that are acquired in a social context: interest here lies not in classifying people but in classifying situations that bring out certain reactions.

Many psychologists reject both the concept and the reality of personality. They argue that how people behave, when consistent, is a function of habits learnt or conformity to the social norms and expectancies that apply in the situation. Somewhat similar are views which maintain that, whatever is called by the name "personality," it is something that just emerges from interactions between a person's dispositions and the environment as it is the environment which influences the way behavioral tendencies manifest themselves.

There are a number of research areas relating personality and buying. One area relates consumer cognitive processes to various aspects of personality while another area relates personality measures to product or brand purchase. The relationships tend to be weak, partly because the personality tests are typically designed for some other purpose than buying. In any case, if the buying involves serious decision-making, no personality test is likely to be highly predictive of specific brand purchases since such decision-making usually involves a creative element as the consumer reflects and resolves conflicts in motives.

DECISION VARIABLES, INFLUENCES, AND PROCESSES

Perception

In the marketing literature, the information processing approach of cognitive psychology describes the various antecedent steps to decision-making such as exposure to stimuli; giving attention; interpretation of stimuli and storing in memory. In the broadest sense of the term, perception covers this entire sequence of events from the presentation of a physical stimulus to the experiencing of it, so embracing the various physical, physiological, neurological, sensory, cognitive, and affective processes. But because this use of the term is so broad, more specialized and restricted uses of the term perception are common.

Like many other terms, the word "perception" can be used as a result ("her perception is . . .") or as a process. As a process perception is commonly defined in marketing as the process by which individuals organize and interpret sensory impressions to give meaning to the world around. What is always recognized is that what is perceived is not uniquely determined by the physical stimulation itself but depends on other things such as the degree of attention; motivation; beliefs and emotions. In other words, we do not all experience the same stimulus in the same way but interpret it according to our goals, interests and expectations based on past experience. Expectations can distort perceptions as expectations (as well as attitudes) influence interpretation. We will return to a discussion of some of these factors in the chapters on advertising.

Marketing is vitally concerned with buyer perceptions since judging what to buy essentially involves two processes:

1 perceptions of the offering;
2 making the logical choice based on those perceptions.

Marketers want perceptions to match those that would trigger buying. Another reason for interest is that sometimes perceptions can be changed without trying to change basic attitudes or, where no firm attitudes exist, a change in perceptions can be the basis for the formation of a favorable attitude.

Related to perception is the concept of *schemata* (the plural of *schema*). Schemata are categories of ideas or general frameworks for interpreting and relating information about any particular stimulus whether person, product or event. For example, a schema about the IBM PC might include opinions of others about it; impressions of media portrayals of IBM; personal experience with using IBM products and so on. Once a schema is established it is used to interpret new information (e.g. about the IBM PC) and so influences perceptions. Existing schemata result in selective perception which can give rise to bias. Schemata are organized hierarchically from, say, general impressions of a product or brand, next being personal feelings about the brand and then, say, to anticipating what it would be like to own, use and consume the product. Schematas are tied to concepts like attitude and brand image.

Motivation

Another concept, related to influencing perceptions, is the question of motivation. Motivation refers to the process of motivating, that is, of providing others with a motive(s) for doing something. The term "motive" should be distinguished from the process of motivating though the term "motivation" is sometimes used as a slightly pretentious synonym for motive. A study of motivation is important since people need to be motivated to buy. But, to actually buy a specific brand, the consumer needs not only the motive but to also possess the ability (financial at least), the opportunity (product availability) and, last but not least, the appropriate set of beliefs about what to buy. This relates to the view that performance is a function of MOA (motivation plus opportunity plus ability) but with the addition of beliefs since motivation is directed as to means by beliefs.

In the literature on motivation, there is the usual split between those who see all human behavior as simply a response to the pull and push of past impressed forces and immediate stimuli, and those who argue that this is nonsense when it comes to human action since people are free agents, acting within constraints certainly, but otherwise free to choose. Within the group of those viewing the consumer as a free agent, there is nonetheless debate over the extent to which the consumer is highly rational. Marketers typically assume a fairly high degree of rationality. This is consistent with the marketing concept though this is changing to a more realistic (but less manageable) concept of flawed and bounded rationality. This is discussed more fully in the next section.

Decision processes

Decision-making, as an area of study, is generally regarded as falling within the field of cognitive psychology. Allied to the study of *actual* decision-making is "decision theory" which seeks both to describe and explain decision-making; studying such things as problem solving, choice behavior, utility theory, game theory and so on. Not surprisingly marketing academics have drawn both from cognitive psychology and decision theory.

Where there is deliberation on which brand to buy (or any other aspect of buying and consuming), there is a need to weigh up the pros and cons. Deliberation occurs in buying when there are risks or uncertainties and the purchase justifies the effort involved. Buying risks and uncertainty may or may not arouse anxiety. A consumer may spend a good deal of time deciding on which TV to buy without any accompanying anxiety about making a serious error. Much buying does not necessitate much in the way of decision-making or deliberation or even acute awareness of what is happening until something happens to jolt the buyer into more conscious thinking.

There are descriptive, prescriptive and normative models of decision-making. Descriptive models purport to show how decisions are actually made and are usually expressed in the form of the heuristics (rules of thumb) used. Some of these are discussed in the next chapter. One way of discovering such rules is through the use of verbal protocols which are records of buyers as they think-aloud as they go about buying. A good deal of the next chapter was based on over 2,000 such protocols. But protocols like these are of limited value if a researcher is not just interested in heuristics and reasons for buying but wants to identify the actual mental processes involved in accessing these reasons and weighing and applying them to reach a decision. Thus if I ask a respondent what comes to mind on being faced with the brand-name, Coca-Cola, and the reply is "soft drink," neither the respondent nor the interviewer will be able to identify the mental *process* by which this response arose. (Nonetheless, for predicting subsequent action, it is useful to know what beliefs were recalled first!) Verbal protocols are most useful for generating reasons for buying and for discovering the inferences that are most likely to be made. As Ericsson and Simon point out, verbal reports are best when buyers are simply asked to report their thoughts as they happen rather than be asked later to remember what they thought.[15]

Prescriptive models are designed to show how we *ought* to make a decision. Many of these models consist also of useful heuristics. But to determine what is best for our purposes, we might think first of some *normative model*. Thus one normative model we may draw on is game theory discussed in Chapter 7 on competitive strategy. In any case, normative models are typically too demanding and this is why prescriptive models, of the sort used in Decision Support Systems (DSS), discussed in the chapter on marketing research, usually differ somewhat from the normative.

To what extent is the idealized conception of rationality, commonly assumed in both economics and marketing, descriptive of actual behavior? Both information search and thinking have costs while there is often time pressure or memory limitations. Herbert Simon speaks of *satisficing* rather than maximizing, that is, selecting a solution that is good enough on the ground that people have *bounded rationality*. Bounded rationality acknowledges that people's ability falls below that demanded to solve many complex decisions and, as a consequence, people fall back on simple rules that yield a satisfactory solution most times. Consumers can be incompetent, inefficient, forgetful, and silly and their rationality flawed. Consumers are not always even consistent but tolerate a good deal of inconsistency in what they say and do. One reason for this suggested by cognitive psychologists is that different (inconsistent) beliefs or cognitions seem to be organized in the mind in different "files" so that inconsistencies may not be recognized until exposed.

Definitions of rationality in decision-making or actions vary. One definition in economics simply defines rationality as that decision that maximizes utility which tells us next to nothing about how to undertake rational decision-making. Others judge rationality of actions as simply those that are consistent with objectives. Others focus on the method of arriving at a decision with validity depending on the method's objectivity and being shown to be helpful in achieving ends. In marketing many equate rationality with some procedure like that of the multiattribute model discussed below. Others would insist on the beliefs entering into the decision being sound and in line with long-term interests and would reject rationality being demonstrated by just having an ordered set of preferences, or action just being goal directed. Thus the philosopher rejects as rational the use of inputs into decision-making that reflect:

1 nothing more than what has been done traditionally;
2 simply advice accepted uncritically merely because it is offered by some celebrity;
3 past experience without assessing its continuing usefulness.

Rationality in decision-making suggests at least establishing the right goals; identifying the most appropriate alternative courses of action; collecting and assessing the evidence and making the right inferences about the relevance of the attributes for the goals being sought. These are hard demands of the consumer as many buying decisions are just made on the basis of social appropriateness, or the result of unexamined advice or even on the basis of the feelings aroused by imagining buying, possessing and consuming the product.

In identifying brand alternatives, brands familiar to the buyer are the *awareness set* and those the consumer actually evaluates are called the *evoked set*. In evaluating alternatives, buyers are often viewed as drawing on certain models or set rules. One such model is the *multiattribute model* or compensatory model where the consumer is viewed as acting "as if" he or she weights each attribute like durability, economy, taste, or whatever and rates each brand on the basis of how much it has of the attribute. The overall relative scores resulting from the sum of the weights times ratings gives the relative evaluation of each brand. These relative scores are sometimes treated as measures of relative attitude toward the various brands or even as the relative motivating power of the brands to stimulate purchase.

The model was first used in social science as a way of describing attitudinal structure. It is known as a multiattribute, compensatory model because several attributes are involved, with a brand's weakness on one attribute being compensated by strength on another attribute. The list of attributes should be those reflecting bases for variations in choice and should preferably be obtained from consumers themselves. The attributes need to be independent (to prevent double counting) and free of vagueness and ambiguity. This may not be difficult to do when the attributes are physically based but can be more problematic when the attributes are abstract such as brand image and the status potential of each brand of, say, car. The validity of the consumer's information and inferences is not questioned. Hence what attitudes consumers might have under full knowledge conditions and what they display under the model may diverge somewhat. In any case, when the consumer is minimally involved with the purchase, he or she may learn somewhat randomly, picking up information rather than actively seeking it. In such conditions, the consumer may passively accept information in an uncritical way, simply seeking to avoid trouble and problems.

The multiattribute model is, of course, the same rational procedure that was used in the last two chapters in using the GE business screen, to select a strategy and in economics as discussed earlier. If this is what occurs naturally in decision-making, it seems odd that it has to be taught so formally! In answer it is claimed it is "as if" such a model is being followed in that attitudes measured in this way are significantly related to purchase and purchase intentions. There is no way of actually "seeing" that this model does in fact describe what happens in the head. Studies of information processing and the analysis of protocols cast doubts on whether the consumer actually does organize information in the way suggested by the model though no one can be sure since so much interpretation is involved.[16] Certainly, few of us seem conscious of fully following such a process though we are all conscious of making trade-offs. The major reason for using the model is not because simpler measures are poorer at prediction but because it claims to offer insight into attitudinal structure, allowing a "diagnosis of brand strengths and weaknesses on relevant product attributes."

Given that organizational buying is likely to be more systematic, it would be reasonable to assume that the model would be more likely to apply to such buying. This may be so but the position is complicated by the fact that in so much organizational buying, multiple participants are involved with competing interests so the strengths and weaknesses of the product may not be the same for all. The multiattribute model is considered in more detail in the next chapter.

Another model is the *implicit favorite model*. Here consumers do not enter into the difficult task of seriously evaluating alternatives until one of the alternatives can be identified as an "implicit favorite" which is the tentative preferred alternative. The rest of the decision process becomes essentially a confirmation process with the decision-maker simply selecting or weighting evidence to support the implicit favorite as the right choice.

There are several decision rules that are *noncompensatory*. In other words, unlike the multiattribute model which is a compensatory model, they do not assume that a brand's weakness on one attribute can be compensated by strength on another. Two of these noncompensatory models—the "conjunctive" and the "disjunctive"—simply separate the options into acceptable and unacceptable groups; they do not necessarily provide a ranking of preferences. Under the *conjunctive decision processing rule*, the consumer establishes *minimum* levels on all attributes or choice criteria. An alternative is accepted only if *every* attribute or choice criterion equals or exceeds the minimum cutoff level, that is, all brands are acceptable that surpass the minimum standards. Thus in Table 4.1 the subject (a student) accepts the two Hewlett-Packard brands of calculator and rejects the other brands in his evoked set. Under the *disjunctive rule*, the consumer establishes acceptable standards for each attribute or choice criterion. An alternative is acceptable if it exceeds the minimum level on at least one attribute or criterion.

Table 4.1 Conjunctive model

Features	Hewlett-Packard	Others
Min. financial functions	yes	yes
Easy learning	yes	yes/no
Immediate availability	yes	no

Table 4.2 Lexicographic model

Features	HP 17BII	HP 19BII
Min. financial functions	yes	yes
Easy learning	yes	yes
Immediate availability	yes	yes
RPN	yes	yes
Key touch	yes	yes
Extra functions	no	yes

Table 4.3 Compensatory model

		Relative points		Total points	
Features	Weight	HP 17BII	HP 19BII	HP 17BII	HP 19BII
Min. financial functions	3	3	3	9	9
Easy learning	3	3	3	9	9
Immediate availability	3	3	3	9	9
RPN	3	3	3	9	9
Key touch	3	3	3	9	9
Integrative functions	3	1	3	3	9
Extra functions	2	1	3	2	6
Speed of calculations	2	3	3	6	6
Price	2	3	1	6	2
Alternative power source	2	1	1	2	2
Size and weight	1	3	1	3	1
Easy opening	1	3	1	3	1
Battery access	1	1	2	1	2
Separate alpha keyboard	1	1	3	1	3
				27	32

A third decision processing rule is known as the *lexicographic rule* which does lead to a unique choice. Under this rule, the consumer ranks attributes or choice criteria from most to least important. The consumer then first chooses that which is the best on the most important criterion. If a tie occurs the consumer selects the best alternative on the second most important criterion and so on until just one alternative (brand) is left. Table 4.2 illustrates the lexicographic rule as the student seeks to choose between the two Hewlett-Packard calculators. Table 4.3 shows the wider range of criteria considered in the multiattribute model and illustrates the procedure whereby the HP 19B11, selected under the lexicographic rule, is also selected under the (compensatory) multiattribute model.

These are not the only decision processing rules that could be in operation but they are the ones most commonly quoted. There are also simple heuristics employed by consumers to avoid heavy computation and hard thinking. As a decision ranks alternatives, these rankings can be viewed as the consumer's relative attitudes toward the brands in the evoked set, as exemplified by the multiattribute model. This leads to a brand preference and (hopefully) the intention to buy.

One final comment. In Figure 4.1, social attachments, individual characteristics and decision variables are connected by arrows leading from one to the other. But in many texts it is common to bring together the social attachment variables, individual characteristics and decision variables into some overall system, with each variable in a box linked to other boxes. This can be misleading if causal linkages are suggested since the linkages are typically conceptual in that the variables can often be linked through having overlapping meanings which is implicit in their definitions. Also many of the variables come from different theoretical orientations so linking one with another can be an illicit graft. In any case, linking together all the various concepts introduced by social scientists gives the impression that these concepts are pieces in a jigsaw puzzle which, when put together, will constitute the complete explanation of buyer behavior. The fact is, of course, that the concepts overlap, or are at different levels of abstraction and come from different theories so that, at best, we have no jigsaw puzzle for completion but different photographs of the same terrain from many different angles. This criticism is not meant to condemn all linking of behavioral concepts as this must inevitably occur to show relationships. But thoughtless linking together of concepts can easily degenerate into misleading boxology.

NOTES

1 Lindblom, C. A. and Cohen, D. K. (1979) *Usable Knowledge: Social Science and Social Problem Solving*, New Haven, CT: Yale University Press.
2 Bruner, Jerome (1990) *Acts of Meaning*, Cambridge, MA: Harvard University Press.
3 Pinker, Stephen (1994) *The Language Instinct*, New York: William Morrow.
4 Foxall, Gordon R. (1990) *Consumer Psychology in Behavioral Perspective*, London: Routledge.
5 Gilovich, Thomas (1991) *How We Know What Isn't So*, New York: Free Press.
6 Ortony, Andrew, Clore, Gerald L., and Collins, Allan (1988) *The Cognitive Structure of Emotions*, Cambridge: Cambridge University Press.
7 Heath, Anthony (1976) *Rational Choice and Social Exchange*, Cambridge: Cambridge University Press.
8 Harré, R. and Secord, P. F. (1973) *The Explanation of Social Behavior*, Totowa, NJ: Littlefield, Adams.
9 Leiter, Kenneth (1980) *A Primer on Ethnomethodology*, New York: Oxford University Press.
10 Blumer, Herbert (1969) *Symbolic Interactionism: Perspective and Method*, Englewood Cliffs, NJ: Prentice Hall.
11 Geertz, Clifford (1984) *Local Knowledge: Further Essays in Interpretive Anthropology*, New York: Basic Books.
12 Hall, Edward T. (1989) *Beyond Culture*, New York: Anchor Books (Doubleday).
13 Hebdige, Dick (1991) *Subculture: The Meaning of Style*, London: Routledge.

14 Katz, D. (1960) "The Functional Approach to the Study of Attitudes," *Public Opinion Quarterly*, 24.
15 Ericsson, K. A. and Simon, Herbert A. (1980) "Verbal Reports as Data," *Psychological Review*, 87.
16 Bettman, J. R. (1979) "Issues in Designing Consumer Environments," *Journal of Consumer Research* 2 (December).

Chapter 5

Understanding the buyer/consumer

This chapter brings together within an overall framework some sensitizing concepts for understanding buying. The aim is to provide a coherent, recognizable picture of the buyer by describing behavior and behavior patterns in terms of concepts that are affirmed by buying experience. The basic framework is shown in Figure 5.1. The chapter follows this basic framework in its headings so it should be referred to constantly. Behind all human intentional action lies a structure of goals/wants and beliefs. In line with this Figure 5.1 shows the consumer's decision to buy as emanating from the consumer's goals/wants and beliefs leading to one or other states of:

1 "wanting without buying";
2 "buying without deciding"; and
3 "deciding before buying"

and subsequent stages of establishing preference, buying intentions, a "will" to buy, buying and post-purchase behavior.

Whereas Chapter 4 considered, among other things, the psychological forces at work in buying, this chapter focuses on describing buying states, choice criteria and reasons for buying. There are alternatives to this approach. Thus some marketing texts just adopt a problem-solving approach, along the lines of John Dewey's problem-solving stages and the planning stages set out in Chapter 3. Still other texts view buying as following some hierarchy of effects model moving, say, from cognition to evaluation to conation (disposition to action). Still other approaches arrange the various concepts discussed in the last chapter into a model of information processing stages. Usually the rational model is assumed. Thus, in respect to one well-known such model, the claim can be reduced simply to saying that beliefs about a brand and its benefits in relation to wants, combined with the confidence in those beliefs, lie behind whatever action is taken.[1] The approach discussed here was developed to introduce more realism, more richness into the description of buyer behavior while getting round the limitations of traditional approaches e.g. that all buying can be described in terms of some formal problem-solving model; that buyers always deliberate on the pros and cons of buying this brand rather than that; that there is only one set of mental processes involved in buying and so on. More of interest, the discussion below and the framework described is geared to aspects of behavior most likely to be of interest to the marketing manager.

GOALS IN BUYING

Buying behavior, like all human action, is purposive. Consumers in their purchases seek "the good life." This vision of the good life reflects a sensitivity to contrasts in the human condition (see Table 5.1) with the more agreeable polar extreme representing the preferred life vision. Consumer purchases track this vision. This preferred life vision is composed of the goals to which consumers implicitly strive. Thus people prefer to be healthy rather than unhealthy; to be loved and admired rather than hated and disliked; to be excited rather than bored; to be beautiful rather than to be ugly and so on.

The good life is the preferred life vision, but not all the elements of the good life can

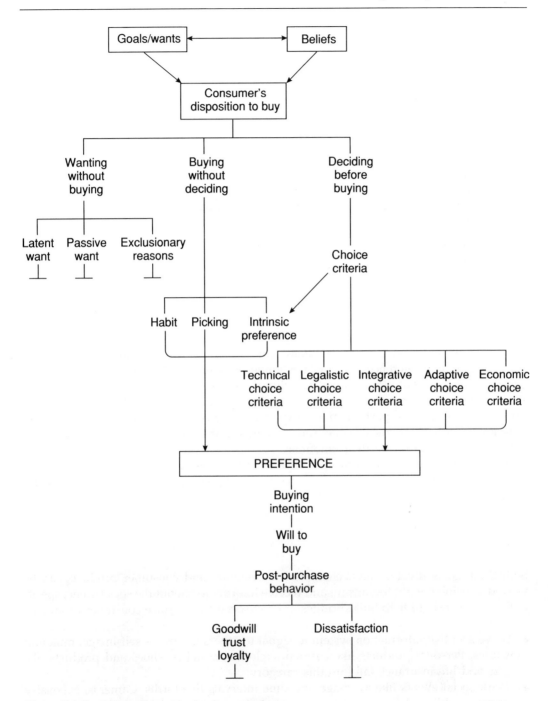

Figure 5.1 Concepts affirmed by buying experience

Table 5.1 Contrasts in the human condition

Track the good life	Avoid the poor life
To be healthy	Being unhealthy
To be loved/admired	Being hated/disliked
To be secure	Being threatened
To be full of life	Being sluggish
To be an insider	Being an outsider
To be confident	Being insecure
To be relaxed	Being tense/anxious
To be beautiful/handsome	Being ugly
To be knowledgeable	Being ignorant
To be in control	Being subject to others
To be entertained	Being bored
To be free of guilt	Being guilt ridden
To be consistent	Being inconsistent
To be rich/powerful	Being poor/powerless
To be a person of integrity	Being unethical

be pursued with equal vigor. The priority ranking of the various elements of the good life represent a person's *system of values*. This system of values manifests itself in a person's product preferences since values guide preferences. How we come to promote certain values and not others is tied to cultural values and past emotional experiences. What weight the consumer gives to being, say, rich and beautiful depends on the culture's values and on past emotional experiences. This does not mean that people are conscious of what they most value, unless some event in life (e.g. the loss of freedom) reminds them by arousing their emotions.

Douglas and Isherwood claim that, beyond just hedonism and buying to keep body and soul together, consumer buying expresses social goals and values.[2] To Douglas and Isherwood priority in buying is tied to values that reflect:

- community with others;
- making sense of what is happening in the world around.

Both these goals involve the exchange of information and consumer products can be viewed as being bought to transmit and receive information about the social scene, specifically information to help build bridges or erect social fences since consumer products:

- Serve as a live information system to signal to others the user's self-image, rank and values. Personal products like cosmetics, clothes, watches, shoes and products like cars and life insurance fall into this category.
- Mark social events like marriage and time intervals like births. Cameras, expensive wines, wedding dresses, and so on are bought to mark social occasions.
- Increase the time available for social involvement. Lawnmowers, washing machines, telephones and TV dinners come under this heading.

- Give order to events. Under this heading come newspapers, magazines and other products that help make sense of what is happening in the world around.

The Douglas and Isherwood thesis explains *patterns* of consumption and the *classes* of products bought. They claim that, as income increases, consumers in buying stress products that release them from constant chores to increase the time for social involvement. They point out that individual purchases are always coordinated with other purchases as goods assembled in ownership "present a set of meanings, more or less coherent, more or less intentional." The consumer's pattern of consumption signals to the world what he or she wants the world to believe he or she stands for. Symbolism is paramount. Consumers are anxious not to give the wrong signals and so choose signals via their buying that are neither vague nor ambiguous but clearly recognizable or standardized in the culture. An exclusive Gucci handbag must stand out as such to transmit to others "who know the code" the message the owner wants conveyed. Typically, advertising is linked, however obliquely, to the consumer's diffuse longings for the good life. In general advertising appeals to values currently held but occasionally seeks to change priorities (e.g. public service advertising). This may on occasions be successful since not all people's values are firm but may be pliant enough to be modified. In fact all values that are relevant to buying are probably conditional as there is unlikely to be any single value that could not be overridden by another value in certain circumstances. Even though a system of values is strongly linked to culture and past experiences, value systems do change with fresh thinking and new experiences.

REASONS (WANTS AND BELIEFS)

Wants

To want "X" is to have a disposition towards using, consuming or possessing "X." To say Jane wants a Mercedes is to say something about Jane's potential future action; it is to attribute to her a certain disposition. A want viewed as a disposition contrasts with the idea of a want being a type of inner tension pressing for relief which is a throwback to the idea of all behavior being determined by some set of drives. Although having a want can be accompanied by a strong feeling of deprivation, this is not generally so; most product wants are not like pangs of hunger. Thus:

- I may want a sports car over a period of many years without being continuously conscious of that want.
- I may plan to buy a product without wanting it immediately.
- Many wants operate simply at the intellectual level as we seek products to perform functions better.

A want, unlike a wish, takes account of feasibility so that neither wants nor goals are entertained that are impossible to fulfill. Also, a want for a product is not just wanting that product regardless (e.g. in poor condition) but is wanted under some description of benefits sought. This is why marketing focuses not on marketing a product but on marketing benefits.

The consumer's preferred life vision gives rise to product wants. But wants stemming from the preferred life vision are usually just *notional* wants in that they simply conjure up the general type of satisfaction that is sought. But not always, since some wants are biologically based, like sex, where the want is a drive giving more direction as to what is sought. However, wants, whether notional or biological, combine with beliefs to provide reasons for buying a specific product or brand.

A "want" is represented in the mind as benefits sought, while a "belief" is a disposition to accept that certain things are true (or false) or that certain things should be done (or not done). Wants are always comparative in that whatever is wanted, it is wanted through comparison with the alternatives displaced. Several propositions can be put forward regarding wants. These are shown in Table 5.2. There are also many terms in popular usage that are variations of the term want. Of interest to marketers are those shown in Table 5.3.

A manufacturer or service provider can seldom cater to a want in all its detail but nonetheless seeks to meet or exceed buyer/consumer expectations. Whenever expectations are seriously violated, the disappointment is apt to inhibit repeat purchase. It is also true that when expectations are more than realized, favorable reactions can increase sales.

Table 5.2 Propositions regarding wants

- Each consumer has a multitude of wants.
- Different consumers have different wants or want priorities.
- Every consumer would prefer to satisfy more rather than less of a want.
- There is a strict limit to the number of wants that can be met by any one product.
- There are always costs attached to the satisfaction of any want, and such costs are best reflected in the alternatives displaced.
- The way the consumer satisfies his or her wants is constrained by perceptions of what is an efficient and socially appropriate way of meeting the want.
- The same lifestyle can find expression in many equally acceptable ways, so many different products are substitutable without any corresponding sense of loss.
- The consumer is *not* always conscious of his or her wants.
- *Active* wants take account of the feasibility of satisfying the want, so that expressed wants do not necessarily take account of all "secret" wishes. Hence asking people what they want in a product or offering is unlikely to generate truly innovative ideas. Perhaps asking them about their secret wishes would stimulate more novel suggestions.
- A want for a product can be thought of as a *cluster of attributes* being sought to generate certain satisfactions, not all of which must be possessed by the firm's offering for the consumer to feel the want is being met satisfactorily. Every individual want will have unique aspects that the standard mass-produced product will have had to ignore.
- Consumers may actually want something they do not consciously believe they want or may think they want what in fact they do not want.
- An *active* want is not just a want for anything that would meet the core want. Thus water may quench the consumer's thirst but the active want is for a cold beer.
- A consumer's *total* want is not necessarily captured by any product, not just because some of the benefits sought are absent but because of the presence of things not wanted (e.g. carcinogens in cigarettes).
- Some wants seek immediate satisfaction; others are intended to be realized in the future.

Table 5.3 Variations of the term "want"

1 *Desire*. A desire is a want that the consumer is acutely aware of not having realized. One aim of advertising is to elevate wants to desires so that the consumer thinks often about the product, inquires about it, and is moved by facts about it.

2 *Need*. A need is an absolute requirement. On this basis we may need things we do not actively want (car safety belts) and want things we do not really need (cigarettes).

3 *Impulse*. An impulse is a strong notional want that finds expression in a response to some stimuli without the consumer being acutely conscious of what is being sought. Product attractiveness when allied to seemingly effortless, low-cost buying can activate impulse buying.

4 *Wish*. A wish, unlike the typical want, is a yearning for some state of affairs regardless of the feasibility of attainment. Emotional stimulation is often tied to appeals to wishes.

5 *Craving*. A craving is a desire that is biologically compelling.

6 *Lust*. Lust is a biologically driven desire that has the potential to lead to actions that defy social norms and morality.

7 *Obsession*. An obsession is any cycle of repetitive behavior from which a person finds it difficult to break free.

8 *Addiction*. Addiction is the paradigm case of obsession when the object of the obsession is some consumable product.

Beliefs

A belief is a disposition to accept that certain statements (for example, about a product's performance) are more likely to be true than false, or that certain things should be done (for example, to shop around before choosing) or not done. The consumer's system of beliefs can be viewed as a map by which she steers with any individual belief being a potential guide or an inhibitor of action. For consumers to want a product they must normally *believe* that the product will help them achieve the good life. If advertising seeks to change or reinforce attitudes it does so by changing or reinforcing beliefs. There is no way of implanting a belief as beliefs are adopted. Although beliefs are held with different degrees of confidence, they are always important to marketers since they generally point to what brand, given some want, will be preferred. Once beliefs are fixed about what is wanted, all options incompatible with these beliefs can be ignored. Beliefs always exclude some possibilities in a particular context though, in another buying context, such possibilities might not be excluded. Thus I may believe that I should not buy a car while living in New York City, but not when I move out to the country.

The demand for a product rests on wants and beliefs. The wants consumers seek to satisfy though, are not necessarily the strongest but perhaps those that cohere with beliefs about what is wise, or the sensible thing to do. Thus I may long to smoke a cigarette but believe this to be bad for me long term. There is thus this conflict between the desire for "instant gratification" and beliefs about what is best for the future. Although changes in beliefs (e.g. about the relationship between health and weight) can lead to not wanting some specific product (e.g. ice cream loaded with calories), there will still remain the general want awaiting satisfaction. This is why a product may at first fail but be successfully reintroduced by eliminating or adding some ingredient, component, or feature. Beliefs lie behind attitudes and control and inform action all the way from shaping wants into specific brand preferences to guiding post-purchase actions such as returning an unsatisfactory product. It is beliefs that convert a notional want for a certain type of satisfaction into a specific want for a certain product and brand.

Beliefs and information

One way of visualizing beliefs is to view them as internal mental structures that steer and control actions in line with their informational content. As more information is acquired about a product, beliefs become more refined and specific in steering action. Initial beliefs at the start of buying may be few and general but, when shopping is a learning experience, beliefs become more detailed and firm. Beliefs are tied to information as new information affects beliefs. Beliefs are thus parasitic on the interpretation of the information that beliefs encode. Of particular significance in changing beliefs is information that adds to the consumer's repertoire of concepts. Just as concepts learnt from reading this book can change the way the reader looks at marketing, so concepts about how to perform a task (word processing versus traditional typing) will change the buyer's beliefs and probably buying preferences. When radical changes in beliefs occur, concepts are replaced, added or abandoned and new relationships among concepts arise. For instance, when beliefs about the long-term consequences of smoking cigarettes changed from the view of effects being benign to the long-term effects being lung cancer, people came to grasp the concept of carcinogens and relate it to the tar in cigarettes and to lung cancer. The learning of new words to describe a brand or the meaning of product features can lead to the consumer endorsing a new set of beliefs. Thus in learning about the mouse as an add-on feature of computers, I may come to endorse that feature, that is, come to believe in its benefits. *Where consumers fail to grasp the concept of the product and its differences from rivals, they cannot develop a genuine preference for it.* All consumers wish their beliefs to be based on the best information available, but time pressures and cost factors usually rule this out. *Consumers are therefore likely to collect just enough information to determine a brand preference but not to become experts on the product class.* This relates to the concept of satisficing behavior mentioned in the last chapter.

Beliefs and emotions

Beliefs are not always based on objective facts but are linked to loyalties, hopes, fears, self-interest, and social conditioning so they only imperfectly relate to supporting evidence. Some beliefs merely reflect wishful thinking. *Self-deception* occurs when false beliefs are accepted for the sake of some goal to which the individual is attached. Wanting something to be true (e.g. a cure for baldness) influences the selection of facts, so that the consumer selectively perceives, remembers, and interprets, filtering out disconfirmations of beliefs emotionally held. Also, consumers do not generally have the time, the ability, or the desire to retrieve and canvass all their beliefs, so that, when disposed to believe X, the result can be an automatic endorsement and choices in line with that endorsement. This is one reason why appeals to emotion can, on occasion, be so effective.

Belief networks

Beliefs are seldom isolated beliefs but are part of a system of beliefs. This is why some beliefs are more fixed and less easily given up or imagined to be false than others. It is also a reason why attacking a single belief (e.g. that smoking is not bad for the health) may be ineffective when it is part of a supporting network of beliefs. It is also the reason why the retraction of a false statement in an advertisement may not undo the damage. Those consumers who believed the falsehood are likely to have retrieved other beliefs in support: these other beliefs remain in place. New beliefs are more easily endorsed when not in competition with other sets of beliefs.

Tacit beliefs

Most beliefs involved in buying are tacit beliefs. Memory stores the resources out of which beliefs come into being with most overt beliefs being probably "manufactured" from information possessed, just as the consumer arrives at her belief about the overall cost of shopping by calling on the rules of addition. But how a consumer acts will depend not just on having some particular belief but on the whole of his or her beliefs, wants and emotions. When we provide reasons for someone's actions, we are supplying the reasons which we believe are the major ones, rather than the only ones at work.

WANTING WITHOUT BUYING

Wanting a product may be a necessary but is not a sufficient condition for buying it. Wants are not in themselves reasons for action; the relevant beliefs need to be present. When the want for a product is "latent" consumers have yet to acquire the relevant beliefs about the product's potential for them. When a want is "passive," consumers are aware to some extent of the product's potential for them but are held back from buying by beliefs about the wisdom of buying. Finally, when a want is "excluded," there are exclusionary reasons precluding buying, that is, reasons that have nothing to do with the relative merits of the offering itself.

Latent wants

Consumers may not be conscious of wanting a product but would want it if made aware of what it could do to enrich their lives. In other words, the want for the product is *latent*. Consumers can overlook, misconstrue, or be unable to visualize what the pursuit and attainment of certain goals/wants would be like. Advertising can give new meaning to a product by inducing *self-persuasion* through getting consumers to imagine the pleasure from possessing, using or consuming the product. This is because *conceiving* the potential of a product comes before actively wanting it. Thus we may be aware of a product (e.g. anti-lock brakes) and the functions of the product (allowing the driver to retain control of a vehicle while stopping on a slippery road) yet still not know enough about the benefits to buy it. A latent want is activated by inducing perceptions of the offering as desirable. A latent want for product X is easier to activate if the consumer already possesses a favorable attitude for the category of products to which product X belongs. Thus SONY would have found it easier to activate a latent want for its newly developed camcorder because consumers would first categorize it as a SONY product, and second categorize it as a Japanese electronic product. Such categorization plus the novelty (at the time of the market launch) undoubtedly would have helped get the product off the ground.

Entrepreneurship lies in identifying latent wants. Thus there was no demand for portable stereo cassette tape recorders before the Sony Walkman nor for the myriad other new-to-the-world products that enter the market every year. If consumers are currently buying the product, they may still increase their consumption of the product if made aware of other benefits. Previously consumers may have thought simply of the overall core-use of the product without thinking about specific attributes and corresponding benefits. Thus my consumption of potatoes may increase dramatically after being told by some nutritionist that the potato has "almost no fat with a laundry list of vitamins and minerals that makes it come close to being the perfect source of nourishment." Consumers, in perceiving a product or brand as serving function X (e.g. baking soda for the baking function), are often blind to seeing radically different other functions (e.g. baking soda as a refrigerator deodorant).

The consumer is often viewed as a bundle of wants which act as a filter determining what products he or she will buy. This ignores the fact that consumers can be stimulated to imagine what something really would be like to possess, consume, or use and in the process come to want it. But wants are not created but activated, since the underlying motivational disposition toward the preferred life vision is already there. Reasoning itself can lead to wanting something since rational deliberation involves making oneself aware of the relevant facts and assessing what they mean in terms of one's system of values. Thus I can come to want a sun protection lotion purely as a result of a process of deliberation on information about the effects of the sun's rays on the skin. Such deliberation in consumer decision-making can be viewed as a process of *coming to prefer* something. This is not to suggest that activating a latent want necessarily involves reasoning in this way. Thus I may simply be reminded of some fact with which I was already familiar (e.g. it is cheaper to go by train than to fly) for a latent want to be aroused.

The appeal to the imagination aims to change perceptions, whereas the appeal to rationality is to provide justification. The problem lies in grabbing the consumer's attention since, when wants are latent, there is not the interest. It is easier if the product is novel since novelty arouses curiosity. Advertisers must necessarily be concerned here with attention getting. When advertising is not directed at what consumers are actively seeking, consumers are not disposed to expose themselves to it. "Word-of-mouth" though is often very effective since, hearing friends talk enthusiastically about the product or seeing them use it (e.g. compact disc player) can dramatize the potential of the product. *We can never be certain whether consumers would come to want the product unless we know what they would do after being made completely and vividly aware of what the product can do for them.*

Activating wants links benefits to the good life. Generally, there is an appeal to values without necessarily an attempt to change values. This is *not* because values or priorities among values are impossible to change but because it is possible to change value judgments without the underlying values being affected. *This is so since value judgments are contingent upon descriptions of the situation.* Thus it may be possible to redescribe situations to fit values. This is essentially what is meant by changing perceptions. Thus the very titles of the "pro-choice" and "pro-life" groups are attempts to influence perceptions by using words that conjure up the perceptions.

Passive wants

A latent want, when activated, may become a passive want in that the prospective customer may know about potential benefits yet still be inhibited from buying. When the consumer has a passive want, buying is inhibited as there is uncertainty over the action to take, given the situation is confusing, full of conflicts, or just obscure. The consumer is in effect saying, "Though I want product XYZ, I do not intend to buy it."

Inhibitors to buying include the following:

1 *Price* may be more than the consumer is willing to pay; that is, the relative weight given to price is higher than the perceived benefits.
2 *False beliefs* in that the evaluation of benefits may be based on erroneous information.
3 *True beliefs* about the product and its performance can inhibit purchase.
4 *Doubts* about the claims made for a product. Doubts can be aroused over any claims but particularly in circumstances where the buyer is highly involved with the purchase. Doubts abound about
   a) "revolutionary advances" in a product's functions,
   b) the performance of multiuse product, (unless versatility is sought);
   c) product advances not being at the expense of losses elsewhere; and
   d) the possibility of the firm having competence across several product areas.
      An interesting example of encouraging doubts about a "revolutionary" advance is the well-publicized claim made by P&G about Unilever's Persil Power detergent in Europe, to the effect that it would damage clothes washed with it. The attack enhances what would be existing doubts about the product while channeling attention after the wash to seeking confirming evidence of the P&G claim.
5 *Social norms* in that consumers often act as if big (social) brother is watching their purchases, even when the product is not visible socially. Thus sales of men's cosmetics are still inhibited by doubts about their social appropriateness.

Sellers overcome inhibitors by choosing an appropriate promotional focus:

- *Price*: Minimizing the impact (e.g. offer of credit) or perceptions of importance (e.g. suggesting the price is an investment).
- *False belief*: Challenging the *set* of beliefs of which the false belief is a part.
- *True beliefs*: Depreciating the importance or compensate for the loss.

- *Doubts*: Showing untenability or nonapplicability.
- *Contrary to social norms*: Showing social approval and/or depreciating the importance. Why beliefs about social appropriateness are resistant to change is because consumers believe their own view about what is socially appropriate is more generally upheld than is in fact the case. If such erroneous beliefs are inhibiting buying we need to show that the consumer's view is not widely endorsed by those constituting their positive reference groups.

Activating latent and passive wants is part of the cost of market entry for any new-to-the-world product and the difficulties involved in doing this can affect the diffusion process, that is, how quickly the innovation spreads. Estimates of what can or will be done to overcome latent and passive wants are also key to forecasting sales.

Exclusionary reasons

Consumers may want a product but incapacities take them out of the market. Exclusionary reasons for not buying are those reasons that have nothing to do with the objective merits of the offering:

- Authority-based factors. An industrial buyer, for example, may be under orders not to buy on merit alone but to buy from local suppliers. Alternatively, consumers may refrain from buying in obedience to their religion.
- Promise-based factors. Promises can override the decision that would normally be made as when a teenager promises his parents not to buy a motorcycle even though it would seem the best answer to his transportation problem.
- Situational factors. Consumers may refrain from buying through being unsure of their ability to judge due, say, to time pressure, lack of expertise, or inhibiting physical and social surroundings, as well as shortage of cash.

Although the above are the general factors that keep people out of a market, there can be product-specific factors like not buying a car radio for fear it will be stolen. But the most important reason everywhere is limited resources. There are so many products we would buy if we had more money. This is why increases in discretionary income (i.e. income over and above basic needs) is so important in predicting increases in sales across the board. Exclusionary reasons are overriding and exclude the consumer from the market. Whereas a marketing strategy may be designed to activate latent and passive wants, marketing strategy is generally impotent for removing exclusionary reasons.

CHOOSING WITHOUT DECIDING

Although "deciding" and "choosing" are often treated as synonymous, they should be distinguished. Whereas deciding involves choosing, not all choosing involves deciding. The core meaning of deciding is deliberation over risks and uncertainties on the costs and benefits attached to options. On this view of decision-making, consumers cannot say what their decisions will be before they have actually deliberated. It makes no sense to speak of "programmed decisions" which suggests the results of tomorrow's deliberation can be known today. This does not rule out trying to forecast the outcomes of decisions but it does rule out knowing the answer with certainty.

Choosing without decision-making involves making unproblematic choices, that is, no practical uncertainties have to be resolved. Choosing without decision-making follows three distinct rules:

- *Habit*: buy the same brand as before.
- *Picking*: buy any brand within a cluster of brands as any will do. Here the consumer is indifferent as to which brand to buy from some group of brands.
- *Intrinsic liking*: buy the brand that appeals most to the senses: that sounds best, feels best, smells best, or tastes best.

Habit

With habit, current choices are the same as past choices, that is, repeat buying is the rule. A habit is like a personal policy-based rule not to reconsider some current choice so there is no weighing up of the pros and cons at each buy. Habits save time and effort, for if the consumer deliberated every purchase, there would be little time for anything else. Every decision has the potential to become a precedent for making a like decision in similar circumstances. This is because there is an investment of knowledge in the habitual buy. Habits in buying refer typically to brand buying since explaining the habitual buying of a particular brand is of more interest than explaining why people buy the product class itself.

Habitual buying suggests a one-to-one correspondence between a want and a purchase. Habitual buying should be distinguished from *habitual picking* from some cluster of brands. It is common in many product categories for consumers to choose one brand on one occasion and another brand on another occasion. This can be termed habitual picking. However, it is not clear that such buying is always "picking" since it may reflect not indifference as to what brand is bought, but

1 a desire for variety, or
2 buying for different use-occasions, or
3 a desire by the shopper to cater to the different demands of members of the household.

Although habit buying or habitual buying is associated with day-to-day buying, it can apply to infrequently bought products like annual vacations. Habitual buying is also not confined to products where there is low involvement: sticking to the "tried and true" can reflect high involvement with the purchase and the desire to avoid unnecessary risks. With habit, choice is more or less automatic. In other words, learning is no longer active; current actions follow rather than improve upon past practices. But because there is low concern with the purchase does not mean the product itself is not salient to the consumer. A product can be of central importance to the consumer but with no risks or doubts associated with the purchase, there is no high involvement with the purchase.

Acting on habit can be a rational strategy. Instead of weighing the options, the consumer falls back on the generalization that there is no better way to meet a particular want than to act as in the past. But once a brand becomes an habitual buy, there is less attention to seeking and evaluating information about rival brands. Consumers are unlikely to seek disconfirming evidence but are more attuned to accepting the brand's advertising copy.

A brand habitually bought need offer no objective advantage over rival brands since the habitual buy always has an advantage over a rival that is objectively equivalent in all relevant respects. This is because the consumer has more familiarity with the habitual buy and so has more confidence in it and liking for it. We may even continue to buy a particular brand when it is at a disadvantage (e.g. on price) so that loyalty alone explains the habit. However, there are always counterpressures to change, including

- social norms on appearing progressive ("don't be an old stick in the mud"),
- toward enjoying variety,
- curiosity about that which is novel, and
- toward making sure today's choices are still the wisest.

But because consumers have more experience with the habitual buys and wish to believe they are already buying the best available, this makes it generally easier to retain customers rather than to convert from rivals. Habits receive support through their integration into a particular way of life just as someone may feel lost without a wristwatch. To retain customers we must reassure customers they are already buying the best while upgrading the offering to match or preempt competition. The tendency to form habits helps the pioneer brand. As the first brand on the market, buyers become accustomed to its particular combination of attributes and with this familiarity comes liking and habit.

Picking

Puzzled consumers tend to have no set allegiance and consumers are often puzzled about differences among brands. One strategy for choosing among such brands is to choose at random or on whim. This is *picking*, just as cigarettes are picked from the pack. The buyer is unable to explain why one brand was picked rather than another. In fact, the case of picking is often selected to demonstrate that people have poor insight into what influences their choices. Thus when consumers are asked in a shop which of four identical pairs of stockings they prefer, the pair on the far right is chosen far more frequently than the pair on the left but, when asked to explain their choices, no one mentions position. Similarly, shifting a brand on the supermarket shelf from eye level to a lower level can have a dramatic effect on sales though consumers are not conscious of shelf-level influence. However, in both cases, the conservation of energy may be a hidden factor at work, guiding picking behavior.

Picking occurs for several reasons. First, there may be a belief that all offerings are alike, that is, whatever differences there are, these differences are not discernible from inspection or from the package information. When all brands are similar on some prominent dimension (e.g. like the packaging), it is the similarities that are noticed and not so much the differences. *This is what makes it so important for the seller to stress the differences.* Second, there may be the belief that the rival offerings, even if not undifferentiated, are not sufficiently different to undertake deliberation. This is not uncommon when product differences are opaque until the product is used or the description of the brand is just too technical to understand (e.g. drugs). Third, the consumer's want for a product may be "holistic," in that there is no want for any refinement. The *holistic want* mirrors the concept of *cluster brands*, where each brand within the cluster is equally acceptable. When wants are holistic, price is usually key. Finally, picking is a way of coping with an overabundance of choice which makes consumers anxious. For example, in some food stores there are as many as 55 types of coffee beans and roasts; too intimidating to try and decide which one is best. When it is said that much buying is mindless, it refers to the large amount of picking behavior that occurs. But where differences among brands are not regarded as significant, picking is as rational a solution as any.

Consumers hate to just pick: this resort to seemingly nonrational choice actions makes us generally uncomfortable. There is also the risk of later discovering that a difference among brands was significant though they did not know it at the time. Although what the consumer actually "picks" can be said to represent the picker's preference, the picker cannot genuinely be said to have a preference, since no preference is implied when several offerings are equally attractive. And with this absence of preference comes a lack of resolve in the choices that are made, which means that the choice itself is devalued. Consumers who initially pick a brand on whim might go on to rationalize the choice and so continue to buy it on an habitual basis. There is pressure to rationalize since one social norm is to justify choices and avoid making errors. Some implications follow from this discussion of picking:

- When picking is extensive, the firm that provides a relevant difference and *proclaims* it will catch the pickers. In psychological terms, the firm needs to teach "stimulus discrimination" so the consumer does recognize a significant difference between the firm's brand and its rivals.
- When a firm cannot distinguish its offering, it may still catch the pickers by increasing brand familiarity and/or associating it with an attractive image or giving it visibility in the store.
- When a brand makes no claim to possessing a significant advantage over rivals, it will lose out to the brand that does.

Intrinsic liking

The buyer may buy purely on intrinsic appeal. If technical features were always top priority, there would be little talk of products like cars becoming psychologically obsolescent. Consumers often trade off higher quality associated with, say, longevity for more aesthetic appeal. When brand preferences reflect nothing more than intrinsic liking, they are based on nothing more than anticipated pleasure or enjoyment. Intrinsic liking involves the senses—the smell of flowers, the looks of a package, the feel of the material, the sound of the brand-name and so on. We speak of the *choice criterion* being intrinsic liking or intrinsic preference. Thus I may like an apple rather than an orange. If I am asked why, my answer will not tell the questioner why I want what I like. With intrinsic liking, no further purpose is involved beyond pleasure or enjoyment. If someone is asked why they enjoyed a particular show, the reply will be in terms of the enjoyment experienced, for example, exciting, funny, novel, soothing. Products bought solely on this basis are bought to provide enjoyment or pleasure. The reasons for buying are purely subjective. There are no objective reasons for choosing since pleasure is an end in itself, so reasons for buying describe the enjoyment expected or the form of pleasure experienced:

- The *taste* is refreshing.
- The *smell* is fresh.
- It *looks* appetizing.
- The name *sounds* soothing.
- It *feels* pleasant.

Intrinsic liking is not always an automatic reaction to what is sensed since imaginative reflection may be at work on occasions, for example, when we get excited about some piece of pottery just because it dates back to ancient Greece. Similarly, a Rembrandt would look different after we were told it was a fake. This perhaps is a reminder how cultural norms affect liking. Products can symbolize something and be enjoyed because of their symbolic meaning. When the utility of something we buy is equated with the utility of what it symbolically means, the action is often classified as irrational, but Nozick, the philosopher, in denying this, points out that a large part of the richness of our lives consists in symbolic meanings and their expression.[3]

The senses are used not just to assess likely sensuous enjoyment but mainly to judge the functionality of attributes (e.g. the sturdiness of the product). But for a product to be pleasing to the senses is still very important. As Sheldon and Arens said in the 1930s:

> Every day the average person makes hundreds of judgments in which the sense of touch casts the deciding vote. Acceptance of a towel, hairbrush, underwear, stockings, hinge on how things feel in their hands ... Designs should be executed with an appeal to the tactile senses.[4]

High intrinsic appeal offers instant gratification that can determine a tentative preference for a brand, with efforts directed at justifying buying it. Excitement may attach to a product's aura as occurs when the product is an original painting by one of the great masters. In line with this, a perfect (but known) counterfeit is never the same as possessing the original: there is a difference in their symbolic meaning.

Taste in food is so often determined by culture, so differences between cultures can often restrict global sales or the product may have to be modified to suit local tastes as occurs with drinks like Coca-Cola. The sound of a brand-name can be important. Some names are just unpronounceable, others may connote meanings in other cultures antithetical to the projected brand's image while still others may project a lifeless image. If the target market includes both men and women there may be a problem too of choosing a gender-neutral name since men tend to prefer a masculine sounding name and women a feminine-sounding name.

Some writers distinguish pleasure from enjoyment. Thus Csikszentmihalyi, a psychologist, defines "pleasure" as that feeling of contentment that arises whenever expectations set by biological programs or social conditioning are met.[5] "Enjoyment," on the other hand, is more complex than pleasure, involving both pleasure and a sense of having achieved something unexpected, adding to one's sense of psychological growth. On this basis, advertising may provide pleasure on occasion but seldom enjoyment. Although pleasure is sought for its own sake, Csikszentmihalyi argues that pleasure does have a function, being a reflex response built into the genes for the preservation of the species. Thus eating is an efficient way of ensuring the body gets nourishment, while listening to music for pleasure brings order into consciousness to ward off boredom and the tendency to dwell on unpleasant images.

Pleasures do vary. Csikszentmihalyi draws on the work of the French anthropologist Roger Caillois in analyzing the type of pleasure provided by games. Thus

- with competitive games, pleasure arises from meeting the challenge of an opponent;
- games of chance give pleasure by creating an illusion of controlling the future;
- games like riding the merry-go-round provide pleasure by transforming the way we perceive reality; and
- games involving pretense and fantasy create the feeling of being more than we actually are.

Films and novels provide pleasure by conjuring up curiosity about answers to the questions implicitly raised by the narrative as well as by the fascination evoked by the characters themselves. Human beings, when not in fear or fearful, are naturally curious and seek novelty as novelty relieves boredom and promises excitement. But novelty is not attached to all that is new but only to those products that are neither too similar nor too dissimilar from what is currently being bought. If too similar, there is an absence of novelty and curiosity is not aroused. If too dissimilar, there is the problem of understanding and accepting the utterly strange.

Liking enters into all buyer evaluations from brand-name, to brand advertising, to the stores themselves, and is often the final court of appeal in determining acceptance or rejection. Consumers avoid shops and shopping districts that make them feel uncomfortable like those in run-down areas of town. When bored we seek excitement and shopping can provide this. When anxious about what to buy, consumers simply want everything to go smoothly and efficiently: excitement just does not come into it.

Although many products are bought purely on the basis of intrinsic preference, as a percentage of all consumer purchases, they are likely to be only a small proportion. Even with food items, anticipated relative pleasure tends not to be the sole criterion: consumers typically take account of calories, convenience in use, nourishment, health, and, last but not least, price. Yet anticipated pleasure is typically one criterion. Thus a major reason for choosing a "luxury" brand is not just belief in extra quality or snob appeal but the fact that luxury gives intrinsic pleasure beyond any utilitarian function.

Pleasure generated by a product diminishes over time unless addiction is involved. In other words, variety is needed to put off the point of satiety. The more frequently the same reward follows purchase, the less rewarding is the purchase and the broader the search for other types of reward. The search for variety is one component of pleasure and equivalent pleasure can be found in a wide range of offerings which are interchangeable from the consumer's point of view. As D. H. Lawrence once said, "I love trying things and discovering how I hate them."

Intrinsic likings present a problem in marketing. In the first place, consumers have difficulty describing their likes and dislikes in a concrete way. Second, expressed likings can reflect socially prudent or socially appropriate replies rather than true intrinsic preferences. It is difficult to change likings but easier to change choices from being purely intrinsic by

1   associating the brand with people, symbols, events, and so on, with which the consumer can identify, or
2   to add features appealing to other criteria (e.g. fewer calories).

Habit, picking and intrinsic liking would favor the brand leader in that: those buying on the basis of habit see no reason to change; those just picking are likely to pick the most available brand, while the most popular brands have intrinsic appeal just by their familiarity.

CHOICE CRITERIA IN BUYING

Deliberation involves canvassing and assessing reasons. Such reasons constitute *choice criteria*. There are just six categories of choice criteria that enter into buying, singly or in combination: technical, legalistic, integrative, economic, adaptive, and intrinsic (enjoyment and pleasure). We have already discussed intrinsic preference. The other five categories are discussed below.

Technical criteria

Core-use function

Ignoring the case where a product is bought simply for its appeal to the senses, products serve some function or functions. The *core-use function* is the primary function for which the product was designed. The name of the product typically suggests the core function. Thus a seat is to be sat upon and toothpaste is to clean teeth. The core technical function is instrumental. It is instrumental to achieving the performances that are sought even if those performances are instrumental to pleasing the senses as with hi-fi speakers or air conditioning. But because the core-use function may be achieved with different degrees of attainment, performance level can be a factor in evaluating the product in its core-use function as in the case of a computer.

Ancillary-use function

Ancillary-use functions are permanent or optional technical functions associated with the performance of the core function. If the core function of a clock is to measure time, an ancillary-use function would be an alarm.

Convenience-in-use functions

Convenience-in-use functions are designed to make the performance of core and/or ancillary-use functions more convenient as is the toothpaste pump. Inventors are often negligent when it comes to considering user convenience. A delightful example is the instructions on a tin can in 1824: "Cut round on the top with a chisel and hammer." It was not until 34 years later and 48 years after the invention of the tin can that someone obtained a patent for a can opener! A major factor today in selling a product will be convenience-in-use and this includes the instructions for use. Consider, for example, these convenience-in-use functions for a vacuum cleaner: ease of assembly; compact design for easy storage; large wheels for better maneuverability; indicator lights for power and other adjustments; foot operated controls; automatic cord rewind; furniture guard around the cleaner and power nozzle for furniture protection; multiple tools and brushes for better cleaning.

Marketers consider

1 the core function for which the product was designed versus the function for which the product is used, so that the two coincide;
2 the level of performance sought by consumers versus the level technologically possible: technological performance must not become an end in itself; and
3 the way consumers infer performance and quality versus the way the firm signals them.

Many a market leader has taken the lead in a market by discovering the true core functions sought or by adding ancillary-use and/or convenience-in-use functions: Thus "Viva" obtained a high market share by stressing the durability of its paper towels when competitors focused purely on absorbency. Convenience-in-use can have a major appeal as in the case of the automatic camera.

Although technical criteria are meant to dominate in most product evaluations since technical functions are viewed as key to the performance for which the product is bought, the fact is today for many products, consumers commonly take the quality and range of technical functions for granted, viewing all brands within some price range to be equivalent technically. Where this is so, manufacturers must either have something technically better to offer (and can be seen to be so) or focus on other choice criteria.

Legalistic criteria

The consumer evaluates brands against some criteria to judge relative merits. But sometimes the buyer is not free to choose, and acts in accordance with the choice criteria imposed by others. The term "legalistic criteria" is adopted to suggest being imposed from outside. Thus doctors legislate medicines while government regulations demand people buy safety belts for their car. There are also situations where consumers buy on behalf of others, like members of the family, and act according to their wishes.

Buyers take account of legalistic choice criteria whenever their buying is determined by some authority or the desires of those *directly* affected by the purchase. On the other hand, my purchase (e.g. of an apartment) might be for the family where I give priority to what others seek since I believe

- it means more to them; or
- they will use it more; or
- others are perceived as just being more knowledgeable about such purchases.

It may be that other members of my family just have "concurring" authority over what I buy as occurs in the buying of a house. Advertisers recognize legalistic criteria whenever advertising reminds its audience of what others (for whom the purchase is being made) really want.

Legalistic criteria enter into household decision-making where the buyer may not be the user. The buyer may simply act as a sort of agent for other members of the family. Although the literature on consumer behavior typically classifies household decision-making into husband-dominant, wife-dominant or joint decision, such categories are not exhaustive since children or relatives in the household can be most influential. In any case, the term "dominant" with its image of power rankings seems generally ill-chosen to represent a process whereby partners gauge how strongly the other feels about the purchase and concede the final decision or veto to the partner to whom it means most.

Integrative criteria

Many rational models of decision-making treat the individual as a nonsocial being, divorced from social pressures and communal controls that affect the choice process. The fact is that some brands have more appeal because

- they promise more social integration; or
- more status and recognition; or
- they facilitate better integration with a person's ethical values or personal integrity.

There is constant tension between these three. We need other people for emotional, intellectual, and material sustenance yet we also seek status, individuality, and independence. A major value is to be accepted; to have a sense of "belongingness." But such a value can conflict with other values like wanting to rise above the crowd, and to be guided by values such as self-governance, and having integrity. People do not passively conform but seek to present themselves ("impression management") in a way that enables them to appear to be conforming to social norms yet achieving status and/or preserving integrity. Advertising, in appealing to integrative criteria, tends to stress just one of the three values: the joy of a supportive network of friends, or the promise of status/distinction, or the satisfaction of being independent of others.

Social integration

Under social integration comes adherence to conventions, fashion, fads, and the desire for status/recognition and prestige. The pressure to conform varies as between cultures. In Asia the tendency to conform is greater than in, say, the United States and Western Europe where individualism is stronger. But in every community there are pressures to conform. In fact many social scientists argue that the only way to obtain a deep understanding of human behavior is by studying that behavior within its social and cultural context rather than thinking in terms of the solitary rational individual.

Convention and social norms.   Consumers, like everyone else, have a conception of appropriate social conduct. Indeed, they must have if they are to function effectively in society. An outstanding peculiarity of human beings is the influence that social conventions and norms have on their behavior, and they will typically trade off the satisfaction of making a completely independent decision for social acceptance. Convention carries the notion of conformity to some societal rules, the following of which serves some common interest, just as driving on just one side of the road facilitates coordination.

The chief identification for most people is personal identification with various reference groups and such identification is a guide to much behavior. Following conventions and other social norms, unlike habits, is not the result of any initial deliberation but emanates from the socialization process. There are conventions about dress; about what to wear at a wedding, at a funeral, and at work. Convention dictates that men avoid dressing like a woman while numerous conventions govern day-to-day activities. More generally, convention influences the type of house chosen, its location, its furnishings, and whatever we eat and how we eat it. What makes a convention a convention is that violations of convention are viewed by others as wrong behavior. Thus columnist William Safire (*New York Times*, October 25, 1990) finds wearing a tie "a pain round the neck," but nonetheless finds himself compelled to wear one "when going tieless would make a fashion statement discomforting other guests, and cause them to think me a too-secure slob."

Sometimes a distinction is made between conventions and social norms. Conventions are viewed as instrumental to coordinated action (e.g. driving on the right hand side of the road) and as being backed by sanctions in the event of violation. On the other hand, social norms need not necessarily aid coordination or be enforced by external sanctions so much as by internalized rules whose violation causes embarrassment or guilt. But social and geographical mobility in Western societies is weakening the hold of society's norms in favor of specific group norms, and what may be socially appropriate for one group, like buying an expensive car, may not be socially appropriate behavior for those in another group where such buying is viewed as distancing rather than sharing behavior.

Fashion.   There are conventions in fashion, but whereas we adhere to conventions to avoid conflict and coordinate our actions with others, we adopt certain fashions as part of image management to signal social aspirations and identifications. People have a preoccupation with personal identity and fashion helps to establish that identity. Fashion can also give a group a sense of public identity that marks them off from the public at large, just as happens with youth gangs. Fashion in clothing helps camouflage our deficiencies and savor the fantasy of being like some famous figure or part of some lifestyle. This helps people cope with life and sustain hope in the face of adversity.

Fashion today can come from any group in society and spread widely after suitable modification e.g. blue jeans and even tattoos, while the "grunge" look seems to have come from those unable to afford anything beyond what *The Economist* calls "Oxfam gear." Innovation in films, too, can trickle upwards; many low budget films damned for being "video nasties" have been redone and repackaged for a more up-market audience. But the concept of fashion need not be confined to clothing as it is popular to speak of fashionable ideas etc. Investors, too, like to be in fashion—"biotech stocks being 'in' last year and China funds this" (*The Economist*, April 23, 1994).

Fads.   Faddish products, unlike fashion, are noncyclical. They are adopted with intense zeal when, as is typically the case, they generate some in-group feeling and a sharing of status emanating from mastering skills associated with the product (e.g. the hula hoop). But there is not always the skill aspect. One fad among teenagers in New York schools was the wearing of a pacifier made of hard plastic in bright colors, interpreted by one psychiatrist as a yearning for dependency! No skills seem to be involved.

Status and recognition

A concern for status is a concern for social recognition and prestige. A search for purchases that signal social distinction goes on relentlessly in spite of societal demands for equality and democracy. This is because status symbols can be a social passport. The desire to be different, to rise above the crowd, can be in conflict with the desire to conform. In such cases, if the desire to be different dominates, then whatever is the most popular brand may be viewed as a reason for not buying it. As one woman said in a protocol of her buying episode: "I want it to be me so it should not be used by many people." The desire for status affects not only what is bought but where it is bought and even how it is paid for; the particular credit card or bank. The desire for status is directly linked with the desire for power, fame, and wealth.

The extent to which there is support within the culture for status differences, the greater will be the desire for status. When objective knowledge about an individual's standing cannot be easily known, status symbols are a substitute for the real thing. But symbols of status can differ between cultures and within the same culture at different time periods. Thus in the sixteenth century Europe, to serve sugar was a sign of status. There is the hope in possessing the symbols of either escaping being treated as a nobody or, "at the very least, avoiding the shame of being thought poor." The desire for status/recognition is tied to the concept of self discussed in the last chapter under the headings of self-concept; self-esteem; self-confidence and ideal-self. Consumers collect what is called *symbolic capital* by collecting status goods. Status helps shift the power balance when we deal with others, which, in turn, increases the likelihood of getting our way.

People wish to signal their status; possessions lessen the danger of that status going unrecognized. A good deal of advertising is concerned with associating the product with status, social recognition, and a certain lifestyle. A key to most services is the symbolization of status through customized execution involving personal recognition. Good service is very tied to massaging egos.

We have talked of the tension between wanting to be part of the group yet wanting recognition and to be above the crowd. Yet sometimes people seem willing to transfer their desire for status and recognition to the group; to accept their own status and the group's are one and the same. This can happen in cults but also in religion and the army.

Ethical values and integrity

We now turn to the third component of integrative criteria, the desire for products that fit ethical values. Consumers have a sense of themselves as moral agents with their buying behavior expressing ethical values. We have what has been called *second-order desires*, that is, desires to have certain desires such as to be ethical in our dealings with the world. Buying, like all social conduct, includes not only self-interest but promotion of ideals. The particular balance that is adopted is intimately tied to an individual's self-image and emotional nature. Support for firms believed to act in a social and morally responsible manner makes consumers feel good about contributing to a better life while at the same time getting a glow of pleasure arising from living up to an idealized self-image.

There is a connection between adherence to some set of community values and respect for oneself. In pursuing intersubjective community social values, consumers not only perceive themselves as fostering such values but are expressing an identification with others. To quote *The Economist* (May 16, 1992):

A growing number of consumers now base their buying decisions on "non-commercial" concerns. Does a product harm the environment? Was it tested on animals? Is it recyclable? Was it made in a Surinam sweatshop? If a firm can answer "no" to all the above, it can make an ethical killing.

To sum up, one way of enhancing a brand's value to the consumer is by building into the offering (product, price, promotion, and distribution) whatever signals social acceptance, social esteem, fashion, status, and consumer values. Integrative criteria can be key in buying socially visible products. Sometimes integrative criteria are called nonrational. This is because

1 social norms may dictate buying without attention to utilitarian functions;
2 the search for status seems empty; and
3 sacrificing material (legal) gain for conscience seems purely emotional.

But most buying that takes account of social norms and status can be done in the most calculating way, while practical rationality does not dictate exclusive concern with selfish ends.

Adaptive criteria

Adaptive criteria reflect the desire to minimize risk and uncertainty in buying. Uncertainty occurs when the situation is unique so risk cannot be estimated (though those who accept the concept of subjective probability deny there is anything but risk). Uncertainty can arise from having to cope with too much information as well as too little and can also arise from the unpredictability of a service or the complexity of the purchase. With risk, there is financial risk as in the buying of the wrong product for the application envisaged and also social risk in not buying what is most socially appropriate, and emotional risk arising from a sense of being cheated. But what a buyer considers risky is not necessarily what objectively might be considered risky. Individual perceptions differ while the social norms of society enter into everyone's perception of risk since many actions have the potential of incurring social disapproval. In any case, there can be prepurchase fear of making a mistake. Adaptive criteria relate to the fear of *regret* or the frustration that occurs when the buyer learns a past decision has proved wrong. Adaptive criteria apply particularly in buying big infrequently bought consumer durables like a house. On the other hand, experience in buying a particular product reduces uncertainty and the fear of making a mistake.

Buyers do not want their choices to be problematic yet uncertainty is inherent in buying. They have to adapt to information overload and uncertainty. Yet choosing wisely to avoid error is a social norm, and violating this norm can lead to a sense of guilt and a loss of self-esteem. Although consumers inspect products where possible, inspection is seldom all-revealing. It affords some certainties (presence of some feature) while typically just providing probable truths (e.g. on quality) or telling us nothing at all (e.g. on the effectiveness of some nonprescription drug). Even when investors are saving for the long-term future, they still worry about any short-term losses in the value of their shares. They dislike a fall in value more than a corresponding gain. This tendency has been described as *myopic loss aversion* in the financial literature. It may well be that on occasions habitually buying the same brands may represent nothing more than feeling too insecure to experiment due to a lack of education and money.

In adapting to uncertainty consumers adopt a number of strategies. One is to *imitate* those "in the know." Consumers typically have limited knowledge about many products they buy and expanding that knowledge may involve too much time and effort so resort is made to imitating others assumed to be "in the know." When it is found that the majority of consumers are taking a lead from just a few judged to be in the know, the process is sometimes called an *informational cascade*. Following social norms or convention is "normative conformity"; imitating those in the know is "informational conformity." Normative conformity is the acceptance of the positive expectations of self and reference groups to obtain approval and avoid rejection. With normative conformity there is public acceptance in that behavior follows the norms but not necessarily private acceptance, so there may be inner rejection of the norms. On the other hand, informational conformity achieves both public and private acceptance as the consumer is genuinely persuaded. But the distinction is less distinct than this suggests since both normative and informational conformity are tied to reference group beliefs. In fact it may be that both normative and informational conformity are simply strategies for coming to terms with uncertainty.[6] Informational conformity is common in certain product categories like stocks and bonds. In tennis, golf and other sports, consumers are attracted to brands that are used by professionals in the belief that the brand must be good or the professional would not use it even if paid to do so. In imitative behavior, there may be no extensive information search though the consumer may be highly involved with the purchase. Buying simply the most popular brand is like dealing with someone about whom you have heard a lot of good things.

A second strategy is to seek *advice*. Advice is sought to clarify beliefs as well as to seek social affirmation of tentative choices. But advice can be given by a manufacturer in recommending another manufacturer's product as occurs when a washing machine manufacturer recommends a detergent. Consumers may believe others know better than they do (e.g. a pharmacist) what is best for them (e.g. in cough medicines) and they may implicitly accept the advice of service station attendants as to the selection of motor oil. Consumers are typically uncertain about trade-offs and will seek advice on major purchases to avoid unpleasant surprises. Advice is particularly influential when those giving advice are known to have a long-term interest in the product class (e.g. garage mechanics for certain car products or hairdressers for hair products) as such interest can make them *opinion leaders*. But the advice of salespeople frequently presents a problem. Interactions with strangers who may or may not be impartial advisers is fraught with uncertainties revolving around the risk of losing control of the situation. Where the salesperson is much more knowledgeable, the power balance can be perceived by the prospective buyer as on the side of the seller with a consequent sense of powerlessness and fear of embarrassment, humiliation, and subjection to pressure tactics.

A third strategy is to look for *guarantees* such as the Chrysler Corporation's money-back guarantee that buyers who change their mind within thirty days or one thousand miles can get their money back. Guarantees are important when information is lacking. Guarantees have been getting more extensive in services. One hotel chain guarantees "no charge" if a room fails to meet the customer's standards of cleanliness, comfort, and safety; AT&T guarantees free calls and rebates if an 800 line fails, while one agency supplying temporary workers provides the temporary help free of charge if the service does not prove satisfactory. Guarantees may not be formally declared but assumed just as I may take it for granted that I can return goods if dissatisfied. When a prestigious retail outlet displays and promotes a certain brand, there is an implicit guarantee.

Often consumers buy the best simply because doing so provides a sense of guarantee. Thus I may consult a top lawyer or doctor even if I am told the problem does not warrant doing so but I do it nonetheless for that sense of guarantee from employing the best.

The fourth strategy is to *sample*, which offers an opportunity for direct experience: the product is tried at minimum cost. Hence the offer of trial sizes to accelerate adoption. Finally, buyers may fall back on *reputation*. There are preconceived images about different brands' reliability and quality, so that a firm that is known and respected (as was IBM when it entered the PC market) has a distinct edge over firms that are not. The well-known brand is usually first to be considered when a new product is being bought.

All the foregoing strategies substitute to some extent for *comparison shopping* and extensive homework, which are costly not only in mental and physical effort but in the postponement of gratification. Yet keeping options open until the consumer knows about the options and the risks involved can be a sensible strategy. In fact it is usually considered essential in, say, buying a house or furniture. Comparison shopping can be a means of getting further advice from sales people. But in shopping around, buyers may also look at the more expensive brands to judge what features to seek when buying a less expensive model.

Comparison shopping is not done just to discover what is available but is often used by consumers to discover what it is they want by seeing what is on offer. Because this type of comparison shopping can take place over an extensive period of time, it can result in consumers deciding what they want months ahead of buying so that, when they actually come to buy, it appears something hurried and unthinkingly done when it is nothing of the kind.

Economic criteria

A buying situation is an approach/avoidance situation. The approach is the anticipated benefits; the avoidance is the sacrifice consisting of the price and the effort expended. Economic criteria take into account anticipated sacrifice. Sacrifice is interpreted in the very broadest sense since a buyer may view as a sacrifice the sunk cost of tapes when thinking about the purchase of a compact disc player. Hence the not uncommon sales tactic of giving something on the old razor, old TV etc. Consumers instinctively rank brands on the basis of price and other sacrifices. Sacrifices are usually measurable, so indecision is more associated with uncertainty about benefits. Even so, consumers constantly balance benefits against corresponding sacrifice.

There are two types of price-conscious consumer. There are the *deal sensitive* who switch among their favored brands, buying that which is on special offer and the *price sensitive* who, regardless of brand, simply choose the cheapest. The maximum price obtainable (if the rest of the sacrifice is of no consequence) depends not just on the importance of the product but on the consumer's dependence on the brand and other factors:

- the brand's centrality in relation to the consumer's goals;
- the brand's uniqueness to the seller;
- social perceptions of the wisdom of the purchase at that price: spending too much may be viewed as foolish by peer groups;
- where the brand is purchased, since location and outlet make a difference in willingness to pay a premium price: paying a high price in a low class outlet is regarded as "getting stung"; and
- the sense of its being a fair price.

Consumers in shopping for an infrequently purchased product will have expectations as to what they will have to pay. But their tentative reserve price, based on these expectations, can change during shopping as they learn about real prices and the extras that can be got by paying more. A high price, given the right product, supportive promotion, and appropriate distribution, can help project a desirable social image, signaling exclusivity/scarcity and status for a socially visible product. But with standard (equal performance) products for standard applications, price becomes key. A *commodity product* such as gold is an extreme example. This is a product that can be traded under a description without actual inspection. In the absence of added value by way of service or whatever, price will tend to be uniform among competitors. However, any well-established brand in a sense can be termed a "commodity-brand" in that units of the brand are considered tokens of each other and hence sold by description by, say, mail order.

The problem with all bargain offers is making the offer credible, for big bargains create suspicion, that is, the feeling that the price is just too good to be true. On occasions, there is no way to dominate a market by low price. Purchases relating to fashion, to mark occasions, to signal status, and so on, are seldom if ever dominated by the lowest priced brand. Perception of price can be key and this can depend on the framing of the choice situation. Thus a 3 percent charge by the retailer for payment by credit card is perceived differently from an offer of a 3 percent discount for cash.

Services are notoriously varied in execution. All qualified doctors do not give the same level of service; all brokers do not offer the same quality of advice and all plumbers are not equal in performance. Yet prices may be fairly uniform as none will admit to being inferior to others while each of the service organizations may be identical in promising what is sought. This is why appearances and why "word-of-mouth" can be so important for the growth of any service business.

The cost of the product is not the only sacrifice. There is also the effort involved. Although shopping can be a highly pleasurable activity, day-to-day shopping generally lacks the novelty aspect and can be a chore. When the consumer is subject to time pressures doing day-to-day shopping, it is difficult not to be free of anxiety which works against finding excitement in shopping. Hence consumers demand regularly bought brands be readily obtainable in the local store. For products bought infrequently or for the first time, there is also the effort involved in learning about rival offerings. Yet a good deal of shopping is pleasurable. Casual shopping is often done to ward off boredom and stimulate excitement. Think of how people like to shop when on vacation!

CHOICE CRITERIA AND COMPETITION

Brands that perform the same core-use functions are substitutes for each other, but brands are close segment rivals only when they cater to the same overall choice criteria. If offerings are perceived as undifferentiated, habit, picking, or just liking (say of the brand-name) will direct choices. Since these processes favor the market pioneers, market shares can be uneven, making little sense given the objective differences among brands. Whatever criteria are stressed, the target audience is being invited to believe these are the important ones. Thus if only economic criteria are emphasized, the focus is on value for money. Hence it should not be surprising if allegiance is merely rented.

THE DECISION

Those buying on habit or just liking or just picking are not engaged in much deliberation and can be said to choose rather than decide. To what extent buying in these cases can be said to be mindless or the consumer viewed as on automatic pilot is debatable. Routine habitual buying might be without thought but with intrinsic liking it depends on whether such likings can be said to be instantaneous, occurring without reflection. Picking involves some deliberation in initially choosing brands from which to pick and/or making sure differences among brands do not justify deliberation.

Deliberation in buying consists of canvassing reasons and assessing them to reach a decision. In the process, reasons that were initially given little consideration may come to be weighted heavily so views about product attributes and combinations of attributes can change. This is not only because deliberation involves rational calculation, but it puts us in touch with our gut feelings (emotions) about the salience of various product attributes.

Rational deliberation is not necessarily cold since it is rational to take account of emotions (e.g. the anticipated future regret if a mistake is made) in making a decision, while an emotional attachment to a product can be sensibly quoted to justify a purchase (e.g. of a sports car). But emotions can distort deliberation by affecting confidence. Thus when we are in a state of excitement (e.g. in seeing the house of our dreams) there is a heightened sense of confidence in decision-making with no sense of anxiety until the excitement wears off!

We commonly assume that consumer decision-making, as practical reasoning, is means-end reasoning. But this is an oversimplification as it suggests that wants (ends) are already in place and fixed. In fact, rationality involves reflecting on the wants themselves and modifying them if there are good reasons to do so. Thus, as I think about future wants, I may change my mind about a second car being a station wagon. The means-end type of decision-making is perhaps less frequent than consumers having no *precise* goals/ends in mind but simply look to what is available (e.g. in houses) so that goals are not tied up in advance. There may be difficulties in evaluating alternative offerings to meet ends. A buyer may have difficulty in saying how much of the ends (e.g. engine capacity) in question is required; how much of the goal/end (e.g. status) will be provided by the various makes or brands (e.g. of cars). There is also the problem of the trade-offs the consumer is prepared to make. Another problem with the means-end model is that it neglects to take account of initial decisions that limit the alternatives evaluated. The consumer may, for example, simply decide to shop in one outlet.

Rationality *proscribes* rather than *prescribes*, pointing, for example, to inconsistencies between immediate desires and long-term goals and distinguishing real differences from distinctions without a difference. The actual trade-offs themselves are value-laden. If the consumer's values form a coherent set for the purpose of buying, the weighing of options and trade-offs is made easier. When value systems are vague, however, and the outcomes sought are vague, decision criteria are correspondingly vague and, unless such vagueness is recognized and corrected, deliberation will inevitably be perfunctory and open to manipulation by persuasive communications. But even when such vagueness is absent there is still the problem of determining how much of any particular product attribute is wanted and how much of it will be provided by each of the options considered. The process of deliberation is often a learning process that moves from some initial (antecedent) set of wants and beliefs to a new or modified set. Thus beliefs about what is practically feasible can affect wants (the "sour grapes" phenomenon) in that consumers may end up desiring only what they know is possible for them.

Marketing, like economics, has tended to accept the convenient assumption of high rationality on the part of the consumer. But even if consumers, on average, were capable of being highly rational, the costs in terms of time spent in thinking and information collection would be a limitation. Consumers have "bounded rationality" with limitations of memory, information access and intelligence. This is not to suggest that everything depends on what is in consciousness. A major claim of some cognitive psychologists is that much of our total behavior is governed by implicit knowledge rather than conscious knowledge. This is in line with Galton in the nineteenth century, who claimed that we would be at the level of idiots if our brain work had to simply depend on what was completely in consciousness. Thus consumers may not be aware of how packaging or brand image influences their choices. This means that the reasons people give for their actions even when reasons are real (and not just rationalizations) can be incomplete.

The standard model used in combining wants and beliefs into a disposition to buy is the multiattribute (compensatory model). This model, introduced in the last chapter, is the model of decision-making that best exemplifies the rational consumer. The model assumes that consumers, in line with the logic of the marketing concept, choose most rationally from among products and brands. The model is again illustrated in Table 5.4. There is no doubt that consumers, when in a situation which induces a rational approach (e.g. in experiments with MBA students), can act as if following such a model. In fact any choice may be interpreted as following this model. For example, suppose the buyer in Table 5.4 simply chose the lawnmower on the basis of brand-name alone. It could still be interpreted as following the compensatory model; just giving the whole weight to the brand-name. However, if we assume that adherence to the model means mentally going through the steps shown in Table 5.4, there are many criticisms that could be made as shown in Table 5.5. The typical defense of the multiattribute model as reflecting buying decision-making in general is to argue that it is "as if" consumers' mental process follows this model. But it is not clear what it means in this case to say it is "as if" the process is followed. We say that it is "as if" attitudes or motives exist because both

Table 5.4 Multiattribute model applied to brands of lawnmower

Evaluative criteria	Criterion weight	Brand Hayter	Brand (Landmaster) Stoic	Col. (2) × Col. (3) Hayter	Col. (2) × Col. (3) Stoic
(1)	(2)	(3)		(4)	
Technical					
Powerful	2	1	3	2	6
Rotary	2	3	3	6	6
Starting convenience	1	3	3	3	3
Economic					
Price around $400	1	1	1	1	1
Maintenance	1	3	3	3	3
Trade-in price on old machine	1	3	3	3	3
Adaptive					
Reputation of brand/name	1	3	2	3	2
Bought by experts	1	1	3	1	3
				22	27

Note: Assumes buyer may act "as if" following a process of rational evaluation (Landmaster Stoic receives highest overall score, therefore preferred).

introspection and observation supports the claim but this is not the case with the multi-attribute model. Although we can witness trade-offs being made and decision-makers are conscious of having goals, evaluating attributes and making, say, trade-offs for a lower price, we are not aware of and cannot observe consumers undertaking anything as complex as the multiattribute model though, in experiments with students, we can set up the experiment in such a way that the model is followed and can be shown to be predictive (not surprising since, once undergoing the process, the choice would be compelling). We can work back from any decision to claiming an appropriate multi-attribute model. But we could work back to an infinite set of mental process models from which the decision could have arisen; the multiattribute is selected because it seems to best represent rationality. Also it is questionable whether consumers, as a rule, under-take comparative evaluations of brands on the basis of their attributes.[7] Also, as Nozick says, the model is a theory of best action, not of rational action since there is no rational consideration of beliefs and goals, both being taken for granted, though rationality might point to the inadequacy of information on which beliefs and goals rest. The model says nothing about how the decision comes to have the beliefs and goals ascribed to it.

Two alternatives to the multiattribute model are the "satisficing model" and the "implicit favorite model," though neither of these models is incompatible with the multi-attribute model. The satisficing model assumes people have "bounded" or limited ratio-nality and so settle for the first solution to their problem that is good enough. With the "implicit favorite model," consumers do not try to evaluate various rival brands until they identify an implicit favorite. The rest of the decision process consists of confirming the implicit favorite as the winner. Alternatively, noncompensatory rules may be involved. Noncompensatory models, unlike the multiattribute (compensatory) model do not assume that a brand's weakness on one attribute can be compensated by strength

Table 5.5 The validity of the multiattribute model: some considerations

- Psychologists point out that when trade-offs are difficult to make, people shift back and forth, first favoring one option and then another, so that preferences can differ depending on when preferences are solicited.
- Some psychologists argue people generally try to avoid making what they perceive as trade-offs so that, when faced with a clear conflict between price and quality, the consumer often dismisses the importance of one or the other altogether.
- Experiments as to the validity of the multiattribute model can be misleading not only because subjects know they are expected to behave rationally, but because, whatever product is being evaluated, there will be some accepted standards for evaluating such products as a good one of its kind. Hence there is always room for any person's preference to reflect that person's knowledge of standards of merit rather than his or her own ways of choosing.
- Where the model is regarded as an optimizing model, it assumes all options are known and preferences for attributes are clear and constant. But these assumptions are unjustified. What consumers actually choose and what they would choose with perfect knowledge will differ.
- Consumers may on occasions simply follow social norms in buying, not necessarily being concerned with the purchase being a means to some end beyond adhering to these social norms. There may be deliberation here but not in the form of weighting attributes and rating rival brands.
- It is not clear that the weightings consumers attach to choice criteria or brands typically reflect firm views about relative merits.
- When physical reality testing is ruled out, consumers are more uncertain and likely to fall back on advice or the brands that are most popular.
- Consumers often lack the motivation, information and ability to undertake the process typified in the multiattribute model. Consumers may use quick and simple heuristics (rules of thumb) rather than complex reasoning and may trade off reliability for speed.
- Brand attributes in practice have symbolic and intangible dimensions not easily captured in laboratory experiments. Faith in a brand-name, not reasoning, may often dominate. What a brand subjectively symbolizes for the buyer is important since "a large part of the richness of our lives consists in symbolic meanings and their expression."
- Preferences are to some extent contingent upon the context and upon the focus of attention of the consumer to particular features of that environment. Consumers often change their minds about the relative importance of attributes when some brand comes along with an outstanding attribute.
- There is the assumption that the importance of one attribute is in no way dependent on the value of other attributes and the importance of an attribute that is variable does not differ for different parts of the range.
- What we have said about the biases and the flawed reasoning of the consumer and the amount of picking and habit etc. that occurs in buying would not lead us to believe the multiattribute model is descriptive of buying in general.
- Awareness of the offering as a whole can be dissolved by focusing on each attribute of the offering in turn.[8] What a product means lies in relating the parts to the whole. Consumers not very knowledgeable about the product class may initially evaluate attribute by attribute but will need to follow up with a brand-based evaluation later.
- As a theory of rational choice, the multiattribute model assumes settled values, wants and beliefs but all of these are subject to choice themselves.

on another. The conjunctive and disjunctive rules relate to the satisficing model while the lexicographic can be related very roughly to the implicit favorite model.

Under the conjunctive rule the consumer insists on minimum acceptable levels for each attribute of interest. For example, in buying a computer: "must have at least an 80486 processor as standard; speed at least 25 MHz; at least 4 megabytes of internal memory; not less than 80 megabytes of hard disk memory; fax capabilities." But are rules like this unconditional? The buyer is likely to insist on a high performance level only when paying a corresponding price. An offering is acceptable under the disjunctive rule, if it exceeds the minimum level on at least one criterion or attribute of interest, for example, "exceeds 4 megabytes of internal memory." Both the conjunctive and disjunctive rules can be regarded as attempts to reduce the total set of options to consider. Where the purchase is important too many options can create anxiety as a wide range of choices is intimidating.

The lexicographic rule does have the advantage of leading to a unique choice. It assumes that alternatives are first compared on the most important attribute or dimension. Any product or brand that is "in a class of its own" on the most important dimension is selected. If several brands are equally as good on the particular dimension, the next most important dimension or attribute is considered and so on. Of course, after using conjunctive and disjunctive rules, consumers could use both compensatory and/or lexicographic rules. Before the choice stage the consumer eliminates brands that do not fall into the segment of the market of interest. Although humans can be described as rule-following animals, it is not clear when consumers use stored rules (e.g. always look along the side of a used car before buying it to see if a ripple effect indicates panel-beating for a past accident) or construct new ones as they go about buying. In terms of the framework of Figure 5.1, intrinsic liking and habit roughly follow the lexicographic rule while picking probably occurs after conjunctive and/or disjunctive rules are applied. Where the various choice criteria are listed, weighted mentally, and options rated against those criteria, then it is "as if" the multiattribute model applies. Even where rationality comes into its own in proscribing options, deficiencies can arise in *receiving information* through functional illiteracy, expectations, wishful thinking, or time pressure. Deficiencies can also arise in *processing information* through lack of competence, faulty reasoning habits, wishful thinking, erroneous beliefs, emotions, the overweighting of more recent events, and just plain fatigue.

Choices are not necessarily in line with the relative strength of wants. Wants are not so much compelling forces as key information to be taken into account. However, the strongest desires start with an advantage as their pursuit seems to promise instant gratification. If there is one thing we have learnt from behaviorist psychology it is the urge for instant gratification.

SURROGATE INDICATORS AND OPENNESS TO PERSUASION

Surrogate indicators

Why should buyers believe that the products they are about to buy have the benefits they seek? More often than not, they have bought the brand or make before and regard the next purchase as identical. But there are problems with a new or infrequent buy when inspection is not all revealing. The buyer is obliged to use *surrogate indicators* of the attributes sought. Thus I may judge the quality of a carpet by its feel; the material of which it is made; its thickness; the closeness of the pile as well as the name of the manufacturer and the retail store stocking it. With sunglasses, I may judge their optical properties by trying them on to see if I have comfortable vision without frowning or a narrowing of the eyes as I look towards the sun, as well as looking at the brand-name and price. In choosing stock, consumers may assume (erroneously) that growth stocks will be those of growth companies and so on. In many product categories brand-name can be the key indicator that benefits as promised will be realized. In choosing a service the perceived knowledge, attractiveness and competence of the service provider may be the key surrogate indicators used to gauge future likely satisfaction with the service.

Even when consumers apply the same choice criteria, the process may not lead to the same preference since applying the criteria is a skill and not a straightforward process of measurement. Visualizing the outcomes of choosing one brand rather than another typically necessitates the use of surrogate indicators. We may accurately gauge the sacrifice but estimating potential benefits is something else. Consumers who seek prestige from a car purchase will differ somewhat in deciding which of the makes is most likely to provide this. The consumer has to estimate such benefits from seeing the product, the promotional material, and from tapping information sources.

The surrogate indicators consumers use to make inferences need to be identified. Thus consumers may associate plastic parts with cheapness and have all sorts of indicators to suggest low quality in foods. In one focus group, transparency and homogeneity in honey suggested artificiality of manufacture, which inhibited purchasing the brand. A firm's indicators should be in line with the symbolization consumers use to indicate what they seek. A firm may even be providing the highest quality but the consumers' surrogate indicators fail to capture that.

Openness to persuasion

Consumers in general are open to persuasion right to the point of sale because:

- Shopping is a learning experience and consumers can learn right to the point of sale.
- Consumers are rarely experts but simply collect enough product/brand information to state a preference. This does not mean that they would not like to be experts but sacrifices are involved. However, not being experts, consumers have less confidence in their judgments.
- Where buying involves deliberation, consumers are uneasy about trade-offs as there is no objective way of doing the weighting.
- Even when satisfied with past choices, consumers recognize that things could have changed.
- New facts, new appeals that bring the consumer's attention to the potential of the product may swing the sale right up to the point of buying.

- Until people have tried all brands, they cannot be absolutely convinced about their preferences.

Some combination of the six choice criteria discussed enter into every major decision. An acid test might be whether they would have relevance in choosing a husband or wife!

- *Intrinsic*: looks, appearance, voice.
- *Technical*: high performance in work, sport, conversation—whatever performances are considered.
- *Economic*: wealth or wealth potential.
- *Integrative*: spouse's link to desirable reference groups, potential to enhance status and self-esteem.
- *Adaptive*: safe "buy."
- *Legalistic*: to comply with family wishes.

If there is something missing here it is the emotional climate that surrounds the decision, emanating from the intrinsic appeal of the partner, the perceived praizeworthiness of his or her actions and the strong feeling of desirability associated with the marriage event.

PREFERENCE

Buying action involves

1 reasons(wants and beliefs);
2 preferences;
3 buying intention;
4 will to buy; and
5 intentional buying.

Here we consider the concept of preference. The output of a buying decision is a preference (comparative desire) where consumers state their choice. We expect preferences to be transitive; that is, if I prefer A to B and B to C, I would prefer A to C. But an intransitive preference (preferring C to A) is irrational only if it can be shown that A is better in all respects and at all times and on all occasions. Intransitive preferences involve inconsistency only when it can be shown that the judgments cannot be simultaneously maintained without contradiction. But preferences are not absolute but vary over time and occasion.

INTENTION

Consumers can have a brand preference without any intention to buy since intention is a commitment to action. Buying intentions can lead to other intentions just as my inten-

takes place over a long period of time and it may not be possible to conveniently record the whole buying episode but resort may have to be made to recording different consumers at the different stages of before, during and after. At the time of taking the protocol, any situational factors that might have unconsciously influenced the consumer should be recorded. Similarly, it is useful to note the consumer's actions since sometimes thought manifests itself in what consumers do and not just in what they say.

All interpretation involves "theory" of a sort, however inchoate and the interpretation of protocols is no different except it is hoped the interpreter will make extensive use of social science theories as discussed in the last chapter.[11] Every protocol throws up the problem of how to relate the parts to the whole. A single statement or even a word in the protocol can be key to explaining the buy. The analysis of the protocols involves reading the whole protocol (including remarks made by the researcher at the time) and studying the parts in relation to the whole. In studying each statement, the analyst notes the key words used by the consumer as the basis for identifying the rules being followed. Thus if someone says she bought the brand because it was the most "familiar," it is in the idea of familiarity that we look for the rule used (for example, "I buy that which is most familiar"). Behavior follows rules, either in the sense that the behavior could be shown to fit some rules or the behavior is actually guided by rules; fitting is simply a matter of true description while guiding suggests deliberate compliance. To interpret a protocol is to make what is said intelligible in the context of where, how, and when it was spoken. One way of making it intelligible is to explain as well as possible the logic behind it. Of course there can be different interpretations of protocol statements but the aim is to choose "from among various competing interpretations on the basis of the evidence provided by a close reading of the textual details."[12]

The meaning of the situation for the individual emerges in the form of the reasons given to justify decisions or actions taken. But when consumers are asked about their reasons, not all the answers reflect the real reasons since some will be rationalizations or socially appropriate, prudent replies. If we want to capture as many of the real reasons as possible, it is more likely to happen if we record at the time what people have to say ("off the back of their heads," so to speak) before buying, during buying and after buying. It is better to just let consumers talk rather than question them or ask them to recall later what went through their minds. Verbal reports are less useful when subjects are asked to remember what they thought, rather than report their thoughts as they happen. At the end of the chapter there is a protocol and an analysis of it (see Appendix 5.1). If the respondent's goals, wants and beliefs were typical of those within the market segment, this would have fundamental implications for the firm's marketing.

The whole process of protocol recording and analysis should be based on rules that guide objectivity, rules such as

1 meticulous observation and recording of what is said without any leading questions being put to the respondent;
2 even-handed review of the social science literature for concepts and findings that would seem to be relevant to the analysis;
3 scrupulous attention to the evidence contained in the protocol and the observations made at the time, whether supporting or not the analyst's evolving interpretation;

4 choosing among rival interpretations on the basis of the best information and evidence available; and

5 a resolution not to go beyond the evidence in suggesting marketing implications.

It is sometimes suggested that the consumers' own account of their reasons for buying or whatever should be taken as decisive. This is the doctrine of "privileged access" but it should not be taken to be universal. An observer or protocol interpreter may have insight which the respondent lacks. If humans are rational animals, they are often also rationalizing animals, protecting their egos.

Within any particular segment, a fairly small sample will quickly yield the choice criteria being used. However, if interest lies in discovering how the various choice criteria are weighted, then a proper sampling procedure should be instituted.

ORGANIZATIONAL BUYING

Organizational buying occurs in:

- commercial enterprises (users, distributors, and manufacturers);
- institutions (hospitals, hotels, schools etc.);
- government (national and local); and
- chain stores (central buyers).

In industrial or organizational buying there is always some explicit or implicit process such as that described below.

Recognition of the need/want

There is first some recognition of a need or want for the product. Organizational buying occurs because buying furthers the goals of the organization by:

1 **Exploiting opportunities to:**
   • increase efficiency, that is, do some job at less cost;
   • increase the salability of the firm's offerings, say, through better packaging, better components etc.;
   • protect the firm's assets e.g. security systems, maintenance or repair services etc; and
   • increase flexibility e.g. in production through the purchase of more versatile machinery.
2 **Overcome difficulties due to**
   • material shortages;
   • obsolescent or worn out equipment;
   • the taking on of new projects such as a plant extension; and
   • poor current suppliers.

Buying situation

The next stage in organizational buying might be a decision on whether to buy or make. If the decision is to buy then the buying situation can be a *straight rebuy, modified rebuy, or new task*.[13] The straight rebuy corresponds to the habitual buy situation in consumer buying in that the buyer simply reorders whatever has met the situation in the past. With straight rebuys, existing suppliers are likely to have the advantage for much the same reasons that are given for the consumers' habitual buys. The modified rebuy occurs when buyers seek some modified version of the offering they have bought in the past to meet slightly changed goals or to improve on what is being offered by current suppliers.

With a new task buying situation, there is more uncertainly about products and suppliers, which is likely to give rise to more of a search for options (products/suppliers) than in the case of the modified rebuy. We say "likely to be" because buyers, like consumers, may just rely on advisers or some reference group such as the lead user rather than undertake the costs of identifying and evaluating alternative offerings/ suppliers. With uncertainty about what exactly is wanted, adaptive criteria are apt to be dominant rather than economic criteria, which means that those with technical expertise are likely to be highly influential. With new task buying, the buying firm will be interested in the seller's total offering since there is a need for reassurance not only about whether the product will do the job, but about continuity of supply, training services and so on.

Buying decision

Finally there is the buying decision itself. The major key phases in the buying decision are:

1 The specification of the offering wanted.
2 The identification of suitable vendors.
3 The evaluation of vendor offerings and the actual selection of the vendors from whom to buy.

How thoroughly each phase is completed will depend on the importance and complexity of the purchase, the size of the organization and its particular "culture." Where the purchase is important and complex and the organization is large, more people with specialist knowledge are likely to be involved, with buying being more formally regulated. When several people are involved in the buying decision we speak of the Decision-Making Unit (DMU). When members of the DMU represent different departments of the firm, they come to the DMU with their own individual responsibilities and attachments to their own department and so are likely to promote those interests. Differences in viewpoints are likely to result in different weights being given to the various choice criteria. Thus the purchasing department is more likely to focus on the commercial aspects of the buy and so be more interested in the economic aspects of the purchase than engineering. Members of a DMU will vary in influence depending on their role, position in the management hierarchy, technical expertise and on their position in the communications network, as a central position close to top management adds to influence.

The core definitions of each category of choice criteria remain as before though what exactly is included under each criterion may have to be modified to suit the application (see Table 5.6).

Within a DMU there may be some (constructive?) conflict arising from differential interests, differential perceptions of reality, differential information possessed, and differential views about the consequences flowing from choosing one offering/supplier rather than another. Conflict may be resolved:

- by mutual compromises, or
- by conformity to the views of the most powerful clique, or
- even going along with the minority viewpoint to avoid destructive conflict.

The idea of the minority view predominating in a conflict seems contrary to common sense but does occur when the minority clique seems unprepared for compromise and the buying decision seems not important enough to indulge in unpleasant conflict.

Different members of a DMU do not have equal influence in the overall decision or at each stage in the decision. The influence of individual participants is deduced from their role in buying which may differ from what would be inferred from their job titles. From a seller's point of view interest centers on the deciders or those who have a say in

- determining the specification of the offering;
- determining sources of supply (the list of suitable vendors); and
- choosing the actual vendor or vendors.

Table 5.6 Choice criteria as applied to organizational buying

---

- *Technical performance criteria*: these include technical performance in the core function for which the product was designed; ancillary functions (or features) and convenience-in-use functions. The core of the concept here is fit for the application.
- *Economic criteria*: these include the total sacrifices incurred to obtain the product, including the price and other costs such as life cycle costs, operating costs, credit terms, etc.
- *Adaptive criteria*: concern with uncertainties as to the supplier capability and risks in dealing with the supplier. These include post-sales services, guarantees, reputation, etc. that provide reassurance to the buyer. Adaptive criteria are likely to be particularly important in dynamic technical environments where there is uncertainty about the stability of the technology being bought.
- *Integrative criteria*: concern with the extent to which the supplier can be viewed as integrated with the buying organization in terms of the services to be offered like presales service by sales people, training and installation services, follow-up and monitoring to ensure post-sale satisfaction. The supplier's support is the core of the concept.
- *Legalistic criteria*: the need to conform to organizational policies or government laws.
- *Intrinsic criteria*: liking for the styling of the product and the individuals with whom the buying organization comes into contact.

Salespeople seek to influence the specification and to ensure they are on the list of approved vendors to have a chance of being chosen as a supplier. This is one reason why salespeople adopt a "forearming" approach by making regular calls on major potential customers to keep up-to-date on future plans. We return to this topic in Chapter 13.

NOTES

1 Howard, John A. (1989) *Consumer Behavior in Marketing Strategy*, Englewood Cliffs, NJ: Prentice Hall.
2 Douglas, Mary and Isherwood, Baron (1979) *The World of Goods*, New York: Basic Books.
3 Nozick, Robert (1993) *The Nature of Rationality*, New Jersey: Princeton University Press.
4 Sheldon, Roy and Arens, Egmont (1932) quoted in Stuart Ewen's *All Consuming Images*, New York: Basic Books (1988).
5 Csikszentmihalyi Mihaly (1990) *Flow: The Psychology of Optimal Experience*, New York: Harper and Row.
6 Choi, Young Back (1993) *Paradigms and Conventions: Uncertainty, Decision making and Entrepreneurship*, Ann Arbor: University of Michigan Press.
7 Foxall, Gordon (1990) *Consumer Psychology in Behavioral Perspective*, London: Routledge.
8 Polanyi, Michael (1958) *The Study of Man*, Chicago: The University of Chicago Press.
9 Gardial, Sarah Fisher, Clemons, D. Scott, Woodruff, Robert B., Schumann, David W., and Burns, Mary Jane (1994) "Comparing Consumers' Recall of Prepurchase and Postpurchase Product Evaluation Experiences," *Journal of Consumer Research*, 20 (April).
10 Hoch, Stephen J. and Deighton, John (1989) "Managing What Consumers Learn from Experience," *Journal of Marketing*, 53 (April).
11 Tracy, David (1994) *Plurality and Ambiguity*, Chicago: University of Chicago Press
12 Holbrook, Morris B. and Hirschman, Elizabeth C. (1993) *The Semiotics of Consumption*, New York: Mouton de Gruyter.
13 Robinson, Patrick J., Faris, Charles, and Wind, Yoram (1967) *Industrial Buying and Creative Marketing*, Boston: Allyn and Bacon.

APPENDIX 5.1   VERBAL SELF-REPORT (PROTOCOL STATEMENT) AND ANALYSIS

Protocol Statement:
Buying Shampoo in Portugal, by Lisa

Anticipatory account
I'm running out of shampoo and I must not forget to buy a new one. For some months I've been using Johnson & Johnson baby shampoo but I don't think I will purchase J&J this time. In fact I have been paying special attention to the TV advertisements for a new product: Ultra Suave from Garnier.

I liked the advertisement so much that I asked my hairstylist her opinion about the quality of the new shampoo. Her opinion was very favorable. She thinks it's very gentle for those who shampoo frequently and she told me a lot of other clients had been asking her opinion about this new product.

I'm specially careful when buying a shampoo. I really need a gentle one because, as you probably know, I am active in sports and so I have to wash my hair almost everyday. I can't bear to think of my hair losing its brightness and strength.

And, you know, in the Ultra Suave advertisement they say it is a shampoo that can be used every day because its formula is based upon natural plants. I even remember the young woman saying: "My shampoo is linden based; choose your type." That makes me think they are of reliable quality and they probably have other varieties. One special kind for each type of hair, I guess.

Apart from this, I have known Garnier for a long time because I have used some of their products. I used their hair softener (Amaciador Garnier) for quite a long time but now I don't need it any more because J&J's shampoo leaves my hair very soft. I also know Garnier because my daughter currently uses their new "wet look" gel. It's fashionable, you know.

[Garnier] being a very well-known French brand makes me confident. You know I suspect those cheap and large bottles of shampoo. I love my hair too much to try such a risky change.

Contemporaneous account

Here it is. I'm happy to find it in my usual supermarket. I don't think I would go looking for it if I couldn't find it here.

Oh! They have a lot of varieties. And really good looking. Very attractive and modern plastic bottles. Surely the nicest on the shelf.

Let me see . . . white nettle, wheat germ, chamomile and linden, of course. All natural plants in fact. Each type has a different color label and cap that goes with it. And they advise as to what type of hair they are suited. I think the chamomile is the right one for me. (She picks the bottle from the shelf.)

They say here that it is best suited for blond hair. Let me see . . . (She looks at the back label) yes, they provide some information here: ingredients, results. They say here this shampoo can be used as often as you want. I didn't realize the shampoo was "made in Portugal" for Garnier. I should have realized. After all this is not an expensive perfume. All of these shampoos are made in Portugal. But at least I believe Garnier must control the quality of its original formula and all such things.

The bottle is translucent and it seems to be perfectly full. That's one thing I really appreciate. Almost all the other bottles of shampoo are opaque but here we can see that nothing has been taken out. I know it's silly to think that supermarkets or other retailers steal the product from the bottles. But the real truth is that when bottles are not full I can't avoid thinking of it.

What about the price? Well, it's not cheap. In fact it's a bit more expensive than my usual Johnson & Johnson but it doesn't really matter. I'm going to try it.

Retrospective account

I'm really satisfied with this new shampoo. I've been using it for a week and I think my hair has nicer flexibility and much more volume – and as you can see I have a short-cut hairstyle. Its smell is fresh and pleases me a lot.

Although my previous shampoo was also designed for frequent use and recommended for kids, I think this Ultra Suave has given my hair a much softer look. No matter how often I use it, and I have been using it daily, my hair always becomes very soft. I always knew Garnier was an expert in this kind of product. With such a wide line of hair products I was sure they were experts.

One thing I noticed, it's the easy way you can comb your hair, and also the easy way you can rinse the shampoo out of your hair. But I think the reason for this is the fact that the shampoo is not very concentrated and so you need a lot of shampoo to make some foam. I cannot understand why this happens because my old shampoo was much more fluid and nevertheless it made a lot more foam. Perhaps that is why I feel my hair needs more frequent washes. In fact with the J&J's I could go two days without washing my hair because it continued to look clean and nice. With this new shampoo the results are much better but the hair loses its bright and soft look after playing sports (you know I play tennis almost every day).

After all I will adopt this new shampoo. My hair is prettier and has a lot more volume. And I really think Ultra Suave suits my hair perfectly.

Analysis

1 Goals
   a) *life vision*: to be beautiful not ugly
   b) *social*: to signal preferred self-image

2 Wants
The advertisement for a shampoo with a plant extract-based formula activated her *latent* want for a true natural product shampoo for high frequency use (low risk or risk free) within the constraint that the shampoo must also make the hair soft. The advertisement was for a shampoo recently introduced in the market (Ultra Suave from Garnier) which she saw advertised on TV.

3 Beliefs
   a) A soft and high frequency, natural shampoo would let her wash her hair almost daily without damaging it (i.e. without losing its brightness and strength).
   b) Her hairstylist could provide expert advice about the quality of shampoos.
   c) She believes Garnier, a French brand, has a full line of hair products which gives her confidence about their expertise.
   d) Shampoos must have different formulas for different types of hair.
   e) She is suspicious about cheap shampoos or those with a low cost/high quantity relationship.
   f) Switching to a new shampoo is a risky matter.
   g) Switching to the new brand would not justify extensive search to find a store stocking it.
   h) Products made in Portugal are perceived to be of low quality. This problem can be overcome by foreign firms.
   i) There is a danger with opaque bottles that some of the contents will have been stolen.
   j) Shampoos must make "enough" foam to be efficient. (Positive correlation between foam and washing effectiveness.)

k) Concentrated shampoo produces more foam for less shampoo.

4 Choice criteria (on which rules of buying based)

Technical criteria
1   Core-use function: to wash the hair clear. Although Lisa had not yet tried Ultra Suave and so was unable to evaluate its effectiveness in performing this function she inferred effectiveness from the perceived expertise of Garnier in hair products.
2   Ancillary-use functions
   a) Softness (avoids the use of hair softeners)
   b) High frequency use without harm to hair (needed because consumer plays tennis every day)
   c) Brightness and strength
   d) Volume look
   e) Flexible/less brittle
3   Convenience-in-use functions
   a) Easy to wash out the shampoo
   b) Easy to comb the hair after use
   c) Allows daily washes
   d) Advice on package about suitability for different types of hair

Integrative criteria
1   Convention (cleanliness)
2   Ego (self-image)

Economic criteria
1   Prepared to pay a premium price to avoid risk: low cost/high quantity shampoo to be avoided
2   Sensitive about the effort that might be involved in buying the product

Adaptive criteria
1   Advice
   Advice of hairstylist
2   Reputation
   Reputation of Garnier as a trustworthy French firm with a wide expertise on hair products
3   Guarantees
   (a) Bottle translucent (perfectly full bottle)
   (b) Shampoo made of natural plants

Intrinsic (subjective liking) criteria
1   Pleasant smell after use
2   Attractive bottle

Chapter 6

Markets, segmentation, and positioning

If the seller is interested in securing a customer and not just a one-off sale, the design of the offering must be grounded in customer wants. There is a need to think about what the market wants and the variations sought by subgroups (segments) within the market. This chapter deals with this issue, being concerned with:

- Market definition and market identification.
- Segmentation: the process of forming subgroupings within the market on the basis of similarities and differences in what people want.
- Targeting: selecting segments in which to market.
- Positioning: describing an offering's intended position (image, associations and benefits) in the market segment vis-à-vis competition and (hopefully) in the mind of the consumer.

SELECTION OF MARKETS

Definition of the term "market"

An organization defines its markets to estimate their size, identify competition, and select the parts (segments) to cultivate. The term "market" has several senses. It can denote the network of institutions, like wholesalers and brokers, dealing in a product. This is the market *in* some product, like the market *in* coffee. It can also refer to the demand, within some territorial area, for those products designed to serve the same function or application, as when we speak of the market *for* coffee. The two meanings are related but distinct, so a change in one does not necessitate a change in the other. Thus, a change in the market *for* coffee (meaning a change in the volume, level, or type of demand for coffee) may have little impact on the market *in* coffee (in that communications and exchange networks may remain unchanged). It is the market *for* goods and services that is of interest in this chapter.

In general, the market *for* soap, banking services, or whatever is defined as the demand for those goods and services serving the same use function. When products in the same market serve the same function, they potentially compete for performing that function. Thus all motor vehicles that cater to the transportation function compete directly or indirectly for performing that function.

Defining a market: function versus generic need

We define "market for ..." in terms of the demand for products serving the same function(s). This definition not only reminds us of the purpose the product serves but is useful for identifying the rival offerings with which the firm competes. The definition also simplifies splitting the market into segments or subgroupings based on variations in what buyers want.

Products catering to the same function are in the same market and consequently, closely or remotely, in competition with each other. Defining a market in terms of

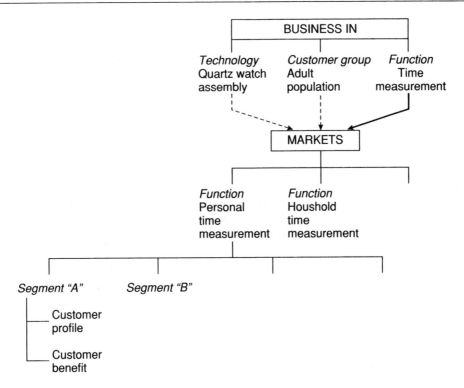

Figure 6.1 Market hierarchy

function(s) served (or more accurately, the demand, within some territorial area, for those goods and services that serve the same function) ties the definition of a market to the definition of the firm's business, describable by technology, customer group *and* function(s) served. However, the function used in the definition of a business may embrace subfunctions sufficiently distinct to be regarded as separate markets. This is illustrated in Figure 6.1 where the business is defined as:

- Function: Time measurement.
- Customer Group: Adult population.
- Technology: Quartz watch assembly.

The overall function of time measurement is split into markets such as "personal time measurement," "household time measurement" and so on, each of which could be regarded as distinct functions defining distinct markets. Defining a market in terms of function served is essentially the same as defining a market in terms of "generic need," the phrase used by Theodore Levitt. In a classic *Harvard Business Review* article, Levitt advocated defining a business in terms of the generic need for which the firm catered.[1] He argued, for example, that those in the film industry failed to recognize that they catered to the generic need for entertainment and so were insensitive to the likelihood of competition from television: "It (*the industry*) thought it was in the movie business when it was actually in the entertainment business." Competition, it was argued, embraces all those products that cater to the same generic need, e.g.

Product	Generic Need
Mini-calculators	Need for a portable device to make speedy and accurate calculation without cumbersome manipulation or effort.
Elevators	Need for vertical transportation that is convenient, fast and safe.

For Levitt, defining a business in terms of generic need not only defines the competition but removes the temptation to enter a market without first considering the wide range of possibilities available. A firm that defines its generic need as "getting rid of rats" recognizes many more options than if it defines its business (function) as just "killing rats."

As with the term function, generic need can be defined widely to embrace competition from many different industries. This is to remind us, say, that paint competes with wall paper, freeze-drying with canning, and so on. However, different industries are typically in different parts (segments) of a market since they offer different benefits even though fulfilling the same core-use function e.g.:

Mode of Transportation	Usual Differential
Airline	Time
Bus	Price
Ship	Comfort
Rail	Dependability

The Levitt article was seminal to thinking how best to define a business. Current thinking defines a business, though, not just in terms of generic need (function) but to embrace customer group and technology used. But there are other reasons to debate Levitt's position.

First, the word "need" is ambiguous. It could refer to some list of needs developed in psychology (like Maslow's hierarchy of needs), or, if used as in day-to-day usage, "need" suggests some absolute requirement. Unfortunately, there is no generally accepted list of human needs in psychology apart from biological needs, while marketing does not confine itself to catering to absolute requirements. On these grounds the term "function" is to be preferred as both more descriptive and carrying less dubious theoretical baggage.

Second, in the notion of catering to a generic need, Levitt is either erroneously assuming there is only one market for a firm's product or, more likely, that the many "needs" that might be served will come under a still higher level need that embraces the many different purposes for which a product is bought. Such an assumption is not justified. What, for example, is the generic need served by a postage stamp? There is the market related to the transportation and delivery of mail and that related to the collector's motives. Can both markets be embraced under *one* generic need? They are really different businesses.

Levitt's examples suggest that the appropriate overall generic need is a one-level abstraction from the specific function being carried out by the firm's product. But, is a one-level abstraction *always* appropriate? Thus, is it always best to regard the movie industry as catering to the generic need for entertainment, as Levitt suggests? It all depends on our purposes. There are many rival claimants. One claimant might be the generic need to occupy leisure time. This second-level abstraction embraces entertainment as a subcategory and may be useful for identifying the widest range of substitutes for moviegoing. However, for the smaller film maker, a definition of the business that confines itself to movies may be much more useful to help it find its niche. Thus, Hammer films catered to a segment of the "movie market" that wanted horror films, while Disney has successfully concentrated on films for the family. How widely or narrowly we define generic need, business function or market function will depend on our purposes. Thus, for certain purposes, Coca-Cola may define its generic need as carbonated soft drinks which include not just colas but, say, ginger ale, citrus drinks, seltzer water, tonic water, club soda. Such a broad definition is a reminder of the broader market competition. However, for most purposes, Coca-Cola is likely to be more vitally concerned with competition from other colas.

Third, while the use of the term generic need or the term function is helpful for identifying competition, it is not sufficient for this purpose. This is because products may appear to serve the same generic need or function without actually being in competition. Both sundials and watches appear to cater to the generic need to measure time, but they do not compete in the same market. In reply it would be claimed that this is because the primary function of a sundial is ornamental and not to measure time. *But to reply in this way is implicitly to acknowledge the need to fall back on facts about the market.* The competitive arena or set of competitive brands is not identified by any armchair reflection on the generic need served. Brands must actually compete and this needs to be established by empirical inquiry. Thinking about generic need or function served offers guidance but is not in itself sufficient to identify what organizations and what products will be in competition.

Although defining a market in terms of function served helps in identifying competition and market requirements, the concept of function is not without its difficulties, over and above how wide "function" should be defined for marketing's purposes. One problem lies in defining a market when the product serves several distinct use functions *simultaneously*. To what market does "Clearasil," a product that seeks both to cover and heal skin blemishes, belong? It would seem to be in both the market for skin ointment and for cosmetics. If there are products similar to Clearasil, then we have a distinct market with the distinguishing function of providing a healing mask. In other cases, the major use function served defines the market, while minor use functions typically are the ancillary-use functions or convenience-in-use functions. In any case, we would need to discover consumer perceptions of substitutes to get a better handle on how the market should be defined.

Another problem occurs when use function is not the key function sought by those in the market. Thus the key function could be the integrative function in that the product is primarily bought as a status symbol. But this is really a pseudo-problem as the true market definition is that most useful to management. Hence we define a market by use function to link it to the firm's definition of the business but may broaden the definition to embrace other functions like the integrative function.

A similar problem arises when the market caters primarily to some form of enjoyment as enjoyment or pleasure are ends in themselves. For example, what is the use function of chocolates and ice cream? One way to define the market is to define the type of enjoyment experienced. Although there are no distinct categories of enjoyment, the name of the product class itself usually conveys the type of enjoyment promised, for example, opera, fragrances, chocolate, Impressionist paintings, and so on. Where the integrative functions are primary, market definition may focus on this fact. Thus the definition of a market might be something like the following:

> The actual or potential market for product X is the global, national, or regional (actual or potential) demand for those products that meet the designated use function and/or other functions that product X serves; the level of function being determined by the purposes for which market definition is required.

The marketing manager looks for markets within the boundaries set by the definition of the firm's business. But identifying exact market boundaries can on occasions be much more involved than just looking at a definition of the firm's business, and a number of research approaches have been developed to help in this.[2] If a firm defines its business as catering to all the adult population (customer group), for time measurement (function) through quartz assembly (technology), the firm will seek markets within this definition that seem most likely to exploit the firm's business system and build on its thrust and core competencies.

CONCEPT OF A SEGMENT

By definition, buyers in the same market seek products for broadly the same function and, in the early stages of the life of a product, both the firm and its competitors may compete by catering to that basic function. But, as a market develops, sellers try to provide more attractive total offerings. Sometimes the improved offering has appeal throughout the market but later, offerings are developed that cater just to subgroups or segments of the market. The appeal is to segments because different buyers in that market want or come to want different configurations of benefits. Even if this were not so and everyone simply wanted, say, the most technologically advanced computer or whatever, it would be impossible to provide what everyone would like to have within an acceptable price range. Thus if everything that was technically ever wanted could be provided in the one computer, it would still only appeal to a segment of buyers because of price. There is a big difference between what buyers find to be ideal and what the seller could feasibly and profitably provide; ideally, the best price for the buyer is no cost at all.

In real markets, different sets of buyers seek different configurations of benefits even though they all seek the same basic function. What this means, for example, is that while all lawnmowers will appeal to some degree to those in the market for a lawnmower, some brands will appeal to some groups more than to others. In other words, although all buyers in the market want the seller's offering to perform the basic function(s), they will differ in what else they seek from the seller's offering. Some will want ancillary-use functions, or convenience-in-use functions, more services, a lower price, certain styling or will respond better to some appeals than to others. Of course, if there were only one brand of lawnmower, buyers would just have to "make do" with that one or do without. As consumer incomes rise, consumers press for offerings more suited to their particular circumstances. In the extreme case, the product is completely customized.

Product customization is becoming more feasible.[3] The new generation of flexible manufacturing systems promises "the marriage of cheap, mass production methods with all the variety of bespoke engineering." There is an incipient trend in manufacturing toward being able to produce customized products at low cost. Programmability of production operations via the computer chip is enabling one machine to produce a wide variety of models. It is argued that such will fragment the market into unit segments, that is, segments with just one member as every buyer gets exactly what he or she wants. But this is misleading in that buyers do not just seek a customized *product* but preferably a customized *offering*. In services the "segment-of-one" has always been common but the storage of information about a customer in computer records has made it even more common to offer customized service packages. An interesting example is how selective binding technology has allowed the customization of magazines. At the most detailed level, every buyer's "want" is distinct but costs usually rule out catering to each distinct want in all its particulars so, on the basis of similarities and differences, the unique wants are grouped into subclasses. The aim is to ensure the wants within a subclass are more alike than wants between subclasses. A true segment consists of a family of closely related wants. The wants in each segment are related in that each want within the segment family solicits the same offering and, ideally, those in the same segment will respond in the same way by buying that offering. However, wants within the same segment will differ in detail, in intensity and sometimes differ in the weights assigned to different components of the offering. But even if everyone within the segment had *exactly* the same want, it would not mean each person would buy the same offering since beliefs might differ as to what offering comes nearest to their ideal. In other words, for all to respond similarly, all must have the same wants *and* beliefs as to what (surrogate?) indicators demonstrate the presence and performance level of each attribute that is sought. We cannot just assert that those with the same want will respond to the same offering by choosing it. For all practical purposes, they need to have roughly the same beliefs as to what to look for and to have the intention and a will to buy.

Each subgroup possessing the same want is generally termed a "market" segment with the process of conceptually distinguishing segments being known as the process of "market segmentation." However, some definitions of a segment would demand that all those within a segment respond positively to the same offering. This is a normative definition as it states what would be ideal for a segment to be, but it is doubtful whether present methods of segmentation do this. We will later return to this topic.

A market segment consists of buyers with more of a similarity of "want" than they have with any other segment that might be formed in the market. The relationship of a segment to its market, though, is not just of subset to set but also one of means to goals, and this has certain implications:

- Those in different segments of a market may seek slightly different goals while pursuing the same function and, as a consequence, seek different means (offerings), with buyers in one segment not regarding what is being offered in another segment as being an adequate substitute (for example, electric razor versus the razor with a blade).
- The function that defines the market will be a means to some higher level function that may be served by other markets. When this is so, there is the possibility of buyers switching among the markets, leading to instability in sales in individual markets. As Levitt's example of the film industry was designed to show, firms in the many markets catering to the need for entertainment must be aware of the competitive impact of those other markets.
- Though buyers must choose from what is available, they are not necessarily satisfied with what is available. A possibility thus remains of designing an offering better suited to the segment.

Those within a segment are more similar in their market want(s) than are those in the market at large, but differences will remain. Thus some of those within the horror segment of the movie market prefer horror movies which have some literary merit, make acute social observations and so on. Horror movies that offer such additional benefits have a competitive advantage within this segment for these movie goers. We can always achieve more homogeneity by subdividing the segment until, say, we have just unit segments. How far the process of segmentation is carried depends on the commercial viability of small segments and the competitive practices of rivals. As we move from market to segment and so on to individual wants, there is an increasing richness in description of what is sought but a decrease in the number of people whose want fits that description. There is a tendency to think of a segment want as defined by a single criterion, but it can usually only be described in terms of a cluster of attributes, not all of which must be possessed by the offering for the consumer to feel the want is being met.

SEGMENTATION VERSUS PRODUCT DIFFERENTIATION

Economists view an offering as differentiated if it differs from rivals in one or more of the following ways:

- Physical attributes.
- Services offered.
- Convenience in using or buying the product.
- Brand image.

All segmentation, except segmentation involving price alone, entails differentiation as defined by economists. Segmentation, however, implies more than product differentiation. The aim of segmentation is not just to divide the market into subclasses based on some differentiation but to distinguish want-categories that correspond to distinct groups in the market. Since those within a segment seek a similar offering, they are moi to respond to that offering as expressed in the marketing strategy.

Some writers view product differentiation as embracing any physical or nonpi attribute (including price) that is perceived by the consumer as making an of different from rival offerings.[4] On this basis they argue that the processes of segmentation and differentiation should be separated from the processes of trying to persuade consumers. There is a recognition here that, while a group may be homogeneous in what benefits members want from a product, they may not be homogeneous in the messages they find persuasive. However, particularly if the market is composed of undifferentiated products, segmentation seeks a basis for identifying segments that require different persuasive appeals. This in particular is the idea behind psychographic segmentation discussed below.

ADVANTAGES OF SEGMENTING A MARKET AND CRITICS OF SEGMENTATION

The advantages of segmenting a market are not always apparent since sellers wish to sell to everyone. There is a failure to appreciate that in a competitive market: "There's no market for products every one likes a little, only those someone likes a lot." More difficult to answer are marketing managers who dismiss segmentation analysis on the ground that they simply look for a competitive advantage or distinctive benefit. A little reflection shows the weakness of this vis-à-vis formally segmenting a market in the way to be described:

- It ignores the importance of considering the range of options open to the firm in relation to its core competencies and thrust and the rest of the firm's business system.
- The firm still needs to determine: whether the competitive advantage is perceived as such, by whom and in what numbers and whether the competition could imitate it. The firm still needs to evaluate the advantage.
- It is an opportunistic and not a proactive planning approach.

Ehrenberg and Goodhardt criticize the effectiveness of much segmentation, or at least the segmentation that occurs in markets such as those for cereals like corn flakes and shredded wheat.[5] They point out that, though corn flakes and shredded wheat differ in product form and seem aimed at different segments, the same people buy both corn flakes and shredded wheat. On the basis of such evidence, Ehrenberg and Goodhardt reach a number of conclusions that require comment.

1 One conclusion is that markets are not made up of segments with different wants because buyers of one brand buy other brands as well.

Comment. The fact that the same people buy both shredded wheat and corn flakes does not in itself imply the absence of meaningful segments. Products in different segments of the market may be bought simultaneously by the buyer for different use-occasions, for different family members, or for variety. Segmentation does not mean that those within a segment buy only brands in that segment of the market. *It is just a shorthand way of writing that gives the impression of segments as mutually exclusive groups of customers.* Speaking more exactly, it is the anticipated wants of those in the market that are grouped, not buyers being placed in one and only one segment. Segmentation is an attempt to get the same effect as supposing everyone in the market submitted a separate request for each of his or her future wants in the market, detailing exactly what will be sought. Since it is typically too costly to design an offering for each and every variation in requests, the firm would group together requests that might be met by a single offering. If the group of similar requests formed a viable volume of business, other things remaining equal, the result would be the formation of a segment. The same individual might submit a request, say, for both cheap and very expensive wine. To just assume that a consumer can be in only one segment is to assume that use-occasions etc. are constant. This is not so and the same consumer can be described differently for different segments.

2 Another conclusion is that buyers choose from a repertoire of brands and, if a new brand measures up to the others, it is added to the buyer's repertoire or list of acceptable brands. Given the fact that consumers alternate between the brands on their list, it may be self-defeating to believe that a brand can successfully be positioned to appeal to a very narrow segment.

Comment. There are markets where consumers just pick brands from different "segments." This is because the segmentation is not very meaningful to these consumers. Such behavior may also reflect different use-occasions, or variety seeking, or various family wants. Thus a woman might want a fresh light perfume during the day and a strong sophisticated scent for the evening. In contrast to the Ehrenberg/Goodhardt assertion many consumers buy just the same brand, week in and week out. The consumer's daily newspaper is a good example but other examples are brands of cigarettes, toothpaste, makeup, cold remedies, and many toiletries.

3 Another criticism is that brands may be indistinguishable in product form yet differ widely in market share. Hence no concept of brand differentiation is needed to explain market success. It is not denied that having a real product-plus is an advantage, but it is argued that this is a matter for the consumer and not just something marketing people tell themselves ought to matter.

Comment. As to the point that "this is a matter for the consumer," it applies to their own claim about the various brands being indistinguishable in product form, as its implicit assumption is that no difference among the brands will be perceived by the consumer. Anyhow, meaningful differences are not confined to product form even for cereals. There is the brand image differential and there is the question of distribution. Segmentation can be on the basis of distribution (e.g. Avon cosmetics) or price, or promoted image (e.g. Smirnoff vodka). Lower price and better distribution save on costs (economic criteria), while image can cater to both integrative and adaptive criteria. The

A focus on integrative criteria is likely to come later. This is not necessarily the pattern that should be adopted by the seller since not every seller can compete, say, on improvements in performance. There is a danger of benefit segmentation not paying enough attention to what the competition is offering. The fact that the same product may offer different benefits to different groups of people means that the same product (but not usually the exact same offering) might serve different segments or even different markets. Thus the same margarine might be promoted to one group for its easy spreading and to another group for health reasons. Alternatively, we might reposition the same product from one market or market segment to another just as Listerine has been promoted as a breath freshener, gargle, after shave and more recently to combat plaque. But there are serious problems. As already pointed out (Chapter 3), the consumer may find it difficult to recategorize the brand in the new way. Similarly when the seller tries to reach additional segments/markets, there is a danger of alienating current buyers. For example, this is what seems to have happened when consultants recommended that *Punch*, a British satirical magazine, make changes to appeal to another group of readers than those currently buying: it failed to attract the new group and simply alienated the old.

The benefits sought by the buyer may not be constant but vary with the use-occasion. Hence it may be that the different benefits sought might be inferred from the different use-occasions.

Once we have identified different sets of benefits, the next step is to identify who wants what by identifying who they are and/or what they do. For example, Russell Haley, who coined the phrase "benefit segmentation," claimed that the oral hygiene market divided into four distinct benefit segments:[7]

a) benefits of flavor and product appearance;
b) benefit of brightness of teeth;
c) benefit of decay prevention; and
d) benefit of low price.

It is not likely that many consumers would be *exclusively* interested in just the benefits cited for the segment, these being simply the key benefits sought. In any case, Haley argued that the segment seeking brightness of teeth was composed largely of young people in their teens with a personality disposed toward sociability and an active lifestyle. Here was the recognition that a segment must be defined both in terms of the buying inducement and a useful description of those doing the demanding.

New segments can be formed by combining the benefits offered by two or more of the current segments, for example, pre-prepared meals that cater to both weight reduction and health. But there can be problems with this. In the first place, it must be established that the benefits can be combined without loss of perceived effectiveness in the individual benefits. Second, a large enough group must want the combination since buyers may believe the brand that shouts loudly about just the one set of benefits is more likely to do a better job than the brand combining benefits.

Benefit segmentation is generally viewed as being concerned with tangible, utilitarian product attributes rather than other aspects of the offering. Thus psychic benefits (usually associated with integrative criteria) are apt to be ignored. However, this need not be so. Thus women buy panty hose not just for utilitarian reasons: in one study in the United States "how they looked to the opposite sex" was the determining factor in 85 percent of purchases. Such benefits can be taken into account. The more serious defect of benefit segmentation is that it takes account of wants but not beliefs about the surrogate indicators used to judge product attributes. This is important given that brand image is commonly used as a surrogate indicator of benefits.

Benefit segmentation in services is typically in terms of benefits like customization, convenience, comfort, reliability, consistency, and personalized execution. What is often forgotten is that in many services there is a very unequal distribution of power between service provider and buyer, in that the buyer is dependent on the provider of the service (e.g. a medical or financial consultant) for advice. Thus those taking out, say, a mortgage can feel very vulnerable, and it is good for business if the provider can do something about redressing the perceived power imbalance.

Demographic segmentation

Instead of focusing directly on benefits sought, we might classify buyers on the basis of age, gender, education, occupation, income, type of dwelling, location or religion and *infer* from such demographic variables the likely variations in what is sought.

Age.   This variable is frequently used since with age comes a change in interests, activities and finances. Younger people in fact may demand something different (e.g. in fragrances and clothes) from what older people are buying, to distance themselves from their parents and the elderly. Even one yogurt firm is using age as a major segmentation variable with its yogurt for children. This is a hybrid yogurt culture that significantly reduces the tart taste while the addition of candy bits and the packaging makes the yogurt appear very different from that eaten by adults. Yet older consumers in Western societies are more numerous than in the past and more wealthy and healthy. Well-off older people in some advertising agencies are classified into four age groups corresponding to distinct spending patterns: 50–64, 65–74, 75–84, and 86 and over. The older groups are regarded as price-sensitive and more concerned with having substantive information about brands than just imagery advertising. Message appeals in advertising to older consumers should focus on reasons to buy that appeal to older people, namely (according to one specialist): comfort, security, convenience, sociability and old-fashioned values.

Gender.   Here is another variable used to segment markets though it may have little to do with product use but be more a matter of appearances. Thus, the strong nineteenth-century division between the sexes was reflected in the production of everything from combs to watches in masculine and feminine models: the masculine rugged and tough, the feminine delicate and refined. This still occurs so that hand calculators designed purely for women may have jewel-studded keys while the Smith & Weston Corporation has launched LadySmith, a line of guns for women! Virginia Slims cigarettes targets only women. Gillette's Soft & Dry deodorant is aimed at young women. Its deodorant Dry Idea was repositioned to appeal to women directly on finding out that most of its users were women, though Procter & Gamble's Secret ("strong enough for a man but made for a woman") was the first to target women and still remains the leader in that segment in the United States. It is not uncommon to choose a gender segment on finding the brand is already appealing to just either men or women. Thus some cars (e.g. the Nissan Micra) seem to have more appeal to women even if they are not targeted exclusively. But some products are difficult to sell, like makeup for men. Such products come up against social norms as to what is socially appropriate behavior.

Education.   This can be fundamental in dividing many markets such as markets for magazines and other reading matter. One market research firm in the United States claims that what people read, particularly their choice of magazines, can better predict buyer behavior than other demographic variables.

Regional location.   This variable can be important not just because of climatic conditions but because of local cultures. Thus, the British drink, Pimms Number One, hardly sells in the North of England and there are examples in every country that are similar. The use of post office zip codes also comes under this heading. Thus PRIZM (Potential Rating Index for Zip Market) in the United States has sixty-two consumer segments based on demographics tied to postal ZIP (area) codes.

Occupation.   This is also a common segmentation variable with specific insurance packages for teachers etc., with even one brand of fragrance in the United States called Long Haul Cologne being promoted just to truck drivers.

Social class.   Demographic advertising is common when the demographic group is likely to be receptive to distinct appeals or have distinct media habits. The part of the offering that is distinct will be the promotion. In any case, keeping up with the demographics of customers is always important as these change dramatically at times. Thus, in the United States, while traditionally sewing machines sold to low-income housewives, today's buyers are young, well-educated and relatively affluent who sew for creative expression and not just to save money.

Demographic factors can be combined to define each social class which in many societies is a good guide to values. Social class can be defined by a single indicator like occupation or the use of a combination of factors like occupation, source of income, type of home or residential area and used to explain gross differences in buying patterns, like broadly distinguishing who buys what price of car. One sociological classification divides society into: upper class, upper middle class, middle middle class, lower middle class, skilled working class, unskilled working class, and underclass. On the other hand, one marketing research firm classifies into: professional/senior managerial, middle managers/executives, junior manager/nonmanual, skilled manual, semi-skilled/unskilled manual, the unemployed/state dependent. No single classification thus serves all purposes. Even the use of occupation runs into difficulty with one market research society providing a 71-page job dictionary to allocate jobs to classes. Household income, as a single indicator, tends to be better for many segmentation purposes, but consumers in many parts of the world find such a question out of bounds. In any case, household income is not always a straightforward guide to the priority with which products are bought throughout the world. Thus the British, by no means having the highest per capita income in Europe, are nonetheless tops in the ownership of household durables like TVs, VCRs, home computers, and so on. We have to go to culture and history to explain this.

Family life cycle.   Another basis for segmentation that draws on demographic data is the family or household life cycle, where each stage in the cycle is a combination of age, marital status and age of children. At each stage, financial conditions change. Also a household with a young family has different product wants, and is responsive to different promotional appeals than a retired couple whose family are grown up. Traditionally, a family life cycle was:

a) young single
b) young married, no children
c) young married, youngest child under six years of age
d) young married, youngest child six or over
e) older married, children
f) older married, no children
g) older single.

But in some countries the stages are no longer this progressive and a more realistic set might be:

1 young single living alone or with family
2 young married, no children
3 young married, with children
4 single parent
5 middle-aged single
6 middle-aged married with no children
7 middle-aged married, with children at home
8 older married, about to retire
9 older single.

Where the household is the decision-making unit, there is interest in discovering the roles played by different members to see whether roles vary or generalizations can be made for different product categories. These roles can be the same as the roles played in any decision-making unit (DMU) as discussed in Chapter 13.

Demographic segmentation is popular because it is often suggestive of real differences in the benefits sought by different groups. Demographic segments also have the additional advantage of being a possible basis for advertising appeals. But demographics in many countries offer only the broadest guide either to what might be sought by way of benefits or what might constitute persuasive appeals: demographic variables are much less defining in Western societies than they used to be.

Psychological and psychographic segmentation

Psychological variables are used to segment markets to identify those most likely to buy the product and to identify the appropriate media and promotional appeals.

Personality.   There is a long history of correlating personality measures to various aspects of buyer behavior. One early study in the United States showed a congruence between the car owner's perception of his car's image and his perceptions of self.[8] Certainly, people often classify others on the basis of what car they drive. One study in Britain showed people associated the Porsche driver with being flashy; BMW drivers as show-offs; Ford Granada drivers as family men and Range Rover drivers as exciting outdoor types of above-average means.

The assumption that buyers seek a match between ideal self-image and brand image is implicit in advertising appeals directed toward certain types of personality. But standard personality tests have been of little use in predicting brand choice. Specifically designed personality tests may have more success. Thus one study claimed that a specifically designed personality test separated the household cleaning market into those who judged their worth by cleaning and those who did not, and that a firm increased its market share by having different promotional strategies for the two segments.[9]

All sorts of characteristics have been included in personality inventories but, according to one study, only four basic dimensions have emerged from over 50 years of research.[10] These are:

- extroversion (sociability, openness, outward-looking) versus introversion (inward-looking, aloof, inhibited)
- neuroticism (the tendency to worry and be anxious)
- psychoticism (tough-mindedness, sensation-seeking, cruelty) and
- obsessionality (including neatness, control, pedantry, rigidity).

Lifestyle/psychographic segmentation.   Segmentation may make use of lifestyle (mode of living) data. Lifestyle influences attitudes and buying patterns. Thus those who live in the city and those who live on a farm have different lifestyles and are likely to seek different things when buying a car. But often of more importance, is the lifestyle to which the consumer aspires. Consumers identify with a favored lifestyle and buy products that exemplify that way of living. Demographics can be suggestive of both lifestyle and values so that we have magazines specifically to appeal to teenage lifestyle and values.

Claritas, one US research firm, has developed the PRIZM system consisting of 40 lifestyle clusters, classified into 12 social classes, based largely on demographic data supplemented by consumption and media usage data. Where there is roughly equal parity in performance among rival brands, then other components of the offering assume greater importance. Thus the firm may offer more service like longer warranties but, for many products, the focus is on associating the brand with specific values so that, in buying the product, consumers see themselves as upholding such values and receiving support or spiritual camaraderie from those buyers with similar values. Lifestyle approaches to segmentation are reflected in *psychographic* segmentation which initially was based on research into Activities, Interests, and Opinions (AIO):

Activities	*Interests*	*Opinions*
work	home	social issues
hobbies	job	politics
entertainment	community	education
clubs	food	culture
sports	media	
shopping		

But psychographic research, drawing on data from self-administered questionnaires, typically embraces not just AIO but measures of motives, attitudes, aspects of personality and values. Psychographic research can be product specific or nonspecific and can be combined with demographic data for advertising purposes. The most well-known system of nonspecific psychographics is VALS (Values and Life Styles), developed by SRI (formerly the Stanford Research Institute). The initial VALS was criticized from many points of view and recently SRI has brought out VALS 2, which is claimed to be a better predictor of purchase decisions. VALS 2 classifies consumers into eight segments along just two dimensions:

1 self-orientation and
2 resources available to sustain the self-orientation.

Self-orientation.   SRI from its research identified three primary self-orientations:

1 *Principle-orientation,* where individuals look within themselves to make choices rather than just reacting to physical experience or social pressure, that is, the individual is inclined to base his or her decisions on strongly held principles, following established codes of family, church, or nation.
2 *Status-orientation,* where individuals make choices guided by the opinions, actions, and the anticipated reaction of reference groups. Such individuals seek a secure social position and act accordingly.
3 *Action-orientation,* where individuals make choices guided by a desire for physical and social activity, variety, and risk-taking.

These three orientations are meant to be suggestive of the type of motives likely to be pursued in buying.

Resources the consumer can draw on to sustain the self-orientation.   Such resources include education, income, health, energy level, self-confidence, interpersonal skills, inventiveness, and intelligence.

The self-orientation and resources available combine to form eight segments within the three primary self-orientations:

- The *principle*-oriented can be either
  1 *"fulfilled"* or
  2 *"believer,"*
  with the fulfilled just having more resources. The fulfilleds as a segment are reasonably active in community and politics but leisure really centers on the home. Values relate to education, travel, health, and tolerance. The believers are a segment with less resources, respect authority figures, and societal rules. They socialize within family and other established groups and are conservative in politics though fairly well-informed.
- The *status*-oriented can be what are called
  3 *"actualizers"* or
  4 *"achievers"* or
  5 *"strivers"* or
  6 *"strugglers"*
  with the actualizers having the most resources and the strugglers the least. The actualizers as a segment are highly social and apt to be politically active. They are well-informed and value personal growth, education, intellect, and varied leisure activities. The achievers as a segment are politically conservative, with lives centering on career and family, with formal social relationships. Strivers as a segment are politically apathetic and look to peer group for motivation and approval while being easily bored, with narrow interests, not including health and nutrition! The strugglers as a segment are conservative and tied to organized religion. With limited interest, their values center on safety and security while often burdened by health problems.
- The *action-oriented* are the
  7 *"experiencers"* and the
  8 *"makers,"*
  with the experiencers having most resources. Experiencers as a segment are politically apathetic, value wealth, power, and fame and the new, risky, and the offbeat. They like exercise and sports, and although concerned about image, they are nonconforming. Finally, the eighth category, the makers, as a segment, just distrust politicians and avoid joining organizations except unions. They value the outdoors and "hands on" activities while spending time with family and close friends.

VALS measures relate somewhat to product ownership and media use. One claim is that VALS 2 will point to one or more of the eight categories most associated with the product class and it will be then up to advertising to design category-relevant appeals for the particular brand. As this is the major psychographic system in the United States with imitators in other countries, it deserves some comment.

The self-orientations are motivational categories in that they are categories of dispositions to seek certain goals:

1 The *principle-oriented* already hold beliefs about what rules (principles) ought to be followed in many areas of life while believing they should follow such principles. But how predictive will this be in buying since there are likely to be doubts as to what principles to apply?

2 The actions of *status-oriented* consumers will depend on what they consider in buying to enhance status or social acceptance. Can it just be assumed that there will be a general consensus on what products or brands symbolize status?

3 *Action-oriented* consumers do not seem as if they would be preprogrammed in any way but will vary with their individual beliefs about what fits best to their desire for activity, variety and risk-taking.

While the VALS categories seem to be describing distinct personalities, grouping into categories depends on who passes what mark on a scale as the categories of self-orientation are not discrete but continuous. Looking at the categories would suggest that the segments are not mutually exclusive. We often exhibit different lifestyle behaviors in different situations or different buying occasions. Thus in buying books and newspapers, I might behave like an actualizer but in buying clothes I might behave like an achiever. Another question: Is not the content of a principle decisive before we can say people can be fulfilled or believers? There is a richness in the segment descriptions that cannot be just deduced from the relevant basic dimensions.

VALS 2 seems to be based on a one-factor theory of motivation, namely self-esteem. Self-esteem is important since it relates to the emotions of self-assessment like pride, guilt, and shame. But it is not the only motive at work in buying though no doubt it is a major one when nothing distinguishes brands in the market beyond their image. But, it is not clear that VALS 2 does distinguish categories of consumers with distinct orientations and it ignores household decision-making altogether.

There have been attempts to develop lifestyle systems that are cross-cultural. Thus Backer Spielvogel Bates Worldwide has developed GLOBAL SCAN, which is based on annual surveys of consumers in 14 countries (in alphabetical order these are: Australia, Canada, Colombia, Finland, France, Germany, Hong Kong, Indonesia, Japan, Mexico, Spain, the United Kingdom, the United States, and Venezuela). GLOBAL SCAN seeks to measure and capture 250 value and attitude elements as well as incorporating demographic data, buying preferences and media usage. GLOBAL SCAN posits five global lifestyle segments. The percentage of the population within each segment varies from country to country. The five global *lifestyle* segments are:

1 *Strivers*. Median age 31. Those in this segment strive hard to achieve success but are stretched. Values are materialistic, looking all the time for pleasure, instant gratification, and convenience.

2 *Achievers*. Slightly older than strivers and ahead of them in affluence. Values relate to status and quality. They are trend setters and tend to shape the mainstream values of society while together with strivers they create the youth-oriented values in society.

3 *Pressured*. Those in this segment are pressured by problems and are mainly women from every age group. Economic and family problems are apt to drain their resources.

4 *Adapters*. These are usually an older crowd content with their lives. While tolerant of new ideas they are attached to their own standards and value whatever would seemingly enrich the more mature years.

5 *Traditionals*. These uphold the traditional values of their culture or country. Very conservative, they prefer the old ways of thinking and living.

What is interesting about GLOBAL SCAN is its implicit assumption that there is perhaps a universal human nature when it comes to social living. We are so accustomed in anthropology and in marketing to reminding ourselves of cultural differences that we forget there are universals e.g. people throughout the world smile when they are happy, are influenced by social norms, love to gossip, and so on.

Other bases of segmentation and the granfalloon technique

The bases of segmentation already discussed are those most frequently suggested. But they are not exhaustive. Any basis that is pragmatically useful for identifying distinct customer groups can be a basis for segmentation. Thus with a new product, the seller might classify those in the market into innovators (to be targeted first), early adopters, late adopters and those likely to be laggards (see Chapter 9).

One common but controversial method of segmentation is the division of the market into "heavy users" and those who are not, with the idea of targeting the heavy users (e.g. the detergent Dash). The typical criticism here is that heavy users are not likely to want anything different from the rest of the market. Even if the 20 percent heavy users buy 80 percent of the product (the so-called 20/80 rule that so commonly operates) the question remains as to what to do differently. The answer lies in the so-called "granfalloon" technique, with the word "granfalloon" meaning a meaningless association.[11] The granfalloon technique is commonly employed in advertising. The technique is based on the finding that, when complete strangers are placed into groups and/or talked about as a group using the most trivial of criteria, individuals are apt to act as if they and those who share the meaningless label were friends or at least have something meaningful in common. It seems that simply knowing you belong to some group disposes you to liking other members of the group. Because belonging to a group can be perceived as supportive of self-esteem, heavy users may accept the granfalloon of heavy user as being meaningful in terms of their having special requirements. The categorization of others as being like oneself can produce shared expectations of agreement, in this case of wanting something different. But much depends on how the heavy user is portrayed. Thus the heavy beer drinker group as portrayed in some commercials, may not be a group with which all heavy drinkers would wish to belong. Also heavy users are not always the heavy buyers or deciders since, for example, though teenagers are the heaviest users of soft drinks, it is mothers who do the buying. Finally, heavy users, such as heavy users of the telephone, may form a *benefit* segment based on their being able to obtain special discounts.

Another common basis quoted as distinct is "brand loyalty." This could be just straight value segmentation and so classified under psychological segmentation; appealing to those disposed to be loyal with the suggestion it is the firm's brand that attracts the most loyalty e.g. "I'd rather fight than switch," the slogan of one cigarette advertisement. But the segmentation could also be regarded as benefit segmentation with the benefits being tied to integrative criteria (belonging to a distinctive group) and adaptive criteria (loyal customers suggest to new users both satisfaction and no risk). It is only because benefit segmentation is so tied to the idea that the benefits must be tangible product benefits that the nontangible satisfactions are not recognized as benefits, which they certainly are. In any case, the stress on loyalty is essentially brand image building: the image of a loyal group of customers helps to retain current customers (the granfalloon effect) and to attract others to a product with such a loyal following. There are still other bases like the propensity to switch brands.

In one approach, questionnaires are administered to measure the "propensity to change brands;" questions covering such items as satisfaction with the current brand, views about alternative products and (in the case of prospects for the product category) the ambivalence about the product category. Actual and prospective users of the product category are grouped into eight categories based on their propensity to change. When combined with demographic data about those in each category, it becomes feasible to decide which consumers will be receptive to what messages.

Sometimes "situation segmentation" is proposed on the ground that benefits sought can vary with the situation. However, different situations can represent different use functions and hence different markets. Where the situations do in fact represent different use-occasions (for example, a dinner party vs. the usual evening meal), situation segmentation seems adequately covered by benefit or lifestyle segmentation.

Segmentation in international markets

The first step in segmentation in international marketing is to group countries regionally on the basis of commonality of culture and language. This is not easy. Even where there is a commonality among countries like, say, Germany and Austria, there are important differences. The same motives, though, may operate when it comes to buying the firm's product. In fact, sometimes the same motive will be at work throughout the world. Many luxury, designer brands trade on the same integrative (status appeal) and intrinsic liking throughout the world, with little need to change from that done in the domestic market. Similarly, for industrial products, the same applications may be common throughout the world and only the degree of service support may vary.

Motives for buying can, however, vary or seem to vary in different parts of the world. Thus the motive (as judged by the advertising) for buying Levi's jeans varies in different parts of the world: in some countries buyers seem to be motivated by the desire to parade the label to identify with American culture; elsewhere the desire is for a "sexy" image and in still other places the desire is to buy a pair of blue jeans that are durable and well-made. The problem lies in determining whether all such motives are at work in each of these places, with particular segments in the various countries having been selected more or less by chance or whether *dominant* motives do in fact vary substantially in different parts of the world. In any case, the seller must decide whether to market the same offering throughout the world or modify the offering when reasons for buying are different. Sometimes advertising agencies develop their own psychographic systems for a particular country. Thus D'Arcy, Masius Benton & Bowles segment Russian consumers into five categories:

1   "Merchants" are reliant, nationalistic, practical and seek value. These are likely to prefer the Volkswagen as a car.

2 "Cossacks" are ambitious, independent, nationalistic and seek status. They are likely to prefer the BMW.
3 "Students" are passive, just scraping by, idealistic and practical. Their car preference is likely to be the Citroen 2CV.
4 "Business executives" are ambitious, Western-oriented, busy, and concerned with status. They are likely to prefer the Mercedes.
5 "Russian Souls" are passive, follow others, fear choices, and are hopeful. They prefer the Lada.

Whether such stereotypes are meaningful for marketing or just categories of dubious validity is a matter of empirical inquiry as they have no theoretical basis. However, being a business executive type does not seem incompatible with being also a cossack or a merchant while the categories themselves seem to be based on no clear criteria, beyond saying the bases are at different levels of abstraction and within a narrow band of values and motives. There is general acceptance that advertising messages must be tied to the culture: something recognized by Unilever in its successful advertising in Poland of Pollena 2000 detergent. On the other hand, its advertising campaign for OMO was mocked in Poland with the audience being unable to accept the idea of a grateful housewife thanking a laundry detergent!

Most US and European firms, in considering expansion abroad, focus on just the wealthy nations. But what is commonly forgotten is that in countries with large populations (e.g. China and India have between them a population greater than 2 billion), there will be many people who can afford to buy whatever takes their fancy. Thus Unilever's business in Asia in 1991 contributed $40.8 billion in sales, amounting to 11 percent of total Unilever business.

Segmentation in industrial markets and not-for-profit

In industrial markets, benefit segmentation is common with benefits embracing:

- product performance in specific end-use applications or speed of service;
- comprehensiveness of service;
- experience with the product;
- post-sales service requirements; and
- quality/reliability needs and uncertainties facing buyers.

One suggestion for mature markets is to divide customers into four segments based on price (high to low) and cost-to-serve (high to low).[12] Each of the four cells suggests different benefits. Thus low price and low cost-to-serve suggests a "no frills" product while a high price and high cost-to-serve suggests an augmented product accompanied by intensive value-added services. The problem with benefit segmentation here is that, if several people are involved in the buying decision, each may want something different. Thus when a decision-making unit (DMU) consists of strategy, operational, and tactical personnel, differences are likely and there is a need to recognize this.

Demographic descriptors such as location, size of prospects, industrial classification (SIC code) can each be a basis of segmentation as can the buyers involved in terms of their age, gender, position and role. The way a company buys is a basis for segmentation. Here, instead of speaking of psychological segmentation we speak of the wider unit of *behavioral* segmentation as industrial segmentation can take account of the size of the typical order; whether decision-makers are central or local; group buying or individual; financial condition; leasing versus buying and so on.

Although there are those who deny there are any significant differences between industrial and consumer market segmentation, others stress the need to recognize real differences in the decision-making process and choice criteria being more grounded in technical and economic criteria.[13, 14]

Segmentation in not-for-profit organizations can use benefit segmentation as do museums and symphony orchestras, and even fund-raising may use not only demographics (e.g. wealth, occupation, year of graduation, and so on) but also integrative criteria (group affiliation, personal recognition, and values) in forming segments requiring different offerings even if such offerings vary no more than in the promotional strategies used.

Which basis is best?

Which of the bases is best? Whenever such a question is asked, we should ask: best for what? as everything depends on our purposes. *Typically, we use some combination of the bases*. If only one basis is used, *benefit* segmentation would seem the most direct approach and the most customer oriented. But there are problems. First the benefits sought may not easily be identified for the whole offering. Second, the want for some benefit may be latent or people may be quite unable to articulate what they want until they get their hands on it and even then they may be unsure. In any case, there is also the problem of how the buyer will judge the presence or absence of some benefits in that, in applying choice criteria, the buyer comes up against the problem of gauging what indicators best demonstrate the degree to which some choice criterion is being met. For example, if reliability, durability, and wearability are the benefits sought, how does the buyer judge the degree to which the product has these attributes? Thus car buyers "may not know enough to talk about a '32-valve V-8' but when they touch the pedal, they want response quickly." Different buyers judge in different ways. Hence, two consumers may have exactly the same choice criteria yet choose different brands. *The solution to this problem of benefit segmentation embracing only wants but not beliefs as to what consumers look for to check that the benefits are present, is for benefit segmentation still to focus on choice criteria and the relative importance of these criteria but ensure that advertising and the product itself put across the relevant surrogate indicators.* Finally, there may be no difference among rival brands in performance and availability so promotional appeals and the development of brand image might seem the way to go using, say, psychographics. Certainly where there is product parity among rivals, the firm with the strongest brand image has an advantage.

When a market matures, performance in use functions gets taken for granted and minor benefits become the basis for preference. Minor benefits, however, can be legion. With a hand lotion, any of the following can be the basis of preference: smells nice; nonsticky; long lasting; convenient dispenser; attractive container; works on dry skin etc. If benefits were to be extended to other elements of the offering, the list would be very long indeed. Some writers argue that, for products where there is low involvement, benefit segmentation is not common. If this seems to be true, it is probably because benefit segmentation is so closely associated with *product* benefits but there are other offering benefits that can be stressed.

While *demographic* data do correlate positively and significantly to buying patterns, demographic data as a whole have not been highly predictive of *brand* choice. Just grouping consumers into income category, social class or whatever does not compel them to behave as expected. Though single people are one of the fastest growing demographic segments they may not want to be reminded of the fact by consumer offerings. Thus single people did not buy Campbell's Soup-for-One. In any case, organizations may have the demographics of the market but still not be sure what is wanted. For example, newspapers find difficulty in knowing what their readers want. It may be on some occasions that we find that those with the same want do have the same demographics though we may also find that many of those belonging to that demographic category do not buy the product. The use of *psychographic* advertising might be most appropriate when there is little differentiation in the product itself so there is more need to appeal to integrative criteria (with self-esteem currently being considered the "hot button"). But psychographic segmentation presents difficulties to mail order firms seeking, say, the principle oriented or the strivers.

It needs to be emphasized about both demographic and lifestyle segmentation that, just because individuals have similar ways of life, similar jobs, similar experiences, similar class and income, it does not follow that similar *standards of judgment* will emerge in making buying decisions. Much that passes in segmentation seems to be accepted on face value and sometimes too easily accepted by academics who are delighted at the idea of industry applying (however crudely), the behavioral sciences and quantitative techniques to marketing. What should be rejected is adopting standard systems when standard conditions do not exist. More thought should be given to developing *customized segmentation* schemes, looking to what is currently done as merely offering ideas. A good example here is P&G's Pampers Phases which consists of 13 different sorts of diapers (nappies), one for newborns and then six for boys and six for girls as they grow from infant to toddler.

How is a basis for segmentation selected?

Selecting the right basis for segmentation is important. Thus when Ford developed the Edsel car (a disaster for Ford) in the 1950s, it still thought of segmentation in terms of price only (high, medium, and low) and saw the Edsel as providing Ford with a car for the medium price segment (new to them) so "they would no longer be growing customers for General Motors" when the low-priced Ford car owners traded up. But a much more appropriate segmentation would have been a benefit segmentation tied to different lifestyles, just as the Rambler car of American Motors successfully catered to the lifestyle of urban dwellers.

It is an elementary truth that the appropriate basis of segmentation depends not on logic alone but on having a substantive knowledge about the buyer. It is common, however, to think of segmentation within price ranges. Firms may even offer exactly the same product at different price levels. Take the anti-arthritis branded drug Dolobid by Merck. It is sold far cheaper by Merck as a generic drug under its generic drug name (diflunisal)!

A market can be divided, but the basis selected may be irrelevant to evoking purchase response, or at least too weak to justify cultivating the segment. Marketers may invent divisions of the market and call each division a segment but, if the invention is to be meaningful, if must fit some recognizable features of the market, reflected in actual or potential buyer behavior. If it were easy to identify all aspects of an offering that would motivate various members of a market, segmentation would present few difficulties. But a major problem lies in determining these aspects or benefits and the optimum values of these for different buyers within some particular price range. It takes research or much experience to discover that consumers discriminate among soaps along the attributes or dimensions of price, image, cosmetic power, size, packaging, hygienic effect, smoothness and other variables. An additional difficulty arises because consumers are not necessarily seeking what they would buy if it were available. We are all open to new offers.

Any grouping into classes (e.g. segments) is theory-loaded. In the case of segmentation, the "theory" is the connection between consumers in the segment and their likely response to different offerings. There is no standard answer as to how to select the best basis for segmentation and firms resort to one or more methods:

- *Intuition and experience.* Many marketing managers have a feel for the market and on this basis choose which demographic, psychographic or benefit combination is likely to distinguish true segments. There is a need to check such intuition against the evidence.
- *Trial and error.* Based on common knowledge about the market, the manager can break down the market into many tentative sets of segments and check which are meaningful in terms of buyer behavior. This is indirectly discussed below under the heading of segmentation by *logical division.*
- *Research on consumption systems.* Observing the total consumption system from the buying of the product through storage, display, use, consumption and disposal, using a random sample of consumers to generate ideas for benefit segmentation.
- *Research on attitudes and perceptions.* This is an area of most current interest with *perceptual mapping* (see later) being one technique for such research.

We need to explain why the bases of segmentation being proposed are likely to give rise to different buyer responses. With benefit segmentation we think in terms of the consumer's actual or potential wants or choice criteria and group these to form benefit segments. The explanation here is that it is rational for consumers to choose in accordance with their wants (and beliefs) and the choice criteria that these imply. But expressed wants may not be firmly held or, when expressed, may not be based on any reflective understanding of the consumer's own situation or the product so there is still a need for some double checking. Beliefs, though, must not be forgotten since knowledge of wants alone is not enough to predict response to the benefits offered.

When we look at demographic and/or psychographic segmentation, we need to understand why such differences should give rise to different buying behavior. The reasoning is:

- If consumer X is, say, an *Achiever*;
- Brand choice will probably be that which reflects status/quality goals;
- Consumer X can be categorized as an *Achiever* on the basis of GLOBAL SCAN;
- *Therefore*, Consumer X's brand choice is probably that which offers most status/quality.

Alternatively we could talk in terms of what advertising appeals would be most effective with Achievers, knowing their demographics and primary motivation. However, all such reasoning is not well grounded unless the probabilities can be justified either empirically or from a theory that is better grounded than what is currently available. What should be said is that segments need not differ in terms of objective product attributes or the benefits reflected in those attributes but can be based on other components of the offering.

What is the process or processes of segmentation?

Segmentation can proceed top down or bottom up. If we proceed from the top down, we start with the market and carry out a division into more and more refined market segments. This process is known as *logical division*. On the other hand, if we proceed from the bottom up, we start with the individual consumer wants and group them into categories. We agglomerate like wants. If logical division is a sort of classification from above (deductive classification), bottom up grouping is classification from below (inductive classification).

Logical division or deductive classification

If we could get out a matrix showing every buyer in the market against every possible offering and let each buyer mark what offering or offerings he or she would be buying, it would simplify segmenting the market but would not eliminate all problems, unless buyers were to get exactly what they wanted. Otherwise there is a problem of grouping wants and buyers.

The key problem lies in identifying "like wants" and "like buyers." Whenever we ask "Should this type of buyer/consumer in this market, who has this want, be included under this group label?" the answer depends both on our purposes and the set of alternative segments we have developed. Thus when asked to classify poison ivy within the system of categories animal/vegetable/mineral, we would classify it as a vegetable but not when we mention vegetables for the purpose of cooking! In segmentation the purpose is to categorize into groups that are ideally most predictive of response to different offerings or different aspects of an offering like various promotional appeals. Like all groupings, the aim is to enable generalization to be made about the items (wants/buyers) in a group (segment). Thus when we group consumers into social classes, we are claiming this implies something about their buying behavior. What can be said right from the start is that there is no one optimum set of segments out there just waiting to be discovered. There are certain major restraining facts but, beyond this, the system of segments used by management are systems they have devised as ways of seeing the market.

We have said that the segmentation of a market can be accomplished by two routes: by logical division or by agglomerating like wants. Logical division is essentially classification "from above" or "deductive classification" while agglomerating like wants is essentially classification from below and may be termed "inductive classification." In practice, the segmentation process is likely to combine something of both approaches just as it is likely to combine several bases.

Segmentation by logical division (deductive classification) partitions the market into mutually exclusive subclasses. The usual way to proceed is by means of a diagram with each path forming a subclass that is a potential market segment (see Figures 6.2, and 6.3). Each subclass is assumed to represent a potentially distinct demand or segment. Division occurs in a series of steps. At each step one attribute (property) or set of

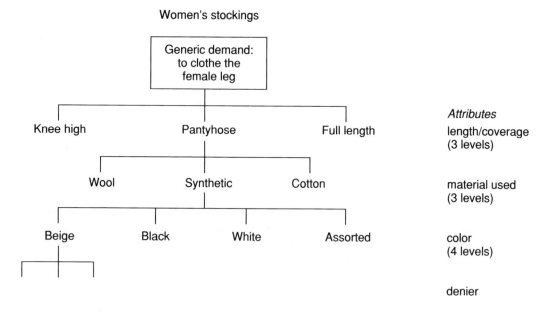

Figure 6.2 Hypothetical hierarchical definition of the women's stocking market (partial representation)

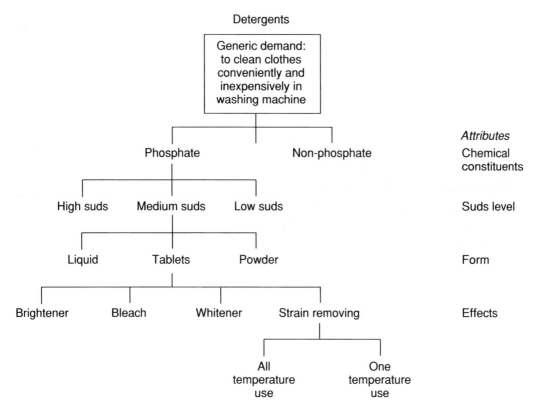

Figure 6.3 Hypothetical hierarchical definition of the detergent market (partial representation)

attributes (properties) is used to distinguish subclasses. Thus in the case of women's stockings (Figure 6.2) the relevant product attributes are, say, assumed to be length/coverage, material used and color, (though there could be other divisions using such attributes as density, texture, etc.) while in the case of detergents (Figure 6.3) the relevant attributes are assumed to be chemical constituents, suds level, form and effect generated. Ideally the hierarchy of attributes and attribute levels should reflect market behavior in that buyers would first decide (in the case of women's stockings) on length/coverage, then on the material, then on the color and finally on the denier (thickness). Where logical division does result in real segments of the market, diagrams such as those in Figures 6.2 and 6.3 are termed *hierarchical market definitions*.

When logical division is applied to an existing market (which it frequently is), the resulting subclasses may already be known to be segments of the market so the aim is to discover whether the process of subdivision can be continued or extended, e.g. the idea of designer deodorants. However, when used without such knowledge of actual buying practices, the deductive classification that emerges may not represent real segments. Much depends not only on the basis (or criterion) used at each step but on the order in which the bases (criteria) are employed. Unfortunately, all too often, the simplicity and clarity of logical division is not matched by its realism. In developing segments by this method, we have to place each criterion in order of significance to the buyer and this assumes we already know a good deal about buyer behavior. When logical division is used in situations where we know little about buyer wants, its very precision can mislead.

The Hendry model developed by the Hendry Corporation has been one way of trying to make sure the subdivisions are meaningful, so that true hierarchical market definitions are obtained.[15] The essence of the model is to use brand switching data to establish the branches of the hierarchy. Distinct branches are regarded as distinct segments. However, just because there is switching between, say, two branches does not prove that the two branches cannot be distinct segments of the market since consumers can switch from one segment to another for different use-occasions. This limitation has led many marketers to use data on consumer perceptions for identifying market and segment boundaries (see below).

The examples just given might suggest the focus be purely on brand or product attributes, which is just not so since other aspects of the offering may be a basis for segmentation. Consumers, too, on occasions can be so brand conscious that they select the brand label first. Firms with highly preferred brand-names are fortunate in that they need not compete in every segment when enough buyers insist on buying from them, regardless of the fact that other sellers are offering tangible product attributes more geared to what buyers want. Thus I may buy from IBM because I trust them, even though I acknowledge that some other brand of computer seems to be a better buy for me on purely objective grounds.

Inductive classification and ordination

As an alternative or as a complement to logical division we may seek to identify either the individual brands in a market and group them into segments or identify the individual wants and group them into segments.

Perceptual maps.   Various perceptual mapping techniques have been used to show the various products or brands on a map, with the relative positions of the brands being based on the consumer's perceptions of similarity and dissimilarity. The result is a *market structure analysis* (see Figure 6.4) since the result shows the relative perceived positions of the brands on the dimensions of interest. Perceptual maps are very attractive to managers since they portray all the competing brands in a market in one or more of the four segments of the map. Figure 6.4 shows the relative positions of brands of lawn-mowers on the dimensions of versatility and reliability. If the attributes of versatility and reliability had been perceived as actually negative for some brands, the other three quadrants would not have been empty.

On such a map we can also plot the preference or *ideal point* of some significant group of consumers. Thus one ideal point for one group is shown in Figure 6.4. In looking at Figure 6.4 it is assumed that:

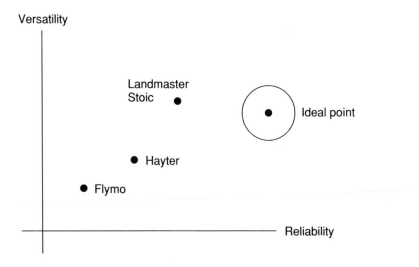

Figure 6.4 Market structure analysis (lawnmower market)

1 The closer the positioning of two brands on the map, the more likely they are to compete as they are seen as closer by the consumer.
2 The closer a brand is to a consumer's ideal point, the more likely it is to be preferred.
3 Gaps on the map near the ideal point can be identified that represent potential market segments.

The first step in constructing such a map is to identify the dimensions (characteristics) by which those in the market evaluate the product. This can be done by using, say, in-depth interviews, or protocol statements as discussed in earlier chapters. Consumers are then asked to rate each brand along each of the dimensions identified. Where there are a large number of dimensions, statistical techniques such as "factor analysis" are typically used to reduce the large number of resulting dimensions to the few under-lying dimensions. Thus in our lawnmower example (Figure 6.4) the dimensions were reduced to versatility and reliability. In any case, the buyer/consumer ratings determine the position of the brands on the map in Figure 6.4.

Another approach simply asks consumers to judge the overall similarity of brands, moving the brands about on the map until satisfied that the relative positions of the brands represent the respondent's perceptions of relative similarity. Just a map is given, without the axis being given any names, and consumers are simply asked to position the brands in the market according to perceptions of similarity. Later, an attempt is made to identify the likely axis dimensions as actual attributes are needed to give real substance to the map. Although consumer perceptions are always useful, there is a problem here in that consumers classify brands in different ways. One consumer may focus on *characteristic features* of the product class in classifying brands, another consumer will have a mental prototype of what the product should be like and judge individual brands as deviations from the *prototype* while, finally, some consumers simply have an

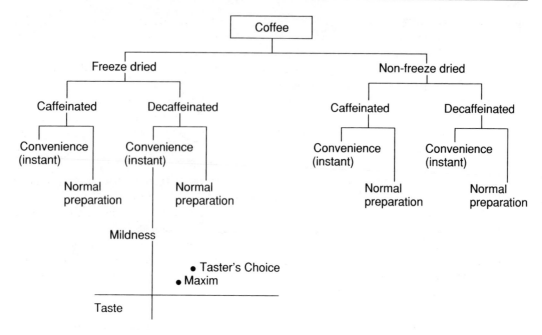

Figure 6.5 Integrating hierarchical market definition and perceptual mapping for decaffeinated instant coffee

Source: After Urban, Johnson, and Brudnick, 1979

exemplar (actual remembered example) in mind of the product class and classify brands on that basis.

Perceptual maps such as Figure 6.4 are used to identify segments by clustering together brands close to each other on the map. But judgment remains. Thus are the three brands shown in Figure 6.4 distinct segments or can Hayter and Flymo be put together? But perhaps perceptual maps are used more often in *positioning* a brand (see later). The hierarchical market definition resulting from logical division or brand switching data can be combined with perceptual maps as is shown in Figure 6.5.[16]

Perceptual maps have not escaped criticism. The term "map" rather than "graph" was introduced because the two end points of each of the axes do not necessarily represent polar extremes. Thus on one perceptual map of selected automobile brands, the two ends of the vertical axis are: top end "has a touch of class, a car I'd be proud to own, distinctive looking" versus the bottom end "very practical, gives good gas mileage, affordable." The two ends of the horizontal axis are: left end "conservative looking, appeals to older people" versus the right end "spirited performance, sporty looking, fun to drive, appeals to young people." Does this mean that car buyers see a contradiction in a classy, distinctive car being also practical, affordable, and giving good mileage or does it (as typically assumed) represent what buyers see as the relative emphasis of the various makes of car? In any case there are a number of considerations to bear in mind in opting to use perceptual maps:

- Two brands may be similar on dimension A, and dimension B etc., but only for buying in context Y or occasion X and not for buying occasion or context Z. How we classify depends on our purposes and purposes differ.
- Two consumers may have the same location on the map but arrive at that position by very different attitudinal routes.
- Just because two brands R and S are closest on the map and the position occupied by R is the ideal point for a certain group, it does not follow S will be chosen if brand R becomes nonfeasible. The consumer may prefer to keep out of the market altogether. Similarly, there is no guarantee that the removal of just one brand may not bring about a reordering of the rest. Thus, for example, the removal of a brand from a price segment on the ground that its chief ingredient is now too expensive for use in that segment, can lead consumers to reorder their preferences to give more weight to the scarce (more expensive) ingredient simply because it has come to signal scarcity.
- To ask a consumer about ideal points can be ambiguous—do we mean always prefer? usually prefer? prefer just now? prefer for this occasion? Answers can vary depending on the context in which the consumer imagines using the product and how the consumer construes the term "ideal."

There are problems in making sure that all the relevant dimensions are included, particularly when other attributes of the offering, and not just product attributes, may be a crucial factor in the buying decision. The procedures of factor analysis used for reducing the number of factors or dimensions to just, say, two are all purely statistical: the factors that emerge still have to be subjectively assessed to judge whether they really do represent meaningful dimensions.

Classifying wants and ordination. We can distinguish here between classification proper, in which it is possible to classify wants into homogenous classes (whether top down or bottom up classification) and *ordination* which involves forming segments or subclasses from divisions along a continuum. A weakness of logical division is its assumption that segments have hard boundaries. It may not be possible to classify market wants on the basis of the possession or absence of distinct characteristics. The dimensions of reliability and durability, for example, are not an all-or-nothing affair but a matter of degree: each is a continuum or gradation.

The criterion or basis for assigning wants into one segment rather than another is often not just a "yes" or "no" decision but a matter of *ordering* where neat pigeon holes are replaced by references to spaces of several dimensions as is the case with perceptual maps. Each segment that is constructed in this way is likely to be composed of wants that are *polythetic* in that no want in the segment must possess all the characteristics and attribute levels used to identify the segment. But because grouping wants here to form segments depends on *degree of affinity*, cases arise in which one want could just as well be grouped in several different segments. Such difficulties have led statisticians to devise rational procedures for identifying similarities for assigning, say, wants to segments, in particular the techniques associated with perceptual mapping like *multidimensional scaling* (MDS). Of course, in many cases, particularly in service marketing, wants can be grouped into segments that have hard boundaries like the segments in education, airlines, accounting, legal services, security services, commercial banking, software, shoe repairs, and so on. But the more interesting and difficult cases are those where segments involve no hard boundaries.

We shall illustrate the problem of *ordination* by an example that requires no sophistication of technique. Suppose there were six (any other sample, however large, could be used) people in the market for chocolate bars and we are asked to group them into segments. The only two product attributes or dimensions considered by the six consumers are sweetness and milkiness. Since sweetness and milkiness are matters of degree, we could ask each of the six to indicate on a scale the level of sweetness and milkiness preferred. We would have to provide the six consumers with a common frame of reference so each would know from exemplars what each part of the scale denoted in terms of sweetness and milkiness. Suppose the results of our inquiry were as follows:

	Buyers					
	B1	B2	B3	B4	B5	B6
Sweetness	1	6	2	2	7	4
Milkiness	2	5	1	3	6	4

The measures can be plotted on a graph as in Figure 6.6. The points on the graph represent the preferences or ideal points of the six consumers. We can now proceed to group them into segments. There are statistical techniques available to do such clustering when the numbers and situation warrant but, in our example, clustering can be done by judgment. If we look at Figure 6.6, there are two distinct groupings if we ignore B6, who is the odd one out. The question arises whether B6 should be grouped into one or the other of the two groups or be regarded as a distinct segment. To group B6 into one or the other of the main segments can be an empty exercise if some competitor is prepared to treat B6 as a separate segment by designing a product specifically for B6.

In identifying a market segment, we must both define the differential benefits sought and draw up a profile of those in the segment that distinguishes them from members of other segments. Although techniques are very useful here, the process of segmentation cannot be entirely mechanical but requires insight into market motivations.

TARGETING: SELECTING SEGMENTS IN WHICH TO MARKET

Some organizations do not attempt to segment the market but adopt what is called a *market aggregation* strategy, whereby the firm just sells to the whole market. But this is misleading since it suggests that segmentation does not occur. In a competitive market, the seller who tries to sell to the whole market, by focusing on what is common to the wants of all those in the market, will still only appeal to some buyers within that market and these will constitute a market segment of some sort, usually that which is satisfied with a product that just meets the core (threshold) want. The seller who avoids

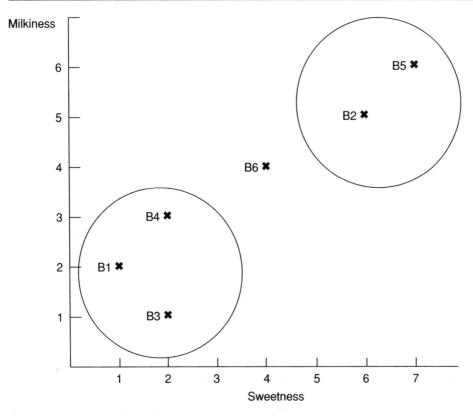

Figure 6.6 Preferences or ideal points of six consumers on the dimensions of milkiness and sweetness of chocolate bars

segmenting the market is in effect, in a competitive market, leaving the segmentation to the market and chance that the product will have a substantial number of buyers. Where an organization does actually segment the market, it may just select one segment, or several or seek to enter all segments to keep out competition. In any case, the selection of segments is against some criteria. In selecting segments, we consider both the general factors used to evaluate any economic opportunity and factors more specific to the selection of segments.

1 General factors:
   • company capabilities and thrust
   • size of segment and growth potential
   • level of investment needed
   • level of profitability
   • risks involved
   • competition
2 Specific segmentation factors:

- segment durability
- segment mobility
- segment distinctness
- segment reachability and cost
- segment ease of entry and bargaining power of buyers and suppliers.

Company capabilities and thrust.   We choose segments that are likely to be responsive to what the firm has to offer. Since what it has to offer is related to its core competencies and thrust, a firm will wish to select segments where the critical success factors and the requirements for success match the firm's thrust and competencies. Thus the firm needs to define the requirements for success and, of these, those that are most critical to success in the segment are used as a basis for deciding whether what the firm has to offer is capable of yielding a competitive or critical advantage. Where the firm is to exploit an existing brand-name, it should choose segments interested in those associations that have attached themselves to the brand. In other words, the segment should be receptive to what the brand is perceived as exemplifying.

Size of segment and growth potential.   The size and growth potential of the segment is an important consideration. Although a firm may do better catering to some niche segment where there is less intense competition, it is also true that the largest segments have the potential of experience curve effects, and economies of scale. But firms can be deceived by the size of current demand. Thus, before the Model-T Ford in the 1920s, many people wanted a car but the demand was inhibited by high prices.

Investment needed.   There are entry costs to any market but there are also the costs incurred after entry. These are the costs of building market segment share. If the segment is new there is the problem of activating what may be only a latent want for the product. If competitors are already in the segment, there is the problem of creating awareness, attracting the new users and converting from rivals.

Profitability of the segment.   There is a problem in estimating likely future sales and likely future costs. Such estimates are best made in terms of different scenarios: optimistic, most likely and pessimistic. Where there is little room for error, it suggests caution.

Risk.   There are the usual risks associated with market receptivity but these are not the only ones. There is the risk of *cannibalism* if the firm already has a major share of the market as sales to the new segment may come at the expense of the firm's sales to other segments. This was Procter and Gamble's (P&G's) worry when it introduced Luvs, a premium priced diaper, that it would take its sales mainly from P&G's Pampers. Risk is certainly lessened when the firm is entering the segment exploiting its thrust, like Coca-Cola and Pepsi exploiting their distribution system.

Competition.   A major error is to select segments without adequate investigation of competition. This has been common for those adopting benefit segmentation. When a firm selects a segment or segments it also selects rivals with whom it will do battle, either immediately or in the future. Though a segment may be a very large one, it may already be well served and dominated by well-entrenched suppliers. There is a need to analyze the offerings of these rivals vis-à-vis the firm's own offering to establish that some sustainable competitive advantage exists. It may also pay to question the rules currently accepted by competitors in the market to see if they can be broken with advantage. Thus the new firm may consider entirely new distribution channels while one bank became established by querying the need of a service charge on deposits and extending bank hours for customer convenience.

The segmentation strategies of rivals should be inferred since a rival may have fragmented the segment it proposes to enter.

Segment durability. There are fads and fashions in every market. Segments based on these are ephemeral and plans need to take this into account. Thus scores of manufacturers in the United States mistakenly believed the cowboy fashion of the 1980s was there to stay and invested accordingly, only to find it was a fad.

Segment mobility. Segment mobility refers to the frequency of customer turnover within a segment. Thus there is high mobility in hair dyes, baby products, teenage magazines, and so on. This means that, if sales are to increase or remain stable, there is the constant problem of attracting new users.

Segment distinctness. Segment distinctness refers to the separateness of the segment from the other segments in that market, that is, the extent it deviates from what would be regarded as the prototypical offering for that market. If what is sought is perceived as very different from what is sought in other segments, the "loyalty" of those in that segment is likely to be greater while those outside the segment are most likely to regard the segment's offering as something not for them. This was once the case with decaffeinated coffee. Such highly distinctive segments may be more stable than other segments of the market.

Reachability. Those in the segment should preferably be easily reached at reasonable cost through established communications and distribution channels.

Segment ease of entry and bargaining power of buyers and suppliers. These are additional factors introduced by Porter's model that need to be separately considered.

How the various criteria described above should be weighted will depend on objectives and which problems are judged to be most important.

POSITIONING THE PRODUCT

Whether the product is already developed or proposed, it has to be positioned. The positioning of a product refers to the process by which the firm decides how it should best depict the product in the market/market segment vis-à-vis competition and hopefully in the mind of the consumer. The term "position" simply refers to the product's place vis-à-vis competition. The usage is similar to the military usage of the term "position" in that a position is always taken against the position of the enemy. Positioning implies a frame of reference and this is usually competition. The aim of positioning is to give a brand a distinctive meaning for the buyer. Positioning implies a segment commitment, namely, to that segment interested in the advantages selected for the brand. Thus one soap depicts itself as a germ fighter. This contrasts with other soaps stressing their skin-softening advantages or cleansing abilities. Similarly, one brand of dish washing liquid stresses its mildness to the hands; another its ability to put a shine on dishes, while the third says it is the best for cutting through grease. The position selected by the firm must be consistent with brand advantages and with current or anticipated perceptions of consumers. It should also offer a reason to buy.

We have argued that a segment should define both what and who: what is being sought and by whom. When we define what is being sought, we may first distinguish the segment want from other wants related to the market function. But, whether we do this or not, we need to answer the key question: "Why should those in our *segment* buy from us?" The answer to this is given by positioning. *Positioning reflects the core of the buying inducement or competitive advantage.* As such it should preferably be something competitors cannot imitate or do not want to imitate or, if they do, they will be less successful at it.

The procedure in positioning is first to identify the competition and their offerings in the segment. The next step is to compare their positions with the proposed position for the firm's brand to make sure the brand has something on which to build a distinctive image or position whether this be some product benefit, or the brand-name, or value appeal. It is inviting failure to enter the segment with just a me-too offering (not necessarily a me-too product) in which there are well-entrenched competitors. If the firm's brand is already in the market, there is the need to discover the position of the brand in terms of current buyer perceptions and the intensity and sharpness of those perceptions. This is very important if repositioning is considered, in that strong associations can set limits on repositioning or, indeed, on expanding into other segments. In fact before considering repositioning, it may be wiser to update the brand since repositioning always carries the risk of losing current customers and not attracting new ones because of the difficulty of recategorizing a brand that is strongly associated with a particular position.

CONCLUSION

The output of any segmentation strategy is:

1 a profile of the customer group, focusing on those profile details that are needed to develop product, promotional, pricing, and distribution strategies.
2 the set of benefits sought and the firm's buying inducement so the firm can develop what is sought and provide the buying inducement. There are the benefits that
   a) define the segment and those that

b) define the position of a brand within a segment to provide a competitive or critical advantage.

A marketing strategy is a strategy for a market, not a strategy for off-loading a product. The most basic element of any marketing strategy is the segmentation strategy, because the segment requirements determine the firm's offering. Until a firm knows in some detail what is wanted and by whom, it cannot develop the other strategies of promotion, pricing and distribution. We can seldom be sure that we have segmented a market in the best possible way. Just as the classification of living things into species is not entirely an arbitrary process or simply the discovery of fact in nature, segmentation of a market does not consist of arbitrary groupings, but neither is there a unique set of segments to be discovered. The normative ideal for segmentation is to achieve what amounts to a "relational classification" in the sense that all those in a segment should be related, via similarity of response, to the same offering as manifested in marketing strategy. No method at present can be sure of achieving this. As we have become aware of the nature of the segmentation problem, we are using more and more sophisticated quantitative techniques, but no such techniques will ever compensate for a lack of understanding of how the consumer "ticks."

NOTES

1 Levitt, Theodore (1960) "Marketing Myopia," *Harvard Business Review*, 38 (July–August).
2 Day, George S., Shocker, Allen D., and Srivastava, Rajendra K. (1979) "Customer-oriented Approaches to Identifying Product Markets," *Journal of Marketing*, 43 (Fall).
3 Piore, Michael J. and Sabel, Charles F. (1984) *The Second Industrial Divide*, New York: Basic Books.
4 Dickson, Peter R. and Ginter, James L. (1987) "Market Segmentation, Product Differentiation, and Marketing Strategy," *Journal of Marketing*, 51 (April).
5 Ehrenberg, A. S. C. and Goodhardt, G. J. (1978) *Market Segmentation*, New York: J. Walter Thompson.
6 Winter, Frederick W. (1984) "Market Segmentation: A Tactical Approach," *Business Horizons*, 27 (January–February).
7 Haley, Russel I. (1968) "Benefit Segmentation: a Decision-Oriented Research Tool," *Journal of Marketing*, 32 (July).
8 Birdwell, A. E. (1968) "A Study of the Influence of Image Congruence on Consumer Choice," *Journal of Business*, 41 (January).
9 White, I. S. (1966) "The Perception of Value in Products," in Joseph W. Newman (ed.) *On Knowing the Consumer*, New York: John Wiley.
10 Kline, P. and Barrett, P. (1983) "The Factors in Personality Questionnaires Among Normal Subjects," *Advances in Behavioural Research and Therapy*, 5: 141–202.
11 Pratkanis, Anthony and Aronson, Elliot (1991) *Age of Propaganda: The Everyday Use and Abuse of Persuasion*, New York: W. H. Freeman and Company.
12 Rangan, Kasturi V., Moriarty, Rowland T., and Swartz, Gordon S. (1992) "Segmenting Customers in Mature Industrial Markets," *Journal of Marketing* 56 (October).
13 Fern, Edward F. and Brown, James R. (1984) "The Industrial/Consumer Dichotomy: A Case of Insufficient Justification," *Journal of Marketing*, 48 (Spring).
14 Shipiro, Benson P. and Bonoma, Thomas V. (1984) "How to Segment Industrial Markets," *Harvard Business Review*, 62 (May–June).

15 Kalwani, M. U. and Morrison, D. G. (1977) "A Parsimonious Description of the Hendry System," *Management Science*, 23 (January).
16 Urban, G. L., Johnson, P., and Brudnick, R. (1979) "Market Entry Strategy Formulation: hierarchical model and consumer measurement approach" working paper, Cambridge, MA: Sloan School of Management, MIT.

Chapter 7

Competitive (rival-oriented) strategies

When a firm enters a market, the objective is growth. With the passage of time, the firm may be content to hold and defend its market share. In either situation, however, the firm's objective may be frustrated by competitive action. To try and avoid this happening, there is a need to think out a competitive strategy, that is, some conception of how the firm's resources are to be deployed to anticipate and overcome competitive activity that frustrates the firm's objectives.

A necessary condition for success in a free market is to have a sufficient number of buyers perceive one's offerings as superior to rivals'. If this condition is to be achieved, it must be actively sought through attempting to stay ahead of competition. The recognition of the need to consider what competition is doing has led to criticism of the concept of customer orientation when interpreted to mean marketing's goal is merely to satisfy customers. But, if we interpret customer orientation to mean meeting or exceeding customer expectations, this does imply the need to stay ahead of competition since buyer expectations depend substantially on what competition is offering. But to change the basic focus of marketing from buyers to competitors would be wrong since getting ahead of competition comes from understanding buyer wants and not just from trying to do better than competition. While competition and competitive offerings provide a good deal of the motivation to improve, "doing better" means doing better for the consumer. Trying to do better by focusing on competition rather than the customer may result in providing extras over competition that are just not wanted or not wanted as much as something else, which focusing on the customer might have discovered. In fact, we do not need to beat competition on all aspects of the offering. We need to beat competition where it counts, that is, counts with the customer: *knowing* what does count or is likely to count comes from focusing on the customer. This does not mean that competition can be ignored. The trend toward giving more emphasis to competition than the customer occurred as a reaction to the marginalizing of competition by companies who acted as if talking about competition gave competition too high a profile. There is a need to keep a constant eye on competition but not at the expense of losing sight of the customer.

This chapter approaches the problem of developing a competitive strategy in four stages:

1 defining the firm's competition
2 collecting and analyzing information on competition
3 identifying the strategic options open to the firm
4 choosing a competitive strategy.

DEFINING THE FIRM'S COMPETITION

A firm's competition is defined as those firms competing in the same market. However, Porter's concept of extended rivalry embraces a wider system since he views competition as including the five forces of:

1 threat of entry

2 rivalry among competitors
3 pressure of substitutes
4 bargaining power of buyers and
5 bargaining power of suppliers.[1]

For corporate planning purposes this is useful as it reminds us that the level of profit involves keeping out competition and substitutes; lessening the dependence on any supplier and having a real critical advantage for the buyer. This chapter, however, will focus just on rivalry among competitors (which can include those selling substitute products) on the assumption that the wider system has already received attention when developing a business-wide strategic plan.

Competition is not restricted to firms in the same business, as competition embraces all competitors catering to the same function. In defining competition as embracing all those catering to the same function, we acknowledge competition could come from outside the industry. Thus the fax machine and payment by automatic bank transfers affect traditional mail while interactive TV is likely to challenge direct mail selling. Competition also embraces foreign competitors operating in the national market or in the overseas markets served by the firm. Competition can come from firms in other businesses that have a different technological base. Hence if the only information is on competitors in the same business, the firm becomes "locked in" to paying attention only to these competitors with a failure to assess the wider range of potential rivals. The maker of leather goods would thus ignore what was happening in plastics. This would be wrong. But much depends on how broadly the market function is defined. For example, if an airline defines its market function as transportation, this is different from defining its market as air transportation, or air passenger transportation.

Nonbusiness organizations (not-for-profit) seldom pay much attention to competition as it seems so "commercial" to do so and conflicts with the image of such organizations as being only concerned with cooperating with others and certainly not trying to compete in any way. But all organizations that depend for their existence on raising revenue from their supporters in the world outside are inevitably competing with organizations in the same "business". Whether just fund-raising for a cause, offering a service or something tangible, a not-for-profit organization must come across as more worthy of support as far as each particular gift etc. is concerned, to enough people than other not-for-profit organizations. The successful are those with *relatively* more appealing offerings, that is, relative to some competitor group.

Large firms define the market function more broadly than smaller firms, which would feel the wider function embraces competition over too wide a net to be useful. In any case, most interest will focus on those in the same segment, e.g. "air travel for middle-class adults traveling on vacation to the following areas . . .". Within that segment most attention is paid to rivals who have positioned themselves similarly.

Sometimes firms speak of the *generic* market when the market function is defined widely, just as General Foods Coffee Division might speak of the generic market as being the demand for beverages. In such a case, coffee would constitute the immediate market with, say, decaffeinated coffee being a segment of that market. Each of these three levels provides a different competitive set, useful for different purposes.

Measures of rivalry vary. There are *purchase-based measures* such as brand switching data. But a high level of brand switching between two brands may or may not indicate rivalry since, when based on household panel data (as is usually the case), it may simply indicate different preferences by different household members or simple variety-seeking. *Consumer judgment methods* tend to be better. Thus perceptual maps of relative brand positions may present a better guide to which brands are close rivals. Or more simply, customers can group brands into different sets based on their perceptions of similarity or on the basis of what brands they would willingly substitute. With a new-to-the-world product, where the market is not yet established, competition is likely to be viewed as wide but, as the market moves to maturity, competitors are more likely to be defined as those in the same business or those operating in the same segment of the market.

Given the objective of growth or hold/defend, which competitors could frustrate that objective? We need to identify such competitors. Where a competitor is part of a large multidivisional firm, there is a need to know this since the parent company's policies may be of equal interest. In fact, size and type of company ownership are important when it comes to likely competitive action. The multidivisional firm that is also multi-national is apt to impose rules on its subsidiary companies which reduce their flexibility, slowing down their response to attack. While the conglomerate may impose less rules, it is likely to be concerned with immediate profit, ruling out strategies that involve heavy investment for long-term payoff. Privately owned firms and local competitors are some of the most fierce defenders of their market position. In any case, we would like to know our competitors' thrust, capabilities and core competencies, current strategies, and financial position. Knowledge of thrusts, capabilities and competencies is important as it is indicative of what the firm *can do*. But of equal importance is what competitors are *likely to do*, that is, their intentions. Such intentions are not likely to be entirely idiosyncratic but are likely to be influenced by how the firm views its position in the market and the characteristics of the market itself, such as the number of firms competing, market growth rate, cost differentials among the competitors, and so on.[2]

COLLECTING AND ANALYZING INFORMATION ON COMPETITION

In competitive intelligence, the most basic questions are: "What is the profile of each competitor? What is each likely to do?" Information on competition is designed to help in:

1 comparing relative strengths and weaknesses in capabilities/competencies vis-à-vis competition;
2 monitoring competitor actions;
3 warning management of rival moves and countermoves, actual or contemplated; and
4 developing competitive strategies.

Intelligence is a prerequisite for strategy formulation but it is never a substitute for good judgment, and it is important only to the extent that it is believed and deals with real issues for management. In gauging capabilities and core competencies, there is usually no difficulty in finding out about product lines, technology, financial resources, physical resources, number of employees, and even the quality of management. The real problem lies in evaluating what these things *mean* for future action. In particular there is a problem in evaluating the potential of any newly introduced substitute for the firm's product based on a new technology. The tendency is to dismiss any incipient new technology as of little potential significance or as merely catering to some faddish segment of the market.

Intentions are more difficult to infer than capabilities and resources. Yet intentions reveal themselves in intentional movements and declarations: all planning takes time and not all of its manifestations can be hidden. But interpreting the significance of a competitor's resources and inferring a competitor's intentions are never free of bias:

- forcing the evidence to fit preconceptions
- being hostile to evidence at odds with beliefs
- predicting the most feared competitive intentions as a defense in any future post-mortem
- as a way of getting support for a favored strategy, predicting that the competitive action will be that to which the favored strategy is an effective counter-strategy.

In general, firms concentrate on the biggest competitors on the ground that a competitor's effectiveness is related to a firm's command over resources. But competitive intelligence should also include competitors with the *capacity to mobilize* resources and those who have displayed *resourcefulness* in developing and implementing strategy. Resourcefulness embraces the stamina to persist in the face of adversity and the inventiveness to do more with less. Resourcefulness should not be confused with ambitious management since, particularly when it comes to global marketing, it is not uncommon to find management ambitions are well beyond what their resources and capabilities can deliver. Resourcefulness is a competence and all competencies are of interest. Spotting resourcefulness in small growing firms is a way of spotting potential rivals even though currently such firms represent no serious challenge. Competencies are a class of capabilities but not all capabilities are competencies since (unlike competencies) not all capabilities are based on human skills and abilities. Thus we speak of a machine having capabilities but not as having competencies. Unlike many resources, competencies are not used up in application but are enhanced through additional learning and sharing. Thus every manufacturing company has competencies in the design and conception of products; in marketing; in production; in finance and management. All thrusts and core competencies ultimately rest on the skills and abilities of management and other employees.

To assess a competitor's response profile, Porter suggests that information be collected on:

1 *Goals*. From past statements and actions, what appear to be the competitor's goals? What would it mean to the competitor to have these goals frustrated (since the relative importance of the goals is a guide to the likely intensity of competitive action or reaction)?

2 *Current strategies*. We can usually identify a firm's investment objective from its actions, while its marketing strategy is reflected in its segmentation, promotion, pricing and distribution. We may also look at a competitor's past strategies to discern some pattern. However, reading a pattern into a series of past strategies can be misleading in suggesting a degree of rationality and a consistency that may not be there.

3 *Beliefs*. Beliefs held by a competitor about itself, competition, and the industry generally form the premises on which competitive decisions are made.

4 *Capabilities*. Information about competitor capabilities for initiating and reacting to competition is needed since the "will to act" may not compensate for weaknesses in resources.

Information of the type discussed by Porter is not readily available. Porter recommends screening what he terms "market signals" though this is a problem when competitors deliberately set out to bluff and deceive. Nonetheless, he argues that much can be discovered from public announcements and what competitors say about the industry and how they explain their actions. But what a competitor says may be of less significance as a guide to intentions than knowledge of past actions. In the most general terms, past history suggests which competitors are:

- *product innovators*. Those with a record of technological breakthroughs are often the most worrying since such innovation threatens others with technological obsolescence.
- *adroit marketers*. Equally to be feared are rivals whose success is based on their having acquired a deep understanding of the market and its wants.
- *followers-of-the-leader*. Some of these may make money, depending on their efficiency but are not so worrying.
- *drifters*. Drifters merely drift, reflecting the power plays within the organization, not uncommon in large organizations that have lost their way.
- *potential invaders from other industries*. Firms in this category may be contemplating entering the market with a new product with a different technological base. These may be dismissed as fad marketers without seriously considering the potential of the technology to reach performances beyond that which can be achieved by the firm's existing technology.

A competitor's history is relevant as a guide to future intentions since organizations tend to be loyal to certain recipes for success that have served them well in the past. Thus we have BIC with its recipe of mass production and mass distribution with a bit of excitement at the point of sale and the Japanese with their recipe of providing more reliability for less cost with miniaturization as a common entry strategy. One problem with the adoption of any generally promoted strategy like that of BCG is its being easily read by competitors, allowing adequate time for counter-measures.

What is also important to know is a competitor's history of progress as reflected in a capacity to *adapt* to changing environmental conditions, to *anticipate* trends, and to *learn* the new skills such changes demand. Thus Chaparral Steel in the United States and

Lucas Industries in the UK attribute much of their success to the ability to anticipate technological trends. An organization's capacity to adapt by upgrading its existing skills and learning new ones is a key competence for competing successfully while an organization that fails to anticipate events that could and should have been anticipated will not adopt a proactive posture. The fact that only a few elements in the external environment can be influenced, makes it imperative for an organization to have the flexibility to adapt.

A common element in the design of a competitive strategy is to develop a strategy that preempts competitors from taking effective counter-action, perhaps because such action would affect broader interests. For example, when American Motors (AMC) first brought out its Buyer Protection Plan, General Motors, Ford, and Chrysler did not copy it since it would have obliged them to offer the protection plan on all their cars and not just on the models in competition with AMC. Since then, even though AMC no longer exists, extensive warranties have become the rule. An effective competitive strategy is tied to developing a sustainable advantage, for example, by having competencies that operate widely over many product categories or by maintaining and upgrading the firm's brand image. In line with this, it follows that understanding the nature of competitors' competencies and brand franchise can be key. We need to know what competencies underlie a competitor's successes and whether the competitor's brands evoke brand loyalty.

Instead of collecting detailed information on competitors as just described, it is common to simply focus on competitor products and their functional performance for imitation or to do some *benchmarking*. Benchmarking is the process of trying to improve some weakness by analyzing the firm or firms that are known to be leaders in what needs to be improved. There is obviously much to be gained from doing this since the gap between the best and worst can be very great indeed. Of course, the best firms may not accept requests to analyze their system particularly if they are direct competitors! But benchmarking does not help in finding entirely new process innovations or entirely new markets while it cannot substitute for understanding the competitor potential through analyzing competitor competencies.

More attention is being given to intelligence gathering. Even small firms are coming to recognize the great advantage in knowing competitor positions in the market and the likely moves of competitors, given their capabilities and implied intentions. More ethically dubious, however, are the many types of *industrial espionage* that are commonly employed. Whatever the ethics involved, the rewards of industrial espionage can be high while the legal penalties in most parts of the world can be minuscule by comparison. But espionage does provoke law suits, with such companies as IBM and GE constantly filing suit against people who, it is claimed, stole their patented ideas or secrets. But espionage need not be this blatant. *Fortune* (May 14, 1984) lists the following legal, but sometimes ethically questionable ways of finding out competitor secrets:

- milking potential recruits;
- picking the brains of competitors' employees at conferences;
- conducting phony job interviews;
- hiring people away from competitors;

- debriefing competitors' former employees;
- encouraging key customers to talk;
- grilling suppliers;
- hiring consultants to interview competitors;
- infiltrating customers' business operations;
- pumping buyers;
- help wanted advertisements to interrogate those replying;
- analyzing labor contracts;
- studying aerial photographs;
- obtaining Freedom of Information Act filings;
- reading uniform commercial code filings;
- taking plant tours;
- doing reverse engineering, i.e. tearing apart the competitor's product for analysis; and
- buying a competitor's garbage.

While the above tactics may raise ethical and legal issues, a campaign of "dirty tricks" always does. There is the case involving British Airways waging a dirty tricks campaign against its small British rival, Virgin Atlantic Airways. Such alleged tricks included computer break-ins; poaching passengers by deception; break-ins of homes and cars of Virgin staff and a public relations firm hired to propagate unfavorable information on Richard Branson, the owner of Virgin. What is so surprising here is that BA had risen from the ashes to become the world's most profitable airline, with Virgin no more than an irritant.

The ethical issues raised in the gathering of intelligence are when misrepresentation occurs, documents are stolen, bribes are offered for information, or spies are used. Although little is known about the use of "spies," their effectiveness can be questioned, quite apart from the ethics of using them. Spies have an incentive to exaggerate the importance of their work and distort information that throws doubt on their previous revelations. But firms can become obsessive about protecting themselves against such spying. They become too secretive and label every single plan "top secret." This weakens attempts at coordinating work among departments and divisions of the company and with outside bodies like advertising agencies. Also it may result in too little effort being made to guard plans that really should be kept secret!

DETERMINING STRATEGIC OPTIONS

Competition denotes a struggle to equal or excel rivals. But competition is not the only way of settling conflicts among competitors. There are in fact three ways to resolve inter-business conflict:

1 legal resolution;
2 resolution via cooperation; and
3 resolution via competition.

All ways of resolving conflict should be considered, so competitive strategies are not confined to beating competition in the open market.

Resolution of conflict via the law

A firm may take legal action to protect its market on the ground that its rival's actions are illegal. Intel has instigated a barrage of lawsuits to hold its dominance in the computer chip market, though it lost its monopoly of the X86 market after failing in its legal fight with Advanced Micro Devices (AMD) of California. P&G petitioned the US Food & Drug Administration (FDA) demanding that Benefit, a ready-to-eat cereal made by General Mills, be pulled from the shelf because of its claim to lower blood choles-terol by at least 6 percent. It was irritating to P&G, which had failed to get approval from the FDA to have its own Metamucil brand of laxative advertised as a cholesterol reducer. In Europe in 1992, there was the case of Mars appealing to the European Commission that Unilever's distribution methods violated EC competition law by preventing Mars ice creams from being stocked in Unilever cabinets in retail outlets! Manufacturers of branded goods are in fact increasingly taking legal action to protect their profits. They are particularly incensed by "look-alikes" which are appearing on the shelves of supermarket chains. They claim that many "own-label" (store) brands hitch a free ride on the brand leader's advertising and want to ban all such look-alikes. We have already mentioned the fight between Unilever and P&G, with Unilever accusing P&G of defamation in claiming that Persil Power (Unilever's breakthrough new deter-gent) is so strong that it damages clothes. These cases are illustrative of many others where there is recourse to the law to resolve conflict, though in practice the law does not so much settle conflict as stabilize it. Of course, resort to the law is not confined to goods manufacturers. Thus dentists have been lobbying the Food and Drug Administration in the United States over the possible health side-effects of peroxide-based whiteners though the lobbying is self-serving in that such whiteners affect the market for the dentists' own professional bleaching service. Trade associations often press for more regulation if tighter controls will mainly affect new entrants or impose higher costs on other industry competitors. Competitive strategies are often constrained by legislation covering the prohibition of monopolies, price discrimination or "unfair" competition. As many firms test the boundaries of the law, rivals will continue to sue to keep them in check. There are also, of course, the attempts to reduce competition by seeking government help in restricting imports of competitor products.

Resolution of potential conflict via cooperation

Competition is concerned with winning and avoiding defeat. Where firms are guided by no other goals than winning, competition is labeled "cut-throat." But a focus on winning *at any cost* can translate into "being relatively better off" than rivals (but not prosperous) rather than being prosperous in an absolute sense.

Being competitive is not equivalent to a fight to the death. Cut-throat competition is not common. A market characterized by cut-throat competition can be a jungle where lions and foxes prevail over rabbits. Perhaps because there are more rabbits in industry than lions and foxes, firms generally prefer not to enter such a jungle. Hence there is usually some cooperation among rivals to bring about some coordinated action either because they have shared interests (for example, in keeping out new entrants or substitute products), or because further battles are not worth the bloodshed. Thus airlines cooperate over airport facilities even when they have their own terminals. The fewer the number of firms competing in the market and the greater their similarity in age, size and ownership, the more likely will be the recognition of shared interests and the desire for cooperation though there is never any certainty as it depends on what type of cooperation is being suggested as well as additional situational factors. If competitors belong to an active trade association, competition is likely to be less cut-throat, since this suggests members have a strong sense of common interests and perhaps even a sense of mutual role responsibilities (for example, leader/follower). In conditions of market growth and product standardization, retaliatory behavior, at least in industrial markets, is perhaps likely to be more common.[3]

Voluntary self-restraint is a form of cooperative behavior. And there may be good reasons for it. Thus Heublein welcomed another firm entering the bottled cocktail field on the ground that the additional advertising would increase total consumption, more than compensating for the increase in competition. Similarly, Gerber welcomed new entrants into what was then the emerging baby food market because it helped get across the message about the convenience and nutritional advantage of commercially prepared baby food. The presence of several competitors in a new market add credibility to a new product's authenticity. More well known are the occasions when various department stores cooperate in going into regional shopping centers on that ground that the traffic they collectively draw is worth more than the business they take from each other.

The above examples can be categorized as examples of *peace based on (tacit) integrative agreements*. Such agreements are accepted because there is a belief that they lead to an increase in the size of market, enough of an increase for all to do better. Peace can also be based on implicit *distributive agreements*, where the distribution of the pie reflects the relative power of rivals. It is thus *peace based on power*. There are three distinct categories of peace based on power:

Equilibrium or balance of power

When there is a balance of power no firm is so dominant that rivals feel unable to maintain their market share in the event of a competitive attack. In such conditions, and given a mature market, firms accept stable market shares not because they are necessarily happy with their shares but because they can do nothing about it. If they promote aggressively, they believe they will be copied by rivals, with a consequent increase in costs, much brand switching and no stable increase in market share. This view has some substance.[4] But there will always be those who want to dominate the market and will look for some way to do so. Nonetheless, fear favors cooperation since it is in everyone's self-interest not to enter into an unwinnable battle. Everything though depends on whether a firm believes its rivals will continue to cooperate.

Hegemony

Hegemony arises through the dominance of one firm. Rivals accept the leadership (for example, in pricing) of the dominant firm because equity suggests that this is where leadership should lie. But perceptions of equity are tied to the dominant firm's being perceived as having a major stake in the prosperity of the industry as a whole.

As with any other group, the behavior of companies in cooperation, via hegemony or whatever, follows norms or rules. Just as those competing in games accept the rules, competition in business is often constrained by implicit rules that set limits to competition, for example, not to indulge in advertising that deliberately denigrates a competitive brand. Orderly restrained competition makes for a "quiet life" as competitive actions become more predictable.

Rule violation is *defection*, but competitive reaction to defection will depend on how serious and how intentional the rule breaking is perceived to be. A strategy of rewarding cooperation and retaliating against defection is called "tit-for-tat." It is defined as "cooperate on the first move then on each successive move do whatever the other player did on the previous move." Though firms do cooperate with others who cooperate, it may also be that they have no qualms about exploiting a "sucker" as firms "keep on defecting against an opponent foolish enough to go on cooperating."[5]

Direct competitors may even cooperate on not recruiting each other's employees and may tacitly accept prevailing levels of advertising expenditure. What firms are trying to avoid is *entrapment*, which occurs when a conflict is allowed to escalate to the point where it becomes destructive of the interests of all competitors. Firms initially seek to maximize gain but, with entrapment, sights are lowered to simply minimizing losses and finally just saving face. It is this danger of entrapment that is frequently quoted as an argument against being too focused on competition. There may on occasions be overt recognition of the rules that are meant to regulate competition. One writer quotes the late Paul Getty as having written a letter to the Jersey Standard Oil Company suggesting that the social norms of competition should rule out a large corporation such as Standard from having a controlling interest in a smaller competing company such as Tidewater.[6] This is in line with an article in *Fortune* pointing out that, because of its size, IBM's actions are judged by different standards from those applied to smaller firms.

Empire

In the case of empire, the dominant firm tries to absorb its rivals or have them completely subject to its dictates. The subject companies do not merely compromise but yield completely, for example, in fear of the dominant firm using selective pricing in their markets. The antitrust or antimonopoly laws of most countries are designed to prevent empires from emerging.

There are four motives that can operate in social cooperation:

1 altruism
2 sense of equity or fairness
3 self-interest
4 fear.

Cooperation among rivals will have a basis either in *fear* or *self-interest* and these are the motives to which to appeal. Similarly, there are three modes of cooperation. There is first the *communal mode*, where everyone just helps without keeping score of each's contribution. This is not the mode used among cooperating competitors. Second, there is the *authority mode*, where there is acceptance of some sort of ranking as to who has most say. This is the empire situation with public compliance without private acceptance. The third mode is the *equity mode*, where cooperation is governed by rules as to what appears fair and reasonable given the situation. This does not necessarily mean equal shares as equity may demand that some competitors are more equal than others. The equity mode operates in equilibrium and hegemony. But when firms within an industry accept equilibrium and hegemony, it is likely to be a sleepy industry. In such a situation, it is not the industry's opportunities that determine the profitability of the industry but the passive members of the industry ensuring low profitability. Fortunately, with competition becoming more and more global, we are likely to see fewer sleepy industries. An interesting and surprising development has been the emergence of co-branding. For example, General Mills Inc and the Kellogg Co. in the United States have co-branded cereals while General Mills has licensed the Reese's Peanut Butter name from the Hershey Foods Corp. for a children's cereal called Reese's Peanut Butter Puffs. Such agreements are viewed as ways of reducing the cost of developing new brands, by building on an already established brand-name. The question, as always, is whether, for example, the Reese name will carry over into the cereal market since there is a danger of the licenser diluting the brand image by extending it too far.

Resolution via competition

A key feature of any market is the degree of competition in it. This is because competition generally determines market shares and influences product form, price, promotion, and distribution. From the point of view of the individual seller, the extent to which a market is competitive depends to a great extent on the difficulty of expanding or holding on to market share. Competition is the spur to customer orientation as the best performance sets the standard. Whenever competition is absent, firms become smug and complacent about their performance: competition gives every firm a truer picture of its accomplishments. Yet as in all competitions, the absolute difference in performance between the winners and the runners-up may be tiny yet the difference in rewards enormous.

Cooperation implies mutual action for achieving common goals. Competition, in contrast, is typically viewed as taking action to win some prize which, if won, deprives others of it. But there is no simple dichotomy between cooperation and competition since there can be *competitive cooperation*. This is the situation where firms must cooperate in order that each may derive any benefits at all, but they disagree over the share of the returns that go to each of them. This may happen in "joint ventures" and in exporting to countries with quotas on imports. An example is Japanese car firms which face quotas in exporting to the EC.

Competition implies some measure of success against which to assess relative performance vis-à-vis rivals. One such measure is market share, which is used as a surrogate for profit. Market competition can be viewed as the process of trying to protect or advance market share. However, market share is only a surrogate since just pursuing market share regardless can be dysfunctional to achieving profitability since high market share may be obtained by selling at cost or at low margins. In any case, there is a need to be clear about what the market is and whether the market is global, regional or just the domestic market. A firm's market need not be determined by just the product itself but be influenced by the seller's promotions. Thus one firm producing sparkling waters promotes itself as an alternative to soft drinks, ignoring firms in the same product category. Whether such a strategy succeeds or not ultimately depends on consumer perceptions and whether other sparkling water firms decide to act similarly. To Porter, the purpose of a competitive strategy is to achieve a sustainable competitive advantage, rather than to protect or advance market share. As stated earlier, for an advantage to be sustainable, the offering must continue to be of central importance to the function for which the product is bought and for that advantage to be unique to the firm because

- competition cannot imitate, or
- competition does not want to do so, or
- if competition did imitate they would be less successful at it.

The following five approaches may be used to <u>develop a competitive advantage</u> or a competitive position in the industry:

1 Choosing market segments where the critical success factors fit the firm's thrust and core competencies. Since a competitive advantage is a relative advantage, there is a need to assess also the thrust and core competencies of rivals to ensure the firm is not outclassed.
2 Comparing the firm's offering with rival offerings to identify relative strengths and weaknesses, for example, in performance, reliability, style, maintenance, and delivery to time and specification. In this way, it is hoped to turn strengths into a sustainable advantage.
3 Questioning the basic rules of the competitive game to see if violating them could result in some advantage that can be retained. Such rules could cover pricing, distribution or anything else about the offering.
4 Seeking new uses or novel applications for the product.
5 Identifying latent wants and developing new products to cater to such wants.

Creating synergies, regarded by Porter as a major source of competitive advantage, is being questioned as it is claimed that synergy seekers "have failed to achieve higher average operating margins then non-synergy seekers."[7] Pioneers in a market often seem to acquire a sustainable advantage and remain dominant when the industry has matured. There are many reasons advanced for this.[8] The theoretical reasons relate to the entry barriers facing the nonpioneers (experience curve effects, market information, effectiveness of advertising, reputational effects, uncertainty about what to imitate in the pioneer brand, the pioneer's technological lead or preemption of resources to late comers). Another theoretical reason is that buyers use the pioneering product to define the product category and so use it as the standard against which to judge rival brands. Still other reasons are that pioneers have had time to build up and establish a highly favorable brand image, establish good distribution and competitive pricing. At the empirical level, PIMS data point to higher product quality, better differentiated products and broader product lines. Followers are often at a disadvantage in being obliged to choose smaller segments to avoid head-on competition with the pioneer. All these factors may indeed be at work. But this is not to suggest pioneers will maintain their dominance. New entrants displace pioneers when pioneers make errors, or lack the resources for expansion or later entrants may manage to leapfrog the pioneer technologically. A competitive advantage (particularly a critical advantage) is difficult to sustain so that most firms rest content with moving from one temporary, *contestable advantage* to another. But having a competitive advantage in the product itself is not the only way of beating competition, since there are other ways, like restricting a competitor's access to basic supplies or by additional "goodwill" services to customers such as supplying computer systems or marketing services.

To return to Porter's point about the purpose of competitive strategy being to achieve a sustainable advantage, one key measure of having achieved a significant, sustainable advantage must surely be market share or *served* market share. Using a market share figure as the goal, a firm seeks either *market share protection* or *market share advancement* (see Figure 7.1 (a) and (b)). Where "market share protection" dominates strategic thinking, there is a danger of adopting a too reactive posture as far as innovation is concerned, with the firm waiting for others to do the innovation. Where "market share advancement" dominates strategic thinking, the firm is more proactive, seeking to preempt competition by being first with new products or other innovations. A proactive strategic posture typically seeks growth as an investment objective through new products and markets. This does not mean that companies should be proactive all the time. As with any other strategic posture, much depends on the firm's resources, capabilities and competencies. The proactive firm needs resources and the ability to innovate, and the rest of the business system needed to achieve, say, distribution and erect barriers for those who would follow.

A set of strategic options is shown in tree diagram and matrix form in Figures 7.1 (a) and 7.1 (b), distinguishing between market share protection options and market share advancement options. The options are not exhaustive nor are they mutually exclusive since several of them may be adopted simultaneously. Which (if any) are adopted, depends not just on what the firm itself is capable of doing but also on the current actions, capabilities and intentions of competitors.

(a) Tree diagram

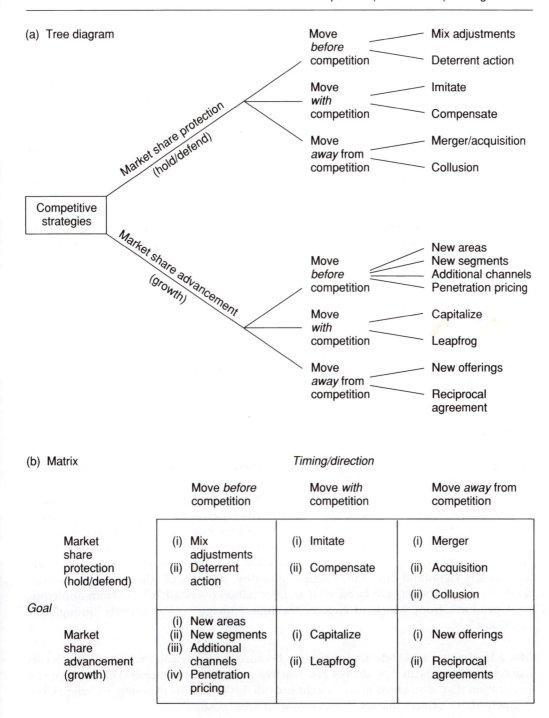

(b) Matrix

Timing/direction

Goal	Move *before* competition	Move *with* competition	Move *away* from competition
Market share protection (hold/defend)	(i) Mix adjustments (ii) Deterrent action	(i) Imitate (ii) Compensate	(i) Merger (ii) Acquisition (ii) Collusion
Market share advancement (growth)	(i) New areas (ii) New segments (iii) Additional channels (iv) Penetration pricing	(i) Capitalize (ii) Leapfrog	(i) New offerings (ii) Reciprocal agreements

Figure 7.1 Competitive strategies

Whether the goal of the firm is to protect or enhance market share, the firm must decide whether to:

- *Move before competition.* Should the firm act ahead of competition? Such a leadership role is not just a matter of taste but depends on what the firm has to offer and the possibilities of retaliation.
- *Move with competition.* If a firm moves with competition, it reacts immediately to competitive moves. This assumes the firm possesses the capacity and the flexibility to respond.
- *Move away from competition.* A firm may decide not to meet competition "head on" but to seek its goals in a more roundabout way.

One thing should be emphasized; there are no simple recipes for overcoming competition that are not just truisms, such as saying a firm's offering must have more appeal to the target market. Those pushing formulas can simply mislead. Contrary to popular belief, Clausewitz (1780–1831), the legendary writer on military strategy, denied any intention of telling generals how to conduct war. He argued that the job of the theorist is simply to educate the minds of commanders in how they might think about issues, not to try and do their thinking for them; otherwise there is the danger of blindly following standard principles when standard conditions seldom exist. In any case, there are enemies on different fronts so a competitor in one segment of the market may not be the same competitor in another segment. Yet when the enemy varies so must the battle plan!

Market share protection

A defensive strategy is generally easier to orchestrate than an offensive one. This is because it is much easier to hold onto current customers (if the product is a regular purchase) than it is to attract new ones. The market share leader seeks to retain existing customers while attracting the same proportionate share of new entrants to the market. Retaining customers is made much easier if the firm has a critical advantage. Where genuine product advantages are difficult to sustain, the loyalty to the brand can still be substantial. The brand image conveys information that may still be decisive in securing a customer. The brand image may signal reliability, status, and other desirable associations. As long as buyers are faced with an information overload, arising from numerous rival products from which to choose, the brand image "offers a route through the confusion."

Mix adjustments and deterrent actions.   Because a firm wishes simply to protect its market does not mean it is always just reactive to competitive moves. Where there is a recognition that competitor moves might provide little time for planning, moving before competition to protect market share appears a wise posture.

One way of moving *before* competition is by *mix adjustments*, or constantly updating the offering or marketing mix. This is probably the most common strategy of market share leaders intent on retaining the loyalty of current customers. The type of updating varies at different stages of the life of the product since there comes a time when product differentiation is no longer significant and buyers become more interested in price and service. It is also true that, with so many firms today focusing on low cost and quality, it may be that these variables may come to be seen as simply the price of staying in the market with new ways being needed for a competitive advantage. The other way of moving before competition is by *deterrent action*. Deterrent actions come somewhere between defensive and offensive actions. They are not merely defensive, since deterrence implies having the capability to strike back. They are not offensive, since they are designed to prevent attack and not to render rivals impotent. However, a deterrence can be active or passive. A *passive deterrence* signals a capacity to deter, while an *active deterrence* proclaims the intention to deter. Thus a passive deterrence to potential market entrants would be to signal the firm has excess capacity while an active deterrence would be a declaration to undersell all newcomers.

An active deterrence might be the introduction of a product similar to that about to be introduced by the competitor. Thus Gillette's Good News could have been introduced to warn off BIC. A *fighting brand* is an active deterrence. Thus when Folger's (a P&G brand of coffee) entered its market test, Maxwell House (General Foods) introduced Horizon, a brand copy of Folger's. The US Federal Trade Commission (FTC) later claimed that Horizon was a "fighting brand" which led to the definition of a fighting brand as "one used to siphon off profits from a competitor through price discounting so as to deter the competitor from competing." In practice there can be a fighting brand without price discounting. The introduction of fighting brands assumes appropriate resources and so tends to be the action of big players. Thus when P&G introduced its Extend, a mouthwash, to compete with Warner–Lambert's leading brand Listerine, Warner–Lambert introduced Depend as a fighting brand to undercut the P&G introduction. For a deterrence to be successful, it must at least be credible. If the signal is costly to fake it is likely to be highly credible, such as a guarantee to all buyers that, in the event of price reduction in the next six months by a competitor, the difference in price will be refunded.

Imitate or compensate. If a firm protects its market by moving *with* competition, it counterbalances the actions taken by competition. The firm may *imitate* competition (for example, in pricing) or it may offer some *compensating benefit* (for example, better service). Imitation is the most common since it requires no creativity and is considered sufficient to retain those likely to move. Thus when the first savings bank in New York offered "gifts" to new depositors, most other banks did the same. The problem with imitating is that, when implemented, the imitator may still be behind when competition has moved on. This has been a complaint against the American car companies, that they have managed to imitate the Japanese of ten years ago in making more reliable cars at less cost but that the Japanese are still ahead.

The "compensating" strategy does allow the firm to project a more favorable image by being different. But compensating may amount to no more than reminding the target audience of the virtues of the present. For example, Curity, a cloth diaper firm, sought to protect its market from inroads by disposable diapers by advertising the soft, flexible, natural nature of cloth diapers as opposed to the unnatural components of disposables (for example, synthetic top sheet, polyethylene film barrier, chemical binders, and so on). This is an attempt to change customer perceptions without doing anything to the product itself.

Mergers, acquisitions, internal development, collusion, concentration. When a firm protects its market by moving *away* from competition, it may do so by merger, acquisition, internal development, collusion, or concentration. *Mergers* and *acquisitions* are often adopted when the industry is under attack from other industries. Mergers can be a way of building a broader base for borrowing and provide advantages of operating on a larger scale. A small firm can be at a serious disadvantage when "everything the small firm does, the big firm can do better." Internal development can lead to defending market share in unusual ways. Thus the purpose of AT&T's Universal (low-cost credit) card is primarily to strengthen its relationship with its nonbusiness long-distance callers in the belief that these customers will want to use just the one card for all credit card purchases including long-distance telephone calls.

When competition between industries increases, firms within an industry often come together for mutual support. Such intimacy provides a climate for formal agreements. If dividing up the market is banned by law, firms may band together in industry associations to, say, pressure the government into erecting tariff barriers. However, open *collusion* is generally prohibited as "in restraint of trade." Even so pricing cartels are constantly being uncovered. Thus the 19 European carton-board makers operated a cartel for four years. The European Commission alleged that the carton-board makers managed to push through rises of 6–10 percent twice a year from 1987 to 1990 in spite of the decrease in the costs of raw materials.

It is not uncommon to speak of competition as occurring between *focal nets*, defined as a firm's customers, its suppliers, and other stakeholders with the firm itself at the focal or hub of the network of players. The reason for promoting this view is to emphasize that the firm is not an isolated unit but draws strength from relationships with stakeholders. Providing managers of the firm appreciate this and acquire the skills to exploit the network and protect it from competitors seeking to undermine it, a network has potential for synergy in production and marketing.[9] There can be a move *away* from competition through "concentrating" on fewer products or market areas. Thus Hotpoint (a subsidiary of GE in the United States) scaled back in the UK to market just a few products, finding itself unable to coordinate its former markets. The international markets for appliances varied so widely in consumer wants and distribution channels that neither standardized parts nor standardized marketing strategies were feasible. While Hotpoint's rivals, Electrolux and Philips, were exhausted trying to manage all these markets, Hotpoint grew in the UK by further segmenting the market, learning in an easier way the process of managing diversity, making it now the most formidable competitor in Europe.

Market share advancement

In seeking to advance market share, it is usually ill-advised to take on the giant company head-on. It is wiser first to try to eliminate weaker rivals and perhaps come from behind in tackling the bigger ones. This is essentially what the Japanese did in entering the motorcycle industry, avoiding the major segments dominated by entrenched competition but building up segments for smaller bikes until the requisite resources and experience had been acquired. But much depends on how dynamic the industry is. Just because a firm is well ahead of its rivals does not mean it is good in any absolute sense since the industry may be a particularly sleepy one and this may offer the new entrant an opportunity right from the start to take on the leaders. The competitive advantage, though, of any new entrant must not be trivial. This needs to be said since new entrants often elevate minor improvements, whose significance eludes the consumer, into major breakthroughs as if the consumer could be "conned" into believing anything.

In challenging the leaders,

1 an offering should have something extra as an advantage;
2 the firm should have sufficient resources to support the challenge with the rest of its business system being at least equal to the rival's other advantages; and
3 the firm's overall offering should be perceived by enough consumers as sufficiently better to overcome the cost to buyers of switching from rivals.

The danger of making price the competitive advantage is that the firm must have established low-cost leadership and this is not easy to prove. Thus Eagle Snacks in the US food snack market has managed to increase its market share and expand its sales by 25 percent per annum from 1988 to 1992 largely by offering more for a lower price. But Frito-Lay, the brand leader, reduced both prices and profit margins and seems intent on preventing further inroads by Eagle Snacks. Since Eagle Snacks has yet to make a profit, it would seem Frito-Lay will win. But this is where Frito-Lay needs to consider not just the Eagle Snacks but the parent company: Frito-Lay will have to assess the patience of Anheuser-Busch, which owns Eagle Snacks.

It is easier to advance market share in an emerging market, before brand loyalties and corresponding buying habits form and rivals become more sensitive about what share they believe they should have. Also early market share gains tend to be more valuable as initial customers are easier to retain than new customers acquired.

If a firm chooses to move before competition to advance its market share, it can do so by:

• new geographical areas;
• new segments/markets;
• new distribution channels; or
• penetration pricing.

New areas.   A successful move into new geographical areas assumes enough people in the new area have a latent or passive want for the offering and that competitors are ignoring the want or they can be beaten. There are many stories of companies in the United States being tempted to market in Europe because the competitors there were firms they soundly beat in the United States. Examples are Campbell's in soups beating

Heinz in the United States and P&G in detergents beating Unilever in the United States and so believing they could do so in Europe, only to find they could not: a failure to sufficiently understand the tug of habit and old, familiar brand-names. But firms do not just move to other countries to sell to those countries and to neighboring ones. The big car companies in the United States have set up subsidiaries and joint ventures in Mexico and the East to produce lower-cost cars for import into the United States to compete with the Japanese.

New segments/markets.   A move into new segments is a frequent strategy as a market matures. It offers the possibility of increasing the total market while being the first in the segment. The expansion of the chewing gum market since 1970 has been largely due to opening up new segments (for example, sugarless gum, center-filled gum). Generally, the first firm to enter the segment is in a strong position to maintain dominance there, for the same reasons that the market pioneer has advantages. The order of entry, in general, is positively related to subsequent market share. Although there may be real competitive advantages in quality, price, distribution, and variety, it is also true that, in a market or market segment composed of largely undifferentiated offerings, buyers are apt to fall back on habit, picking, and gut liking; processes that tend to favor the early pioneers retaining market share. But, as with market pioneers, success is never guaranteed since the second entrant to the segment may enter with a product even more finely tuned to the segment.

New segments may be true new segments, or a combination of existing segments or a splitting of some existing segment. Many a company has chosen to market in all known segments (like P&G in diapers) to keep competition from dominating any segment. And new entrants can start by dominating an ignored segment. Thus in the United States Ben & Jerry's ice cream offered 39 offbeat flavors. This would seem something easy to imitate and certainly no sustainable advantage. But this is to ignore the power of imagery. The firm presented its target audience as "real" Americans who wanted a product having "real American ingredients" while the firm was one of the first to stress its social responsibility credentials and last, but not least, to offer service with a very big smile! Intrinsic and integrative criteria are commonly exploited in forming new segments since pioneers may simply focus on technical and economic criteria and ignore the matter of design and snob appeal.

So many of the so-called competitive advantages in long established markets are quickly copied. This means there is very little time to establish goodwill and a brand image and, without a strong favorable brand image, there is an absence of that emotional bonding that is the basis of customer loyalty. Sometimes this bonding is done by extending a brand-name. Thus Anheuser-Busch in the United States was only successful in attacking Miller's Lite beer when it used its most famous brand-name (Bud Light). Another way of gaining some sort of emotional bonding is by establishing clubs (helped by the granfalloon effect), like those established among children for toys like the Barbie doll. The basic aim is to build up a continuing visible relationship between the firm and the customer to establish that emotional bond. There is also the opportunity to sell more merchandise related to the core brand, for example, Barbie clothes.

Although in seeking new segments we tend to think of tangible product benefits, one form of benefit segmentation is that of *time-based competition*. This is a matter of having the latest designs or whatever to reach the market before rivals; achieved

1 by cutting down on the number of production processes involved;
2 by increasing flexibility in manufacture as Honda and Fiat have done; or
3 by having lots of excess capacity like Crown Cork & Seal in the manufacture of steel cans.

Examples of *splitting a segment* successfully would be the development of an "energy" drink just for sportsmen while an example of *combining segments* would be the Quaker Oats' Tender Chunks whose target segment draws from the segment buying traditional canned dog food and the segment buying dry dog food. This does not mean that the original segments disappeared but simply that new segments were formed.

An important competitive strategy, particularly in industrial marketing, is to think of new uses for the product since new uses correspond to opening new markets with their potential for high sales and less dependence on existing markets where competition is intense. Identifying new markets for a product usually requires having knowledge about different industries for possible applications. The typical error is leaving it to sales people to discover these new market applications since they seldom have the time or the expertise to do a good job.

New channels.   The opening up of new channels or additional channels is another way of seeking to advance market share. The sale of magazines through supermarkets, shoes through drug stores, milk through machine dispensers, door-to-door cosmetics and so on were all radical departures when first introduced. The problem lies in determining channel suitability. Thus jewelry stores were not a good channel for the Swatch watch while Coach, a leather goods company, has to watch its US high-class image in selling through so many channels, for example, catalogs, discount outlets, department store boutiques, and free-standing retail stores.

Interesting channel selections still occur. Thus Bandag Inc. in the tire-retread business, in anticipation of more European competition, dismantled its distribution network and started a franchise system, increasing Bandag's market share in Europe from 5 percent to 20 percent in a tie with France's Michelin. What is so interesting here is Bandag's service system. Customers no longer come to Bandag outlets but Bandag sends out trucks after hours, filled with tires and equipment, as perambulating workshops, so truckers can keep their rigs on the road throughout the day.

Penetration pricing.   The final strategy listed for advancing market share by moving before competition is penetration pricing. When low prices are coupled with quality, penetration pricing is one way of competing through value. Experience curve pricing was recommended by BCG for the lowest-cost competitor. The claim being made was that, if the lowest-cost competitor converts his lower costs into lower prices, he gains market share, other things remaining equal. But as already argued, even if the concept of the experience curve is fully accepted without modification, the advice assumes that price is the key buying inducement. Sometimes it is, often it is not. In any case, there is always the danger of a price war. "Schismogenesis" is the term used to describe a situation in which one party provokes another to go further in the behavior to which the first party is reacting. A price war can be an example of "symmetrical schismogenesis." The first firm, A, reduces price and this provokes B to reduce price still further, which provokes A to go still further and so on. The net result is profitless sales.

Capitalize, leapfrog.   If market share is advanced by moving *with* competition, the firm may *capitalize* on the efforts of rivals or it may *leapfrog* competition, that is, take a leap ahead of competition. RCA capitalized on the promotional efforts of SONY in video-cassette recorders. SONY, through a massive advertising campaign did a great deal to establish the primary demand for the product but RCA capitalized on this, using print advertising to compare its own brand favorably with Sony's. A leapfrog strategy can be a market entry strategy as when P&G brought out the Pringle brand of potato chip as less perishable than the existing brands on the market. A leapfrog strategy can also be used to regain market share. For example, when the tin can was threatened by aluminum, the steel industry developed a light weight "skinny" tinplate to combat the lightness of aluminum.

New offering.   When a firm elects to advance market share by moving away from competition, it may introduce a "new offering" that competes less directly with those currently on the market. New offerings are very much tied to product innovation but not necessarily. Thus one pump maker in the UK, failing in its efforts to sell complete pump systems, turned successfully to selling just pump components. An example that did involve innovativeness is Toddler University Inc. in children's footwear. There are up to 11 sizes in children's shoes which, when combined with five widths, represents having 55 pairs of any particular model in stock. Toddler University brought out a single shoe with five inserts for width, which, not surprisingly, caught on with retailers. But the new offering may have plenty of tough competition if the offering is merely new to the firm. Thus IBM in Europe, under a subsidiary called Individual Computer Products International (ICPI), has entered the low end of the PC market which has been growing at around 45 percent per annum against 21 percent for the whole PC market. This new computer range, called Ambra, does not have the IBM logo through fear of undermining the IBM image. The question arises as to how such a product can be successful. It is a me-too product and, although it will be distributed extensively through dealers and retailers and direct, others are doing the same. Many would argue that PCs now are just a commodity product and, since IBM is not the lowest priced, it will not be all that successful. There is some truth in this argument but first, many doubt that a PC can ever be a true commodity product since consumers suspect that all PCs are not assembled with equal attention to reliability etc., and second, in spite of the nonuse of the IBM logo, everyone will regard Ambra as an IBM product with all the assurances that name offers.

Reciprocal agreements.   The final strategy of *reciprocal agreements* is an application of the saying, "you scratch my back and I'll scratch yours," in that firms agree among themselves to buy from each other or to favor the other as a supplier.

CHOOSING A COMPETITIVE STRATEGY

Relative capabilities vs. strategic requirements

For a strategy to succeed the firm must have the business system to exploit the strategy. The strategy itself indicates the business system needed. Thus, just as an acquisitions strategy assumes the firm has adequate financial resources, an "imitate" market protection strategy assumes the firm has the ability to imitate and the flexibility to do it quickly. A distinction should be made here between actual strengths (abilities, competencies, capabilities etc.) and potential strengths. *Potential strengths* are the strengths on paper, while *actual strengths* are those that can be immediately mobilized. Big organizations seem to be able to do most things on paper but their very size and complexity may be a drag on putting that potential immediately to work. Coordination problems and organizational foot-dragging is a frequent explanation of battles lost. Bureaucratic inertia may also explain the slow response of a company (for example, Gillette in the past) to an attack on its market. In any case, in choosing a competitive strategy, we are concerned with actual strengths in reacting to attacks and with potential strengths for long-term competitive plans. What resources an organization is prepared to devote to a competitive strategy depends on what is at stake, namely, the gains or losses that are likely to result from applying the strategy with different degrees of intensity. But behind any such analysis is the firm's own assessment of its "assets" and the assets of competitors. An asset is something the firm has that is likely to be a strength in competing in the market. A firm needs to list its assets and judge whether, as compared with its rivals, the firm is plus, minus or equal in respect to that particular asset, as illustrated in Table 7.1. Thus the profile of the firm that emerges from Table 7.1 suggests choosing a strategy that exploits the firm's marketing expertise, goodwill/image and financial strengths.

Seldom is there a perfect match between the firm's assets and a competitive strategy and the firm is obliged to choose the best fit between what it has to offer and the total business system ideally needed to make success a practical certainty. Of course, the attacker can also be attacked, so every firm needs to know whatever weaknesses it has that would make it vulnerable. For example, firms making plug compatible/copycat

Table 7.1 XYZ's assets vs. competitors A, B, and C

Asset	Competitors		
	A	B	C
Financial	+	+	+
Raw material reserve	−	−	−
Physical plant capacity	−	+	+
Patents	−	−	−
Customer goodwill	+	+	+
Marketing expertise	+	+	+
Production expertise	−	−	−
R&D expertise	+	+	−
Distribution network	−	+	−

versions of IBM's computers were highly vulnerable to design modifications by IBM and they were caught off-guard in the early 1980s when IBM did just that. But IBM was highly vulnerable, too, on mainframe computers and on outside suppliers like Intel and Microsoft for key components. A "vulnerability analysis" is meant to identify such weaknesses, just as Table 7.1 suggests the firm is vulnerable to certain competitor strategies through inadequate production expertise or an absence of patent protection.

Anticipating competitor reaction

Any competitive strategy should anticipate competitor reaction, but a major problem lies in predicting the counter-strategies (if any) likely to be adopted by competitors. Sometimes firms undertake partial action to try and anticipate that reaction, such as declaring certain intentions or reducing prices in just one part of the country. But basing decisions on *immediate* competitor reaction to some partial action can be misleading as competition needs time to reflect. Much in fact will depend on how competition assesses the probable cost and benefits of fighting back and whether they perceive core values and interests as being threatened.

Both sides in a competitive battle can easily misunderstand the actions of the other. The attacker often overestimates what the firm brings to the battle while the attacked are prone to underestimate the significance of what is happening: both misperceptions arise from the self-aggrandizement to which organizations are disposed. There is also the emotion aroused by any competition if viewed as a test of who is best. When passions are involved, the stakes are not weighed objectively.

The theory of games.   A competitive strategy should try to preempt effective counter-measures. But, just as in the case of a critical advantage, a preemptive competitive strategy may work for the immediate future but cannot guarantee against the long term: a preemptive strategy, like a critical advantage, is difficult to sustain. Ideally, a firm in a competitive market will draw up a list of the options open to it and seek to identify counter-strategies. *Game theory* provides a conceptualization of the problems involved.

Although game theory had its origins early in the century and the 1920s, it is pre-eminently associated with the mathematician John Von Neumann (and, for economists, John Von Neumann and Oskar Morgenstern). Game theory attempts to analyze rational strategic behavior in situations of uncertainty. The primary goal of the theory of games is to determine, through formal reasoning alone, what strategies the players ought to choose in order to pursue their interests rationally and what outcomes will result if they do. The theory of games provides rules for deciding on a strategy that need not be altered to achieve its goal, even if rivals acquire new knowledge in the course of the game.

One well-known application that was developed around 1950 is the game known as the "prisoner's dilemma" which has been used extensively to study not competition per se but cooperation and defection. In brief, two prisoners, partners in crime, are given the chance of turning state's evidence. Each may implicate the other. If neither informs on the other, each will serve just one year; if both inform on each other then each will serve two years but, if only one informs, the informed-against will serve three years with the informer being let off altogether. Each prisoner must choose in isolation. The situation captures the frequent conflict between individual self-interest and collective group interest as often occurs in ethical issues.

The theory of games applies to the study of any situation where:

- There are two or more decision-makers (called "players") choosing from among two or more courses of action, called "strategies" for the purpose of the game.
- Outcomes depend entirely on the strategic choices of the players.
- Each player has a well-defined preference from among the possible outcomes so that numerical payoffs reflecting these preferences can be assumed.

Let us suppose that firm A's major rival is firm B and that the strategies open to them are:

- penetration pricing (pricing for rapid penetration of the market);
- product adjustment; and
- a technological leapfrog innovation.

If firm A adopts penetration pricing, firm B might choose simultaneously any of the above three strategies as counter-strategies. Similarly, if firm A adopts either the product adjustment or the leapfrog innovation strategy, firm B can also retaliate by adopting any of the three strategies as a counter-strategy. It is assumed that firm A can make some estimate of likely market shares resulting from adopting any of the three strategies, given that firm B can choose any of the strategies as well. Figure 7.2 shows all nine market share estimates for the nine pairs of strategies. Thus, if firm A adopts penetration pricing, its estimated market share will be 58 percent if firm B also adopts that strategy, but will be 64 percent if B adopts a product adjustment strategy and only be 53 percent if B adopts a leapfrog strategy.

In the theory of games, we assume that Firm A has no idea about the probabilities

| | | Firm B's strategies | | |
		Penetration pricing	Product adjustment	Leapfrog
	Penetration pricing	58%	64%	53%
Firm A's strategies	Product adjustment	43%	56%	46%
	Leapfrog	57%	67%	55%

Figure 7.2 Game matrix: Firm A's estimated shares

of B's counter-strategies, in which case it is argued that the attitude of the decision-maker in firm A alone will determine which strategy to adopt. A pessimistic attitude entails assuming the worst. Thus firm A looks across all the rows of market shares in Figure 7.2 to choose the strategy that gives firm A the maximum of the minimum payoffs. The minimum payoffs in each row are:

Strategy	*Worst market shares*
Penetration pricing	53 percent
Product adjustment	43 percent
Leapfrog	55 percent

The maximum of these minimum payoffs ("the best of a bad lot") is the leapfrog strategy with a market share of 55 percent. The criterion used to select the 55 percent is known as the *maximin criterion*. An optimistic attitude would lead firm A to choose the maximum of the maximum payoffs. This rule is known as the *maximax criterion*. The maximum payoffs in each row are:

Strategy	*Best market shares*
Penetration pricing	64 percent
Product adjustment	56 percent
Leapfrog	67 percent

The maximum payoff is 67 percent which (coincidentally) again corresponds to the leapfrog strategy.

In line with game theory, the argument so far has assumed that firm A has no idea about the probabilities of firm B's actions. But it is argued that we can always treat a problem of decision under uncertainty (as above) as a case of decision under risk by simply supposing that each possible outcome is equally likely. But suppose that firm A can do better than this because it believes that it understands the rules that seem to govern firm B's competitive actions so that it can estimate the probabilities (likely intentions) of each of the strategies being adopted by firm B. Suppose these were the probabilities:

Strategy	*Probability of adoption by B*
Penetration pricing	0.5
Product adjustment	0.2
Leapfrog	0.3

(The probabilities add up to 1, because it is assumed that one of these strategies will definitely be adopted by firm B.)

If we multiply the market shares in each row of Figure 7.2 by their probabilities of being adopted by firm B and then add the products, we get firm A's expected market shares for each of the three strategies as shown in Table 7.2. The leapfrog strategy yields the highest expected market share and so has first claim to adoption.

To return to game theory proper, game theorists define "strategies" in terms of a set of prior, comprehensive statements of the decisions to be made at every stage of the

Table 7.2 Firm A's expected market share for each of three strategies

Firm A's strategy	Market share payoff (1)	Probability (2)	Expected market share (col. 1 × col. 2) (3)
Penetration pricing	58	0.5	29.00
	64	0.2	12.80
	53	0.3	15.90
			57.70 %
Product adjustment	43	0.5	21.5
	56	0.2	11.20
	46	0.3	13.80
			46.5 %
Leapfrog	57	0.5	28.50
	67	0.2	13.40
	55	0.3	16.50
			58.40 %

competitive game. This differs from the concept of strategies used in this text where strategies are categories of options and cannot be reduced to "some set of prior, comprehensive statements of the decisions to be made at every stage of the competitive game." The typical criticism of game theory is that it is too simplistic and has produced "no hypotheses and understanding beyond common-sense." But from our point of view, its very formality has the advantage of bringing out the basic problem of making strategic decisions in conditions where success depends on the reactions of rivals.

How should a firm then compete? The answer is that a firm should seek to anticipate the actions and reactions of competitors and to beat competition by only competing in those segments of the market that exploit its relative strength and creativity. Take for example, a growing but relatively small company. It needs to build on its strengths, capitalizing on the advantages of being small: the ability to grow in small segments (market niches); the ability to enter such segments without disturbing market equilibrium while still having the ability to react quickly to changes in the market. It must avoid strategies that are likely to put the firm at a disadvantage, for example, where state of the art research is costly, yet needed to succeed; where heavy capital investment is needed to reach optimal size and to avoid acquisitions that can threaten the control of the firm's common stock. Often for the small but growing company, it is wiser to expand geographically, exploiting more fully the firm's product line or only expanding with convergent production and convergent marketing.

It must be recognized that every competitor cannot be the technological leader. Such leadership tends to go to the giants with the most to spend on research and development (R&D) since, once the technology is off the ground, it is usually possible to predict likely performance against expenditures of resources. But once a firm realizes that all segments of the market are not demanding the latest in performance, it can shift toward focusing on other criteria than technical performance in the core-use function. Thus while competitors all stressed the quality optics of their sunglasses, Foster Grant made a successful market entry by emphasizing the glamour of theirs.

If we only had to worry about buyer reactions and passive competition, the development of a competitive strategy would be much simpler since the focus would be on developing an offering that had the edge on what competition was currently offering. But where competition is not passive but actively aggressive, the problem becomes one of staying ahead of competition by developing an offering and further offerings that minimize the impact of retaliation. Success, though, cannot be guaranteed: for success to be certain, the whole world must cooperate.

NOTES

1 Porter, Michael E. (1980) *Competitive Strategy: Techniques for Analyzing Your Business and Competitors*, New York: Free Press.
2 Ramaswamy, Venkatram, Gatignon, Hubert, and Reibstein, David J. (1994) "Competitive Marketing Behavior in Industrial Markets," *Journal of Marketing*, 58 (April).
3 Ibid.
4 Metwally, M. M. (1978) "Escalation Tendencies of Advertising," *Oxford Bulletin of Economics and Statistics*, 40 (May) 153–163.
5 Beardsley, Tim (1993) "Never Give a Sucker an Even Break," *Scientific American* (October).
6 McDonald, John (1977) *The Game of Business*, New York: Doubleday.
7 *The Economist* August 20, 1994 page 21, for a review.
8 Kerin, Roger A., Varadarajan, P. Rjan, and Peterson, Robert A. (1992) "First Mover Advantages: A Synthesis, Conceptual Framework, and Research Propositions," *Journal of Marketing*, 56 (October).
9 Cunningham, M. T. and Culligan, K. (1991) "Competitiveness through Networks of Relationships in Information Technology Product Markets," in Stanley J. Paliwoda (ed.) *New Perspectives on International Marketing*, London: Routledge.

Part III

Marketing intelligence

Chapter 8

Information, marketing research, and the marketing manager

This chapter deals with the problem of providing marketing management with the marketing information it requires. And information is required since marketing cannot be conducted without plenty of it. Information is critical to decision-making since the quality of the decision depends vitally on the validity of the information on which it is based. This chapter describes the role of information in marketing and reviews the procedures and methods of marketing research to understand its techniques and limitations.

The chapter covers:

1 *information for the manager*. This section discusses the nature of information, management information systems (MIS), and decision support systems (DSS) as well as the various logical decision processes for which information is needed, namely, description, explanation, prediction, prescription, and evaluation.
2 *stages in doing a marketing research study*. This section covers problem diagnosis, research design, evaluative criteria, and data collection methods. (The term "marketing" research is used here to reserve the term "market" research for research into some specific market. However, some writers use the term "marketing" research for that research that seeks to expand on fundamental knowledge about marketing.)
3 *techniques of analysis*. This section deals with the analysis of data and the role of quantitative techniques.

INFORMATION FOR THE MARKETING MANAGER

Definition of information

Information is a special type of knowledge. It is knowledge that has utility for the user. In the case of marketing management, this utility is the value of the knowledge for managerial decision-making. Information shapes a decision or affects the confidence with which it is made. Where this does not happen, it is not information to the manager but merely data. Equivalent to this definition are those definitions of information that define it as data with meaning: "Information can be defined as data that have been organized or given structure for the context and thus endowed with meaning."[1]

This pragmatic definition of information carries implications:

1 Managers receive vast amounts of what market researchers might classify as information but which is not information to managers as it means nothing to them: information is very much a function of the recipient. Managers have their own ideas (representations, models) about how the market works so data that is useful to them is very tied to how it illuminates management's understanding. Any information system must not just be relevant to the marketing manager's problems from the "expert's" point of view but must either:
   a) fit the manager's current models of how things work or fit together, or
   b) the manager must be re-educated in some way to understand better models.
2 Information is only information if managers believe it is relevant to their problems so it has the potential to affect their decisions or the confidence with which they are

made. To be information, data must have the potential to *change expectations*. However, what changes the expectations of one manager is not necessarily what will change the expectations of another: information must to some extent be customized.

3 At least at the conceptual level, a cash value can be put on information as equivalent to the difference it would make to the quality of the manager's decisions if such information were not available. In general terms, that value varies with the criticalness of the decision and the unexpected nature of the content of the information. We define a critical decision as one that is unique yet of central importance. As a consequence, the more critical the decision and the more the content of the information is unexpected (changes expectations), the more the value of the information.

4 The information sought depends on the "theories" held by the manager about the nature of the problems faced. The more the marketing manager understands his market and marketing, the more selective and relevant will be the data he or she collects.

Although information is so vital to decision-making, it has proved difficult to convince nonbusiness organizations (except political organizations) of its value, though the difficulty here of conducting research has been a barrier. Professional service firms, too, have tended to rely on internal sources of information and rarely attempt external surveys. In industrial marketing, marketing research is most concerned with forecasting or obtaining information on those involved in buying and the products bought. Marketing research is much more common in consumer markets, particularly among the big package goods manufacturers.

Management information systems (MIS) and decision support systems (DSS)

In the 1960s, it was anticipated that the use of computers would expand beyond simple routine jobs like payroll and order processing to encompass managerial decisions. The vision was of a company-wide, totally integrated information system to serve the needs of the organization. The description *management information systems* (MIS) was used to distinguish this vision from mere data processing. The MIS movement had some success in using the computer to automate a number of decisions (like inventory control) that could be routinized and programmed. In general, however, the computer had little impact on management decision-making. The failure lay in misunderstanding the nature of most management decisions.

What MIS presupposed was that management decisions could be programmed: that most decisions could be reduced to following algorithms. For this to be so, the problems faced by managers would have to be sufficiently structured for rules to be developed to solve the problem. Where problems are structured, computers come into their own:

- the use of computers to facilitate the management of large databases;
- systems and procedures analyses to simplify procedures and methods for transfer to the computer;

- management/marketing science employed in developing optimization models or simulation models to help predict the consequences of actions.

However, most problems faced by marketing management are only partially structured or they are even unstructured. Where a problem is completely unstructured, management is at a loss about how to go about solving it as they do not know where to start. On the other hand, if a problem is partially structured, that part can be attacked in an analytic way even though judgment is needed to solve the whole problem. The description *decision support systems* (DSS) covers the use of computers to help managers come to grips with partially structured problems. The emphasis is on the word "support." Unlike with data processing, the aim is not efficiency (cost cutting) but to complement and supplement management judgment by helping the manager make more effective decisions with the help of computer programs, embodying various user-oriented, problem-specific, partial decision models. Decision support systems are likely to consist of a number of software programs developed in conjunction with the manager. In general, these software packages handle information processing chores such as monitoring financial performance, which were formerly carried out manually by highly skilled people. Managers themselves should be involved in their design to confirm their relevance and user-friendliness. Many decision support systems have been standardized and developed for marketing managers, such as Brandaid, concerned with helping the manager evaluate proposed strategies and Statport used in formulating and evaluating business portfolio strategies.[2, 3]

The movement away from centralized data processing to distributed data processing means marketing managers are more active in the organization of MIS/DSS within the marketing function. The regular reports and analyses from marketing research are part of MIS. However, a good proportion of marketing research is concerned with semi-structured problems. This offers scope for building a DSS resource. There are always unique problems or problems that occur in unique circumstances which cannot be solved by standard programs but need a tailor-made approach. Computers are a key resource today for management. But as one authority on the use of computers says:[4]

> While computers afford humans much valuable help, they offer little serious competition in the areas of creativity, integration of disparate information and flexible adaptation to unforeseen circumstances. Here the human mind functions best. Machines only manipulate numbers, people connect them to meaning.

We can do a great deal with the aid of computers but problems can still remain. Thus a supermarket chain can have instantaneous data on sales but collecting and transmitting reports from thousands of cash registers across the country is one thing but converting such data into a form that can be used to make decisions can still present serious problems.

General purposes served by information

At the most general level, information serves the purpose of decision-making by describing some state of affairs; explaining some happening; predicting some event;

evaluating some proposed course of action and, finally, the prescription of some action plan. Figure 8.1 illustrates.

Description

The collection of descriptive data about customers, competition, markets, and other aspects of the external environment is a major function of marketing research. No amount of psychological theory will predict, say, that the average American household sends out thirty-eight Christmas cards a year or that less than half of American adults do not brush their teeth up and down. There is also research on the level of customer satisfaction. This is particularly important in services where wide variability in service quality is common. Hence the importance to hotels, airlines, etc. of constantly researching the level of satisfaction.

Figure 8.1 shows the type of descriptive data collected. Thus marketers want to know sales data, buying motives and buying practices, competitive success and performance data. More recently, there has been the growth of *relationship marketing*, with marketing departments building *databases* on their customers to customize their offerings and target their messages. Companies now are developing computer-based programs to store customer details, particularly details on purchases. Some of this is a spin off from political marketing in that such databases allow differentiated messages to be sent to individual households. The whole idea is to reinforce or develop loyalty. Targeted marketing means companies can reward loyal customers and cease wasting time on promoting to unlikely buyers. Another trend is the collection of performance data (other than market share data) to include measures of service quality using traditional statistical quality control techniques.

Explanation

Explanation in daily life is viewed as something that reduces the unfamiliar or unexpected to something that is familiar or to be expected. In the sciences, explanation is viewed as the conditions under which some event (described in a certain way) varies, fits into some known system or follows from some principle accepted as true. This may take the form of showing the causes, the origins, the effects or the function of that to be explained. The explanation sought depends on the purpose of the inquiry. For example, if we were to ask why people buy a product, there are a number of possible answers—reasons for buying, how the decision evolved, influences at work that led to the decision, and so on. We must first determine, therefore, what is to be explained. For example, we need to decide what aspect of behavior is of interest since seeking an all-embracing explanation of buying behavior is like seeking an explanation of holes in the road. An overarching theory of buying behavior, can be, at best, simply an orienting model that points (like a laundry list) to the factors at work. Thus a decision under conditions of certainty is different from deciding under conditions of uncertainty. Once we determine what has to be explained, the next step is choosing the appropriate type of explanation.

Description of:	Explanation of:	Prediction of:	Prescription for:	Evaluation of:
External environment	Social, technological, and economic events	Social, technological, and economic trends	Business-level planning: business in, investment objectives thrust	Business-level sales market share(s) earnings earnings per share return on investment/equity, etc.
Market	Market growth/decline, demand fluctuations, industry profitability	Market demand and sales forecast market share marketing costs	Market strategy product competitor segmentation promotion pricing distribution	Marketing level *Sales* products territories customers channels sales people method of sale delivery size of order, etc. *Costs* promotion selling transportation warehousing and order handling credit and collection, etc.
Customers	Customers' buying processes, preferences, perceptions, attitudes	Buying behavior values attitudes perceptions		
Competition	Competitors' behavior and performance	Competitors' actions and reactions		
Company	Company success/ low performance, relative market share	Performance(s) e.g. market share level of service		

Figure 8.1 Logical decision processes

One of the most common questions asked of marketing research is to explain why some product failed or is selling below expectations. On occasions, the answer is all too apparent; a consequence, say, of a rival market entry that was simply overwhelmingly superior and backed by a huge promotional budget. The question that would be asked here is not why the product failed but why the firm failed to anticipate the competitor's entry.

In general terms, failure can be attributed to one or some combination of:

- higher costs than anticipated: costs cover entry costs and the costs of building market share.
- competitor actions: this may not be a matter of competitors coming out with something better, but (if the product is new-to-the-world) not spending sufficiently on building up primary demand for the product.
- change in wants and beliefs so that the market is less than expected.
- capacity limitations not anticipated.
- deficiencies in marketing strategy, analyzed in terms of product, price, promotion and distribution.
- organizational deficiencies leading to poor implementation.

The requirements for success involve all the above. If any of these six go wrong, the consequence could be failure. Postmortems about what went wrong are useful, not in laying blame but in establishing failure to learn, failure to anticipate, or failure to adapt, so such failures are noted and action taken to prevent their recurrence.

Less commonly requested are explanations of success because of the assumption that success arises from marketing expertise. If this is true, it is good to document it; if chance factors brought the success, it is even more important to reveal this, so that management is not lured into complacency and an unjustified faith in its strategy. The analysis of success establishes the contribution of product, price, promotion and distribution to that success, special attention being paid to how these elements were interwoven and coordinated; the role of marketing research in providing the informational base; the contribution of changes in the environment like government policy and last but not least, the management of the implementation.

Prediction and forecasting

In science, prediction takes the form of: "If conditions A, B, C, occur then consequences X, Y, Z occur". While *explanation* starts with some effect and looks to see what brought it about, *prediction* states what events will come about as a consequence of some situation or set of conditions.

Prediction is not mere forecasting. Prediction makes statements about future events by considering the *effects* of some set of conditions, while forecasting is a statement about the future based on historical extrapolation. But the distinction is not that clear in that forecasting by trend extrapolation implicitly makes assumptions that certain conditions will remain constant and that there is some momentum in the trend that will carry it forward to the next period of the forecast. Perhaps, a clearer distinction between the two would be that prediction in science stems from some underlying theory that is something more than that which underlies forecasting.

One reason for seeking explanations in marketing is to help predict behavior. For example, if we had a law to the effect that: "If the price of a product is raised, then sales of that product will decline in proportion," such a law would sustain the following:

- If the price of brand X were to be raised, the sales of the brand would fall in proportion, and
- if the price of brand X had been raised in 1992, sales of brand X would have been less than they were in 1992, in proportion to the price increase.

Unfortunately, no such universal laws (or universal principles!) exist in marketing. What makes prediction and forecasting hazardous is beliefs and wants change as well as other things in the environment. Although forecasting is something more than a projection of ignorance, it is inherently uncertain and approximate since both databases and erratic environments make it impossible to support forecasts of perfect reliability. Their accuracy depends on the validity of the underlying assumptions such as that the underlying causes of the trend will persist or that exponential smoothing in trend extrapolation is correct in giving more weight to recent data.

It is not uncommon to find firms like Keuffel & Esser, once a leader in the slide-rule market, whose 1967 forecast did not foresee that the electronic calculator would make its product technologically obsolescent within five years. The big problem in extrapolating from trends is the prediction of turning points. As one economist's ditty has it: "A trend is a trend is a trend, but the question is will it bend? Will it alter its course through some unforeseen force and come to a premature end?" Naive models like trend extrapolation obviously perform better in stable conditions and for short-term forecasting.

What helps forecasting is that:

- much buying is habitual;
- many statistical regularities like the percentage of people catching cold in winter do not change in the short term;
- there is the persistence of social conventions like weddings and wearing ties at business; and
- "causal" type associations like the level of education and the type of magazine read.

Forecasts about products found in magazine articles have had a low record of success. They seem to be more influenced by what is novel and technically feasible than what will be bought.

The sort of events marketing seeks to forecast are shown in Figure 8.1. It is difficult to forecast future environmental conditions and most firms do not attempt such forecasts. What is of universal interest is forecasting sales and market share. But first a few definitions:

- *Market potential.* Market potential reflects the *market opportunity* and answers the question: How many will buy (or can be persuaded to buy), in what amounts and how often in the next twelve months? Sometimes this figure is calculated on the basis of present sales, modified by trends or expectations of promotions activating latent and passive wants. While this definition conveys the general sense-meaning of market potential, actual estimates of potential can vary widely within that definition.

- *Sales potential.* Sales potential reflects the *actual sales opportunity* for the firm. It is the firm's estimate of its likely share of market potential, given an all-out effort.
- *Sales forecast.* This reflects *company expectations.* The firm's sales forecast differs from sales potential in that it assumes usually something less than an all-out effort. The sales budget is usually based on the sales forecast.

Market potential, sales potential, and the sales forecast make many assumptions about customer behavior, competitor behavior, company strategy and environmental trends. There is no certainty about any of these. Hence it is common to indicate this in the estimates by suggesting a range of error.

The forecasting of new-to-the-world products is particularly difficult. Thus the market potential for 3M's Post-It notes was only estimated to be around three quarters of a million dollars at the very best. Faith in Post-It had more to do with the extensive use being made of it by people within the 3M company than data provided by marketing research. Similarly, market research did not support Hewlett–Packard's introduction of the first "scientific" hand-held calculator. Where there are no past sales to go on, the firm may receive some insight from the sales of analogous products: insight on the rate of diffusion and adoption of the product and the likely pattern of sales. Another approach is to identify *suspects* for the product and estimate how many of these are likely to be *prospects* and how many of these prospects' latent demand can be activated from latent to passive to active demand. Estimates of the market are also made from survey data based on presenting the target audience with a statement of the product concept, demonstrating the product or letting people use the product (see Chapter 9).

There are many approaches to forecasting. The main ones are shown in Table 8.1. Some combination of these methods is usually employed, together with more unorthodox methods. Take, for example, the subject of predicting or forecasting the actions of competitors. The techniques that can be used are game theory, the opinion of experts, past behavior of competitors in like situations, declared intentions, but there is also role playing. *Role playing* is essentially a simulation or the acting out of the role of the competitor. It does not seem to be much used yet there are good theoretical reasons for thinking it to be most useful.

Forecasting methods are judged on the basis of their "usefulness" and "accuracy." *Usefulness* relates to the reliability of the forecasts and how they help in decision-making while *accuracy* refers to how precise the forecasts are when compared to what actually happened. None of the methods shown in Table 8.1 make highly accurate forecasts as most market situations are characterized by environmental changes and a high level of "noise" which makes interpretation of data difficult. However, the more recent the data, the more useful is it likely to be. It follows from this that the accuracy of forecasts is improved by constant updating. Other advice is to draw on as many sources as possible

Table 8.1 Methods of forecasting

A. Sales force composite method

This method of forecasting is based on the sales force's own estimates. It is a bottom-up approach in that the total forecast simply aggregates the individual forecasts of each member of the sales force. It has the advantages of being easily understood; involves the participation of the sales force; can be built up from individual estimates of what is likely to be sold in each outlet. On the other hand, if used as a basis for sales compensation, it is subject to bias while it needs to be modified to take account of promotional programs etc.

B. Survey of buying intentions

This method is based on a survey among the target group about buying intentions. For example, if a sample of firms in the target group report likely purchases of the product in the next year to be $1,600,000, and collectively the sample of firms employs 3,200 workers, this means that the average sales per worker will be $500. If the whole industry employs around 100,000 workers then the estimated sales will be $50,000,000. Intentions are always conditional so the method is risky in times of large economic change.

C. Group of experts

It is common to use experts for technological forecasting. For example, the Delphi technique discussed in Chapter 10 or techniques like decision calculus discussed in Chapter 12. Several judges should be involved. However, forecasts tend to be influenced by the expert's attitude at the time (whether pessimistic, optimistic, or just conservative) and by what information has most recently been brought to the expert's attention. For certain types of forecasting, it may be possible to discover the rules used by the judges by recording what the judges say "off the top of their heads" during forecasting. The resulting rules constitute a formula that is more reliable as following rules eliminates many of situational biases to which judges are subject. This method is called "bootstrapping"; we pull ourselves up by our own bootstraps, that is, we improve our judgments by modeling ourselves. Thus a model is derived from the expert's analysis but use of the model alone actually improves decisions because the model is not subject to the distractions and fatigue that affects humans. Bootstrapping of consumer intentions typically uses the technique of conjoint analysis as described in Chapter 10.

D. Time series analysis

The extrapolation of the time series of past sales is probably the most common method of forecasting, with recent sales being given additional weighting by the technique of "exponentially weighted moving averages." It has the advantage of being reducible to a routine but is not much use when sales are subject to erratic swings.

E. Econometric models

An econometric model forecasts using one or more algebraic equations that reflect some underlying theory. This contrasts with time series, which simply treats sales, say, as a function of time. The coefficients are the "constants" in the various equations in the model (such as "a" and "b" in the equation $Y = ax + b$). Econometric models are designed so that all the coefficients can be measured. They are essentially simultaneous systems of multiple regression equations. Current interest lies in the econometric models of logit and probit. Econometric models are best used for long-term forecasts though they are commonly used for short-term forecasting. They assume the firm has access to a great deal of historical data.

F. Ad hoc relationships

There is, for example, the so-called "hem line indicator" in finance that relates the stock market to the length of women's dresses; buy when they are long, sell when they are short. No comment!

and to make one's assumptions as clear as possible. Finally, study old forecasts to see if something can be done to make improvements in the future.

It is common to predict buying *intentions* from attitude measures. Among marketing academics, the term "attitude" is commonly viewed as embracing three components: cognitive (beliefs about the object); evaluative (liking for the object); conative (readiness for action toward the object). Some writers substitute the word "affect" for the term "evaluative" while others argue the two are distinct dimensions thereby suggesting that there are really four components of attitude. But the term "affect" in psychology embraces emotions, feelings, mood, and temperament. The term "affect" in this sense presupposes some attitude in that I only get emotional, say, at the burning of the flag because I already have a certain attitude toward the flag as a symbol.

There are many different measures of attitude in social science and in marketing research even more! Most focus on the evaluative component of attitude. The debates over definitions and operational measures of attitude are essentially debates over how best to view the concept of attitude for our purposes. Attitude cannot be studied like parts of a machine but until something better comes along, we simply assume it is "as if" people have something like attitudes. In any case, in whatever way attitude is measured, measures must be reliable which means there must be consistency in test–retest, or in split-halves or in equivalent tests. More important is the predictive validity of attitude measures. Predictive validity assumes reliability since high predictive validity means the measures do predict as intended.

The multiattribute model discussed in Chapters 4 and 5, has become a popular way of measuring attitudes among marketing academics. It aims to capture the judgmental process and so is considered useful in diagnosing the beliefs that underlie attitudes. The multiattribute model focuses on the cognitive component of attitude, but implicit is the idea that relative overall scores reflect the evaluative/affect dimension of attitude. The trouble in using the multiattribute model to measure attitudes is that

1 there is the possibility of interaction among the factors which means that the importance weights can become distorted; and
2 the importance of a factor might be different for different parts of its range.

It is assumed that the subject or respondent takes account of these factors implicitly when rating some brand. But the researcher may take more explicit account in designing the questionnaire.

In Table 8.2, choice criteria are shown in Column (1). In Column (2), the choice criteria in Column (1) are weighted with the sum of the weights totaling 10. The ratings of brand X are shown in Column (3) on a seven-point scale. But because, beyond a certain point, more (or less) of the criteria may not be sought, Column (4) shows the respondent's ideal rating, that is, her ideal level. Column (5) shows the absolute difference between the actual rating and the ideal. Column (6) multiplies the weighting in Column (2) by this absolute difference in Column (5). The sum 17 is the attitude score. It is a relative measure as it needs to be compared with the attitude scores for rival brands to gauge its significance.

An attitude toward some brand may not be strongly related to specific buying action;

Table 8.2 Evaluating the attitude toward brand "X"

Criteria (1)	Weighting (2)	Rating (3)	Ideal (4)	Absolute difference (5)	Score (6)
Economic	1	4	3	1	1
Technical	3	6	2	4	12
Intrinsic	2	5	3	2	4
Integrative	4	1	1	0	0
Total Col. (6)					17

a measure of "intention" is likely to be more predictive. Fishbein's "theory of reasoned action" is an extension of the multiattribute model to relate attitudes to intentions. This model views intention to take an action as a function of:

1 the individual's attitude toward taking that particular action. This is measured in a multiattribute way that takes account of beliefs about the consequences of taking the action and an evaluation of these consequences.
2 the individual's perceptions of the social and group norms relevant to the behavior, given the situation; and
3 the individual's motivation to comply with these group norms.

Although, when divorced from its algebraic formulation, this "theory" appears somewhat pedestrian, it can be criticized for assuming attitudes are independent (not influenced by) perceptions of social and group norms and independent of the motivation to comply with these norms. Social and group norms clearly influence the evaluative beliefs entering into attitudes while the motivation to comply with such norms is likely to influence the intensity of attitudes. It is also doubtful as to whether the Fishbein formulation takes sufficient account of a person's sense of integrity and any perceptions of risk attached to the action; both of which can influence behavior.

Of increasing interest is the identification of *values* as a basis for predicting behavior as well as a basis for advertising appeals. Notwithstanding whether systems like VALS are the best way of capturing and utilizing values, it is recognized that values are fundamental to marketing. All brand images and other symbolization are grounded in values. There are values which seem universal in emotional appeal like motherhood but there are also the values of the target group to which appeals are made. It is these that are key. This, of course, is the basic insight of psychographics but the problem lies in establishing

a) first that the target group does indeed have distinct values and
b) how to discover the most salient values distinguishing the group.

It may be that such values are best discovered by being a *participant observer* within the group; listening and observing rather than going out with some questionnaire.

Evaluation

In general terms evaluation is the process of determining the relative position of something against some criteria. More specifically, in business, evaluation is the process of determining how successful some plan or action was or is likely to be in achieving the goals laid down for it. Information for evaluation either helps management evaluate a proposed course of action to determine its future potential or it is information for the evaluation of past performance. Evaluation of past performance involves a comparison of actual performance against some standard or criteria to judge degree of attainment. Thus actual market share is compared with the market share that was set as an objective or the salesperson's monthly sales might be compared with the individual's sales quota to judge the level of performance. The evaluation of proposed strategies and other courses of action is essentially an evaluation of their future potential against the criteria and so involves the prediction and ranking of likely performance.

All evaluation is evaluation against some criterion so evaluation always raises the issue of appropriate evaluative criteria with debates over the dividing lines between excellent, good, satisfactory, and poor performances for the criteria selected. In marketing there is dispute over the use of sales or market share as overall measures of performance in that neither are sufficiently tied to profitability. The first step in resolving such disputes lies in being clear about the *objectives* of the evaluation in that all criteria must reflect objectives. Whenever universal performance criteria are proposed, universal objectives are assumed to be valid.

Prescription

Prescription means prescribing some specific course of action. The process involves decision-making: setting objectives; identifying the relevant alternatives and their likely consequences; evaluating these consequences; and, finally, the prescriptive decision itself. But stating the stages in decision-making in this way hides the role played by the description, explanation, prediction, and evaluation. For instance, the relevant alternatives depend on the problems to be solved, and the collection of data and the explanation of occurrences are often a prerequisite to the specification of alternatives while asserting consequences is in the nature of prediction and assessing their significance involves evaluation. Although prescription links back to the descriptive base for action, descriptive facts do not suggest what action to take: the prescriptive cannot be derived from the descriptive since prescription is tied to values and objectives.

Success in marketing is never guaranteed so showing that actions are warranted by the evidential information available is of particular importance. In fact, when the evidence and reasoning are exposed, others can make a critical assessment. However, in evaluating past decisions, it is easy to look back and point to evidence that was indicative of what was happening but was unfortunately ignored. While failures to anticipate are common, it is also true that, at the time, there may have been other evidence that was more supportive of what was actually done. Evidence in the case of prescription consists of any information that helps in judging the extent to which a suggested course of action will achieve goals. The inference process consists in the use of information (evidence) which in effect raises or lowers the attractiveness of the alternatives being considered. But goals affect the way information is used as it is against goals that some particular item of information is judged to be relevant.

In general terms, marketing research is concerned with description, explanation, and prediction with the marketing manager focused on prescribing plans and evaluating performance. But nothing in practice is this tidy as marketing management must give direction to marketing research by:

1 defining objectives;
2 defining the problems and advancing ideas as to what data might be relevant;
3 suggesting how marketing research might go about collecting some specific type of information;
4 questioning the assumptions lying behind the techniques being proposed and reports issued; and
5 providing cost and time constraints.

None of these management responsibilities can be adequately accomplished unless the marketing manager knows something about the methods and limitations of marketing research. Similarly, those doing marketing research must know how to interview, construct a questionnaire, know how to observe behavior and to conduct an experiment. Figure 8.2 illustrates some of the problems with which marketing research is typically concerned while Figure 8.3 suggests the phases in planning and control together with the type of information associated with each particular phase, whether descriptive, explanatory, predictive, or evaluative.

STAGES IN MARKETING RESEARCH

This section discusses the typical stages in a market research study. These stages are:

1 setting objectives
2 problem diagnosis
3 research design
4 establishing evaluative criteria
5 data collection
6 data analysis

Michael Polanyi, the physical scientist turned social scientist, claims that scientific knowledge and personal knowledge are no different in kind while George Kelly, a psychologist, in rejecting behaviorism, came to view humans as going about their lives as if engaged on scientific inquiry as they are pattern-seeking and inquiring individuals.[5, 6] What at a minimum is being stressed here is that going about something in a more scientific way does not involve alien ways of thinking but simply taking more

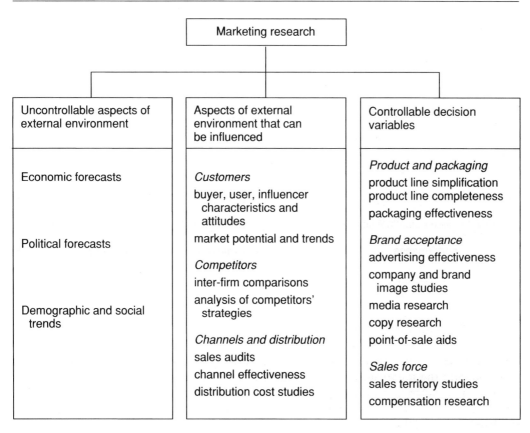

Figure 8.2 Information from marketing research

safeguards than are normally taken. It was in fact Albert Einstein who stressed that science was nothing more than a refinement of everyday thinking.

Setting objectives

Decisions presuppose problems and problems presuppose objectives. If there were no objectives, there would be no problems and no need for a decision. Thus a firm that does not seek growth, has no problem about how growth might be achieved. All marketing research studies have some objective such as finding out who buys the product, how often, and how frequently, but such objectives ultimately connect with overall marketing goals or objectives.

There are objectives, however, that do tend to be neglected. These relate to testing our ideas. Too few managers use marketing research as research is used in science, that is, to systematically test hunches (hypotheses) rather than to collect information likely to be supportive of some favored course of action. Also, all objectives operate within

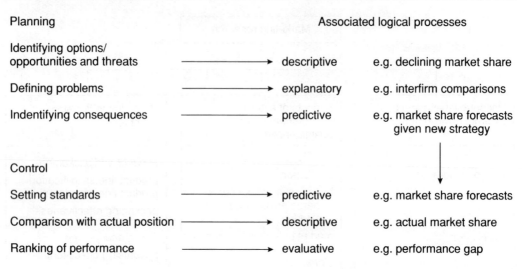

Figure 8.3 Planning and control information

constraints such as ethical ones. The major ethical issue is dishonesty when deception is used to gain cooperation or the use of information in a way that violates confidentiality (protecting the identity of respondents from public exposure) or anonymity (no one knowing the identity of respondents).

Problem diagnosis

Problems are reflected in the difficulties encountered in attaining the goals of marketing. But recognizing that a difficult situation exists does not always mean that the exact nature of the problem is known. To interpret the difficult situation as a problem is to indicate the way the difficulty should be attacked. Thus I may recognize that the loss of market share is a difficult situation suggesting some underlying problem, but I still need to define the exact nature of the problem. Have tastes changed? Has the competition done a leapfrog? and so on. Sometimes, of course, we define the problem so it in no way reflects on what we have done or intend to do but is simply a problem, say, of "unfair" competition.

Sometimes the problem is a recurring one, such as a fall off in demand due to a recession, but information is still needed on the problem; how it is changing; what efforts in the past have been successful in dealing with it and what still needs to be known through research. In problem diagnosis, expertise and experience direct attention to likely causes. The novice in contrast will often act like the mechanically incompetent driver seeking to discover why the car does not work. Unless the driver has some mechanical knowledge, he simply does not know what to look for in trying to understand how things are related. Similarly, the marketing manager needs to know the market, since the idea that X might, say, be the cause of this is only tenable against some background idea (theory/model) of why this might be so.

Most marketing research studies address specific problems for which information is needed in the form of

1 estimating some characteristic of a target population (for example, what brand(s) of detergent do they use?); and
2 identifying relationships among variables such as the relationship between income and brands bought.

But sometimes marketing researchers are asked to test hypotheses and managers need to assess how well it has been done. The hypothetico-deductive method of testing a hypothesis, (for example, that point of purchase (POP) material does increase the level of brand purchase), consists of asking what consequences would follow if the hypothesis were true. Confirming that these consequences do in fact occur helps corroborate the hypothesis. However, there is always a need to assess the significance of the confirmation for the truth of the hypothesis. This is not simply a matter of using statistics to check whether the results could be explained by chance but the consideration of rival hypotheses. Ideally, we would wish to predict consequences which, if confirmed, would rule out all other rival hypotheses. Since we can never be logically certain of ruling out all other possible hypotheses (not even after conducting a controlled experiment), we can never be logically certain a hypothesis is true, but this does not rule out our being confident enough to act. In fact, we are not always certain that the predicted consequences are something that must occur if the hypothesis is true, only that it seems reasonable to assume so.

In assessing whether the hypothesis should be accepted given the evidence, the marketing manager considers the likelihood of getting the predicted (and confirmed) consequences (results), if the hypothesis were not true. The manager has to ask herself or himself whether, if the hypothesis were *not* true and the various assumptions about conditions are in place, then would the result or consequences obtained be highly improbable? The more improbable the results or consequences if the hypothesis were *not* true, the more confidence the manager can have in the hypothesis being true. Of course, we would like to measure on some scale the degree to which a hypothesis is confirmed where absolute truth is the end of the continuum. This is beyond what is logically possible; particularly when researchers and managers may have different views about what evidence to accept, what evidence is most relevant, and how different bits of evidence are to be weighted in reaching a decision. But it is easy to exaggerate the conflict over the weighting of evidence in that accommodation is usually reached in practice because a business background establishes certain conventions.

Research design

Whether the purpose is to describe, explain or predict, marketing research is generally associated with the collection of data either from records (internal or external) or through surveys. Surveys are popular as they provide quantitative data and, for most routine work, the best evidence is often quantitative as the questions asked (for example, what percentage of the target audience are women? How many of the target audience saw the advertisement?) demand numerical answers. This is one reason why marketing research is so associated with the discipline of statistics. Yet most of the stupidities that occur in marketing research like sampling the wrong population or using an ill-designed questionnaire, can usually be attributed more to a lack of common sense than a lack of training in statistical techniques. Although carrying out a census among the target population is by no means unusual in, say, industrial marketing, the more common type of research involves soliciting the views of actual or potential buyers, customers, clients or users through some form of sampling. This means getting out a "sampling plan." The first step is to define the *sampling unit*.

The sampling unit

The "sampling unit" defines the population of interest. Until the population is defined, it is impossible to select a representative sample from it. But selecting the target population needs careful attention. For example, suppose the company makes men's ties and wants to determine its market share. What is the population of interest? Is it all those men who buy ties? This could be misleading since women buy a very large proportion of ties for men.

Probability sampling

The next step in the sampling plan is the *sampling procedure* which determines how the sample of respondents is to be selected. The basic choice is between probability and nonprobability sampling. In *probability sampling* each individual has a known or equal probability of being selected. Thus in *random sampling*, each member of the population has an equal chance of being chosen. Random sampling presupposes we have a sampling frame whereby each member of the population can be located and selected in some random way. For example, if we wanted a sample of medical general practitioners (GPs), we decide on the sample size needed to provide an acceptable estimate and then we could choose a random sample using the doctors' medical register as the sampling frame. While this is fine theoretically, problems arise when we try to interview members listed in the sample in that some will be away or not at home while others refuse to cooperate. Nonetheless, the random sample is the safest way of getting a *representative sample* though it is expensive and does not necessarily achieve representativeness.

The expense of random sampling has led to other methods of probability sampling. *Systematic sampling*, which consists of choosing every 10th or 20th name or unit (e.g. every 10th house in each street) after some random start. *Stratified sampling* involves dividing the population into strata (for example, social classes) and drawing random samples from each stratum. In this way we remove that part of the variation caused by the differences between the strata. If the population is heterogeneous, stratified sampling is a way of ensuring greater precision for any particular sample size. In *cluster* or *area sampling*, the population is first broken down into convenient subgroups (usually geographical areas). A number of these subgroups are then selected at random (on the assumption that spatial patterning reflects other differences), and an appropriate part of the sample is selected from within each subgroup.

Nonprobability sampling

Nonprobability sampling is most common in marketing research. One form is purposive or *judgmental sampling*. This is essentially the case study approach whereby we generalize from what we regard as the typical case. This is not uncommon in industrial marketing research when we generalize from the "typical" user. But the assumed homogeneity needs first to be established before generalizing.

The most common form of nonprobability sampling is *quota sampling*. In quota sampling the interviewer is given a description of the types to interview and the number required of each type. Usually, the proportion of each type to interview is the same as the proportion in the population but not always since some types may include only a very small proportion of the population. In any case, the interviewer is left to locate, select and interview those with the prescribed characteristics. Thus she may be given 10 interviews to make and told they must be distributed as shown in Table 8.3 with the 0s representing the quotas. Quota sampling is cheap while the problem of nonresponse does not arise. On the other hand, it is risky since the freedom to select respondents gives rise to unknown biases so that (theoretically at least even if not followed in practice) statistical analysis cannot legitimately be used to estimate the probable error. There also tends to be a difference between the *target population* (the population we would like to interview) and the *sampled population* (which is all we could get). In fact the gulf between target and sampled population can be very wide indeed as the following quotation indicates:[7]

In the earliest days of polling, people were questioned in public places, probably excluding some 80% of the total population. Shifting to in-home interviewing with quota controls and no call-backs still excluded 60%—perhaps 5% inaccessible

Table 8.3 An example of a quota sample

Description of sample and number of interviews

Men	*0 0 0 0 0*
Women	*0 0 0 0 0*

Age characteristic		*Socioeconomic characteristic*	
21–29	0 0	Av+	0
30–49	0 0 0 0	Av	0 0
50–64	0 0 0	Av–	0 0 0 0 0
65+	0	Group D	0 0

Note: 0s represent a quota of 10 interviews to be distributed according to the above age and socioeconomic characteristics.

in homes under any conditions, 25% refusals, and 5% through interviewers' reluctance to approach homes of extreme wealth or poverty and a tendency to avoid fourth floor walkups. Under modern probability sampling with call back and household designation, perhaps only 15% of the population is excluded: 5% are totally inaccessible in private residences (e.g., those institutionalized, hospitalized, homeless, transient, in the military, mentally incompetent and so forth), another 10% refuse to answer, are unavailable after three call-backs, or have moved to no known address.

It is difficult today to just knock on doors or to obtain an unbiased sample in a household survey while in any case timing is key to contacting various family members. For street or local shopping mall interviews, police permission is commonly required while the interviewer should look the part with the right dress and clipboard prominently displayed. Very important is the ability of the interviewer to establish immediate rapport and to project respect for the prospective respondent. Advice on the extent of eye-to-eye contact and physical distance while interviewing, varies with the culture since some cultures accept close proximity while others avoid eye contact as a sign of respect.

Some methods of carrying out surveys like shopping mall and telephone surveys are apt to underrepresent poor people and minorities while in general there is a growing refusal by the public to cooperate. Some of this noncooperation arises from the obvious abuse by sales people gaining attention by pretending to be doing genuine market research. There is also a certain disillusionment with surveys when rival companies publish so-called research findings that are in direct conflict with each other. This arises because many studies are undertaken simply to lend support to advertising claims, political lobbying, or mainly to help polish up a company's tarnished image. It is usually easy to get any results we want if we are prepared to bias the sample and the questions asked.

Establishing evaluative criteria

What happens when the results of the study are in? There is a need to anticipate the different results that might be obtained and to decide what the different results would mean in terms of actions. Doing this provides a check on the pragmatic value of the proposed study and the relevance and adequacy of the data collected.

What difference would it make to decision-making having the results of the study? Too many studies are proposed and carried out simply on the ground that such a study sounds interesting, without any attempt being made to think through the study to the possible findings and their likely value to planning and control. All proposed studies need to be evaluated against criteria such as the following:

1 the relevance of the study to marketing or corporate decisions;
2 the adequacy of the study for the purpose for which it is being undertaken;
3 the cost of the study in relation to its likely value;
4 the timeliness of the study for the decisions to be made; and
5 the user-friendliness of the study.

Data collection

Data collection often presents a problem. This is particularly so in many nonindustrialized countries of the world where some of the more traditional methods of data collection can be ruled out because of

1 a general unwillingness to respond as being socially inappropriate e.g. women in many Muslim countries;
2 the literacy level of the target population; and
3 inadequate information on who constitutes the target population.

In any event, a method or methods of data collection have to be selected by the researcher. If the firm does not employ some outside research organization, it will also have the problem of selecting and training interviewers and drawing up a time schedule for the completion of the work.

The various methods of data collection are shown in Figure 8.4, though no doubt some methods do not fit perfectly into just one category.

Techniques of observation

Observation of behavior is useful in itself but can also usefully precede other methods of data collection to give a feel for what to expect. As a method of conducting marketing

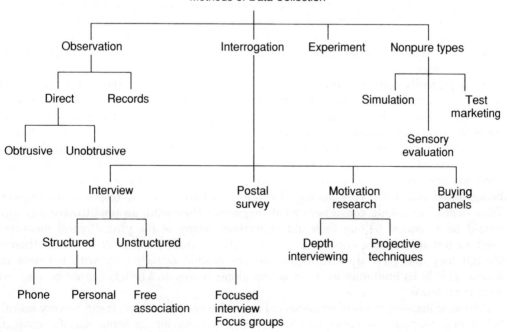

Figure 8.4 Methods of data collection

research, observation can be direct or take the form of examining records. In any case, before any observation starts the researcher must decide on what is to be observed, where, who, when, and how to record what is seen and heard. Direct observation might be the observation of a product in use or of the buying process. The major marketing research agencies are too wedded to surveys to do much by way of direct observation of consumers in how they behave. Advertising agencies, however, seem more willing to undertake direct observation in the hope of getting some insight for advertising themes. In any case, direct observation should occur more often to understand the context in which the product is bought, used and disposed of. Research-type, systematic observation (as opposed to casual observation) is not simply just looking:[8]

- it is planned;
- it is tied to some purpose;
- the observations are directed at checking ideas and are subject to checks themselves; and
- it uses prearranged categories and scoring systems.

Of particular interest to service organizations is the situation where the observer becomes part of whatever is being studied just as a researcher may be a service worker in a hotel or on an airplane to study the service given and customer reactions. In each of these cases the researcher becomes a *participant-observer*. A participant-observer has a defined role in what is happening and so is not just a spectator or customer.

Another approach is the study of specific groups and places. The approach is called *ethnography*, with the observer looking, listening, asking questions and recording it all. Ethnography, unlike participant-observer, is not a specific research method but combines observation and interviews. However, the value of both ethnography and participant observation very much depends on the researcher's skills in observation and description of what occurred.

What probably restricts the use of direct observation is not just the cost or the fear of nonrepresentativeness but the belief that the presence of an observer will bias behavior. This may occur, at least until those being observed grow used to the presence of an observer. However, all observation need not be obtrusive. Thus, instead of asking drivers about their radio listening habits (which can invite a biased reply), an unobtrusive measure could be obtained from noting the station to which the car radio is tuned. Methods are said to be unobtrusive when they do not affect the answers to questions being asked when the very asking of a question may distort a respondent's answer. Thus instead of asking consumers what magazines they read, an unobtrusive measure would be a request to buy their old magazines. Many of the physiological measures used to test advertising copy (e.g. pupil dilation) could be regarded as unobtrusive though they also have disadvantages. All observation deals purely with behavior or action. This is its limitation as, from action alone, wants and beliefs cannot be inferred with confidence.

Behavioral mapping tends to be neglected in marketing research yet it can be very useful. Behavioral mapping is concerned with people's behavior in some specific context. For example, we might map out the area of a museum (called the "behavior setting") and record the kinds of behavior observed to occur, who participated and for how long. A "place-centered" map shows how people in the museum arrange themselves while a "person-centered" map shows people's movements and activities. With a place-centered map, observers watch the action from a specific vantage point but with a person-centered map, a specific number of people are first selected and their activities charted throughout the day. If the objective is to evaluate a location, room or building, the place-centered method is better. However, if the goal is to learn about some specific group like the handicapped, the person-centered approach is better. Observation in either case can be continuous or follow some sampling procedure such as activity sampling as used in industrial engineering.

If the term observation is used to cover the examination of records then the observation of internal and external records is a major source of research data. There are the "internal secondary data sources" such as sales orders; "external secondary data sources" such as census data and "internal primary data sources" such as salespeople's reports. More specifically we have:

1 *Internal e.g.*
   - geographical division of sales
   - sales by size of order
   - sales by type or size of customer
   - trend of sales by region
   - seasonal fluctuations in sales
2 *External e.g.*
   - US Department of Commerce (rich source of information on both countries and markets for products within those countries)
   - United Nations "Statistical Year Book"
   - chambers of commerce
   - foreign banks
   - trade association publications
   - competitors' announcements
   - etc.

Computerized databases are spreading throughout the world. The latest example is the American Information Exchange (AMIX). AMIX lets potential buyers look over descriptions of its offerings from suppliers of information. This, of course, is what usually happens with information providers but AMIX has gone beyond this. The intention is to encourage buyers to advertise their informational needs to allow sellers to offer what they believe will meet the need or for the buyer and seller to negotiate a consulting contract to collect the information.

Techniques in interrogation

Interrogation is "conversation with a purpose" and is the most frequently used method of obtaining marketing research data. This is understandable since direct observation, for example, cannot provide information on attitudes or perceptions or past buying practices. On the other hand, all interrogation assumes members of the target audience are accessible and willing to supply information. We will discuss each variation of interrogation as shown in Figure 8.4.

Interview.   There is first the interview which can be either *structured* or *unstructured*. The structured interview is associated with closed (multiple choice) questions. In the structured interview there is a set wording of the questions in a set sequence which limits the freedom of respondents in replying. The questions may require a "yes" or a "no" answer, that is, a dichotomous answer or, alternatively, the respondent may be free to choose from several possible answers as shown in Figure 8.5(a). The unstructured interview is associated with open-ended questions where respondents write their own answers.

The structured interview need not, of course, be face-to-face but can be conducted over the telephone. *Telephone interviewing* is common in advertising research with consumers being asked about their recall of commercials or magazine advertisements. It has the great advantage of speed. In many countries now there is computer assisted telephone interviewing (CATI). The interviewers sit in booths with the questions to be asked being flashed onto computer screens. As the answer is recorded and tabulated by the computer, the next question automatically flashes on the screen. This facility makes it possible to do, say, 2,000 interviews in one night and have the data on the desk of the manager the next day. The problem is that more and more consumers are coming to resent the intrusion so there is a high rate of refusal to cooperate.

Many interviews in marketing research are concerned with asking respondents what they would do or how they would act in such and such circumstances e.g. in the event of a price decrease. There are problems here in obtaining correct answers, even if the respondent answers honestly. In the first place, we are asking our respondents to think about "counterfactuals", that is, about things which may occur but so far have not. Respondents commonly find counterfactuals difficult to think about. In the second place, we are taking for granted that respondents have the self-knowledge to report accurately about their thoughts so as to predict accurately their future actions.

Questionnaire design.   Questionnaires have both *content* (subject matter) and *format* (structure *and* appearance). Content should preferably focus on a single issue while a basic problem in format is whether to have open-ended or closed categories of questions which, in turn, revolves round whether the interview is to be structured or unstructured or something of both. Questions that ask respondents to mark their choice along some scale from strongly agree to strongly disagree, or very important to not at all important, usually have some middle position that is regarded as neutral or undecided though it may be better to label this the position of the "don't knows." General advice is to set a strict limit on the number of questions asked to avoid respondent fatigue; avoid loaded and emotive language (unless deliberate); provide balance in the questions so that the number of questions tilted to one view are counterbalanced by an equal number for the opposing view.

The design of the questionnaire is still something of an art. A whole host of factors

(a) *Structured interview*
Dichotomous questions, e.g.,
Q3. Have you ever had a book published?
        Yes   1   Please answer Q3–Q7
        No   2   Skip to Q8
Multiple choice, e.g.,
Q4. When was your first book published?
      (Circle the appropriate number)
      1950–1959   6   1970–1974   9
      1960–1964   7   1975–1979   10
      1965–1969   8   1980–1984   11
Open ended question, e.g.
Q5. What prompted your to write your first book?

(b) *Semantic differential*
Question format, e.g.

High |
quality | | Poor
        | | quality

Portrayal of results, e.g.

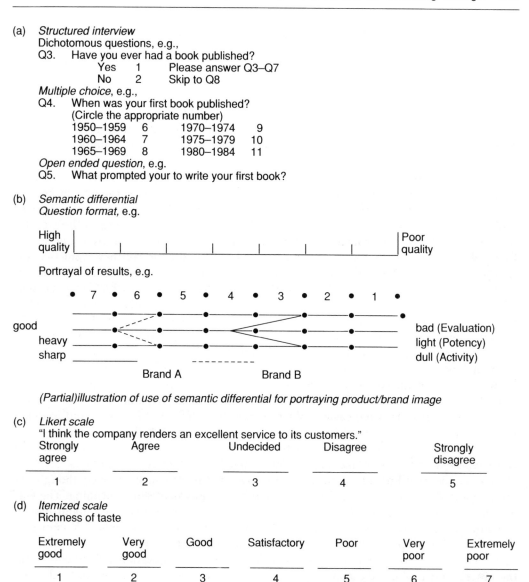

(Partial)illustration of use of semantic differential for portraying product/brand image

(c) *Likert scale*
"I think the company renders an excellent service to its customers."

Strongly agree	Agree	Undecided	Disagree	Strongly disagree
1	2	3	4	5

(d) *Itemized scale*
Richness of taste

Extremely good	Very good	Good	Satisfactory	Poor	Very poor	Extremely poor
1	2	3	4	5	6	7

Figure 8.5 Questionnaires: types, scales

can bias while no amount of statistical manipulation can make up for the unknown error of dishonest replies. Of course, we can check the consistency of replies by repeating the question in a different form but this is not enough. Bias can arise through the design of the questionnaire, the way the questions are asked or through the complexity of what is being asked. Questionnaires begin with the more interesting questions being put first (or some question to determine whether the respondent is part of the population of interest) with the simple routine questions (e.g. on occupation) placed at the end. One question should follow another in logical sequence with a *"bridge"* statement to introduce any change of subject.

The way a question is worded and asked can in itself shape the reply. Thus when an issue is presented in one way, we get one answer and when presented in another way we get an entirely different answer. In fact, when people are not highly involved with an issue, opinions are apt to lack stability and fluctuate according to the way the question is worded. Thus consumers in the United States seem quite happy in one survey to say they want to see Japanese imports curbed but in another say they want freedom to choose between Japanese and American so as to get the best deal. People are also concerned to give the "right" (socially appropriate) answer, which may be why 80 percent of adults in the United States claim to be environmentalists in surveys! When nothing is at stake for the respondent, the answers can be just off "the back of the head." Daniel Yankelovich, the well-known pollster, suggests that when polling the public on issues we should ask them: how personally involved are you in the issue; how much thought have you given to the issue; how likely are you to change your mind? The answers to these questions are used to construct a "volatility index" or "mushiness index" to determine which opinions are likely to be fickle (volatile) and which firm.[9] Yankelovich argues that the basic problem is not the problem of sampling but to determine whether we are measuring the target audience's real attitudes and opinions.

Question asking is in itself a persuasive device in that it helps structure the respondent's decision-making processes by framing the issues and by limiting possible answers. A slight change in the wording of a question can elicit a different answer even though the original and the revised question may seem to be of equivalent sense-meaning. The way a choice is framed can influence the answer e.g. consumers are worried about, versus consumers have not been worried about. This is particularly so when it comes to inquiring about wants and beliefs as respondents may not see the equivalencies in the questions being asked. For example, consider these two questions: "Do you agree the law should prohibit the manufacture of consumer products that are not biodegradable?" Versus "Do you believe manufacturers should be prohibited from producing disposable diapers?" These two questions produce very different degrees of support. Alternatively, the respondent may not see the connection so appears to be inconsistent: For example, "Do you want a fairer distribution of wealth?" Versus "Do you want an incomes redistribution policy?" Respondents may favor the former while condemning the latter. There is also the emotiveness of the words themselves. Thus just substituting the word "warm" for "cold" in a long description of a person, leads to a much more positive judgment of that person. Similarly words in questionnaires can have emotive meaning which can bias replies.

In general, it is taken for granted that respondents will be truthful; are able to understand whatever is asked; have stable opinions; have an excellent memory (embracing an effective information retrieval system), and last but not least have a very cooperative disposition. In practice, there are problems in determining whether replies will be truthful and whether respondents will understand the questions in the way intended. The sources of bias commonly given are:

- the grammatical form in which the question is worded;
- the words used;
- the number of response options provided;
- the order in which the questions are presented;
- whether there is or is not a socially appropriate reply;
- whether alternatives are presented pictorially or verbally;
- the interviewer's race, gender, socioeconomic level;
- the interviewer's manner and the guidance he or she offers; and
- the personality of the respondent since there are those who tend to be nay or yea sayers.

There is the further problem of ensuring respondents have the same frame of reference. There is no difficulty if we merely ask whether someone owns a car. But suppose we ask, "Do you consider yourself a very heavy, moderately heavy, or light drinker?" Answers to such questions do not allow meaningful comparisons as we do not know the frame of reference being used by respondents, that is, with whom are they comparing themselves? There is a need to ask about actual quantities drunk and even then we have the problem of memory.

An *anchor* is a reference point against which other choices are compared. Thus in asking, say, respondents whether they would be prepared to pay a certain sum for the product, this figure can become the anchor used by the respondent as a guide to its value so that when asked the amount they would pay for the product, their answer is influenced by this anchor.

This review of the problems involved with interview surveys draws attention to the fact that the method is not just a matter of getting the right sample size and choosing a random sample but the much more difficult task of human communication.

Many questionnaires are designed to measure attitudes toward a brand or its attributes. We have already discussed the multiattribute measure but there are many more measures and it is not altogether clear that all such measures provide equivalent results. We will discuss some of these other measures.

Semantic differential scale.   There is first the "semantic differential" scale (Figure 8.5 (b)). It was developed initially by Charles Osgood and co-workers for evaluating the sense-meaning of individual words. The subject or respondent rates the meaning of each item on a seven-point scale (sometimes a five-point scale to ease tabulation) along a number of dimensions such as like–dislike, weak–strong, tense–relaxed, and so on. A brand or company image, for example, can be evaluated on a seven-point scale for each of a series of bipolar attributes. Factor analysis of the data emanating from many applications of the scale have generally revealed three distinct dimensions:

a) evaluation: good–bad (extent to which the object judged favorably or unfavorably)
b) potency: strong–weak (the amount of strength needed to deal with the object)
c) activity: fast–slow (how quick the activity should be in relation to the object)

In marketing it is the value (evaluative) dimension that is most important since this is what makes the semantic differential scale an attitude measure. But the scale does assume intelligent and cooperative respondents since errors in using the scale are otherwise common. The essence of the technique lies in selecting a sample of descriptive but polar terms covering the three dimensions. In capturing "meaning" the semantic differential measure is more embracing than the usual attitude measure since attitude, as typically measured in marketing, is but one factor (mainly the evaluative factor) of meaning. A linking of the choices made by a respondent can be charted to depict pictorially the meaning of the object for the respondent (partially illustrated by Figure 8.5 (b)). For researchers who use the semantic differential in the way described, meaning is viewed as the mediating variable between the input of the stimuli and buying action. In this way, it is hoped the semantic differential will be a better predictor of action than other measures of attitude. But most marketers deviate from this conception of the semantic differential and use the term semantic differential to cover any scale that uses bipolar adjectives as end points!

Likert scale.   Another well-known scale is the "Likert scale" (see Figure 8.5 (c)) which is used primarily in the measurement of attitudes. The respondent is given a number of opinion statements, for example: "I think the company renders an excellent service to its customers." The respondent is asked to rate the statement according to his or her degree of agreement or disagreement. Usually there are five levels, running from "strongly agree" through "uncertain" to "strongly disagree," although, in marketing, scales with just three or more than seven choices are used and called Likert scales. The respondent's attitude is the summation of the individual ratings on each statement. The advantage of the Likert scale is that the resulting data are amenable to the statistical technique of factor analysis to determine the basic underlying dimensions of the attitude.

There are other scales, such as the itemized scale (see Figure 8.5 (d)) and the Guttman and Thurstone scales, which, although offering distinct advantages in terms of measurement, tend not to be used in marketing because of their complexity.

Pretesting of questionnaires.   Questionnaires always need to be pretested by interviewing a sample of the target population. A pretest covers all aspects of the questionnaire: question content; question sequence; question format and wording to identify likely problems associated with

- vagueness (not sure about the exact reference meaning of a term, say, like heavy drinker);
- ambiguity (likely confusion of terms); and
- meaningfulness to the respondent (to gain cooperation).

The protocol technique can be used in pretesting questionnaires by asking respondents to "think aloud" as they fill in the questionnaire. This can be a good way to discover likely problems particularly if followed by asking respondents to explain the meaning of the question and to elaborate on their replies.

Unstructured interviews. We now come to the question of "unstructured interviews." As these can be expensive in terms of time and cost, they need to be justified. Their justification is based on the limitations of standardized questionnaires.[10]

The questionnaire reflects the researcher's way of viewing of the "reality" of interest and assumes the researcher knows exactly what questions will elicit the information sought. But the subject's world and the world of the researcher can differ widely, with the distance between the respondent's world and that reflected in the questionnaire being increased by forced-choice questions which limit options and miss the richness of opinions. We expect respondents to reply to questions in a set way and not elaborate as would be the case in normal conversation. As a result, the full meaning of things to the respondent can get lost in the answers.

Critics claim that standardized questionnaires are least useful when the need is to understand some target customer group. This is because understanding some target group does not result from asking some set of predetermined questions but from "lengthy interaction" with individual members of the target group. This is where the unstructured interview is better. Unstructured interviews, where the respondent's replies are recorded exactly as spoken, have the advantage of utilizing "the respondent's own categories and world of meaning" though they give rise to problems in coding and interpretation. There are problems in interpretation because a person's answers yield both a *manifest* content (the unambiguous literal interpretation) and *latent* content (the underlying, tacit, concealed information conveyed by both what is said in the context and also by the tone of voice and nonverbal behavior).

Unstructured interviews are recommended when the range of possible answers is either unknown or too numerous; when the researcher wishes to avoid influencing answers by predetermined questions; and the researcher wants to understand respondents' own worlds of meaning and what is salient to them.

With unstructured interviews, there can be *free association interviews*, where respondents just give free rein to their thoughts, or there are *focused interviews*, where there are formalized introductory questions but otherwise respondents are free to answer any way they wish. Unstructured interviews are associated with qualitative research. They are key when a researcher needs to explore a topic and define likely areas of importance. They can also be an essential preliminary step before conducting a structured interview.

One such qualitative technique is that of recording the consumer's thoughts as he or she thinks aloud before, during and after buying as discussed earlier in talking about protocol analysis, and interpretative social science (*hermeneutics*). If we just asked people for their reasons for buying, several types of reasons could be given: reasons that are not the real reasons but rationalizations or simply justificatory reasons that did not enter into the buying decision. More of the real reasons for buying are likely to be captured when we record at the time what people have to say as they go about buying: before buying; during buying and after buying. It is better to just let subjects talk since questioning can direct attention to factors that played no role in their decision but which they might feel they should endorse. Verbal reports are less useful when subjects are asked to remember what they thought rather than report their thoughts as they happen. In recording what people say, tape recorders may be used since they record the hesitations and tone of voice which, when added to interviewer notes on situational factors and nonverbal behavior, can greatly assist in interpreting what was actually said. However, the transcription from tapes can be very time consuming while some respondents are uncomfortable speaking near a tape recorder.

Focus groups.   A major technique in qualitative research is the "focus group" interview which brings together, say, six to ten consumers for an open-ended discussion about some product or product-related behaviors. Focus groups have been used to help, say, define the shape, features, and performance of products like cars. But focus groups have many critics. Participants can be influenced in their replies by group influences while relying on a fickle long-term memory. Critics argue that focus groups are best used to try out ideas, and cannot be expected to throw up radically new ideas but only incremental improvements. As one researcher in the auto industry says: "Drivers have a difficult time imagining something better than what they already own." Advocates of focus groups, on the other hand, argue that focus groups are good for gauging what consumers think is important and are an excellent source for advertising themes or words to use in advertising to give an advertisement authenticity while providing a symbolic link with the subculture of some target group (e.g. the use of the word "zits" instead of "skin blemish" in an ad directed at US youth).

Postal (*mail*) surveys.   Surveys need not be carried out by interview but by mail using self-administered questionnaires. The major advantage of a **postal survey** is usually the saving in cost. But cost may not be the main reason for adopting this method. A problem with the personal interview is that a respondent may give a different answer if she had time to reflect or consult records. This is important on occasions particularly in industrial marketing. The mail survey gives time for the respondent to reflect and consult others. But these advantages seldom outweigh the disadvantage of a low return rate, its slowness and the impersonal imprint. The low return rate is reinforced when the researcher uses a lengthy questionnaire. Thus one lifestyle questionnaire sent to consumers consists of 64 questions, covering 20 pages with each question split into many subquestions. The first question on activities undertaken lists 38 activities with the respondent being asked whether he or she watches TV, swims, or whatever, "at least once per week," "twice a month or so," "once a month or less," or "not at all in the past two months." In any case, there is no way such a questionnaire would get a random sample of the population to reply. There is a need to contact personally a sample of those who do not respond to gauge whether, and in what way, they might differ from those who did respond. It is better to send questionnaires by first class mail so those not delivered are returned while hand addressing the envelope and the use of attractive stamps as opposed to franking, may at least stimulate people to look at the contents.

Whether surveys are conducted through the mail or by interview, there is a problem of the "don't knows." A high percentage of "don't knows" results in serious bias unless we can assume they occur randomly over all the categories into which the respondents are grouped. The "don't knows" may reflect a genuine "no preference," in which case the answer should be recorded as such. In other cases, the "don't knows" may reflect a deficiency in the way the question is worded. One author, for example, cites the case of a question demanding a too precise answer ("How high is your heel?"), which needs to be made less precise to reduce the percentage of "don't knows" (for example, "Would you say your heels are high, medium or low?").[11] Respondents may also be helped by a funnel approach, where an initial broad question leads to more narrowly focused ones. For instance, "How many loaves of bread did you buy last week?" can be reduced to two questions: "How often did you buy bread last week?" and "How many loaves did you buy each time?"

Motivation research.   The next technique in Figure 8.4 is motivation research. This refers to the use of intensive, disguised, qualitative, clinical procedures for discovering subconscious motives. Group discussions and depth interviewing are the main techniques used. At one extreme is the fairly structured approach with predetermined opening questions followed by nondirective probes. (A *probe* is a comment or question to elicit more information without biasing the reply.) At the other extreme is the psychoanalytic-type interview designed to explore the emotional context and symbolic meanings associated with products, brand-names or whatever. Focus groups are often used to generate motivation research data, usually employing *projective techniques*. The basic assumption lying behind projective techniques is that, the more ambiguous the stimulus, the greater the scope for respondents to project their basic motivations into their answers. The motivations and personality characteristics of the respondent are said to be revealed as the respondent is ostensibly engaged in, say, telling a story around some figures presented by the interviewer. There are several projective techniques:

- *"association"* techniques such as word association tests where the subject is presented with a word and asked to say immediately what it brings to mind;
- *"construction"* techniques such as picture interpretations, where the respondent is asked to construct a story about some picture;
- *"completion"* techniques such as sentence completion, where the subject is asked to complete a sentence at high speed;
- *"expressive"* techniques such as play therapy where the emphasis is on the way subjects express their emotions as they play.

In focus groups, construction techniques and completion techniques used in combination are probably the most common forms of projective techniques used. Thus, one bank interested in the buying behavior of those taking out a mortgage gave each member of the focus group a drawing of two figures (a man and a woman) looking at advertisements for mortgage loans and asked them to talk about what was going through the minds of the couple. They were asked also to complete sentences such as the following: "Buying a home, I worry most about . . ." and "The worst thing about getting a mortgage . . ." Verbal self-reports, too, are used as a basis for clinical psychoanalytic interpretation if it is suspected the self-reports are mere rationalizations concealing the true unconscious determinants of behavior.

Motivation research reached the height of its popularity in the 1950s and 1960s based on its claim to identify unconscious motives for buying. But the problem lies in demonstrating that motivation research findings are reliable in that a common training of analysts does not guarantee that interpretations of the data from, say, projective techniques will not differ widely. Apart from this, there is a bias against psychoanalytic interpretations as they seem to undermine the view of ourselves as having personal autonomy and being capable of exhibiting a high degree of rationality. But advertising agencies commonly draw on motivation research techniques as a source of ideas, usually in conjunction with focus groups.

Buying panels.   The final technique under the heading of interrogation is the buying panel which is commonly used to determine buying habits and shifts in buying. Buying panels can be very large with panels in the United States having a base from which to draw of around 300,000 households.

Buying panels have received a new lease of life with the development of the Universal Product Code (the block of black stripes known as the bar code that goes on over 90 percent of goods in many countries). More than half of supermarket purchases in the United States (around one third in Western Europe) are made at stores with scanning devices that read these codes. This allows stores to know what brands are selling and to compare store sales. But, more important, it allows the seller to learn a good deal also. Members of a panel can be given store cards. When they shop, the cashier at the store types their identity code into the computerized cash register. When the bar codes on the items bought are scanned, the computer records the purchases and records the information on the customer's file. In this way the buying patterns and preferences of the families are recorded. Such information can be correlated with the shopper's TV viewing and reading habits. It may even be that the cable TV programs watched by panel members do not always carry the regularly scheduled commercials but send out test commercials to gauge the effect on buying.

Buying panels are controversial. There is first the problem of generalizing from a sample that may not be very representative. Even if panel members were initially representative of the target population, they may not continue to be since membership of the panel may change behavior, for example, in making them more sensitive to prices etc. But, in respect to supermarket data, the very richness of the data has up to now muted much criticism.

Experiment

Experiment should be preceded by observation of the behavior of interest so as to avoid the laboratory experiment being too remote from the real world. In the controlled experiment the interest lies in, say, establishing the precise relationship between independent variable X and dependent variable Y. A variable is any quality, property, or characteristic that differs in degree like income or in kind like gender. Some variables are continuous like age and others categorical like gender where the categories (male, female) are mutually exclusive instead of continuous. However, some variables can be treated as either categorical or continuous. For example, we can categorize hair color into exclusive categories (dark, light) or measure hair color along a scale from dark to light. In an experiment, the *independent* variable is the one manipulated or given the treatment while the variable it is assumed to influence is the *dependent* variable.

The effect of some stimulus, X, on the buyer's response, Y, can be influenced by:

1 other contemporary events affecting the buyer;
2 the buyer's wants and beliefs changing during the period under consideration; and
3 the actual measurements made by the observer.

These three sets of variables are *extraneous* variables as they need to be eliminated or controlled so as not to distort the effect of the independent variable. In order to control or eliminate the effect of these three factors, we set up "control" and "experimental" groups that are matched either through random selection or some formal selection procedures. The group exposed to the different levels of the independent variable is the *experimental group*, with the *control group* being exposed to all the factors or variables that influence the experimental group *except* for the independent variable. We seek to isolate the differential effects of X on Y by seeking to eliminate the effects of other factors. For example, suppose:

E_1 = the state of experimental group before the experiment e.g. performance = 110
E_2 = the state of the experimental group after the experiment e.g. performance = 120
G_1 = the state of the control group before the experiment e.g. performance = 110
G_2 = the state of the control group after the experiment e.g. performance 115;

$$\text{Then the effect} = (E_2 - E_1) - (G_2 - G_1) = (120 - 110) - (115 - 110) = 5$$

The statistical technique of "analysis of variance" can now be used to check whether this result could have arisen by chance. But there is still no certainty. In the first place, matching control and experimental groups by age, gender, etc. makes the assumption that we know what factors are relevant, but this may not be so. There may be other factors (genetic, biochemical etc.) of which we are presently unaware. In any case, contrary to what is commonly believed, the controlled experiment does not prove some cause. Although experiments can be highly corroborative, they may still fail to distinguish true cause from mere coexistence. Also consumers themselves change. For example, I may undertake an experiment and find that putting a chocolate on the pillow of each hotel guest has a positive effect on their attitudes and good will toward the hotel. But it may be perceived as rather "corny" and mechanical when imitated by every other hotel.

The effects of several independent variables (for example, the gender of the buyer; whether or not exposed to the advertisement) on a dependent variable (for example, the number of purchases made) can be measured by "factorial analysis of variance." A factorial design sets out all the combinations of the factors. If there were just two factors (for example, gender and exposure to advertisement) and each factor has two levels (for example, male or female or exposed or not exposed to the advertisement), then the

		Exposure	
		A_1 (exposed)	A_2 (not exposed)
Sex	B_1 (male)	E_2 (male)	G_2 (male)
	B_2 (female)	E_2 (female)	G_2 (female)

Figure 8.6 Factorial design

number of combinations to test = 2^n where n = the number of factors and 2 = the number of levels. The position is illustrated in Figure 8.6.

In considering the effect of several different stimuli or factors on several different groups, we can use one of many so-called Latin square designs. For example, if we aim to gauge the effect of four different point-of-purchase aids, A, B, C, D, in each of four towns 1, 2, 3, 4, for each of four socioeconomic groups, I, II, III, IV, the number of combinations to be tested is shown in the matrix in Figure 8.7. The experimental results, which would be inserted in each of the cells, are checked by analysis of variance to judge whether the results could be explained by chance. The particular Latin square design in Figure 8.7 was used to determine the effect on apple sales in conditions where:[12]

- no promotion was undertaken
- a promotion campaign was undertaken stressing the uses to which apples could be put
- a promotion campaign was undertaken stressing the benefits to health of eating apples.

Six towns, similar in size and economic profile, and twelve types of food stores within each town were selected, and the three different "treatments" of no promotion, health-theme and use-theme were given in six towns. The result indicated that the "use-theme" was the better strategy.

Although *field experiments* like the above are much more realistic than those conducted in a laboratory, the control is less, as a field experiment is subject to many potential influences. But with laboratory experiments there is more doubt about "external validity." *Internal validity* is concerned with whether the tools used measure what they are supposed to measure like attitudes, while *external validity* is concerned with the generalization of the findings to the marketplace. Often the answer is that results cannot be generalized to the world outside the laboratory but to insist on generalization is often to miss the point of much experimentation which is to show that certain relationships

Town

		1	2	3	4
	I	D	A	B	C
Socioeconomic level	II	C	D	A	B
	III	B	C	D	A
	IV	A	B	C	D

Figure 8.7 Latin square design

do or can in fact exist even if they can only be detected in laboratory conditions. Research findings should also be *reliable*, that is, findings should be replicable. Validity presupposes reliability, though studies can be reliable but not valid.

There are also *natural* experiments or studies of naturally occurring events where it is impossible to divide groups into experimental and control groups. A natural experiment might consist of comparing the performance of two sales force teams where the financial incentive scheme was different. For differences to be meaningful the two groups would have to be alike in all significant respects except for the way they are paid.

Nonpure types

Simulation. The final category in Figure 8.4 is a miscellaneous set, covering computer simulation, sensory evaluation, and test marketing. All are common in new product development and will be discussed more in our discussion on product management. But a word about simulation. *Simulations* are imitations of real situations in which the many variables are just mixed together to see what happens with no attempt at systematic control. Business games are simulations while board games like chess and Monopoly are simulations of conflicts. In computer simulation the computer is programmed to behave in a manner analogous to thought processes or behavior. But the critical element is the program since this represents the theory of behavior which is under examination. Simulations are typically used when situations are complex but simulations with people as players can be artificial as those involved are not involved in the same way as they would be in real life.

The *shopping game* illustrates both the laboratory-type simulation and an experiment. In one such game, participants were asked to simulate a shopping trip.[13] Each was told the amount she or he would have to spend, the brands available for purchase and their prices. However, the prices of the brands were systematically varied to gauge the effect on the amount bought as a basis for estimating demand at different prices. It is difficult to judge whether such games sufficiently represent real-world behavior for the purpose of prediction: there is a need for follow-up studies to establish whether subsequent behavior was in fact in accordance with what the results of the game would have predicted. But not all simulation studies are interested in demonstrating predictive power but merely with understanding how the factors in a situation are likely to interact.

Sensory evaluation. Sensory evaluation to test the psychophysical properties of products are common particularly in the food industry. Judges may be asked to rate items along some scale (sweet to nonsweet) or asked to compare two versions of the product or participate in blind tests where the judges are not given the product's identity or a double blind test where neither judge nor researcher knows the identity. This topic and the topic of test marketing are considered in Chapter 10.

Typical uses of the various methods of data collection are shown in Figure 8.8. All methods have shortcomings: for interrogation it is the possibility of bias; for observation it is the possibility of unreliability, while for experimentation it is artificiality. Hence it is preferable to use several research techniques, each with different shortcomings.

DATA ANALYSIS AND TECHNIQUES OF ANALYSIS

Editing, coding, tabulating, and interpreting

The data collected in surveys must be "edited," "coded," "tabulated," and "interpreted." The purpose of *editing* is to eliminate data that are irrelevant or unsatisfactory in some other way. *Coding* refers to the process of categorizing answers and allocating to the different categories a numerical code to facilitate the transfer of the answers for computer analysis. Since coding is facilitated by a set of options that are exhaustive and mutually exclusive, open-ended questions make coding difficult particularly when responses are recorded verbatim. However, with the multiple choice type of questionnaire, scoring is straightforward and can be done by hand (if need be) which has the advantage of providing a better grasp of responses. Finally, when the data are coded, they are *tabulated* and *interpreted*.

Information is like headlights to a night driver: it illuminates the road ahead but does not rule out the need for good judgment. It is in the interpretation of marketing research findings that good judgment is important. On the other hand, what data are collected and by what method will shape that interpretation in that marketing research findings will mirror the procedures used to collect data. Thus data collected on customer choice criteria are very different if collected through questionnaires as opposed to protocols, recording the consumer's thoughts before buying, during buying and after buying. Interpretation judges the meaning and significance of the results. But the results are structured by the way the basic data are collected. A common bias in interpreting all marketing research data is "attentional bias" where the analyst focuses on that which lends support to existing beliefs and fails to look for the evidence against such beliefs.

Managers often feel more secure with figures as these seem to represent the hard evidence. As Yankelovich words it:[14]

1 *Observation*

a) Obtrusive e.g. Study of how product is used and with what.
      e.g. Study of shopping behavior at supermarket, say, effect of location of
      brand in store on sales.
b) Unobtrusive e.g. As above but when observation or interrogation might give rise to bias.

2 *Interrogation*

Interview

a) Structured
 • Personal interview, e.g. factual data about consumer of not-too-personal nature.
 • Phone interview, e.g. when less inhibited replies sought, cheapness counts, and every
  member of target audience has a phone.

b) Unstructured — getting ideas from customers.
 • Free association, e.g. image research, establishing associations.
 • Focused, e.g. to give free reign to thoughts but within some time constraint.

Postal
Industrial marketing usually, e.g. about buying intentions. Allows consultation but difficult getting
replies.

Motivation Research
You believe in unconscious motivations in buying and want to tap them for advertising ideas.

Buying Panels
For continuous monitoring of buying behavior in relation, say, to TV viewing.

3 *Controlled experiment*

Desirability research—for identifying and comparing consequences/effects of different mix
options, e.g. packaging, pricing options, or sales force actions.

4 *Non-pure types*

Simulation — see ASSESSOR model pp. 395
Test Marketing — see p. 397–399

Figure 8.8 Typical uses of various methods of data collection

They can accept as genuine knowledge only those data that can be quantified. Some
business clients, if an insight cannot be expressed in the form of a statistic, cannot
deal with it. They are just plain uncomfortable with qualitative insights. Even when
these express an important truth and the statistics are superficial, they prefer the
statistics. The quantitative approach to knowledge seems more scientific to them, and
it promises greater objectivity and control. The qualitative approach undermines their
feeling of mastery and control; it makes them anxious.

But many insights and feelings, important for understanding the consumer, cannot be captured in figures. Figures in any case do not speak for themselves but have to be explicated and interpreted: figures always leave a good deal of scope for exercising judgment as to what the figures mean for marketing.

Mathematical/statistical techniques of analysis

Statistics and mathematics inevitably play a role in marketing research. In the first place, sample data is typically presented in the form of percentage estimates like estimates of market share, brand awareness and so on. An important part of the interpretation of these estimates involves statistical analysis.

If we interviewed a random sample of 400 of our target population and 120 of them said they were familiar with our brand, we would want to ask: How probable is it that the figure of 120/400 or 30 percent represents the position rather than something that could have come about by chance? Alternatively, we might ask how many interviews must be made to establish this percentage with a plus or minus 2 percent accuracy, at the usual 95 percent level of confidence? As most reading this book will probably know, it is simple to calculate the answers: that at the 95 percent level of confidence, the true population figure would be 30 percent plus or minus 4.6 percent while the sample size needed to reduce this to 2 percent accuracy, at the 95 percent level of confidence, would be 2,100. But all this assumes a random sample has been taken which may not be the case. In fact it is most common in marketing to draw conclusions from nonrandom samples but to treat them as if they were! Also there is the question of the confidence limit selected. A conclusion is always relative to the preassigned confidence level. Unfortunately, a more rigorous confidence level requires a more expensive investigation, which must be set against the fact that a low cost investigation can result in relevant effects remaining concealed.

The role of mathematics and statistics in marketing is to bring out the implications of the data: implications that remain hidden unless such techniques are employed. Quantitative analysis expresses in succinct symbolic form the pattern of relationships found among the data collected while measurement is needed to make comparisons between actual results and those predicted as well as trying to make qualitative distinctions more precise. In fact, although it is common to talk of mathematics ignoring all qualitative distinctions, both mathematical and statistical techniques presuppose that qualitative differences exist and help make it possible to recognize many qualitative distinctions that would otherwise be ignored. However, mathematics is not some miracle tool for creating knowledge out of nothing. *To bring out the implications of data is not to create but to infer. No amount of quantification can make up for a poor conceptual base: much qualitative thinking and conceptualization precedes fruitful quantification.* Poor marketing thinking does not become sound simply by being expressed in mathematical terms, but neither does poor marketing thinking become convincing by showing disdain for all mathematical reasoning.

At the problem diagnosis stage, the market researcher may build some mathematical model to test some hypothesis. Whenever the study of the structure of system X is useful for understanding that of system Y, the structure of X is a model of Y. In practice, the term model is used much more loosely in marketing to mean any representation of some or all of the properties of the larger system. But a model will always have features that are unique to the model itself, just as the written word, as a model of the spoken language, has unique features. If a model were a perfect match to reality, there would be no need for the model. Models are analogies that, like all analogies, break down at some point. When this is forgotten there is a danger of identifying warranted assertions about the model with warranted assertions about the system being modeled. This can happen with game theory and the use of the computer as a model of the mind. Also, in the case of mathematical models, it is all too easy for original, creative insights to be buried, as far as the manager is concerned, "under a cenotaph of technical virtuosity and unacknowledged sterility."

In marketing, we draw on existing models in mathematics to see if such models can be used to represent marketing processes, just as marketers used the Markov chain from mathematics to simulate brand-switching behavior, or borrowed from statistical theoretical distributions. Such existing models are known as *synthetic models*, as they exist abstractly quite apart from any relevance they might have for marketing. However, they are only appropriate to the extent that their structures do in fact correspond to some real marketing situation. There is always a need to check. In checking a model, the manager needs to confirm that the model contains the relevant and only the relevant variables while checking that the assumed relationships among the variables makes sense.

Scales.   Numbers can stand for a number of properties in the real world:

a) *identity*: numbers can be used as labels to identify items. Where numbers are used just to identify, the scale of measurement is called a *nominal scale*.
b) *order*: numbers can be used to show the rank order of items. Numbers that order items use an *ordinal scale*.
c) *intervals*: numbers can be used to reflect distances among items. Numbers used to reflect distances between items use an *interval scale*.
d) *ratios*: numbers can be used to reflect ratios among items. Numbers used to reflect ratios use a *ratio scale*.

Each of the above scales has its own characteristics that affect what mathematical manipulations can be carried out:

1 *Nominal scale.* Any data obtained from a dichotomous question such as "Would you or would you not shop here?" fall into the nominal scale. The nominal scale also covers any data that are simply in categories, as occurs when, say, an interviewer asks a respondent to place a brand in categories such as old-fashioned, trustworthy and so on. The nominal scale allows us to count numbers to show frequency distributions or bar charts but not much else.
2 *Ordinal scale.* In an ordinal scale, items are ordered from "most" to "least." For example, the data obtained from the request to the respondent to "Arrange the

following brands in order of preference" would fall into an ordinal scale. We would not, however, be able to measure the distance that separates one preference from the next. The Likert scale discussed earlier is an ordinal scale, although it is usually treated as something more for the purpose of statistical analysis as, strictly speaking, an ordinal scale only permits the calculation of correlations on the ranked data and the calculations of medians: it does not allow addition or subtraction and so rules out multiplication and division.

3 *Interval scale.* This is a true metric scale justifying the use of the term "measuring" rather than just "scaling." The intervals between the successive measurements are represented by the distances between the points. Nonetheless the starting point is arbitrary. Thus the time interval between the year A.D. 100 and A.D. 200 is the same as that between A.D. 400 and A.D. 500, but the year A.D. 200 is an arbitrary starting point, so that it makes no sense to say that the year A.D. 200 is twice as much time as the year 100. Temperature (Celsius and Fahrenheit) and IQ are similarly intervally scaled.

4 *Ratio scale.* This is the type of measurement we do with a ruler since there is a true absolute zero point. Because this zero point is not set in an arbitrary way, multiplication and division and all other mathematical manipulations are possible.

Most statistical manipulations assume that data are at least measured on an interval scale. Thus in treating the Likert and the other scales shown in Figure 8.5 as interval scales and ratio scales, we are violating the rules of mathematics. But all researchers in marketing do it as they opt for the advantages of using sophisticated statistical tools against the unknown error arising from transgressing the rules of measurement. When added to the fact that the sample is not likely to have been a true random one in the first place, it should make researchers hold back from dogmatic claims.

There is another important reason for discussing measurement and this has to do with the weighing up of evidence in favor of some hypothesis or theory. No one has yet succeeded in developing a way of measuring on an interval or ratio scale the evidence to measure the truth of some theory or hypothesis. Thus we cannot say the difference between the evidence for theory "A" and the evidence for theory "B" is 20 points in its favor or that there is 20 percent more evidence favoring "A" over "B." If we could there would be little need for juries in criminal cases! What we do expect is for those who have examined the evidence to agree on a ranking so as to be able to say that there is more evidence (but not how much evidence) favoring "A" than "B" so we will go with "A." But the fragmentation of the social sciences, resting on even basic disputes as to the nature of the human animal, shows that even this, on occasions, seems to be asking too much.

The interval and ratio scales assume that whatever is being measured has a single, unidimensional, underlying *continuum* (for example, going from very sweet to very sour). However, many attitudes, for example, toward a product or whatever, do not lie along a single continuum. They are really multidimensional but are often made to fall along a continuum by using indices. For example, the IQ is really multidimensional (being composed of several dimensions such as comprehension, reasoning ability, spatial ability and so on) but the IQ index allows the ranking of intelligence scores along a continuum. But instead of being represented by an index, intelligence could be represented by a set of aptitude scores. In such a case, there is no single IQ score but as many numbers as there are dimensions of intelligence.

What has been said about intelligence can be said about, say, preference. There are many reasons for preferring one brand to another, and the various factors or attributes entering into preference can also be represented by points in space with as many numbers as there are dimensions of preference. Such representation and measurement fall under the heading of "multidimensional scaling." *Multidimensional* refers to variables and factors that lie along more than one dimension. While *multidimensional analysis* is a method of identifying the small number of dimensions that may account for the variability observed in a large number of scales in respect to, say, some preference, *multidimensional scaling* is the statistical procedure for making a multidimensional analysis.

In marketing, multidimensional scaling typically starts with the judgments of consumers as to their preferences for certain brands or their judgments of similarity among brands. The aim of the analysis is to identify the underlying dimensions behind these judgments. As shown in the chapter on segmentation, multidimensional scaling can be used to produce perceptual maps where brands perceived as most alike are placed closest to each other on the map while consumer preference data produce maps that show the consumer ideal points. But the underlying dimensions are not always easy to interpret while the technique assumes at least eight brands are involved.

Multivariate analysis is common in the analysis of marketing research data where the term has come to mean those techniques which consider simultaneously the effects and the influences of a number of different variables. "Simultaneously" because the variables may be interrelated and these interrelationships cannot be established if the variables are examined individually. The most widely used multivariate techniques are *multiple regression* and "correlation." Multiple regression is used to obtain a relationship between just *one* "dependent" variable and one or more independent variables. In establishing such a relationship, it is hoped that the value of the dependent variable can be predicted when the values of the independent variables are known. While the actual values of the dependent variable are given in the multiple regression, the purpose of *correlation analysis* is to measure how well the regression equation fits the data from which it was obtained. The overall fit is measured by the *multiple correlation coefficient*: the closer this is to 1, the better the fit. The Pearson product-moment coefficient is one correlation measure for continuous variables while the Spearman rank-order coefficient is a correlation measure for ranked data.

Partial correlation coefficients may also be calculated to measure the degree to which the variables are interrelated or are redundant to each other. This allows us to examine a large number of variables and screen out the ones that are redundant. Of course, what is being established in multiple regression and correlation are purely mathematical relationships. Thus, as every course in logic and elementary statistics stresses, establishing a high correlation does not establish causation. However, it does provide evidence in that causation is one reason for correlation. Nonetheless, it is all too easy to assume a cause and effect relationship exists when none in fact does.

X and Y can be related without influencing each other. They may, for example, be expressions of the same thing such as an expression of the same lifestyle. Thus, in the 1980s, among a certain group of young male adults, we were told there was in the United

States a strong association between the possession of a Rolex watch and the buying of a BMW car; not cause and effect but the expression of the "yuppie" lifestyle. In any case, the relationship between X and Y may form an interacting system where X affects Y and Y affects X. Just as mental illness can cause physical illness and physical illness can cause mental illness, attitudes can affect behavior and behavior can affect attitudes. An even more relevant issue, when it comes to looking at high correlational data is the question of *stability* in that relationships found in past data may not project into the future, given a dynamic market with wants and beliefs changing all the time.

Multiple regression and correlation are the tools most commonly used in academic research for most pedestrian studies. For example, someone suggests a credible measure of some construct such as brand loyalty and, with the measure of loyalty in place, dozens of other researchers seek correlations with variables such as age, social class, and so on! *Yet correlations are important since together with probability theory and hypotheses testing, they are the foundation for most of our beliefs in social science.*

What are the factors underlying intelligence? The technique of *factor analysis* was first developed by psychologists to answer such questions. The term "factor analysis" serves as an umbrella term for a number of statistical procedures whose function is to identify such underlying factors. One major application in marketing has been to try to find the basic factors underlying the consumer's preferences, that is, the most salient attributes involved in evaluating brands within some product category. Factor analysis seeks to establish the underlying factors that can mathematically account for the correlations between, say, a sample of consumers' attitude ratings on the salient attributes of each of the brands. Those that correlate highly with each other become identified as representing a single factor. The actual correlation between a particular variable (brand rating) and the particular factor presumed to underlie a set of variables is called the *"factor loading."* The variables that do not correlate with each other are identified as representing orthogonal (or independent) factors. The aim of factor analysis is to identify a small number of factors each of which would be orthogonal to each other which means they would lie at right angles to each other when graphed.

One of the earliest studies in marketing tried to find the basic factors underlying consumers' preferences for various kinds of meats; beef, lamb, fish, pork, and poultry.[15] The consumers' attitudes to each of the meats were measured and the correlations between the attitude ratings for each type of meat with every other kind of meat were calculated, so we had the correlation between attitude ratings on, say, beef with the attitude ratings on pork and so on. The next stage was to analyze the array or matrix of correlation coefficients to isolate the underlying factors. The procedures after this are all strictly statistical while the factors that emerge from the analysis rest purely on interpretation. The factors that emerge from the analysis have to be judged subjectively to determine if they make sense since it is always possible to think of other factors that could be equally valid given the data.

A *cluster* in statistics is any group of contiguous elements (e.g. a group of people living in the same house) of a statistical population. *Cluster analysis* in statistics is similar to factor analysis in that both involve the search for unitary elements, in this case clusters rather than factors to account for the variability observed in the data. Cluster analysis in marketing is used to demonstrate that members of subgroups like those in market segments are more similar in relevant respects to each other than to members of other subgroups or segments.

Another technique that uses the same basic input data as factor analysis is *discriminant analysis*. This brings statistics to bear on a major problem in classification. Given that some item could have come from one of several clusters or populations, the problem is to allocate it to a population with the minimum likely error. Thus, which set of attributes best discriminates among brands? For example, discriminant analysis has been used to distinguish between Ford and Chevrolet buyers on the basis of nine attitude scales and to distinguish between creditworthy and credit-unworthy loan applicants.

One final technique to which we will be returning in the chapters on product management is *conjoint measurement* which is measurement where that which is being measured like consumer preference is composed of two or more elements, which can trade off for each other. For example, a consumer's preference for a particular make of car is made up of elements or attributes like price, styling, size such that, for example, an increase in price may shift preference dramatically even though all else has remained constant. In marketing, conjoint measurement is being used primarily to determine which combination of attributes the consumer most prefers.

International aspects

Companies often wish to repeat the same survey in international markets as done at home. There are problems in that a questionnaire can be distorted in translation or, at least, the questions may not have precisely the same meaning. The rule here is to have someone else translate the questionnaire back into the original language. There is, too, the matter of cultural values, the unwillingness of consumers to respond, and business firms being reluctant to give any information about themselves. There is also the matter of literacy level as this restricts postal surveys while telephone surveys are restricted in most countries to the wealthy. No marketing executive can assume consumers abroad are just like those at home and that organizational buyers are similarly motivated.

Some general comments.   A problem in all marketing research is the problem of "dirty data." Whenever multiple sources of data on the same phenomena are tapped, it is common to find much inconsistency among the different data sources. Thus one survey among consumers might suggest the brand has a 30 percent market share while a store audit might put the figure at no more than 18 percent. This is not uncommon which makes many marketing managers somewhat skeptical about techniques that assume perfectly valid data on which to build a superstructure of statistical inference. Valid information is expensive and, at every stage, the manager is balancing off the value of more valid data against its cost. A marketing manager, too, must recognize that all marketing problems are not simply puzzles that can be solved by marketing research. At every stage judgment has to be exercised; judgment that has been sharpened by immersion in the market and not just by acquaintance with the figures. Although textbooks on marketing research focus on method, usually quantitative methods, methods alone are not enough: there is also the need to ask the right questions which goes back to our understanding of the market. Such understanding does not just come about from an accumulation of past research findings but from hard thinking, being human, and part of the target audience. Such understanding and insights should not be cast to one side in the belief that marketing research is some final authority. Sometimes it is but sometimes it is not as we may have other evidence from our own experience. There is no infallible knowledge generated by marketing research or any other method and all research findings should be viewed critically if we are not to substitute formula for thought. It is commonly pointed out that much of the conventional wisdom in marketing is not backed by the sort of empirical studies (validated theory or generalizations of high probability) that are needed. There are no universal laws when it comes to behavior in the market so empirical evidence consists of statistical generalizations. But statistical generalizations may not go beyond the population from which they were drawn; the product and country involved; the time at which the study was conducted and so on. Where generalizations are theoretically grounded, we have more confidence in them and can perhaps identify the conditions under which they are more likely to apply. For example, take the generalization that people seek to avoid risk. Further investigation has shown that risks imposed on consumers or appear to be beyond their control are more salient to consumers than those they assume themselves. Similarly, natural risks are less threatening than man-made risks while the risks arising from exotic technologies generate more dread than those involving familiar technologies. While generalizations are useful in drawing attention to factors, applying such generalizations to the individual case is a matter of judgment as to representativeness. Thus to say that half of all new product launches, of which X is one, will fail, says nothing specific about product X. Product X may fail or it may not fail, but saying the probability of failure is 0.5 predicts neither one nor the other of these two possible outcomes.

As the situation determines what applies, marketing "genius" often appears a matter of selecting, what after the fact, seems like a truism. Much in marketing is a matter of applying marketing concepts and a trained marketing mind to the situation. If I say that a small firm should preferably seek a niche and avoid taking on the giants head on, the reader, on reflection, would view this as a common-sense generalization, with the logic of the situation determining the exceptional cases. Although this example is too simple, much in marketing is of this nature. In any case, those marketing managers who would demand empirical evidence for every statement made would wait for ever. While pure rational reflection is not enough, nor is mere empirical data: neither the rational nor the empirical can function without the other even if the combination is nothing more than a rational assessment of experience. But it is the balance that is debated and the question of what counts as evidence (as an extreme consider the atheist versus the Christian). The behaviorist would have a very narrow concept of acceptable empirical evidence while the game theorist would fall back on simply the rational thing to do.

The report

A report is always written with an audience in mind. This means that researchers must put themselves in the reader's place and imagine the reader's needs, given that person's responsibilities. In this way, researchers can identify what the reader wishes to know in line with those needs. The most significant findings should be put first. Statistical detail is inappropriate for the body of the report and most of the statistical analysis can be put into an appendix. Although we think of marketing research reports as fairly factual and incontroversial, this is not always so. Findings are not necessarily welcome and readers may pick on minor errors to discredit the whole report. Hence time spent in turning out a thorough report is time well spent.

NOTES

1 Glazer, Rashi (1991) "Marketing in an Information Intensive Environment: Strategic Implications of Knowledge as an Asset," *Journal of Marketing*, 55 (October).
2 Little, John (1975) "Brandaid: a Marketing Mix Model part 1 and part 2," *Operations Research*, 23 (July–August).
3 Larréché, Jean–Claude and Srinivasan, V. (1982) "Statport: a Model for the Evaluation and Formulation of Business Portfolio Strategies," *Management Science*, 28(9) (September).
4 Penzias, Arno (1989) *Ideas and Information*, New York: Touchstone Books, Preface.
5 Polanyi, Michael (1962) *Personal Knowledge*, Chicago: University of Chicago Press.
6 Kelly, George (1963) *A Theory of Personality*, New York: Norton.
7 Webb, E. J., Campbell, D. T., Schwartz, R. D., and Sechrest, L. (1966) *Unobtrusive Measures*, Chicago: Rand McNally, p. 24.
8 Bickman, L. (1976) "Data Collection; Observational Methods" in C. Selltiz, L. S. Wrightman, and S. W. Cook, *Research Methods in Social Relations*, New York: Holt, Rinehart and Winston.
9 Yankelovich, Daniel (1991) *Coming to Public Judgment: Making Democracy Work in a Complex World*, Syracuse University Press.
10 Reinharz, Shulamit (1991) *On Becoming a Social Scientist*, New Brunswick, NJ: Transaction Publishers.
11 Zeisel, Hans (1968) *Say It With Figures*, New York: Harper Row.
12 Henderson, P. L., Hind, J. F., and Brown, S. E. (1961) "Sales Effects of two Campaign Themes," *Journal of Advertising Research*, 1 (December).
13 Pessemier, E. A. (1960) "An Experimental Method for Estimating Demand," *Journal of Business*, 33 (4).
14 Yankelovich, *op cit.*, p. 188.
15 Gatty, R. (1966) "Multivariate Analysis for Marketing Research: An Evaluation," *Applied Statistics*, XV (3).

Part IV

Marketing mix eleme

Chapter 9

Product management: needs, policies, and strategies

These next two chapters deal with anticipating and adapting to changes in demand. If an organization is to continue to exist, it needs to anticipate the impact of technological developments, increasing competition and changing fashions. Seldom do organizations have the luxury of developing an offering and continuing to sell it, unchanging, for the working life of the firm's managers: standing still is not an option. With the passage of time, competitive advantages erode as competitive offerings emerge, improve and intensify their appeal. Sometimes the firm can prevent such erosion but sometimes the firm is unable to prevent a product's decline, with the possibility that harvesting or divesting might have to be considered. Even if a firm does continue to hold a dominant market position, growth for a one-product firm is limited by the size of the market, and further growth may depend on the development of new products.

This chapter considers:

1 the extent to which the idea that products have a life cycle, offers guidance for product planning;
2 the need for policies to direct product management; and
3 ways to upgrade the firm's offerings.

The next chapter deals with the whole process of developing new products.

THE PRODUCT LIFE CYCLE

As a specific pattern of sales over the life of the product

The belief that a product follows a life cycle has been around since the beginning of the century. The pattern of this life cycle assumes that either a product dies at birth or passes through a specific sequence of stages corresponding to the life phases of infancy, growth, maturity and decline. The whole concept of life cycles is part of "organismic theory," developed in the nineteenth century to draw attention to the idea of evolution and developmental processes in contrast to the mechanistic model of nature associated with Newtonian physics.

The concept of a product life cycle is reflected in the shape of the sales curve. Figure 9.1 shows the assumed shape of the sales curve over its life with the stages of introduction, growth, maturity and decline. This pattern is usually viewed as applying not only to the product category (for example, automobiles) but also to product forms (for example, sports cars) and to a brand (for example, the Rolls Royce Silver Cloud). The acceptance of the life cycle brings with it the recognition that:

1 *Products can be displaced.* A product category (like the slide rule) can be partially or completely displaced by an entirely new product (the hand calculator). Consider the following:
   a) the quartz crystal plus the microchip replacing the mechanical watch;
   b) perspex (a plastic) replacing glass because it is lighter, and virtually unbreakable with excellent optical properties;

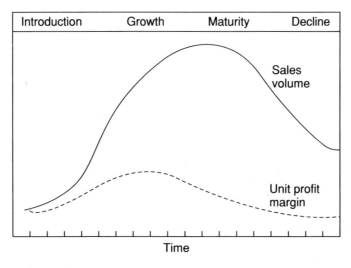

Figure 9.1 Product life cycle

c) cassette tapes and compact discs replacing records; and

d) cash machines replacing bank tellers.

Many of the products that play a major role in our lives were unknown or just a novelty at the beginning of the century. Usually these new products represent a much better way of doing an established function, for example, cars and aircraft in transportation; television in home entertainment, and satellite links in communication. Some new products simply perform a use function in a more convenient way (for example, the automatic camera) or in a different form (for example, paste instead of powder in bathroom cleaners) or improve on efficiency (for example, the computer reading of bar codes in supermarkets, sending the price to the cash register and updating the stocklist). But it is not always easy to anticipate the future of innovative new products even by those within the technology itself. For example, the large engineering firms saw no future in the motor car and left the development to others.

2 *Profit per unit follows the sales curve.* It is claimed that, though absolute profit may be at its highest at the maturity stage, profit per unit is likely to reach its peak before the maturity stage, reflecting competitive pressures.

3 *Market conditions vary at different stages.* The life cycle as illustrated in Figure 9.1, suggests different opportunities and threats at each stage. Hence attempts are made to prescribe the most appropriate strategies for each stage. Generally, the advice relates to the life cycle stage of the product *class* rather than the product form or brand. The advice offered is not usually empirically based but logically deduced from the market characteristics assumed to prevail at each stage (see below).

Marketers do not regard the product life cycle (PLC) as just a sales curve though this is how it is often depicted. There are those marketing academics who sought to justify the *shape* of the curve by pointing to the diffusion process (see below) and other market forces likely to be at work. While different products take different amounts of time to pass through the cycle of introduction, growth, maturity and decline, some products such as light bulbs and aspirin seem to remain indefinitely at the maturity stage, while other products just come and go. Also, because of consumer ignorance, many products can be a long time dying. Just as countries, too, are at different stages in economic growth, a product can be at the infancy, or maturity stage in one country and in decline elsewhere. But change is occurring and one of the big trends in international marketing is for the product life cycle to be the same in both domestic and international markets.

Although the overall market can be mature, some part of that market (e.g. some product form) may be revitalized into a growth segment. Thus in 1993 in the United States, while toothpaste sales overall remained fairly static, toothpaste with whiteners rose around 25 percent to $51 million. Baking soda toothpaste is included in this sales figure. Even though no brand of baking soda toothpaste has claimed to whiten teeth, consumers of toothpaste strongly believe it does!

Although *brand* life cycles are shorter than the life cycle of the product itself, there are brands that have changed little, except in packaging, over the last hundred years. These include, for example, Ivory soap, Arm and Hammer baking soda, Heinz Tomato Ketchup and Maxwell House coffee. The sustainable advantage here has been the power and image of a long-established brand.

Status of the product life cycle concept

There is a need to discuss the status of the PLC to understand how it functions in marketing. Some claim it is a truism, others that it is a universal fact or "law," while others that it is just typically what occurs. We will consider each of these, finally arguing that the PLC is best regarded as an *ideal type* akin to perfect competition in economics.

A truism

There are those who regard the PLC as simply a truism. After all, if a product gets off the ground, sales must start and finish with maximum sales in between. This view trivializes the concept since to say that a product follows a life cycle, is to say something more than sales must go up before they come down.

A universal fact or law

It was once commonly believed that all products passed through the pattern of sales as shown in Figure 9.1. While exceptions would disprove such universality, these were thought to be so rare that, for all intents and purposes, they could be ignored. But, when the evidence was in, there was no difficulty in finding deviant life cycles. Hence the next step was to identify various categories of life cycle. One attempt is that in Figure 9.2, which shows:[1]

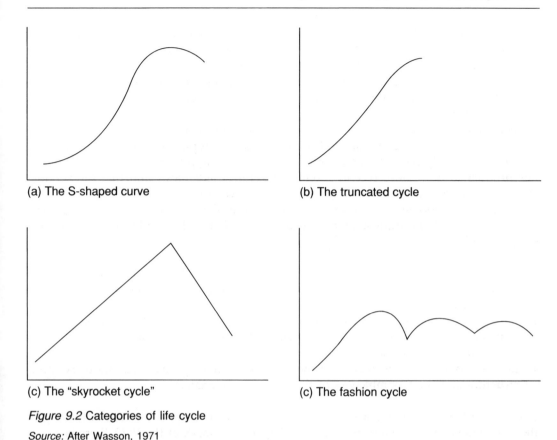

(a) The S-shaped curve

(b) The truncated cycle

(c) The "skyrocket cycle"

(c) The fashion cycle

Figure 9.2 Categories of life cycle

Source: After Wasson, 1971

- *the life cycle as normally described*: this covers products that need to be pioneered
- *the truncated cycle*: this has no introductory stage because the product has "lasting substantive appeal but not a substantial learning requirement," for example, television
- *the "skyrocket cycle"*: this is the true fad as sales plummet after the novelty has worn off
- *the fashion cycle*: this produces oscillations in sales as fashions come and go and come and go again.

Such different life cycles call for different plans. The life cycle as normally described (Figure 9.1 and Figure 9.2 (a)) has high learning requirements and so needs heavy expenditure in market development, promotion and distribution. Similarly, the truncated and the skyrocket cycles demand intensive distribution at the introductory stage, large inventories and promotion. The fashion cycle demands production flexibility. If the explanations for each curve are accepted, there is logic in this advice. But the shape of the curve has many explanations, not confined to those suggested. Thus, even if the sales of a product followed the alleged standard pattern depicted in Figure 9.1 and Figure 9.2 (a), it could arise from other than a high learning requirement. For example, it could arise from the market having to await, say, an increase in income per capita. For the PLC to be a universal law, we would want to know the *development law* or mechanisms that bring about the stages. At present it is not even easy to identify stages since this assumes we know the necessary and sufficient conditions characterizing each stage. We do not know this with any level of confidence and certainly there is no relevant development law.

There is also debate over whether the PLC applies to the product class, product form and/or brand. Some argue that the traditional pattern applies better to product forms than to product classes or brands, while others argue it applies to neither product class nor product form.[2,3] More recently some marketing academics claim that the product class is the most appropriate candidate since product forms and brand sales reflect the competitive developments within the life cycle rather than the overall life cycle pattern itself.[4] These authors argue that the evolution or shape of the PLC for the product category reflects:

- the *demand system* since the rate of acceptance of a product is likely to increase as product performance, availability and communications are improved and the perceived risk of buying is reduced;
- the *supply system* in that the pattern of development is likely to be influenced by the number of other firms that enter the market, the speed of their arrival and the level of resources they invest; and
- the *resource environment* including the needed technology, materials, industry infrastructure and the favorableness of the regulatory climate.

They argue that the focus normally is exclusively on the demand system in looking at the PLC. However, if we are to try and anticipate the stages of the PLC, there is also a need to consider the supply system and the resource environment.

The idea that product forms and brand life sales are more likely to reflect competitive developments within the life cycle of the product category, is very pertinent to what has been happening in the computer industry. Thus Wang focused on minicomputers, failing to anticipate the large impact a new generation of more flexible personal computers would have on its sales. IBM's success was linked to its hegemony in large mainframe computers. But the technological breakthrough with personal computers undermined IBM as it did Wang. IBM, like Wang, failed to see the threat that PCs posed to its mainframe business, thinking PCs would merely be connected to these. In the late 1980s, new chips made the PC so capable that PCs could be brought together in a network as a cheaper alternative for many mainframe applications. Also, when IBM did enter the personal computer(PC) market, it used Intel for its supplies of chips and Microsoft for its operating software. These companies supplied the same components to all IBM's rivals. What IBM failed to learn was that a good deal of its mystique was tied to the belief that it had something exclusive to offer.

The PLC has no lawlike status and each stage does *not* entail the next stage. The decline stage can be indefinitely postponed by an unfolding succession of innovations and, just as the Stone Age or Bronze Age can be skipped in archaeological evolution, so products may skip or repeat stages. If the PLC concept is to have explanatory value, it would have to go beyond the inadequate metaphor of the cycle of birth, growth, maturity and decline. Goods and services are not biological organisms. We would need to know the external factors or processes acting as causal mechanisms in bringing about the sequence. To show sales varying with time is not enough since time in itself is not a forcing variable.

The most typical type

The traditional PLC as depicted in Figure 9.1 is regarded as the most typical PLC. This is not easy to prove. There is first the problem of obtaining a random sample of life cycles over all classes of goods and services. We then have to allow for population changes during the life of the product as well as price changes and the level of discretionary income. There are problems, too, in defining product classes as well as operationally defining each stage of the life cycle. Nonetheless, there have been attempts at establishing whether the typical PLC is as depicted. One study covered 258 brands of ethical drugs.[5] As this was no random sample of products, it can only be regarded as exploratory. Some 28 percent followed the traditional PLC pattern, while 39 percent followed a two-hill pattern, suggesting that a product's life can be renewed by marketing efforts. Other types of life patterns were also found. Another study measured the PLC stages in terms of the percentage change in sales during the life of the product and found less than 50 percent of the products followed the traditional pattern.[6] But another researcher found the traditional pattern applied to the industrial products he studied.[7] While all these studies were weak for establishing the relative frequency of the traditional PLC, the pattern may be more common than any other pattern. But the pattern has not been shown as applying to the majority of products (not to mention brands and product forms) so following strategies on the assumption that the pattern holds just cannot be justified. This is not to suggest there is no need to think about the life of the product. This type of forecasting is mandated for calculating likely profitability. However, we should not just assume a certain pattern always prevails.

An ideal type or fictive term

The PLC is probably best viewed as an *ideal type*. An ideal type is an abstraction that may or may not correspond too closely with the real world but is assumed to represent core features. Pure competition, as defined by economists, or bureaucracy, as defined by the sociologist Max Weber, are ideal types since concrete cases can be expected to deviate from the ideal. The ideal type is not something arbitrary but rooted in plausible assumptions suggested by experience. A failure, however, to establish the truth of the ideal type does not disconfirm the ideal type because, as an abstraction, it is always to some extent false to reality. The plausible assumptions for establishing an ideal type of product life cycle are:

1 At the introductory stage, knowledge/awareness of the product's potential spreads among the target customer group. Adoption is slow at first then accelerates.

2 At the maturity stage, market penetration is complete, leading to just replacement sales and the attraction of new users to replace those going out of the market.

3 Decline comes about as the result of better substitutes coming along.

From these assumptions we could deduce the traditional PLC as the ideal type for PLCs. The ideal type is used to compare with real life sales curves to find out why the ideal type assumptions do not hold. In this way, we learn more and more about the forces at work in the real world. The PLC, as an ideal type, is a standard against which to compare real life cases. For example, during the pioneering (introductory) stage of a new-to-the-world product, there may be deviations from the smooth PLC traditional curve because growth often depends on the solution of a wide range of technical problems. Thus, growth in the automobile industry showed erratic fluctuations in sales as passive demand was inhibited until certain technical problems had been solved by pneumatic tires, a light engine and a convenient system of ignition. Even today the revival of the electric car awaits the solution of a long-life battery.

What complicates the concept of the PLC even as an ideal type is that products can be revived through finding new uses for the product. Thus the steam engine in the eighteenth century was just used to pump water out of mines. It took a long time for it to become a source of power for industry, then for railway transportation and then as a way to generate electricity. The fact is that the potential uses for some new invention are seldom immediately apparent. This is why finding new uses (new markets) can be so key to success in industrial marketing. In the physical sciences there is the same concept, sometimes called a *fictive term* such as "an ideal gas." A fictive term (as with the ideal type) is a simplification whose function is to highlight features that are taken to be the most significant. Thus the PLC as a fictive term draws our attention to the features of infancy, growth, maturity and decline. These features highlight potential future problems. A criticism of the use of fictive terms or ideal types is if they are based on inappropriate simplifications, implicitly treating some aspect as unimportant when in fact it is an important characterization of the behavior of interest.

The product life cycle versus Porter's evolutionary stages

Research has focused on the shape of the PLC because the PLC concept is often viewed as a *sales* life cycle. But should the shape of the curve be the key issue? If all product categories followed the typical, traditional formula PLC, it would suggest the same causal factors were at work. We might thus be able to show the necessary and sufficient conditions at each stage that are needed to produce that particular stage and to induce movement onto the next stage. No such set of necessary and sufficient conditions exists. A particular shape of sales curve can be explained by a myriad possible causal (market) conditions. It is probably for this reason that Porter focuses not on the shape of any curve but on the conditions underlying the evolutionary stages he distinguishes, namely, emerging, transition to maturity, and decline.[8] Porter obviously sees the PLC as a sales curve and rejects the idea of sales (demand) as necessarily following some exact pattern. But the fact is that marketers have not just confined their attention to the PLC as a sales

Table 9.1 Porter's evolutionary stages vs. traditional PLC approach

Stage description		Strategic action	
Porter's categories and descriptions	*Traditional PLC descriptions*	*Porter's suggestions*	*Traditional PLC advocates*
Emerging industry Uncertainty among buyers over product performance, potential applications, advantages of rival brands, likelihood of obsolescence Uncertainty among sellers over market wants, technological developments	*Introduction (pioneering stage)* Customer awareness of product low Limited distribution Sales slow Few competitors	*Emerging industry* Strategy to take into account 5 forces of: • threat of entry • rivalry among competitors • pressure of substitutes • bargaining power of buyers • bargaining power of suppliers	*Introduction* Stimulate primary demand (among early adopters?) Selective distribution Advertising to create awareness of product's potential
Transition to maturity Falling profits for industry Slowing growth Customer knowledgeable about the product Less product innovation Competition in non-product aspects of the offering	*Growth/maturity* Competition intense Slowing growth Consumer knowledge and preferences mature Widest ever distribution	*Transition to maturity* New segments or cater more closely to wants of some segment More efficient organization	*Growth/maturity* Market penetration or hold/defend via market segmentation Service emphasized Selective demand advertising Closer dealer relations
Decline Competition from substitutes Changing wants Demographic factors affecting markets	*Decline* Competition from substitutes Customer changing to new products Distribution shrinking	*Decline* Seek pockets of enduring demand *or* Divest	*Decline* Seek new product uses Changes to revitalize product Simplification of product lines

curve. They have been concerned, like Porter, to specify the conditions typifying each stage and to deduce the marketing strategy implications from these conditions.

The descriptions of Porter's three categories (emerging, transition to maturity, and decline) are shown in Table 9.1 which contrast these with the descriptions of the traditional PLC given by PLC advocates. Some judgment has to be exercised, as Porter's transition to maturity stage is a category that overlaps the PLC stages. Table 9.1 also contrasts Porter's suggestions on strategies at each stage with the strategies traditionally advocated by marketers. Although there is much that is vague in Porter from an operational point of view, his descriptions and suggestions are sharper, crisper, and clearer than those typically found in marketing texts. On the other hand, an examination of Table 9.1 should make us hesitate to speak of the revolutionary nature of Porter's work: it has historical antecedents not only in industrial economics but in marketing as well.

Product life cycle and marketing

Table 9.1 lists some suggestions on strategies for coping with stages in the PLC. Table 9.2 shows additional suggestions in respect to elements of the marketing mix. Textbooks and articles on marketing are full of such suggestions. It is not always clear whether the suggestions are intended to be descriptive of what happens or prescriptive advice. In any case, the suggestions should not be taken seriously. It is always possible to think of circumstances where the opposite advice should be taken just as there are circumstances where low prices rather than high prices might be more appropriate at the product introductory stage. Often the advice is just platitudinous. For example, one of the latest bits of advice tells me that during the growth stage I should try to increase my competitive position which is, of course, something we should be trying to do all the time. Another article puts forward a table which sets out a matrix with the stage in the life cycle along the horizontal and the company's relative strength (from dominant to weak) along the vertical with the recommended strategies filling each cell. Thus the dominant firm is advised to push for market share during the introductory stage, and hold/defend during the other stages. This sounds like the BCG advice! On the other hand, if the firm merely has a favorable competitive position, the advice at the introductory stage is to selectively push for position; at the growth and maturity stage the advice is to find a niche and hang onto it, while at the decline stage the advice is to

Table 9.2 Typical suggested strategies relating to mix variables in the product life cycle stage

Stage in life cycle	Product	Pricing	Promotion	Distribution
Introduction	Iron out product deficiencies	High	Create awareness of product's potential Stimulate primary demand	Selective distribution
Growth	Focus on product quality Variations of product introduced		Selective advertising of brand Heavy advertising to create image	Extend to coverage sought
Maturity	Product adjustments for further brand differentiation		Image build and maintain Sales promotions Facilitate changes in product, etc.	Seek close dealer relationships
Decline	Simplify product line Seek new product uses Changes to revitalize product	Low	Primary demand may again be cultivated	Selected dealers cultivated

harvest or divest. Porter's advice here! What is wrong about such advice is the belief that there are specific strategies which can be recommended without regard to market conditions other than the (difficult to establish) life cycle stage.

Even the generalizations that are typically made about the market at each life cycle stage can be queried. Thus it is commonly claimed that, at the maturity stage, brands become so alike that prices become fairly uniform. Whatever the statistical evidence behind this statement, it may or may not have relevance to the individual brand or the individual market. For example, perfume is a mature market but prices vary widely, as do the prices in many mature markets for services (even hairdressing!).

Even more erroneous is the implicit assumption that stage in the life cycle should completely determine the strategy adopted. Behind this assumption lies some futility hypothesis to the effect that it is futile to attempt to accelerate, change or reverse the forces that bring about the PLC. Those who accept this position feel they have history or some lawlike generalization on their side but this discourages them from seeing whether marketing efforts can reverse the decline stage and so on. But, on occasions, particularly when talking of the life of a brand, management may adopt strategies that seek to influence the stage itself by, say, rekindling primary demand, while the growth stage can often be prolonged or decline postponed or even reversed. Thus we have the revitalization of the fountain pen market and the bicycle. The mountain bike attracts a new type of bike buyer: young adults using them to stay in shape, not for transportation. Bennetton almost single-handedly reversed the decline in wool outerwear garments by catering to the latent want for more fashionable and colorful wool garments. The individual seller need not be persuaded to divest just because the overall level of demand is in decline. Thus in the United States, total beer sales are in decline but one brand, Rolling Rock, has been increasing its sales by around 15 percent per annum helped by its in-bar promotions. Similarly, the US consumption of coffee is on the decline with only about half of adults in the United States consuming coffee, down from three fourths in the 1960s. Yet the gourmet coffee segment is growing at an average of 13 percent per annum. It cannot always be assumed that market decline will continue as there are often limits to substitution. Thus man-made fibers did not drive out cotton, wool, and silk as had been predicted, and plastics did not completely drive out leather. Similarly the popularity of videocassette recorders and pay movies on television led many to predict the final demise of moviegoing. But it seems to have stimulated interest in films and has resulted in an expansion of the total market for films. It is not only easier but more dramatic to claim that the advent of some substitute will lead to the total demise of the product being displaced than to think of how the two might eventually coexist and come to occupy different segments of the market.

It is still possible to enter a mature market and do well. Thus Arm & Hammer entered the most difficult of mature markets—the differentiated oligopoly in the toothpaste market—but still managed to get a nearly 9 percent market share in the United States, a high share in such a market. Not only that but its success was largely *word-of-mouth* about the taste of the toothpaste: sharp, gritty taste that gives an after-use feeling that consumers either love or hate. Nor can it just be assumed that, at the mature stage, the focus of consumers will be on price with products becoming "commodity-like." Thus a current belief is that the PC is a commodity product. This may be so but it need not be: it just reflects the imitative behavior of the competitors. Even if nothing can be done about the product over and above what others are doing, the key thing is to avoid having a me-too offering even if obliged to have a me-too product. Thus in the PC market, service is making a difference while it is doubtful that any product so ill-understood by buyers will ever be just a commodity. Brand image/reputation is likely to count given the importance of adaptive criteria. The more the various brands look alike, the more consumers will seek something distinctive in the offering. But substitutes do on occasions wipe out a market, just as the calculator destroyed the market for slide rules. Sometimes the substitute is also not that obvious. Thus the sale of Heathkits, which were kits that allowed amateurs to build their own radios, televisions, and other electronic equipment was destroyed when such electric equipment became so easy to buy while the target customers for do-it-yourself electronics became enamored with computers!

The specific conditions operating at any one stage in the life of a brand can vary widely from the *general* conditions operating for a product class. While each stage of the PLC will always be accompanied by certain market conditions, knowledge of these conditions is just informational input into thinking about strategy. Simply to take account of the life cycle stage and devise strategies geared simply to meet life cycle stage conditions is to assume that:

1 knowledge of such conditions is the only type of environmental information that is relevant;
2 stage conditions should be completely determining of strategy; and
3 we can accurately identify each stage and know the nature, intensity, and potential impact of the conditions at each stage.

None of these assumptions is true. What we do need to do is to estimate sales over time of a new product or brand; try to estimate growth rates and whether the pioneering period will be short or long, smooth or erratic. Forecasting the actual future of a product or brand cannot be avoided if cash flows are to be estimated and future needs for facilities anticipated.

There will continue to be strong debate over the extent to which the stage in the product life cycle or Porter's evolutionary stage should influence the marketing mix and hence the marketing strategy. But until we are able to operationally define and measure the conditions that will operate at each stage, we cannot be sure we have unambiguously identified the stage in the life cycle. Nonetheless, we do know something about the likely conditions and recognize them as factors that have to be taken into account in strategy formulation. Moreover, in defense, the concept of the PLC directs our attention to the concept of portfolio balance and the need to monitor the ups and downs of sales and seek their explanation.

THE DIFFUSION AND ADOPTION PROCESSES

The diffusion and adoption processes are quoted as supporting of the S-shaped curve of the traditional PLC. The term *diffusion* refers to the spread of information about an innovation or the spread of the innovation itself throughout a market. Whereas the PLC takes an overall view of the sales cycle and underlying market conditions, diffusion theory is at the *individual* level, focusing on the likely behavior of individuals in the market. The term *adoption* refers to the assumed mental process through which a consumer passes in deciding to adopt a product. In the introductory stage of the PLC, diffusion and adoption relate to the need to activate a latent want and/or to activate a passive want. In any case, both diffusion and adoption take time and this is used to explain the early shape of the PLC curve.

Diffusion

The speed or rate at which diffusion occurs has been of central research interest. The diffusion process is generally assumed to follow an S-shaped curve as in the case of the traditional PLC. But, as in the case of the PLC, there are other possibilities depending on what assumptions are made. Also, as with the PLC, interest has centered on describing the diffusion process in the expectation it will help guide marketing strategy. It is hoped that understanding diffusion will help us forecast the whole diffusion curve from early diffusion data. However, there is little research to date on the validity of such forecasting.

If a firm introduces a new-to-the-world product, it is naturally concerned with the rate of its diffusion. Early work suggested the following factors were involved in the rate of diffusion of an innovation:[9]

- the relative advantages of the innovation, since relative advantage is one guide to relative interest;
- the compatibility of the product with existing lifestyles and consumption systems. This raises the issue of the nature of the innovation. The literature distinguishes "continuous innovation" from "dynamically continuous innovation" and both from "discontinuous innovation." The classification is based on the degree of corresponding behavior change that is needed to use the product. With a continuous innovation, little change in behavior is needed. With a dynamically continuous innovation, the product requires a major change in behavior, but the change is of little significance to the individual, as was the case of the compact disc player. On the other hand, with a discontinuous innovation, major changes in behavior are required and the behavior change does matter to the individual, for example, the PC for the typewriter. Although useful for thinking about compatibility, this classification, by focusing on the innovation's impact on behavior, is confusing in that the general understanding of, say, a discontinuous innovation is not the behavioral impact but simply the innovation being very different from what exists already;
- the lack of product complexity, since complexity imposes problems of learning. Thus diffusion may be a problem with discontinuous products because they are more likely to be complex;
- the divisibility of the product, for example, the possibility of trial and the availability of trial sizes. Such divisibility reduces risk in buying; and

- the communicability of information on the product. The communication of what the product is and its advantages may not be easy. One vacuum cleaner with the advantage of lightness was perceived as "poor" since its lightness to many consumers meant "it was not pressing in" for it to do its job. In the case of 20/50 motor oils, the advantages were finally communicated by word-of-mouth rather than advertising.

Foster adds to this list:[10]

- the timing of the introduction in that a product may be a little ahead of its time. On the other hand, the timing can be just right. For example, Helene Curtis introduced its Salon Selectives shampoos in 1987, just in time to take advantage of rapidly increasing interest in salon-style hair-care products and reinforced this with the advertising line: "Like you just stepped out of a salon." Timing is very much tied to the times. For example, many marketers are finding in the 1990s that consumers in the United States are abandoning the 1980s love of excess and ostentation in favor of brands that do not claim ostentatious snob appeal such as the Gap stores. If this is so it will certainly hurt French exports as France, more than any other country, is associated with luxury, snob-appeal markets;
- the pricing strategy since a high price increases the risk and reduces the size of the target group;
- whether investment is required by the user in that a heavy investment is a major inhibition to trial;
- the financial resources of the innovator since costs are involved in entering a market with sufficient critical mass;
- the number of people involved in the decision since the more that are involved the more difficult it is to get agreement on buying something new;
- the sprit of entrepreneurship which influences the attitude toward risk;
- ease in judging the innovation's effectiveness; and
- whether *gatekeepers* are involved. (The term "gatekeeper" was first used by the social psychologist Kurt Lewin. It arose from the observation that, as news flowed through channels, certain points serve as gates through which news might or might not pass. The term today is used more generally to refer to anyone who can block information or access, for example, doctors for prescription drugs and teachers for textbooks.)

The above is not comprehensive. We can add others:

- the role of government regulation. This can be important. Thus, as a result of pressure from compact disc makers (who fear the digital audio tape will be used to copy from compact discs) in the European Common Market, the diffusion of digital tape technology has been stymied around the world. Similarly the Federal Communications Commission's demand that any High Definition Television (HDTV) marketed in the United States be compatible with existing domestic receivers has delayed the introduction of HDTV. The introduction of new communication technologies is often delayed in this way; even the introduction of commercial television was delayed in the United States for around ten years because of fears of disrupting existing social and economic structures;

- buyer expectations in that, the more innovations are expected to emerge in any particular market, the smaller the rate at which any are likely to be diffused since users are likely to wait for the next improved version. This happens with personal computers; and

- perceptions of buyers since whether someone calls something an innovation or not depends in part on what classifications (pigeonholes) the buyer has. Does the new product fall into the category of some existing product class for the buyer or does it require a new category of its own? For a new product to be considered a major innovation by its prospective buyers, it is likely not only to have to differ from other products but have no direct, obvious relationship with other products.

Does the diffusion process explain why the PLC is likely to have an S-shaped curve as in Figure 9.1? The factors, that are said to determine the rate of diffusion, only suggest why the initial part of the curve might be slow or quick getting off the ground and even here they are of limited explanatory value. As the study quoted earlier in the chapter showed, current diffusion theory at present simply reflects the demand factors at work and not the position of supply nor the infrastructure that also impact on diffusion. (In fairness, diffusion studies in spatial geography have taken account of infrastructure, supply and other physical, economic, cultural, linguistic, and political factors.)

The role of *word-of-mouth* communication and personal influence in diffusion (and adoption) have been of continuing interest. The role of word-of-mouth in accelerating the diffusion of an innovation is not uncommon but it presupposes that the passer-on of information is enthusiastic enough to pass on the information or the receiver is concerned enough to inquire. This generally assumes a high degree of involvement with the purchase decision. When a new product or service does solve a problem better than any other and the problem is sufficiently important to stimulate high involvement by users, they are pleased and usually anxious to share their discovery with others. But much depends on the culture. Thus anthropologists speak of high-context cultures, which are cultures where people are highly involved with each other (e.g. Japan). In such cultures information flows freely and is widely shared, whereas in low-context cultures (e.g. Switzerland), this is not so. Word-of-mouth can be related to the concept of social contagion in social psychology which is the process by which behavior patterns spread across many people as the result of their interactions.

In the case of personal influence (advice etc.) it is not surprising that it increases in conditions where adaptive criteria operate, that is, in conditions of information overload, decision uncertainty and risk. A traditional view of the personal influence process is the *trickle-down effect* where influence flows down from the upper classes. Sometimes such upper classes were the aristocracy and sometimes the middle classes. No doubt in some cultures this may still be true but the trickle-down hypothesis is less apparent today in industrialized societies unless trickle-down is from prestige groups like movie stars and football stars rather than from the upper classes. There can be even *trickle-up* as witness the "grunge" look ("I couldn't seemingly care less how I look") which appears to have come from the streets.

The next view was the *two-step flow hypothesis* that the mass media first influence *opinion* leaders who then influence their followers.[11] This can and does happen, but it is not universal. We are influenced by people within our groups who are not opinion leaders while there is *opinion sharing* as well as opinion seeking and giving. With respect to influencing us about products, negative comments are apt to be more persuasive than positive ones. The current view is a *multiflow view*, where it is accepted that, while most personal influence is exercised at the peer group level, different social levels can influence each other and the influence exercised need not be one way. Thus we have the diffusion of youth styles from subcultures to the fashion market: "Youth cultural styles may begin by issuing new challenges but they end by establishing new conventions; by creating new commodities, new industries or rejuvenating old ones."[12] In fact information about products floats around most societies without any hard and fast communication channels.

This whole debate about information flows reflects sometimes a belief in there being just one universal explanation. The search for universals (laws) is an article of faith in scientific research even if, in human affairs, things are messy and varied. The danger lies in a reluctance to look for variety and prematurely assuming a unity that does not exist. But, more important, is the *source* of information all that important? It is thought to be, as it opens up the possibility of marketing influencing that source. But what is neglected are

- explanations of what makes one individual more fertile ground for the information than another, and
- why in some cases information spreads not just rapidly but *effectively in influencing sales*.

The adoption process

The most frequently quoted model of the adoption process falls into the category of a "hierarchy of effects" model as it views the buyer as proceeding through a series of mental stages:

1 *awareness*: the consumer knows of the innovation but lacks enough specific information about its functioning etc;
2 *interest/information*: the consumer becomes interested enough to seek information, for example, how the product works, what it costs and how it compares with substitutes;
3 *evaluation*: the consumer uses the information collected to evaluate the product;
4 *trial*: the consumer experiences the product on a trial basis; and
5 *adoption*: the consumer decides to adopt the product.

Whatever the applicability of this model, it refers to purchase decisions with which the buyer is likely to be highly involved. For example, does a consumer go through such steps in thinking about buying a new candy bar? The consumer is more likely to say "It appeals to me, therefore I will try it." For many purchases steps will be skipped and for some decisions the sequence will be changed. Thus, for the many products with which the consumer has low involvement, the process might be Awareness ⇒ General Information ⇒ Trial ⇒ Evaluation ⇒ Adoption with the information being very general and the evaluation being just a superficial confirmation that the product is fine. Of course, we can design a questionnaire to get respondents to answer "as if" they go through a specific set of stages but this does not prove anything about the actual mental processes involved in adoption. In any case, the process of adoption can be a learning experience where evaluation criteria change through trial.

In looking at the process of adoption or, in fact, any of the many other hierarchy of effects models discussed in advertising, there is always a danger of confusing a logical process with a mental evolutionary one: to observe a set of stones in ascending order of magnitude is to identify a logical order but not necessarily an evolutionary one. Adoption in fact is likely to be a very complex set of processes for major purchases of new products rather than a single unitary one as suggested, while the adopting unit could be some group or decision-making unit rather than an individual.

Assuming that diffusion leads to adoptions that, when plotted on a graph, follow the normal (bell-shaped) distribution curve, then adopters can be defined and classified as follows:

a) *innovators*: these are the first 2.5 percent of the adopters;
b) *early adopters*: these consist of the next 13.5 percent of adopters
c) *early majority*: the next 34 percent of adopters;
d) *late majority*: the 34 percent following the early majority; and
e) *laggards*: the final 16 percent.

This distribution is sometimes quoted as lending support to the PLC as being S-shaped. But the above categories are just divisions into which *any* sales data collected over time can be put. The labels attached to each class of adopter misleadingly suggest that each category has certain attributes in common. But just making arbitrary statistical divisions along an assumed distribution does not necessarily yield any meaningful groups from the point of view of marketing. For example, can we be sure that there are any differences or, at least any recognizable differences, between innovators and early adopters beyond the buying sequence? Buying sequence may reflect nothing more than the order in which consumers heard about the innovation. Many among the early adopters, if asked to classify themselves, might think of themselves as innovators if they were unaware of not being among the first to buy. What prompted them to buy may be no different from that which influenced the innovators. But research has continued in the belief that the categories are highly meaningful in terms of consumer behavior. Thus initially it was claimed that innovators are likely to be younger, more educated, more exposed to the mass media and more upwardly mobile than the average adopter. But other studies have cast doubt on innovators being a special group that can be described in specific behavioral and demographic terms. Different people may be innovators for different products depending on how similar or dissimilar the product is relative to those previously available.[13]

Early adopters have been the major focus of attention as it is this group and not the innovators that is suspected of being the *opinion leaders*. As opinion leaders are considered to be people who have had more long-term interest and experience in the product category than others, it is not clear why they should not also be a major part of the innovator category. But certainly in absolute terms there are likely to be more opinion leaders in the category labeled early adopters since there are many more of these. What can be important is getting the innovators and early adopters to buy big ticket items early in the brand life cycle since later entrants to the market are likely to follow the brand choices of early buyers. The term *market mavens* has been used to describe those opinion leaders who provide considerable information to others across a wide range of product categories. (A "maven" or "mavin" is a Yiddish word for an expert in everyday matters.) Perhaps market mavens cannot consistently be the innovators! A general view has been that the introductory market plan should be geared to the early adopters. But others have challenged this strategy on the ground that, although early adopters may in some contexts be identified, they may still not be the best prospects to target as early adoption propensity may not go with either heavy buying propensity or the propensity to influence.[14]

Do these categories of adopters relate to the PLC? It could be argued that the introductory stage covers innovators and some early adopters, the growth stage embraces other early adopters and some of the early majority, while the maturity stage covers the rest of the early majority plus the late majority, leaving the laggards to the decline stage. But this simply demonstrates that views about the adoption process are not incompatible with the traditional concept of the PLC. However, these views about the adoption process lend little support to anything we might say about the product life cycle. If we acknowledge the weakness of the evidence for generalities about the diffusion and adoption processes, we will recognize the even weaker support these processes offer for the traditional views on the product life cycle.

Concepts such as the PLC, diffusion, and adoption are important, however, even if these concepts do not lead to simple "laws" we can use in marketing. This is important because, within the guidelines so far provided, we have to think about these concepts and research them for application to our own products. But product life cycles, diffusion, and adoption processes need to be supplemented by research that seeks to describe the competitive market dynamics throughout the life of a product or brand. For example, here is one possible scenario that can be supported by many case studies.

Whenever a new-to-the-world product enters the market both the innovating firm and other early market entrants focus on beating competition by performing better in the core-use function. The situation may be described as *product parallelism* in that competitors are all going in the same direction in seeking a competitive advantage. But this is the road to disaster for many companies. Foster of McKinsey, the consulting firm, provides the explanation as to why this might be so. He points out that increases in technological performance depend on how quickly the underlying technology can be exploited, which in turn depends on the level of expenditure on R&D. The relationship between expenditure on R&D and progress in increasing performance follows an S-shaped curve: progress is slow at first then there is rapid progress and finally a plateau as the technology matures. Thus the firms with the most R&D resources are likely to attain technological leadership with the technological laggards dropping out of the market. This explains the early fall-out of competitors at the growth stage: they had wrongly believed that they could compete on performance when they were ill equipped to do so. If the remaining competitors continue to be exclusively concerned with performance in the core-use function, there will ultimately be what might be termed *product convergence* as the technology matures and all competitors are technologically mature and equal. The result is a market of undifferentiated products. If product convergence occurs in conditions where price, promotion, and distribution are all comparable in appeal, consumers will choose on the basis of habit, picking, or subjective liking. What this means is that, since every firm cannot be a technological leader, those that cannot must compete in some other way right from the start. They may try what might be termed *product radiation* where the product is modified by adding ancillary and/or convenience-in-use functions that fit the demands of some specific segments. Thus in toothpaste, in the 1940s it was ammonia; in the 1950s it was chlorophyll; in the 1960s it was fluoride; in the 1970s it was gels; and since then plaque fighters, tartar fighters, and whiteners! A good deal of competition alternates between product parallelism, product convergence, and product radiation where the focus is on the product itself. But if *product* competition were the only type of competition open to a firm, most of the current leaders in the PC market would be out of business. But many consumers are willing to trade off high technical performance for a lower price. Still technical and economic criteria are not the only basis of a competitive advantage. Many companies have grown rich by the styling of their product and cultivating an aura of exclusivity.

BRANDS AND BRAND EQUITY

Concept of a brand and brand image

It was argued earlier that the brand itself is often a most sustainable critical advantage. This is why Marlboro was estimated at one time to be worth $31 billion to its owner Philip Morris. The Coca-Cola brand is estimated to be worth $24 billion to the Coca-Cola company; Nescafé to be worth $8 billion to Nestlé; Pampers to be worth $6 billion to Procter & Gamble (P&G); Johnnie Walker Red Label whisky is estimated to be worth $2.6 billion to Guinness; Smirnoff Vodka to be worth $2.3 billion to Grand Metropolitan and so on. Such values stem from the fact that top brands tend to remain top brands. Thus the Boston Consulting Group showed that of thirty product categories studied in the United States, twenty-seven of the leading brands in 1925 were still the leading brands sixty years later: Eveready in batteries; Kellogg in breakfast cereal; Kodak in cameras; Wrigley in chewing gum; Gillette in razors; Lipton in tea and so on. As one commentator said: "It is difficult to kill a strong brand franchise."

The *referential-meaning* of the term *brand* is simply the name and any accompanying markings (distinct trademark or logo) that identify a particular company's product. Manufacturers' brands came about with mass production and the need to assure customers that all units of their product were always the same. The brand-name served two purposes. One to identify the brand and two as a reassurance about quality. As far as the customer was concerned, trust in the brand-name replaced the former trusting relationship with the local supplier. But a brand has a *sense-meaning* as well as a refer-ential-meaning and this is where the added value lies.

A brand-name is a sign (i.e. it represents something) that *signals* membership of a certain product category but it also *symbolizes* something. Just as fire signals burning but also symbolizes life, the sense-meaning of a brand is what it symbolizes: generally and specifically for the individual. What a brand symbolizes *generally* is called its "brand image." The brand image consists of the impressions (like we have of a book's contents after reading it) or associations linked or conjured up by the brand based not just on the brand's physical attributes (including its logo and packaging) but all other associa-tions built up through advertising, word-of-mouth communication, observation, and experiences in using the product. Consumers are apt to evaluate rival brands through a looking glass consisting of the various brand images. A brand image is like a picture in the mind, not a literal picture but a synthesis of impressions; a summation that can take the form of a gut reaction or some mental flash reflecting attitudes toward the brand or its attributes as well as perceived benefits. What makes brand image so impor-tant is that it is part of the awareness of a brand that is *recalled* before contemplating buying or part of that awareness occurring when a brand is *recognized* in the store. Actual *knowledge* of a brand is all the information possessed about a brand and so is more specific and more embracing than brand image. Sometimes the whole of brand aware-ness never gets beyond brand image so brand image can be the basis for buying. Buying based solely on brand image has the advantage of conserving mental effort in judging whether to accept or reject a brand.

Brand image, as operationally measured, is based on some overall community consensus on the impressions of a brand. What a brand symbolizes for the individual, however, is the configuration of benefits it promises for her or him. Thus Rolls-Royce projects a brand image of, say, smooth elegant driving, luxurious living, wealth, snob-bery, and so on, but what it symbolizes is not something that has significance for most of us since we are not part of that market segment. A brand image must symbolize something positive to the consumer if he or she is to contemplate buying it. What sellers try to do is to make their brand a *significant symbol*. A significant symbol is one that is the same to those perceiving the symbol as it was intended by the producers of the symbol. If sellers want the brand to symbolize a certain type of experience (since imagining that experience can be a form of self-persuasion), they will stress this experience in all their persuasive communications. A positive brand image is linked to positive brand equity.

Brand equity

Brand equity, if positive (brand equity can on occasions be negative), is the additional value put on a brand by its customers over and above any value it has relative to the brand's objective performance vis-à-vis its rivals. Aaker, in a very persuasive text on managing brand equity, defines brand equity as the set of assets such as name aware-ness, loyal customers, perceived quality and other associations that are linked to the brand (its name and/or symbol such as a logo, trademark or package design) that add or subtract value to the product/service being offered.[15] An allied term is *brand power*, one measure of which uses two criteria: "share of mind" or the consumer's familiarity with the brand and secondly consumers' "esteem" for the brand in terms of how good they thought it was. If we look at power as the basis of influence and influence as the exercise of power, the concept of brand power as measured here only captures some aspects of the potential power of a brand to influence purchase. It is not surprising that on this definition the Rolls-Royce motor car ranked fifteenth in its share of the European consumers' mind but first in esteem. Much more indicative of the power of a brand occurs in blind tests. Thus in one well-known blind test among consumers, Kellogg's Corn Flakes got a 47 percent approval rating but, when consumers were given the brand-names, the approval rating shot up to 59 percent. This type of brand power is some-times included in the definition of customer-based brand equity: "Customer-based brand equity is defined as the differential effect of brand knowledge on consumer response to the marketing of the brand."[16]

There have been many attempts to measure the value of a brand. One complex formula breaks down company earnings by brand and then subtracts what it calculates would be earned on a basic, unbranded version of the product. To that figure it applies a "brand strength" multiple based on factors such as market position, degree of internationaliza-tion and trends in the sector. This formula is very far removed from the perceptions and buying behavior of customers who collectively decide the valuation in their demand. Prominence was given to this formula (and so to the sponsoring company) when it was claimed that IBM's name now has negative value. Any approach to valuation that is remote from actual buyer evaluations, based on much that must be just analysts' judgment and throws up such results must necessarily be treated with a good deal of skepticism. Another measure of brand equity uses a matrix defined by brand stature (defined in terms of familiarity and esteem) and vitality (defined in terms of relevance and differentiation). This at least seems more tied to consumer perceptions lying behind brand equity.

The obvious question is: "Why positive brand equity?"

1 In the first place, the most well-known brand (high brand recall and recognition) within the product class provides a reason for selecting it in what would otherwise be a picking situation. And situations, where people cannot really judge differences among brands, are probably more common than some marketing academics care to admit. The well-known brand also has great appeal in situations where adaptive criteria (need to adapt to information overload, uncertainty and fear of making a mistake) dominates. What is being bought here is a reassurance, a guarantee, a promise that the buyer will not be disappointed.

2 The second reason has to do with brands easily recognized by "those in the know" and oozing up-market symbols of taste, class and status, for example, wearing Ferragamo shoes, a Hermes scarf, a Rolex watch, Chanel perfume, a Louis Vuitton bag, and so on. It is interesting to reflect that the successful Chanel No.5 ($195 an ounce), created in 1921, has minimalist packaging and a name that was chosen by Coco Chanel simply on the ground that it was the fifth bottle presented to her by the perfumier, Ernest Beaux!

3 The name itself may project its benefits like Chicken of the Sea, the most famous brand of tuna in the United States, which is an advantage when brands are difficult to differentiate.

4 The most important reason of all has to do with loyalty to brand leaders. Successful experience with a product inspires goodwill and trust, and the more the experience, the more the trust. At some stage loyalty develops. This is not the more simplistic concept of loyalty as measured by buying the brand consistently and having a favorable attitude toward it. This is more a measure of devotion to a brand than loyalty. Where there is loyalty in a relationship, it means "sticking to the other party through thick and thin" so that unequal exchanges are in the short period accepted because there is trust that the other party will put things right long term. The same goes for a relationship with a product. This type of loyalty has an emotional base: there is an emotional bond between brand and customer. It is this type of loyalty that is the best protection against competitive inroads. Even if buying is halted, the emotional tie remains. Thus local East German breweries are getting back market share as they get access to better quality materials and packaging. In other words, even when desertion of the brand occurs (perhaps through abuse of the brand by the owner), the emotion often remains, just waiting to be rekindled. This accounts for the revival of old brand-names which can still carry a recognition value and an emotional appeal that would be costly to achieve for any new brand-name. Increasingly, consumer product companies are reintroducing extinct brands that are still known to the consumer. There is the realization that the favorable associations attached to the old brand-name should not just be abandoned when such associations can represent a foundation on which to build the brand anew.

It may be much easier to resurrect an old brand than to build a new one. In fact some companies have in-house entrepreneurial units concerned solely with resurrecting old brands. This is not to suggest the name is enough: it is not but, when allied to an updated product, it may quickly establish itself. As Aaker points out, many extinct brand-names are recalled by consumers as if still going and this provides a basis for resurrecting brand-names with success. While Aaker is right to point to the nostalgia and emotion that can attach to old brand-names, nonetheless this does not mean enough consumers will go on buying the memory. While old names can be exploited by good marketing, it is also true that many old brands are just marginal tenants on supermarket shelves. In the United States such brands are Ajax and Rinso detergents, Vitalis hair products, Maypo cereals, Yuban coffee, and many more. One reason for this is because the large retailer chains (through the use of the Universal Product Code) know how quickly brands sell. It is also true that many marketers fail to revive a brand regardless of the marketing. Thus the Liggett Group failed to revive its Chesterfield cigarette in spite of a lavish attempt to do so. One solution is to try and revive the brand only where there are strong regional loyalties. While it is true that when some product is wanted, buying may be done on brand image alone (where the brand image becomes a surrogate indicator) but it is also true that some buying is based on a more rational evaluation, even if not as thorough as the multiattribute model would suggest.

It should not just be assumed that the market leader will necessarily have the highest loyalty rates, however measured. Thus Bayer is the brand leader in headache remedies and the most well-known brand, but the consumers of Tylenol are much less inclined to substitute. The more distinctive the segment benefits, the more likely the loyalty. However, we suspect that not all product categories have the same inherent capability of generating loyal customers. The more intimate the type of relationship with the product; the longer the use of the product and the more the product is the type associated with pleasure or excitement, the more likely the emotional (strongest) type of loyalty. Thus products that are consumed (e.g. alcohol) or applied to the body (e.g. cosmetics), are perhaps more likely to generate brands to which consumers are emotionally loyal.

5 Allied to the last point, is the possibility of using the brand-name on other products. Many firms paid outrageous prices for acquisitions to possess certain brand-names, obviously believing the brand-names were not being sufficiently exploited. This seems the only satisfactory explanation of Philip Morris's $3.8 billion purchase of the Swiss coffee and chocolate firm of Jacob Suchard, or Philip Morris's purchase of Kraft for $12.9 billion, which was four times its book value, or the Nestlé purchase of Rowntree for $4.5 billion, which was five times its book value. Any extension of the brand-name should exploit whatever it is that gives core meaning to the brand as the name should not be used indiscriminately. As Aaker says, a brand can help get new customers, recapture or hold onto old ones, enhance brand loyalty, allow higher margins with premium pricing, provide a platform for growth via brand extensions, provide leverage in distribution channels and provide a sustainable advantage. Chiquita bananas and Perdue chickens illustrate that alleged commodity products can, on occasions, be successfully branded.

International brands

There are brands that sell unaltered around the world, for example, drugs, certain electronic products, and many industrial ones and some services like hotel management. But there are not many brands that are well-known throughout the world, Coca-Cola being one of the exceptions. There is still a tendency for Europeans to like European brands, the Japanese to prefer their own brands, and the Americans to choose their own brands.

Although there has been much talk about global markets for standardized offerings ever since Theodore Levitt proclaimed this was the way to go, products and offerings have typically been adapted to local markets. If Heinz's ketchup is a global brand, it is still made sweeter for the British market, spicier for the Continental Europe and more tart for the United States. The same product is not always even used for the same purposes around the world. Thus consider the two major products of Cadbury-Schweppes: chocolate and tonic water. Chocolate is a snack to consumers in some countries and a pudding to consumers in other countries, while tonic is drunk straight by the French but mixed with gin by the British. In fact a standardized product does not always yield the economies predicted. Production costs may not be that major, for example, consider perfume and cigarettes where production costs are a very small part of total costs. In any case, there are relatively few globalized *standardized brands*, and relatively fewer global markets for *standardized offerings*. But some can be found. For example, educational, reference, medical and other scientific books in English sell as global products around the world. Simon & Schuster has stressed this side of its publishing business while Time-Life's international sales are a large part of its success.

Building new brands

Building new brands is really the subject of the next chapter but some things can be said here. New-to-the-world products that aim to displace an inferior, substitute technology may have brand-names that come to exemplify the technology. Examples are Hoover in vacuum cleaners, Singer in sewing machines, and IBM in data processing. The problem lies first in displacing the existing rival technology to establish the new brand. This takes time. Products, new only to the company, can have even more difficulty in establishing their brand-name. This is particularly so in markets like detergents, and toothpaste that are essentially differentiated oligopolies. Rival firms rush to copy anything new before a new entrant can get a foothold while the cost of effectively promoting the brand may be too costly. Only big companies enter the big segments of mature markets to take on the giants and even then they need to have some distinct, sought-after competitive advantage such as Unilever did with its Lever 2000 soap. We are reminded of what was said earlier: What can the little guy do that the big guy cannot do better? The little guy enters niche segments that do not disturb the giants, uses its relative flexibility rather than muscle, and avoids areas where size and muscle count.

Destroying the brand

Aaker makes the point that killing a brand is hard without its owners doing a lot to help. Thus he takes to task promotional strategies that focus on price promotions; or using the brand-name on products that do not exemplify what the brand stands for, resulting in a confused and inconsistent image; or diluting the brand image by going downscale with the brand-name; or failing to upgrade the brand; or failing to support the brand with advertising dollars resulting in the brand gravitating toward being a faceless, lifeless product. Aaker puts a lot of the blame on the short-term orientation of product managers and suggests companies should hire "brand-equity managers" to monitor the status of their brands and ensure they retain some advantage. Perhaps some of the sunset status brands currently include P&G's Camay, Kraft General Foods Sanka, and Coca-Cola's Tab! While Aaker is right to stress management's culpability, it is also true that technological developments can just displace a competitive advantage. Thus the MacIntosh computer, which when first introduced had the critical advantage of "painless" computing, was undermined by the development of Microsoft's Windows.

PRODUCT POLICY

Scope for "new" products

Booz, Allen & Hamilton Inc, the consulting firm, uses the term new products in the very widest sense to embrace:

- new-to-the-world products that create new markets;
- new product lines that allow a firm to enter established markets, that is, new-to-the-firm product;
- additions to existing product lines;
- repositionings;
- improvements in existing products; and
- cost reductions.

These options are illustrated in Figure 9.3.

Every organization needs policies to guide its new product additions. Underlying these policies should be an assessment of the firm's actual or potential capabilities/competencies and thrust so that, whatever new products are sought, they build on the firm's strengths in seeking a competitive advantage. Not every firm will have what it takes to develop "new-to-the-world products." As has already been pointed out, a small firm should avoid new products that depend on state-of-the-art research or heavy capital

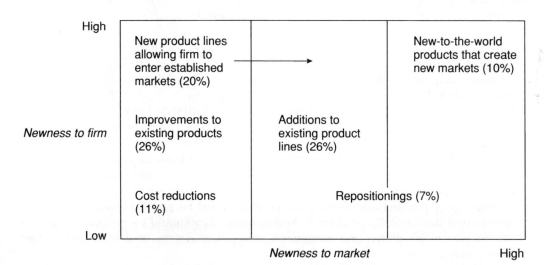

Percentages denote number of
introductions relative to total

Figure 9.3 New product directions

Source: After Booz, Allen & Hamilton Inc., 1982

investment but seek segments in which it can grow without disturbing the giants and where relative flexibility and speed of response are an advantage. Even if only product improvement is anticipated, such improvements must be meaningful in terms of consumer perceptions.

How should a firm select additions to its product portfolio? At any one time, a firm seeks products for markets that fall within the firm's definition of its business and where the firm's total business system and its particular competencies and thrust match the requirements for success. If the firm no longer has what is needed to provide some advantage in the market, not even the advantage of location, it may have to think about divesting or, if some potential remains, a turnabout to bring its capabilities in line with some segment requirements.

The purpose of getting out a product policy is to give guidance on what to look for in a market or market segment and what to avoid. In other words, a product policy has links with the concept of industry attractiveness (see Chapter 2). But it is difficult to draw up a product policy statement as it can be a premature closure of options when drawn up in advance of experience. It may be too rigid and lack sensitivity to opportunities. However, there must be some constraints on the search for new products; constraints such as those suggested by "business in" and company thrust.

Product policy elements

The following suggested elements of a product policy (that might apply, say, to a firm like BIC) are not meant to be definitive but merely illustrative.

1 *Business(es) served*: the boundaries within which to look for markets.
    Example: Additions to the product portfolio will be consumer products that are inexpensive, disposable and mass produced and capable of being sold through the existing distribution network.
2 *Financing*: method of financing and the maximum amount to spend.
    Example: The development and marketing of any new products must be financed primarily from earnings with the goal of being self-financing in 3–4 years.
3 *Degree of risk*: the acceptable risk level. Expected payoff is an inadequate criterion as it ignores the risk for a company with limited resources; legitimate risks must, though, be distinguished from gambles that can threaten the firm's survival.
    Example: Any product additions to the portfolio must be products that have proven themselves domestically or abroad. Additionally, they should be products that lend themselves to integrated and automated production systems and tight quality and cost controls.
4 *Degree of innovativeness*: This is important as a reminder that the various cells in Figure 9.3 are apt to carry different types and degrees of risk. Thus in general, a new-to-the-world product innovator would need to have an R&D thrust; the follow-my-leader an efficiency thrust; a leapfrog strategy a strong development resource and flexibility to respond.
    Example: No product will be added to the portfolio that is not already established

elsewhere. The company's brand when introduced will mostly compete on lower price and wide distribution as befits a low cost producer with worldwide distribution.

5 *A balanced portfolio*:
   Example: At present the firm's portfolio consists mainly of products at the maturity stage of the life cycle. The focus should be on seeking growth markets in which the firm can develop some stars.

Product policy gives direction to the search for product additions and so is associated with the investment objectives of growth, hold/defend, and turnabout. But product management is not just concerned with these objectives since at some stage there might be a need to harvest or divest.

PRODUCT STRATEGIES

Product considerations enter into all major company decisions. What products are produced, for example, affects investment decisions about what facilities will be needed to make and market products in the future, while recruitment, selection and training must consider the tasks that producing and marketing such products will impose on the business. It is for this reason that many of those teaching business policy regard product strategy as the major strategic focus for the firm with finance, personnel and production strategies being seen as emanating from the basic product strategies.

The investment objectives for the business and the thrust of the business are major determinants of product policy and strategy which, in turn, relate to product goals or objectives as shown in Figure 9.4. These goals/objectives are in terms of the earnings stream that is needed:

1 immediate earnings;
2 steady earnings; and
3 future growth in earnings.

If the goal is immediate earnings, the firm focuses on present strengths and avoids projects that call for extensive technical development or necessitate high capital investment. Management is likely to find cost reduction and product improvement the most attractive strategies for achieving immediate earnings. Where a steady earnings flow or steady net cash stream is sought, the search for new products is likely to be more passive than active in that the search is more likely to be undertaken as a reaction to competitive attacks. Management in such a situation is likely to be more reactive than proactive and focus on line development and product improvement. With a proactive strategy, the focus is on preempting competition by being the first to market a new-to-the-world product or some product variation that has a competitive advantage. Management is thus likely to focus on future growth in earnings through innovation which typically means having its thrust in R&D for product or process innovation and/or marketing for developing new markets.

Figure 9.4 illustrates some of the possible options in cost reduction; product improve-

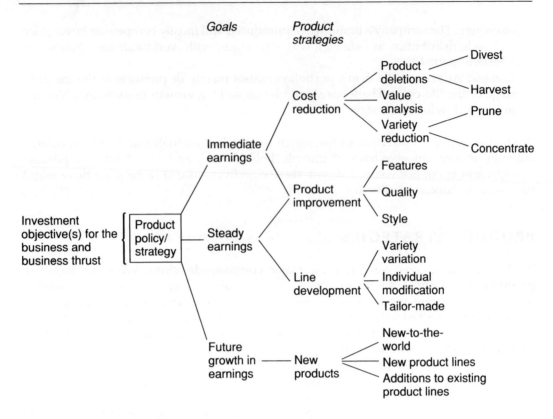

Figure 9.4 Company goals and corresponding product strategies

ment; line development and new products. The strategies shown in Figure 9.4 embrace the Booz, Allen & Hamilton categories shown in Figure 9.3 except for "repositionings." If in repositioning a product, the product remains unchanged, the problem is a market segmentation one and only secondly one of product strategy. However, if the product is changed in some way, it is covered by the strategies shown in Figure 9.4 and it will be dealt with below.

Cost reduction

One of the major programs adopted in turning around a company from a position of unprofitability is *cost reduction*. Such cost cutting is likely to involve a reduction in the number of products both in the product mix and the product line. The *product line* refers to the firm's products that fall within the same product class (for example, the different coffee products of General Foods). The *product mix* refers to the set of product lines produced by a business or division (for example, Gillette's various men's products). We speak of the *"breadth"* of a product mix in reference to the number of different product lines produced by a business and speak of the *"depth"* of a product line in reference to the number of products in the line. Cost reduction as a way of achieving low cost production is particularly important to those adopting a follower strategy. Thus Helene Curtis's success with its Suave line rests on the company's ability to spot likely competitor successes like herbal shampoo, and introduce the same product under the Suave name at a lower price.

Product deletions

Product mix expansion which is unrelated to the firm's thrust and competencies is a major reason for business failure. Firms increase the breadth of a product mix to exploit a perceived market opportunity, but the strategy fails not because there is no market opportunity but because the market opportunity is not an opportunity for the firm since it did not exploit what the firm had to offer.

Product deletion is an attempt to remedy the error of unwise product proliferation either by immediate divesting or more slowly via harvesting. Product deletions are often resisted by the Sales Department, whose attention is frequently more channeled to producing revenue than profit. Yet retaining even marginally profitable products can be costly in terms of opportunity cost. This is not to suggest that profitability be the sole criterion for retention. Sales people are not always just concerned with revenue but also concerned with past commitments to others. Some product deletions involve breaking implicit promises on servicing those who have already bought the product. Breaking a commitment is the breaking of a promise (violating a trust) and can reduce the firm's ethical image. A product may make no contribution to profit as conventionally measured, but still be retained on the grounds that:

- it is an integral part of the firm's product line in that customers expect the firm to carry it;
- it keeps out competition from getting a foothold in the market;
- it meets the demand of certain key distributors;
- it contributes to corporate image; and
- it is expected eventually to be profitable.

The more unprofitable products can be eliminated first with promotional support being gradually withdrawn from the rest in a harvesting strategy. But some thought might be given first to whether the marginal product can be made profitable. In practice, a major problem lies in knowing whether a product is indeed unprofitable in that true costs may not be revealed by the firm's costing system.

Variety reduction

Product variety (sizes, colors, shapes, etc.) within a product line must relate to segment demands and justify the extra cost involved in manufacture and marketing. But again it is often difficult to measure the extra cost and losses involved particularly when variety is advocated as a way of facilitating sales: sales of particular product variations may be uneconomic but their presence in the line may facilitate sales.

Value analysis and value engineering

Both value analysis and value engineering are standard techniques for reducing the cost of a product without sacrificing market appeal. They are techniques with which marketing management are frequently involved and can be used in the improvement of quality and not just reducing costs. The *value analysis* approach typically follows the following steps:

1 *information collection* stage. Information is collected on the functions performed by the product; materials used; tolerance limits; processes used in manufacture; surface finishes; standardized parts used; cost breakdown of parts and materials. Functions are defined by just a verb and a noun. For example, the use function of a pen cap may be defined as "protect nib." This definition emphasizes the contribution the pen cap makes and also suggests alternative means for the same function, for example, retractable nib.
2 *brainstorming*. A team consisting of (say) the designer, a marketing executive, a production engineer, cost accountant and a purchasing manager analyze the information collected and speculate as to what might be done to reduce cost (or improve quality?). One member records the ideas put forward. No attempt is made to evaluate the ideas on the ground that criticism applied too early unduly inhibits the free flow of ideas. Can functions be performed with less costly materials, less tight tolerances, cheaper processes and finishes?
3 *evaluation*. The ideas are ranked according to their estimated potential to reduce costs and examined in this order on a good-bad basis. For example, in one case, the idea of a power cable being made of sodium was put forward on the ground of its being the cheapest material to use as an electrical conductor: the good and the bad of the suggestion were put forward. The good aspects were the low cost, plentiful supply, being flexible and light. The bad were that it reacts instantly on contact with water and oxidizes rapidly in the air. The bad may present a seemingly insurmountable obstacle but attempts are made to overcome such obstacles without adding more to cost than to savings (for example, the bad points of a sodium conductor were overcome through the use of a plastic coating).

Value analysis is applied to existing products. The technique when applied at the design stage is known as *value engineering*. In recent years value engineering has been used to design products to reduce quality errors, for example, by designing the product so that wrong assembly is impossible.

Product improvement

Product improvement involves changing the features, quality or style of a product to give a better fit to the (new?) demands of the market or market segment. It is difficult to draw a sharp line between an old product that has been improved and a new one. Things about the old product may change but the promise, the character, the total image of the offering does not. One operational rule is to ask whether basic changes in strategy are required. Thus, while DYMO did not add much to the established method of labeling via relief lettering (simply using colored plastic tape instead of metal strips) and the cassette innovation was merely a convenient way of holding a magnetic tape, both these products required very different marketing strategies from the originals and so were considered entirely new products. Brands change through time but to be recognizable as the same brand there must be some core that remains in brand image.

Product improvement is never-ending. Even if a firm invented the product and created the market for it, there is every likelihood that product improvement is necessary for the firm to continue to hold on to its market. Yet the product improvement strategy is not without its dangers. For example, P&G's Prell brand of shampoo was changed from green to blue as they added a conditioner. This alienated the existing users of Prell (green) who demanded its return. As Prell (blue), however, had attracted a different segment of the market, P&G restored the original Prell (green) but continued with Prell (blue). In doing this P&G seemed to follow Coca-Cola in restoring Classic Coke. It was not that Prell's customers did not seek any improvement in Prell. In fact, Prell had successfully undergone at least eight major improvements since it was first launched in 1947, including at least three changes in the product's fragrance, but apparently the color was part of the core meaning of Prell for many of its customers. Many other examples could be quoted. Even cat box filler is not exempt as witness the outcry from customers when Kitty Litter tried to improve its formula, giving them no option but to return to the original formula.

Features

One writer describes a feature as any "physical and functional characteristics or component of the basic product that may be used to distinguish it from competing products of similar quality."[17] He distinguishes the following bases:

- *material of construction*, for example, the glass-lined water heater;
- *method of construction*, for example, the "unitized" automobile chassis;
- *kind of performance*, for example, television combined with a VCR;
- *construction or performance of one part*, for example, power steering; and
- *arrangement of component parts*, for example, the freezer at the bottom of the refrigerator.

These bases are appropriate for physical products but have little relevance to services. Yet the service industries are very much concerned with features since many service firms have one core service but add on many features to distinguish themselves. The addition of features is, together with any other add-ons, what is called the *augmented product*.

Typically successful features are copied by competition fairly quickly. Why then add features? Features can evoke intense preference and so attract and convert from rivals during the time the firm has the feature exclusively. Firms that are innovative in new features project a progressive image and can attract a great deal of free publicity. Features are also a flexible competitive tool since often they can be added, dropped or made optional. Features can also be used to attract distributors and provide the sales force with something distinctive to talk about. Thus in watches we have multi-featured diving watches, new lines of trendy art watches as well as the more established jewel-encrusted fashion watches.

Features are commonly identified with ancillary and convenience-in-use functions. But by no means is this always so. At present in the PC market, a good deal of competition revolves around the provision of features. While many of these, such as screens for notebooks, video and audio chips, and built in software, are concerned with technical functions, there are also the features that relate to the total offering such as extended service contracts and warranties. This latter example also illustrates something else about features; that the addition of features often favors the industry giants who have the resources and capabilities to add features without necessarily having to increase price. In this way the leading brands push out those who, while able to compete on price for the basic product, are unable to compete on features or offer sufficient of a price cut.

Features can be used as a basis for creating new market segments. Thus the filter in cigarettes created a new market segment. However, because smokers may buy filter cigarettes for different reasons (to keep particles of tobacco out of the mouth and/or for less tar intake) these different reasons can be used as a basis for promotional segmentation in that promotional appeals can stress either one or the other.

Quality

To say a product is of high quality is to evaluate it as having high standing relative to similar products. The key then to understanding what the term means in some particular context is to identify the criteria used in the evaluation and to identify the other products against which the product is being ranked. There are no standard criteria since criteria vary with product category. However, a distinction should be made between the professional's criteria and the buyers' since they may not completely overlap. The professional is likely to be concerned with technical criteria such as the materials used, attention to detail in the construction and so on. Not all such technical aspects will necessarily enter into the buyer's own indicators of quality. Although the focus should be on customer perceptions and surrogate indicators of quality, a distinction should be made between what buyers may view as quality and what they will come to view as quality after using the product. A firm is concerned both with what indicators buyers use to suggest quality and also what will be meaningful to them as they come to use the product.

"Quality" can cover:

- *factual properties* of the product, for instance, known durability of structure and serviceability;

- *success properties*, for instance, known performance, and reliability, consistent conformance to established standards etc.; and
- *response properties*, for instance, image, aesthetics.

"Quality" must relate to the performance of functions but a quality product is not necessarily good in every discernible part. Some use the term product quality as a synonym for *customer value* but the two can be distinguished as product quality does not include all that would enter into customer value: product quality does not include the whole of the offering but the term customer value does. In terms of choice criteria, product quality relates to intrinsic, technical, and integrative criteria but does not include economic (price, easy availability), service quality, and perhaps not adaptive criteria which can revolve around factors incidental to the product itself.

We said that talk about quality presupposes the existence of criteria against which to evaluate. But talk about quality is not only relative to some criteria but to some comparative set of products against which the product is to be ranked on the criteria. This set can only be the products that are rivals. When consumers speak of a brand being of high quality, they are not generally speaking of quality in some absolute sense but against other brands within that segment, within that price range. Thus when we speak of a firm making a quality product we mean that, within its class, it is a good product with "class" being wide enough to embrace the brand's segment rivals. Sometimes, of course, consumers do compare a downscale brand with an upscale brand and talk about the downscale brand being of low quality, but this should not divert us from recognizing our product's true comparison group. In respect to nonservices, improvements in quality are most often in terms of improving those technical attributes like performance in core-use functions:

- Not everyone seeks the highest level of performance in the core functions for which the product was designed. Even if consumers would like the extra quality, they may not be prepared to pay for it: quality is generally quality within some price range.
- High performance in core-use functions may be incompatible with having other functions and the consumer may be willing to trade off performance in the core function to achieve these other benefits. Thus, in general, consumers refuse to sacrifice glamour for a more water-repellent raincoat and gladly sacrifice high wearability/ durability in order to get the benefit of a minimum iron shirt.
- Consumers often cannot gauge quality directly and may use the wrong indicators. Thus the optical properties of sunglasses may be judged purely on the sturdiness of the frames or on the basis of brand familiarity. If manufacturers find that buyers are using the wrong indicators to judge quality, they cannot ignore providing such indicators even while educating consumers on how to truly gauge the quality they seek. Sony has a quality image slightly higher in the United States than its rival Panasonic, allowing it to charge a higher price over Panasonic in the United States, but not in Japan, where the two firms are considered equal in quality. Quality is very much a matter of using surrogate indicators for many consumers. This is somewhat analogous to judging whether something is water. Consumers establish that it is water by indicators: it is wet, colorless, and tasteless but, we

have known since 1750 that the essential property of being water is being made of H_2O.

- There may be no objective measures of quality beyond the reactions of consumers. Thus there are no known chemical tests for measuring the quality of coffee beyond taste tests.
- Not every firm can be the technological leader in performance in the core-use function. Such firms might find it wiser to seek segments that weight other choice criteria more important than high performance in the core-use function.
- Improving the core-use function assumes that this function is the true function for which the product is being used. It may not be.
- The key functions on which the buying decision is made can vary over time just as watch accuracy ceased to be a discriminator with the advent of the quartz watch.

One technique for improving service quality is that known as *blueprinting* in which the whole network of service processes is mapped; points of weaknesses (likely failures) noted, failsafe procedures instituted and, finally, standard execution times established. In general, where service is purely instrumental, as in banking, quality of service is tied to its being an efficient one and the satisfaction that comes from a feeling of progress being made toward achieving goals. What the customer wants to avoid are any apprehensions, anxieties, fears and frustrations that might arise in the process of rendering the service. The customer wants the service provider to "just get the job" done without fanfare or bells and whistles. What we term a businesslike atmosphere is what is sought where the customer perceives the service provider as reliable, competent and responsive to his or her special needs, with sales people being perceived as courteous and accessible. On the other hand, when service is to provide enjoyment, customer satisfaction will come from excitement and the avoidance of boredom. Whereas providing an exciting atmosphere in a bank would not be in keeping with that type of service, the atmosphere of any place of entertainment must be concerned with stimulating intrinsic liking and enjoyment.[18]

A *quality image* is generally hard to earn but easy to lose and difficult to regain. Poor quality is not just a cost in terms of reduced sales but can be costly in terms of returns, allowances, loss of goodwill, product liability claims, servicing and repair under warranty and customer complaints. The maintenance of quality is essentially concerned with the absence of variation over the standard laid down and this can be expensive in terms of process control, training, quality reporting systems, inspection and testing. This has led more firms to go back to the drawing board to basic product design to make rejects, errors in assembly and use of the product less likely: what might be called inspecting a product before it is made.

Other concepts that have come into vogue are *total quality control* and *just-in-time supplies*. With total quality control (TQC), quality-control principles are applied not just to manufacturing but to every operation, every facet of the business. The aim is to continually improve all aspects of quality for every customer in the chain of customers right through to the final consumer. There are what are known as "extended design teams" composed of customers at each level and "quality function deployment" that involves (following the multiattribute model) customers weighting the various quality dimensions as to relative importance and how the company compares with its competitors. Finally, continuous efforts are made to avoid what is termed "tolerance stackup" or second order variation, resulting from two or more within-specification parts not fitting, which is exacerbated as the number of process stages increases. The need for high quality becomes a necessity when buyers insist on "just-in-time" (JIT) deliveries. JIT deliveries cater to integrative criteria in that the buying institution becomes more integrated with the supplier to achieve the benefits of reduced inventory; reduced lead times; increased labor efficiency; smoother material flow; increased space utilization; and simplified production planning and control. But the burdens on the supplier in respect to meeting production schedules and making sure of quality are immense. Yet speed of delivery can be a key competitive advantage in some industries, like that part of the clothing industry that caters to the whims of fashion. To date the evidence would suggest that total quality control programs have not had the impact on competitiveness as envisaged. One reason put forward for this is that firms, in concentrating their efforts on improving the quality of their processes, have not kept their sights on the customer. Some firms have merely gone through the motions while others have used the approach simply for cost cutting (Motorola, for example, claims its total quality program reduced its manufacturing costs by $700 million). What is needed is feedback from the customer in terms of matching results against customer expectations. There are also organizational issues in that responsibility for quality is a universal one.

Services. Service quality is as important as product quality and one study claims that the five most significant factors that influence the overall evaluation of service quality are

1 reliability;
2 responsiveness;
3 assurance;
4 empathy; and
5 tangibles such as physical facilities and equipment.[19]

But the question arises as to whether these five criteria apply or are relevant to all service industries. One question raised by another study is whether the causal relationship is:

- service quality ⇒ satisfaction *or* (as the evidence seemed to suggest);
- satisfaction ⇒ perception of service quality; *or*
- prior expectations of service quality ⇒ satisfaction ⇒ current perceptions of service quality; *or*
- performance ⇒ service quality ⇒ satisfaction.

Satisfaction appears to have a stronger and more consistent effect on purchase intentions than does service quality.[20] But we can query the meaningfulness of these relationships.

Common sense suggests that unless service quality is construed to be equivalent to overall performance, it cannot be assumed that service quality is guaranteed to lead to satisfaction with the service. A buyer may acknowledge the dress is of low quality but be highly satisfied with it because it suits. Similarly, she may regard the dress as of high quality yet be highly dissatisfied with it. If satisfaction with a service leads to perceptions of high service quality regardless of the objective facts about the service, then service (as it is construed) is either not important or consumers are more given to self-delusion than anyone thought. Finally, the causal chain of: performance ⇒ perceptions of service quality ⇒ satisfaction is unlikely unless service quality is construed as overall performance. More defensible is the view that both perceptions of high performance and perceptions of service quality are conceptually undifferentiated in the respondent's perception of satisfaction. In other words, the relationships between performance, perceptions of satisfaction and service are not causal but simply represent conceptual equivalencies. Thus what else would respondents *mean* by satisfaction with a service but having received quality service/good performance overall?

Most offerings include some pure service component. Although product quality is typically key, the service component can swing the sale. Thus one mattress manufacturer offers delivery within twenty-four hours but, in addition, takes away the old mattress. This has proven to be a major buying inducement. Further along the continuum, there are the pure service industries like banking and insurance. Quality here relates to technical factors such as the expertise of the service providers, and their reliability; integrative factors such as responsiveness to the customer, courtesy and understanding; adaptive factors such as consistency of the service quality and trustworthiness of the service provider. The aim of quality control is customer retention and/or good word-of-mouth communication about the service. Since word-of-mouth communication is apt to be more important for services than for goods, bad-mouthing a service can undermine any attract or convert strategy. Customers are far more likely to tell about their bad experiences with a product than their good experiences. This can be very destructive of brand image. As a consequence, more and more firms are concerned to remedy any fault found with their product. Particularly with respect to services, the key lies in getting customers to voice their complaints to the company so that the complaining customer is made to feel the firm is anxious to make amends. The setting up of some unit to handle complaints usually more than pays its way in getting repeat sales and avoiding the lost sales from customer complaints to other potential customers.

A good service or overall service quality/performance can mean different things to different people which suggests a basis for segmentation. Thus consumers shopping for bargains can be irritated by extra services since they may believe this sends up the price, or resent elaborate treatment or sales pitches as wasting their time. On the other hand, there are consumers only too willing to pay extra for pampering. Even when sellers know what constitutes a quality service to the buyer, there is the problem of controlling the service to avoid substandard variations since people are not machines. There will be variation among the employees and it is not as easy to measure this variation as it is with a machine-produced product. But certain ingredients are always present when the service involves interpersonal communication as all people wish to protect their self-esteem and like to be recognized and treated with courtesy. Thus, as

British Airways found, addressing passengers by name ("Have a good day, Mr. Smith") considerably increased customer satisfaction with their treatment and flight.

Encounters with service providers often means dealing with strangers which can be fraught with uncertainties revolving round our having less control over the situation. A strong sense of an absence of control gives rise to a sense of powerlessness, a sense of being less able to cope leading to:

- entertaining the possibility of confrontation;
- fear of embarrassment, for example, through being conscious of being observed, perhaps critically, and yet not knowing how to respond; and
- fear that service people will not be supportive of the customer's sense of personal worth or self-image so holding out the possibility of being humiliated (sense of being reduced in status).

Self-service for some people is more preferable. It can also be time-saving and customized to the consumer's browsing habits. Self-service can be desirable when the product is a well-known standard product with known applications (for examples, groceries). Self-service is convenient and the addition of indifferent service can do more harm than good. But many products are not standard and need to be explained, like mortgage loans, or need to be customized as in the case of insurance and financial planning, while the use of sales people always holds out the possibility of the customer being persuaded to buy or buy more.

The computer is doing much to improve service. Thus industrial buyers can tap their rebuy orders directly into their supplier's computer; Federal Express uses a computer system that can tell customers exactly where their packages are at any time, and the new Otis elevators automatically report anything going wrong with them to the Otis's computer system, without any human intervention at all. Perhaps one of the best uses of the computer in services is where it results in service workers' devoting more time to building relationships with customers and allowing the firm to focus more on the recruitment of those with human relations skills. Thus American Express now uses the computer to help employees at every step from the receipt of applications, to managing credit, to collecting overdue accounts.

The service industries are more and more concerned with customer perceptions of their service. Instead of just advertising claims about service that build up expectations among customers that are never realized, the aim is to deliver more than promised so that expectations are exceeded. But this has meant changing the attitudes and skills of service people through education, indoctrination and incentives. Attitudes often need to be changed since service persons who regard the job as demeaning will automatically think of themselves as being perceived as inferior to those being served. With the conception of helping others to meet their goals, rather than serving others, service people can feel more adjusted, with each interaction an opportunity to help. But training is needed in how to deal with critical incidents; how to make people feel good about themselves through supportive comments, seeking common ground and favorably mentioning what is worthy of mention; avoiding overt flattery or pressuring through "advice" so that people buy without reservations.

Style

Style preferences are generally thought to reflect intrinsic liking but need not do so in that certain styles might just be perceived as more socially appropriate or more geared to use function. A strategy based on style tends to be common when it becomes difficult for the company to stress a differential advantage in terms of the core-use function. However, smart marketers recognize style is a powerful motivator at any time in the life cycle. Thus Reebok and L. A. Gear have shifted their emphasis in footwear from performance to innovative fashionable new styles.

Frequent style changes may be essential to keep up with current tastes. In fact, a common strategy in the car industry in the past was not to improve the quality of the product but to plan changes in style to make the older models appear psychologically obsolescent. But style changes typically require investment in design and equipment so that many small firms eschew a policy of frequent style changes to concentrate on classic designs.

Where a style preference is simply a matter of taste, it is difficult to predict market reaction or promote the style exclusively to those who might prefer it. Complicating matters even more is when a nonoptional feature is added to a change of style. This can narrow the market for a product if the liking of the feature is independent of liking the style. Hence there is a need to know not only how many prefer the new style and how many prefer the new feature but *who* prefers what. Yet style can be a major buying inducement as consumers seek a style that fits their surroundings or coordinates with their other purchases. The introduction of style has induced women to buy several purses (handbags), pairs of shoes, and so on while the innovation of the Swatch watch did much to revive the Swiss watch industry. When an attractive style seemingly also helps increase performance in the core-use function, the market appeal can be very high indeed. But, as the example of the Swatch watch shows, the core function may not be the key function but the display of the style itself as signaling some set of values.

Style does not just refer to the style of the product itself but also to its packaging. Many a company, by improving the packaging, has had a dramatic effect on brand image from being a lifeless and dull one to being lively, exciting and modern. Thus, McCormick & Co., the largest producer of spices in the United States, gave a new look to its product, freshening it up by replacing the red and white cans with clear plastic bottles. Consumers may love the product inside the package but restrict buying because of the packaging. This was the situation with Cadbury's "Milk Tray," where consumers would say they would never give it as a present because the package conveyed a boring, old-fashioned image. Needless to say Cadbury did much for sales by updating the package.

Because style is so subjective in its appeal, it has tended to be ignored when it comes to studies of quality such as the relationship between quality as "objectively" measured and price. On this basis consumer advisory magazines can sound naive. For example, one such magazine tested sunglasses ranging in price from $12 to $230 and concluded the best buy was at $15, though there are few who base their purchasing of sunglasses just on keeping out ultraviolet rays.

Market repositionings are usually accompanied by some changes in the product to stress the change in target segment. Sometimes the change may be such that the repositioning is more a case of market development in that the product use has changed. A good example here is in the market for cold medicines such as antihistamines, decongestants, analgesics, and cough suppressants. These same remedies have been repackaged by some firms, given a new name and a higher price and called flu remedies. The medicine's association with treating influenza suggests something more powerful than just a cold remedy. Unethical advertising suggests the flu remedies have therapeutic value though they offer nothing more than symptom relief. The usual problems associated with repositioning do not arise here in that current customers are not alienated (typically they are unaware of what has happened) while there is no problem for the new customers having to recategorize old cold remedies as remedies for influenza (since they, too, are typically unaware of what has occurred).

Line development

Buyers within a market segment more resemble each other in their market want than they resemble those in other segments. However, they may still differ in ways that can be accommodated by introducing some variety in the line. Thus we have variety variation, modifications on request and tailor-made products, all accommodated within the same market strategy.

Variety variation

Variety variation occurs when there are variations of the product within the line, for example, number of sizes and different colors of the same shoe. Such variations can proliferate unless controlled since there is always pressure from sales to widen choice. Sometimes the variations can be made to appear so fundamental that the variation is no longer variation within a segment but each variation becomes a separate segment. Thus we now have flavor segmentation in coffee. Another example, is with athletic shoes. At one time consumers considered one pair of shoes suitable for tennis, basketball, and running. But some firms, citing medical authorities, claim that different types of activity give rise to different stresses on the feet. Avia now designs shoes for these specific athletic activities.

Individual modification on request and tailor-made products

The basic product may have to be modified to fit the specific, if not unique, requirements of the individual or buying organization. This is common in the service industries. Airlines draft travel documents to fit the individual's requirements; doctors treat according to specific symptoms; lawyers' advice is tailor-made to the case; banking loans and mortgages are tailored to the individual and so on. The exemplar case of a service in fact is the case of the customized service carried out in a personalized way. While many products bought by industry are standard with standardized applications, many products bought are not. The more an industrial product moves away from being a standard product with a standard application toward being a nonstandard product with various applications, the more the need for the service supplied by a sales force.

In some cases, computers are now allowing tailor-made products where previously only a standard product was available. An interesting example here is Rocky Mountain Log Homes, builder of prefabricated dwellings, which lets its customers be architects using computer-aided-design (CAD) so the computer can send the customer's own design straight to the factory. McGraw–Hill offers professors the chance to create their own textbook tailor-made for their courses, by choosing individual chapters from a database of texts. The National Bicycle Industrial Co., which makes bicycles under the Panasonic brand-name, builds one-of-a-kind bicycles through the use of flexible manufacturing. The process starts with the individual customer's order. CAD produces blueprints from the order in three minutes and the custom bicycle takes three hours to make. The small factory of 20 employees can produce any of 11,231,862 variations on 18 models of racing, road, and mountain bicycles in 199 color patterns in any size. The problem of determining the optimal composition and size of a product line is very complex as it involves what features to add, styles to adopt, flavors to produce and so on. Little has been written on the problem until recently.[21] In any case it may not be the product itself that is improved but some other component of the offering. Appendix 9.1 illustrates suggested improvements in an offering that did not involve any change in the product itself.

The product audit

In assessing whether a product should be improved or eliminated, a product audit can be a useful preliminary. This consists of a detailed analysis of the market position of one or more of the company's products, covering the makeup of the product, its packaging, its image, its performance in use functions, the market and its pricing. Table 9.3 is a checklist of the typical information collected to answer such questions as the following:

- Does the product fit the marketing and production system of the organization?
- Is the product likely to be displaced by some new technology or innovation? What are the strengths, or weaknesses of the product and the opportunities and threats facing the product?
- Is quality based on technical or commercial criteria?
- Is the value of the product to the user decreasing?
- How are the product's sales, profitability, and market share over the years?

These are just some questions that may be addressed. What should be emphasized is that the product audit is not just another cost reduction approach but firmly grounded in information relevant to the product's current position in the market and its likely future.

Table 9.3 Product audit information

Product	Market

Characteristics of product
• description
• principal users
• role played by product in company objectives and strategy, e.g. complete existing line
	Segment
	• description
	• size
	• location
	• growth potential
	   numbers buying
	   amount bought per occasion
	   frequency of purchase

Production of product
• raw materials and their availability
• warehousing needed
• inventories required
• whether product requires specialist plant, specific skills, aptitudes and attitudes
• technical know-how
	Customers
	• reasons for buying
	• use of product
	   how? when? with what?
	• relative importance of quality, price, convenience, shape, weight, size, style, packaging
	• how reached?
	   media
	   channels
	• coverage
	• goodwill

History of product
• time series of sales
• seasonal pattern of sales
• costs and profitability
	Competition
	• names of rivals
	• comparison on the following:
	   share of market
	   pricing
	   policies
	   prices to different groups
	   warranties
	   credit policy

Future • vulnerability to obsolescence • anticipated future sales trends • anticipated future costs and profitability	*advertising* expenditure by region and media
Product performance compared with objective set for it	*distribution* channels sales organization accounts where strong
Effect of withdrawing product • on strategy • on profit • on suppliers • on customers • on employees	*service* services offered training of staff quality of service
	flexibility in speed of response to competitive action

NOTES

1 Wasson, C. R. (1971) *Product Management: Product Life Cycles and Competitive Marketing Strategy*, St. Charles, IL: Challenge Books.
2 Rink, David R. and Swan, John E. (1979) "Product Life Cycle Research: a Literature Review," *Journal of Business Research*, 7 (September).
3 Dhalla, N. K. and Yuspeh, S. (1976) "Forget the Product Life Cycle," *Harvard Business Review*, 54 (July–August).
4 Lambkin, Mary and Day, George S. (1989) "Evolutionary Processes in Competitive Markets: Beyond the Product Life Cycle," *Journal of Marketing*, 53 (July).
5 Cox W. E. (1967) "Product Life Cycles as Marketing Models," *Journal of Business*, 40(4) (October).
6 Polli, R. and Cook, V. (1969) "Validity of the Product Life Cycle," *Journal of Business*, 42 (October).
7 Cunningham, M. T. (1969) "The Application of Product Life Cycles to Corporate Strategy: Some Research Findings," *British Journal of Marketing*, 3 (Spring).
8 Porter, Michael E. (1980) *Competitive Strategy: Techniques for Analyzing Your Business and Competitors*, New York: Free Press.
9 Rogers, Everett M. (1962) *Diffusion of Innovations*, New York: Free Press.
10 Foster, Richard (1986) *Innovation*, New York: Summit Books.
11 Lazarsfeld P. F., Berelson, B., and Gaude, H. (1948) *The People's Choice: How the Voter Makes Up His Mind in a Presidential Election*, New York: Columbia University Press.
12 Hebdige, Dick (1991) *Subculture: The Meaning of Style*, London and New York: Routledge.
13 Donnelly, J. H. and Etzel, M. J. (1973) "Degrees of Product Newness and Early Trial," *Journal of Marketing Research*, 10 (August).
14 Kotler, Philip and Zaltman, Gerald (1976) "Targeting Prospects for New Products," *Journal of Advertising Research*, 16.
15 Aaker, David A. (1991) *Managing Brand Equity*, New York: Free Press.
16 Keller, Kevin Lane (1993) "Conceptualizing, Measuring, and Managing Customer-based Brand Equity," *Journal of Marketing*, 57 (January).
17 Stewart, John B. (1959) "Functional Features in Product Strategy," *Harvard Business Review*, 37 (March–April).
18 Apter, Michael J. (1989) *Reversal Theory*, London and New York: Routledge.
19 Parasurman, A., Zeithaml, Valerie and Berry, Leonard (1988) "Servqual: A Multiple-Item Scale for measuring Consumer Perceptions of Quality," *Journal of Retailing*, 64 (Spring).
20 Cronin, Joseph J. and Taylor, Steven A. (1992) "Measuring Service Quality: A Reexamination and Extension," *Journal of Marketing*, 56 (3) (July).
21 Green, Paul, and Krieger, Abba M. (1985) "Models and Heuristics for Product Line Selection," *Management Science*, 4 (1) (Winter).

APPENDIX 9.1 MEMO ON BRAND EXCEL OF SUNFLOWER COOKING OIL

Some suggestions for upgrading the offering.

A. Marketing objectives

1. *Long-term mission:* market leader in the sunflower oil segment of the market.
2. *Goals*
   (i) Reversal of the decline in market share.
   (ii) Increase in market share by X percent in the first year.

(iii) Sustained growth.

B. Competitive strategy

Market share advancement will be achieved by:

1. *Enhancing product* attractiveness *through product improvement.*
   (i) Redesign of the bottle for convenience in use
      (a) no messiness in handling
      (b) no leakage
      (c) instant recognition
   (ii) Redesign of the label to project an image of modernity and promise of good flavor.
   (iii) Addition of personalized logo or scene with which the consumer can identify emotionally. The aim is to give personality to the product; a personality suited to the product, distinctive and attractive.
   (iv) Provision on the label of Excel's advertising assertions.
2. *Enhancing brand* visibility *through consumer promotions.*
3. *Reducing Excel's current uneven distribution and out-of-stock occurrences by trade promotions.*
4. *Advertising to project a distinctive personality with distinctive benefits.*

Note on rationale

Advertising alone – however creative – will not be enough to do the whole job of substantially increasing Excel's market share. It is essential to upgrade the product and/or its packaging. A paler oil would most connote the desire for purity and absence of injurious substances. The product or its packaging must be seen to be updated or otherwise advertising will have little credibility. Excel at present when on the shelf looks like the rest – a tired brand with unimaginative packaging and promotion.

Given that around 50 percent of the target market have never even tried Excel we need sales promotions to add visibility to the product and trigger trial buying.

Consumers identify with brands that seem more "alive" (there is a streak of animism in all of us) with an attractive personality. In this case we need a personality that reflects aspects of the good life that cooking oil promotes: fresh, clean, serene, confident health and friendship.

C. Core (segmentation) strategy

1. *Customer targets*
   (i) Primary group: housewives who care about food preparation sufficiently to seek a high quality product.
   (ii) Secondary group: wholesalers and retailers.
2. *Buying inducement*
   (i) Housewives
      Excel will be positioned in the sunflower segment of the cooking oil market as having the following advantages over rival brands

(a) brand *endorsed* by well-known chefs (or chefs attached to famous restaurants) as being best for cooking, enhancement of food taste, absence of smell and convenience in use
(b) general convenience in using the bottle
(c) attractive (not lifeless) image or a lively (not tired) brand
(ii) Wholesalers and retailers
   (a) stocking incentives
   (b) performance incentives
   (c) individual incentives

Note on rationale

In an undifferentiated market consumers look for advice from those in the know. There is a tendency to informational conformity. There is also a desire to buy the most socially approved brand. There is thus also a tendency to social conformity. The chef endorsement concept should satisfy both those who seek the best advice and those who seek social endorsement of their purchases.

The highlighting of convenience in use is a dominant buying criterion particularly for the upper and middle classes.

The development of an attractive personality for Excel is to appeal to those for whom buying oil is a low involvement exercise. In such circumstances they react rather than evaluate the pros and cons of rival brands.

It is essential that the "pull" strategy of product updating and advertising be supplemented by a "push" strategy by inducements to wholesalers and retailers. In an undifferentiated market the power of wholesalers and retailers increases enormously allowing them to increasingly discriminate against brands that slight their position as "gatekeeper."

D. (Brand) supportive strategies

1. *Advertising*
   (i) Competitive objective
      (a) Primary: To *convert* from rivals and promote the return of former users of sunflower oil now buying cheaper soybean oil.
      (b) Secondary: To *attract* new entrants to the market on the benefits of Excel.
   (ii) Message appeal
      (a) Conversion objectives: Show top, modern chefs using Excel and endorsing the brand. Aim is to appeal to consumer motivation to
      – informational conformity
      – social conformity
      Animation of the product to emit personality in line with values promoted by the product. This is a better way of suggesting the product is supportive of health and is pure—both taken as general attributes of sunflower oil.
      Message appeal should answer question "Why should the consumer buy Excel?"
      (b) Attract objective: Dramatize importance of
      – convenience-in-use

- absence of smell
- importance of "right" oil for appetizing food
- Excel for cooking the modern way

Both the convert and attract competitive objectives can be captured by "top chef using" approach

(iii) Message format

(a) reason giving as to why consumers should choose Excel

(b) emotional element

- Chefs should have openness as if revealing all while at the same time showing feelings. Intimacy is important.
- Demonstration should suggest how cooking competence can be enhanced.

Note on Rationale

Emotional element is often enough to swing a sale in an undifferentiated market. Emotional aspects of advertisement convey:

- Vitality versus sluggishness
- Close warm relationships versus loneliness
- Inner harmony versus tension
- Sense of competence/accomplishment versus being unable to cope

(iv) Media

Television is the ideal medium but cost may limit its use.

TV facilitates chefs' demonstrations and enhances emotional content of advertisement.

Magazines Good for reason giving copy and for showing food products.

Posters – for visibility?

(v) Geographic coverage. Perhaps initially those areas where loss of market share greatest *providing* uneven distribution system corrected.

(vi) Scheduling. Concentrated initially then intermittent.

2. *Distribution*

The dependence on wholesalers to distribute Excel in country areas is the weak link in the chain. In this segment of the market, there is no strong consumer insistence on obtaining any particular brand. Hence the retailer is usually content to accept what is made available by the wholesaler. This means the wholesaler is in a powerful position vis-à-vis the manufacturer. Options available:

(i) A long-term solution is to escape this dependency by selling noncompetitive products to retail making it economic to hire additional salespeople to call on most of the outlets *or* to add to the product line.

(ii) A short-term solution is trade promotions. This is the solution adopted here.

Missionary salespeople calling on retail to obtain orders for transfer to local wholesalers are not likely to be effective when wholesalers can make better deals with other manufacturers. They are likely simply to "drag their feet" to sabotage the effort.

(i) Objectives

(a) To encourage wholesalers (particularly those no longer carrying Excel) to distribute and push the brand.

(b) To encourage extensive retail distribution of Excel as ready availability in every food store is a prerequisite for such a convenience food product.

   (ii) Methods of achieving wholesaler cooperation
              Material incentives are probably essential. Suggestions?
              – Stocking incentive—quantity discount
              – Performance incentive—count/recount method
              – Individual incentives—push money
   (iii) Methods of achieving retailer cooperation
              – Stocking incentive—promotional allowance
              – Performance incentive—space allocation allowance
              – Individual incentive—premiums for dealer
3. *Consumer promotions*
   Premium offers are most likely to give visibility to Excel. Such must fit the housewife's interest and cohere with advertising campaign. Suggestions
   (i)   Chef's recipes
   (ii) Contest having chefs select best recipe sent in
4. *Pricing*
   Current premium price suited to the image of a quality product.

Chapter 10

New product development

Product strategies

Investment objective(s)		New products	Line development	Product improvement	Cost reduction
	Growth	✖	✖	✖	✖
	Hold/defend		✖	✖	✖
	Turnabout	(?)		✖	✖
	Harvest				✖
	Divest				✖

✖ = major relationships

Figure 10.1 Product strategies relating to investment objectives

THE NEED FOR NEW PRODUCTS

As shown in Figure 10.1, product strategies relate to the investment objectives of growth, hold/defend, turnabout, harvest, and divest while Figure 10.2 shows how product strategies relate to the various competitive strategies.

While the investment objective of growth relates to all product strategies (see Figure 10.1), it is preeminently associated with the development of new products. But a firm's very survival, not just profitable growth, may depend on introducing new products though new products may be introduced for still other reasons, e.g. to utilize excess capacity or to make use of waste by-products. Both these latter purposes can also contribute to profitable growth providing the firm possesses the other requirements of success.

The technological performance curve

There are usually just a few technologies crucial to achieving high product performance, for example, the semiconductor chip in the computer. Foster of McKinsey argues that performances based on any technology follow the S-shaped (Gompertz) curve when plotted against expenditures on R&D: slow progress during infancy; then an explosion with breakthrough developments; next a gradual maturation of the technology resulting in diminishing returns as the technology reaches some limit on the performance(s) sought.[1]

For Foster, knowing the limits to the technology is vital:

Product strategy

	Cost reduction	Product improvements	Line development	New products
Market share protection (hold/defend) — Mix adjustments, Imitate, Compensate	Value analysis Variety reduction	Features Quality Style	Variety variation Individual modification Tailor-made	
Relevant competitive strategies — Penetration pricing	Value analysis Variety reduction			
Market share advancement (growth) — Capitalize, Leapfrog		Features Quality Style	Variety variation Individual modification Tailor-made	
New offerings				New-to-the-world New product lines Additions to existing product lines

Figure 10.2 Product strategies relating to relevant competitive strategies

1 Recognizing the technology is reaching its limit, as this signals the need to develop or look for a new technology.
2 The maturing of an old technology opens up the possibility of a competitor entering the market with a new technology that is at an early stage of its S-curve, with the potential to surpass the market leader by producing a product that is sufficiently superior to give it a competitive edge (see Figure 10.3). Alternatively, the new technology may add something else of value to the customer, like ancillary or convenience-in-use functions. Foster accepts that when customers take for granted a high performance in the core-use function, this triggers the demand for additional benefits which the newly emerging technology might be able to offer.

Foster acknowledges it is not always easy to identify the maturity stage of a technology since there can be temporary plateaus in the S-curve. There is also a problem in seeking the technological limit on performance to ensure it is of interest to customers and not something going beyond what is wanted. Thus in the 1950s, detergents made clothes as

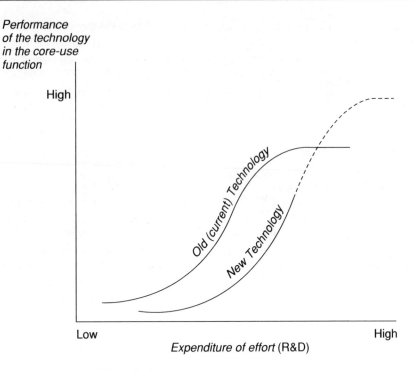

Figure 10.3 The technology life cycle S-curve

Source: After Richard Foster, *Innovation,* New York: Summit Books, 1986

clean as it was possible to get them but, because old clothes acquire a gray, dingy look, consumers were not satisfied that their clothes were as clean as they could be. P&G capitalized on this misconception by adding "optical brightness" to the detergent. These were chemicals that make clothes appear brighter – and cleaner in the eyes of the customer though not in fact. But well before the limit was reached in making clothes optically the brightest, the customer's desire was sated and customers went on to demand other things.

Foster claims that firms need to estimate the S-curves of their technologies and the S-curves of competing technologies as a basis for investment planning. They should consider adopting the competing technology if discontinuous from the firm's own as discontinuous technologies are invading old markets all the time. The conventional wisdom of "sticking to one's knitting," while generally sound advice, may not be a viable option if a firm is approaching the limit of its own technology and the invading technology has some way to go before reaching its own performance limit. It is wrong to ignore the new technology. Thus Michelin radials were initially sold in the United States to the tire replacement segment of the market because the car manufacturers dismissed them on the ground that customers would not trade off a smoother ride for a longer-lasting tire. The tire manufacturers dismissed the new technology, making them less prepared later to meet competition.

As Foster points out, firms exploiting the new technology have an advantage over incumbent firms using the older technology. Incumbents err in not learning about the new technology and anticipating its impact, but instead go all-out to protect their business based on the old, becoming-obsolescent technology. In 1971, NCR went on refining its obsolete electromechanical technology even when the computer revolution was about to overwhelm it. However, if incumbent firms seek to enter the new technology, there are problems of

- obtaining the needed skills;
- making traumatic changes;
- investing enough in the new technology to be a winner; or
- adopting the new technology with such haste that disaster is inevitable as with Addressograph Multigraph in moving into electronics.

Failures then are the usual ones: a failure to anticipate the new technology; a failure to learn what is happening, and a failure to adapt adequately when making the transition. With any new technology, it is important to judge its potential; to identify potential applications and to learn how to produce and market—and later to make improvements in offerings faster than competition.

Competitive posture

Foster focuses on the case of a firm with an old technology being innovative enough to adopt the new technology. But this is not the common situation. Most innovations are incremental additions in performance rather than discontinuous (sharply different), going up the S-curve of the technology such as Intel in going from the 80286 chip to the 80386 to the 80486 and so on. This may still revolutionize markets. What is interesting about the Intel case is the way Intel discourages buyers from waiting for something better, because of the speed of advances. Thus in 1988, when talking about the advent of the 80486 chip in 1990, Intel predicted the price of a desktop computer incorporating the new chip would be around $20,000. Whether by accident or design this announcement certainly got many buying what was then available!

There can be a market push or a technology push toward innovation. New, non-revolutionary products often arise as a reaction to competition and the shorter PLCs than to basic changes in technology. The firm with a self-image of leadership will seek to be proactive, innovative and be quick to respond to competitive attack. Early entry to a market can mean reaping experience effects, early customer patronage, and the opportunity to keep ahead in innovation. A generally innovative firm like the 3M company (with around 32 percent of its $11 billion sales in new products) is innovative by design and not by chance. Its innovative posture is supported by:

1 *Strategies/policies*:
   a) High R&D as befits a pioneer;
   b) The 25 percent rule which says that one quarter of any division's sales should

come from products introduced within the last five years;

c) The 15 percent rule which states that up to 15 percent of an individual's time can be spent on developing new ideas which, if approved, will receive financing in support; and

d) Managers from R&D and elsewhere to make frequent visits to customers and routinely invite customers to "brainstorm" ideas.

2 *Organization*:

a) Divisions kept relatively small (under $200 million in sales);

b) Task teams recruited from technical areas, marketing, manufacturing, and so on to develop any promising new product; and

c) Financial incentives for meeting standards and exhibiting entrepreneurial behavior.

3 *Culture*:

a) Tolerance of failure;

b) Sharing of knowledge among the divisions; and

c) Innovators as heroes and entrepreneurship as a value to be upheld.

Product innovation is not the only way of innovating. There is innovation in finding new markets and in other aspects of the offering itself. An interesting example here is General Motors' and General Electric's entry into the credit card market with specially tailored MasterCards. In the United States, the credit card market is mature so how do these companies hope to attract and convert? The GE Rewards card costs $25 per annum but offers discounts on GE appliances and rebates from participating retailers, airlines, and hotel chains. The GM card has no annual charge. It, too, allows the holder to get discounts from participating firms. What is distinct and interesting, though, is that the card offers consumers a 5 percent rebate on purchases for use against the purchase of a new GM car or truck. This suggests that it is not the profitability of loans via credit cards that is of interest to GM but the use of the card to sell more GM vehicles. The scheme has since been copied by Ford and others.

New product failure

More and more attention is being given to devising procedures and techniques to secure more winners among new product introductions. This is because, in whatever way "new product" and "failure" are defined, surveys point to a high percentage of new product failures. Some of the most newsworthy failures are Ford's Edsel, Dupont's Corfam, Polaroid's Polavision, and RCA's Videodisc. Some organizations seek to reduce the failure rate by bringing out modified versions of their successes. But these, too, often fail as witness the failure of baby food for single adults, liquid brown sugar, low calorie cake mix, and shampoo laced with yogurt. It may be that competition is getting tougher rather than that companies fail to improve, or it may be that firms take a specific level of risk which corresponds to a certain failure rate. After all, a firm that never has a failure suggests it either never introduces any new products or it is not taking enough risk.

We can define *"new product failure"* as occurring whenever management regrets the decision to introduce the new product. If a firm regrets the introduction, it believes resources could have been better employed. This seems a better definition than defining failure in terms of product withdrawal since sunk costs may result in a firm continuing to market the product. Similarly, this definition seems better than defining a failure as failing to meet profit and other objectives since initial objectives may subsequently seem ill-conceived (e.g. too high a projected level of sales).

Why do products fail? It is not easy to identify the reasons for failure. The reasons given by companies are seldom based on any thorough analysis, and single factors are often quoted when several factors are likely to have been at work. Even if an analysis seeks to be thorough, it may be impossible, ex post facto, to eliminate all rival hypotheses or to measure the contribution of each of the causal factors. The true cause may be unknown or just imperfectly understood. At the most general level, reasons for failure come down to the factors listed in Chapter 8:

- *marketing strategy*: Any of the elements of product, pricing, promotion or distribution might have been sufficiently ill-conceived or ill-coordinated as to bring about failure. Sometimes failure lies in not solving some technical problem. Thus one Japanese firm in the 1970s spent $46 million in bringing out an electric car but was (like others before and since) unable to make a battery that met buyer expectations;
- *product and market entry costs*: After spending $36 million, the Japanese firm that brought out a remote-controlled undersea oil-drilling rig in the 1970s failed on costs as it was no cheaper (or better) than conventional offshore rigs;
- *competitive actions and reactions*: RCA did not anticipate the competitive reaction of IBM in providing its 145 computer range with a larger memory and a lower price tag;
- *size of the segment*: One Japanese firm in the 1980s, at a cost of $11 million, brought out integrated circuits to withstand cold weather but the market segment for the product was too small; and
- *organization*: Organizational deficiencies can frustrate successful implementation of strategies.

The Japanese examples are deliberate to show failure is truly worldwide. But unlike these examples more than one factor is usually at work. Take for example, the Epilady leg-hair remover, which reached sales of $200 million before sales crashed. There was first the response of well-established rivals like Remington Products, which introduced a similar product, but there were also complaints that the product's rotating coils were apt to pull hair out by the roots, while the market proved to be much smaller than was anticipated.

Market conditions conducive to entry success are:

- a product with a critical advantage tied to the firm's competencies and thrust;
- suppliers numerous and lacking market power;
- a growing market; and
- competition fragmented and nonresponsive.

The most difficult market to enter is one dominated by a *few* market-oriented firms with differentiated offerings. New entrants often have to buy their way in via acquisition. If the market is just dominated by *one firm*, it may be possible to be a "runner up" by producing something different for segments being ignored. Finally, where there are *numerous* sellers, it may be possible to become the market leader with a breakthrough in technology or marketing.

THE PROCESS OF NEW PRODUCT DEVELOPMENT

When a strategy of growth via new products is chosen, the risk of failure is of central concern. One way to reduce the failure rate of new products (the evidence on failure rate in the United States [as opposed to anecdote] suggests around 20–30 percent for industrial products and 30–35 percent for consumer products), is to tighten up the process of new product development to weed out likely failures.

Between the decision to seek new products and the decision to launch a new product in the market is the process of *new product development* which at every stage is concerned with filtering out likely failures. The following are the stages in new (physical) product development. But like all such steps or stages, some can be skipped, some combined, and some done in a different sequence altogether:

1 idea generation/opportunity identification/new product conception;
2 screening new product ideas;
3 business analysis;
4 testing: concept testing; preference testing; home-use tests;
5 product brief; building the product prototype;
6 developing the tentative marketing mix of product, price, promotion, and distribution;
7 market testing;
8 commercialization/product launch; and
9 monitoring/management of the product.

The development of a new *service* proceeds similarly through idea generation, screening, and business analysis, but many firms at that stage just try out the service since there is usually less at stake financially.

Idea generation/opportunity identification

Companies do not investigate every new product idea. They will encourage ideas for products that fit the markets and market segments they are already in or propose to enter. The requirements of these markets channel the search for new products.

Sources of ideas can be distinguished from the methods used to generate ideas.

There are external and internal sources of ideas. External sources are customers, suppliers, competition, and published information. Internal sources can be R&D, marketing (in particular sales and marketing research) and other units of the organization. But, whether we are talking of industrial or consumer products, probably the biggest source of ideas (but not necessarily the most rewarding) is internal. According to one study by one high-tech consultancy firm, successful *breakthroughs* (radical innovations) are often technology-pushed, not market led.[2] In another study, for 74 percent of the 137 product innovations studied in two industries, the source of the innovation was the supplier's customers.[3] In any case, the introduction of major technological innovations often happens outside the industry. Thus mechanical typewriter manufacturers did not introduce the electric typewriter and the electronic typewriter manufacturers did not invent the electronic typewriter. In one study of twenty-two companies in seven industries, the first commercial introduction of the product occurred from outside the industry in four out of the seven industries.[4] The older technologies did not decline immediately as it took 4–14 years for the new technology to exceed the old technology in dollar sales.

The customer.   The *customer* can be one source of ideas.
What the customer *says*:

- expression of likes and dislikes;
- expressions of preferences/attitudes; and
- expression of beliefs, wants, choice criteria.

What the customer *does*:

- in using the product;
- shopping habits;
- viewing patterns; and
- buying patterns.

What the customers *is*:

- role responsibilities;
- personality; and
- demographic characteristics.

How the customer is *changing*:

- trends influencing wants;
- two salary families; and
- disproportionate growth in age group over 65 years.

There is debate over the fruitfulness of using customers as sources of ideas. This is inevitable as experiences vary. All agree that customers are useful for suggesting product improvements but many deny their usefulness in suggesting new products. However, many companies are recommending the use of customers as "collaborators" in design. For example, Hewlett–Packard depends on these so-called *user-groups* to help create and identify new technical opportunities. Instead of just listening to customers or observing them, companies encourage customers to build a conceptual model of their suggested innovation and how they would want to use it. A computer simulation of the idea, or a cardboard mock-up, facilitates further customer collaboration.

Competition.   An understanding of competitor strengths and weaknesses and how competitors segment the market can help identify market gaps. Abe Plough, of Plough Inc., is reputed to have watched a pharmacist cut a regular aspirin into parts for the lower-level dosage required by children. This led him to develop an aspirin specifically for children. The gap in the market, though, may not relate to the product. When Remington Rand moved into copiers, its strategy depended less on developing a better product than those of Xerox, IBM, and Savin so much as on developing a superior network of independent dealers and serving them "as if they were the company's own branch offices." Observing the competition and trying to capitalize on their efforts or leapfrogging their technical performances are a major source of new product ideas. But frequently, competitors are just copied which is seldom a way to beat the competition.

Published information.   Technical discoveries, as reported in technical journals and elsewhere, are an important source of ideas. Technical discoveries in oil-refining led to an enormous number of new products, including plastics, man-made fibers, synthetic chemical fertilizers, and detergents. A technical discovery can stimulate new product versions of old products that have remained unchanged for years. The telephone is one of the most recent examples. It changed little in a hundred years. However, the microprocessor is having its effect: phones today have a whole range of new functions, like reminding you to make a call, dialing the number, and persisting in dialing if the line is busy.

Internal sources of ideas.   We typically associate new products with R&D. "Basic research" is fundamental research while "applied research" establishes the link between fundamental research and the customer. R&D, though, is expensive with a payoff perhaps every ten years. Furthermore, if new product ideas come from R&D alone, the failure rate tends to be highest. The failure rate drops significantly when ideas come from marketing but, in many industries, the success rate is best of all when both R&D and marketing cooperate and agree.

Methods

Except conceptually, it is difficult to separate sources of ideas from the methods used to generate them as sources often point to methods. Nonetheless it is useful to remind ourselves that knowing sources is not enough since we need a system for tapping those sources.

Problem identification and creativity.   One method used to generate ideas is problem identification since the solution to a problem may generate ideas for new products. A number of approaches are used to identify problems:

- *activity analysis*. This involves directly observing the performance of some function such as washing the dishes, shaving, or whatever activity is relevant to the market area.
- *product analysis*. This involves examining the whole of the buying cycle from the purchase of the product to its use and disposal. In protocol analysis, researchers note dissatisfactions expressed and which of the six choice criteria discussed in Chapter 5 are insufficiently exploited.
- *problem analysis*. This starts off with a list of frequently mentioned customer problems and asks respondents with what products or brands or activities they associate the problems.
- *ergonomics* (human engineering). Ergonomics is the study of the "fit" between jobs and people. It is used to deduce the limitations of human capabilities as a pointer to likely problems. Ideally, the problems identified should be major unsolved ones identified by asking how annoying the problem is; how frequently it comes up and its consequences on the performance of the function for which the product is bought.

Identification of a problem is one thing, a creative solution to it is another. The degree of creativeness relates to how novel the idea is and how valuable the idea is likely to be. Creative approaches need not produce something *highly* novel and *highly* valuable but simply be better at doing so than alternative approaches. There are no standard procedures for being creative. If the mechanical application of rules produced valuable ideas, the person producing the ideas would not be regarded as creative: by definition, creativity is more than a conscious following of procedure. Thus while brainstorming (see Chapter 9) is classified as a creativity technique, it can do no more than produce a mental set favoring the creative individual: it guarantees nothing.

What is typically involved in discovery is reasoning by analogy: creative people, as well as being optimists and anxious to do something novel, are able to recall patterns from elsewhere which have similarity with the problem at hand. In fact, intuition may operate through reasoning by analogy. Some psychologists claim the creative person is marked by an ability to think of an idea that is improbable, unusual or remote, yet exactly right for the situation (though this seems to be no more than a definition of creativity). Others talk of the "divergent" personality. Divergence, as it relates to creativity, is sometimes measured by how many novel ideas a person can think of, for using, say, an old hat. The best predictor of creativity, though, is past creative achievement. Psychologists, while no longer viewing creative ability as like a creative IQ, are studying the "creative moment" and creative individuals in terms of their background and attitudes but substantive results for marketing are still in the future.

Ayres claims that the great inventions leading to technological revolutions are new combinations (patterns) of tools devised for different purposes.[5] Thus the airplane was a combination of kite plus internal combustion engine, while the automobile was a combination of buggy plus internal combustion engine. Even the internal combustion engine was a combination with a gaseous fuel substituted for steam. This view sees each invention as the end of an evolutionary series of inventions and implies increasing technological progress, since, as tools increase, so does the number of potential combinations.

Technological forecasting.   Technological forecasting (TF) is concerned with predicting advances in technology and science. Such forecasts are relevant to possible future products. The most popular TF technique in business is the Delphi technique. Project Delphi was the name given to a study commissioned by the US Air Force from the Rand Corporation in the 1950s concerning the use of expert opinion. What has come to be known as the Delphi technique is a way of tapping the opinions of experts while avoiding the possibility of conformism that might arise through bringing them together. One procedure is as follows:

- Experts are asked to list the developments that are likely in their field during the next, say, ten years or to name inventions or other breakthroughs urgently needed and realizable.
- Next time round, the experts are asked for the probable dates of the developments predicted.
- Third time round, the data are fed back to the experts, noting where a consensus has been reached. Dissenters from the consensus are asked to give their reasons. This third stage gives an opportunity for participants to rethink their opinions and the forecaster to reword the questions if there is ambiguity.
- In round four, the experts are given both the majority as well as the minority opinions and asked to record their estimates of when the events are likely to occur.

There are limits, of course, to technological forecasting. It is easier to predict a technology's future when the technology has got off the ground. But to predict a technological invention based on an entirely new concept, is to actually invent it!

Gap analysis.   Once a firm selects a market, gap analysis is used to identify gaps in market segments. If such a gap is found it represents a market opportunity that might be an opportunity for the firm. Thus Lean Cuisine, a low calorie, gourmet frozen dinner, filled a gap in the market that has led to sales of over $400 million per annum. Perceptual maps are the basis for identifying gaps (see Chapter 6). There are several ways of getting out such maps. For example, we might ask respondents to rank brands on the basis of similarity: pairwise (two at a time) comparisons over all the two-member subsets on the basis of similarity and dissimilarity and proceed from there to build the map. Another approach is simply to ask respondents to position a set of brands on a map as in Figure 10.4. In Figure 10.4, the dimensions of reliability and versatility have been determined from factor analysis to be the two dominant dimensions. But some marketers prefer to show the quadrants of a graph without showing any dimensions and ask respondents to say into which quadrant each brand should go on the basis of similarity and dissimilarity and to space them within the quadrant, on the basis of similarity and dissimilarity.

The reason for leaving the classification to the respondent rests on the supposition that *folk classifications* reflect how the consumer communicates about the various brands and so retains meanings rooted in the purchase/use context, whereas researcher systems are designed for information retrieval and ease of fitting every brand into its pigeonhole. Consumers classify in several ways. One method uses *defining features* so that a toothpaste containing fluoride is grouped with other brands containing fluoride. Another approach uses *prototypes*, which represent, for the consumer, different subcategories of the product, with consumers classifying brands on the basis of their similarity to the prototypes. Because people classify on the basis of prototype they have more difficulty, say, in classifying a kiwi as a bird than they have classifying a robin. A final way of classifying, which has similarities to the prototype, is through the use of *exemplars*, which are remembered actual examples with brands being classified or clustered on the basis of their similarity to remembered examples. All these consumer ways of classifying suggest that the consumers' segment distinctions may be tied to their way of classifying. This is why the consumers' own classifications may be so important particularly when the attributes or variables are numerous. However, we would always need to identify the underlying dimensions if we are to understand what the gaps are about.

Because it is important to identify underlying dimensions, a favored approach to getting out perceptual maps is a quantitative one. One approach asks consumers to rate or rank brands on a number of key dimensions or attributes. These dimensions are identified through focus groups, protocol analysis, or any other technique used to stimulate thoughts on what attributes consumers associate with the brands in the product category. Where many dimensions (attributes) are mentioned, factor analysis is used to identify the underlying key dimensions. Multidimensional scaling techniques are then used to determine the relative positioning of the brands on the dimensions (attributes). The respondent's *evoked set* (that is, the brands that the respondent has used, would consider using, or has rejected) seldom comes to more than five brands, so respondents are rarely called upon to perform feats of memory.

Sometimes the relative importance consumers attach to the dimensions of the perceptual map (e.g. reliability and versatility in Figure 10.4) can be measured by *preference regression*. Consumers first rank order the various brands. These rankings then become the dependent variable with the independent variable being, say, degree of reliability

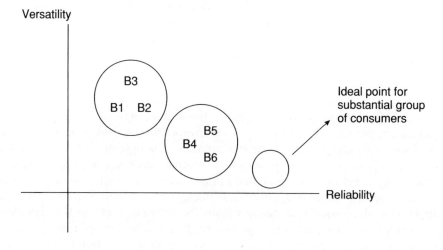

Figure 10.4 Market structure analysis: brands in lawnmower market

and then versatility to get the two regression lines, their relative slopes being taken to be the relative weightings on the two dimensions.

Perceptual maps are not without problems. In the first place it is not easy to determine key attributes and factor analysis may not reduce their number to some manageable number without some forcing, while the names given to the factors always involve judgment. There is also the question of coping with the intangible attribute of image unless we assume that image is just a summation attribute. In any case, every consumer in the market does not have the same perceptions of key attributes or seek the same level of performance in an attribute.

On the assumption that we have surmounted the above problems, and produced a map showing a perceptual positioning for the various brands (e.g. of lawnmowers represented in Figure 10.4 by B1 to B6) on the two key dimensions (e.g. of versatility and reliability), we have a representation of the structure of the market or what is called a *market structure analysis*. If the two dimensions are the key ones used to evaluate rival brands, it seems reasonable to assume that competition among brands is likely to depend on how closely they are positioned in relation to each other. For example, in Figure 10.4 we might cluster the brands into two groups: the brands B1, B2, and B3 cluster as one group and the brands B4, B5, and B6 cluster as the other group.

On Figure 10.4 we can add the consumer's preference or *ideal point*. If the dimensions of versatility and reliability are the key attributes used to evaluate and select a brand, ideal points can be equated with preferences. If a firm's brand is closer to some group's ideal point than competitive brands, then, (if other things about the offering remain equal), it is more likely to be bought by members of that group than any of the alternative brands.

In examining a perceptual map on which the preferences or ideal points of consumers are recorded, we might find a wide gulf between perceptions of current brands and the ideal point of a substantial group of consumers. For example, in Figure 10.4 we might find some group giving absolute priority to reliability. Our firm might consider developing a product to fill the gap to match the ideal point of that group. Alternatively, if our brand is already near the ideal point, we might improve the reliability of our product to position it better for this segment of the market. Figure 10.5 illustrates the process as described. It is a process that is helpful to spotting possible gaps in the market rather than being a mechanistic procedure for identifying definite market opportunities for the firm.

Positioning. Allied to the concept of gaps in the market is the question of positioning. Positioning a product in the market vis-à-vis competition is a way of trying to give a brand a distinct meaning for consumers so they distinguish it from rival brands. Identifying a gap as a market opportunity means either identifying a segment or identifying a way of better positioning one's brand within an existing segment. A number of problems arise in positioning within a segment vis-à-vis competition. For example, let us suppose that, although everyone within the segment seeks milky chocolate, the milkiness level sought by particular consumers differs. The first entrant into a market segment should consider the effect of his positioning on the positioning choices of subsequent entrants. Figure 10.6 shows three distributions of preferences.

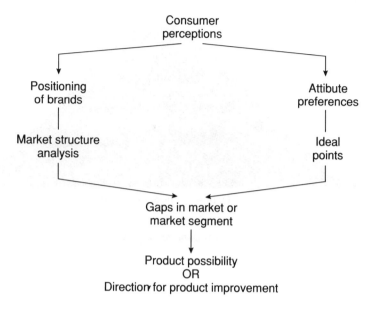

Figure 10.5 Gap analysis: process

Figure 10.6(a) shows a distribution of preferences that follows the normal curve in statistics. If the first firm to enter the segment positions its brand at the center, the second entrant could position its brand just left or right of center to capture all those consumers to the left or right of center. In Figure 10.6(b), where the distribution of preferences is bimodal, the first entrant might be advised to bring out two brands right from the start to cater to the two cliques within the segment. In Figure 10.6(c), where the distribution is polymodal, there is even more incentive to cater to a number of segments, if the first entrant is not to find its market position seriously eroded by subsequent entrants. If a new segment is attractive, it should be considered. This is so even if *cannibalism* (that is, some sales going to the new product coming from the firm's other brands) is feared, as the opening up of the segment by competitors is likely to have that effect anyway. The advantage of having a position in each segment is to protect the firm's lead brand since it is common (consider, for example, the Japanese entry into the motor cycle market) for competitors to break into a market by first establishing themselves in a segment ignored by those already in the market.

The above assumes the firm wants to position its brand on some *tangible* basis to differentiate the brand from rival brands and be a basis for preference. But sometimes, positioning a brand is complicated by its existing associations. Positioning within a market segment may mean on occasions locating the brand within the segment to appeal to those with a preference for the associations attached to the brand: tangible product qualities may not always be the major associations that determine such preference.

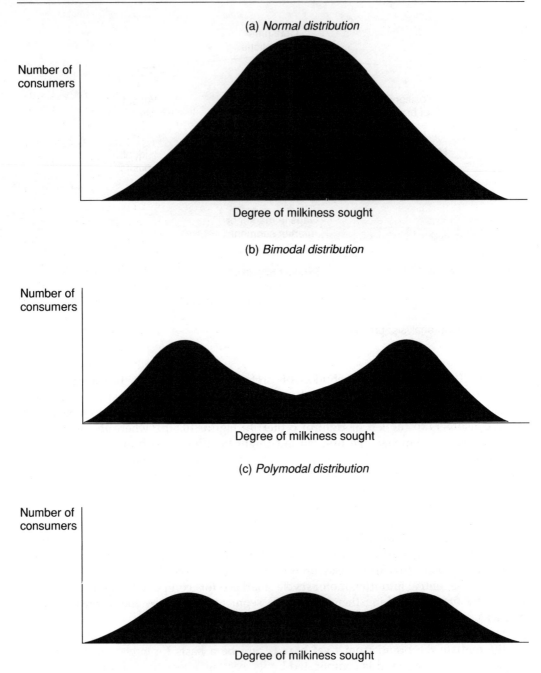

Figure 10.6 Possible distributions of preferences on a key attribute

Screening new product ideas/opportunities

Prescreening

A new product idea is just that—an idea. Ideas need to be evaluated. This is particularly important when the new product involves considerable financial investment since mistakes could on occasions be ruinous to the firm. There are always the two types of error; the error of accepting a product that turns out to be a failure or rejecting a product that would have been a success. And the latter does happen. For example, Xerox failed to recognize the potential of Alto, the first personal computer, built by researchers at Palo Alto Research Center in 1973, before Apple and IBM got into the market. Sometimes the product manifestly has potential but the timing is wrong just as deep frozen food only became a commercial proposition with the development of the domestic refrigerator.

There is usually little difficulty in conceiving of better products (for example, foods that add nothing to weight; clothes that never need cleaning; burglar alarms that never give false alarms and so on). But what is logically conceivable may be neither technically feasible nor commercially viable. Even if technically feasible, a new product idea, while eliminating old problems, may introduce new ones. It is also easy to conceive of products that are technically feasible that do not have the other attributes that are necessary for commercial success (for example, a reasonable price). Consumers do not beat a path to the door of the manufacturer who develops a technically better mousetrap if, additionally, it is too pricey, or too bulky, or messy or just socially inappropriate as, say, being too cruel.

A prescreen is sometimes all that is needed to rule out some proposal. The idea may be too novel and socially inappropriate as was the case with the idea of someone at 3M who suggested selling sandpaper as a replacement for razor blades. Shavers would just rub their cheeks clean, with the product being cheaper and without the risk of "nicks" to the skin! Another novel product that failed was dry beer; beer drinkers were just not prepared to find out about it. An initial screening may avoid enthusiastically "backing technological horses before they are really fit to run."

Initial questions relate to product policy:

- Does the proposed product fit corporate objectives?
- Are the risks acceptable?
- Will the product contribute to a balanced product portfolio?
- Does the new product fall within the firm's business?
- Is the firm capable of building and marketing the product and has it got what it takes to be a success in the market?
- Does the proposed new product exploit the firm's thrust?
- Is the firm capable of obtaining a sustainable competitive advantage with the product?

On occasions, a proposed new product may violate product policy but still be appealing. Like all policies, a product policy can be a premature closure of options or may have outlived its usefulness in the light of fresh developments and more imaginative thinking. On the other hand, prescreening points to factors that suggest likely success such as

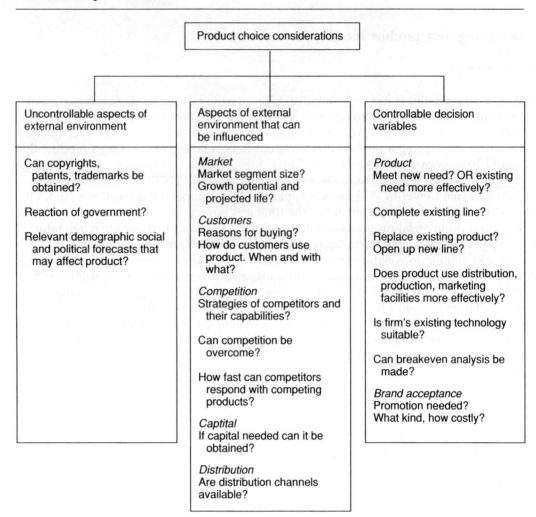

Figure 10.7 Screen for new product ideas

sleepy, fragmented competitors; high growth market; little buyer or supplier power; no substitutes; economies of scale possible; core benefit proposition strong, and so on. If the new product idea coheres with product policy, a checklist such as that shown in Figure 10.7 can be used to prescreen.

Professional screen

A professional screen will, as a minimum, take account of:

a) sales potential, likely market share, and likely costs;

b) business requirements for success; and
c) competition.

Sales & costs. Estimating potential sales may be postponed until various tests such as concept and preference testing have occurred. But even with such tests, there is no certainty. However, if we have data on similar products, we may be able to calculate the probability of purchase from knowing what percentage of our respondents express a first preference for the suggested new product and what percentage express a second preference. Suppose 20 percent of our sample of targeted consumers express a first preference for the proposed product and 30 percent express a second preference, and *past experience* with products within that product category indicates that 80 percent of first preferences buy the product, and 15 percent of second preferences buy the product, then:

(20 percent * 80 percent) + (15 percent * 30 percent) = 20.5 percent

of those in the market are likely to buy the new product.

Other ways of linking expressed preferences to buying have been developed that take account of the *intensity* of preferences but results are always somewhat problematical. This is because such estimates are made without regard to the total marketing mix. Thus a certain percentage of those who would buy may not be reached so the want remains "latent" while for others the want may remain "passive" in that price or distribution may inhibit purchase. In estimating sales, account must be taken of likely cannibalism arising from the new product siphoning off sales from the firm's existing brands. Thus, Anheuser Busch, the brewer, accepted that around 20 percent of the sales of its new beer, Michelob Light, would come from other Michelob brands. This did not stop them from going ahead because the segment would otherwise be served by competitors. Even with cannibalism, a firm may increase its market share and stem the sales of rivals. Nonetheless, an important question in all cannibalization is whether the new product is cannibalizing upscale or downscale, that is, whether sales are coming from the higher priced brands or the lower.

While firms may pay insufficient attention to the size of the served market and their likely share of it, costs can also be neglected. Raw material costs are deduced from the product specification but there are also processing and capital investment costs plus packaging and overhead costs. All such costs go into the breakeven analysis and calculations of the annual profit budget. The relevant calculations are illustrated in Appendix 10.1.

Business requirements. The firm must have the business system to meet the requirements for success. The question to be answered is: What are the requirements for success in terms of supplies, production system, finance and marketing (including distribution)? Answering this question is not as easy as it sounds since knowing what the marketing mix should be amounts to having a strategy in mind. At the time of the new product's conception, there may be doubt as to whether the firm can actually develop the product or market it successfully, while it is difficult to make a realistic estimate of the costs involved in going from product conception to product launch.

Competition.   Some attempt must be made to anticipate competitive reaction. If the firm can match what is being sought by the market, it possesses the minimum for success but, for a firm to have the most meaningful advantage, its offering must have criticalness for enough people. Criticalness, as already said, consists of centrality plus uniqueness. The criticalness need not reside in the product but in some other aspect of the offering. Products, for example, may be built to sell at a price advantage (for example, the Model "T" Ford in the early part of the century); to fit an image; to exploit a distribution system. It is wrong to assume that a me-too product must fail for lack of criticalness, as a me-too product does not entail a me-too offering. This simple truth tends to get obscured by the tendency, when a new product fails, to attribute its failure to its being a me-too product, dismissing differences from competitive makes as irrelevant to the consumer. On the other hand, if the new product succeeds, minor differences between the new product and rival brands are made to seem highly significant when it may have been something else in the offering that made for success.

When a new-to-the-world product is launched, the entry of competitors is not always bad in that competitors can give legitimacy to a novel product and increase primary demand while sharing the cost of developing the market.

Business analysis

Considerable investment might be needed to develop the new product. In justifying a heavy investment, the economic gain that is set against the capital outlay is "operating cash flow." In this case, it is the net cash inflow (or outflow) resulting from the difference between the additional revenue generated and the additional expenses. In considering the relative desirability of new product proposals, there is a need to estimate future cash from data on likely sales and costs. The major problem lies in estimating future sales (demand) as sales depend, within limits, on price, while price is influenced by costs, and costs in turn are influenced by cumulative sales over the life of the product! Not surprisingly uncertainties abound. There are several decision support systems that have been developed to help here such as Risk Analysis, the Sprinter model, the Ventur model, and others that have been designed as rational approaches for coping with such uncertainties.[6,7,8] Until recently none of the models coped well with cost declines with output (sales) but this is changing.[9]

Testing: concept testing, preference testing, and home-use tests

Depending on the product, a whole series of premarketing tests may be undertaken to check the likely acceptance of the proposed new product. Examples of such tests are:

- *concept testing*, where new product ideas are described to potential buyers to test their appeal;
- *preference testing* to assess whether potential customers prefer the new product to current substitutes in numbers that will make the product worthwhile to produce; and

- *home-use tests* to assess acceptance after usage as a guide to likely repeat sales

The problem with these tests is the absence of the rest of the marketing mix so that consumer judgments are made in the absence of commercial influences such as advertising, packaging and distribution. In support, many marketers argue that this is as it should be in that the test is of the product itself: whether it has the power to attract and motivate on its own. Others claim that a product's appeal cannot be separated from the context in which it is sold so that the suggested new product may fail these tests yet be a success because of what the rest of the marketing mix has to offer. It might also be added that many a suggested new product has passed each of these tests only to be a failure because the rest of the marketing mix was inadequate for the job.

Concept testing

In concept testing, a description of the proposed new product is set out in a *concept statement*, which describes the idea in terms of benefits and values, and in language the consumer can understand. For example, the concept statement of Tang, an orange drink, was in terms of its orange flavor, high vitamin content, ease of preparation, and the fact that it needed no refrigeration. Although the primary purpose of concept testing is to measure consumer reactions to the product idea before going ahead with its development, concept testing can be a help in the product's development:

- identifying additional uses or markets for the product;
- identifying target segments and positioning within the segments;
- identifying the relative importance of the various product attributes or choice criteria;
- suggesting its pricing by including in the concept statement questions on the price respondents are prepared to pay;
- noting criticisms made;
- predicting cannibalization; and
- predicting likely sales.

Likely sales are generally predicted from asking respondents about intentions (definitely would buy; probably would buy; may or may not buy; probably would not buy; definitely would not buy). While a number of studies have found purchase intentions to correlate highly with subsequent buying, the evidence on the relationship between purchase intentions and actual behavior is, as one research team worded it, "rudimentary at best" while the evidence on the predictive accuracy of intentions data for new products is not strong.[10] Given the huge number of different types of products, the variation in the representativeness of the samples of respondents, the possible contexts, the subsequent marketing mixes, it is doubtful whether definite stable generalizations are even possible. But a firm should collect data on intentions to see if it proves useful for prediction. Every answer, indicating *some* likelihood of buying, should be taken into account because those subsequently buying are not just those who stated they would definitely buy.

Concept testing can involve individual consumers, focus groups or even employee panels. Ideally, each concept statement for each suggested positioning is tested on around 300 respondents. Several concept statements might be explored in group discussion and with unstructured interviews to test the appeal or improve the product idea and its positioning. Tang, for example, was perceived as a breakfast drink and was subsequently marketed as such. There can be probing about price, possible additional uses and benefits while judging the degree to which the suggested new product idea is perceived as different. While a novel new product is sought, too much novelty can simply puzzle and inhibit buying, at least in the short term.

There is *omnibus testing* where a series of concept statements is put forward for evaluation or there is *monadic testing*, where only one concept statement is put forward so it can be explored in depth. There are also *competitive environment tests* (CET), where the concept statement for the proposed new product is presented to the consumer together with concept statements describing the current leading brands with which the new product will be competing. However, such comparisons cannot be made for truly novel products.

The first step in concept testing is to answer the following questions:

- What will the product be like?
- What function(s) will the product perform?
- How will the product be used?
- Where will it be used?
- When will it be used?
- Who will use it, with what and with whom?

Concept testing relies on descriptions of the product and its benefits including experiences in using the product (e.g. one concept statement for a new fragrance spoke of "makes you smile when you put it on"). Hence everything depends on the skill of the copywriter and the interpretation of the concept statement by respondents. In any case, respondents may have difficulty in visualizing a nonexistent product.

The use of concept testing for predicting sales has its dangers when applied to "discontinuous" innovations as reactions based on first exposure to a discontinuous innovation tend to be a poor predictor of the numbers buying after prolonged exposure to the product. This point is similar to that made earlier about a *highly* novel product being difficult for the consumer to classify and understand. Novel stimuli are liked better if relatively less complex, or, if complex, then liked better if familiar, that is, less novel. It seems strange though to regard the novelty of 3M's Post-It as being the reason so few consumers and retailers endorsed the product when it was first tested with them!

The results of concept testing are seldom good for predicting repeat (as opposed to trial) purchase because people seldom know in advance about future buying. However, this does not mean that predicting from data gathered from a large sample of respondents might not have *some* predictive value.

Preference tests

A major criticism of concept testing is that it does not tell us the best concept; preference testing is much better for this purpose. Certainly, if the proposed product can be made available, preference testing is more meaningful. Such tests can be:

- *direct comparison tests*, where potential users compare the new product with competitive substitutes;
- *staggered tests*, where potential users alternate between using the new product and rival makes; and
- *monadic tests*, where potential users evaluate the new product in isolation. Usually, one half of the sample of respondents is given the new product and the other half a rival product.

Direct comparison tests are criticized on the ground that respondents are being asked to encode a good deal of comparative data, which rarely occurs in a natural learning setting. This criticism applies less to staggered tests but still has some applicability. On the other hand, monadic tests inhibit making comparisons and dispose the respondent toward favoring the product. All these criticisms are concerned with the artificiality of preference tests. But they can be overstated. Thus while it is true that respondents are being asked (but not obliged) to digest more comparative data than they would when out shopping, it does not follow that respondents *do* encode more than they do when actually buying a new product and comparing it with similar ones. In fact some marketers make the opposite criticism: that, in testing, respondents feel no obligation to try the product, examine it closely, or compare it with rivals except superficially. This does not mean that only one or other of the critics must be right: both could be right but in different situations. With regard to monadic tests, many buyers in actual buying look at specific brands in isolation without making comparisons with other brands. Much more is being asked of respondents by way of encoding if they are asked to rank brands through the use of the multiattribute model since the procedure itself obliges a good deal of encoding of comparative data. Yet preference scores based on the multiattribute model sometimes predict 40–60 percent of the consumers' first choices. But preferences expressed in preference tests do not necessarily have much relationship to choices after the product is launched.

Has psychology anything to say that might be relevant to the fact that expressed preferences may have little relationship with actual choices made after the product is launched? When decisions are difficult people suffer from indecision: shifting from favoring one option and then the other. Thus which option we prefer may depend at which particular time the question is asked. On the subject of consumers being asked to encode a mass of comparative data, whether in a laboratory buying experiment or in real life, consumers may follow the *elimination-by-aspect* rule, where the decision-maker searches for attributes that will eliminate options to reduce them to a reasonable number. Whatever attribute the consumer latches onto, he or she eliminates all of the options in the choice set that lack that single attribute. This rule is a noncompensatory rule (see Chapters 4 and 5) without the suggestion that the attributes involved are necessarily of major importance. This style of decision-making leads to ignoring many minor differences in attributes that *collectively* might favor some other option than the one finally chosen. Finally, high preference may be a poor predictor of trial since consumers, though they may prefer the suggested new *product*, they may still prefer the *offering* of some rival firm.

Even if we accept that preference tests are far from perfect, preference tests can still provide all sorts of useful information, such as:

- weaknesses in the product;
- the identification of potential customers, potential markets, and market segments; and
- likely promotional appeals.

Home-use tests

It may be possible to provide consumers with a kit, consisting of the new product and its closest competitor, and to finance the consumer's weekly "buys" at a generous usage rate. Researchers note the choices, purchase patterns, preferences and reactions to taste, texture, odor, and appearance. Consumers can be asked about the degree of liking, about overall satisfaction with each product, and preferences can be ranked and attitudes assessed. The limitations of home-use tests are that those participating are not faced with the full range of competitive offerings and advertising, selling and distribution do not play the role normally allotted to them. When the brands in the kit do not have brand labels, the home-use test has the advantage of focusing attention on the physical aspects of the product. But it also means that product quality has to be inferred from physical cues, when out in the market, rival products might have the advantage of a brand-name as an indicator of quality.

Product brief and building the product prototype

At some stage the product idea has to be developed into a product brief and an actual product. A *product brief* is drawn up to help the designer and/or manufacturer to build the product. Such a brief might cover:

- the objective in developing such a product;
- the market or market segment for which the product will cater: target customer group; buying inducement; positioning;
- functions served by the product and performance characteristics;
- likely pricing, distribution and promotion; and
- cost estimates.

Sometimes the product brief is elaborated into a market brief by providing much more information on the market: size, trends, competition, market structure, distribution, and pricing. In any case, at the product brief stage, the original product idea is apt to change through more knowledge of consumer wants, the market, and what is technically feasible. A firm may know, for example, how the product is to be positioned on the perceptual map, but the combination of characteristics that best achieves that positioning may still need to be discovered. In general, a proposed new product cannot be better on every dimension than competition, so there is the question of what dimensions to emphasize. The technique of *conjoint analysis* helps the manager to determine the relative importance to the consumer of the many attributes (properties, dimensions, characteristics) of a product as well as the desired attribute levels. In essence, conjoint analysis, as defined by Green and Srinivasan is "a set of techniques for measuring buyers' tradeoffs among multiattribute products."[11] It is a way of estimating the relative values, utilities or partworths of the various attributes of the product as a basis for determining what overall set of attributes will be preferred. It is a way of helping the marketer gauge consumer trade-offs among the various product attributes, for example, between a lower price and higher quality if we define the product to include its price.

The purpose of conjoint analysis is to identify the most preferred combination of attributes without a firm having to set out every possible combination to see which would be most preferred. Conjoint analysis starts with the list of relevant (independent) attributes and their levels. For example, we might have price, and technical performance as the attributes sought, with price being at three levels, and technical performance at two levels. With a large number of attributes with different levels for each attribute, the possible combinations become immense. There are statistical procedures for reducing the combinations to a reasonable number, say, just ten combinations. Respondents then rank the ten combinations according to preference or likelihood of purchase. From such global rankings, the technique of conjoint analysis decomposes the rankings into utility scales for each attribute. It is possible to plot the utility curve of each attribute on a graph, for example, to show the relationship between the decrease in price and what it means in terms of utility (value) to the consumer. Figure 10.8 illustrates. Assuming the consumer is using the compensatory model of decision-making, we can vary the levels of some attribute, for example, performance, and offset it by a change in another attribute to maintain the overall utility (value), or preference level, or alternatively we may search for the combination of attributes and levels that maximizes preference. The Marriott hotel chain started with fifty attributes, each ranging from two to eight levels to determine which combination of attributes at specific prices was most preferred.

In a survey of commercial uses of conjoint analysis, one study found that conjoint analysis was not used when attributes were "perceptual" (like image) as opposed to physical and less used when there were a very large number of attributes or the attributes were highly correlated.[12] More recently, the authors suggest the use of the technique is probably growing with the development of appropriate software.[13] Applications were not only in consumer and industrial goods but also in services. Data collection is mainly carried out using the personal interview but not necessarily face-to-face interviews since telephone interviews are being used to obtain a wider sample.

The authors discuss the reliability and validity of the technique. The authors claim that the reliability of conjoint analysis varies with the number of respondents, number of trade-off judgments made per respondent, the number of attributes and the

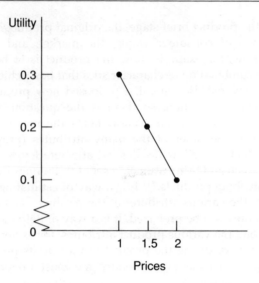

N.B. Arbitrary zero point

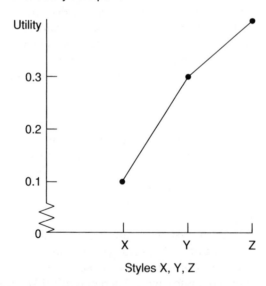

Figure 10.8 Typical illustrations of utilities in conjoint analysis

number of attribute levels. The authors point out that the closest conjoint studies come to testing for validity is by comparing predicted market shares *from a simulation* with actual market shares. The authors do not measure the predictive validity of the technique but instead point to the tremendous technical difficulty of getting out such a measure in practice. It might also be added that similar difficulties have hampered any demonstration of the reliability (consistency of results) and predictive validity (predictive inferences justified) for techniques like concept testing and preference testing. Green and Srinivasan in the article mentioned earlier, while acknowledging the difficulties of using the technique to predict market shares ("because of the confounding effects of marketing mix variables") do quote the case of AT&T where a simulation forecast a share of 8 percent for AT&T four years after the launch and the actual share was just under 8 percent. Given the problems in establishing validity this result is surprising.

The most common method of conjoint analysis assumes preference is determined by adding up the individual attribute utilities. The assumption is that the factors in combination do not interact but are merely additive. But can we always just assume that because attribute A at level X is most preferred and attribute B at level Y is most preferred and so on, that the combination of each of these attributes would be the combination that would be wanted? Thus it is doubtful whether using this technique to select the most beautiful woman in the world would result in the combination of features that was most appealing, since the whole would be something more than the sum of the parts. With products that have an organic whole, the value of the whole does not have to be the sum of the values of the individual components. The theme of a play or the plot of a novel are emergent qualities that only make themselves meaningful at the collective level of structure and are fairly meaningless at the component level. Another question relates to the stability of the measures. Conjoint analysis assumes that beliefs and wants are relatively well-developed and fixed. It assumes that buyers know their goals, down to how much of the goal should be sought and what different trade-offs mean in terms of likely satisfaction. But the conjoint analysis process makes respondents evaluate their desires and this in itself can lead to changes in wants and beliefs. In fact, far from having fixed preferences, the problem for the respondent may be that of choosing what attributes are preferred. Preferences are not static. Consumers learn as a result of experience and are often (if not always) open to persuasion right to the point of sale. Consumers, too, may not be fully informed as to the significance of each product attribute (or, for that matter, any particular combination of attributes) for them. The fact that consumers are unaware is hidden from the researcher by the confidence with which respondents fill in questionnaires or rank in order of preference twenty-four 3" × 5" cards, each describing some combination of attributes. Do consumers always detect combination differences and, if so, do they imagine what each combination would mean in terms of benefits? There is also the problem of intangibles like image (and perhaps other criteria falling under the heading of integrative and adaptive criteria) since few respondents recognize what image they want or accept that image is important for them. In any case, two consumers could indicate a preference for a certain combination of attributes but still choose very differently because they settle on very different surrogate indicators for recognizing the presence and level of the attributes. There are finally a number of technical questions, for example, the difficulty of extrapolating preference measures for attribute levels falling outside the ranges covered by the original measures. But, in spite of these limitations, conjoint analysis is a useful procedure when the design problem involves identifying new-product designs and determining the most appealing combination of physical attributes for the product. As with all such techniques, the question is not whether it is perfect but whether it is better than what it displaces.

After the design of the product, the next step is to build a prototype that meets the specification to check on production and design feasibility. How long this will take will depend on the product. There may have to be laboratory tests, further consumer tests and government authorization. Sometimes the product brief is necessarily vague as when the brief talks about intrinsic benefits. For example, while the product brief for a new perfume may include the demographics of the target audience, whether the perfume will be top of the market etc., the description of the scent itself might be in terms of the mood or the image it is meant to capture. There is usually no way to meet this specification except by trial and error as various perfumes are developed and put forward for evaluation against the specification. This can take up to two years while additional time may be needed for testing among the target customer group.

In respect to services, new product development is likely to be easier. What has to be developed are "blueprints" of the proposed service. Getting out such blueprints is typically what systems and procedures specialists do already. Some writers on service marketing argue that developing a service involves much more detail than just the flow charting of systems and procedures specialists. In fact, systems and procedures personnel (organization and methods or work study in Britain) have more detailed techniques than flow charts if such are needed. However, what can be said is that, if systems and procedures are used to develop a service, they should be clearly told what level of service has to be achieved and also that effectiveness, not efficiency, is the primary goal.

If we are building a service from scratch, the first step is to specify the inputs and outputs. The outputs of the service, for which a procedure has to be developed, are the objectives of the service and the standard of performance to be achieved. Take, as a simple example, devising a procedure for refunding money to customers. The first step would be represented by a simple block diagram as in Figure 10.9(a). The second step would be to set out the "processing" functions that are necessary to achieve the objectives. These can be drawn within the single block diagram as in Figure 10.9(b). Each processing function is then expanded to show its own inputs and outputs in the form of information and supplies. This is shown in Figure 10.9(c). The functions can now be synthesized into a multi-block diagram by joining the appropriate inputs and outputs as in Figure 10.9(d). Flow charts (Figure 10.10) can now be developed on this basis and the procedure tried out in a pilot scheme.

For some services, the firm might offer different versions of a service for different market segments though the problem of catering to different quality segments is the problem of maintaining a consistent brand image.

Developing the marketing mix

The product is just one element in the offering or marketing mix. It is usually the core part so typically the product concept is developed first. However, there are some occasions when the product is designed to fit some other element of the offering, for example, to fit into a price range, fit some brand image or distribution system. But this is a simplification. Given that the various parts of an offering must be interdependent, there must be a procedural interconnection in the design of the various parts so they

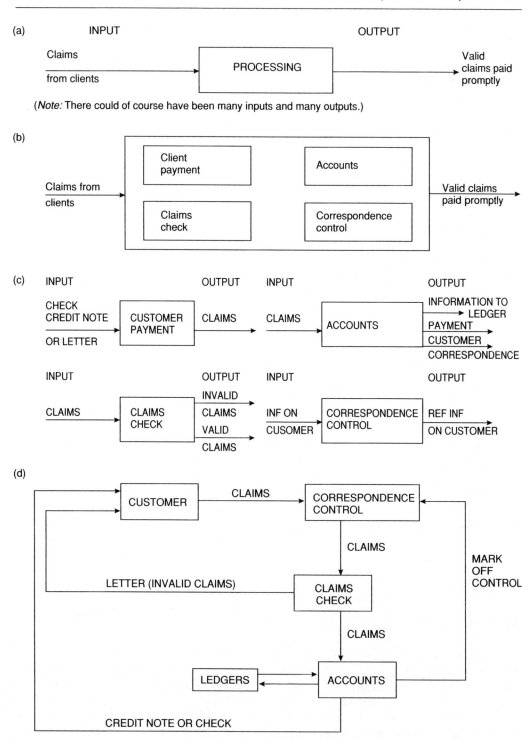

Figure 10.9 Devising a procedure for refunding money to customers

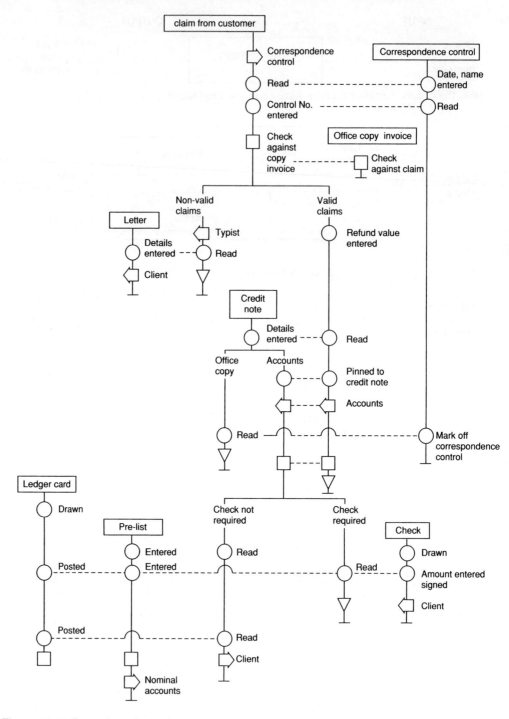

Figure 10.10 Procedure chart of refunds procedure

fit together. This can be difficult since, during the time spent developing a product, the market can change. The marketing manager has to constantly anticipate the direction of that change and the implications of this for the offering being developed.

The main thing is to think early about the complete offering: drawing up a tentative marketing strategy is part of new product development. Thus when Giorgio Armani chose his latest scent, he had to choose a name (Gio), the bottle, its shape, the parchment packaging, the display advertisements, the sales assistants' mustard coat dresses, the scent samples, the advertising media, the scent strips for the magazines, the advertising budget, and so on.

Lever introduced its Lever 2000 soap to fill a perceived gap in the market, positioning it as a deodorant soap with distinctive skin-care properties. Although a multipurpose soap, it was not promoted as "an all-things-to-all-people" soap. The reason was the belief that the brand must fit a category that already exists in the consumer's mind (the folk classification concept discussed earlier), otherwise the product would have problems getting understood. Whereas the general tendency when adding functions to products is to add just one ancillary-use function (e.g. a complexion soap or an antibacterial soap) to indicate a credible advance and a specialized thrust, versatility through multipurpose can be sought when several family members are using the product. Lever 2000 filled this gap for an all-family soap. Interestingly P&G has repackaged its Safeguard brand of soap with the slogan "mild enough for the whole family." Since the formula has remained the same, P&G is hoping that upgrading the image will help it compete, though it is doubtful whether this is sufficient.

The following comments on promotion, pricing and distribution simply sketch the surface since they are considered in detail in later chapters in the book.

Promotion

If the want is latent or passive or if integrative and adaptive criteria are important, promotion is key. In general terms, the buying inducement (sometimes called the *core benefit proposition*) points to the benefits that should be stressed in promotional appeals. But the first problem is to determine the advertising budget or what it will take to create the level of awareness needed. There are also other promotions to consider such as enticing consumers to try the product through the offer of free samples or trial offer. For certain industrial products, personal selling might be the major means of communicating benefits so that selling time must be considered, whether through the use of the firm's current sales force or by hiring a *"flying force."*

When Lever 2000 came out, Lever spent $25 million on advertising alone and the next year $40 million on promotion generally. Even when a product has a very definite advantage (at the time) like Gillette's Sensor blade, sales cannot rely on word-of-mouth (unless it is something central to the function, unique, *and salient to the buyer* like a cure for Aids). Apart from advertising, Gillette spent $75 million on public relations, packaging, and design to help in the promotion. What was interesting, though, was that the advertising had to be withdrawn because demand could not be met. Gillette had grossly underestimated likely sales.

Pricing

Price is important not just for its potential to inhibit purchase but because it contributes to the image of the product. Some idea about how demand is likely to respond to differences in price might be obtained during concept testing, preference testing, or through the use of conjoint analysis. Where full production capacity has yet to be built, rationing by price might be considered while fear of competitive reaction might lead to considering a *penetration price strategy*. However, although the introductory price is of immediate interest, management has to think out the overall pricing strategy to be adopted as the market develops. This pricing strategy need not envision either lowering prices in parallel with the experience curve or ensuring prices cohere with the life cycle stage as assumed by those who regard the PLC as determining marketing strategy.

Distribution

If distribution to the target segment cannot be assured then much else fails. Distribution channels do something more than make the product available since they do much to promote the product or define its image. This means that, not only has the marketing manager to identify distribution channels, but also needs to consider consumer promotions, trade promotions, point-of-purchase material and perhaps even a "missionary" sales force to sell the customers' customers. There is also the question of the other services that need to be provided by the distribution channels. Thus when the Huffy Corporation in the United States, a successful bicycle manufacturer, brought out its Cross Sport bicycle, which was a combination of the mountain bicycle and the thin-framed, nimbler racing bicycle, it found sales frustrated by the distribution channel. Because of the higher price and the product's newness, it required knowledgeable sales people to sell it but this did not happen.

Promotion, pricing and distribution strategies are brought together to form a coordinated overall marketing strategy. The design of each of these strategies requires lengthy discussion and is dealt with in subsequent chapters.

Packaging

Packaging in itself can constitute a competitive advantage in any of the following functions:

1 *Protection*. The traditional function of packaging is to protect the product against dirt, damage, theft, mishandling, and deterioration.
2 *Promotion*. Attractive packaging increases product appeal and can differentiate a brand from competitive makes. Sometimes protective outer packs may be made to unfold into an attractive display or dispenser for the retailer. In any case, packaging has become a major vehicle for projecting the brand's image and may have to be evaluated for its promotional impact:

- *Design*. A distinctive package design can be crucial to merchandising at the point of sale. Tests might focus on the time required to find or recall the product in various types of packages.
- *Content*. A package may mislead as to its contents. A can of stewed steak should not be mistaken for dog food. The contents suggested by a package can be measured by, say, flashing the proposed package on to a screen and questioning a carefully selected audience about likely contents.
- *Image*. The image and general connotations of a product are key factors when integrative criteria dominate, for example, in perfumes. The image projected by the package needs to cohere with image being sought. A package that is to project an image of quality and softness must not be perceived as cheap and hard. Every component of the packaging communicates something even the color. Some colors are warm and some are cold, some happy, some sober etc. In cigarettes for example, white packaging suggests low tar while red packaging suggests a strong flavor. Colors have come to symbolize *general* qualities in all cultures. In the West, these qualities are: White: delicacy; Black: mourning or business; Red: strength, vitality, excitement, danger; Yellow: youth, hope, and cheer; Blue: harmony, honesty, and calmness; Green: outdoors, and country life; Brown: friendliness, trust, and reliability.

3 *Visibility*. A striking package can draw attention to itself in the store. This is essentially a promotional role but it is given separate billing here because of its importance.

4 *Convenience* (including ease of disposability). Packaging imposes demands on the user and these demands should be minimal. The antiquated method (still in use) of opening a can of corned beef by twisting with a key, is a sure sign of a sleepy industry. Since World War II, the demand for convenience in the use of all products has been one of the major movements affecting marketers (the others are fashion and health). Some products, like hair sprays were only made possible by developments in convenient packaging, namely, the aerosol. The convenience of the package may in fact determine the use to which a product is put, just as tub brands of margarine are largely used for spreading while wrapped margarine is largely used for cooking.

5 *Provision of information*. Packaging provides information on contents, instructions on use and (if necessary) information required by law. The convenient provision of information is important. Instructions are often hard to read without a magnifying glass while they are frequently vague and ambiguous. All too often instruction manuals are poorly written. The Japanese are some of the worst offenders, producing booklets which would challenge any reader. With regard to computer software instruction manuals, a mini industry has grown up providing alternatives to the manufacturers' manuals, which computer users find incomprehensible. This should not be. Instructions need to be tested for understanding since any instruction embraces all those methods of using the product not excluded by the instructions! The lack of instruction clarity leads to errors and is a reason for nonrepeat purchase.

The same package may be required to protect its contents in the factory, in transit to distributors, in storage and at the place of use. Alternatively, "outpacks" may provide the initial protection to the point of sale.

Packaging can be deceptive, although sometimes it is not easy to determine whether the intent is to deceive. For example, packaging designed purely to be attractive and convenient can be deceptive. Thus, ten cold capsules seem poor value for money when in a bottle but not so when attractively and conveniently displayed in a sleeve with a film covered window. A good deal of packaging can also be dangerous, with 50,000 people a year in the UK (where figures are kept) being badly injured while trying to open food packaging.

Service supply/demand

Many services cannot be stored as physical products can. This raises a special problem of whether to

- expand the service to cater to the high demand period;
- cater to some other level of demand; or
- try to manage the demand so that demand fluctuations are less extreme.

Managing demand fluctuations may be done through pricing, just as cinemas may price differently during some days or in the afternoon than for their regular shows at night. The aim in fact might be to have different target segments use the service at different times just as airlines do. In any case there is a need to think in terms of the revenue arising from different utilization levels so that the cost of underutilized capacity is known.

Branding, brand image, brand persona, and brand personality

Whenever we speak of a "brand" in marketing its *referential meaning* is the name, sign and/or the design used to identify a firm's product. Although a "trademark" is that sign or parts of the brand that are registered to provide legal protection, an American submission to GATT defined it more broadly to cover any "sign, word, design, letter number, color, shape" that can be used to distinguish a product as belonging to one producer as distinct from another. Trademarks are usually registered in each country where the product is likely to be sold.

Initially a brand is just a name but over time it comes to acquire definite associations or *sense meaning*. What the brand symbolizes is part of this sense meaning. A symbol is a sign that not only denotes something but connotes some value. Whereas the brand image is the impression created by the brand in the minds of consumers, what a brand *symbolizes* are the associations conjured up by that image: what the brand stands for; what it exemplifies. Gut reactions to symbols like brand-names can be viewed as *identification reactions* since reactions (e.g. favoring or not favoring buying) occur on identification without further investigation. A brand's image, as a collection of qualities, properties, attributes, characteristics, attitudes, benefits and feelings associated with the brand, encapsulates a brand's overall connotations as shared by the public at large or by some particular group of buyers. A favorable brand image can be key in buying since it signals benefits without involving the consumer in exhaustive information processing. A brand image may speak to the imagination in a way that drowns out whatever speaks for substance. However, at the level of the individual consumer, brand image will always vary somewhat since experiences that shape that image are never quite the same for any two people. In particular brand image constitutes a profile of beliefs and impressions about the likely performances of a product. When these embrace what the consumer seeks, the brand is perceived as a "good" product. Goodness (as Aristotle points out) rests on a "conditional wanting rule," so that to call a product a good one is to say that it will do for us whatever we want from that type of product.

How does brand image enter into choice? Although brand image can be decisive in choosing from the consumer's evoked set of brands or in what would otherwise be a picking situation, there are other possibilities. Brand image could act as a conjunctive rule in eliminating all brands that do not have a favorable image. Brand image may lie behind the implicit favorite model, with the rest of the evaluation process being essentially a decision confirmation exercise where consumers make sure their implicit favorite is the right one for them. Brand image may also enter into evaluating a brand against choice criteria. Thus I may credit the brand with a good image as technically better, being less risky to buy, being value for money and more socially appropriate.

Although we said that initially a brand is just a name, it can still have meaningful associations because of the name. The initial selection of a name is important since, even in the absence of experience with a brand, the name still conveys some sense meaning. *Names help shape perceptions.* Every brand-name evokes a mental image and should preferably be a means by which the consumer perceives a brand's unique qualities. This means that attention must be paid to the selection of a brand-name right from the start to try to convey the desired associations. But the question arises as to what associations? Thus a recent perfume is DNA, which is certainly not a sensual, fashion-glamour type name as would be expected. The advertisement purports to explain the connection: "DNA ... it's the reason you have your father's eyes, your mother's smile and Bijan's perfume." The name draws attention to itself and the copy will excite enough curiosity to be read and these are real advantages but it is a big price to pay for inappropriate or obviously forced associations.

Brand images change as associations change. But what should be rejected is the idea that a particular name has the same sense-meaning regardless of context. Thus it was claimed that the name of the Oldsmobile car should be changed because the name had associations with "old." The fact is that the Oldsmobile car has collected its own associations as the connotation of a name is relative to the semantic system within which the name functions. Thus DieHard batteries does not convey the meaning of diehard as meaning a person who "vigorously maintains a hopeless position, outdated attitude" as per the dictionary definition. The DieHard name, when related to batteries, was meant to suggest they last a long time and no doubt such a name was helpful when the brand was first launched. However, an established brand acquires a meaning that can be very remote from what the brand-name suggests. For example, "Times," "Post," "Telegraph" are used in many parts of the world as names of newspapers. When first introduced, these names did convey some sense of "being there with the news" but each of these names has come to acquire connotations specific to each newspaper so few readers are likely to reflect on the name but simply use it to distinguish their order.

George Eastman was reputed to have called his camera Kodak simply because the name was "short, vigorous, incapable of being misspelt ... and meant nothing." He would be wrong about the name meaning nothing; names of brands do not just register on the mind but conjure up some set of associations. Thus Kodak would not have been a suitable name for, say, facial tissues as the name sounds more hard than soft. Similarly, the name "Nintendo" (which means hard-working in Japanese) would not be a good sounding name for, say, a moisture cream. Names incorporating "L" and "M" (like Lam) give off images of gentleness, in contrast to names involving "T" and "K" (like the word Tak) which suggests sharpness. If brand image is important then suggested names should be evaluated through, say, association tests, remembrance tests and preference tests.

The brand-name is important in launching a new product. *The unity and uniqueness of a name suggests the unity and uniqueness of the brand itself.* As stated earlier but needs repeating, every name conveys a host of impressions and these impressions are the starting point for conceptualizing the brand itself. Also an easily remembered name helps recall, and those with favorable images tend to be recalled first. Names are considered attractive if they sound somewhat familiar and are easier rather than difficult to pronounce. But names do not appear to have lasting influences on consumers though they can affect a consumer's willingness to collect information beyond the name itself.

Advertising presupposes a brand-name to promote. But the brand-name serves purposes other than to identify. As suggested earlier, a name can draw attention to a brand's major buying inducement, for example, Ultra Brite toothpaste. When a brand is still trying to get off the ground, this can be important; people tend to act on the labels. What the seller is in effect trying to do is to get the consumer to accept a certain definition of the product: a definition to arouse buying action in line with the definition. An example here would be "Self Tanning Milk" made by Clarins. It says it all: concept and promise are in the name.

When there is nothing else to go on in choosing among brands, the consumer may choose the brand with the most appealing name. Brand name allied to brand recognition can be particularly important in a "picking" situation. Also a brand-name can signal information as to quality, provide confidence in buying and so can be decisive when adaptive criteria are dominant. Brands can come to have a *persona* (the public face presented to the world) that fits the preferred image of the target audience so that buying the brand becomes part of the consumer's system of *image management*. This is one reason designer labels may be perceived as bestowing a distinction on the owner. But where this is so, it becomes important for the persona to be consistent as consistency of image projected symbolizes *certainty* and a *commitment* to whatever the image suggests.

The persona of a brand can be sharpened by the addition of a logo or other symbol such as the package, a picture, the shape of the product or an associated character. A logo can be a particularly useful way of differentiating a brand in a market composed of me-too products. A *logo* tends to affect brand image as a logo can be one of clearest sensations received that enter into the composite picture constituting the brand image. One survey in the *New York Times* (September 16, 1992) showed that 55 percent of brand or company logos showed to consumers evoked different reactions from just being shown the brand or company names alone. Seventeen of twenty-four logos tested evoked more positive responses than the brand-names alone. Thus in the case of the Buick car, the score for trustworthiness and quality (on a scale from 1 to 100) increased by sixteen percentage points when consumers saw the full-color Buick logo instead of the name alone. In six cases, however, the logos scored less than did the brand or company names when shown alone. However, the study was not confined to those in the target markets so, although the same general picture might have emerged, the exact results might have differed. What might be said is that the logo itself should connote something the brand wishes to project and be updated with any overall image change.

The persona of a brand is the image presented to the public as intended by the firm while the brand image is the actual image the public has of the brand. The term *brand personality* is often used interchangeably with brand image, though brand personality focuses on aspects of brand image that distinguish the brand from other brands, usually by describing the brand as if it were a person ("If the Mercedes were a person, how would you describe that person?"). The firm seeks to have brand persona and brand image coincide. But this may not be easy when experience teaches otherwise or other factors, like the country of origin, have a significant effect on brand image. And the country of origin can affect brand image since *stereotypes* exist about products from different countries. Although the term stereotype is used to refer to a generalization about a category of people that sets them apart from other groups, it can be used for products also. Thus part of the Japanese car stereotype is reliability and value for money. Stereotypes magnify differences between similar products from different countries and minimize differences among manufacturers of the same product from the same country. A stereotype, like a brand image, allows mental short cuts and therefore quicker (but not necessarily wiser) judgments. Stereotyping can be remote from reality today given the advent of so much offshore manufacture. Nonetheless, if the law allows, information about products is often manipulated to exploit the stereotype.[14] Yet many products succeed in spite of their "inappropriate" country of origin because they manifestly (or are known to) offer substantive qualities. In general, consumer confidence in the stereotype for a well-known country of origin is unlikely to be the same as confidence in the meaningfulness of a well-known brand image.

A firm can adopt an *individual brand-name* (for example, Ultra Brite toothpaste) or a *family brand-name* (for example, Lux soap, Lux dishwashing liquid) or a *corporate name* (for example, Heinz or Kellogg) or some combination. Family brand-names and company (trade) names are not equivalent in power. A family brand-name can be more descriptive of the set of symbolic properties or attributes possessed by the brands it covers, but a corporate name has that extra value that comes from the corporate image. As markets become more crowded with brand-names, adaptive criteria become important and so do corporate names and symbols for getting new products off the ground. This stress on the symbolism attached to a brand or a logo (e.g. the lamb as a symbol of gentleness and meekness) can be important as symbolism is so basic to the human mind. One only has to think of the symbolism in religious rites: without some understanding of the symbolism, the rites seem pointless exercises or superstitious mumbo-jumbo.

Companies in the same market do not necessarily adopt the same branding policy in that market. P&G adopted the individual brand-names Pampers and Luvs for their diaper lines to connote the feelings of a mother toward her baby. Johnson's Disposable Diapers in contrast sought to benefit from Johnson's general reputation for quality goods. But the use of a company or family brand-name can accompany an individual brand-name as in the case of Kleenex Huggies. The name has a dual role

1 suggesting the value stemming from the Kleenex quality reputation in paper products; and
2 suggesting the benefit of the close fitting, gentle feature of its diapers.

Brand extensions and line extensions

An individual brand-name can be selected to reflect the product's unique advantage or to promote the product as completely new, without worrying about any inappropriate connotations associated with a family or corporate name. But the cost of establishing an individual brand-name may be prohibitive. Hence a firm might use an established brand-name for the new product. When this occurs, it is known as *brand extension*. Of course, the established brand should not be in decline or its name might be a disadvantage rather than an advantage for the new product.

A brand extension tactic is adopted to reduce the cost of building a new brand as it facilitates buying by reducing perceived risk. Given the large number of products, there is more than the consumer can digest so using a trusted family brand-name can help a firm get through the clutter. Even firms traditionally adopting individual brand-names like P&G are now embracing brand extensions. Thus up to around 1984, P&G sold only one type of Tide but now there is Liquid Tide, Tide with bleach and so on. In 1988/9 P&G came out with around ninety new products and none of them carried a new brand-name. Some writers, and perhaps P&G itself, would not regard all these as brand extensions but as *product-line filling* within the existing product line or, alternatively, *product-line stretching* downward to the lower end of the market or upward to serve the upper end of the market or *two-way stretch* if current market position is at present mid-way. This is because some marketers reserve the term *brand extension* as using a brand-name established in one product category to enter *another* product category or market. Thus we have Helene Curtis's extension of the Suave name into skin cream and deodorants. Equally common is the extension of the corporate name to all its products, however different. This problem with terminology arises from a confusion over "brand extension" and "line extension": product-line filling and product-line stretching are *line extensions* (see Figure 10.11).

In the 1980s many firms were taken over at prices that made little sense unless the buyers believed that the acquired firms had many well-established brands whose names could be further exploited in brand extensions, that is, the brand-names could be used in many other product categories or markets. There are many cases on record of firms not realizing the value of their brand-names. Exploiting the name means broadening the range of products under that brand-name, to the full extent of the connotations of the name.

Product category

	New	Exists
New	New company product	Flanker brand
Exists	Brand extension	Line extension

Brand-name

Figure 10.11 Product category/brand-name combination

A brand extension should exploit what the brand is meant to exemplify, otherwise there is a diluting of the brand image. Thus if the brand-name is synonymous with reliability, then such should be a key selling point for the brand extension. This means that firms need to have a very deep understanding of what a brand stands for; what it means to the consumer, what it connotes, and its image. A question instantly arises about what a corporate name like GE stands for when it is used to cover so many different product categories. The answer is "good in its class" or "always a quality product." In any case, the brand extension should not stray from the original brand's associations. For example, Hallmark Cards and Benson & Hedges cigarettes tried brand extensions into luxury ball-point pens but tests predicted failure. Gillette's Silkience did not extend well from haircare products to facial moisturizers while sales of Coca-Cola clothes are hardly getting off the ground. Arm & Hammer, which succeeded in extending its name from baking soda to toothpaste and a refrigerator deodorant, failed in trying also to extend the name to personal deodorants.

The constant danger in brand extensions is the risk of diluting the image of the original brand (family or mother brand) by spreading it over too many products, too loosely connected with the associations of the mother brand. It was for this reason that IBM called its low priced entry into the European PC market Ambra, rather than risk diluting the upscale image of the IBM name. Cadbury-Schweppes has extended the Cadbury name from chocolate to Marvel dried milk and Smash, a mashed-potato mixture. Both Marvel and Smash have benefited from the Cadbury image of value and quality but unknown is the effect on the Cadbury chocolate image. The MG name, once the exemplar of the dashing young person's sports car, was thrown away by Rover putting the name on family hatchbacks. The conditions under which a brand extension dilutes beliefs associated with the family brand-name have been studied.[15] Not surprisingly, brand extensions can dilute beliefs when the brand extension attributes (e.g. durability) are inconsistent with the family brand beliefs. Family brand beliefs can be diluted if the brand extensions are viewed as moderately typical, that is, the extensions were consistent with some expectations about the family brand-name but not others. In contrast, brand extensions that are perceived to be clearly different from products offered under the family brand-name carried a more moderate degree of risk with virtually no dilution in cases where the brand extension's typicality was salient to consumers. What is important is what associations carry over from the family brand to the brand extension and how favorable and how relevant are these associations for the brand extension.

If a firm brings out an additional product within one of its product categories but the product is given an individual brand-name, it is called a *flanker brand*, for example, Brim coffee of General Foods. If the same product were given the existing brand-name, it would be a line extension (see Figure 10.11). Flanker brands are a common way of catering to different segments of the market to keep out rival entrants. Both flanker brands and line extensions are a common way of erecting barriers to entry reducing marketing costs, and increasing perceptions of value by having wide price gaps.

Line extensions are far more common than brand extensions though they are not free of risk. There is the danger that the line extension will dilute the brand image. If the line extension is lower priced and fails to establish itself as catering to a distinct segment, then extensive cannibalism might result. Ideally, a line extension should be at the same level of quality, the same price level, the same persona as the established (mother) brand otherwise there is a danger of antagonizing the buyers of the established brand. This was the problem with General Motors when it extended the Cadillac name to the Cadillac Cimarron. Those who owned Cadillacs were annoyed at GM putting out the diminutive model.

A good deal of image dilution has come about through licensing. This has happened with many designer labels like Christian Dior, Yves St Laurent, Pierre Cardin, and Gucci. As brand-names, they are not the same today as in the 1970s, largely as a result of the names being allowed to appear on too many shoddy licensed goods in the case of Pierre Cardin, and just too many unrelated (by snob appeal) products. This licensing of a name should be distinguished from the licensing of a technology which may be undertaken to help standardize the technology, tap certain markets, or attract resources to exploit the technology further.

A common problem in service industries is the question of *bundling*, that is, whether the consumer has to buy the whole bundle of services or can pick and choose. Thus consultants or investment bankers may offer some unbundled package of services. A firm might wish to sell only its whole package as it believes that only in this way can it demonstrate its expertise and avoid direct competition with firms specializing in just one part of the bundle. On the other hand, consumers would prefer to pick and choose or assemble their own bundle from various other specialist firms.

Product service and services

The word product service refers to pre- and post-sale services offered to customers, organizational users or channel intermediaries. Service here is essentially the backup a firm gives to its customers to satisfy them, retain them or secure a sale. It covers guarantees, maintenance, repairs, delivery or availability, credit terms, technical help, and training: it can even be extended to include market studies, assistance in product planning and development, advice on materials handling and help in production layout and design. It goes without saying that a service offered by one firm may be the product of another firm, for example, repair under guarantee as opposed to repair being the business of the firm.

Some firms simply make service the dealer's responsibility or restrict service to the minimum. Although there is an implied warranty in law to protect the consumer from fraud and there are the customary warranties given by all firms in an industry, additional guarantees can give an important competitive advantage when the customer is worried about the risks of purchase. There are typically perceptions of high risk in buying high priced products; when the negative consequences of failure are high; when the market has a bad reputation on quality and the buyer's ego or job is on the line. A customer-oriented guarantee would be unconditional; easy to understand; would cover what is significant and collecting on the guarantee would not be difficult. Maytag unconditionally guarantees its washing machines for ten years which has allowed Maytag in the past to charge a premium price.

The promise of service can be what swings the sale. This is not uncommon in industrial marketing. The seller first wins over an industry leader by the promise and delivery of a higher level of service than that given by competitors. Recommendations follow, with new accounts being taken on as long as the additional servicing requirements do not outstrip the service resources available. A system built to deliver an efficient service (for example, Federal Express) cannot be copied overnight and may never be equaled. But a policy on quality service is not always adopted as a competitive tool. It may be a way of spotlighting production defects (for example, during factory repair service) or it may be a very profitable sideline (for example, spare parts).

Customers expect a firm to live up to promises on service. Everyone who has contact with a customer provides service. Whether we are speaking of those answering the telephone, field maintenance repair men or sales people, they are all potentially ambassadors of goodwill. When service functions do not all come under marketing, it makes coordination difficult which can be undesirable if service is intended to give the firm a competitive edge. The management of a purely service organization like a bank recognizes that service quality depends on people whose interpersonal skills and other behavior vary widely even after training. This, when allied to the fact that service is often intangible, means it is more difficult to develop an effective quality control system than with machine output. Also as the production and consumption of a service often occur more or less simultaneously, this stops the suppliers of services from making minor adjustments or replacements when defects show up in production. What adds to the problem of trying to avoid unevenness in the quality of service is that customers are less likely to complain about poor service (nothing to show, only a disputed description of incidents) so management fail to recognize the extent of poor service. In general, services are often difficult to evaluate in advance which means new customers tend to seek past users for advice. If the service did not meet or exceed past users' expectations then the service will be criticized and criticism is much more effective in deterring usage then is praise in encouraging trial. Innovation in service organizations can either involve units that have direct contact with customers or units that provide the back up support like the kitchen in a restaurant. Design of systems in both units may be demanded. In the design of a service, the key is to focus first on quality not on productivity. Improvements in efficiency without effectiveness is tantamount to thinking of cheaper ways of achieving unsatisfactory results. Services are typically individualized or customized. Where such customization requires the service provider to process quickly and accurately a good deal of information, computer information systems come into their own. Once the system is designed, there is a need to check feasibility before documenting it in written manuals, video presentations, or thinking about indoctrination, education and incentives for those who render the service.

Most service industries have relatively high fixed costs as labor cannot usually just be hired and laid off as needed. When this is so, the service organization is highly vulnerable to fluctuations in demand. As a consequence, service management is vitally concerned with demand management to try and even out the fluctuations through price discounts, appeals to different market segments and so on.

Forecasting sales prior to test marketing

At every stage in new product development organizations are interested in predicting market potential and likely sales and costs so as to check whether further development and marketing are justified. In general, in industrialized countries the big uncertainty is the likely demand for the product though in many other countries of the world, the uncertainty lies in supply and producing to time and specification.

Buying intentions and preferences.   Early estimates on sales are made on the basis of buying intentions, preference data, or more recent approaches like logit analysis. In *intention-to-buy surveys* (as we have seen) consumers are asked to make a subjective estimate of their probability of buying and sales estimates are built up from the replies. For example, from past data assuming 70 percent of the "definites" will buy; 35 percent of the "probables"; and 10 percent of the "might buy" and then extrapolating from this sample of replies to the total target group of customers.

In respect to *preferences*, consumers are asked to rank their choices. Again past data on the product category or analogous products might suggest that, say, 80 percent of those ranking a brand as first choice will buy it and, say, 20 percent of those ranking it second will buy it. Logit analysis or the logit model is based on preferences but takes account of the relative intensity of the preferences so as to obtain better estimates of purchase probability. The inputs to the model are both the values of the preferences and data on the actual brand choice for existing products.

Forecasting based on buying intentions and preferences may be a poor predictor for a new-to-the-world product as discontinuous innovations take time for the consumer to adjust to them. But all surveys as to intentions and preferences have weaknesses. Intentions, as measured, are always conditional and are not the same as someone saying they *will* buy, or they *promise* to buy, and future preferences are always uncertain when competitive actions are unknown, while promotional campaigns can affect both intentions and preferences.

Historical data on relationships.   Data on similar new products in the past may be used to establish the relationships between marketing inputs (for example, advertising expenditure, pricing, extensive distribution) and the number of consumers made aware of the product, the number trying it, and the number repeat buying. The approach assumes that relationships that held on some analogous product in the past can be applied to the new product. We assume, say, that the introductory history of the new product will be similar in "all relevant respects" to the analogous one; that the market conditions that will prevail are also similar and so on. Such assumptions are more likely to hold when the new product is merely a line extension.

Laboratory simulation tests.   Laboratory simulation has been used to predict trial, predict repeat buying, predict the long run market share of new *packaged* goods, to estimate likely cannibalism, to screen out undersirable elements in the product and suggest promotional strategies. Laboratory simulation forecasts are based on exposing a sample of around 300 target customers to commercials for the new product and a small set of established rival products. Next the consumers enter a simulated store with the opportunity to purchase the new product or the established competing ones. Follow-up interviews with those who bought the new product are conducted to measure attitudes toward the product and repurchase intent. Typical such tests are Comp and ASSESSOR.[16, 17] The ASSESSOR model is the most well known. It both aims to forecast sales and test market shares for new consumer products and also to provide a structure to help evaluate alternative marketing strategies. As with other simulations, the basic data comes from enticing shoppers passing through a shopping mall to watch competing commercials, including the one for the new product, with shoppers being given the opportunity, after the commercials, to select one of the brands from a shelf display.

Laboratory simulation is unsuited for truly new-to-the-world products. It assumes that purchase rates are the same as for established brands and that preferences quickly stabilize. It is not suited to industrial products or those to be sold through personal selling rather than being promoted through advertising. However, similar models have been developed to deal with *durable* consumer goods.[18] With consumer durables like washing machines, penetration of the market can be very slow with sales saturating only after many years. The question, though, is to what extent the process mirrors what happens in the real world? Being asked to watch commercials in an artificial situation is not the same as watching them on TV. Nor is buying in a simulated store the same as buying in a supermarket or other real store. There are other real life deficiencies but the basic question is: Does it predict? ASSESSOR has been shown to predict test market shares with a high degree of accuracy in certain defined conditions.[19] It could be argued that practitioner consultants only parade their successes and there is a need to survey a sample of users to gauge the overall effectiveness of the technique. But whatever the limitations (inherent or practical), the question also to be answered is whether the technique is better than alternatives.

Sales wave experiments. Consumers may be sent the product or details about the product and offered an opportunity to purchase it at a favorable price. Typically, the consumers belong to a panel who receive a monthly catalog. When a product is to be tested, the advertisement for it is placed in the catalog. It is assumed that the demand for payment combined with the opportunity to repurchase will simulate the consumer behavior that occurs. This approach is not suited for all products and would perhaps be invalid for the truly innovative product. The buying behavior resembles the awareness $\Rightarrow$ trial $\Rightarrow$ repeat order process that occurs through selling via mail order, not through the stores.

Other methods.   Sometimes none of the above techniques can be applied to forecasting likely sales. Marketing management in this case may

- look at the sales curve of products that are analogous in some way;
- management may select from the target customer group those likely to be "suspects" and then screening for likely "prospects"; or
- by considering the likely diffusion process.

We still need to develop pretest market models for forecasting sales of industrial products and services though some progress has been made. Services are typically just tried out on a pilot basis and expanded throughout the market with a "roll-out" strategy, that is, from one area to the next until the whole country/area is covered.

When it comes to forecasting sales for a new product there is always the unknown factor of competitive retaliation. A pioneer firm may seek to protect itself for a while through the law. There are essentially four ways. The first is the law that covers *trade secrets* in respect to formulas. The second is *copyright* so that the individual or organization gets paid for use of the material. Copyright, though, protects the particular expression of an idea but not the idea itself. Nonetheless, this is ideal for products such as software and semiconductors. The third is *trademark law* to prevent other firms from using the organization's identity. Number four is *patent law* to protect innovative products or processes so that the owner has a temporary monopoly in each country where the patent is registered. But patents today tend to be immediately exchanged for royalties or other patents as otherwise competitors tend to get around them in some way.

The eight or so signatories to the International Convention for the Protection of Industrial Property (the so-called Paris Union) agree to register the trademarks of other signatory states as registered in the country of origin and acknowledge the property right residing in trade names. The Madrid Agreement is also concerned with the international registration of trademarks, permitting the registration in just one of the twenty-two or so participating nations to qualify as registered in all member countries. There are many other such international organizations.

Market testing

Mini-market tests

There is debate over the use of test markets. Certainly, companies are tending to skip test marketing for line extensions. Thus P&G saw little risk in taking its instant decaffeinated version of Folgers coffee to market without any market testing. More surprising was Gillette's decision to launch its new Sensor razor throughout America and Europe at the same time without any traditional market testing. One fear is competitor sabotage or providing an opportunity for the competitor to copy. For example, when P&G began testing a ready-to-spread Duncan Hines frosting, General Mills saw a winner and brought out its own Betty Crocker brand, which now dominates that product category. Also some of the techniques like laboratory simulation are being substituted for market testing. But sometimes companies simply do *a mini*-market test.

In a mini-market test, the product may be placed in several stores and areas to observe buying. Alternatively, there may be direct marketing through mail order or sales through mobile vans. Such tests are used to check different aspects of the proposed market plan:

- repeat purchase pattern and seasonality of sales,
- buyer profiles,
- price/quality relationships,
- likely shipping breakages,
- how stores display and position the product,
- packaging appeals,
- possibilities of distribution, and
- likely sales.

The mini-market test can include experiments. For example, a city can be divided into control and experimental zones for testing several variables simultaneously. Such experimentation has been greatly facilitated by scanner data and cable television. A panel of consumers in a selected area is given identification cards, which they present at cooperating supermarkets checkout counters. Checkout counter scanners of the uniform product codes (UPC) on products record each person's purchases, and how much and how often a product/brand is bought. When such data are linked to the buyers' TV viewing habits and which commercials were seen, a great deal of information is assembled about likely sales and likely advertising effectiveness. But there are still many limitations. In no country is cable universally used by all buyers, while no one suggests that participants are a representative sample of the target market. There are still doubts, too, about whether the process itself alters buyer behavior.

Full market testing

In full market testing, the new product is put on sale in several areas with a marketing strategy as near as possible to the one it is proposed to use in the national launch. Ideally it is the national launch in miniature. A full market testing is a check on the:

- feasibility of the marketing strategy,
- viability or likely commercial success, and
- desirability of the various elements of the plan.

These purposes are illustrated in Table 10.1 together with a listing of many of the limitations of test marketing. Some of the criteria used to select the actual test market areas to be used are:

- *Number*: where experimentation is to be carried out, then two areas are needed for each test, for example, four test areas for testing two levels of advertising expenditure;
- *Size*: large areas may be selected to reduce bias;
- *Place/location*: television areas may be required if television is to be the advertising medium and commercial retail audit areas if results are to be projected to the national level. The test area that is ideal from a location point of view may not be ideal from, say, a media planning point of view. And where comparative testing is the chief goal, matched areas may be more important than representative ones. Where the primary goal is sales forecasting, emphasis should be placed on getting a cross-section of the product's ultimate users;
- *Demographics*: factors to consider are: age distribution, socioeconomic level, consump-

Table 10.1 Full market testing

Purposes	Limitations
Testing for feasibility, viz: - revealing shortcomings in proposed marketing strategy - whether distribution goals can be achieved - whether proposed systems and procedures (e.g. order handling system) are effective and efficient *Testing for commercial viability*, viz: - frequency of purchase - cannibalism - positioning as perceived by the consumer - volume of sales - source of sales - level of distribution *Testing for desirability*, viz: - product features and packaging - service - advertising copy - pricing - distribution	Expensive (sales typically do not cover the cost) Time consuming (around a year) Exposure to competitive imitation or disruption No ideal test area Usually a "spillout" of sales into other areas, which distorts sales patterns Special treatment (for example, sales force focus) often occurs to inflate sales Often not feasible for industrial products since production may require equivalent investment to full launch Testing for desirability often frustrated because of the practical problems in achieving sound experimental designs or experimental controls

tion pattern, income per head, type of industry/employment, channels used, climatic conditions, and so on;

- *Stores selected*: a cross-section of stores that will handle the product during the national launch.

The uses of test marketing are a matter of dispute. There are those who see it as a dress rehearsal to test all the elements in the marketing strategy, while others argue that test marketing should be an aid to budgeting costs and facilitating planning on the ground that winners and losers should have been identified earlier. Cadbury of Cadbury–Schweppes argues that test marketing is frequently used to discover facts that can be obtained more efficiently in other ways.[20] He provides some illuminating examples of failures in the food/confectionery business, for example, how the product finally launched may not live up to the test market sample; how products that were liked in the test market failed because they did not fit the rest of the consumer's consumption system; or even how the packaging (inability to stack) can make the product unpopular with channel intermediaries.

There are problems in projecting the results or predicting from a test market as all future marketing stimuli are not present; areas are not representative, while marketing management often undertake extraordinary actions to ensure success, like offering large incentives to retailers.

The problem of "grossing up" to sales after the product launch is complicated when the firm aims to launch the product worldwide. The simplest way is to assume that results in the test market (including likely market share) are what will be obtained in other countries. But this is seldom a safe assumption and the firm should test market in each of the major countries or, from past data, work out what the relationship might be. Many firms simply launch the new product in other countries after it has been launched in their own country but there are advantages in market testing the product in each of its largest markets. In this way the firm has a better idea as to what modifications to make to the offering. One factor that is apt to enforce some modification in the offering and that is the law.

The legal environment in international marketing.   Throughout the world, nations tend to have laws covering product quality, packaging, warranties, trademarks, and patents. There may also be laws about products having a percentage of local content. This is not surprising in that what many of the importing countries seek is technology transfer as well as employment opportunities for their citizens. Price controls in many countries also operate as a (deceptively) easy way to limit inflation, though some countries allow price agreements among competitors. In respect to advertising, commercial TV may not be allowed (e.g. Sweden) while premium offers may be banned (e.g. in France) or comparative advertising may not be allowed (e.g. in Germany). Distribution can be a nightmare in many countries. Sometimes wholesalers are in a legally powerful position, making it difficult to bypass them (e.g. Germany). Certain types of distribution may be prohibited (e.g. door-to-door selling in France) or existing channels may legally restrict entry (e.g. in France) or distribution agreements may tie the manufacturer long term or be broken only with severe penalty. In some common law countries the ownership of a trademark depends on who is the first to use it while in code law countries, the first company or person to register the trademark is the rightful owner.

A number of models have been developed to forecast future sales from test market data. The Parfitt–Collins model, which relies on housewife panel data, is purely concerned with forecasting sales.[21] But other models like Tracker and NEWS, which rely on survey data, can be used not only to forecast sales but to evaluate the product's marketing mix.[22, 23] Each of these models, however, applies mainly to inexpensive, frequently purchased products. What is monitored in test markets depends on whether the test is concerned with feasibility, viability, or desirability or some combination. A primary interest in *feasibility* leads to a focus on distribution, production, service and coordination problems. There is a recognition here that any strategy can be frustrated by poor attention to operations. An interest in *viability* focuses on such factors as the repeat purchase pattern, frequency of use, and the amount purchased on each occasion. It also leads to the collection of store audit data, average sales per store, dealer attitude surveys, and whether the product is being put to the use anticipated. Finally, an interest in *desirability* leads to the detailed observation of buyer behavior. Under the heading of desirability we might include ethical issues raised in product management:

- Is the product safe to use?
- Is it easy to accidentally misuse the product and, as a consequence, injure the user?
- Are warning labels prominently displayed?
- Is the labeling in any way misleading?
- Is the package in any way deceptive as to what quantity or contents are being purchased?

A complicating factor in all market testing is competition. It is all too common to under-estimate competitor reaction. Competitors may buy large quantities in order to mislead. They may bring out a rival product or adopt dubious tactics aimed at sabotaging any attempt to break into the market. It is odd that many companies see nothing unethical in some of these practices.

If a product is to be introduced throughout the world the test market may be a region consisting of a cluster of countries that are fairly similar in "relevant" respects. What is primarily of interest here is the extent to which the product should be modified to suit the local market and how far other elements of the marketing mix have to be changed. An example here is the market for diapers in Japan. In selling its Pampers in Japan, P&G overlooked a key cultural difference in that Japanese mothers change their babies' diapers about fourteen times a day, which is probably more than double the figure in the United States and Europe.

The product launch

It is the *product launch* that requires the largest commitment of resources which means that, before launching, the product must be judged to have a high probability of success.

However, the product may still fail in the market, not because of any inherent deficiency, but because the launch was poorly conceived and executed.

Goals in the product launch are influenced (but not fully determined by) whether the firm is a pioneer or a follower. Although the pioneer is free to choose any segments or positionings, without the immediate need to consider rivals, the pioneer must consider what it can best defend long term which depends on its basic competencies vis-à-vis likely market entrants. The goal, though, of any pioneer is likely to be to dominate the market and develop early brand loyalty (some studies even point to early buyers being more brand loyal). They also have an opportunity to establish ways of doing business in the market in respect to pricing, distribution, warranties and so on. Thus IBM, in following Xerox in office copiers, found that customers expected them to be leased with a charge per copy. In order to achieve the goal of market leadership, pioneers commonly enter the market with a broad product line, extensively promoted and distributed. However, while the pioneer may also have an advantage in the new technology, the danger lies in not recognizing the possibility of being leapfrogged.

In the early stages of a growth market, market dominance may be sought by focusing on attracting new users as the easiest way of gaining market share. Firms in a growing market can increase sales without increasing market share, but attracting new users will aim to increase market share because market share gains that are achieved in the growth stage are likely to be worth more later on.

A follower in the market has the goal of either usurping the leadership position or being a major runner-up. This all presupposes the follower can

a) capitalize on any wrong moves taken by the pioneer whether in the product, the positioning, the promotion or the distribution;
b) leapfrog the pioneer in technology;
c) choose a more promising segment or several smaller segments that encircle the market leader; or
d) produce a better price/quality relationship.

The actual campaign for launching the new product will consist of:

• a program giving the sequence of tasks to be done;
• a schedule that relates the program to a time schedule; and
• budgets that allocate resources to the program and schedule.

Some typical things to be done prior to the product launch are:

• production facilities to be built; equipment to be ordered, delivered, and tested;
• inventory to be in place;
• credit facilities to be arranged;
• an order handling system to be devised; stationery specified, delivered, and distributed;
• sales people to be selected and trained;
• sales materials to be designed, ordered, delivered, distributed;

- dealers' service personnel to be trained;
- an advertising agency to be selected and the agency educated about the product;
- a promotional campaign to be drawn up, the printing of the literature, the design and production of point-of-sales aids and packaging materials.

The key organizational issue is coordination to synchronize production and marketing activities. Hence the usefulness of techniques such as *critical path analysis* for coordinating the timing and scheduling of activities. The manager responsible for the product should be responsible for this coordination and for planning the launch generally while the actual launch is carried out by the various operating personnel, with the planner in the background playing a supportive, coordinating role.

When a launch on a national or international basis is predicted to outstrip production and training facilities, the product may be launched on *a roll-out* basis, area by area, or industry by industry. Whether to use the firm's own sales force may be a problem since obtaining initial orders can be very time consuming, while the sales force itself may not be attuned to the pioneer-type selling that may be demanded. The firm, as a consequence, may hire some "flying (sales) force" from the various agencies specializing in such services.

Various models have been developed to predict sales after the campaign has begun. For example, the Ayer New Product Model uses the historical data/regression method discussed earlier.[24] This assumes the firm has the data for analogous products; data, say, about the relationship between media impressions and advertising recall, and between product satisfaction and repeat purchase. But given a reasonable distribution and a realistic advertising and promotion budget, getting consumers to try a new product may not be too difficult. The real problem lies in getting them to buy again and again.

Managing after the launch

During the transition to maturity there is likely to be a "shakeout" of the weakest competitors. If a firm is to survive this period it needs some competitive advantage to develop new segments, cater better to existing ones or to win on costs. For most firms, there cannot be a technological advantage in performance so that they cannot appeal to technical criteria as their buying inducement. Even the technological leader must recognize that, as the technology matures, it, too, may have to think of additional ways to maintain leadership as the brand-name may not be sufficient to overcome a competitor's advantages. As growth levels off, the goal of the market leader is to hang on to his customers as it is usually easier to retain customers than to attract new buyers or convert from rivals though this does not mean that attracting and converting must be ignored.

CONCLUSION

Product management is a major area of research by academics as good product management is seen as a condition for survival. But in spite of all this research, product management is still a risky business. Some writers put the blame on the elaborate system of new product development in regarding it as too slow to be responsive to changing customer wants and competitive activities.[25] It is argued that if more time and attention were given to mastering the firm's basic technology, understanding the firm's core competencies and its target customer group, allied to integrating the customer into the product design phase while constantly monitoring competition, fewer product failures would occur. There is an assumption here that firms do not try hard enough to acquire the extensive knowledge base being advocated and that customers are homogeneous enough to dispense with the wide tapping of opinions as currently recommended. What is true is that, in certain industries, there are *lead users* who are customers who "not only have new needs but can state the problem and suggest a solution" and sometimes create a product to solve the problem. It has been suggested that partnering with lead user customers will be a common way to go in the future.

While firms have got better, the competition has got tougher. The various management (marketing) science models pushed by consultants have done much to diffuse knowledge of them and to create a better climate for their acceptance and use. What many of these models do is expose a line of reasoning about a problem and how it might be solved, when previously there were only solutions based on darkness as to the underlying model. But many of the new models do not stem from any deep understanding of buyer or market behavior as all too often the management scientist and the specialist in buyer behavior go their own ways. Management scientists tend to focus on prediction without being too concerned with underlying theory, beyond assuming some sort of rational model of behavior. But at least they make their assumptions clear and open to debate. What is often difficult to do, however, is to evaluate the limitations of the models. Both sides depend more on pure logic to defend and attack rather than collect the relevant empirical evidence and demonstrate how the technique is an advance of what has gone before. Not that such evidence is likely to entirely underwrite some technique as universally valid but at least such evidence would provide more insight into the conditions that favor the use of a technique. At present, to get a hearing, benefits tend to be exaggerated with only successes reported in the literature accompanied by an unwillingness to concede any criticisms are other than nit-picking. This leads the opposition to be all too dismissive of what are in fact the only games in town.

NOTES

1 Foster, Richard (1986) *Innovation*, New York: Summit Books.
2 Nayak, Ranganath P. and Ketteringham, John M. (1994) *Breakthroughs*, New York: Mercury Books.
3 Von Hippel, E. (1977) "Has a Customer Already Developed Your Next Product?," *Sloan Management Review*, 18 (Winter) 63.
4 Cooper, A. C. and Schendel, D. G. (1976) "Strategic Responses to Technological Threats," *Business Horizons*, 19 (February) 61.
5 Ayres, Clarence E. (1944) *The Theory of Economic Progress: A Study of the Fundamentals of Economic Development and Cultural Change*, Chapel Hill, NC: The University of North Carolina Press.
6 Hertz, D. B. (1964) "Risk Analysis in Capital Investment," *Harvard Business Review*, 42 (January–February).

7 Urban, G. L. (1968) "A New Product Analysis and Decision Model," *Management Science*, 14 (April).
8 Pessemier, E. A. (1977) *Product Management: Strategy and Organization*, New York: John Wiley.
9 Bass, Frank M. and Bultez, Alain V. (1982) "A Note on Optimal Strategic Pricing of Technological Innovations," *Marketing Science* (Fall).
10 Jamieson, Linda F. and Bass, Frank M. (1989) "Adjusting Stated Intention Measures to Predict Trial Purchase of New Products: A Comparison of Models and Methods," *Journal of Marketing Research*, XXVI (August).
11 Green, Paul E. (1990) "Conjoint Analysis in Marketing: New Developments with Implications for Research and Practice," *Journal of Marketing*, 54 (October).
12 Cattin, Philippe and Wittink, Dick R. (1982) "Commercial Use of Conjoint Analysis: A Survey," *Journal of Marketing*, 46 (3) (Summer).
13 Wittink, Dick R. and Cattin, Philippe (1989) "Commercial Use of Conjoint Analysis: An Update," *Journal of Marketing*, 53 (July).
14 Papadopoulos, Nicolas and Heslop, Louise A. (eds.) (1993) *Product-Market Images: Impact and Role in International Marketing*, New York: International Business Press.
15 Laken, Barbara and John and Deborah Roedder (1993) "Diluting Brand Beliefs: When Do Brand Extensions Have a Negative Impact?" *Journal of Marketing*, 57 (July).
16 Burger, P. C. (1972) "COMP: a New Product Forecasting System," Working Paper, Evanston: Northwestern University.
17 Silk, A. J. and Urban, G. L. (1978) "Pre-test Market Evaluation of New Packaged Goods: a Model and Measurement Methodology," *Journal of Marketing Research*, 15 (May).
18 Urban, Glen L., Hulland, John S., and Weinberg, Bruce D. (1993) "Premarket Forecasting for New Consumer Durable Goods: Modeling Categorization, Elimination, and Consideration Phenomena," *Journal of Marketing*, 57 (April).
19 Urban, Glen L. and Katz, Gerald M. (1983) "Pretest Market Models: Validation and Managerial Implications," *Journal of Marketing Research*, 20 (August).
20 Cadbury, N. D. (1975) "When Where and How to Test Market," *Harvard Business Review*, 53 (May–June).
21 Parfitt, J. H. and Collins, B. J. K. (1968) "Use of Consumer Panels for Brand-Share Prediction," *Journal of Marketing Research*, 5 (May).
22 Blattberg, Robert and Golanty, John (1978) "Tracker: an Early Test Market Forecasting and Diagnostic Model for New Product Planning," *Journal of Marketing Research*, 15 (May).
23 Pringle, Lewis G., Wilson, Dale R., and Brody, Edward I. (1982) "NEWS: a Decision-Oriented Model for New Product Analysis and Forecasting," *Management Science*, 1 (Winter).
24 Claycamp, Henry J. and Liddy, Lucien E. (1969) "Prediction of New Product Performance: an Analytical Approach," *Journal of Marketing Research*, 6 (November).
25 McKenna, Regis (1991) "Marketing is Everything," *Harvard Business Review* (Jan–Feb).

APPENDIX 10.1 INITIAL SCREEN OF SUGGESTED NEW LINE

Grosvenor House Suit Company

MEMO

1. Product policy on men's suits

The suggested new line fits the product policy on men's suits. It furthers the objective of increasing defensive flexibility by becoming less dependent on the current G. H. line and the one market segment for which the line caters.

The NEW LINE also coheres with our policy of minimizing risk since it uses existing production and marketing facilities while exploiting the firm's thrust.

2 . Market (segment) potential for the NEW LINE in men's suits

At this stage no firm market research data are available, but preliminary inquiries in the trade suggest the following:

(i) *Potential*

(a) Upper-quality segment . . . . .3,000,000 suits p.a.

(b) Those likely to buy a suit within price range (3 percent) . . . . .90,000 suits p.a.

(c) Sales estimate for NEW LINE . . . . .30,000 suits p.a.

These figures are only a rough order of magnitude.

(ii) *Profitability*

Breakeven analysis

Selling price to retailer	$120	
Variable cost per unit	$ 70	
Contribution to fixed cost and profit	= $ 50	per unit
Addition to fixed cost:		
Advertising	$100,000	
Salaries	$60,000	
		$160,000

Breakeven point: $\dfrac{\$160,000}{\$50} =$ 3,200 suits

Annual profit budget

Total revenue (30,000 × $120)		$3,600,000
Total variable cost (30,000 × $70)	$2,100,000	
Fixed cost	160,000	
		$2,260,000
Profit before tax		*$1,340,000*

The low breakeven point provides a large safety margin for errors in the tentative sales forecast.

3. Requirements for success in the segment

The following appear to be the requirements for successfully marketing to the segment:

(i) *Product*

(a) *Brand-name*

For a high quality clothing product, a well-known brand-name would help the product get off the ground.

(b) *Characteristics*

Grosvenor House current qualities of workmanship.

(ii) *Channels*

(a) Need for retailer to provide advice and reassurance.

(b) Individual retailer to carry full range.

(c) Need for "push" selling by retailer, in particular good display and retailer recommendation.

(d) Exclusive distribution to encourage push selling.

(iii) *Advertising*

Push strategy by retailer more important than any attempt to "pull" customers to the product via advertising.

(iv) *Personal selling*

(a) Development selling initially.

(b) Sales people to become merchandising consultants for retailer staff training, display and trade promotions.

4. Capability of Grosvenor House relative to the requirements for success

(i) *Product*

NEW LINE is a good quality product but the brand-name needs to be established. There will undoubtedly be customer acceptance problems initially.

(ii) *Channels*

Most existing Grosvenor House stockists can handle the product and provide the needed advice and "push." But merchandising and education at store level will be the major problem in promoting the NEW LINE.

(iii) *Personal selling*

The existing sales force are not skilled in development selling or even sufficiently skilled to carry out the major merchandising/education job to be done.

(iv) *Competition*

We have no profile of likely competitors and whether they will react, and, if so, how. Information is urgently needed before making the final decision.

(v) *Congruence with existing endeavors (synergy)*

The line:

(a) fits existing skills and resources;

(b) fits current distribution channels;

(c) can be sold by existing sales force (after some initial training);

(d) has the advantage of risk spreading.

In conclusion, there is as yet no established market segment for the NEW LINE. The segment has to be created. Prospective members of this segment are not people to whom the Grosvenor House name is a sufficient factor to get them to try the NEW LINE. They are the people, though, who can be persuaded to buy a better-quality suit. Such persuasion requires exposure to the NEW LINE and, often, education. In the main, those buying the NEW LINE will be less affluent, less sophisticated, less knowledgeable than those currently buying Grosvenor House. Hence the greater need for a push strategy and in-store merchandising.

5. Sketch of possible marketing strategy to fit the requirements for success

A. Customer targets
(i) *Final customers*
   (a) *Primary*
      Demographically, customer targets are centered around the mid-thirties; the emerging executive with aspirations to senior management or high advancement in his career; salary level $40,000–50,000; lifestyle of the established professional middle class.
   (b) *Secondary*
      The young well-educated, unmarried, in the professions or management.
(ii) *Intermediaries*
      Buyers in outlets catering to patrons who seek service and advice in choosing a quality suit. Such outlets are the better-class department stores and men's outfitters. Exclusive distribution since patrons will want an exclusive suit and will be prepared to look around before choosing.

B. Customer benefits provided
   A high quality suit, viz:
(i) traditionally made, needle sewn;
(ii) distinctive feel when worn; can be contrasted with the feel of a fused suit;
(iii) excellent cloth value that can stand up to wear;
(iv) well-styled—conservative and currently fashionable.
   The primary and secondary targets are likely to place different values on these benefits.

C. Customer appeals (benefits to be promoted)
(i) Focus on quality benefits.
(ii) Attention to problems of educating and reassuring buyers who lack confidence.
(iii) Education as to what factors to look for in a quality suit.

D. Promotional campaign
Mainly in-store merchandising and cooperative advertising. A benefit of cooperative advertising is that the store announces publicly its commitment to the brand.

E. Sales campaign
(i) *Persuaders*
   (a) Show the NEW LINE matches the demand of the store's patrons.
   (b) Show the profit margin is high to cover the service offered. (There is a need to give guidance as to likely sales for a store of a particular size in that location so quote likely gross profit.)
(ii) *Selling task*
   (a) Maintain business in existing retail outlets by regular calling and joint promotions.
   (b) Increase business by concept selling in reference to the NEW LINE.

(c) Attract new outlets by quoting the profitability of NEW LINE. (Is there any way of allowing a trial period?)

F. Service
The new outlets will expect service, as to them the NEW LINE is the most expensive product they handle. Customers will have similar expectations. As retailer goodwill is all important to solicit push selling from them, everything must be done to win their support by offering a two-day delivery on any item in the NEW LINE range.

G. Distribution system
Exclusive to gain retailer support. Additional incentives are needed if maximum support is to be obtained.

H. Pricing
The main competitive objective is to convert buyers who are currently buying suits around $175. Such buyers have expectations about the price to be paid for a better-quality suit and will hesitate to pay 30 percent more than they are currently paying. Price, even though it will be a surrogate indicator of quality, is a major hurdle to be overcome in marketing the NEW LINE. With a regularly bought consumer product of small value, the strategy would be to make a temporary price offer to encourage trial, but this is not appropriate in this case. We need to think out some unusual form of guarantee and product description to encourage a trial buy.

Conclusion
The company must recognize that it is creating a new market segment based on the assumption that a gap in the market exists between the quality level represented by the fused suit and the high-quality level of the current Grosvenor House Line. In the case of a suit, superiority in quality is not immediately apparent and relative advantages need to be communicated. The active cooperation of retail sales people in creating awareness and interest and helping the prospective customer evaluate the product is of particular importance.

We anticipate a gradual increase in business. We might speculate that early sales might be confined to innovators, constituting around 3 percent of ultimate customers. These are likely to belong to our secondary target group—the young unmarried, of good status and income, possessing a cosmopolitan outlook. The next 14 percent of customers are likely to be the main opinion leaders, belonging to our primary target group and well established and respected in their spheres. If the NEW LINE lives up to expectations, those interested in buying will follow this first group of innovators and early adopters. Sales can be anticipated to build up over a four year period. The use of the Grosvenor House name could contribute to the speeding up of the adoption process but is neither a necessary nor a sufficient condition for success; the NEW LINE will ultimately stand or fall on its own merits as to whether it fills a true gap in the market.

Chapter 11

Advertising, sales promotion, publicity, and corporate communications
Their roles and how they work to persuade

This chapter explains the roles and function of advertising, sales promotion, publicity and public relations (PR), in communicating information to influence the actions of target audiences. Without some understanding of how communications induce changes in wants, beliefs, attitudes, and behavior, the marketing manager possesses no explicit criteria against which to evaluate communications programs.

Most marketing managers possess a good deal of implicit knowledge about persuasive communications, as such knowledge is a necessary part of social living, whether in business or society at large. In fact we should not abandon common-sense intuitions or uncritically accept something because it is labeled "scientific." This assumes social science has all the answers, which is just not so. However, social science offers a number of models and "mechanisms" relating to persuasive communication and provides a vocabulary of concepts that facilitate discussion in the design of effective communications.

Communication is the transfer of message meanings, feelings, and tones from one person or group to another. In their persuasive communications, marketers seek to transfer a set of meanings, feelings, and tones about a product to some target audience so that the audience's perceptions of the product mirror those that they want to convey. Take as an example, the slogan "Reach out and touch someone," which was the basis in the United States of AT&T's advertising campaign to increase its telephone business:

- *Meanings*: The target audience is reminded of how much it can mean to close friends and family to receive a phone call. And all *they* have to do is reach for the phone. The message is not transparent and so invites us to think about it.
- *Feelings*: The slogan stimulates the target audience into visualizing (helped by the rest of the commercial) the effect of phoning a certain someone. Feelings are evoked through its implicit appeal to the values of friendship, family and close human relationships.
- *Tones*: The tone of the message is gentle and warm, like a concerned friend. There is no harshness and no command.

The slogan (and the rest of the commercial) is designed to endear the audience to AT&T as something other than a huge bureaucracy. Persuasive communications act to establish wants (motivations), beliefs, and attitudes among the target audience by helping to formulate a *conception* of the promoted brand as being one which people like themselves would or should prefer.

The tools of persuasive communication are:

- advertising,
- sales promotion,
- publicity and public relations (PR),
- personal selling (to be discussed in Chapter 13), and
- packaging, displays, store ambiance, and so on.

These represent different ways of influencing the target audience and a communications program has to be coordinated to give each its due weight.

Although the old adage "good wine needs no bushel" suggests that word-of-mouth or forms of publicity are all that is needed to attract customers if the product has a competitive edge, this is not generally so. Even where word-of-mouth communication is key, as in many services, persuasive communication can increase the level of business and accelerate the diffusion process. Where a firm neglects persuasive communications, late market entrants are admirably positioned to capture the market with a me-too product backed by persuasive communications. Nonetheless there are situations where few paid-for communications by the seller are necessary. Even where paid-for communications are necessary, there may be little need for persuasion. Buyers may already be actively looking for such a product (e.g. a cure for baldness) or may instantly see the potential of the product on being informed about its existence. Where there is extensive dissatisfaction with current products, or the firm is catering to a function salient to the lives of consumers, little may be needed to get people to try a new market entry. But getting consumers to try a new product is one thing; repeat buying is something else since relative product performance is what secures a customer, not an isolated sale.

While it is common for industrial products to be promoted solely by the firm's sales force, there are also consumer products that have found success without advertising except at the point-of-purchase. This was so when Wilkinson Sword stainless steel razor blades first came out where the company relied on word-of-mouth about the product's advantage. Hershey, the US chocolate firm, did not advertise for years until Cadbury and other European firms entered the market. Although marketers generally view advertising as crucial for the success of brands of fragrances, the Youth Dew fragrance of the Estée Lauder Company was not supported by advertising from 1976 until 1993 and yet was bringing in $25 million a year in sales. Another example is the Scoresby brand of Scotch which became, without advertising, the fifth largest brand of Scotch in the United States, though it now does advertise. Current customers may habitually buy the same brand without advertising support as the habitual buy has a subjective advantage over any rival that is objectively equivalent because the consumer is more confident and comfortable about using it. Typically, the habitual buy, though, does have objective advantages in the eyes of the buyer. Thus, if we take the following national brands in the United States that do not spend on national advertising, Barbasol shaving cream, Lux soap, Bon Ami scouring cleanser, and the many others, each has some advantage (e.g. Barbasol in price) even if it is simply the image of quality and reliability. But how are *new* customers attracted since advertised brands have an advantage in creating awareness, familiarity and image? Even those habitually buying the unadvertised brand need to be reminded of why they initially chose it if they are to continue to buy it. There may be, of course, word-of-mouth and new customers may have been socialized through the family into using the product. But these are seldom sufficient.

It would be very difficult today to introduce new services or consumer packaged goods for national distribution without extensive advertising. Unless the product is being bought by the reseller as private label or the product is to be sold purely on price, resellers want to be assured that the seller will stimulate demand via advertising. Retailers who once allowed sales representatives of well-known manufacturers to restock their shelves with well-established but unadvertised brands, become more reluctant to do so as accurate sales per unit of shelf-space become available. Sellers, though, may have reasons for not advertising. They may be following a "harvesting" strategy (sacrificing market share for immediate earnings) or the market segment may simply be a niche segment that, while generating a loyal following, is too small to justify supportive advertising and relies on word-of-mouth. In general, consumer brands of nationally distributed but unadvertised products are "*dogs*," throwing off just enough cash for the manufacturer to find no urgency about withdrawing them. They are *orphan products* which, through inertia, continue in the firm's product range. Long term, consumer brands that do not advertise tend to sell on price, or cater to some very small niche, or sell as private label.

THE ROLE OF ADVERTISING

There are as many ways to categorize advertising as there are distinct variations in the purpose of advertising. The categories, though, of interest are based first on whether a product category (good or service) is being advertised or the brand. *Primary demand* advertising refers to advertising to promote the whole product category just as some dairy association advertises the benefits of milk. Primary demand advertising is particularly common when high brand consciousness is absent as in the case of food products like milk, fish and meat products. In contrast, *selective demand* advertising focuses on an individual brand. The second categorization of advertising is based on whether the target group are consumers, channel intermediaries, employees, industrial firms, government departments or professional firms. These categories are very relevant to the selection of the advertising message and media.

The role of advertising can be:

- advocacy,
- social diffusion of information, and
- a major or minor factor in the marketing mix.

The advocacy role

The advocacy role is primary, as suggested by the definition of advertising as any paid form of nonpersonal public announcement by an identifiable sponsor whose purpose is to influence behavior. Advertising's short-term advocacy role is to induce a favorable attitude toward the product (good or service), sufficient to arouse interest or persuade the buyer to actually try the product. In the long run, a key role is to retain the customer's loyalty even though advertising alone does not create that loyalty in the first place.

Advocacy in advertising is often viewed as concerned with attitude change on the ground that advertising alone cannot be held accountable for sales since actual sales depend on the whole marketing mix and favorable environmental conditions. Where the focus is on attitudes, goals relate to the beliefs that lie behind attitudes:

- changing beliefs about the brand;
- changing beliefs about the relative importance of attributes;
- changing beliefs about competing brands; and
- adding beliefs

Advertising in this way can activate a latent or passive want or induce the consumer to endorse the belief that the product or brand is the best way to meet the function(s) sought. Another way to describe advertising's advocacy role is in terms of what might be called

a) want-conception,
b) want-development,
c) want-focus, and
d) want-satisfaction.

These goals are shown in Figure 11.1. In Figure 11.2 these goals are related to the competitive objectives of market share protection and market share advancement. Which are adopted depends on the competitive strategy being pursued as shown in Figure 11.2. It will be recalled that competitive strategy is also linked to the firm's investment objectives as market share protection is associated with the investment objective of hold/defend while market share advancement is tied to the investment objective of growth.

If buyers always:

- knew what they wanted,
- were resolute in the product attributes desired,
- knew which brand best met their want, and
- remained satisfied with whatever was bought

then advertising by the seller would be wasteful: it would play no role in increasing

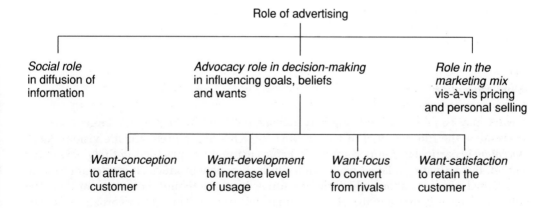

Figure 11.1 The role of advertising

	Want-satisfaction (retain)	Want-focus (convert)	Want-conception (attract)	Want-development (increase)
Market share protection — Mix adjustments	✖			
Imitate	✖			
Compensate	✖			
Market share advancement — Penetration pricing		✖		
Capitalize		✖		
Leapfrog		✖		
New offerings			✖	✖

Competitive strategy

✖ = major relationships

Figure 11.2 Advocacy role

sales. But consumers do not regard themselves as all knowledgeable in buying. In fact, few seek to become product experts but collect just enough information to determine a brand preference. Even when buyers weigh up carefully the pros and cons to reach a decision, that decision is probably the result of many uneasy compromises with the possibility of new information leading to a change of mind. This is because trade-offs can seldom be objectively measured using some common unit of measure. As consumers trade off, say, quality for a lower price, there is typically doubt about the wisdom of doing so since the consumer must usually rely on "gut feel" or intuition. This means that buyers in general can reasonably be assumed to be open to persuasion right to the point of sale.

Want-conception

A want may be latent. Advertising may activate the want by helping the target audience to visualize the full potential of the product for achieving a preferred life vision. *Want-conception* is particularly important in *attracting* customers to products entirely new to the market. But activating a latent want is not confined to new products. It is relevant to well-established products about which the consumer is aware though not aware of their full potential. This is commonly the case with financial services. Thus the advertising of insurance is designed to suggest its centrality in everyone's life by generating a different conception of the role of insurance in our daily lives. Advertising in itself is unlikely to sell the product (sales people do this) but it can develop the right mental set for the purchase of insurance, enough, say, to send for more details, see a salesperson or seek advice.

Want-development

A customer may be using a product but be ignorant of the additional uses for the product (e.g. condensed soups as sauces). Advertising may point to these additional uses. The aim of *want-development* is to *increase* or intensify usage of the product. Often this presents no problems but there is sometimes a danger of weakening the brand's image for its original function. The old adage "jack of all trades master of none" can also be applied by buyers to a product unless versatility is what is sought.

Want-focus

Advertising may demonstrate a more perfect match between the firm's offering and what is being sought than can competition. Alternatively, it may seek to change the buyers' choice criteria or alter the nature of the trade-offs made by the buyer. The aim of *want-focus* is to *convert* from rival brands. There is some evidence, however, that advertising in itself is less effective at stimulating brand switching than reinforcing existing preferences.[1] This is tied to the difficulty of changing habits and a reluctance of consumers to switch permanently to another brand that has no major advantage over the habitual buy. Advertising can only project a promise of performance: it is experience that is meant to confirm it.

Want-satisfaction

Advertising can reassure customers that they have bought the best or are buying the best, as a reminder to repeat buy. The aim of *want-satisfaction* is to *retain* customers by allaying any doubts that undermine satisfaction with the purchase. Retaining customers is a major reason for advertising since brands that do not advertise are likely to lose market share to those that do, since such brands may fail to attract new users and tend to lose their sharp brand image. It is commonly accepted that General Foods' reduced advertising support for Maxwell House coffee led to Nestlé and P&G's Folgers catching up. It is easier to retain customers than to win over the customers of rivals. This is what makes advertising for customer retention so important. Advertising's effectiveness long term may be through reinforcing customer satisfaction so they continue to buy.

Social role

Advertising plays a major social role in the diffusion of information about products even though there is debate over what should constitute "informative advertising." The act

of informing is successful as soon as the audience understands the words while information is something that changes beliefs or the strength of beliefs. What critics mean,
though, is that advertising does not put across objective information that would prevent
the buyer from making an error. Some critics argue that advertisements are becoming
less and less informative.[2] This is understandable in mature, established markets
where brands may only be distinguished in image, but the criticism is not restricted to
advertising in mature markets. Critics argue that advertising should be confined to the
normative role of providing "facts" that prevent consumers from making a mistake. But
advertising restricted to the provision of "neutral" information, unrelated to brand
promotion, would not be advertising as we know it.

Role in the marketing mix

Direct competition among rivals competing in the same market segment is commonly
confined to just a few firms. In such oligopoly situations, many firms prefer to increase
demand through advertising than to reduce prices, since distinctive advertising or advertising that creates a distinct brand image, can be more difficult to match than a price
cut. However, this assumes that a firm can achieve a competitive edge in advertising
and that it does not possess such a large cost advantage over competition as to make
price competition an attractive strategy.

As to the role of advertising vis-à-vis personal selling, advertising generally has an
advantage in cost per person reached over personal selling when the job is to create
brand awareness among mass audiences. Advertising can also have a wider reach and
establish an image for a product that cannot be matched by personal selling, since
personal selling does not have the technology for communicating an aura. On the other
hand, advertising cannot close the sale nor ensure an audience; nor can it distinguish
suspects from prospects, give personal attention to individual buyer problems and
personalities, or act as a liaison between the company and the firm's customers.

THE WAYS IN WHICH ADVERTISING WORKS

Does it work?

If the sole purpose of advertising were to create awareness of a brand, no one doubts
that mass advertising (television, newspapers, magazines, radio, and cinema) could
achieve that purpose. But in asking whether advertising works we are usually asking a
different question, namely, whether advertising is a major factor in moving a target
audience into buying action. We know that advertising is neither a necessary nor a
sufficient factor in producing sales but would like to know how major it is in the
marketing mix. The short answer is that sometimes it is a major factor and sometimes
it is not.

Some writers credit advertising with the ability to manipulate the consumer at
will, providing huge enough funds are available. Marketers respond that advertising,

unsupported by product performance, may gain an initial trial but, when in conflict with the realities of experience, it leads to the bad-mouthing of the product and non-repeat sales. That advertising must be supported by brand performance is *almost* always true since there can be exceptions as occurs when experience with the product is ambiguous about the brand's performance. Also, consumers do not always buy primarily for high performance in the product's use function since consumers may buy the fantasy or image created by advertising. However, if we are not to go beyond the evidence, we would merely say that some advertising, directed at certain kinds of audiences, under certain conditions, has led some people to buy the advertised brand in preference to another. Advertising, whether primary for the product class or selective for the brand has, in general, a positive effect on sales, but particularly in the case of primary advertising, any sales increases directly attributable to advertising cannot be guaranteed.[3]

Nobody knows how advertising works?

It is frequently asserted that nobody knows how advertising works. In support, examples are quoted showing that advertising works on one occasion and fails to work on another and that what works for one product does not work for another. What is meant here is that there is no theory for the design of advertisements that can be guaranteed to justify their cost. But such a guarantee is an impossible goal in a dynamic world where neither the buyers themselves nor competitors can be guaranteed to be fixed in their ways.

We can understand the problem better by way of an analogy. Suppose we randomly scatter plant seed around the world. Some seed would not grow because of the infertile soil or unsuitable climatic conditions. Advertising, too, must fall on ground that is fertile, that is, reach minds that are predisposed to favorably interpret the message. *Every advertisement invites a certain interpretation but it is an invitation that can always be refused.* Each member of the target audience interprets the advertisement against his or her own individual background of experiences and knowledge. Advertising assumes that the backgrounds of those in the audience for any specific ad will have high commonalities: there is a need to check that the relevant commonalities are there so that the intended meaning will be the one conveyed. Also just as the climatic conditions must be suitable for a seed to act, so the rest of the marketing mix must be suitable for advertising to work. In any case, advertising, as we have seen, is not always necessary for producing sales, just as seed is not always necessary for producing plants.

What we would like to be able to make are statements such as the following: "Given a certain type of distribution, pricing, competition, etc., then an advertising campaign in the form ABC in this market structure will attract (convert, etc.) so many customers whose combined sales would amount to $X per annum." We have no theory that allows us to make such predictions. When such forecasting occurs it is apt to rest purely on statistical correlations that have held up reasonably in the past. Even assuming we do have some highly validated theories about the ways in which advertising works, we would still have problems:

- we cannot always control factors like competition that may frustrate our plans; and
- we may not be able to develop advertising to fit the theory.

But no theoretical framework is ever likely to be detailed enough. Advertising, like interpersonal influence in selling, depends not just on the validity of some grand theory but on attention to detailed tactics, each having its own theoretical support. Still more complicating is the fact that interpretations of any particular ad will vary with differences in social experience. "Aberrant decoding" of ads is common and predicting how an ad will generally be interpreted is rendered still more difficult by having to take some account of the media used; the pictures, music and the paralanguage accompanying the ad plus other situational factors.[4] Nonetheless, we must seek theoretical underpinnings to effective advertising since the more we understand, the better position we are in to devise better advertising.

Each of the various systems of psychology makes a contribution to understanding the ways advertising works to change behavior. These are:

- Associationism, Conditioning/Reinforcement;
- Cognitive approaches: Hierarchy of Effects models; the Elaboration Likelihood Model; Communication Approaches;
- Consistency theories: Balance Model; Congruity Model; Cognitive Dissonance/ Attribution Model;
- The psychoanalytic approach; and
- The emotional approach.

Associationism, conditioning/reinforcement, repeated exposure

Association, the basis of conditioning, is still a major thrust in all types of advertising. The association of the advertised product with pleasant places, people and situations is something we expect to find in advertising. Less obvious is the association of the advertised brand with a way of life.

Associationist psychology preceded the concept of conditioning. Hartley in the early part of the eighteenth century developed associationist psychology focusing on the contiguity of events; contiguity being one of the trio mentioned by Aristotle who proposed three relations between elements that lead to establishing an association, namely, contiguity, similarity, and contrast. But the principles of association can suggest links anywhere. The problem lies in identifying those likely to be compelling. What complicates the problem is that associations can be very contextual so that a particular association is not evoked for every context, just as a particular piece of music does not always evoke the same memories on every occasion a person hears it played. Pavlov's studies on conditioned reflexes were believed at the time to have suggested an answer by seemingly having provided the mechanism of the reflex to explain the power of association. In the early days of behaviorism, most theories of learning were expressed in terms of associations between stimuli (S) and responses (R) or $S \Rightarrow R$ connections. While no school of psychology in modern times has called itself associationist psychology, the concept of association has been one of the most enduring mechanisms in discussions on learning.

Behaviorists advocating operant conditioning see advertising as concerned with retaining customers (the want-satisfaction discussed earlier). What advertising does is remind customers of the benefits of the brand that have acted as reinforcers in the past, that is, it is advertising's job to remind the audience of the association of brand to benefits.[5] For behaviorists, converting from rivals or attracting new users is less meaningful, given that prospects have no experience with the brand. Similarly, increasing the level of usage (for the same function) does not require advertising since this occurs naturally if the brand offers sufficient reinforcement. All this is very much a minority view among marketing academics while it would be difficult to find support among marketing managers for such a restricted view of advertising's function. But conditioning is not the only way that people learn since people can observe what happens to others, learn through other forms of direct observation and experience, or can learn through imagining or just being told to do something.

It is not just behaviorists who can be linked to the power of association. The various projective techniques seek associations as when consumers are asked to complete a sentence ("Coca-Cola went to a party last week and . . .") or asked to match companies or brands with various animals, colors, places, or types of music and so on. Consumers become comfortable with names and trademarks, and advertisers accelerate the process by associating the brand with attractive logos and pleasing ads.

Leymore accepts that people throughout the world are sensitive to the contrasts in the human conditions ("the eternal polarities of the human condition") such as being beautiful versus being ugly, being rich versus being poor and that people seek the more pleasant polar extreme.[6] Leymore argues that the relative effectiveness of advertisements depends on the extent to which the advertisement establishes an association between the product being advertised and the highest level of values in the society. She claims that advertising functions in the same way as myths function in society, namely, to reinforce cultural norms, values, and beliefs, to reduce anxieties by promising solutions to the eternal polarities of the human condition. This means that advertising must be sensitive to the changing values of society.

The traditional values in western societies relate to the home, family, children, fairness, respectability, social status, and ideals such as masculinity and femininity. These still count, though more weight is being given to self-fulfillment, autonomy, or more control over one's life which all tend to be a move toward individualism. But is Leymore right in focusing exclusively on values at the highest level? It could be argued that the values to which advertising should appeal should incorporate the specific values of the target group's subculture. As one writer on culture points out, Western cultures are rife with subcultures resulting in plurality of belief and behavior systems with each subculture seeking "self-legitimation" of their lifestyle and members of the subculture being indoctrinated to believe that their subculture alone speaks the language of truth about life and how it should be lived.[7]

If we look at hedonistic values, *reversal theory* argues that people seek to be excited rather than bored, and relaxed rather than anxious so that effective advertising either *associates* excitement with the brand or the removal of some anxiety.[8] This distinction is in line with those in marketing who view buying motives as either being negative (aversive origin like getting rid of a headache) or positive (appetitive origin like going to Disneyland). The most recent stress on association is found in *transformational advertising* which aims at associating the buying, possessing, using or consuming the brand with values and experiences that are highly desirable. The problem, as always, is to make the association compelling since not all juxtapositions of images in an advertisement come to be associated in the buyer's mind. One example of transformational advertising which shocks many people is Calvin Klein's advertisements for Calvin Klein jeans. One advertisement was a *book* insert in Vanity Fair magazine that chronicled a slice of the life of a pop group. How was this to be interpreted? The first problem is that the pages have multiple referents. But we will suppose readers see it refers to the lifestyle of some pop group. Given that lifestyle connotes or exemplifies some set of values, the second problem lies in interpreting what these values are. Strange as it may seem, some ambiguity may be desirable as it can contribute to the richness and power of an ad, with people being able, within the recognizable limits set by the text, to read what they want into it.

If the advertisement exemplifies the sensual, nonconformity lifestyle, how does this relate to the product? There are the following links:

- Ad for Calvin Klein jeans ⇒ Pop group
- Pop group ⇔ sensual, nonconforming lifestyle.

Therefore:

- Sensual, nonconforming lifestyle ⇒ Calvin Klein jeans.

The arrows point to the associations. Lines with single arrows indicate what is denoted; those with double arrows indicate what is meant to be exemplified. Whenever "A" refers to "B", it denotes "B" but "A" exemplifies "B" when "A" both refers to "B" and is an instance of "B." The advertiser would like the prospective buyer to view Calvin Klein jeans as not only denoting but also exemplifying the sensual, nonconforming lifestyle. In other words to make the last line read:

- Sensual, nonconforming lifestyle ⇔ Calvin Klein jeans.

The Calvin Klein advertisement communicates its message nonverbally and in a way that would be outrageously vulgar if expressed in words while no words could capture all the nuances of the advertisement.

The "soft sell approach" and associationism go together. The aim is to fuse the associations and the brand so that the brand is viewed as possessing the associations. The brand is no longer just the original product but comes to incorporate whatever associations can be attached to the brand. Ads that merely entertain with fantasy situations can often be puzzling to the logical mind but the aim is to share the fantasy with the audience as there is a human need for fantasy-satisfaction. Such entertainment can grab an audience's attention and put people at their ease, making them more receptive to the message as well as associating the brand with pleasurable experiences.

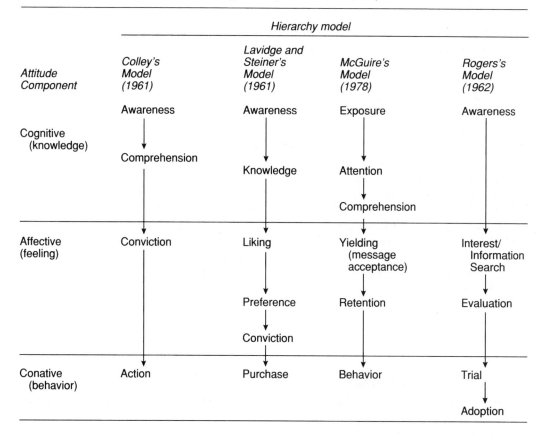

Figure 11.3 Hierarchy models showing mediating processes leading to action and their link with the alleged components of attitude

Cognitive psychology approaches

Hierarchy of effects models

Cognitive psychology focuses on internal, mental processing with the consumer being viewed as an information processor. In explaining how advertising works, the aim is to identify the mediating mental processes between exposure to the advertisement and buying. One such explanation is the *hierarchy of effects* model, which claims to depict the mental stages through which the buyer can be guided in creating a favorable attitude toward the product. We have already mentioned one hierarchy of effects model, namely, the adoption process discussed in Chapter 9 and shown again in Figure 11.3, under Rogers's name.

Any hierarchy of effects model can be regarded as a learning model. The idea of some hierarchy of mental stages is captured by the *AIDA* (*a*ttention, *i*nterest, *d*esire, and *a*ction) model found in courses in salesmanship, developed before and independently of cognitive psychology. The salesperson is seen as moving the buyer along this sequence by rewarding the prospect at each stage, for example, getting beyond attracting attention to generating interest by focusing on what the product can do for the prospective buyer. But it was Carl Hovland and his colleagues at Yale in the late 1940s and 1950s who divided the learning process into four stages:[9]

1 The message must first attract the audience's attention.
2 The arguments in the message must then be comprehended.
3 The recipient of the message must learn the arguments contained in the message and come to accept them as true.
4 The audience will act on this learned knowledge if there is an incentive to do so.

In advertising, the first hierarchy of effects model was Colley's, which views the target audience as being moved along the following sequence of stages:[10]

1 *awareness*: developing consumer awareness of the brand;
2 *comprehension*: consumer understanding of a product's benefits, etc.;
3 *conviction*: getting members of the target audience convinced enough to want to buy the product; and
4 *action*: getting the target audience to take some form of buying action.

Hierarchy of effects models view advertising as having its impact on sales through consumer attitudes, establishing attitudes where none existed or reinforcing attitudes or pushing them in a direction they are already moving. Attitude is conceptualized as having three components:

- a cognitive (knowledge) component;
- an affective (feeling, liking/disliking) component; and
- a conative (behavior) component

The hierarchy of effects through which the consumer is said to pass is related to the components of attitude as each stage falls into one of the three components. This is shown in Figure 11.3, where Colley's model and the other advertising hierarchy models are shown in relation to the components of attitude when conceived in this tripartite way. In general, hierarchy models assume the consumer first learns something about the product, then develops feelings toward it, and then behaves consistently in the light of such knowledge and feelings. The formation of attitudes is thus considered key to understanding the persuasive process, with the various hierarchy of effects models being views about the mental processing steps that comprise attitude development: the mental processing steps comprising the cognitive and affective dimensions of attitude with the conative being identified with some behavioral outcome. Although the hierarchies differ, each of those shown in Figure 11.3 represents a defensible, plausible mental process. Probably McGuire's information-processing model is the one most grounded in cognitive psychology. Thus, unlike the others, he includes a *retention* stage, which is important since advertising is more directed at future action than action at the time of seeing the advertisement.

Even if all the various hierarchy models could be reconciled and shown to be descriptively correct, they would simply show the hurdles to be overcome by advertising but not *how* to overcome the hurdles. Even if advertisers believe that creating awareness and comprehension is technically solvable, they would still be faced with the problem of how to get conviction and action. Hierarchy models do not tell them, beyond recognizing the need for some rewarding mechanism to be at work at each stage. But advertisers need to know about such mechanisms or the appropriate appeals that move the consumer from one stage to the next. Hierarchy models tell us where we are and where we have to go but not how to get there.

Further criticism of hierarchy models stems from an implicit recognition of the arbitrariness of the various stages described and the assumed uniformity of the choice process. On the surface, Colley's mental sequence of

Awareness $\Rightarrow$ Comprehension $\Rightarrow$ Conviction $\Rightarrow$ Action

would appear appropriate for activating a latent want. But creating awareness means nothing unless the product is shown to be relevant to meeting the consumer's goals. If the want is passive, awareness and comprehension have already occurred and the need is to change that part of the offering that is holding back buying or depreciating the factors inhibiting purchase.

Hierarchy models seem to have little relevance to maintaining buying habits or altering a picking situation so that the firm's brand is picked more frequently or bought exclusively. Similarly, if intrinsic liking alone determines choice, the model misrepresents the choice process. There is no meaningful evaluation here or deep deliberation (as implied by terms like "comprehension") since intrinsic choice may consist simply of:

I see $\Rightarrow$ I like $\Rightarrow$ I buy.

A communication (e.g. from one's physician) *can* be persuasive even if arguments are not learned, remembered, and fully understood: impression and faith (unshakable belief) often substitute.

For extrinsic preference, the model also shows weaknesses. Comprehension is interpreted to mean absorbing facts about the product or brand. But if integrative criteria (for example, the desire for group acceptance) dominate choice, is "getting comprehension" a meaningful description of the job to be done? If adaptive criteria (for example, worry over making a mistake) dominate, is "getting conviction" particularly relevant? The term "conviction" suggests being rationally convinced. If so, this ignores the fact that many products are bought on the basis of advice or the brand's reputation/image, or through following the lead of others in the hope (but without conviction) that we have chosen wisely.

Each of the hierarchy models presupposes that consumers first learn something about a product or brand before liking or disliking it, which, in turn, assumes that finding out about a product and finding out whether one likes the product are two distinct mental events. This is doubtful since all conscious awareness involves a form of acceptance or rejection. Finding the facts is not a process separate from or prior to the evaluation of the product: there is a perceptual and procedural interdependence between the two. Just because we can separate the cognitive and the affective at the conceptual level does not mean that they reflect separate mental steps. The various hierarchies simply represent different logical refinements of the process or simply different interpretations of processing stages using the computer as an analogy.

The hierarchies of effects models mislead if treated as universally valid. If a particular stage is not a necessary step for the target audience to go through, resources could be wasted in focusing on it. For example, an advertising campaign launched to generate comprehension errs if buying action can be prompted by some personality recommending the product. Also, an emphasis on creating awareness and comprehension can misdirect if it tempts advertisers into always putting across more and more product information. Buyers are not just persuaded by technical and economic facts and neither are such facts always primary for the buyer.

An answer to some of this criticism is to accept that the standard learning hierarchies illustrated in Figure 11.3, taking the form of learn $\Rightarrow$ feel $\Rightarrow$ do, are more applicable to situations where the buyer has high involvement with the purchase and consequent involvement with the advertisement for the product. Krugman in the 1960s argued that, in respect to TV advertising, there was learning without involvement.[11] As a consequence defenses were down when receiving the message. Krugman defined involvement as the "number of conscious bridging experiences, connections or personal references per minute that the viewer makes between his own life and the stimulus." Although Krugman's article was not a piece of research but more an observation or hypothesis, it had such intuitive appeal (coinciding as it does with the idea of the viewer being just a "couch potato"), that many marketers have come to accept the idea of the passive viewer. But more recently, research has supported the idea of an active rather than passive viewer. But how can something like this be demonstrated either way? Psychological theory is neutral and statistical generalizations are not likely to cover a random, unbiased sample. All we can say is that some viewers may be passive and some will be active.

Krugman's seemingly straightforward definition of involvement has given rise to many different operational definitions as researchers have attempted to measure it. Yet the term "involvement" as defined by Krugman is the same as the term "symbolic meaning" as used in some branches of sociology. When such sociologists say that "meaning" directs behavior, they are saying in effect that it is beliefs about what something signifies for a person's wants that determine his or her actions. If buyers are highly involved with an advertisement for a product, it is the same as saying they believe the advertisement has significance for their wants. The concept of meaning in the sense described has the advantage of combining both wants and beliefs, that is, reasons for action or nonaction, in the one word.

The acceptance of Krugman's concept of involvement, when linked to the recognition that consumers do not all follow the same sequence of stages in attitude formation, has led to the development of additional hierarchies to replace the single process view. Thus Ray posits three distinct hierarchies.[12] These are shown in Figure 11.4:

a) the *standard learning hierarchy* of learn $\Rightarrow$ feel $\Rightarrow$ do;

Decision process hierachies

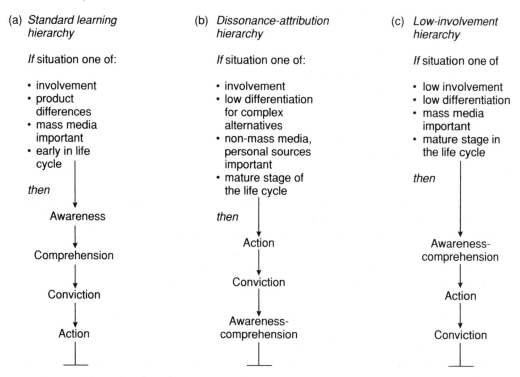

Figure 11.4 Decision process hierarchies
Source: After Ray, 1982.

b) the *dissonance-attribution hierarchy* of do ⇒ feel ⇒ learn, where the action comes first followed by the affective (evaluative) and then by the cognitive; and
c) the *low-involvement hierarchy* of learn ⇒ do ⇒ feel where some learning occurs first then the conative and then the affective. This model reflects Krugman's view and has received some support in the literature but also some skepticism. This is not surprising since it is difficult to visualize learning enough about a product to actually buy it without having feelings toward it.

The conditions listed by Ray under which each of the processes is said to arise are also given in Figure 11.4. Ray does not claim that these conditions are either necessary or sufficient for each stage in the process to be carried along. Figure 11.4 simply shows the *logical* link between situations and processes though it is the *empirical* link that needs to be firmly established. As with the standard hierarchy, it is not clear how the target audience moves from one stage to the next. There is the assumption that marketers know the full potential of each of their promotional tools and so can devise appropriate strategies for moving the target audience through any hierarchy adopted.

Many of the same criticisms made of the standard learning hierarchy also apply to all hierarchies made of constructs similar to those of awareness, comprehension and conviction. We must ask whether these constructs are sufficiently operational and comprehensive enough for depicting the relevant process of attitude formation and coming to buying action. Even if we accept that awareness/comprehension ("learning"), conviction ("feel"), and action ("do") are distinct mental processes, there are additional possible hierarchies:

Ray's hierarchies
a) Learn ⇒ feel ⇒ do
b) Do ⇒ feel ⇒ learn
c) Learn ⇒ do ⇒ feel

Additional hierarchies
d) Feel ⇒ learn ⇒ do
e) Feel ⇒ do ⇒ learn
f) Do ⇒ learn ⇒ feel

Ray would probably argue that his three hierarchies have some theoretical backing but since the other possible hierarchies are easy to visualize as occurring in our mental processing, they should not be ignored as too remote to consider.

One advertising agency that uses the hierarchies classifies the learn ⇒ feel ⇒ do and the feel ⇒ learn ⇒ do as operating in conditions of high involvement, with the first sequence being attributed to the consumer as "thinker" and the second to the consumer as "feeler." The do ⇒ learn ⇒ feel and the do ⇒ feel ⇒ learn are seen as operating in conditions of low involvement with the first sequence being attributed to the consumer as "doer" and the second to the consumer as "reactor."

For Ray the hierarchies are very much tied to promotional strategies and budgeting in that each hierarchy stage is tied to some component or components of the communications mix. Ray argues for what he calls a "balanced, multi-communications-tool approach," choosing whatever tool will do the job most effectively, within some budget constraint, while at the same time recognizing a *compensation principle* to be at work in that setting extreme targets (for example, stressing as the advertising theme, *zero* cigarette tar) tends to have corresponding mental reactions (for example, less credibility about the cigarette's taste). Of course, not all advertising is concerned with moving along some hierarchy, for the focus might be simply on retaining current customers. Also there is the problem that arises when different members of the target segment are at different stages of the same hierarchy or at different stages of different hierarchies which may necessitate different campaigns.

Elaboration likelihood model

Petty and Cacioppo's elaboration likelihood model has aroused considerable interest because it is concerned not just with the development of an attitude where none exists but with changing existing attitudes.[13,14] Petty and Cacioppo posit two routes to persuasion: a *peripheral route* and a *central route*. In the peripheral route, persuasion comes about through simple cues about

• what is socially acceptable;

- the attractiveness of the communicator; and
- the pain/pleasure attached to agreeing with the position advocated.

The peripheral route leads to *short-term acceptance* of the message. Unlike the peripheral route where persuasion is tied to various *affective* cues, the central route involves the receiver of the message in thoughtful reflection on the true merits of the information presented. The central route to attitude change results in *long* lasting, true *rational attitude change* that arises from processing cognitively the information contained in strong (valid) messages. What particular route is adopted depends on the receiver's *motivation* and *ability* to elaborate cognitively the information presented. What determines motivation to think about the informational content is the personal relevance of the issue. We return here to the importance of the level of involvement or meaning of the issue for the recipient of information.

In the elaboration likelihood model, there is the suggestion of central route persuasion arising as an objective property of the arguments used, just a matter of processing "good" information, since Petty and Cacioppo argue that only the cognitive processing of strong arguments persuades in a fundamental way. Their model suggests that social comparison with reference group norms does not influence the perceived validity of the messages being processed via the central route, that is, peripheral factors do not affect the perceived validity of the information being processed. However, the authors acknowledge they do not know what makes an argument persuasive but define an argument as strong simply on the basis of its subjective effects, namely, its rated persuasiveness together with its capacity to stimulate favorable thought in the recipient of the message. Thus real persuasion is identified with information processing: information processing of "good," "valid" and "sound" information with good, valid and sound information being defined as that which persuades!

In seemingly denying the fact that what is considered good, valid and sound is tied somewhat to social norms and conventions, the authors are regarding validity as in some sense an inherent, objective property of the information processed. But is validity a property of the information per se or a function of the perceptions of the recipient doing the information processing? If so, such perceptions are not independent of social norms and conventions. Further there is the question of whether the bulk of consumers have the motivation and ability to process information via the central route. One piece of research relevant to this question found the following:[15]

- the subjects in the study (a wide cross-section of people in the United States), commonly viewed pseudo-evidence (just the plausibility of the argument) as powerful in persuading them as genuine evidence when it came to establishing the correctness of ideas or hypotheses;
- subjects commonly were unable to envision alternatives or counter arguments to their own "theory," just continuing to stick to positions they thought others would endorse;
- even when subjects did entertain alternative explanations, they sought more to rebut them than to seriously consider them as rival explanations. Predisposition to certain beliefs make it difficult to entertain other explanations;
- subjects whose disposition was to see positions as either right or wrong or to see all

alternative explanations as equally defensible, saw little value in even engaging in argument;

- the study found that only 9–20 percent of subjects had the necessary understanding needed to generate and evaluate alternatives to reach a reasoned judgment, with the author of the study arguing that without such understanding "people have little incentive or disposition to develop argumentative skills."

Psychologists interested in reasoning skills claim that people do not normally use logic to solve problems.[16] Of course, we must use some logic to cope with life but we seem to use it sparingly.

It is difficult to believe that there are no communications that are deeply persuasive based on the peripheral route. Thus in accepting the elaboration likelihood model, we are, for example, either assuming that religious conversions are just short-term conversions or that long-term religious conversions, based on strong convictions, cannot arise from or be primarily influenced by

- that attractiveness of the communication source;
- what is socially endorsed; and
- the pain/pleasure attached to agreeing with the position advocated.

We will later argue that complete changes of perspective come about by indirect means of persuasion and it is doubtful if such persuasion can be reconciled with this model.

One reason for the support of the elaboration likelihood model is its seeming support for the distinction between "normative conformity" and "informational conformity"; a distinction used in Chapter 5. But adhering to what is socially appropriate or dictated does not necessarily mean some peripheral route to persuasion but can arise from a good deal of hard thinking as to what would be the prudent thing to do. On the other hand, informational conformity may simply mean following the actions of those considered to have the best information (e.g. as occurs in buying shares) without doing any deep reflection on relevant information which may be beyond the lay person's comprehension. Also in the message-dense advertising environment, who has the time to think deeply about some issue? There is time pressure, information overload, and general lack of expertise in assessing the validity of information which leads to the use of heuristic (rules of thumb) in decision-making.

Most academics would very much like to think there is such a thing as an Olympian examination of information leading to real persuasion (rationally convincing) when consumers are highly involved. But perhaps Cohen and Nagel are right when they say in their classic 1934 textbook on logic and scientific method: "The factual persuasiveness of arguments is more often brought about by properly chosen words, which through association, have powerful emotional influences, than through logically unassailable arguments." It is not often easy to do *physical reality testing* in considering the validity of information but, at least, consumers feel they can do *social reality testing* to gauge the product's social acceptability. It is doubtful that messages that go against the social norms of a group will be acceptable. Some psychologists argue that all arguments, if they are to be effective, should be pro-normative.

The persuasive communication approach

We discuss here persuasive communication whose pioneer was Carl Hovland (1912–1961) who viewed the effectiveness of persuasion as dependent on

1   the individual recipient's mental set and other characteristics;
2   the communicator/information source; and
3   the content and presentation of the message.

The approach does not accept that those being influenced are passive receptors of that influence but, on the contrary, are active participants in the process. We will discuss each in turn.

The individual recipient's mental set and other characteristics.   Traditionally the factors considered here are

a)   audience attention to the message,
b)   message repetition and distraction, and
c)   personal characteristics of the target audience like wants/needs, mood and existing perspectives on the issue.

A necessary condition for being influenced by a message is that the audience should first pay *attention*. This can be a problem since there is "selective exposure" by any target audience as people are disposed to information that is congenial and avoid exposure to information that does not fit existing attitudes. The more ego-involved the audience is with their preexisting attitude and the more emotionally committed to a contrary position, the more exposure to information will tend to be selective.

Constant *repetition* of a message can help on occasions to get acceptance. Repeated exposure to an object (e.g. an ad) generally leads to positive feelings so that the repetition of an ad many times can result in generating a liking for the product advertised because it has become familiar. Although most consumers express annoyance at the constant repetition of an advertisement, the familiar ad can offer the comfort of things being still the same and so found attractive—though the same old corny joke in an advertisement can lead to irritation instead. The repetition of the same slogan suggests truth and a consistency of image. *If*, however, the stimulus (e.g. the ad) is initially evaluated negatively, the more the repetition, the more the stimulus is likely to be disliked. But advertisers worry about *wearout*, that is, of an advertisement ceasing to be effective, becoming like the buildings around, just part of the unnoticed scenery. This is why advertisers often keep the same basic message but add some variety or variation on the theme or more recently the TV advertisement that is a soap opera!

Distraction can interfere with the development of counter-arguments against a position being taken just as loud background noise can make it difficult to reflect and develop counter-arguments to some TV claim. People vary with the ease with which they can be persuaded depending on their interests, beliefs, self-esteem (the lower the self-esteem, the more likely to be persuaded), the stability of current attitudes (children and young adults tend to have less stable attitudes than older people) while people in a good mood are less inclined to process the message but more disposed to simply accept it. However, from the point of view of persuasion, the most difficult situation arises when the target audience's perspective on an issue differs radically from that being proposed.

Persuasion comes into its own when there are doubts and uncertainties about courses of action. Thus we do not talk about persuading people to accept the validity of arithmetic or some theorem in Euclidean geometry where deductive arguments are logically compelling. But perhaps all other arguments will only have validity to an audience that already has the "right" perspective. Communicating with a group that does not share the communicator's basic perspective can be frustrating since the claims and arguments of one can seem perverse and even nonrational to the other. Good arguments are only good from a certain point of view which means that the target audience must be on the "right wave length" or in the right frame of mind to consider the argument. People make their choices within some perspective or perception of the situation. Thus it was difficult for Tip O'Neill, when speaker of the House of Representatives to go along with President Reagan's arguments, with O'Neill regarding government as an agent of change and the solution to many social problems and Reagan regarding government as a problem in itself with its interference in the lives of Americans while at the same time impeding economic progress. What is persuasive to one audience may fail with another whose different perspective makes the argument lack credibility. This is one of the problems in lecturing to various audiences; to adjust the talk to their presuppositions. It is also a problem in selling proposals to management or in making any communication persuasive. Many supporters of moral causes (e.g. animal rights) resort to violence because they do not know how to get agreement except by coercion and do not know how to even think about changing perspectives.

To argue within the *accepted perspective* of the buyer is to try to induce a judgment that is claimed to most cohere with that perspective. But to induce the right perspective in the first place, *indirect* means of persuasion are required. This is because a direct approach typically meets with resistance and counter-arguments. Indirect means of persuasion involve vivid imagery, metaphor, or a slogan that sticks in the mind to challenge the current perspective. But, while individual beliefs, particularly factual beliefs, may be easy to change, the changing of *systems of beliefs* are apt to challenge a way of life, with a corresponding change needed in one of the *conceptual* lenses through which the world is viewed. Concepts mediate between the mind and the world: they are tied to the world by representing it and are linked to the mind by being constituents of it. Even small changes in moral judgments are not easy to make because the moral is interwoven into social life so moral beliefs are supported by a whole system of social beliefs.

One vivid approach to changing a perspective is the use of a metaphor such as "the mind is a computer." A single well-chosen metaphor can sometimes create an inspired image that can transform our perspective by getting us locked into an idea. Thus consider the metaphor in the statement: "He wants to turn the clock back." Although it is now a little tired, the metaphor suggests that time itself will bring about human progress and that it is a delusion to think time can be rolled back. The metaphor resists its metaphorical extension, as the objects to which it applies do not typically belong to its literal extension. But the application also attracts for it arouses curiosity, likening the metaphorical extension to the literal extension. The similarities can be a never ending source for reflection. But once a metaphor gets completely accepted, it dies as it no longer invites comparison. Yet metaphors invite certain comparisons but not others. Thus in talking of the mind as a computer, comparisons are not made with the material of which computers are made or that they feed off electricity. A metaphor is *closed* when comparisons are strictly limited, as saying "men are all pigs." An *open* metaphor is the most effective ("You are my sunshine") as there are no semantic rules that rigidly specify what characteristics are to be imputed to the object.

A metaphor defamiliarizes the familiar so it is seen in a different way. However, a metaphor need not be verbal. Indeed advertising commonly uses nonverbal metaphors like the Marlboro cigarette ad or words plus some nonverbal metaphor like showing the puppy dog next to the brand of toilet paper with the words "irresistibly sequeezable." There are many ads that try to persuade without using language but depend on a metaphor like the gasoline ad focusing on a moving tiger. Names of brands can also be metaphors like the Jaguar car or the name *Poison* for a perfume to conjure up the femme fatale.

What advertising tries to do is to court a viewpoint and a standard of truth by which the advertisement's own message follows in a manner acceptable to the target audience. But advertising also tries on occasions to induce major changes in perspectives. Thus advertising can be undertaken to change a deeply ingrained outlook such as racial and religious prejudice, cigarette smoking, and so on. Those embarking on such advertising recognize it has only long-term effects.

A common way of inducing *a minor* shift in perspective is through the *definition of words or a situation*. Thus one prominent business man, challenged about his bribing government officials in Africa, claimed, "I never bribe. I simply invest in people." Political campaigns are full of definitions of a situation construed to induce a change in perspective (e.g. "Tax and spend democrats"). The definition of the situation that irritates many in the United States is the slogan "Guns don't kill, people do." If this perspective were accepted, it would be very difficult to argue against the proliferation of the nuclear bomb among nations! In marketing, the examples are more mundane. Thus if I can get my audience to accept the "price" as an investment rather than a mere payment, it will facilitate the sale. Similarly, the marketer might speak of a product being inexpensive rather than cheap, while the two sides of the abortion issue are both intent on getting their own particular perspective adopted by defining the situation in the one case as murder and in the other as pro-choice and individual freedom. It does make a difference whether the retailer says she is giving a 5 percent discount for cash as opposed to saying there is a 5 percent charge on credit cards. The labels used to describe a product or name a brand are important as they channel the individual's thoughts into making the association or assuming there is one. This is one of the reasons given for the selecting of a brand-name that declares the brand's advantage. If that advantage over time is no longer valid, it is hoped by then that the name can stand on its own. The Diehard battery and Ultra Brite toothpaste mentioned earlier are examples. Language used within an organization can also mold thinking and one wonders about the cynicism of ad people who refer to the ad copy writer as "liar for hire", the head of public relations as "Goebbels", a focus group as "lab rats" and a new product as "the cancer cure."

Asking questions is another way of directing thoughts toward favoring the brand, particularly if the question itself has ambiguous overtones like the famous advertisement for hair coloring with the question: "Does she or doesn't she?" From what has been said in the chapter on marketing research, the wording of a question can help define the situation for the respondent and subtly suggest the "logical" reply, for example, "Do you favor more government interference?"

Words, images, metaphors, slogans, and questions can all be recruited to structure the thinking of the target audience. Words commonly used in advertising such as "fresh", "new", "discover", "light" evoke promise and potential opportunity while words such as "save" and "extra" point to what might arise from taking immediate action. There can also be the *manipulation of expectations through comparisons*. Since all expectations are relative to some standard, the aim is to change the standard. An advertisement may deliberately depreciate the target audience's expectations by saying that acceptance of such low standards is no longer necessary. In selling there is the tactic beloved of those selling real estate to show some outrageously priced house first or (if selling an estate of houses) to suggest most have been sold (particularly the best, since it is felt these can always be sold when the others have gone). We need not comment on some of the ethics of this except to say that there is more awareness of sharp practice than sellers seem to assume.

The communication source.   The communicator's personal sources of influence in changing behavior reside in the communicator's perceived credibility and attractiveness. Credibility consists of both perceived trustworthiness and technical expertise relevantly applied. Attractiveness relates to the communicator's similarity in background values, openness as if revealing all, physical appeal, as well as the likeability that comes from supportive interaction through time. A credible source means being able to field questions with answers that reveal expertise, sincerity and honest intentions. The company itself seeks to be perceived as a credible and attractive organization as this helps win support from all its constituent stakeholders. A persuasive message founded on facts tends to be more persuasive than an attractive one. However, when the message is about matters of opinion, the attractive communicator will be more persuasive than the one who talks like an expert.

The question of credibility and attractiveness comes up particularly in the service industries, in selling and in the selection of a spokesperson in advertising. The target audience identifies and wants to go along with an attractive personality while a credible one by definition inspires trust. Thus one commercial, depicting an engaging three year old eating a highly nutritious cereal, stimulated sales since there was resistance before to thinking anything nutritious could be tasty (Ray's compensating principle again).

In going along with the choices of an admired actor, athlete or whatever, consumers can enhance their self-image and so their self-esteem by feeling part of the group that embraces such celebrities. In any case, every association of celebrities with the brand gives the brand something of the persona (the public face) of the celebrity. Wishful thinking and fantasy suggest that all the consumer needs do to possess the persona is to use the same products. This is something of an exaggeration of what occurs but it is in the right direction. In advertising on TV, it is common to use models of similar background to the target audience. This has the advantage of the audience finding it easier to relate to the model and hence to view the rewards coming to the model as possible also for them. This all assumes that members of the target audience will self-categorize with the group to which the model belongs. While I may acknowledge I belong to that group (heavy-user, large family housewife) I may not want to be categorized as one of them! It might be noted that the elaboration likelihood model claims that mere attractiveness counts little when people are processing information along the central route!

A source of high credibility is needed, the more the gap between the communicator's message and the perspective of the audience. For credibility, a salesperson or spokes-person should not appear to be trying too hard or should point to things, like the competitor's product, in a way that does not appear to be promoting pure self-interest. This is because any audience being "sold" expects a hard sell and the promotion of pure self-interests: not living up to these expectations reduces the defenses of the audience and facilitates the view of the communicator as sincere, trustworthy, dependable, and knowledgeable. We see attempts to increase credibility in advertising by the adoption of a professional manner in an advertisement for analgesics or the authoritative tone in the advertisement for an antiperspirant that uses the words: "for the first treatment, use on four consecutive nights." The important thing for a communicator is to present a coherent and consistent persona or image otherwise there is only confusion and with confusion come the doubts about attractiveness and credibility.

The message itself.   There has been a lot of research on the message itself:

- position advocated by the message,
- presentation,
- the medium used to put across the message, and
- message content.

This is difficult research to generalize about (particularly to other cultures) since context is so important.

An audience will have only a certain latitude of acceptance for any position advo-cated. If the message falls outside that latitude, then the more difficult is the job of persuasion as it might require a change in perspective. One type of research in *presentation* is concerned with whether a sales appeal should be two-sided or one-sided. Where we are communicating to a well-informed target audience and trying to convert them, the two-sided presentation comes out best: not the completely balanced two-sided but one that culminates in an argument where the communicator's case still has the edge. Whether conclusions should be made explicit or not varies with the selling situation but in general in a message dense environment, the general rule is to make conclusions explicit. Another area of research on presentation is whether the first or last message or part of a message has the most impact. There is both evidence in support of what is called the "primacy effect" and, on occasions, also for the "recency effect."

With respect to the *medium*, printed messages tend to be more critically examined but are better comprehended than audio and audio visual messages. But likable communicators are apt to be more persuasive in audio and audio visual form than printed. With regard to message *content*, simple messages and the avoidance of messages that go against the audience's self-interest, tend, not surprisingly, to be more effective. There is evidence to suggest that long messages (if they get the initial attention) suggest substantive content and can be persuasive, providing the target audience does not examine them too closely.

Some TV advertising persuades not by explicit messages but by getting the target audience to imagine the situation; observe and learn by imagining being in the situation. Imagining oneself using or possessing the product ("Imagine what it would be like, really like to have an MBA") is halfway toward buying it! This accounts for those announcements asking the audience to imagine what such and such a product could do to enrich their lives and asking members of the audience to send their thoughts to the firm for some reward.

Consistency theory

Cognitive consistency theories claim that people value the experience as well as the appearance of being consistent. There are a number of models that assume people seek a coordinated set of values, beliefs (cognitions) and actions. These models are concerned with changing attitudes also but assume that certain attitudes can be changed in the process of getting them to be consistent. The consistency approach lies behind the dissonance-attribution model of do $\Rightarrow$ feel $\Rightarrow$ learn mentioned earlier.

All of us seek some degree of consistency in the ways we think and act, otherwise no one could depend on us which could lead to social ostracism. Thus if nobody kept promises, it would be impossible to make any agreements. Hence we expect people to keep promises and not to lie. It could be argued that such expectations operate in advertising and selling so that we have a disposition to believe what ads say and promise. Also if we are to assume that attitudes, given the relevant goals, are predictive of behavior, this assumes people have a well-structured belief system so that beliefs cohere among themselves and with subsequent action.

There are several consistency models which can on occasions be useful to the marketer: they are the balance model, the congruity model, and the cognitive dissonance or dissonance-attribution model.

Balance model

The basic assumption is that people seek a *balance* or congruence (agreement) between their feelings (affects) and their beliefs (cognitions). For example, if we manage to rationally convince the consumer of the superiority of the firm's brand, his feelings about the brand are likely to change to fall in line with his beliefs. On the other hand, the change of feelings may come first. No doubt when Armstrong Cork years ago set out to provide housewives with a whole range of creative ideas about the entire home and not just about Armstrong products, they sought to enhance good feelings about the company hoping it would lead to more favorable beliefs about Armstrong's products. This is not to suggest that our feelings can change all beliefs: no one will believe black is white just because it would be comfortable to think so. Perhaps the balance model can explain the contribution that role playing (of buyers or rivals) can make to changing attitudes. It seems that playing a part can create attitudes that fit the role, perhaps because the feelings generated by the role can come to change beliefs.

Congruity model

The *congruity model* claims that people seek congruence between their attitude toward a communication source and attitude toward the things linked to the source: "the sources we like should always denounce ideas we are against and support ideas we are for." This is another reason for using well-loved personalities to sponsor our brand. It could also be a reason to justify the abundance of associationism in advertising. While the congruity model has a narrow focus, its central message is the same as that discussed under associationism except the explanation of the phenomena here has to do with the our desire for consistency. The congruity model would explain why the liking for an advertisement can carry over to the brand being advertised.

Cognitive dissonance/attribution model

As developed by Leon Festinger, *cognitive dissonance* occurs when a person holds at the same time inconsistent cognitions (beliefs).[17] Thus the belief that I am doing action XYZ yet I believe that this is wrong can cause discomfort so people try to reduce the conflict. Anyone who makes a difficult decision, particularly one that cannot be reversed, is assumed afterwards to strengthen his or her decision so that it will come to seem more justified than when it was first made. Every choice made by a buyer is a potential source of dissonance, as the perceived loss of an attractive displaced alternative is dissonant with the knowledge that another product has been chosen.

Cognitive dissonance may be reduced by the individual's lowering the value placed on some aspect of the product sacrificed (for example, being told "the 586 has yet to be tested"), or by enhancing the advantages of the product bought (for example, "since you bought, the price has risen 25 percent"), or by stressing the similarity between the product bought and the one sacrificed (for example, "in practice you'll find there is no real difference between the two"). When some not-for-profit organizations deliberately seek to arouse feelings of guilt, behind that guilt is dissonance: the belief that the receiver of the appeal for funds is a person who believes herself to be generous to the less fortunate, and this belief is inconsistent with any belief that the appeal must be ignored. It is the same with those begging in the street: to refuse a request can challenge beliefs about the type of person one is. The response, of course, may not be to donate but to argue to oneself about the unworthiness of the cause relative to others.

Cognitive dissonance is often used to explain market behavior. One study found that buyers of new cars paid more attention to advertisements promoting the brand they had bought than to advertisements for other brands.[18] Cognitive dissonance is usually quoted to justify "keeping the customer sold" by reassuring him about the wisdom of the buy. However, the theory of cognitive dissonance has lost some of its shine. There is the recognition that the disposition toward the reduction of dissonance can be very weak when other interests are at stake. But, a more teasing problem has been the fact that we cannot predict before an experiment which mode of dissonance reduction will be employed, so that it becomes difficult to think of an experiment that would test (seek to try and falsify) the theory as we do not know what predictions are to be confirmed or disconfirmed. This is why some researchers have used *attribution theory* as the preferred mode of explaining much of the same phenomena.

Attribution theory claims people try to understand their entire social milieu in terms of attributions. A person attributes causes to social events that are either internal or external to the person, for example, successes are due to one's ability and failure to uncontrollable environmental causes. Whenever we observe someone else's behavior, we look for causes, meanings and connections. We attempt to determine whether it is internally or externally caused. If the behavior is distinctive, unusual, not generally done by others in a similar situation, then there is an external attribution. On the other hand, if a person routinely does it then we fall back on some internal attribution. In looking at the *behavior of others* we tend to underestimate the influence of external factors. This is the fundamental *attribution error*. On the other hand, we are apt to make internal attributions to explain our success and external attributions to explain our failure. This is known as the *self-serving error*. It is the tendency to make such errors that are exploited in advertising; confirming self-serving attributions (e.g. failure in love attributed to not using a breath freshener) facilitate selling.

Consistency theories have intuitive appeal and we recognize the phenomena in our own lives. But we also recognize we can hold together many beliefs and actions that are inconsistent in order to satisfy various self-interests and conflicting demands. We do not necessarily recognize our inconsistencies as they may be brought into consciousness in different contexts.

The psychoanalytic approach

The psychoanalytic approach to persuasion is associated with discovering the unconscious meanings attached to products so that the advertiser can design appeals that tap the most basic motivations. When Vance Packard published *The Hidden Persuaders* in 1957, the approach received public prominence because of the claims made for subliminal perception which does not refer to perception in the usual psychological sense but simply to the effect of a below-threshold stimulus upon a person's behavior.

As has already been pointed out, the psychoanalytic approach found its fullest expression in motivation research. The use of focus groups is probably the major legacy of the heyday of motivation research. It is claimed that employing projective techniques with focus groups inspired Pepsi to come out with Pepsi Light. A more recent innovation is the staged "piggyback" focus group, illustrated by the ten doctors who watched ten arthritis sufferers discuss doctor–patient relationships (with the ten doctors being amazed at the level of dissatisfaction among the patients at the insignificant voice they had in their treatment).

It is common in focus groups to hear consumers claiming they buy a product not because of its distinctive benefits but because they identify with the type of person they believe uses the product. In line with this, there has been a growth in asking respondents to personify a brand: Man or woman? Car likely to be driven? Music liked? Alternatively respondents may be asked to match various companies with the animals they believe best exemplify the particular companies.

Agencies routinely ask consumers to provide a profile and preferably a sketch of the typical user of some brand. Thus Marlboro smokers are viewed as hard workers and ladies' men; Michelin users as sophisticated briefcase toting Porsche drivers; Pillsbury-cake-mix users as just dowdy and old-fashioned, bedecked in frilly aprons and prim bows. When the Playtex bra was seen as being associated with full-breasted, overweight, old-fashioned women (which many respondents were but denied it), Playtex devised a replacement campaign showing a sexy, svelte, but big-bosomed model with the slogan: "The fit makes the fashion."

What is common to a lot of these techniques is not just the search for hidden meaning but a distrust of the standard type of marketing research with its structured questionnaires, on the ground that they only elicit superficial, unreflective, socially appropriate replies not the unconscious desires that motivate behavior. While many advertisers find psychoanalytic theory much too vague for their purposes, the traditional psychoanalytic techniques are still in vogue even if academics claim projective techniques, say, are notoriously unreliable.

Emotional approaches

Although it makes for a neater classification to treat emotion under one or more of the systems of psychology already discussed, the subject is too important in persuasive advertising not to receive separate treatment. Emotions seem to have evolved to tell us what to think about and so guide our attention.

Mainstream psychology uses the term *affect* to embrace emotions, feelings, mood, and temperament. Although affect is, as we have seen, commonly equated in the marketing literature with attitude, "affect" really presupposes some attitude in that, for example, I only get emotional at the burning of the flag because I have certain attitudes toward the flag as a symbol of the values that I hold. But the term emotion itself has proved difficult to pin down, with probably no term in psychology being so frequently used about which there is so little agreement as to what it is. In both the psychology literature and public discourse, the term is an umbrella term for a "number of subjectively experienced, affect-laden feeling states." Where definitions of emotion in the social sciences appear to be precise, they turn out to be really little mini-theories on the nature of emotion. What seems to be fairly agreed, though, are the factors involved in emotion:

- *Stimuli*: the stimuli giving rise to an emotional reaction can be either from the environment *or* generated by one's own thoughts;
- *Autonomic physiological effects*: the physiological happenings may not necessarily be directly experienced but may take the form, say, of higher blood pressure or pulse rate;
- *Cognitive appraisal*: beliefs to which the stimuli give rise dictate the personal significance of the stimuli;
- *Motivational arousal*: some psychologists argue that there is an emotional basis in all actions. In any case, emotion can motivate action just as fear of cancer can lead people to stop smoking.

We can regard emotions as reactions to real or imagined situations that are tied to highly positive or negative evaluations of that situation, whether some event, some action or some object. If the consumer views a situation in a certain way and, as a result, evaluates the situation in a highly positive or negative way, then that situation has the potential to be emotionally arousing. Because evaluations of a situation differ, the same situation (e.g. the plight of the homeless) may be emotional to some and not to others while the same situation (e.g. success of a football team) may thrill some and depress others depending on their interests.

We can research emotions in advertising by asking subjects to identify the emotions they experience in looking at the appealingness of something in the ad and/or judging the praiseworthiness/blameworthiness of actions of characters in the ad and/or reflecting on the consequences of events depicted in the ad. Consequences can be viewed as highly desirable/undesirable in relation to goals; actions can be judged highly worthy or blameworthy while the imputed attributes of objects can be highly appealing or highly unappealing. The higher the appraisal, the more intense the emotion. Also the more the object of the emotion seems real, close at hand and close in proximity, the more intense the emotion is likely to be. But intensity has to reach some threshold level to be experienced as an emotion.[19]

Values link back to past emotional experiences. The frequent disproportionate emotional response to some incident suggests the incident is a surrogate indicator for some past event so the incident symbolizes some past event to which the emotional response is more suited. When certain actions seem more expressive of values than being calculative and self-interested (e.g. charity giving), these are often symbolic actions tied to the emotions. Aristotle distinguished three modes of persuasion:

1 ethos which relates to the personal characteristics of the one doing the persuading;
2 logos or the logic of the message itself; and
3 pathos or the emotions of the audience.

Aristotle argued pathos relies on putting the audience in a state of mind that stirs the emotions for "our judgments when we are pleased and friendly are not the same as when we are pained and hostile."

One reason, perhaps, for the prevalence of a psychoanalytic dimension in much advertising is the neglect by mainstream psychology (particularly behaviorism and cognitive psychology) of emotion. The focus in much of buyer behavior literature and in marketing science is on "rational" benefits as these are not only easier to handle but seem more consistent with a customer orientation that talks all the time about catering to the consumers' "needs" instead of wants: a definitional strategy designed to arouse good perceptions of marketing. But those with an interest in emotional behavior argue that research into rational benefits may reveal how consumers rationally think but not how they feel.

The typical market survey with its standard questionnaire seems the wrong vehicle for eliciting emotional responses so there is resort to other techniques such as focus groups. Newer approaches include the *benefit probe*, where, for example, respondents may be asked to cite two functional benefits of each product benefit and two emotional benefits of each functional benefit. Thus in a benefit probe of a mouthwash the respondent related the functional benefit of breath cleaning with the emotional benefits of eliminating worry, fostering confidence, moving toward being less anxious and more relaxed.

Another approach tries to measure the consumer's emotional bonds with a brand. Somewhat along the lines of the multiattribute model, emotional feelings are first listed, then weighted for relative importance in terms of a product class and then brands are rated according to their perceived possession of each of the emotions, with a final score being calculated. Current brands are rated against some emotional ideal to judge if there is some emotional gap to be filled. Thus if beer should be linked to camaraderie and friendliness, then the associated emotions need to be generated by advertising. It is claimed that all tangible, rational benefits are highly vulnerable to being copied but emotional bonds are more difficult to break.

What prompts people into buying cannot be decided a priori but is tied to what reasons the individual finds compelling. These reasons can be other than technical, aesthetic or economic. The appeal of any offering for the consumer is tied to his or her preferred life vision which, in turn, is likely to be implicitly tied to values. But the shaping of values is likely to be tied to early emotional experiences and more recent traumatic experiences. In fact, one way of identifying a person's values is through knowing what he or she gets emotional about. However, emotions should not be viewed as something contrasting with rationality. Current and anticipated feelings can be a rational input into any decision. Thus in thinking about risky choices such as buying stock, it is rational to take account of the regret we might feel if the value of the stock were to go drastically down after we bought it.

In contrast to Petty and Cacioppo, psychologists Zajonc and Markus speculate that attitudes may have a strong emotional base, developed before any cognitive elaboration.[20] Such attitudes, they claim, can only be changed by exercising emotional influence that bypass the cognitive. They argue that even when a preference has been built from cognitions in contrast to being built from affect, an affect aspect of the preference may develop that is independent of the cognitive elements that were the original basis for the preference: one begins to like simply as the result of repeated exposure. They claim that cognitive approaches (rational approaches) to attitude change have not met with a great deal of success because they do not reach the "motor system and other somatic representational systems of the organism." All this, if true, undermines the elaboration likelihood model since the central route to persuasion seems implicitly to be stressing the rational. However, much will depend on the basis of the attitude: many may be rationally based. In fact it is difficult to think of any emotion which is not tied to the cognitive (beliefs) involving some antecedent evaluation: the cognitive and the emotions are interdependent. Nonetheless, to claim as per Petty and Cacioppo that the emotional basis of attitudes comes via the peripheral route, so leading to only superficial acceptance of the message, is seemingly to ignore the emotional bonds of personal, moral and religious attitudes that are so strongly held and difficult to change.

A rational argument debates premises. This is difficult to do if the aim is to change behavior that has a basis in emotion since the aim here is not to lead to any inference but to change an interpretation, create a certain perception or conjure up a certain experience. Advertising might try to show the product in a certain light, to make the target audience share a particular perspective. But for this to be done, the advertisement must tie into the values of the audience and evoke the sort of emotional experiences that led to the values in the first place. Many persuasive appeals in advertising use a language that taps values that are strongly emotionally based such as the AT&T advertisement (discussed earlier) to encourage the long distance use of the telephone.

An important question is whether liking an advertisement carries over to the brand. This would be expected from both association and congruity theory. This carry over effect must be distinguished from favoring the brand because of beliefs about the brand emanating from the advertisement. There is apparently a positive relationship between liking an advertisement and liking the product and some of this may come from "image" attributes stressed in an advertisement as opposed to just "utilitarian" attributes.[21] Nonetheless, it should not be concluded from this that liking an ad is a necessary condition or sufficient condition for generating sales but it can help. Thus five of the seven packaged goods brands that were among the most popular and best remembered commercials of 1993 had either flat or declining sales that year (*Wall Street Journal*, July 4, 1994). As one commentator said liking the commercial "can make you feel better about choosing a brand, but only when the other variables are in place." Perhaps sales might have been worse but for the ads! But there is some research suggesting that attitude toward the ad is a significant predictor of attitude toward the brand only for noncomparative advertising.[22] It is speculated that the persuasive impact of comparative ads derives from their being processed via the central route which, if the elaboration likelihood model is correct, would mean they have the potential for being highly persuasive.

Common sense suggests that a communication need not necessarily be liked to have the effect intended. A good example is an advertisement for Radion, a washing powder, which focused on its performance in removing unpleasant, personal odors from clothing. Surveys indicated it was the most disliked ad on British TV but it gained 8 percent market share. However, most people watch TV for entertainment so liked ads are to be preferred for this reason and because of the generally positive relationship between liking the ad and liking the brand.

Although appeals to the strongest emotions like guilt, anger, and pity are done by not-for-profit organizations, commercial advertising does appeal to fears. Within limits, there is a positive relationship between the degree of fear aroused and the amount of attitude change induced. In general, those with high self-esteem, tend to be the ones most likely to react immediately to strong fear appeals but those with a low opinion of themselves tend to follow later. But the communication must offer a feasible way out (for example, in the case of fire fear, buy our smoke alarm system) and source credibility must be high.[23] *All this neatly illustrates how action is a function of motivation (high fear), beliefs (about the recommended action) and ability (able to perform the action recommended) plus the opportunity to act.*

A more general appeal to the emotions, albeit not usually strong, is the attempt to create what was called earlier the granfalloon effect: trying to get a target customer group to think of themselves as a group. Examples are designer labels; clubs for those buying specific makes of cars; identifying the target market with the persona or personality of the brand. People take their identity partly from the groups with which they identify so groups can be a source of self-esteem, provide a sense of belonging with a perceived sense of shared feelings. People with a sense of having little control over their lives are particularly vulnerable to anything that bolsters their self-esteem. But, again it depends on whether the target audience wants to self-categorize itself as belonging to such a group. A good illustration here is the "electronic church" in the United States with its TV ministers trying to get the audience to believe they belong to a close, warm, God-fearing, born-again-to-be-saved family of believers. There are many Christians in the United States who would never want to join such families, regarding much of what occurs as remote from true Christianity.

In marketing, there is a constant debate over the importance of the emotional versus the rational. The "hard-headed" point to a rational consumer, concerned to get the "best bang for the buck" while others claim the "heart rules the head." There is truth in both positions. Some buying situations can generate considerable emotion like buying a house, while in other buying situations like buying groceries we are much more likely to encounter the rational consumer.

THE GOALS OF ADVERTISING

The *mission* of advertising is to influence those whose decisions and actions determine the organization's success or failure. The more general immediate aim is to help create and retain customers at a profit. With respect to specific goals, we might first remind ourselves of the purpose of setting advertising goals. First, they are meant to guide the creative copy work and media planning. Second, they operate as a standard against which to measure achievement and evaluate results. Given these purposes, marketing goals in terms of sales, profits and market share are not suitable since they offer too little guidance to planning. The danger of setting goals in terms of sales is the implication that, if sales goals are not achieved, advertising is responsible. Except for certain cases of direct response advertising, this would neither be meaningful nor demonstrable. Advertising is not the sole factor in the marketing mix while there is the additional problem of calculating the carryover or long-term effects of advertising. This does not mean that an organization can ignore making estimates of sales resulting from different levels and types of advertising. Indeed some such estimates are implicitly, if not explicitly made.

Colley developed his hierarchy of effects model to support the claim that advertising goals should be communication goals rather than sales goals. His systems, called DAGMAR, after the title of his book: *Defining Advertising Goals for Measured Advertising Results*. Colley's reason for substituting communications goals for sales goals was the recognition that sales goals result from the cumulative effects from the total marketing strategy and not from advertising alone. Unfortunately, it could also be said that this is true for hierarchy stages. Thus, how often (say) can "conviction" be regarded as solely due to advertising without consumers taking account of the product itself, its pricing and availability?

The superordinate *goal* of advertising is to establish a distinctive, memorable, favorable identity and image for the product or brand. While brand image is derived from the product itself, its name, its packaging, its type of distribution, its price and style of advertising, it is advertising that typically does more for the development of the brand's identity than anything else beyond the appearance and the performance of the brand. The goals that relate to establishing the identify of a brand should be tied to the competitive task(s) to be achieved, whether the task is to:

- convert from rivals;
- increase the level of individual usage of the brand;
- attract new users; or
- retain existing customers.

If the competitive task is customer *retention*, advertising seeks to develop resistance to change by promoting *want-satisfaction*. Tangible advertising goals would measure the degree to which brand switching might be minimized. Customer retention as the sole goal might apply to a mature market where the firm is satisfied with its market share. The aim is to provide assurance to reinforce habits and strengthen attitudes since the opportunity for increasing sales by conversion from rivals may be more difficult in mature markets composed of well-established brands.

If the competitive task is to *attract* current nonusers, advertising seeks to promote *want-conception* by getting the target audience to perceive the potential of the product for meeting their wants. Tangible advertising goals measure the percentage of nonusers who come to recognize the product's potential for meeting their wants. Customer attraction as the sole goal might apply at the pioneering stage of the product's life cycle. Customer attraction means establishing the brand's purpose and competitive advantage right from the start. This requires some thought since, as already pointed out, repositioning a brand later can be very costly and risky.

If the competitive task is to *convert* from rivals, advertising seeks to promote *want-focus* by showing how the brand better meets the buyer/user goals or choice criteria than rival offerings. Tangible goals could measure shifts expected in beliefs about the competitive standing of the organization's offering.

If the competitive task is to *increase* the level of individual usage, advertising seeks to promote *want-development* by showing the additional uses for the product. Tangible goals could measure the number in the target audience buying the product for the additional uses.

Sometimes several competitive tasks can be set, though this is a move toward using the shotgun rather than the rifle: the spread in goals widens the audience but weakens the impact on each of the different audiences. Sometimes the goals of advertising in terms of competitive task or hierarchy stage may have to be supplemented by specifying certain subgoals (for example, to encourage stocking, induce requests for literature, facilitate a salesperson's call and so on) that could serve as a way of achieving the competitive task or stage in the hierarchy. What goals to set for advertising depends on the market situation. In measuring goal attainment, we need to measure effects that relate solely to advertising as far as that is possible. Both in the case of goals in terms of sales and hierarchy of effects stages, we cannot usually ensure that our measures do not result from other elements of the marketing mix. However, the competitive task measures are not entirely immune from this criticism but are better at distinguishing between the effects of advertising and other forms of influence.

ROLE AND GOALS OF SALES PROMOTION, PUBLICITY, AND PUBLIC RELATIONS

Consumer-goods companies have become more doubtful about the cost-benefits of national advertising and have looked to other ways of building sales and getting across their message. This has led to more resources being spent on sales promotions, advertising through mail shots, event sponsorship and public relations. Thus expenditures in the United States on sales promotion are greater than expenditure on traditional advertising; spending on direct mail is increasing more than any other marketing promotional expenditure while just a public relations campaign (not advertising) has been credited with projecting the Body Shop into a major brand. One reason for all this is the belief among marketers that there is a need to use as many channels of communication as possible to reach and influence the market because:

- Markets are becoming increasingly divided into small segments. With the number of brands in a market increasing and the number of consumers in the market not growing, this also means markets are becoming more and more fragmented.
- With the development of technology that allows the consumer to move from one TV program to another during a commercial or to pass over a commercial in watching a recorded TV program or to switch off the sound in a commercial, consumers are paying less attention to TV commercials which in many countries have been the most important and the most effective way of advertising a national brand. This channel switching is seen as another manifestation of consumer satiation and indifference with the whole "blooming, puzzling mass of advertising messages." In such conditions, there is a serious problem of getting attention. With relationship marketing and all the other trends toward customization, many marketers believe mass media advertising is much less effective than it used to be.

- The decline in audience market share attracted by national (network) TV in the United States during prime time. This has made it more difficult to reach mass audiences.
- With the proliferation of brands in every consumer market, together with the problem of trying to differentiate them, creative advertising has been difficult to achieve. Thus in the United States in 1979 there were eighty-four brands of cereal: today there are more than one hundred and fifty. This makes it harder for the typical consumer to spend time differentiating among the brands with fickle consumers replacing those who were brand loyal. In such conditions, products come more and more to be seen as commodities where picking or price dominate.
- Bar-code scanners in supermarkets are allowing retailers to identify consumer preferences for themselves, to see what brands sell and to allocate shelf-space accordingly. This is accompanied by increasing demands from these retailers for manufacturers to switch money from advertising into price promotions. Bar-code scanners are now used in over half the supermarkets in the United States and the position is somewhat similar in Europe.
- Modern computerized customer lists have made it possible to develop detailed profiles of individual consumers so persuasive communications can be tailored to particular consumers and sent to them through direct mail. For example, General Motors sent out a mailing to 170,000 young affluent consumers offering its video-cassette on its new Cadillac Seville. American Express has used its credit card business to collect vast amounts of data on customers and their buying. All this is leading to more targeting of the individual consumer.

This move away from traditional mass media advertising is reinforced by the pressure on brand managers for short-term profits instead of investing in nurturing and protecting the brand's image. A danger inherent in this move away from image building is the damage it can do long term, turning what was formerly a premium priced product, stemming from its superior image, into just another token of a commodity product. As was said earlier, advertising is still the most effective way of building brand image apart from product performance itself. The more brands become alike, the more the importance of other aspects of an offering and the importance of advertising in giving a brand a distinct identity so as to develop consumer insistence for the brand to "reach over the heads of the retailer and talk to the consumer directly." Creative advertising can still stand out and be noticed from the rest, as witness the recent Taster's Choice "soap opera" serial.

Sales promotion

Sales promotion does not group naturally with advertising as a form of communication. It is discussed here (as well as in the chapter on pricing) because it is nonetheless promotion and has an intimate association with advertising as part of a communications program whose various parts draw on the same communications budget and need coordination.

Sales promotion is the name given to a collection of incentives used to trigger sales.

Table 11.1 Major sales promotions

Consumer	Trade
Free samples	Sale or return
Trial offer	Trial
	POP aids
	Local ads
Coupon offers	Cash incentives
Price offers in special packs	Push money
Branded offers	Promotional discounts
	Credit facilities
	Slotting allowances
Self-liquidating premiums	Premiums
Contests	Staff contests
Collection items	Bulk discounts

Such incentives are *consumer promotions* when directed at the consumer and *trade promotions* when directed to channel intermediaries like retailers to stock or push the firm's brand. However, it is doubtful whether incentives are ever purely one or the other, but the logic of first encouraging the trade to stock the brand and then helping the trade not only by advertising but by encouraging immediate purchase is a useful distinction conceptually. The major sales promotions are shown in Table 11.1.

Appendix 11.1 summarizes the views of one expert on the implicit assumptions lying behind consumer and trade promotions.

Role

The key role allotted to sales promotion is that of triggering the sale or the process of a sale. Ray sees sales promotion as combining the sales closing advantages of personal selling with the mass reach of advertising at a low cost per customer target. There is a danger here of viewing sales promotion as similar to personal selling in triggering a sale but with the possibility of doing it more cheaply. In fact, sales promotion and personal selling draw on different sources of influence: personal selling draws pre-eminently on attractiveness and credibility to persuade, while sales promotion offers material inducements or merely heightened visibility to get action.

Sales promotion or promotional inducements increase marketing productivity in three ways:

- complementing or supplementing the marketer's persuasive communication;
- reshaping the benefits of the basic offer to meet competitive pressures; and
- controlling to some degree the timing and manner of consumer actions.

Sales promotion focuses on providing the prod to action. In general terms, there must be a passive want for the product among the target population not presently buying (even if a previous buyer) or not presently stocking up on the brand. Advertisers need to know what is inhibiting purchase, as such information is a factor in the choice of promotion. For example, if many in the market believe the brand has nothing to offer above the others in a cluster of brands, free samples may be the answer providing the brand really does have an advantage.

Consumer promotions

Free samples.   A key promotion for a new product is the free sample or trial offer, which usually gets over buying inertia and the risk barrier. But sampling assumes that the product has that additional something to create customers. This relates to two errors sellers make in using samples. The first error is to use sampling for a brand that has no competitive advantage but is just a me-too product. The second error is to assume, if the brand does have an advantage, it will be noticed by the user. A sample is meant to exemplify something, but suppose I give out a free sample of my cereal, what is the sample meant to exemplify? Taste? Protective packaging? Appearance? If the sample was a unique vitamin-enriched brand, the consumer needs to be told this at the time of taking the sample, not just assuming the consumer will read the package or feel better after using the cereal.

Not all products lend themselves to sampling. Some products are too expensive or too well-known, or are purchased too infrequently or are just too costly to distribute free. But, where appropriate, sampling can be key.

Price deals in one form or another are the most popular form of consumer promotions for packaged goods (and most consumer promotions tend to be on consumer packaged goods) and what is typically meant when the words consumer promotion are used in an unqualified way. Price discounts assume that price is inhibiting trial because consumers are unsure whether the product benefits justify the cost or see no reason for trying the product. The firm should have evidence that the product has something to justify its continued purchase at the normal price, otherwise the effect of the "subsidies" is short-lived. In one study on established brands of regularly packaged goods like coffee, tea and detergents, consumer price promotions had no noticeable effect on either long-term sales or brand loyalty.[24] Although sales promotion did lead to an immediate boost in sales, the extra sales came from previous customers of the brand rather than from new customers. Within a product category like coffee, there are likely to be cluster brands within which consumers move from one to the other depending on which is currently on discount. Price deals in such circumstances do not buy loyalty; they merely rent allegiance. However, if the goal is merely to reduce inventories to increase cash flow or meet budgeted sales, the renting of allegiance for the period of the promotion may be all that is required.

Constant price deals tarnish an image, with the brand being bought only when it is on special offer. Perhaps excessive discounting, regardless of the amount spent on advertising, is detrimental long term because consumers may attribute excessive sales promotions (vis-à-vis competition) as being caused by the brand's inferiority. If all competitors use sales promotions consumers may attribute this to brands being undifferentiated. It is also a possibility that consumers, buying a brand on special offer, may attribute their buying just to the price incentive rather than to anything about the brand itself. These are interesting speculations on the basis of attribution theory though the evidence still needs to be collected. But it is not easy to investigate this issue in surveys since consumers may genuinely not know how it affects their behavior and are unlikely to admit thinking less of a discounted brand. It becomes difficult for the manufacturer to stop discounting once started. This is the situation with cars in the United States. Car buyers seem convinced that price discounting will go on and if manufacturers call a halt, car buyers simply wait until someone breaks ranks. With more than 350 different models of car on sale in the United States, it is becoming more and more difficult to stand out from the crowd. On the other hand, price inducements have substantial appeal and offer immediate gratification to buyers. Nonetheless, price deals are not generally appropriate for high quality brands sold at premium prices as an air of class can easily be lost when bargain deals are seen as necessary to making sales.

Price deals may involve price offers in special factory packs or *branded offers* where two products usually related in use are sold together at less than their combined individual prices. But instead of a direct price reduction, a *coupon* may be surrendered when the brand is bought. Coupons have several advantages:

- the customer may redeem the coupon before being tempted by seeing her regular brand;
- advertising can be put on the coupon;
- the "trade" is encouraged to buy in if customers are not to be lost (with a price offer, if the dealer is out of stock, the customer is unaware of the offer);
- there is no need for special factory packs; coupons can be used to buy regular stocks; and
- coupons may achieve the benefits of price discrimination for the supplier, for example, in competing with private label brands while maintaining the higher price for the "lazy" consumer.

But coupons can have problems:

- to produce the same sales increase, the coupon value must be greater than any corresponding price reduction;
- dealers may abuse the system by accepting coupons as payment on other products while they demand to be paid extra for handling the coupons. Coupons are also subject to many other abuses such as charities collecting coupons for sale to retailers who return them for cash;
- it is difficult to predict the redemption rate: it can be as low as 1 percent if the coupon is part of some magazine advertisement and as high as 40 percent if the coupon is of high value for convenience packaged goods, and distributed door-to-door.

Traditional coupons are less effective than they used to be because of the sheer number of them. In the United States, marketers gave consumers around 300 billion coupons with a face value of $175 billion in 1993! But consumers only redeemed 2.3 percent of them. Coupons, however, that are distributed in supermarkets are gaining in popularity in terms of being redeemed.

An innovation is the use of the computer in the supermarket to track purchases and offer rebates to regular buyers of brand-name goods. Participants get a list of the hundred or so brand-name products in the rebate scheme, together with a monthly statement showing credit earned. At the end of some period, say, four months, participants receive a voucher for spending at the store.

Premiums (e.g. toilet bag offered with any cosmetic purchase of the company) are often used to get enhanced visibility for a brand to facilitate purchase. The "self-liquidating premium" is sold at a price that will cover the seller's costs and perhaps even yield a small profit. The offers can be an effective way of getting attention for some brand via point-of-sale display. "Contests" are a way of getting point-of-sale display and building interest in the brand by publicizing a contest. Prizes may be large (e.g. a car) or small and numerous. Where there are likely to be too many winners, contestants can be asked to devise, say, a slogan to be used to evaluate the final selection. "Collection items" (for example, sports cards in packets of gum) can similarly create visibility for a brand and, because several trial purchases are needed, there is the possibility of breaking a previous habit and converting from rivals. A problem lies in determining when to stop, since there are always some buyers still completing their sets. A collection item is essentially a free premium offer as it is given away to help sell another product. It is claimed that the premium family of sales promotions are usually more efficient than price deals if the target audience is not brand committed. The premiums offer good value, reinforce advertising, secure visibility and fit the product (e.g. mugs for Campbell's soups).

Sales promotions have the advantage over advertising in seemingly providing measurable results. It also seems the logical thing to do when marketers are told that around 70 percent of brand selections are made in the store. But, as we have seen, there may be a spurt in extra sales but no long-term advantage. Furthermore, just because most supermarket brand purchases are not preplanned but occur in the store, does not mean that, in looking at the brands available, the consumer just picks in the absence of sales promotions. The consumer may have been thinking about buying the product for a long time.

It may well be that many if not most promotions do not pay when costs and forward buying are taken into account. Also promotions are easily copied and so provide no sustainable advantage and, when used as a substitute for advertising, the long-term result may be a brand with a faceless, lifeless, commodity image as price promotions condition the buyer to believe that price is the key buying factor with brands otherwise alike.

Trade promotions

If consumer insistence for a product can be stimulated by advertising then the focus is on a "pull" strategy of pulling the consumer toward the point of sale. However, if dealer participation in the selling process is needed and dealer support is sought then the focus might be on a "push" strategy of pushing the product through to the consumer. In this case trade promotions are important.

The problems with trade promotions can be somewhat similar to consumer promotions. Thus cash and promotional discounts can get the seller "locked in" to giving such discounts, with the retailer buying only when discounts are offered. Delayed invoicing and extensive credit can be very costly. Dealer contests and staff contests, where prizes are won on the basis on sales made, may be attractive to sellers but these are not necessarily the promotions that are attractive to dealers. *Push money* (PMs) to dealer staff who are star sellers of the brand tend to distort the dealer's aim of pushing brands according either to demand or profit markup.

Perhaps no trade promotion is so controversial or a point of grievance with manufacturers than the so-called *slotting allowances* which are payments to the retailer for putting the manufacturers' brand on his shelf. The position of a brand in the store can be a significant factor in sales. Thus in supermarkets, those brands that are placed on the shelves at eye level sell more, as do small-ticket merchandise placed at the end of a supermarket aisle or near the checkout counter. There are also similar payments for displaying any large point-of-purchase material.

Point-of-purchase (POP) advertising material is often considered essential to inform, to remind, to persuade, and to add a little excitement at the point of sale. Thus Timex has a still-clicking watch at the bottom of an aquarium, and Pantene uses a haircare diagnostician in stores, while a cosmetics firm has consumers pressing buttons to respond to questions on a screen about their hair and skin condition to recommend a customized solution to their beauty needs. Although POP is typically associated with mere cardboard displays near the product, there are now far more elaborate aids as these examples illustrate. There are also, of course, those huge signs outside outlets like McDonald's and gasoline stations.

Many of the payments and price discounts given to retailers are no longer considered "promotional" but something coerced from the manufacturer by the retailer. P&G has argued that constant price discounting has eroded brand loyalty and has sought to replace these discounts with "everyday low prices." It has cut its wholesale prices and slashed its spending on trade "promotions." The logic of its new pricing, away from discounts, is

- to stop wide price variations from store to store resulting in the consumer either paying an inflated price or shopping around to locate it on special offer; and
- to stop rewarding retailers for what amounts to their abuse of trade promotions.

What is common is the payment of

- huge "slotting fees" to obtain space in the retailer's warehouse;
- "facing allowances" to obtain premium shelf space; and
- payment for retailer local advertising which is commonly just pocketed.

Retailers are apt to respond to discounting on popular brands by stocking up ("forward buying") during the promotional period and selling what remains after the promotional period at the normal price. American supermarkets have invested in huge warehouses just to do such stockpiling. But P&G's battle against all this is not going to be easy since the big retailers have come to depend on so-called trade promotions for a good part of their profits. The danger is that retailers will not see it as an opportunity, but will deliberately hold back their support of P&G though P&G are relying on their customer franchise to block any moves to stop stocking their products. Another danger inherent in their action is that P&G's competitors will exploit the situation and pay to grab P&G's prime shelf space.

Competitive task goals

The question of when to use sales promotions depends on our goals. The superordinate goal of sales promotion is to trigger purchase or start the process leading to purchase. The competitive tasks are to attract trial; induce brand switching; retain custom; or increase usage in off-peak/off-season periods. Such task goals may be couched in other terms such as to get rid of old stock or to achieve a better geographic distribution, or more adequate stock level, or better point-of-purchase display or to reduce inventories, preempt competition or sustain market share. But whatever the task goal or goals, they should be sought within the constraints that

- whatever is done is in fact consumer-franchise-building; and
- the particular sales promotion adopted should be coordinated with, or reinforce and cohere with the rest of the promotional campaign.

Once having thought about the competitive task goal, there is a need to explain why members of the target audience are not buying and define the difficulties in retaining customers.

In the most general terms, sampling is the best for attracting and inducing trial. Price deals are good for attracting increased usage during off-peak times, although there may be difficulty keeping up the increased usage level unless supportive advertising and use experience induces perceptions of benefits. Premiums can also induce increased usage in off-peak periods, although they will have difficulty maintaining the increased level unless either the promotion gives rise to liking through familiarity with the brand or brand performance advantages are demonstrated during usage.

The promotional costs to the seller consist of both the cost of the sales promotion itself and the losses from being unable to confine the promotion to *prospective* customers. Future business is siphoned away when existing customers take advantage of price deals to buy in bulk. A firm with high market share in a mature market will (if acting rationally) be less tempted to use sales promotion than the firm with a very small share of the market. Also competitors are less likely to retaliate against a small competitor, if the promotions are off-season, or supported only by very nominal advertising. On the other hand, retaliation by major rivals is likely if the promotion is undertaken by a large rival firm with high market share and those not currently undertaking sales promotions have high fixed costs and a perishable product.

Publicity and public relations

Both *publicity* and *public relations* (now often called *corporate communications*) are used to generate supportive information about the firm and its products. In general, both publicity and public relations are used at the start of some campaign to stimulate interest and add credibility to subsequent advertising, sales promotion and personal selling. But often the publicity is not instigated by the firm while public relations are frequently called upon to fight fires.

Publicity covers all those news items about the organization and its products that are not linked to the firm as their sponsor or directly funded by the organization. Not all favorable publicity for an organization is deliberately sought but, if it is, it is typically done through news releases, films, tapes, and press conferences. But there are other ways of generating publicity. For example, there is the stunt to attract attention and teaser advertising (e.g. exciting curiosity by hiding what the car is going to look like when about to be launched). But any product innovation that commands wide interest can generate publicity as occurred in the case of Gillette's Sensor razor. There can also be highly favorable publicity generated by an attractive advertising campaign as happened in the case of the serial television commercial for Nestlé brands of coffee, Gold Blend in Britain and Taster's Choice in the United States. What makes favorable publicity so effective is that it appears to be an independent endorsement which enhances its credibility. The problem with publicity is the lack of direct control over whether the news item will be taken up and, if so, whether it will be publicized when most useful to marketing.

Public relations covers all attempts by the firm to anticipate, monitor and influence the type of "press" it gets so as to enhance or maintain a positive corporate image. Public relations (PR), too, uses the press release, interviews, and press conferences to reach its publics, which are wider than the organization's customers or clients. In PR there is a recognition that all actions taken by the firm communicate something to someone and the effects achieved incidentally may be so profound that they cannot be eradicated by any amount of public advertising. As Edward Bernays, usually considered the father of public relations, once said, there is no detail too trivial to influence the public in a favorable or unfavorable sense. What is meant here is that what an organization might dismiss as unimportant may have high meaning for some groups outside the firm. While a corporation's advertising may reflect what the firm would like its customers to believe, other actions of the firm like its social performance, may shout an entirely different message. However, public relations and advertising tend to overlap in institutional advertising designed to present a certain persona to the public. Thus one TV campaign showed misty-eyed college graduates eager to start saving the world as employees of Dow Chemical. The aim was to change Dow's somewhat tarnished image following its association with producing napalm and agent orange during the Vietnam war.

PR has the broad mission of considering the firm's image and projecting its persona to all its various stakeholders:

- *Employees.* As all key competencies or thrusts ultimately reside in employee knowledge and skills, their morale and goodwill is a top priority. Employees want to work for a firm that is a good citizen and lives up to its claims about what it stands for. If the organization is projecting an image to the world as having a corporate culture whose heroes are ethical and whose ways are democratic then, if this is not to breed employee cynicism, employees need to be convinced that this is so. A bank that boasts about the level of its customer service alerts its employees to its importance while also logically compelling management to do everything it can to make it so.

- *Public interest and pressure groups.* The growth in public interest and pressure groups has, perhaps more than anything else, alerted corporations to the importance of public relations. There have been boycotts of brands of tuna that use tuna caught in nets that also entrap dolphins; boycotts of firms dealing with countries that are considered repressive; boycott of firms that are not socially responsible in their hiring policies or in helping the environment and so on. One case is P&G's Folgers brand of coffee, which was attacked in the United States by a group that accused P&G of buying its coffee beans from El Salvador and so in the process subsidizing the regime and its brutal war. P&G was alleged to have responded by using the threat of withdrawing advertising to prevent the pressure group Neighbor to Neighbor from advertising its complaint. But the use of such coercion simply generated a huge amount of favorable publicity for Neighbor to Neighbor. This is not unexpected, since the public at large in a democratic society is apt to react unfavorably to any suppression of the "little guy trying to persuade the big guy not to support brutal overseas regimes."

- *The government.* Governments now realize that a country's standard of living depends on the success of its industries so, more and more, the government consults company spokespersons on proposals that affect them, for example, proposals about hazardous waste disposal.

- *Shareholders.* It is becoming more and more difficult to ignore the true owners of a company when the large institutional investors own such large amounts of stock in companies and are prepared to exercise their power. It is not uncommon to find, within public relations, some unit specifically concerned with investor relations whose job it is to persuade shareholders that company management is worthy to be in charge.

- *The media.* While the media may not determine what people think about an issue, it affects what people think are important issues. In any case to have the media on your side is half the battle. What this means in practice is showing the firm reacts to dramatic events on a like scale. Thus Johnson & Johnson took Tylenol off the market after some containers on supermarket shelves had been poisoned leading to the death of innocent people. A hamburger chain that failed to learn this lesson and did not close down for a period after its meat was found to be contaminated, lost critical support from its customers. In any such crisis the chief executive should be on the scene to show urgency and concern about the issue, not as in the case of the large oil spill off Alaska, leaving junior spokespersons to do the job.

PR advertising refers to the use of advertising to generate comment in the media about the company or its products. Bennetton uses PR advertising, exploiting social themes, because it believes "modern companies are social-political entities and that all their communications have social, political content." Bennetton seeks an image of being innovative, adventurous, prepared to take risks and as a company that has extended the boundaries of communication. Increasingly, it is argued, that consumers are looking at the values of the company behind the ad to see if it justifies their support when competitive brands are similar.

In the international arena, company image is particularly important with the United Nations developing codes of conduct for all multinational firms. In Canada, for example, there is the Foreign Investment Act of 1976 by which foreign-owned firms are evaluated to judge the extent to which they are "good citizens" of Canada. PR has to assess the likely impact of the firm's operations on the host country against a background of viewing the firm as others in the country see it. Publicity is often easier to get in overseas countries than, say, in the United States since elsewhere there is often a dearth of news items.

THE ORGANIZATION OF THE ADVERTISING BUSINESS

The advertising business is composed of the advertisers, the owners of advertising media and the makers of advertisements, who are usually advertising agencies. Some firms have their own in-house agency, but most advertisers use an advertising agency to help plan the advertising strategy, write copy, produce the advertisement, and buy space from the media. The exceptions tend to be business-to-business advertising and the advertising of services which can be handled in-house. Thus John Deere uses an outside agency for its advertising to the consumer but does its tractor advertising in-house.

There is nothing to stop an agency from employing several other agencies, with one agency being used for TV commercials, another for print advertising and so on or a firm could deal solely with specialist agencies—one agency for creative work, one for media buying and so on. Where a firm has several distinct product groups, it may use a separate agency for each group. Thus P&G employs at least eight major agencies.

The bulk of an advertising agency's income comes usually from the discount given by the media: the agency buys space or time from the media at 15 percent discount but charges its clients the full rate. This has the disadvantage of encouraging high expenditure on media advertising that allows the discount but the advantage is that the commission system does have a built in reward for good work in that a successful advertisement will be used time and time again, generating the commission without the corresponding work. Still neither client nor agency tends to be satisfied with the commission form of payment. The commission system is good for the agency when the market is expanding for heavy media usage but not when advertising campaigns are being cut. On the client side, many firms insist on negotiated commissions. Nissan, the Japanese automobile producer, pays its agency 10 percent commission on the first $150 million of billings and 5.5 percent on the next $100 million. A major exception to this trend is P&G, which except for Philip Morris, spends more than any other firm on advertising. P&G will maintain the base 15 percent but will also pay agencies that create advertisements placed in media that do not pay agency commissions. This move is justified by the spread of other media reaching the public such as controlled-circulation magazines, shopping carts, and video screens, and the desire of P&G to motivate its agencies to reach its customers in as many ways as are effective. The company has also agreed to increase its fees to agencies that develop campaigns for new products, not just the token fee that is currently the norm.

A full service agency is organized into several departments:

- *Copy department/creative department*: Those who create the advertisements are the art director and the copywriters in the copy department, which is typically part of the creative department which includes art, print, radio, and TV production (if such work is undertaken at all). The copywriters write copy after the basic concept has been decided; graphic artists create layouts and so on and broadcast producers are concerned with TV and radio. One problem here is the two audiences: to persuade the consumer and to persuade the client that the proposed advertisement will in fact do that.
- *Account management*: The account executive is the liaison between all agency departments and the client. She or he is responsible for running the campaign while the account planner helps in the collection and analysis of market research data. In any case, account management is responsible for keeping the agency ahead on client wants.
- *Media department*: This department is concerned with media selection and buying. The print buyers work with newspapers and magazines, while time buyers work with radio and television. A not uncommon problem is conflict between the media people and the copywriters who often believe they know best which media is most suited for their creative endeavors.
- *Traffic department*: The scheduling and coordination of the work going through the agency or to outside suppliers is the responsibility of the traffic department.
- *Research department*: Marketing research departments are commonly found in advertising agencies as a service for their clients.

The big agencies like Saatchi & Saatchi, Densu, Interpublic Group, WPP Group, Ogilvy Group, Omnicom Group, Young & Rubicam offer a full range of services. But not all agencies are full-service ones and the trend seems to swing back and forth. In the 1980s the swing was toward being full service and multi-divisional with some of the big agencies adding public relations firms and specialist boutiques to offer a service to their clients on a world-wide basis. However, an agency may rely for collateral services, such as sales promotion, media buying, marketing research, public relations, and tele-marketing firms, on outside suppliers.

The product managers, where such exist, are likely to be responsible for the advertising of the brands under them, with the advertising department in a company acting in an advisory role to the product managers and in a liaison role between the product managers and the advertising agency.

Although an agency will lean over backwards not to lose a major client, there are sources of conflict between advertiser and agency. An agency may, for example, recommend the medium in which it is most proficient rather than the one that is most suitable, or it may stress the advantages of using the same theme in all the media to save creative work when a multiple solution rather than a single solution may be more appropriate. An agency may, in fact, recommend the same theme year after year ("Why not stick to a winning appeal?") when cost saving is the motivation. Finally, an agency may transfer its most creative staff from the client's account once the patronage has been secured. Deception arises if such transfers are presented as being in the best interests of the client ("A person can get stale you know"). On the other hand, some advertisers (firms) are notorious for their cavalier treatment of agencies. Every advertiser should:

- keep the agency informed about the brand and its market segment;
- allow ample time to prepare a campaign;
- state the advertising objectives and provide any other information that will help, for example, on pricing, competition, distribution channels; and
- be courteous enough to listen to the agency's presentation, that is, do not dismiss it without a fair hearing.

It is costly to change agencies because accommodation to a new agency takes time and it is not certain that a new agency will perform better. In choosing an agency, a firm needs to know the thrust of the agency in its creative work, its size and the services it offers. But a basic question is how the advertiser will get along with the agency. Ideally, a potential client would like information on an agency's track record; whether the agency has competitive accounts; who in the agency would be working on their account; and whether the agency agrees that the client should also be involved in the creation and evaluation of advertising proposals.

Presentations to demonstrate an agency's potential ability are still common though they can be misleading. Creative copy work should be based on substantial knowledge about the firm, its brands and its markets, and not just be conjured up in a vacuum and later have to be adopted regardless. As an example, of choosing on the basis of a presentation, there is the case of Subaru of America, who in 1992 dismissed its advertising agency and chose another. What the competing agencies had to go on, apart from their own observations of the car industry, was the description by one automobile magazine of the Subaru having "gritty power, all weather capability with a refreshing emphasis on utility." All the agencies recognized that the car had an identity problem and that current customers tended to be educated people concerned more with the utilitarian function of a car. Subaru's goal was to develop a distinct umbrella image for its cars and had $70 million to spend for the first year of advertising. There were 35 agencies on Subaru's initial contact list which was down to 12 after screening through a questionnaire sent to each of them. Of the twelve semi-finalists, six were invited to make a presentation. A very brief overview of the presentations is of interest.

The first firm suggested an advertising serial in fifteen installments which would follow a fictional driver on a year long journey through bad weather and near disaster. In its advertisements, car buyers would be criticized for their obsession with trends rather than with practicality with the slogan "Get real, get a Subaru." The second presentation was based on the belief that automobiles were essentially "mechanical sports jackets" in that they tell people who you are, how you vote, whether you're available to go home with someone after the bar closes. In addition, the advertising would stress durability, value, and engineering with the slogan: "Subaru. For all the right reasons." The third presentation argued that it was wrong to stress four-wheel drive engineering— the content of its cars, rather than character: the focus would be not on what the car can do but on what it *means*. A dependable car means that the driver is also a dependable person, captured by the slogan: "A car that can. Why should John Doe take his family out on a night like this? Because he can." The fourth presentation suggested that consumers realize that cars are pretty much alike and that conventional advertising can do little to help as consumers hate them. The theme suggested Subaru as the mainstream alternative with the slogan: "Subaru. What to drive." The final presentation was based on a research approach known as "brand keys" which consists of depth interviewing of the form: "If you were your ideal car, would you be a master of ceremonies or a member of the audience?" which purported to reveal which product attributes consumers bond to emotionally. The suggested slogan was to be: "The perfect car for the imperfect world. Subaru."

Subaru of America first debated on whether to go for a traditional campaign that would please the dealers or employ an unconventional agency that might inspire a sales burst but with the danger that the campaign might come unstuck. They felt the "Get real" campaign was simply an imitation of Heineken beer advertising while "For all the right reasons" could apply to any product. The campaign following the fictional driver was too similar to Chevrolet's "Heartbeat of America Campaign." Wieden & Kennedy got the account with its slogan "Subaru. What to drive." Wieden & Kennedy only held on to the Sabaru account for 28 months! The first questionable assumption is that the problem of Subaru's sales is just an advertising one and not something to do with the core offering. The second assumption is that effective copy can just be dreamed up together with a good sales pitch to sell it to the advertisers. But once this is done the agency feels obliged to go along with its suggestions even if further reflection and research on the firm's products and its market makes these original suggestions somewhat premature.

NOTES

1 Tellis, Gerard J. (1988) "Advertising Exposure, Loyalty and Brand Purchase: A Two-Stage Model of Choice," *Journal of Marketing Research*, XXV (May).
2 Leiss, William, Kline, Stephen, and Jhally, Sut (1986) *Social Communication in Advertising: Persons, Products and Images of Well-Being*, New York: Methuen Inc.
3 Leone, Robert P. and Schultz, Randall L. (1980) "A Study of Marketing Generalizations," *Journal of Marketing*, 44 (Winter).
4 Cook, Guy (1994) *The Discourse of Advertising*, New York and London: Routledge.
5 Ehrenberg, A. S. C. (1974) "Repetitive Advertising and the Consumer," *Journal of Advertising Research*, 14 (April).
6 Leymore, V. L. (1975) *The Hidden Myth*, New York: Basic Books.
7 Collins, Jim (1990) *Uncommon Cultures: Popular Culture and Post-Modernism*, London and New York: Routledge.
8 Apter, Michael, J. (1989) *Reversal Theory*, London and New York: Routledge.
9 Hovland, C. I. and Janis, I. L. (eds.) (1959) *Personality and Persuadability*, New Haven: Yale University Press.
10 Colley, Russell H. (1961) *Defining Advertising Goals for Measured Advertising Results*, New York: Association of National Advertisers.
11 Krugman, Herbert E. (1965) "The Impact of Television Advertising: Learning without Involvement," *Public Opinion Quarterly*, 29 (Fall).
12 Ray, Michael L. (1982) *Advertising and Communication Management*, Englewood Cliffs NJ: Prentice Hall.

13 Petty, Richard E. and Cacioppo, John T. (1979) "Issue Involvement Can Increase or Decrease Persuasion by Enhancing Message Relevant Cognitive Responses," *Journal of Personality and Social Psychology*, 37 (October).

14 Schumann, D. W., Petty, R. E., and Clemons, D. S. (1990) "Predicting the Effectiveness of Different Strategies of Advertising Variation: A Test of the Repetition-Variation Hypothesis," *Journal of Consumer Research*, 17.

15 Kuhn, Deanna (1991) *The Skills of Argument*, Cambridge: Cambridge University Press.

16 Watson, P. C. and Johnson–Laird, P. N. (1972) *The Psychology of Reason: Structure and Content*, Cambridge, MA: Harvard University Press.

17 Festinger, Leon (1957) *A Theory of Cognitive Dissonance*, Stanford, CA: Stanford University Press.

18 Ehrlich, D., Guttman, I., Schonback, P., and Mills, J. (1957) "Post-Decision Exposure to Relevant Information," *Journal of Abnormal Psychology*, 54.

19 Ortony, Andrew, Clore, Gerald L., and Collins, Allan (1990) *The Cognitive Structure of the Emotions*, Cambridge: Cambridge University Press

20 Zajonc, Robert B. and Markus, Hazel (1991) "Affective and Cognitive Factors in Preferences," in Harold H. Kassarjian and Thomas S. Robertson (eds.) *Perspectives in Consumer Behavior*, Englewood Cliffs, NJ: Prentice Hall.

21 Mittal, Banwari (1990) "The Relative Roles of Brand Beliefs and Attitude Toward the Ad as Mediators of Brand Attitude: A Second Look," *Journal of Marketing Research*, XXVII (May).

22 Droge, Cornelia (1989) "Shaping the Route to Attitude Change: Central Versus Peripheral Processing Through Comparative Versus Non-Comparative Advertising," *Journal of Marketing Research*, XXVI (May).

23 Leventhal, H. (1970) "Findings and Theory in the Study of Fear Communications," in L. Berkowitz (ed.) *Advances in Experimental Social Psychology* Vol. 5, New York: Academic Press.

24 Ehrenberg, A. S. C., Hammond, Kathy, and Goodhardt G. J. (1991) *The After-Effects of Large Consumer Promotions*, Working Paper, London Business School.

APPENDIX 11.1   SALES PROMOTIONS, CONSUMER PROMOTIONS, TRADE PROMOTIONS

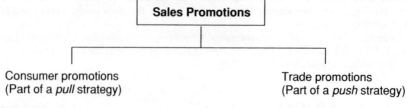

Sales Promotions

Consumer promotions (Part of a *pull* strategy)	Trade promotions (Part of a *push* strategy)
Assumptions	*Assumptions*
1 Consumers have a passive want for the product but are inhibited from buying by one or more of the following (i) Price (ii) False beliefs (iii) Doubts about the product (iv) Social norms	1 Cooperative dealers whether wholesalers or retailers
2 Inhibitors can be overcome by a material incentive	2 Profit per unit (markup) significant to dealer *and/or* shelf location/shelf space significant to sales. Dealer plays key role in the amount bought either by retailer or consumer
3 Offering has something distinctive if the aim is to create a future customer	

Figure 11.5 Sales promotions

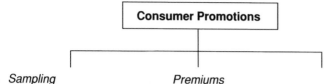

Sampling

(Free samples or trial offer)

1 Quickest way to *attract* customers for *distinctive* new product or *convert* from rivals for *distinctive* new/neglected brand.

2 Not appropriate for well-known brand or where cost is prohibitive.

3 Major problem lies in selecting a distribution system to reach target audience.

- in or near store?
- in high traffic area?
- by mail?
- by van?
- distributed door-to-door?
- via institutions? (e.g. schools)
- via parties? (e.g. food sampling parties)

Premiums

(Free or nominal cost item offered with product)

1 Quick way to give visibility to the brand.

2 Induces brand switching but whether temporary or not depends on consumer's experience with the brand.

3 Problem of selecting unusual item that fits the target audience's interests and coheres with advertising's image/message.

4 Problem of selecting form of delivery.

- in/on package?
- container itself the premium?
- displayed next to product?
- send-away for premium?
- contest? sweepstake?

Price deals

1 Quick way to induce trial where price is the inhibiting factor.

2 Major problem lies in selecting the type of price deal.

- specially priced pack
- cash refund given after proof of purchase
- branded offer (two related products sold below their combined price
- coupon whether distributed by print media, in package, direct mail or by store
- coupons encourage trade to buy in
- no special packs needed
- only coupon customers get the lower price

but

- handling allowance
- dealers can abuse
- redemption rate uncertain
- redemption period uncertain

Figure 11.6 Consumer promotions

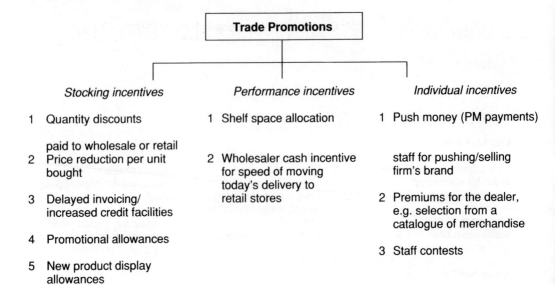

Figure 11.7 Trade promotions

Chapter 12

Developing an advertising strategy

As noted earlier, a strategy is a broad conception of how to deploy resources to over-come "resistance" to the achievement of objectives. Advertising is no exception. But what is the resistance to be overcome? There is first the barrier of ignorance about the product, but there are also the dispositions, attitudes, wants and beliefs that advertisers seek to change or reinforce.

If marketing catered to just absolute needs and buyers knew and recognized on sight which products best met those needs, advertising would simply focus on the provision of information. But marketing caters not just absolute requirements (needs) but to wants which can be latent until activated by advertising. Nor do prospective buyers necessarily understand a product sufficiently to anticipate what it would be like to possess, consume and use. Even with food products, which consumers have tasted and disliked, they may like them done in a different way so that President George Bush (who let it be known he hated broccoli) could have come to like broccoli cooked in a different way or mixed in a certain dish. He might even have tried it if it was put to him how healthy broccoli was. Advertising is a way of getting across a viewpoint, a definition of the situation, an alternative window onto a problem, a new perspective or a message that reinforces a current view. Advertising can fill the gap arising from mere observation and superficial reflection by bringing fresh facts, viewpoints and imagery to augment what is known in a casual way. If the world tomorrow was without adver-tising, it would be a world where there were far fewer perceived choices with all sorts of consequences for jobs and the standard of living. However, advertising is a waste of national resources when it neither informs, reminds nor persuades but simply consumes resources that could do good elsewhere.

This chapter helps us design an advertising strategy to avoid the problem of ineffective communications. At this stage we assume we already know the investment objective for the brand, the competitive strategy and the (core) segmentation strategy (which includes the customer target and the buying inducement) and the way the brand is positioned in the market vis-à-vis competition. Pricing and distribution will either already have been established or be tentatively agreed so we are now in a position to consider adver-tising the brand and determining the promotional budget for incorporation into the marketing strategy.

THE GLOBALIZATION ISSUE

If the organization operates internationally, there are certain questions to be addressed, answers to which determine advertising's spread:

- Is a uniform product to be sold in other countries?
- If so, is it possible to have a single advertising campaign?

Whether to market a uniform product internationally is a question not easily answered. Parker Pen tried to sell the same pens throughout the world only to meet with failure. What seems to be a product bought for the same function everywhere, turns out not to sell in other countries without modification as Parker Pen and a number of manufacturers of women's skin-care products have found to their cost. Even where a product does sell around the world (and there are many such products particularly industrial products, drugs, electronic products, and certain services), it cannot be assumed that the advertising, too, can be uniform. Nonetheless, global advertising is something to be considered since it exploits:

- commercial and production cost savings;
- greater central control over the message;
- the advent of global media like MTV and satellite networks;
- the growth of an international cosmopolitan culture;
- universal motives like the desire for status;
- the nonverbal persuasion of visual imagery;
- the increasing standardization of high-technology products.

As the world gets smaller, there is an increasing need for a consistent brand image so that buyers do not get confused as they move around the world. This is what led British Airways to adopt global advertising under the slogan: "World's Favorite Airline" and Gillette to adopt global advertising for Gillette Sensor under the slogan: "The best a man can get." But usually there is modification to the advertising to allow for cultural differences. As an example, Goodyear Tire and Rubber advertised in thirty-nine countries under the single slogan: "Goodyear, Take Me Home." But the actual commercials differed throughout the world. In Britain, the product's attributes were put over by an unseen husband and wife talking in their car. In the Philippines, there were emotional scenes of families reuniting while, in Brazil, the commercial ended with a visual joke. Similarly, the Kellogg Company's advertisements for its Frosted Flakes cereal are nearly identical throughout the world but not quite; different names are used in different countries. The problems involved in adopting uniform advertising lie in the recognition that:

- *The product may not serve the same function everywhere.* Take the example of bottled water. In Europe, the attraction is the minerals in the water but in the United States people drink bottled water for everything it does not contain! US consumers are more concerned about water purity than its mineral content so manufacturers stress their brand's additive free nature.
- *Cultural beliefs can differ.* The commercial for P&G's Wash and Go shampoo in Poland failed to take account of culture. The commercial showed a woman coming out of a swimming pool to shower though there are few people in Poland with swimming pools while the general population has baths not showers.
- *The stage in the product life cycle differs.* Thus, at the time of writing, toilet paper in Russia is considered a luxury.
- *Wants can differ.* An advertisement for a low-fat margarine as a more healthy substitute for butter was just incomprehensible in Russia, given the longing to buy any decent type of butter. People in different countries can be in different states of readiness to buy which is a problem when considering global themes. People may have similar preferred life visions, but very different wants since people

have different views about efficient and socially appropriate ways of meeting their vision.

- *Attitudes can differ*. Advertisers are finding ironically that advertising in Eastern Europe evokes memories of communist propaganda which makes people suspicious of all forms of advertising. Attitudes that are based on personal experience are stronger than those based on less direct sources. And attitudes influence the reaction to an advertisement. Thus the original and very successful "Charlie" fragrance advertisement in the United States, showing the liberated woman stepping out into the world, was not a success in Latin countries.

ELEMENTS IN ADVERTISING STRATEGY

Although a global, *uniform* advertising campaign may not be the trend, this does not rule out having a global strategy for advertising. "Think globally, act locally" might be the slogan. Kodak speaks of devising global advertising strategies but accepts that its commercials are likely to look very different throughout the world. There is an attempt to find some commonality in the elements of the advertising strategy world wide so that product image retains a *core identity*.

Whether we are talking about advertising or sales promotion, strategy involves the following:

1 a definition of the target audience;
2 a statement of goals;
3 the message strategy:
   a) persuasive focus
   b) persuasive appeal
   c) method of execution;
4 media planning; and
5 the communications budget

Figure 12.1 shows the elements in the detail to be discussed. The sheer complexity of information relevant to devising a strategy suggests that no one person will be sufficiently confident about all the details involved: it is very much a group effort.

THE DEFINITION OF THE TARGET AUDIENCE

Advertising is persuasive communication directed at some target group(s). The first step is a definition of the target audience since advertising must know to whom it is communicating. The more that is known about the group, the more relevant can be the message and the more targeted the media. Psychographic segmentation is meant to simplify the task by defining the target audience in terms of lifestyle so appeals can be linked to corresponding values, to develop a favorable attitude toward the advertisement. This favorable attitude toward the ad is assumed to carry over to the brand.

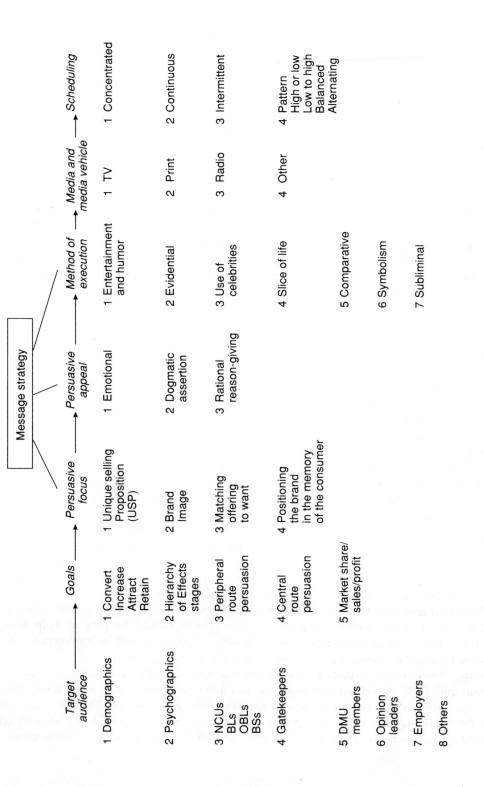

Figure 12.1 Advertising strategy elements

A useful nonpsychographic categorization of the target audience is into:

1 new category users or NCUs,
2 brand "loyals" or BLs,
3 other brand loyals or OBLs, and
4 brand switchers or BSs.

Rossiter and Percy argue these four groups reflect differences in awareness and attitude:[1]

- new category users (NCUs) have a latent or passive want for the product;
- brand loyals (BLs) are habitually buying the brand;
- other brand loyals (OBLs) are habitually buying rival brands; and
- brand switchers (BSs) typically use technical, and economic criteria as the reason for switching, though other choice criteria cannot be ruled out.

But the target audience for advertising need not be buyers as the above assumes. Thus doctors act as "gatekeepers" for prescription drugs, teachers for textbooks, and house-wives for much of the food consumed by the family. On other occasions (particularly in the advertising of services) the target audience may be the firm's own employees as a way to encourage better service. A firm like McDonald's recognizes at least three audiences: its franchisees, their customers and their employees. The target audience may even be opinion leaders or influencers outside the market. Even the advertising agen-cies may not have just the target customer group in mind as an agency tries to please the client or future clients with its cleverness! However, the primary audiences are usually those in the market segments. Advertising preferably should be directed solely at just one audience as "it is hard to communicate frankly with one audience when other audiences are listening in."

Every seller prefers to develop buyer insistence and not have to depend on inter-mediaries for stimulating sales. While drug companies seek to influence the doctor's prescriptions, the advent of health maintenance organizations (HMOs) with their cost-conscious attitude toward doctors on their lists, has led drug companies to advertise directly to the public about their prescription drugs. This allowed the "nicotine patch" (prescribed by doctors to wean people off smoking) to develop into an $800 million market.

A problem often lies in defining the target audience to help in the task of persuasion and media selection. This can be particularly difficult in industrial marketing since it is not always apparent who are the members of the relevant decision-making units (DMUs). Where a direct sales force is employed, sales people should be able to help here, providing they have been taught how to identify those involved in buying who are likely to be most influential; a topic reserved for the next chapter.

Demographic data is usually necessary but not sufficient. We need to know what the demographics mean for advertising. For example, it is not enough to know that the target audience is the well-off who are over fifty years of age. Thus it is known that the spending patterns vary among the age groups 50–64, 65–74, 75–84, and 85 and older. But what about their buying behavior and their reactions to advertisements?

Some evidence suggests that, in the United States, older people do not generally buy brands with their age in mind. Nonetheless, their choice criteria is more targeted to comfort, security, sociability, convenience and they react best to sales appeals tied to old-fashioned values that eschew too much "puffery," seeking genuine information about products. They do not want advertisements to show the discomforts that can accompany old age or try to exploit fears based on this. Thus one advertisement showing a young woman turn into a hunch-backed hag through not taking calcium pills was a disaster. They want themselves depicted as they see themselves: active, trendy, visible, with a good social life.

Gender, too, can be a factor. For example, the language used in selling cosmetics to men differs from selling the same cosmetic to women. Men are more responsive to talk about the cosmetic making them look healthier rather than beautiful. Sometimes men respond better to straight talk. Thus as one beautician says: "If you talk to a woman, you might mention the tiny wrinkles around her eyes. To guys, you can say, 'this product is great for crowsfeet'." Perhaps the right words might also get men interested in bronzing gel, which so far has not caught on!

Whether all the above about age and gender is true or not is not the point. What is important is to recognize that demographics can be highly relevant for advertising. And a change in demographics can lead to a change in advertising messages and media. Thus initially, the advertising of diet drinks was directed at non-working-class women, the category most concerned with weight and appearance. However, since diet drink advertising separately targeted men, the percentage of diet drinks drunk by men has increased in the United States from 25 percent to 44 percent. For those who accept that the buyer can be in various buyer states of readiness to buy, it is useful for advertising purposes to find out the proportion of the target audience in the various buyer states and to consider the advice shown in Table 12.1.

ADVERTISING GOALS

As mentioned in the last chapter, many marketers recommend stating communication goals in terms of hierarchy of effects stages. The typical sequence of stages is viewed as the: Learn $\Rightarrow$ Feel $\Rightarrow$ Do sequence. The cognitive (learn) component of attitude is to be changed by changing beliefs about, say, the relative importance of attributes. The affective (feel) component of attitude might be changed without changing beliefs by, say, linking the brand to pleasant associations. Finally, the behavior component (do) may be changed by, say, some direct experience such as through sampling the brand. But there are problems as different sequences are possible and members of the target audience can be at different stages while hierarchies seem to be much more appropriate to the formation of attitudes when the product is new.

Another approach is to think in terms of goals

- the goal of peripheral route persuasion to attitude change; or
- the goal of central route persuasion to attitude change if the level of involvement provides the requisite motivation.

Table 12.1 Advertising: buyer state and strategy focus

Buyer state (1)	Operational measure (2)	Goal (3)	Strategy focus (4)
Latent want	Estimate of those: • having use for the product • having ability to pay for it • ignorant of product's potential for meeting their wants or additional wants.	*Attract* new buyers or *Increase* level of purchase for additional uses.	*Want-conception* by creating awareness of the product's potential for meeting wants or *Want-development* by showing product's suitability in other uses.
Passive want	Estimate of those who know about the product and want it but are deterred by barriers not considered insurmountable.	*Attract* new buyers	*Want-conception* by advertising removal of barrier (e.g. price reduction) or minimize the importance of the barrier.
Habitual purchase	Estimate of those making repetitive purchase of single brand.	*Convert* from rivals or *Maintain* habitual customers.	*Want-focus* that undermines confidence in habitual purchase (e.g. free sample, etc.) or *Want-satisfaction* that gives reassurance to existing habitual customers.
Picking behavior	Estimate of those who alternate their purchases from among a set of brands on the grounds that there is little to choose among them.	*Convert* from rivals.	*Want-focus* by positioning brand vis-à-vis its current substitutes to establish image of superiority.
Intrinsic preference	Estimate of those buying the product *solely* on the basis of "liking best."	*Convert* from rivals.	*Want-focus* by showing how firm's product is more likely to provide form of enjoyment sought.
Extrinsic preference plus (?) intrinsic preference	Estimate mix of reasons for buying: • intrinsic • extrinsic: technical performance factors integrative factors economic factors adaptive factors.	*Convert* from rivals customers more disposed towards the firm's offering.	*Want-focus* with copy strategy in line with target audience's mix of reasons.

The problem lies in the validity of the claim that the two routes are distinct.

A final approach is the setting of competitive communication goals in terms of:

- convert (want-focus);
- increase (want-development);
- attract (want-conception); and
- maintain/retain (want-satisfaction).

Thus:

- New category users (NCUs) are to be attracted.
- Brand loyals (BLs) are to be retained or brand use increased.
- Brand switchers (BSs) are to be retained (if favorable brand switchers) or converted (if other brand switchers).
- Other brand loyals are to be converted.

There are always facts about the market that might have to be considered. For example, new category users such as the young may not be attracted for no other reason than that they seek something different from their parents. When related to the buyer state or states, the communication goals suggest the strategy focus as shown in Figure 12.2 and Table 12.1. The attract goal can be used to cover cases where the aim of advertising is not to get nonusers to immediately go out and buy. Advertising may just initiate this by creating awareness. Thus advertising for a new car simply creates awareness and enough interest to investigate further while an advertisement for car leasing may be enough to prompt buying. High brand awareness is not the same as having high familiarity with a brand since "high familiarity" means having many direct experiences with the brand. Consumers may have bought the product several times before being regarded as having high familiarity with the brand. Awareness can induce *brand recall* where the brand is recalled when such a product is wanted. If brand choice is influenced simply by what brand comes to mind first, then choice is governed by the *availability heuristic* or the rule of acting on what is first available to the mind. Awareness may instead simply induce *brand recognition* at the point of sale. A given level of recognition is reached with far fewer exposures to an ad than would be needed to achieve the same level of recall.[2]

A focused advertising campaign presupposes an audience is homogeneous in relevant respects. This is the problem, say, for Pepsi-Cola. Its primary audience is youth under thirty years of age yet it recognizes its market also includes older age groups, a segment that could be increased by advertising directly to them. Pepsi tried to do so with its "Gotta have it" campaign which featured more adults with older celebrities like Yogi Berra. The campaign was dropped as it seemed to risk turning the brand away from "its core franchise," the young. The problem remains: how to reach both groups without alienating either or diluting the impact of the campaign.

Many advertisers favor a move away from the softer measures of advertising effectiveness as reflected in communication goals, toward measures that show the contribution of advertising to sales, market share and profit. This is possible if advertising

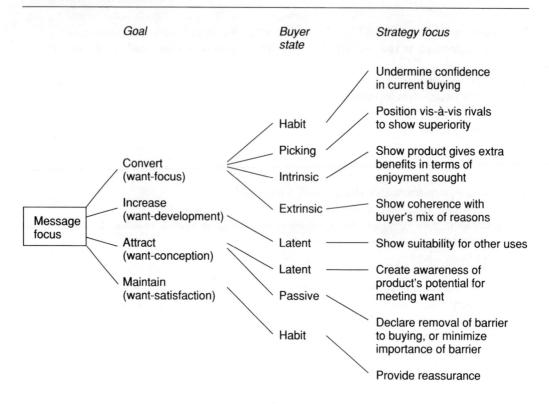

Figure 12.2 Relating competitive goals, buyer state, and strategy focus

is the only factor at work as is sometimes the case with direct marketing. But elsewhere there is the problem of separating the contribution of advertising from other antecedent events. If through surveys we estimate the numbers converted to the brand; the increased usage of the brand by existing customers; the attraction to the brand of previous nonusers and the percentages of customers retained, these can be used as measures of the effects of advertising. The goals of convert, increase, attract and maintain (retain) can be related to buyer state to suggest the focus for the strategy. Table 12.1, column 1 shows the various buyer states relevant to buying the firm's brand. These buyer states are habit; picking behavior; intrinsic preference (liking) and/or extrinsic preference embracing some combination of the choice criteria technical, economic, legalistic, integrative and adaptive. Column 2 suggests how such buyer states and the numbers in each state might be measured. Column 3 suggests the most suitable goal (whether to convert, increase, attract, or retain) given the buyer state. Finally, column 4 gives the suggested focus for the advertising strategy. Thus if the buyer state is that of picking behavior, the goal would be to convert from rivals and the strategy focus would be to position the product vis-à-vis rivals to demonstrate its competitive advantage.

THE MESSAGE STRATEGY

The process of developing a message strategy as shown in Figure 12.1 involves three steps:

1 identifying the most appropriate *persuasive focus*;
2 determining the *persuasive appeal*; and
3 determining the method of *advertising execution*.

The first two steps of identifying the most "persuasive focus" and determining the "persuasive appeal" constitute roughly what in most textbooks are termed the "message appeal" or "copy strategy" since they determine the basic message to be put across. The third step, determining the method of "advertising execution" is typically what is called the "message format" or "copy platform" since it considers how the message is to be put across to the target audience.

All the elements in these three steps form an interdependent whole so that discussion of them separately can be misleading if it creates the impression that each element can be considered in isolation. The whole process of developing the message strategy is an iterative process, as we move back and forth among the elements. Whether we believe in moving the target audience through some hierarchy of effects or just choosing between central and peripheral routes or just focusing on the task to be done (e.g. converting etc.), the elements in these three steps will need to be considered, using the material in the last chapter as a theoretical guide in devising the persuasive tactics themselves.

Whatever the message strategy that finally emerges, it must first capture the attention of the target audience. The emotional content of the advertisement, its novelty, its capacity to arouse curiosity, its repetition are all factors that can draw attention to an advertisement. However, sustained attention (interest), will always depend on the advertisement's tie to the wants of the audience.

The more focused the advertisement, the more effective it is likely to be. The shotgun approach of trying to convert, increase, attract and retain by packing the advertisement with as many messages as possible is seldom an effective tactic. Second, there must also be a recognition of any changes occurring. For example, when the economy is low, there may be a dislike of conspicuous consumption, or the social climate may demand more sensitivity to be shown in the portrayal of women and other groups.

No marketer can predict with any certainty whether the target audience will interpret the advertisement as intended. Thus while Dow Chemicals may seek to project a caring image in its commercials, these advertisements may be interpreted (at least initially) as a cover-up of past and present sins. What persuades is very much a function of the belief systems of the target audience. But beliefs change which means that yesterday's advertising may become unsuitable today for the persuasive task to be done. In any case, the message strategy must take account of the advertising of rivals to ensure advertising is saying something distinctive and to know what competitors have already done to make the market aware of the product.

Identifying the most persuasive focus

Identifying the most persuasive focus means deciding the overall focus of the advertising. For our purposes, this could be any of the following:

- the *unique selling proposition* (USP);
- *brand image*;
- *matching offering to the want*; or
- *positioning the brand in the mind of the consumer.*

The unique selling proposition

Rosser Reeves, a legendary name in advertising, argued that reason, not unconscious hidden desires, was key in buying and pushed what has come to be known as "the unique selling proposition" (USP), that is, a message with a unique promise. The method usually singles out an offering's key demonstrable attribute and hammers it home through constant repetition. Thus Apple Computer is currently proclaiming the Mac is now affordable. This claim is a declaration that the Mac is now the best value for money on the market. This assumes a large passive want in the market that is merely inhibited by price. A promise or USP is more likely to be persuasive when rivals are not promising the same, that is, the promise is truly unique, and there is considerable dissatisfaction over what is on offer. Whether this is so in the Apple case is a matter of dispute.

The USP is likely to be based on the buying inducement as set out in the segmentation strategy and is a focus very much tied to benefit segmentation. The USP avoids confusing the audience with a multiplicity of messages. However, the problem (as Reeves himself saw) is never one of finding some unique thing to say (every offering will have something unique to offer) but of saying something that is not only unique but of central value to the audience. Thus where Cadbury's Marvel, a powdered, dried skim milk, was both unique and of central value to the customer's purpose was in the making of light, white coffee, as Marvel does away with the need to heat milk, avoids the use of cold milk (which cools the coffee), and is conveniently available. But it should not be assumed that the USP has to come across as a blunt declaration since it can be applied in some dramatic way (for example, Maxwell House's "Good to the last drop"). Some centrally important claims in advertising are not unique, like the constant claim of high quality. These can be so general as to lack credibility unless backed by evidence. The USP, though, may not be unique to the brand but simply unique in that the firm alone is making the claim. Thus one firm claims its cigarette is "toasted" which applies in fact to all flue-cured tobacco. Similarly, one airline stresses its safety precautions though they are no different from competition.

Brand image

Advocates of USP claim the consumer is becoming more and more sensitive to functional performance, more concerned about getting value for money and not paying just for brand image. Opponents, on the other hand, claim that, with brand proliferation and the surfeit of advertising messages, the only way to get through the clutter is through creative advertising that focuses on images. Many brands have no USP to put over and a hard sell on pushing minor technological improvements irritates more than it persuades. Feeling positive in response to seeing the brand may determine attitude, not a more objective assessment of direct experience with the brand.

A brand image focus is associated with David Ogilvy. Brand image is the collective perception of the brand that influences buyer views about the brand's performance in the various functions for which it is bought. Sometimes the promise projected by the brand is simply that it will lift the consumer away from boredom, dreariness and toward a more exciting life. The *purpose* of promoting brand image is to associate the brand with desirable qualities and give the brand a distinctive, likable, memorable identity. The *function* of brand image in the communications mix is to provide an informational anchor that conceptualizes the brand as being one which people like those in the target audience would or should prefer. The image projected should be one that suggests the brand was specifically designed with the target audience's values or fantasies in mind. The *role* of brand image in promotion is to obtain a distinctive position for the brand in the mind of the consumer in a way that connotes its benefits. The brand with an up-market image can give its owner confidence, a sense of status, and enhance satisfaction over and above the brand's performance in its use functions. But many companies today are finding it difficult to establish a preferred image for each of their brands so resort is being made more and more to stressing the company name. Thus Heinz, with 300 products, is moving toward stressing the name "Heinz" and what are seen to be fundamental Heinz values.

A focus on brand image is associated with emotional bonding with customers, helping consumers feel better about themselves. Many marketers claim that top brands have remained the top brands not because they have any technical advantage but because of their image. When people in the United States think of McDonald's they think of more things than hamburgers, including cleanliness of its outlets, its social performance, and its symbolism as a core piece of America: all evoking a feeling of warmth toward the firm and its products.

The recalling of a brand-name with a rich image is like recalling the name of a book or film whose contents are well known: both the name of the brand and the name of the book or film conjure up all sorts of images without much cognitive processing (and people wish to conserve mental energy). When brand images are tied to values, this leads the buyer into thinking favorably about the brand. An example here is the promotion of raisins. Before a certain well-known campaign in the United States, research had demonstrated that consumers already understood all the healthy, rational benefits of raisins but people's attitude toward them was either neutral or negative. A campaign was undertaken by the industry to improve the image of raisins, in fact to give them a "hipper" image. The result was a dramatic increase in the sales of raisins.

Some manufacturers in promoting brand image ignore the physical product altogether. This has been true of both Esprit, a California jeans manufacturer, and Bennetton, which both push social themes like ending racism. This is to both get attention and appeal to the values of the young who are less tolerant of the world's injustices. Both firms have had campaigns showing its family of customers around the world to provide the global image of the firm. Another jeans firm, Pepe Jeans, preferred to create a brand image through celebrity association, using Jason Priestly, a TV star, on the ground that "Jason personifies what we'd like Pepe to be . . . an image of romance for Pepe that it doesn't have today." Transformational advertising is a form of image advertising that seeks to create brand associations aimed at changing the use-experience with the brand. A brand image, though, develops regardless through actual experience with the product and this is likely to be the most lasting image.

Though brand images are not just formed by advertising, advertising tries to build a brand image by taking some appropriate attractive image and trying to attach it to the brand. Sometimes the image is an illicit graft that does not take. But the buyer does not have to believe, say, there is some connection between his after-shave and his sex appeal for an advertisement suggesting the connection to work. The advertisement in suggesting this new meaning, that brand X after-shave $\Rightarrow$ sexual attractiveness will have done something to put the connection in the consumer's mind. With constant repetition, the connection may be passively accepted; enough perhaps to influence buying. Image building uses *allusion* as one vehicle for transferring its associations. One ad makes an allusion to another by referring to it indirectly. Thus one advertisement for Shell gasoline alludes to the brand by reference to a tiger whose qualities (e.g. aggressiveness) are meant to denote and/or exemplify the brand. Metaphor makes use of allusion. Thus one brewer refers to one of its brands as the "King of beers"; the metaphor denotes the beer in its metaphorical extension while only alluding to those (kings) in its literal extension. With allusion, we are using indirect means for persuasion. Carefully chosen words here are important in inducing the right perspective or definition of the situation. We are influenced by the way a situation is characterized. Thus Germany's environmental minister refers not to rubbish or garbage but to "secondary raw material" which provides an entirely different perspective as to its usefulness. At the more mundane level we have car sales people who refer not to used cars but "preowned" cars. The recognition of the importance of words to perspectives and corresponding attitudes is what motivates advocates of political correctness on US college campuses.

Brand images are not easy to manipulate. Attempts to establish a prestige brand image can be defeated by the consumer refusing to go along. Consumers recognize projected images can be deceptive and many factors contribute to brand image that are beyond the control of the seller. Consumers are more impressed with information they believe cannot be manipulated for purposes of deception (e.g. the materials out of which the product is made). Manipulating brand image is easier when objective contrary evidence is not available.

Matching offering to the want

The aim in matching the firm's offering to the want is to show the firm's offering is the best fit on the ground that we should not distort the wants of the consumer: "there is more money in just selling them what they want." The focus is saying: this is what the consumer says she wants according to the multiattribute model, or her ideal point on the perceptual map or the noncompensatory rules she employs, and we are going to demonstrate that our offering is the best fit to what is wanted. The focus assumes a fairly rational buyer and an offering that is good enough to make this claim. It is not an uncommon alternative to *image* advertising in the selling of cars and it is a common focus in industrial marketing and the selling of services. However, in the selling of services, because it is often easy to know what constitutes "good" service, it is all too easy to promise the best but completely fail to deliver on the promise.

Positioning the brand in the mind

Positioning the brand in the mind is an attempt to secure a unique position for the brand in the mind of the consumer. This presupposes the advertiser knows via perceptual mapping or whatever, how brands in the market are currently categorized in the mind of the consumer. The next step is to select a unique and meaningful position there: a position that will differentiate the brand from its rivals; be consistent with the core advantage of the brand and provide a reason for buying the brand. Positioning in the mind can be on many dimensions of the product, not just one unique attribute as per the USP though the logic is the same in both cases. The USP certainly says how it would like to be distinguished from competition but beyond that consumers may not distinguish it from competition. Nonetheless, USP can give a brand a unique position in the mind of the consumer vis-à-vis competition but it is not necessarily directed at doing this.

Positioning a brand in the mind of the consumer is important, given the multitude of brands there usually are in the market. When light beer in the United States first appeared, it was positioned as a woman's beer. It failed until Miller brought out a light beer and positioned it for "males under 49 years of age and of a sporty disposition." This is not surprising since the position of the brand in the mind of the consumer affects how the brand is recalled or perceived. Sometimes a way to position the brand in the mind is through the brand-name, just as the name "Nice 'n' Easy," the Clairol brand of hair coloring, conveys the idea of simplicity and convenience. Sometimes positioning is done by contrasting the brand with more famous rivals. In emphasizing how the firm's brand differs, the known brands act as anchor points for a juxtaposition of the brands. Thus 7-Up was advertised as the "Un-cola," while such descriptions as "off-track betting" or "tubeless tires" tend also to be remembered for their contrasts. To say a dog is a mongrel with short legs and droopy ears is less memorable than saying the dog is a cross between a dachshund and a spaniel. Positioning a brand firmly in the mind of the consumer can be effective in what would otherwise be a picking situation since it helps both brand recall and brand recognition.

Determining the persuasive appeal

Persuasive appeals are usually an amalgam of:

- emotional appeals ("feel")
- rational, reason-giving appeals ("learn/think")
- dogmatic assertions ("do")

Emotional appeals

Every manufacturer or seller would like to establish an emotional bond between brand and buyer. Many of the slogans used in advertisements have an emotional ring to them like Campbell's Soup's "M'm, M'm, Good!"; Hallmark Card's "When you care enough to send the very best"; AT&T's "Reach out and touch someone"; Nike's "Just do it" and Gillette's "The best a man can get." These slogans operate as symbols (signs with meaning for the recipient) because they are tied to our values. *Slogans tied to values can be powerful as witness such slogans as: "A war to make the world safe for democracy." This is because symbols give order and simplicity to an otherwise puzzling complexity. Symbols, too, can compensate for present tensions just as symbols of farm life on the packaging of butter have been found to be appealing to those living in cities.*

There are certain community values that everyone absorbs and makes part of his or her value system, like the value of friendship. There is also the universal value of enhancing self-esteem. The desire for high self-esteem is very powerful as it is tied to the self-assessment emotions of pride, envy, shame, guilt, and personal integrity. Pride is tied to self-esteem in that what one is proud of is that which others perceive as increasing one's standing in the world at large. We envy something about others that we would like to have but, when we are consumed with envy, self-esteem is likely to suffer because of the comparison with our own position. Shame results from violating internalized norms of behavior with the result that self-respect suffers, which in turn reduces self-esteem. Guilt arises from violating some rule or norm of an accepted authority (religious taboo or the law). This results in a sense of reduced standing in the relevant community which again is a reduction in self-esteem. Loss of a sense of personal integrity arises from violating one's own code of personal values. This reduces self-respect and so reduces self-esteem. Although we have certain universal values, every subculture also has distinct values and a problem for every advertising agency is to identify those values to make appeals as directly relevant as possible. *The major research task lies in identifying the symbols that express the values, just as the national anthem or the nation's flag symbolize national identity.* One way to show the advertising is on the right wave band is to use the language of the target audience. This explains the increasingly common use of the vernacular: it allows advertisers to use words and phrases of the target audience. Thus the expression "You gotta get this thing" heard in one popular commercial came from focus groups.

Appeals to values via appropriate symbolism are particularly important when there is ambiguity surrounding which brand to buy, in a market where brands just seem to be tokens of each other. Advertisers also seek emotional appeals as a way of drawing attention to the advertisement. Pictures are useful here because of the power of the picture to say things which cannot be said in words without sounding just a little silly. Some marketers see the visual being used much more commonly to replace talk because "visualizing claims in dramatic capsules can by-pass the critical faculty."

It was argued in Chapter 4 that consumers should not be regarded as just a bundle of wants which act as a filter determining what products they will buy since people can come to want something through persuasive communication, particularly by emotional appeals to the imagination. By getting prospects to imagine in an emotional way what something would be like to have and to use, is essentially a method of *self-persuasion*. Value systems and our major attitudes probably result from past emotional episodes. Certainly threats to what we value arouse us emotionally and such emotions can be highly motivating. But this is not the only view as to how values arise. The behaviorist simply regards them as the result of reinforcement schedules while the Freudian tendency is to view them as neurotic rigidities.

It is wrong to view emotion as the enemy of reason. Emotional reasons can be good reasons: rationality does not have to be cold. In any case, emotions are responsive to beliefs in that emotions can change as beliefs change, for example, regarding the safety of traveling by air. But more important, emotions fill the gap left by reason by weighting the factors entering into decision-making.[3] Where there is no way of measuring trade-offs in terms of some common scale like money, emotions come to the rescue in directing the decision. This is not to suggest that strong emotions cannot interfere with thinking objectively. Thus the emotional behavior of investors in bull and bear markets seems to defy prediction. This is probably why professional advisers, acting rationally, do less well in bull and bear markets.

Emotions are like an urgent judgment about a situation judged to be highly unpleasant or highly pleasant. This is why an emotional response is not always in line with inter-ests soberly considered. People are in an emotional state whenever they evaluate some-thing as highly pleasant or highly unpleasant, resulting in some physiological change such as an increase in pulse rate, heart beat, flushing, sweating, or muscular tension. But being in an emotional state does not necessarily cause any bodily feelings of which we are aware. For example, a person may not be aware of his blood pressure rising. On the other hand, it seems wrong to speak of unexperienced emotions except in the case where the emotion has not reached the level of intensity above the threshold required for it to be experienced. Whenever some stimulus exemplifies something in the preferred life vision or is diametrically opposed to it, an emotional response is likely. This is because dramatic portrayals of aspects of the preferred life vision meet with a gut reac-tion of approval while the opposite is repelling. Emotional appeals in advertising seek to induce either highly positive evaluations of some item, action or event *or* seek to induce a desire to avoid future fear or anxiety by buying the firm's product, with adver-tising trying to make the audience worry enough (fearful enough) (e.g. being without insurance) to take action.

It is claimed four cognitive appraisal processes mediate the choice of how an audi-ence is going to react to a fear appeal:

1 the perceived severity and nearness of the threat;
2 the perceived probability that the threat will occur;
3 perceived ability of a coping behavior to remove the threat; and
4 perceived ability to carry out the coping behavior.[4]

As a consequence, advertising should give the target audience information on

a) the severity and nearness of the threat;
b) the probability of its occurrence;

c) the effectiveness of certain coping strategies; and
d) the speed and ease with which the coping response can be implemented.

An advertisement may relate to the social tensions of the age and offer a solution via the buying of the brand. Thus one cigarette advertisement suggests a woman can both be in the forefront of undermining male dominance yet remain sexually alluring with the advertised brand of cigarette solving the conflict! Advertisements may contain themes that reflect the fantasies of the target audience. *Fantasies* are thoughts we entertain that are free of being evaluated for their relevance to our problems or the world around us. Fantasy in psychology corresponds to what is popularly called *daydreaming*. The playful or fearful images and counterfactual propositions that make up our fantasies often accompany the processing of external stimuli and are a way of thinking about different possible futures, goals and past intentions. Fantasies have the capacity to stimulate the emotions and, even though fantasies are known to be false, they can be felt to be true. It is perhaps in fantasizing that our ideal self-image takes shape to influence buying in line with that image or fantasy or gives rise to wishful thinking in which the buying of some product becomes a step on the road toward attaining some dream.

   Typically, the dimensions associated with emotional stimuli are:[5]

- *activation*: associations of being alive, and full of vitality as opposed to being bored and sluggish;
- *relatedness*: associations of warm, close, loving relationships with others as opposed to being lonely, isolated and an outsider;
- *hedonic tone*: association with achieving inner harmony, and relaxation as opposed to being in a state of anxiety; and
- *competence*: associations of being in control of life, and having a sense of accomplishment as opposed to feeling unable to cope.

These dimensions are tied to values or the preferred life vision and when embodied in an advertisement may arouse emotion (however slight) through the mechanisms of conditioning, contagion or identification:

- *conditioning*: conditioning can occur because events can have associations that stimulate a conditioned response (e.g. a loving mother).
- *contagion*: behavior exhibited by others can be contagious. Thus everyone clapping or laughing serves to suggest some social consensus which becomes a cue for others to imitate: it is the thing to do to signify one belongs. Anything that makes for similarity with the characters (like circumstances, age, or background) increases emotional contagion. One advertisement that tries to exploit contagion, shows the product being demonstrated, with the words "I'm impressed," appearing on the screen.
- *identification*: one form of identification in advertising is identification with someone's frustration arising from some *interrupted* plan. Thus in one advertisement we see the hostess's entertainment plans being interrupted by seeing that the wine glasses are "spotty." The audience identifies with the situation and the character's disappoint-

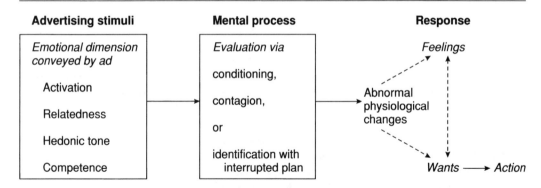

Figure 12.3 Emotion in advertising

ment and glee when Cascade (a dishwasher detergent) remedies the situation. It is not so much that we identify with the fictional characters in the TV commercial than that we assimilate the situation, coming to see the situation both from the point of view of the characters in the situation and from the outside as well. We do not so much identify with the housewife in feeling her embarrassment but understand why she would be embarrassed because of our grasp of the situation. Without this capacity for understanding, no theater would be possible.

Figure 12.3 illustrates the process. Not all of the physiological changes can be introspected as feelings, so a dotted line is shown going from the autonomic physiological changes to feelings. Similarly, autonomic physiological changes need not give rise to wants: not all emotions have an appetitive component. This latter point raises a related issue. *Advertising may activate an emotion but the problem is to channel that emotion in the direction of buying the brand advertised.* The target audience can be emotionally activated but not necessarily into buying the brand advertised. There is also the problem of ensuring advertising *connects to the experiences* that lie behind the values symbolized in the advertisement. Many marketers consider this the most difficult task of all in trying to generate emotion in advertising: the right emotional buttons are not always marked for pressing, though claims are made for focus groups and the use of psychographic data as useful for identifying emotions and values.

Conditioning, contagion, and identification suggest the mechanisms at work in producing a *national mood*. A mood, as an emotional state, differs from normal emotions in being diffused and attached to no specific object, being more a persistent feeling tied to personality or perceived quality of life rather than to any one event or situation. Moods can be the lingering effects of a series of events that are emotionally charged. There are times when sizable segments of the population can coalesce in a common mood. Thus national events such as the crime and unemployment figures and perceptions of the country's international stature (e.g. as, say, judged in international sport competitions!) can affect national mood. Knowledge of moods can be important since moods dispose us to make certain types of evaluation and to be even more selectively perceptive of the facts. Thus during a recession the mood is to evaluate certain types of expenditure as wasteful or as insensitive to the plight of others and to selectively pick product attributes that suggest good value for money. Shoppers in a good mood are more likely to buy and be satisfied with a store. When personal service staff uplift customer mood this can be a factor in disposing the customer to buy or repeat a buy.

There are certain anti-pleasure moods and suggested counter-measures:[6]

Anti-pleasure mood	*Advertisement counter-measures*
Jangled nerves	Something soothing
Feel dull	Something exciting
Feel bored	Something amusing
Life unmanageable	Return to simpler life

The return to the simpler life gives rise to nostalgic feelings accompanied by a desire to relive earlier times. In times of rapid change, life can seem unmanageable as the experiences and informational anchors that give people a sense of security and personal identity disappear. *Nostalgia* is one form of longing for something different from the present: longing for something lost like "paradise" itself. Nostalgia is common during people's lives when careers have leveled off, and values seem to be changing. However, what is nostalgic for one audience is not necessarily nostalgic for another while the objects of nostalgia need not be just places but can be the celebrities who typified the past. This may account for the Ford Motor Company's use of the Beatles' song of 1965, *Help* in its advertising and the return of old slogans like Timex's "it takes a licking but it keeps on ticking" and the revival of certain brands and magazines. However, nostalgic advertising tends to give rise to an anti-nostalgic backlash in advertising appealing to the young though if the young includes thirty year olds, the 1980s can be nostalgic for them.

The power of emotional bonding is best seen in the attachment to a brand that may be objectively undifferentiated from its rivals. This attachment is a feeling, typically built up from past pleasant associations with possessing, using or consuming the brand. Familiarity does not breed contempt of brands that have served the consumer well. On the contrary, it leads to increasing sentiment toward the brand. If, on some occasion, the brand is at a disadvantage (e.g. price remains higher than its rivals) and still the consumer sticks to it, this demonstrates the core concept of what we mean by loyalty. It is the loyalty of the child for its security blanket, refusing to accept a like substitute.

Dogmatic assertion

If nostalgia focuses on "feel" or feelings, the dogmatic assertion focuses on "do" (action). Any appeal can just be dogmatically asserted (for example, Brand X is the lowest tar cigarette; Switch to—; Success starts with—; It's time for—). The dogmatic assertion is a persuasive device when put across by a confident speaker in a self-assured way. The nonverbal, too, can add to that persuasiveness such as body posture, dress, authoritative tone of voice and so on. The dogmatic appeal may be in the form of a slogan, for example, "builds bonny babies." But whatever the type of dogmatic assertion, its aim is to convey conviction to lend credibility to the message. Precision in dogmatic statements (Ivory soap's 99.44/100 percent pure) can add credibility as does the documentary style of presentation.

Rational, reason-giving appeals

If the nostalgic appeal focuses on "feel" and the dogmatic assertion on "do." the reason-giving appeal focuses on "learn/think." Rational, reason-giving appeals explain why the message is right, correct or true. It is a common form of appeal when the product is complex and there is high involvement with the purchase. However, the distinction between reason-giving appeals and the emotional is not as clear-cut as would be assumed, not only because emotional factors can be built into a rational argument as reasons for buying but because reason-giving appeals are modeled not on formal logic but the rules consumers actually use. The logic in decision-making logic is not the deductive logic going from premises to conclusion but from goals/problems to a consideration of alternatives that best meet the goals. Even where some deduction does enter into the decision, it has its own logic, namely:

- the premises in some commercial or advertisement are those already believed by the target audience: they are not necessarily true; and
- the passage from premises to conclusion is of an acceptable kind, being more likely based on analogy than anything resembling formal logic.

Determining the method of execution

The way a persuasive appeal is put across can be decisive. It is not just what one says but how one says it. But whatever way is selected to put across the appeal, its first job is to get attention. For example, in TV, it has long been recognized that viewers are not a captive audience as they zip through commercials when they play back tapes or zap through other channels while a commercial is on. On-screen typography has become one way to capture attention. Thus one commercial for AT&T has screens full of kinetic words in eye-catching typefaces—nine varieties whizzing past in 30 seconds! In magazine advertising, there are many gimmicks like the advertisement for Absolut vodka which played Christmas carols, using a microchip embedded in the magazine page while another advertisement created a globe inside a page filled with plastic snowflakes that would swirl around the tiny Absolut vodka bottle wrapped in a red scarf. Of course, getting attention is one thing but having the message remembered is another. Psychologists (and our experience in reading examinations!) tell us that points put first (the primary effect) and points put last (the recency effect) are most likely to be remembered while the strongest points are best put first if a critical audience is to show interest. Some methods of execution can now be discussed.

Entertainment and humor

There are two reasons why an entertaining or humorous execution is adopted, particularly in TV commercials. First, making commercials fun to watch is one way of holding on to the viewer. The other has to do with the fact that for most of those watching TV, it is a move away from anxieties toward being relaxed or sometimes (e.g. watching sports), it is a move away from boredom toward excitement. In either case, viewers are interested in entertainment, not in heavy thinking. Hence entertaining and humorous commercials fit viewer predispositions. This probably explains the success of serial or *episodic advertising* campaigns like the one for Nestlé coffee where the viewer experiences "the magical, mystical moments of courtship, of possibility." Serials become soap operas, allowing the characters to develop their own personalities with which the viewer can identify. The serials tell a story that builds on the previous one. This contrasts with the usual commercial with everyone carrying out the same routine.

Humorous commercials, a specialty of British commercials, are becoming common. Perhaps, people want to be cheered up when times are tough. Humor (not just jokes) is a way of resisting control and the social pressures arising from everyday life. But humor is also attention-getting and can be a distraction to thinking of counterarguments so allowing the advertising message to be absorbed. However, humor is always tricky to orchestrate and can be trying if the same advertisement is constantly being repeated. While entertainment goes with emotional appeals, we have no conceptual framework for even knowing (beyond our own experience) what will in fact be found entertaining by various target audiences.

Evidential and factual

Evidence under the banner of science has high credibility. Some cynics argue that anything presented as science is believed and nothing believed when presented as religion! In any case, arguments that are evidential and factual are common in advertising to industrial users and in advertising services since buyers in both cases seek something tangible to go on. Long messages tend to be persuasive on the ground that message length suggests the advertiser believes the message is true and important.

Use of celebrities

A high percentage (around 40 percent in the United States) of TV commercials use celebrities. According to the likelihood elaboration model, the use of celebrities is most appropriate for persuasion via the peripheral route, suggesting low involvement on the part of the consumer. What little evidence there is suggests that the use of celebrities tends to produce above average brand awareness but only about half of the celebrities have a positive effect on consumer attitudes toward the product. This suggests more consideration should be given to choosing the celebrity. Ideally, the celebrity should

- exemplify the values being promoted;
- have an intimate nonaggressive style (combative language generally is not suited to TV with an audience more receptive to loving than fighting);
- have a background like that of the target audience; and
- achievements that mirror the longings of the target audience.

Spokespersons categorized as similar to self are likely to be more persuasive as such celebrity spokespersons are more likely to be pro-normative, that is, supportive of the norms or standards of the target audience. Ideally the target audience should have a sense of shared social identity with the celebrity spokesperson. One reason why beliefs are resistant to change by advertising is because the target audience believes such beliefs are those upheld by their peer group. One way of persuading them is to show such beliefs are not in fact held by significant people in their social milieu. A good many social problems are eased by appeals involving spokespersons who are respected by the target group. In consumer marketing, the extent to which people are influenced by celebrities depends on how knowledgeable they are already. In any case, the celebrity might "sell the first bottle of fragrance but the scent has to sell the second."

Slice of life advertising

A play is a slice of life and slice of life advertising is like a miniature play involving some incident (like the spotty glasses described earlier) that demonstrates use of the product. With slice of life advertising, we are able to say things that would otherwise be difficult to express directly and coldly. For example, one advertisement for Chivas Regal Scotch shows a man at a bar requesting: "A Scotch please." When a beautiful and sophisticated young woman sits next to him, he immediately changes his order: "Chivas on the rocks" while she seems to give her approval. What is often forgotten by advertisers is the need for the product-user in a slice of life advertisement to belong to groups with whom the target audience will self-categorize.[7] It is not enough that the target audience belongs by having that particular problem, as seems to be commonly assumed; the group must not be a negative reference group. *Members of the target audience can fit the label but not the stereotype.* Consumers must perceive it as socially appropriate to self-categorize themselves with the group to which they nominally belong. Slice of life advertising is a form of *self-persuasion* through the mechanism of *self-imagining* because slice of life advertising allows the audience to imagine or dream they are these characters who are trying to solve a common problem, helped by using the brand.

Comparative advertising

In the United States, positioning in the mind, dogmatic appeals, reason-giving appeals and comparative advertising go together. Comparative advertising is a tactic for new entrants with some strong competitive advantage who want to make an impact quickly. It has also been used to regain market position, as witness Maxwell House of General

Foods in its aggressive attacks on P&G's Folgers brand of coffee. Comparative ads have been banned in many parts of Europe. Though they are now ostensibly permitted in the EC, restrictions are so severe as to ban them in practice. This contrasts with the United States, where about 30 percent of TV ads shown on network television are comparative. But comparative claims are getting risky; legal suits against the comparative ad are becoming more and more common. While comparative advertising has been found to enhance purchase intentions, the advertising profession as a whole has not been enthusiastic. In the first place, it seems to require no creativity to knock the competition. A second reason is that, when competitors respond, it develops into a shouting match that lowers the credibility of both advertisers and perhaps advertising in general.

Consumers can be put off by strident and offensive advertising claims to brand superiority. This is because many comparisons have nothing to do with how buyers make choices as the superior differences being claimed are not differences that enter into the consumer's choice criteria. Thus one advertisement contrasted "our brand's" fresh ingredients with the dry ingredients of the major rival's brand. In actual fact the dried ingredients were what made the taste so good!

Symbolism

Much image advertising relies on emotional symbolism. This is because image advertising is not concerned with leading the target audience to some conclusion through an inference process but to conjure up a certain perspective so as to get the audience to reinterpret something about the brand. We can take, as an example, the famous Marlboro cowboy cigarette advertisement. To understand the success of this advertisement, we first ask ourselves what associations does the ad conjure up with its symbolism:

- the Western lifestyle as propagated by American movies where life is simple, without the complications of present day living; where the bad and the good are easily distinguished and men are men, engaged in manly pursuits;
- strong masculine image of rugged individualism, independence, and strength; and
- although the cowboy is alone, except for that faithful friend, a horse, the theme projected is not that of isolation or loneliness but of independence of others, a declaration of individuality that is welcome to those feeling dependence on others for emotional sustenance.

Although such ex post facto explanation of the advertisement's success is easy to accept, it is less easy to identify the experiences, the values and the symbols that arouse such emotional bonding. Yet this advertisement took a lackluster brand targeted at women into being the number one brand in the United States. However, all symbols and imagery need to be updated and it is difficult to know at present whether the continuing success of the Marlboro ad has more to do with being tops than through continuation of the same advertising. Another example is an advertisement for Schlitz beer based on the slogan: "You only go around once in life, so go for the gusto." This emanated from a psychographic profile of the heavy beer drinker in the United States as

- more of a risk-taker;
- more self-indulgent; more interested in sports;
- less concerned about responsibilities; and
- with a strong preference for physical male-oriented action.

This slogan links to values (which is what psychographics do) by offering support for following a hedonistic lifestyle. The link is with the specific values of the target customer group, that is, the link is to subgroup values not to society values as a whole.

Symbolism need not involve words and some advertising dispenses with words altogether by just showing pictures, sometimes with animals, babies, beautiful girls and other symbols of things lovable. The full meaning is left to the imagination of the audience. This is true for Japanese consumer advertising, where the advertising focuses on images as analogies for the product such as showing not the Mitsubishi car itself but a speedy lizard. This strong focus on imagery in Japan is defended on the grounds that in Japan quality is taken for granted and the problem is to get attention and "an indecipherable ad may stick in the consumer's mind, if only because he or she is trying to figure it out." If words are used they are "purr" words, that is, words with no reference, lots of ambiguity but rich in overtones of positive connotations; political speeches and advertising are full of them. Ambiguous advertising (as is common in transformational advertising) intrigues those seeking excitement but irritates many others: make sure your target audience belongs to the first group!

Some symbols constitute the trademark. The top-hatted, monocle-wearing dandy on every packet of Planters nuts is typical. It was common at one time to view such characters as too old fashioned for a modern era. But such symbols give identity to the product and its familiarity helps generate liking and with liking can come some loyalty. What was wrong was not the use of such symbols per se but not keeping them fresh and up-to-date. A good example is Beefeater gin. The advertisers wanted to get away from the Beefeater symbol of a white man with a beard looking very stoic in English military uniform, carrying a weapon! On the other hand, they wanted some symbolic continuity to not antagonize those customers to whom the symbol was a bonding. The bright red tunic (worn by beefeaters who guard the crown jewels in the Tower of London) was continued but minus the man and presented in humorous, unexpected ways.

Symbolic characters on packets can at times be too successful. This is the case with Old Joe, the camel appearing in ads for Camel cigarettes. One sunbathing camel asserts smoking is suave while another portrays a group of camels as a jazz band, complete with sunglasses and hip clothing. This attractive camel, with its pro-smoking message, has been all too successful in getting young children to start smoking. R. J. Reynolds, whose brand it is, is having a hard time defending Old Joe camel advertising.

Symbolism, though, can often offend as people interpret differently. Thus we have the Bennetton advertisements that have shocked many people and reveal how different cultures, with their own particular history, will interpret symbolism differently. Thus the white-baby/black-breast advertisement that won awards in France and Italy, outraged many Americans, particularly black Americans who were reminded in the advertisement of how slave girls did in fact breast feed white babies.

Subliminal advertising: The myth and the reality

Many consumers believe they can be influenced by subliminal messages. Many think they are highly effective and are willing to pay money for tapes with subliminal messages to help them lose weight, be more assertive, study harder, enhance their self-image and so on. In 1992, Americans bought 5 million subliminal tapes. Books have been written showing how advertisers put the letters s-e-x in the ice cubes of a gin ad; penises in pats of margarine and so it goes on. It is not that subliminal messages never get through. Research has shown that people can detect stimuli below the level of conscious awareness, though the ability to do so varies along normal distribution lines. It is also true that people can be influenced by suggestions of which they are unaware as occurs when someone acts on a suggestion made under hypnosis. But this is something different from claiming subliminal advertising is an effective means of persuasion. We will return to this topic later in the chapter when we consider the claims about advertising and manipulation.

There have been various attempts to give general guidance on choosing a message strategy. In Table 12.2 are the recommendations of Rossiter and Percy in their text on advertising. The first step in using the table is to categorize the buying by the type of purchase decision and the type of motivation involved. The type of purchase decision can be high-involvement or low-involvement and the type of motivation can be informational or transformational. *Informational motivation* covers negative motives where the motive is to avoid or remove a problem (e.g. a headache), dissatisfaction with current brand or routine replacement purchases. Informational motivation contrasts with *transformational motivation*, which covers motives of a positive or appetitive origin where the motive is to seek additional sensory enjoyment, intellectual stimulation or social approval which roughly corresponds to intrinsic liking and integrative criteria.

If we look at Table 12.2, the low-involvement/informational category of consumers is assumed to want relief but at minimum cost in terms of effort as there is not much at stake. Further, because of the low risk, consumers are not likely to be critical of what is communicated which assumes the target audience has no active contrary beliefs or doubts that are resurrected at the time of exposure to the advertising. For the high-involvement/transformational category, the target audience is assumed to want relief for their problem but because of the high-involvement, consumers believe they need to equip themselves with more information to choose wisely. For the low-involvement/ transformational category, consumers seek the good feelings that are anticipated to arise from possessing, using or consuming the product, and because of the low involvement, are open to believing what they *feel* to be true. For the high-involvement/transformational category, it is assumed consumers want the good feelings anticipated to result from possessing, using or consuming the product but because of the high involvement they need more convincing that what they feel to be true is actually so.

It is not clear that all members of a target audience will fit neatly into just one of the four categories which do not have hard boundaries. However, though the advice will be found to be very general when applied to concrete cases, it is nonetheless useful to consider.

Table 12.2 Type of motivation/type of decision and message strategy

		Motivation	
		Informational (Motives of a negative/ aversive origin)	Transformational (Motives of a positive or appetitive origin)
	Low Involvement	Give Reasons 1 Simple problem-solution format 2 Easy to understand 3 Likeability of advertisement not necessary	Focus on Image 1 Emotional authenticity important 2 Unique execution 3 Advertisement liked 4 Frequent exposure for liking
		Ask a Lot 1 Extreme claims	Ask a Lot 1 Benefits claimed linked to brand 2 Dramatize use/possession/ consumption of brand
Type of Decision	High Involvement	Give Reasons 1 Link to attitudes/beliefs 2 Reasons given via comparative advertisements if competition is well entrenched 3 Likability of advertisement not necessary	Focus on Image 1 Emotional authenticity important 2 Appeal/format fits lifestyle 3 Seek identification with brand 4 Frequent exposure for liking
		Ask only what is reasonable 1 Do not over- or underclaim	Ask only what is reasonable 1 Some information may have to be put across. 2 Do not underclaim: slightly overclaim

Source: After Rossiter/Percy model

MEDIA PLANNING

Media planning is concerned with putting across the message to the target audience in the right media, at the right time and frequency. The problem involves selecting the right mix of media (TV, magazines, radio, etc.), the right media vehicles (the specific TV program, magazine, etc.) and media options (for example, a full page or a half page in the magazine). This is not a simple problem since members of the target audience are very unlikely to be exclusively TV viewers of just certain programs, or a magazine reader or a radio listener. Each member of the target audience will have his or her own network which will not be confined to just the dominant categories of newspapers and TV but is likely to include junk mail, billboards, and so on.

The recognition that buyers are exposed to a multimedia environment has led to *personal media mapping*. This involves charting the working day of a sample of the target audience to discover the media to which each is exposed and at what times. For example, at 8 A.M. it might be a soft rock station, then the newspaper, then another radio station and billboards on the drive to work, with the news TV program at 7:00 P.M. and then some soap opera and so on. What this means is that no one medium can be thought of by itself because there may no longer be a particular medium that will reach the target audience. Once the samples of *media maps* have been obtained these are passed to copywriters to create the advertisements for a specific time and place. Thus media planning is not something always done subsequently to developing the message strategy since the two are interdependent.

Many advertising agencies in the United States believe that media buying should not be separated from the creative side of advertising and this has led them to resist the centralized media buying arrangements so common in Europe. Specialized media buying shops are common in Europe. Working for many clients, these specialized media buying organizations buy in bulk to get cheaper prices in return for a commission of around 3 percent of the advertiser's media budget. Several of the large advertising agencies have come together in *media buying clubs* to compete with the specialists, buying media space or time for their own clients and others. The independent specialists and the buying clubs together now account for over 40 percent of Western Europe's expenditure on advertising.

In the United States, specialist media buying firms tend to be adjuncts for small and medium-sized ad agencies who find it uneconomic to have their own buying organization. But this is likely to change with large media owners like Time Warner offering advertisers large discounts on cross-media deals and big firms like Nestlé seeking to consolidate media buying into a single agency, even though that agency is not the creative agency for all the firm's brands.

Media mix, media vehicle, media options

In selecting the appropriate media mix, it is not enough to know what media and at what times the target audience is exposed, but to ensure advertising fits the medium to get the audience's attention. The size, intensity, color, background, emotional content, and (often neglected) the effort required to process the stimuli have to be considered. This is all in addition to ensuring that the advertising appeal for the brand generates interest in the brand since consumer attention may be elicited without the target audience remembering the brand or what it has to offer. A whole variety of criteria are used in selecting appropriate media:

- the persuasive route and persuasive appeal being considered;
- media habits of the target audience as established by personal media mapping;
- type of product being advertised in that some media are more appropriate than others for the product, for example, TV is less suited to advertising complex products;

- relative cost and flexibility of the media for reaching a particular target audience; and
- rival's advertising. Both the advertising message and media selection must take account of the advertising by the rival brands to which the target audience has been exposed. This is because rival advertising tells us what is already likely to be known about the product class and whether it is wise to directly compete in the same media. Where the brand is new-to-the-world and so constitutes the whole of the product field, brand advertising is obliged to do the whole job of getting the prospect to conceptualize the product and try it.

Television

In general, TV dominates national consumer advertising in most industrial countries as it suits the promotion of simple, inexpensive products. The demonstration, the story, the testimonial, situational predicaments, special effects etc., are all possible approaches in the TV commercial. It is claimed that the typical American "watches" TV over 30 hours a week which potentially means being exposed to around 38,000 commercials per annum. But due to zipping, zapping and being absent during the commercials, estimates are that people see at best around 10,000 commercials a year. In many households, the TV set is on most of the time but seldom fully watched. Competitive media quote figures showing people are watching less and less TV and, even when they do watch, more and more of them do not watch commercials. If they watch commercials, the vast majority do not remember them the next day, though this does not mean the ad has not registered with the brand recognized when next out shopping.

We speak of watching TV not listening to TV. TV is the medium for the dramatic, visual event, making it ideal for linking a brand to target audience values. This is why spokespersons with the ability to dramatize are more effective than fluent speakers who lack dramatic finesse. Commercials that conjure up claims in dramatic vignettes may bypass the critical faculty by focusing the viewer's mind on the advertiser's view of the situation. This is helped by the recognition that it is impossible to justify claims in the time frames involved. In fact a criticism of many commercials is that they are much too complex and subtle to be interpreted correctly by the viewer, even if he or she is fully concentrating on what is happening.

Like radio, TV is essentially an intimate medium so it is better to court the audience than harangue them.[8] This is often the error made by comparative advertising: it makes TV a battleground when it should be wooing them. TV is watched by just two or three people in the intimacy of their home, not by mobs in the street. Celebrities who express their feelings comfortably can create a sense of personal disclosure which can establish an emotional bond with an audience. A TV commercial controls the context of the message to a large extent and, since interpretation of messages is very much affected by context, a commercial is potentially very effective for generating the interpretations sought.

The content of a commercial is a fine balancing act to achieve the right mix of entertainment, information, and persuasive drama. Advertising that accompanies entertaining programs should preferably also be entertaining as a strong, hard sell, and solid informational advertising is apt to go against the mental mode of the audience. Mild distractions like background music, attractive models, songs, comedy, irrelevant scenes can all undermine counter-argument by providing a mild distraction. Whether distractions are deliberate as critics of advertising ethics maintain or an attempt to gain attention as advertisers claim, it should be said that, where an advertiser has a good case, distractions are apt to undermine an ad's persuasiveness. Distractions only increase persuasiveness by undermining counter-arguments when the advertiser has a weak case in the first place.

The problem of getting attention has led to a number of innovations. The *serial commercial* has already been mentioned, though experience suggests that each episode in the serial should avoid having to rely on viewers interest in the serial per se. There is also the *split spots*, two related 15 second spots with an unrelated 30 second spot in between. There are also the more controversial documercials that attract attention by appearing to be an official news item or commentary.

The most interesting innovation is the installing of televisions wherever people have to wait in line for some service such as at airports, banks, supermarkets, fast food restaurants, and so on. In the United States, Turner Broadcasting System (TBS) installs the satellite dishes and monitors for the supportive TV network whose programs consist of a cycle of five minutes of "infotainment" and two minutes of advertising. What has made such advertising attractive to advertisers is that the audience often coincides with the target audiences of many advertisers. This is important since a current criticism of commercial TV is that the coverage is too broad for many advertisers. This use of television away from the home is a good example of the many ways currently being developed for reaching the consumer. As would be expected, the cost of a spot on TV varies with the time of day, the amount bought and the *rating* of the program. Thus a rating of 10 for a program means that 10 percent of all the homes that have TV in the specified area (which could be the nation) were tuned into this program. If one rating point equals one million homes, the rating of ten means ten million households were reached.

The *people meter* (or variations of it) have allowed many useful estimates to be made. This meter is put in a sample of 4,000 or so homes. One meter has eight buttons, six for family and two for visitors. Each member of the family has a personal button to register his or her presence and exits from the room. In sum, the meter allows the calculation of when sets are on, which channel, when channels are changed and who is viewing. Additionally meters may have a laser wand that records purchases when rubbed over the Universal Product Code placed on most packaged goods. Together with the scanner data obtained at checkout scanners in supermarkets and drugstores, there is the potential to better analyze the effects of TV advertising and also consumer promotions like coupons. But there is some way to go before there is a reliable system linking buying information to the TV ads actually watched. The collection and analysis of such *single source* data on a national scale is what package goods companies hope will allow them to make much better promotion decisions.

Other methods of obtaining data on TV viewing are telephoning a sample of viewers and asking them which programs they are watching or asking a sample of viewers to keep diaries on their viewing habits. The people meters seem superior to telephoning or diary keeping. But all have large margins of error. With regard to the people meter, consumer participants get lazy about pushing buttons and they may be conscious of "representing the nation" and this can bias their viewing. A new French system, *Motivac*, overcomes some of these problems. It uses a photonic sensor to record the number of people in a room through the reflection of light from their skin. Motivac uses this information to measure the audience for whatever program or commercial is on. The panel member is not asked to do anything so they can forget they are panel members. Motivac identifies family members by the chair being used in that it appears 95 percent or so of family members sit in the same chair. With a profile of each family member plus a record of his or her spending, a central computer, to which all the information is transmitted, can give instant information on, say, what percentage of Mercedes owners are watching a particular show or commercial.

A key question at present is the future of the TV commercial, given the claim that, in the future, mass broadcasting to a passive audience will be replaced by viewer-controlled interactive channels that will allow the customizing of information and entertainment on demand. There is the danger that viewers will prefer to interact only with those (e.g. pay-per-view) channels that do not show commercials. No doubt commercial TV will adapt since many people will prefer to accept commercials to reduce the cost of TV viewing.

Print

The advertising that appears in newspapers, magazines and so on is referred to as *print*. *Newspapers* tend everywhere to be the primary advertising medium in both the amount of revenue such advertising generates and the number of advertisements newspapers take. Newspapers are important as they capture such a large literate audience but they suffer from poor reproduction and clutter.

Magazines in the industrialized countries rank second to TV for national advertising, with lots of relatively recent innovations such as third page folding out; pop-up 3-dimension inserts and scratch and sniff fragrance ads. Magazines are often tied to a specific audience (for example, magazines on computers) which can be an advantage. Also the readership is often much wider than the circulation figures would suggest. Advertisements in magazines allow long messages and cogent arguments as well as colorful ads when colorful presentation of the product (e.g. clothing, jewelry, and so on) can be important in catching attention and interest. The problem with most magazines is their limited reach, long lead times needed to advertise and the clutter arising from a magazine crowded with ads. Rates are typically based on circulation with a rebate if the numbers fall below the circulation given. But bulk discounts and extra payments for the most popular sections of the magazine complicate the problem of calculating relative costs.

Radio

Particular programs on radio often capture audiences homogeneous from the point of view of advertisers. Hence radio can be suited to segmentation based on lifestyle or demographics. For some advertisers, radio is the only medium that reaches their target audience such as the blind and many elderly people. But radio is limited in creative possibilities and in communicating descriptive detail. Although research data tends to be limited, estimates are available of the numbers listening to programs and the program's share of all those listening to the radio.

The growth of other media

With the decline in the numbers actually paying attention to TV ads, more attention is being paid to reaching them by other than the traditional means. A recent trend is to spread advertising rather than focus on just one medium in the hope that the sum total of ads brings in more business at less cost than expensive TV campaigns. Ads are now popping up everywhere in supermarkets, on videotapes and computer discs mailed to the consumers' homes, and so on. In 1989 Toyota, just before its Lexus went on the market, sent thousands of tapes on the new car to car enthusiasts. Warner–Lambert is experimenting with direct mail (considered later), to even putting ads on blood-pressure monitors in pharmacies. There are also the well-established specialty advertising (e.g. the calendar), and advertising through product placements in movies and advertising in movie theaters. This growth in using multimedia to reach audiences has been accelerated by the recognition by many firms that target audiences are not homogeneous from the point of view of advertising; that different demographic, psychographic or subcultural groups require to be targeted directly in that what persuades one group may not persuade another. This, of course, has long been recognized in political marketing in its use of mailing lists categorized into ethnic groups etc. to allow more tailored messages to be sent. Experimental media include advertising wallboards that are hung in beauty parlors, doctors' and dentists' offices and free magazines placed in waiting rooms plus (more controversially) TV educational programs that also include advertising offered to schools.

Poster advertising has been given a new lease of life. This is partly due to poster companies providing advertisers with better information for the planning and evaluation of poster campaigns and making this medium more flexible for advertisers. Advertisers used to detail audience figures can now get these for posters, for example, the percentage of a specified audience who will see ads on chosen sites and also how many times they are likely to see them over some time period. Of course, billboards, skywriting and other outdoor advertising depend on who passes by, as there is no question of delivering the sign to the audience!

Typical characteristics of the various media are shown in Table 12.3. Consumers do not confine themselves to one medium so there is considerable overlap. But viewing habits do vary: young people tend more to populate the cinema; women as a whole watch more television; men read more newspapers and so on, though patterns can and do change (for example, as fewer women stay at home as housewives).

This discussion of the media can be misleading if it suggests that media selection dominates media planning. In practice more time tends to be spent in selecting the media vehicle (the specific magazine, TV network) and media option (for example, whether to use a one page or half-page advertisement). Although on occasion the message strategy

Table 12.3 Typical characteristics of various media

Television:
- facilitates demonstrations of product;
- sound dramatizes emotional appeals;
- can quickly create awareness of product;
- time limits what can be put across;
- low involvement, so need to be specific and dramatic.

Radio:
- sound dramatizes emotional appeals and can create image;
- listeners to specific radio programs tend to be more homogeneous than those listening to specific television programs;
- inexpensive relative to TV.

Direct mail:
- can deliver message to specific group;
- flexible.

Magazines:
- good for putting across reasons (readers apt to be involved);
- good for showing pictures of product and creating mood;
- all readers can be the target audience if specialist magazine.

Newspapers:
- good for putting across reasons;
- better than magazines for ensuring viewing during a specific time period.

Outdoor marketing:
- good for dogmatic appeals;
- visibility from a distance;
- able to convey atmosphere.

---

forecloses many alternatives, it is still true that the decisions about media vehicles and options are difficult matters where judgment rather than fine theory predominates.

Reach and frequency

Every advertiser wants to know both the *reach* and *frequency* of a media vehicle. The reach of a media vehicle is the number of people exposed at least once to it in a given period while frequency is the number of times people are exposed to the media vehicle (*not* necessarily the ad), given a certain media schedule. Given a fixed total number of exposures to the target audience, reach and frequency are inversely related: as one goes down, the other must go up. The *gross rating points* (GRP) is the reach multiplied by the frequency. Hence a 100 GRP could mean a hundred percent exposure just once or, say, twenty percent exposed five times. A high level of reach is typically sought for new brands.

If we interpret reach and frequency as relating to the vehicle and not the advertisement, perhaps only around 60 percent of those exposed to the vehicle may see the ad.

Another point revolves around the fact that the frequency distribution of exposure to advertising is positively skewed (i.e. a distribution that is not symmetrical but has a longer tail extending toward the higher values). Hence, if we wish to expose most people to the message, say, three times (often considered a minimum number), the average frequency of exposure must be higher than three.

Calculating reach and frequency is very complex and many mathematical models have been developed to aid in the task.[9]

There are also specialist agencies that estimate readership and viewing audiences, but such estimates are apt to be in terms of opportunity to read, see or listen, not in terms of actually having seen, read, or listened to the ad. In any case, not all readers, viewers or listeners are likely to be members of the target audience. But perhaps the most basic problems in media planning are how to identify and calculate the effect and value of repeated exposures and how to cope with a complex system of pricing discounts. It is known that impact and effectiveness can in fact decline at very high levels of repetition of the ad: what has come to be known as *wearout*.[10]

Scheduling

There remains the problem of scheduling or allocating the advertising budget over the campaign period. Repetition of an ad increases the chances of the ad being noticed and reaching the individual in the most appropriate circumstances. For example, a mother may fail to take in or be affected by an ad for hand cream when she is coping with young children, but may pay close attention to the same ad when there are no children to distract her. Also the more frequently the brand is advertised, the more likely it is to be *recalled* first when the product is needed or *recognized* first when buying the product in the store.

How should the ads be distributed? "Continuity" refers to the pattern of advertising whether every day, every week etc., that is, whether concentrated, continuous or intermittent. Also what should be the pattern: high or low; low to high; balanced; alternating? At present such decisions rely heavily on judgment about the effect of different distributions and patterns of exposure on consumer response.

Direct marketing

Direct marketing is usually defined as embracing *direct response advertising* and *direct mail advertising*. With direct marketing the advertiser is more able to control who receives the ad and what is said and when, than is the case with traditional advertising. Where the target customer group is relatively small and can be fairly well-defined and easily reached, direct marketing is commonly considered as the major way to reach the target customer group. It is called "direct" because the relationship between advertiser and customer is a direct one.

Direct mail advertising

Direct mail often supplements a major advertising campaign. Thus direct mail advertising can be used to facilitate a sales call, or support local dealers as well as building up immediate sales. Sending advertising material direct to the prospective customer has a number of advantages:

- the advertising message can be targeted more to those known to be prospects for the product;
- different messages can be developed for each subgroup within the market segment of interest;
- if read, the mailing is not competing with other ads at the same time;
- buying action can be greatly simplified by a stamped addressed postcard; and
- the effectiveness of the mailing can be measured.

A key requirement for success is to have an up-to-date list of prospects. The innovation here is *databased marketing*, which simply means marketing based on having detailed information on each customer so message and product can be more focused. Such information may include not only demographics such as occupation, age, income, and education level but also psychographic information and knowledge of product buying patterns (obtained from credit cards). These mailing lists can be *compiled lists* or actual *response lists*. A compiled list like one compiled from public records is not nearly so useful as lists of people who have actually bought that type of product (or contributed to that type of charity etc.) and about whom the firm has a good deal of relevant information at the individual level. Such lists are developed by the firm itself or are rented. The best prospects tend to be those who have recently ordered by mail, buy similar products, have personal characteristics that make them a prospect and not just a suspect, such as young mothers for baby products and so on.

Some other firms' advertising, requiring a direct response, may be put into packages being sent to the prospect. The package of clothing ordered by mail might contain an insert for some woman's magazine or the bill from the phone company might contain some ad from a car company. All these are "ride-alongs." The tacit endorsement by the distributing organization can give legitimacy to the "ride-along" firm's product.

What so appeals about direct mail is the ease with which it can be tested. There is first the mailing list itself. What type of individual responds? It seems those between the ages of 25–35 years of age are the most likely to throw away such mail without even reading it. There is also the message itself. Direct mail allows the advertiser to experiment with different messages to different groups to see which is most effective. In fact a good deal of advice about writing advertising copy has come from direct mail advertisers. Finally, there is the timing or when to send the ad since so many products are bought on a seasonal basis.

Direct response advertising

Direct response is any advertising that is used to sell products directly to consumers. When direct mail advertising not only sends out advertising but provides an opportunity to purchase direct from the seller, it is also direct response. However, the message tied to direct response advertising need not necessarily be sent through the mail. Direct response advertising is increasing, no doubt because buying products this way is convenient for many busy people. What is still a problem is the number of direct marketing firms who exploit the gullibility of the consumer. From the seller's point of view, although the cost in terms of numbers reached is much higher than for traditional advertising, it can be much cheaper per prospect reached since the advertising can be more finely targeted. This was facilitated initially by combining demographic data with zip code/postal area number and more recently by adding psychographic and purchasing pattern data on each prospect. It is computers that have allowed the collection and utilization of such detailed information at the individual level and also enabled the advertiser to customize and personalize the message.

One term frequently used in direct response is *synchrographic segmentation*, which is simply segmenting the market on the basis of when major lifestyle changes occur, such as marriage, new homeowners, new mothers, retirees. The focus is on when the prospect *must* buy.

Telemarketing.   Telemarketing has grown enormously in the last ten years, helped along by prospective customers being able to use the telephone to make the order at no cost (toll-free). In *outbound telemarketing*, the seller calls the prospect to make a sale, whereas *inbound telemarketing* has the customer making the telephone call to the seller in response to some ad seen on TV, in a magazine, catalogue or newspaper. If outbound telemarketing is to be a success, the customer target list must consist of true prospects; the telephone salesperson must be trained and provided with a well-tested message and answers to likely objections. As this is development selling, the salesperson is essentially trying to activate a latent or passive want for the product. What has currently tarnished the image of outbound telemarketing is automatic dialing recorded message programs (ADRMP) which are automated, computerized systems that randomly dial prospects and deliver a prerecorded sales message. ADRMP cause a great deal of resentment while they undermine the very idea of direct marketing being more finely tuned to particular customer groups. Although under telemarketing comes the home shopping channels on TV, they are sufficiently important to receive separate billing in the next section.

Television.   There can be the typical one-minute commercial offering some low-cost product for sale, asking the audience to call the toll-free number and order the product with their credit cards. The direct response commercials are likely to appear on TV at times when low rates can be negotiated. The second type of TV direct response advertising is the program-length show. Thus one such program has two celebrities discuss and share beauty tips while viewers are encouraged to call toll-free to order, say, the George Hamilton Skin Care System for $39.95. Program-length commercials in the United

States, market everything from courses in financial planning to hair-growth elixirs. In recent years, marketing via TV has gone from the spot commercial to program-length shows to having whole networks devoted to direct response. These are the *home shopping television channels,* or networks that are now a major source of revenue for direct marketing although most of the products currently being sold are jewelry, appliances, and clothing.

We might also consider under the heading of television the growing use of *video-cassettes* in advertising. Videocassettes are being used instead of catalogues. A common complaint is that dresses in catalogues are never the same, when received, as in the pictures. Videos seem to get round this problem. While cassettes are sent on occasions to consumers, more commonly videocassettes are being used for business-to-business advertising. Thus one small firm selling POP sends out a video on its company as a way of introducing itself and company personnel to facilitate a sales call. Firms use videocassettes to explain their product and its application to the industry.

Radio. Although radio is never likely to be a major direct-response medium compared to TV (as no product can be seen and toll-free numbers cannot be shown), radio does have audiences that can coincide with certain segments of a market. However, as currently being used, it serves more as a backup for direct-mail campaigns.

Magazines. Magazines are a major medium for direct-response advertising. A magazine can specialize on a product category like yachting and provide a customer profile that can be invaluable in developing advertising. But magazines also have the advantage of having a long life, and being able to use color while the prestige of the magazine can create an aura useful to any brand advertised within it. As with much of direct-response advertising, the product should be something different from what is sold in the local store unless it is being sold purely on price. In any case it should offer good value, be small enough for mailing and preferably help to secure a future customer.

Newspapers. Newspapers carry the great bulk of advertising and some of this is direct-response advertising particularly the *freestanding inserts* (FSI) that are distributed by local papers. It can be a coupon in the newspaper or pave the way for a future sale.

THE ADVERTISING BUDGET

If we knew the likely sales response to the various parts of the communications mix, there would be few problems in setting the communications budget, as each marginal expenditure could be compared with the resulting gain. Similarly, if we could evaluate the effects of each proposed communications tool, we could choose the best and the optimal communications mix.

With the advent of single-source marketing data, whereby information on actual consumer purchases is correlated to data on TV commercials watched, it is now claimed we will be able to measure the incremental effects of TV advertising, merchandising, and pricing. But this has yet to be established since the interpretation of all such data makes many assumptions.

Estimating the sales response curve

"Advertising," according to Phineas Barnum of Barnum Circus fame, "is like a little learning; a little is a bad thing." Perhaps a firm needs more advice than this in deciding how much to spend on advertising. We suspect, though that Barnum was right and that there is a minimal level of expenditure below which advertising is wasteful but above which advertising gives a spurt to sales, which eventually level off.

Although the relationship between increases in advertising expenditure and resulting sales is not identical for all products, the most commonly assumed shape is the S-shaped curve as shown in Figure 12.4. But other shapes have been demonstrated. In fact one study of the sales performance of 360 different products concluded that only 46 percent of the media advertisements for established brands induced extra sales and only 16 percent of the trade promotions were profitable. However, no doubt it could be argued that sales might have decreased in the absence of advertising; an attractive argument for those who regard advertising for established products to be mainly concerned with retaining existing customers. But even if an S-shaped curve could be assumed, the firm would still want to know the specific curve that might result from different expenditures on advertising.

A firm needs to estimate the sales response to different types and levels of advertising if it is to gauge whether the net profit yielded by incremental sales justifies the corresponding expenditure on advertising. The advertiser also wants to know both the short-term and the long-term effects of advertising on sales and profit so it can be discounted at a rate that reflects the displaced alternative uses for the money, at different levels of risk. Long-term effects are important since an advertising campaign may not immediately influence buying but the advertising can still be significant in affecting

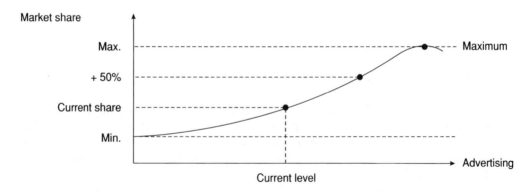

Figure 12.4 Response curve of sales to advertising expenditure (decision calculus approach using executive judgment)

behavior long-term. Although there are advertising models that take account of the lagged effects or carryover effects of past advertising, the long-term effects of a particular advertising campaign, outside of direct marketing, still remain somewhat speculative. Because wants and beliefs among those in the market change over time, the curve showing the response of sales to advertising expenditure will change over time so that past relationships may offer little guidance for the future. Even anticipating the immediate impact of advertising on sales is usually an unknown quantity, lying somewhere between present sales and total market potential, as the level of sales depends not just on advertising but on the other elements of the firm's total offering vis-à-vis competition.

Regression and cross-sectional analysis

Cannot statistical analysis establish the relationship between past sales and past advertising expenditure? Many studies have tried to do this. However, a significant positive correlation may reflect nothing more than the common practice of basing the amount spent on advertising on past sales! In any case any relationship found for one group of products may not apply to another nor to the same group of products in the future. Even where advertising expenditures are varied throughout the country to provide cross-sectional data, the results emerging may still be spurious.

The advent of single-source marketing data from supermarket checkout counters, has led to a number of studies that are trumpeted as being able to establish everything that needs to be known about how advertising works. But relating brand choices to the advertisements to which consumers are exposed, tells us nothing directly about how advertising works as it tells us nothing directly about want and beliefs systems which have to be inferred. In Chapter 4, we pointed out that of the three components of human action—wants, beliefs, and the action itself—we need two out of the three to try and establish the third. Single source data record only actions taken, together with advertisements seen. This does not mean such data cannot be useful but just that it is inadequate for the explanatory purposes adopted. Some of the tentative findings are:

- There is no simple correspondence between advertising and higher sales.
- New brands should be advertised more heavily at their introduction, and they benefit from more prime time advertising.
- The relationship between *standard recall* and *persuasion scores* and the *sales impact* for established brands is tenuous at best.
- Heavy TV advertising is more likely to affect sales when there are changes in brand or copy strategy (so as not to be saying the same things all the time to the same people). Increased sales are more likely in conditions where the message strategy says something fresh and new about the brand.
- Heavy TV advertising is more likely to be effective if the segment is growing with high purchase opportunities.
- Advertising works long-term through customers buying more or more often than through bringing in new customers.

- If advertising has no effect on sales within six months then there is likely to be no long-term impact.

Experimentation

Field experiments have been undertaken to establish the effects of advertising. One marketing area is the control group and another the experimental group or there can be a split run (as occurred in the study reported in the last section). But it is never certain how well the groups are matched in the relevant respects or whether the results are just ephemeral or of substantive value. One early but well-known experiment involving Budweiser beer showed that, beyond a certain sales level, sales became insensitive to additional advertising expenditure.[11] However, no one knows what might have happened with entirely different advertising or a change in competitive activity. This is another problem with correlational data. The data assume that a $1 spent on advertising is a $1 spent on advertising as if the quality etc. of the advertising will be equally good or equally bad now as in the future. Alternatively, there is a belief that, in using a large sample of products, such differences are of no significance. The fact is, of course, we never have a true random sample of all consumer goods and services, while TV advertising is just one medium.

Simulation

Some of the simulation models used in media selection have been used to estimate the sales response to advertising with different degrees of success.

Decision calculus

Decision calculus arrives at a response curve through using executive estimates. Managers, for example, might be asked to estimate:

- the maximum possible sales resulting from a saturation level of advertising;
- the minimum sales level on the assumption that advertising is abandoned;
- current advertising expenditure and current sales level; and
- likely sales if advertising were increased by, say, 50 percent.

All these points are plotted on a graph as in Figure 12.4 to establish the relationship between expenditure on advertising and sales or market share. The strong reliance on management judgment has been criticized on the ground that experience may be of little use in thinking about advertising situations not encountered and, even if it were, things can change. In fact, one experiment found that decision calculus under certain conditions diminishes rather than improves the effectiveness of management decision-making.[12] Advocates of decision calculus in reply claim that, in providing information, managers base their "calibrations on multiple information sources and detailed knowledge of market and consumer behavior." But this is to assume that such knowledge is valid for the purpose.[13] This needs to be established. It is easy to flatter a manager into being a co-conspirator in providing guesses to be used as a basis for rigorous model-building: after all, if the result proves to be nonsense, only the manager can be blamed since everything else depends on his or her input. More seriously, in a final analysis, it is irrelevant how confidently or intensely a manager believes something. It is the content of his or her assertions relative to the evidential facts quoted in support that we need to know.

More recently there has been an acknowledgment that most managers' estimates are both uncertain and inaccurate unless they have experience with varying levels of advertising expenditure and testing various alternatives in the marketing mix.[14] But many argue that, when experience along these lines is available, it would never be enough or rigorous enough to underwrite decision calculus. But as a way of revealing the implications of what managers believe to be the relationship between sales and advertising, decision calculus is useful. It is also useful to try and identify the rules and factors that might be considered by managers to determine likely sales responses to different levels of advertising expenditure so that their rationale can be debated and tested. Attempts have been made in this direction.[15]

METHODS OF BUDGETING ADVERTISING EXPENDITURE

The tentative budget and its allocation

Ray argues that, after marketing objectives are determined, a tentative total budget for communications should be set and allocated among advertising, sales promotion, publicity and field selling. The basis for such budgeting and allocation would be decision calculus for estimating response functions. There is the belief here that guess-estimating by management is what mainly occurs at present but decision calculus can make the procedure more systematic. Apart from the usual problems involved in estimating all these individual response functions under different assumptions, there is the added complication that the response to sales promotion and field selling typically depends on the quality and quantity of advertising: synergistic effects operate. Nonetheless, the need to think about response functions cannot be denied.

The chief division in the communications mix is between advertising and personal selling. Where the mix is weighted in favor of personal selling, it suggests a *push strategy*, since the focus is on "pushing" the product through the distribution channels to the customer. There is a reseller orientation in promotion. A good many department store products are push strategy items. An emphasis on advertising, on the other hand, suggests a *pull strategy*, since it visualizes "pulling" the target audience toward buying the product. A pull strategy is commonly associated with supermarket packaged goods where advertising is used to develop consumer insistence for the brand. Of course, neither advertising nor personal selling might be dominant; both might be stressed equally.

All the communications tools have a functional similarity since they are all concerned with persuasive communication, but they are not equal in potential effectiveness. In one marketing situation, advertising may be preferable to personal selling, while in other circumstances publicity or sales promotion might be still more effective. The mix will in fact differ with:

- *the product*: thus the mix in fragrance marketing will tend to emphasize advertising, while the communications mix for high priced, nonstandard industrial products will emphasize personal selling;
- *the stage in the evolutionary life of the product*: in the case of consumer products, a higher percentage of the communications mix budget tends to be spent on advertising during the introductory/growth stage than in the maturity stage; and
- *the financial resources of the firm*: what might be most desirable from a communication standpoint may not be financially possible.

The advertising budget

As we have seen, the problem of predicting sales effects from advertising can be immensely difficult except in direct marketing. Estimates based on past relationships may not be very meaningful when every new advertising campaign:

- is unique in terms of its qualitative aspects;
- is part of a marketing strategy that has unique objectives;
- is directed at a target audience whose perceptions, expectations, attitudes, and beliefs change and are constantly being changed during the period between advertising campaigns; and
- occurs within a competitive environment that is itself changing.

Where the past, the present, or the future represent very different market situations, prediction from relationships established on past data can be misleading. There is in any case a certain emptiness about statistical relationships that are not rooted in explanatory theory. Yet marketing must have some method of determining what to spend on advertising and some of these are now discussed.

Percentage of sales method

One of the big cigarette companies determines its advertising budget by multiplying each 1,000 cigarettes of forecast sales by 90 cents. Many firms follow a similar practice, allocating a fixed percentage of sales to determine the advertising budget. The approach is defended on the ground that competitors do the same and any attempt to reduce advertising expenditures could dilute brand image while any attempt to increase expenditure would invite retaliatory action by competitors. This ignores the need for advertising to be tied to the achievement of certain goals and to fit the advertising strategy.

Share of market approach

Some marketers claim they can show a relationship between advertising expenditure and market share. While the general validity of such a relationship can be debated, the approach depends on there being little difference between rival offerings to make market share so dependent on advertising share.

Investment approach or payout planning method

In the investment approach advertising is considered an investment on the ground that its effects continue into the future. This approach is sometimes known as the *payout planning method* since advertising expenditure is budgeted for several years ahead. Apart from the fact that the advertiser may be interested only in immediate sales, the approach does presuppose that the sales response to advertising expenditures can be reasonably estimated, since determining future cash flows rests on such estimates.

Competitive parity method

Under the competitive parity approach, no estimates are made of the sales effects of advertising. The amount spent on advertising is based purely on what is spent by competitors. There is the assumption that matching or maintaining a percentage relationship to a competitor's advertising expenditure helps ensure the maintenance of market share.

The maximum affordable method

In launching a new product, a company may spend as much as it can afford on advertising, with the implicit assumption that an even greater expenditure would be justified if the money was available. No estimates are made of the relationship between advertising and likely sales and the approach ignores thinking about objectives to be achieved beyond implicitly pushing for maximum sales.

Marketing science models

Several of the models discussed for forecasting sales in the chapters on product management make assumptions about the level of advertising expenditure and so can be used to relate sales and advertising in new product launches. There is also the decision calculus approach, which is often advocated as the basis for estimating what to spend on advertising.

The objective and task approach

Under this approach the goals of advertising are set out and the strategy adopted. The goals are typically in terms of communication goals in line with one of the hierarchy of effects models. Alternatively, the goals might be in terms of retain, convert, increase, attract and the corresponding task objectives of want-satisfaction, want-focus, want-development, and want-conception. In any case, the approach to setting advertising budgets on a "task-related" basis, that is, according to the job to be done, is finding more and more favor. The weakness of this approach is the failure to estimate the effects on sales, costs and profits for different degrees of task attainment.

If the sales response to advertising expenditure could be accurately gauged, there would be few problems in budgeting. But the whole of competitive activity is designed to frustrate a rival's success. Nonetheless, many firms could improve their budgeting methods; difficulties must not be equated with hopelessness.

EVALUATING ADVERTISING

Marketers evaluate advertising by pretesting it and/or evaluate its performance by post-testing it. In any case the message strategy can be evaluated or the media plan. We focus here on evaluating the advertisement itself.

Pretesting

In evaluating a proposed advertisement, the aim is to predict its likely effectiveness and/or to diagnose its possible weaknesses. There are a number of methods currently being used.

Checklists

The use of checklists is common and some of these are shown in Table 12.4. While many checklists point to logical requirements for any persuasive communication, most implicitly assume a theory of advertising effectiveness: a theory whose assumptions once exposed may have no validity. Even the commonly used checklist "F" in Figure 12.4, which claims an ad should be likable, believable and meaningful can be questioned. Is each of these criteria necessary and are they collectively sufficient for success? Does a persuasive communication have to be *likable* to exert influence in the direction favored by the advertiser? An advertisement like a salesperson can have high credibility without any attractiveness. An advertisement can be disliked yet be effective, as witness some of the advertisements that conjure up fear of being ostracized for "ring around the collar" or not using a deodorant. However, the liking of an ad can carry over to the brand, so likable ads have an advantage, and it also helps if the claims in the ad are "believable" and "meaningful" since an ad that rates high on these two dimensions is more likely to lead to trial.

Table 12.4 Typical checklists in pretest evaluations of a proposed advertisement

---

Checklist "A": Principles of good advertising
1 Involves consumer
2 Consumer-oriented
3 Concentrates on single, most persuasive selling idea
4 Unique and competitive
5 Credible and sincere
6 Simple, clear, and complete
7 Links selling idea to brand-name
8 Takes advantage of medium
9 Makes the sale

Checklist "B": Answer your customer's questions:
1 Is it worth my time?
2 What does it offer me?
3 What good is that to me?
4 Is it better than the alternative?
5 Do I believe it?
6 Do I need it?
7 Do I want it?
8 Can I afford it?
9 What do I do next?

Checklist "C"
1 Does the copy strategy fit the buying motives of the target audience? Does it fit the brand's benefits to those motives?
2 What impression does the advertisement leave with its audience? Is it the impression you intended?
3 How are the emotions touched?
4 Does it get the target audience to reflect on what brand to buy?
5 Does it encourage the response/action that is desired?
6 Does it give the brand a personality? Is this the brand image that is sought?
7 Does it exploit the market opportunity or meet the marketing problem?
8 Is the supporting evidence skillfully exploited?

Checklist "D"
1 Will the advertisement attract the attention of the target audience?
2 Does the advertisement focus on the major benefit of the brand?
3 Are the rational and emotional appeals appropriate given the target audience?
4 Does the advertisement enhance the brand's personality in the direction sought?
5 Are the images or impressions generated by the advertisement the ones that are sought?
6 Does the advertisement encourage the buying action that is sought?

Checklist "E"
1 Does it say something desirable?
2 Does it say something exclusive?
3 Does it say something believable?

Checklist "F"
1 Is it likable?
2 Is it believable?
3 Is it meaningful?

The "Heartbeat of America" campaign for Chevrolet scored high for both recall and liking but did little for sales because, critics say, it was just not *believable* that the Chevrolet, a declining entry-level brand of car, could possibly be perceived as the heartbeat of America. But the ad was not relying on the slogan being literally believable but aimed at tying the car's image to certain cultural values. The ad was not meant to sell cars but simply to get the car considered by those looking for a new car. Some ad claims, of course, must not be disbelieved (though they can be doubted) if the ad is to be effective as buying is prefaced on the claim being true. But not all advertising is like this. Much advertising simply hopes to influence behavior by tying the brand to pleasant associations or values.

We can now come to the criterion of *meaningfulness*. An ad is meaningful if it has meaning for the audience, that is, the target audience believes it is relevant to their wants. The problem here lies in spelling out what would make an ad highly meaningful to the target audience. If "meaningfulness" includes understanding the ad, this can be an important criterion since it is estimated that around 20 percent of print ads are misunderstood by readers and the misunderstanding of TV commercials is even higher. But some ads are deliberately vague, allowing the target audience a good deal of latitude to interpret the ad in a way most pleasing to it.

In sum, checklists are useful providing it is recognized there is no one checklist that applies to all advertisements: much depends on what is being advertised and the persuasive mechanisms that have been adopted. Any checklist it is proposed to use should be shown to have roots in the persuasive approaches discussed in the last chapter.

Focus groups

Focus groups or a panel of potential customers can be brought together to discuss various advertising ideas or to choose among alternative proposals. Such groups might be useful in determining the understanding and meanings conveyed by the ad so as to provide a rough screen. Sometimes projective techniques, associated with motivation research, are used to try and identify perceived inner meanings and the unconscious associations of ideas and words in the ad.

Interpreting the ad for its persuasive content

An ad can be interpreted for its persuasive content, drawing on the various persuasive theories from psychology, social psychology, and sociology for appropriate sensitizing concepts. Take, for example, an ad that appeared in the UK (*The Times*, May 21, 1993) for Linn Hi-Fi. It simply showed a head and shoulders photograph of a young, attractive girl, with the words:

SHE'S TERRIFIC IN BED. SHE'S WITTY, INTELLIGENT AND MAKES HER OWN PASTA. SHE DOESN'T HAVE A LINN HI-FI. BUT HER SISTER DOES, AND SHE'S THE ONE I MARRIED.

We can look at the persuasive content of this ad according to the various approaches discussed in the last chapter.

- *Associationism.* The Linn Hi-Fi is being associated with certain values like self-fulfillment, egocentricism, search for excitement, and hedonism generally.
- *Hierarchy of effects.* The ad is merely drawing attention to the brand and does not offer enough information for the reader to get any sense of the brand's competitive advantage. The aim is to arouse curiosity in suggesting to the target audience that "people like themselves have a high opinion of the brand."
- *The elaboration likelihood model.* Peripheral route is used as the focus is on affective cues. This is because the ad is not meant to be enough to sell the product but simply enough to stimulate sufficient interest for the target audience to inquire further.
- *Persuasive communication approach.* Images used to induce a perspective of Linn Hi-Fi as being part of a certain sophisticated, modern lifestyle.
- *Consistency.*
  a) Balance model—ad conjures up certain feelings that are meant to induce certain favorable beliefs about the brand;
  b) Congruity model—target audience is expected to identify with the communication source and so with the message.
- *Psychoanalytic.* "Hidden" meaning likely to revolve round who would be perceived as buying the brand. The ad conjures up a certain profile of the user (target audience):
  a) male about 25–40 years old;
  b) man-about-town;
  c) upper-middle class (the girl in the photograph seems of this class);
  d) hedonist values; and
  e) women are just a means to gratification!
- *Emotional.* It is assumed the target audience will give a highly positive evaluation of the ad with the emotional dimensions of activation (sexual stimulation) and competence conveyed by the ad with the emotional reaction coming via classical conditioning.

(The Linn ad was rightly considered tasteless by many and offensive to women. The ad was subsequently withdrawn.)

However, the persuasive content of an ad depends on its being interpreted in the standard way, but we can never be certain about whether an ad will be interpreted as expected nor whether the interpretation will be pleasing to the audience. A failure to justify a proposed ad in terms of the theories discussed should not necessarily lead to the rejection of the proposed ad. This would be to assume that we already have full theoretical knowledge of all that might be persuasive. Instead it would suggest going back to those who developed the ad for their rationale. An ad that is evaluated in isolation, divorced from the situation in which it is normally viewed, may give a misleading assessment of its potential effectiveness. In any case, we are a long way from fully understanding and measuring the impact of the paralanguage of gestures, eye movements, posture, voice tone and pitch etc., on likely interpretation and the persuasiveness of an ad. What we do know is that the meaning of such paralanguage can vary from country to country.

Split run technique

Firms may use the *split run* technique for testing print ads whereby different advertisements alternate off the presses to be tested for their attention-getting value in subsequent interviews with readers. With regard to TV ads, it is possible to substitute regularly scheduled commercials for proposed commercials to a panel of buyers and, by monitoring subsequent purchases of those exposed to the proposed commercial compared with those not exposed, some measure of the ad's potential effectiveness will emerge.

Trailer tests etc.

Another test for television and radio commercials (which relates to forecasting techniques discussed in earlier chapters) is the Schwerin test, in which prospective customers select from a list of brands they would choose as a prize. After being shown the commercial, they are asked again to choose a brand from the same list. Any change in brand preference is attributed to the commercial. There is also the ante-room trailer where people in a shopping center are invited into a trailer to watch the commercial and interviewed later for their reactions. With regard to print ads, dummy magazines can be distributed in a random sample of houses where housewives in various ways are encouraged to look at the magazine and later interviewed for reactions to ads.

Physiological measures

There are a number of unobtrusive measures of reaction to ads. Hidden cameras may be used to study both the time spent on different ads and the time spent on different parts of an ad. There is the eye pupil dilation test where pupil diameter may be observed and measured since eye pupil size varies with interest in the subject. Another technique is the "program analyzer," which allows members of the audience watching the TV commercial to press buttons to record indifference, likes, and dislikes. There is the galvanometer (which works like the lie detector test) to measure emotional response. Technical aspects of an advertisement can be tested by equipment such as the "visual testing apparatus" which allows control of exposure, distance and so on to provide measures of visual efficiency of an ad, for example, to consider at what distance each aspect of the ad can be recognized. Although many of these techniques appear objective and unobtrusive, the results are not clear cut, leaving much scope for interpretation. Hence they are being less used.

Hierarchy of effects and the elaboration likelihood model

If an ad is viewed as moving some target audience along some hierarchy of effects to develop a new attitude, the ad is evaluated for its likelihood of moving the target

Table 12.5 Some dos and don'ts on attention-getting advertisements (in print)

1 Pictures of people command attention.
2 Increasing the size of an advertisement increases readership, but not in proportion to size. One approach suggests the following formula:

$$x = N + (100 - N)\ 0.01\ N$$

where

x = predicted percent of those noting ad of twice the size
N = percent who noted original ad of given size.

3 Color is important for getting attention, particularly if color is little used in the rest of the paper or magazine.
4 The most important factors for achieving high attention value in print are:

square inches of ad
square inches of illustration
number of colors.

Putting the ad near an appropriate feature or on the cover page also helps gain attention.
5 Small case is easier to read than when the type is all capital letters.
6 Copy set across the page is not so readable as splitting it into two.

audience onto the next stage. Similarly, if the elaboration likelihood model is accepted as a model showing routes by which attitudes can be changed, then the ad will be evaluated as to whether it engages the central route if there is high involvement and the peripheral route if there is low involvement. However, neither hierarchy models nor the elaboration likelihood model tells the advertiser about appropriate persuasive communications for moving along the hierarchy or persuasive communications via either the peripheral or central route. There would be a need to draw on material in the last chapter.

In whatever way we seek to pretest the effectiveness of a proposed ad, it will always be somewhat artificial, divorced as it is from the actual context in which it will be shown. In practice, a good deal of evaluation relies on the evaluator's judgment about how an ad can best draw attention to itself and also how it can succeed in persuasion. These two purposes are related. Given the numerous advertisements to which any target audience is exposed, there is a need for what has been called an *interrupting idea*. For Rosser Reeves this meant taking his USP and drilling it in by repetition, while for Bernbach, who stressed the need for creative advertising, it was not how often the ad was run but how much excitement it created by its novelty.

No pretesting guarantees to identify effective advertisements or to eliminate all the ineffective. The Avis ad about being number two and so trying harder failed a pretest, while many disastrous ads have passed the pretest with flying colors. We know much more about what an ad should have to gain attention (see for example, Table 12.5) than about how to ensure that the ad will be interpreted as intended.

Post-testing

Sales and market performance

Measures used to evaluate the effectiveness of advertising range all the way from simple tests of recall to attempts to assess the level of resulting sales. There is usually no problem in recording sales before and after an advertising campaign. There are organizations that specialize in tracking product withdrawals from the warehouses of the supermarket chains or in carrying out in-store audits so the advertiser knows whether the product is moving off the shelf.

Except in the case of direct marketing, judging advertising by resulting sales could be misleading if the aim is to discover the true reasons for failure; advertising could be the reason but the fault could lie elsewhere or with advertising plus other elements in the marketing mix. Still some firms insist on accountability in terms of sales. Thus one firm, in consumer products not directly marketed, evaluates the performance of its advertising agencies as follows:

1	share of market performance	60 percent
2	creativity	20 percent
3	cooperation	20 percent

The weighting of 60 percent for market performance means the firm holds its advertising as key to its performance in the market. This assumes that increases/decreases in performance from some base figure are essentially due to advertising. This, in turn, assumes that other things will remain constant like competitive activity, consumer tastes and so on. With regard to the 20 percent for creativity, unless creativity does have an impact on performance in the market, it should not be rewarded. If it has had an impact then it would have been reflected in market performance. The real danger in rewarding so-called creativity is of the advertising agency quickly identifying the rules used by the client for recognizing creativity and slavishly following such rules even though they are not known to produce effective advertising. Finally, in respect to the 20 percent for co-operation, there is a danger here of confusing subservience for cooperation so that the agency fails to stand up for what it believes. No doubt the firm would argue that measures of advertising effectiveness must stem from the objectives set for advertising and that these measures do. Thus we come back to the goals set for advertising.

It is true that measures of effectiveness must relate to the goals set for advertising. Unfortunately, many firms use the standardized measures supplied by research agencies without such measures being tailored to the individual advertiser's needs. The problem lies in judging whether the loss in relevance in using standard, commercially available data is significant enough for the firm to develop its own measures.

In spite of what has been said about the problem of relating advertising and sales, it is becoming more common. One reason is the use of *single-source data* (mentioned earlier) where the participants in the research have their TV viewing habits recorded together with their subsequent purchases. There are also the consumer panels. One panel in the United States consists of 300,000 households who keep diaries. Once a month they keep a record of the TV commercials they see that day; record the channel; the product advertised and their buying intentions after watching the commercial. These buying intentions are then compared with their buying intentions recorded the previous day. Here the goal of advertising is assumed to be the triggering of buying intention. The method ignores any lagged effects of advertising and assumes that viewing habits and buying intentions are not distorted by diary-keeping. It is also possible to continue experimenting with different TV ads using sales as a measure of effectiveness. The system is the same as for pretesting. Experiment in both cases is made possible by the use of a dual cable television system. Cable television subscribers in certain "representative areas" are hooked up to alternate cables. The service uses this dual system to cut in "test" commercials along one of the cables while the other cable carries the normal commercial of the client. Corresponding to the two different cables are panels of, say, 1,000 households each, which keep diaries of their purchases. One panel constitutes the experimental group and the other panel the control group. Data from the weekly purchase diaries are analyzed and passed along to the client, specifying, for example, the differences in purchases of the brand between the control and experimental group. This system of measurement allows the firm to continue experimentation after the product launch. However, the question arises of how far a panel of consumers, drawn from just one or two areas of the country, who subscribe to cable TV and are willing to keep diaries can be truly representative of the target audience.

Communication goals

Where the goals of advertising are set in terms of moving the target audience onto the next stage in the hierarchy then measures can be taken that confirm the extent to which this has happened. Some writers argue that in addition to measuring effects within the hierarchy, measures should be taken of the extent of ad likability, believability, and meaningfulness as a way of trying to explain why the particular effects occurred. This in turn assumes that these three dimensions offer a sufficient basis for explaining persuasive advertising. While we have suggested these dimensions should be considered, they do not offer a sufficient basis for explaining resulting advertising effects, though on occasions they can be suggestive as to why the ad has been ineffective.

Similarly, if the aim is to persuade either by the peripheral route or the central route, measures can be developed that test for this. Finally, if goals are set in terms of convert, increase, attract, or retain, the numbers actually converted, the numbers who increase their level of business, the numbers who are attracted as new users or the numbers of customers retained, can be measured by sample surveys.

One communication test of the cumulative effect of advertising is the extent to which those exposed to the advertising adopt the advertiser's formula for talking and thinking about the firm's brand: the collection and analysis of protocol statements can help discover this.

Recognition, recall, and comprehension measures

A good deal of commercially available data has focused on recognition, recall and comprehension measures. Recognition, recall and comprehension measures reflect stages in hierarchy of effects models and are common measures after launching a product. Creating brand awareness can either be in terms of ensuring brand recognition at the point of sale or ensuring that whenever that type of product is needed, the brand will be recalled. High recognition is achieved with fewer exposures to an ad than is necessary to achieve the same level of recall. Although high recognition is usually regarded as an insufficient measure of consumer response, it is an important measure nonetheless since high brand recognition acts as a signal to the consumer that the brand is well known and established which can be important when having to choose from a number of otherwise undifferentiated brands.

THE SOCIAL CONSEQUENCES OF ADVERTISING

Social benefits

Advertising has two major purposes:

- to communicate factual information about the offering; and
- to induce buying action or reinforce loyalty by modifying beliefs, feelings, tastes, and understandings

There are social benefits in providing information about new and better ways of meeting buyer wants. Without the opportunity to make the market aware of new product developments through advertising, for many companies there would be little incentive to undertake R&D and new product development. Unless the consumer is made aware of new developments, less effective and less efficient ways of meeting wants would be continued. Advertising also provides something like 50 percent of the income of newspapers and magazines and is virtually the sole source of income for most television. However, critics argue that these benefits can be outweighed by the way advertising pursues its second purpose.

Social costs

Advertising, as a tool, is capable of being abused: it is commonly accused of:

- creating false wants;
- distortion of values;
- causing higher prices;
- gross deception; and
- manipulation.

Creating false wants

Marcuse, in his *One-Dimensional Man*, a book that was popular with students in the 1960s and early 1970s, argues that the mass media maintain a form of totalitarianism.[16] They do this by creating false wants, which are superimposed on the bulk of the population by vested interests to assimilate potentially opposed classes into a state of uncritical acceptance of prescribed attitudes and values. This is an extreme view, but the belief that advertising creates wants is commonly held. Advertising, it is claimed, is able to do this by encouraging the feeling that "what we do not yet have" is vastly more desirable than what we do have.

Advertising does stimulate people into buying products they would not otherwise buy and in this sense a want can be said to arise that was not there before. But such stimulation presupposes there is a basic underlying appetite for the product. Marketers sense out latent wants and seek to activate them; consumers are not motivationally empty until marketers come along. If "wants" could be just created out of nothing, there would be no limit to the rate of growth for the firm, since demand would no longer be the problem.

What is a much more relevant criticism is the intensifying of undesirable wants. There is evidence, for example, that children below eight years of age are highly persuaded by advertising, putting pressure on parents constantly to buy what they see on television. Although after that age children are more skeptical of advertising, they can still be persuaded to buy harmful products. The Joe Camel ads have already been mentioned where the central character is always in a heroic pose surrounded by adoring women amid the palm trees. The ads promote smoking as part of the sophisticated, fashionable lifestyle—and children have been the ones chiefly attracted.

Distortion of values

An English novelist at the beginning of the century wrote that you could tell the ideals of a nation by its advertisements. "In advertising, men are taught to judge their happiness by their immediate pleasures, by the beautiful women that pursue them, by their possessions and by their popularity." There is truth in these charges. Money, sex and power are often motives that advertising taps but this is not true of all consumer advertising as critics claim.

The standard answer to charges of value distortion is that advertising responds to trends in the culture rather than initiates these trends. While this may be true, advertising can accelerate an undesirable coarsening and narrowing of cultural values. While advertising may not be able to impose a certain line of thought upon the nation, it is successful, in conjunction with the mass media, in determining what people think about.

The criticism about advertising distorting values has become muted in recent years simply because advertising is no longer the chief culprit: the values proclaimed in TV programs and films seem to make most advertising by comparison seem rather harmless. Nonetheless, there are many countries in the world where responsible opinion worries about the materialistic values being promoted. They would not deny that we have a disposition toward materialism but see no reason as to why we should constantly reinforce these dispositional urges.

Without standards that reflect decent values, a society becomes governed by the laws of the jungle. Without support of these standards in the media, they can in the long run be seriously undermined. Some recent advertising in the United States, in order to break through the commercial clutter, has adopted shock tactics that attract attention but at the expense of good taste. The Calvin Klein ad in *Vanity Fair* magazine, already mentioned in our discussion of transformational advertising, is illustrative. This ad (and others for Calvin Klein products) have been highly offensive to most people but not seemingly offensive to his target audience of young people. The ads put across an image of Calvin Klein being "hip" and contemporary and create a fantasy for the consumer, with a stress on sex and "romance" on the ground that these are the things young people mainly fantasize about.

Higher prices, poorer products

Critics have long argued, like Carlyle in the nineteenth century, that developing consumer loyalty via advertising becomes a substitute for developing better products and lowering prices. Critics point particularly to the pharmaceutical industry, which spends 25 percent of its costs on advertising; as a consequence, one firm can charge for its brand four times the price obtained for Chlorpheniramine, which is the same drug under its generic name. The charge that advertising on occasions allows the firm to obtain higher prices cannot be denied. On the other hand, if advertising substantially increases the amount sold, lower unit cost could result in lower prices. Certainly many products, with relatively high costs of production, could not be produced unless a wide market was assured by vigorous advertising. As one study on the subject concluded: the evidence is convincing that "manufacturer advertising results in lower retail gross margins for the more advertised brands to the unadvertised and less advertised grocery brands in the same product category."[17]

Gross deception

Deception is distinguished from falsity. Falsity is objective fact while deception is subjectively interpreted as injurious to consumers. Daniel Defoe writing in the eighteenth century noted that during the worst horrors of the Plague in 1664–1665, London was plastered with advertisements promising miracle cures. Even coffee was promoted as a cure for eyesores, coughs, and colds. Given the Victorians' preoccupation with their health (to which there has been a return!), deceptive advertisements for patent medicines were common. One nineteenth-century advertisement for a tonic claimed that it "could utterly destroy the death microbe itself" while an advertisement for a lotion claimed to "refresh the mouth and immediately sweeten the breath; fasten teeth though ever so loose, and strengthen tender gums." Nor in the nineteenth century was there any reluctance about just associating celebrities with their product. Queen Victoria was depicted behind the window of her railway dining car apparently enjoying a cup of "Cadbury's Cocoa" while another ad showed the Pope drinking a cup of Bovril and entitled: "The Two Infallible Powers." This sort of exploitation and bad taste still occurs in some countries. One ad used to sell a Japanese car in Holland shows a woman, obviously intended to be Princess Diana, creeping out of bed in the middle of the night to join her lover, passing portraits of Queen Elizabeth and corgis on her way.

To those who draw attention to deceptive advertising and false advertising, there has been some progress. But untrue claims are still all too common. An advertisement for grapefruit claimed that "the more you eat, the slimmer you get." An advertisement, supposedly demonstrating clean car windows, had the window rolled down while an advertisement for soup used marbles to push the soup's ingredients to the top. An article in *Business Week* (December 2, 1985) pointed out that deception was not only common in advertising but not uncommon even among national brands.

Wartime propaganda showed how repeating a lie, if repeated often enough, can influence beliefs so people come to believe the lie. For example, the constant use of the term "anti-aging" in promoting certain facial creams can lead consumers to believe such exists because

- few will attempt to check whether it is true;
- buyers want to believe it is true; and
- the constant repetition starts to create its own reality for the consumer.

Consumers may ridicule the claims made for a brand when talking among friends yet once out shopping, brand recall or recognition may dominate as the only information possessed. Although a government may insist the advertiser stops the deception by some consent decree or insists on the advertiser providing the needed additional facts (affirmative disclosure) or insists the advertiser develops corrective advertising, the falsehood can remain accepted for a very long time, confusing consumers and undermining honest competitors. In the United States celebrities endorsing a brand are not allowed to make claims that cannot be substantiated, the celebrity must be a current user of the brand and have no financial interest beyond payment for services given. There is particular criticism of advertising to children that exploits their vulnerabilities and projects dubious values. But what has also come in for criticism on ethical grounds is ads that exploit associations (the Linn Hi-Fi ad would be a perfect example) that have no connection with the product's benefits.

Printers' Ink, a magazine for the advertising industry, in the early 1900s, published a model statute for the state regulation of advertising designed to "punish untrue, deceptive or misleading advertising." But it still goes on, often in more subtle ways, through the use of words and symbols. Thus advertisers may call their orange juice "fresh" when it is processed orange juice. P&G called its brand Citrus Hill Fresh Choice, adding the phrase "we hurry to squeeze them before they lose their freshness."

The FDA has stopped P&G from using the word fresh in this way. There is some sort of belief that when everyone is doing it, it must be ethical. Thus at sale times, stores will display a sign "50 percent off" and then in tiny letters will be the words "those marked with a red label." This grabs attention through deception and consumers may not comment (as it is so common) but the firms that do not do it become more noted for integrity. One ex-advertising executive points to the pressures that lead to the misleading omissions, false implications, illusions, and nonsense phrases that suggest benefits. As he says, "the trouble with people who think it's all right to tell a little white lie is that they soon become color blind."[18]

Manipulation

Consumers can be said to be manipulated if they act according to the wishes of the advertiser

- without being conscious of doing so, and
- their acting that way would not have occurred if they had been cognizant of the type of influence being employed.

A number of the techniques of persuasion discussed in the last chapter have the potential for being manipulative. The sound bite, the slogan, the metaphor, the emotional anchor tied to values (often hedonistic or materialistic ones) are common in TV advertising where there is little time for informed comment.

The most severe critics of advertising as a manipulative tool have been those influenced by both a Marxist perspective and French postmodernism. Jhally's criticism is typical.[19] He first takes to task those critics of advertising who talk about manipulating consumers into desiring things they do not really need, critics who focus on the purely utilitarian uses of products, ignoring their symbolic meaning. The defenders of advertising, on the other hand, while recognizing the symbolism that can attach to products, do not face up to the social consequences of advertising. Jhally argues that it is control over symbolism, not the contradictions in the means of production (as claimed by traditional Marxist dogma), that has become the key focus in advanced capitalist societies and this control over symbolism necessitates the mastery, control, and manipulation of the symbolic codes through which products are given their meaning. He argues that it is the meaning given to a product by advertising that provides the product with exchange value in excess of what the brand would command for its utilitarian use-value (an echo here of positive brand equity). For Jhally, advertising builds meaning into a product, making a "fetish" out of it. Making a fetish of a product is to invest it with magical powers it does not have but is made to appear to have. There is a human need that searches for meaning and the symbolism inserted by advertising provides this. Jhally views advertising as the major source of product information but argues that with TV there is too little time for "reason-why" advertising so the focus is on entertaining, lifestyle advertising, facilitated by psychographic segmentation. In this way advertising focuses on creating advertising that resonates with the values and beliefs of the target audience to create pleasurable feelings that will be transferred to the brand and recalled when the product is sighted in the store. But all this depends on advertisers knowing the symbolic code (what signs symbolize what) to develop ads that will project the meaning desired and get the audience to interpret the codes of advertising in the way desired. Advertising relates the product or brand to the consumer by way of symbolism; a symbolism that seeks to make a fetish of the product.

What particular meaning does the advertiser try to build into brand advertising? Jhally suggests the following meanings as transmitted by advertising:

- personification (human qualities attributed to the brand);
- positive emotional impact from using the brand;
- brand use as having the power to transform the user, for example, making the user more attractive;
- brand possession/use as having the power to complete social relations;
- brand use as mediating or making certain relations possible;
- brand's mere presence making a situation more meaningful; and
- brand as capturing certain natural forces.

Jhally grossly exaggerates the power of advertising. His characterization of the consumer as

- desperately searching for meaning in a world where traditional informational anchors are no longer in place, and
- looking to the media (mainly TV) as the only source that gives meaning to products (a meaning which the consumer just passively accepts, unconsciously or consciously)

is a very distorted characterization. He seems to go along with Baudrillard, the French postmodernist, in arguing that, through the manipulation of the symbolic code, any object can take on any symbolic meaning regardless of its physical attributes. But whatever symbolic code exists, it still needs to be known (codified) if it is to be used by advertisers; until then advertisers must rely on their own intuitions as to what is likely to symbolize what. Jhally credits advertising agencies and marketers with more knowledge than they possess. Marketers have long accepted the limitations of their persuasive abilities and recognize that it is the total integrated system of product, packaging, branding, pricing, distribution and promotion that constitutes the offering to the consumer and advertising cannot make up for the deficiencies in the tangible aspects of that offering, as US automobile manufacturers have painfully discovered.

The general fear of being manipulated is indicated by the uproar over subliminal advertising. In 1957 in the United States, the words Coca-Cola and "Eat Popcorn" were alleged to have been flashed, below the threshold level of seeing, on the screen in a movie. It was claimed that the sales of Coca-Cola went up one sixth and sales of popcorn by one half. James Vicary, the author of this story, was later to acknowledge to *Advertising Age* that the study was a fabrication intended to increase customers for his failing business.

There is evidence to support the claim for the existence of subliminal perception (some subliminal messages do get through) but this is not the problem. The subliminal perception thesis suggests that such stimuli also affect mental processes like evaluation. There is no evidence to suggest that manipulation can occur via subliminal perception.[20] There is no empirical evidence for strong subliminal effects such as inducing particular behaviors or changing motivations. In fact such a notion runs in conflict with a substantial amount of research and is incompatible with experimentally based conceptions of information processing, learning and motivation. However, the debate continues. Although few today in the light of the evidence would claim subliminal advertising as a manipulative tool, some quote evidence that subliminal advertising can trigger action if the action (e.g. purchase) is already strongly desired!

There is manipulation in advertising but the evidence does not support the strong manipulative effects of advertising. Personal experience with a brand cannot just be ignored. Yet there are products that continue to be sold because of faith in the promotion combined with uncertainty over the effects of using the product. Thus I may continue to take a rejuvenation pill because it is promoted as such and I attribute my good health to it or claim that my illnesses could have been worse without its benefits. However, advertising is just one source of information to the consumer, who is in touch with many other influences—such as friends, reference groups, consumer associations, and institutions such as government agencies. Nonetheless, consumers would make better decisions if they were not fed misleading information.

As far back as 1893, a society known as Scapa was formed to check the abuses of public advertising, while in 1924 at an international advertising convention in Wembley, England, a code of ethics was adopted with the command to "tell the advertising story simply and without exaggeration and to avoid even a tendency to mislead." But no country relies on the ethical conscience of advertisers. The law usually reinforces the will to be good. But the law is notoriously ineffective in regulating moral behavior unless such behavior is part of the regulated group's own set of norms. Legislation must be buttressed and reinforced by the advertising industry itself as well as by the consuming public. Finally, it is worth pointing out that where there is resort to manipulation and deception, it could not occur without the connivance, if not the encouragement, of the sponsoring firm: an indication of the sponsor's marketing bankruptcy.

NOTES

1 Rossiter, John R. and Percy, Larry (1987) *Advertising and Promotion Management*, New York: McGraw–Hill.
2 Singh, Surendra N., Rothschild, Michael L., and Churchill, Gilbert A. (1988) "Recognition versus Recall as Measures of Television Commercial Forgetting," *Journal of Marketing*, XXV (February).
3 De Sousa, Ronald (1990) *The Rationality of Emotion*, Cambridge, MA: MIT Press.
4 Tanner, John F., Hunt, James B., and Eppright, David R. (1991) "The Protection Motivation Model: A Normative Model of Fear Appeals," *Journal of Marketing*, 55 (July).
5 Davitz, Joel R. (1969) *The Language of Emotion*, New York: Academic Press.
6 Gosling, J. C. B. (1969) *Pleasure and Desire: The Case for Hedonism Reviewed*, Oxford: Clarendon Press.
7 Turner, J. C. (1987) *Rediscovering the Social Group*, Oxford: Blackwell.
8 Jamieson, Kathleen Hall (1988) *Eloquence in an Electronic Age*, New York: Oxford University Press.
9 Agostini, J. M. (1961) "How to Estimate Unduplicated Audiences," *Journal of Advertising Research*, 1 (March).
10 Calder, B. and Sternthral, Brian (1980) "Television Advertising Wearout: an Information Processing Viewpoint," *Journal of Marketing Research*, 17 (May).

11 Ackoff, R. L. and Emshoff, J. R. (1975) "Advertising Research at Anheuser Busch Inc (1963–68)," *Sloan Management Review*, 16.
12 Chakravarti, D., Mitchell, A., and Staelin, R. (1981) "Judgment based Marketing Decision Models: Problems and Possible Solutions," *Journal of Marketing*, 45 (4) (Fall).
13 Little, John D. C. and Lodish, Leonard M. (1981) "Commentary on Judgment based Marketing Decision Models," *Journal of Marketing*, 45 (4) (Fall).
14 Lodish, Leonard M. (1986) *The Advertising and Promotion Challenge*, New York: Oxford University Press.
15 Lilien, Gary L. (1979) "Advisor 2: Modeling the Marketing Mix Decision for Industrial Products," *Management Science*, 25 (2) (February).
16 Marcuse, Herbert (1964) *One-Dimensional Man*, Boston: Beacon Press.
17 Albion, Mark S. and Farris, Paul W. (1981) "The Effect of Manufacturer Advertising on Retail Pricing," *Marketing Science Institute* (Cambridge, MA) Report no. 81–105 (December).
18 Baker, Samm Sinclair (1968) *The Permissible Lie, The Inside Truth About Advertising*, Boston: Beacon Press.
19 Jhally, Sut (1990) *The Codes of Advertising: Fetishism and the Political Economy in the Consumer Society*, London and New York: Routledge.
20 Moore, Timothy, E. (1982) "Subliminal Advertising: What You See Is What You Get," *Journal of Marketing*, 46 (2) (Spring).

APPENDIX 12.1 SPECIMEN (HYPOTHETICAL) ADVERTISING STRATEGY (OUTLINE)

Benson's mixed nuts

A. Advertising objectives
(i) *Mission:* to favorably dispose the target audience to Benson's brand.
(ii) *Goals:*
(a) To *convert* from rivals by promoting the match between expressed preferences and Benson's brand. The change in perceptions is anticipated to take volume away from rivals as follows:

A Brand (12 percent)
B Brand (8 percent)
C Brand (6 percent)

This conversion target requires a change in perceptions by 9 percent of current consumers.
(b) To *attract* current nonusers by promoting the desirability of eating a nut with the taste of crisp-dryness. It is anticipated that the campaign will attract 10 percent of new entrant consumers mainly in the age group over 15 but under 18 years.

B. Message strategy
(i) *Primary proposition:* Assertion that Benson's has the enjoyment emanating from a revolutionary crisp-dry taste. Crisp-dryness positions the product as constrasting with competition.
(ii) *Secondary proposition:* Benson's are airtight sealed to preserve and guarantee the crispness as befits a quality product.

(iii) *Image projected:* Brand image of freshness, crunchiness, and light-heartedness.

(iv) *Support:* Support of copy strategy via demonstration of Benson's characteristics and of consumer enjoyment of the product.

C. Media strategy

(i) *Target audience:* All consumers of nuts but with focus on the high income/heavy user category defined as:

(a) young (under 18 years) of middle-class families;

(b) housewives in middle-class households over 30 and under 45 years of age.

(ii) *Media:* TV and magazines (details on media vehicles and options to be confirmed).

(iii) *Reach and frequency:* During the first year introductory period, Benson's seek a reach/frequency of 80 percent/8 against all consumers of nuts.

(iv) *Geographic coverage:* National coverage but weight of distribution to reflect potential.

(v) *Scheduling:* Advertising will continue throughout the year but weighted for peak months June–September.

Marketing Rationale

1. Target audience

Advertising will communicate the end result benefits as:

(i) crisp-dry taste guaranteed by airtight package;

(ii) quality appearance to inspire confidence.

The focus on the high-income/heavy-user category is because:

(a) this subsegment, while composed of only 12 percent of households, purchases 40 percent of sales;

(b) blind tests show this subsegment to be most responsive to the product and its differential advantage.

2. Message strategy

(i) *Primary proposition:* The revolutionary crisp-dry taste is the major appeal as:

(a) taste is the major attribute on which preference is based;

(b) the taste of Benson's is distinctive and in blind tests was preferred by the target audience subsegment in 80 percent of cases;

(c) the taste is not easily manufactured by competition.

(ii) *Secondary proposition:* Price and appearance to convey a quality image as revealed in tests. Airtight seal demonstrated.

(ii) *Image projected:* The image to be projected is congruent with the buying inducement, the quality claim and the occasions on which the product is generally eaten.

3. Media strategy

(i) *Target audience:* The subsegment positioning was based on market research. This to be both the high purchase group and the group most responsive to the Benson product.

(ii) A high *reach* is needed since 90 percent of households purchase the product category at least once every four weeks. Achieving a high *frequency* is important as the product is frequently purchased. A frequency level of 8 is designed to keep the Benson product in the forefront.

(iii) TV will be the major *medium* to achieve reach and frequency. TV is particularly suited to the copy platform to be adopted.

Chapter 13

Sales management

There are many goods and services whose benefits, competitive advantage, and terms of trade are sufficiently unknown and complex as to require personal selling. In fact, as soon as an organization moves away from marketing standard products with standard, known applications, toward marketing nonstandard products with developing or non-standard applications, the more consideration needs to be given to direct selling. The reason has to do with the communications burden: at some point the amount of information to be put across becomes too much for nonpersonal methods of communication.

For many companies, personal selling is a necessary condition for success, with the sales force being analogous to battle troops as their relative quality determines who wins the competitive war. Advertising is not a substitute for face-to-face selling when individually tailored advice and explanations are needed for the customer to appreciate what is being offered. Personal selling has the potential to capture a buyer's attention, retain the buyer's interest, anticipate objections, adapt to the buyer's personality and, through supportive interaction with the buyers, create goodwill and emotional bonds that predispose buyers toward favoring the salesperson. This is why personal selling with its flexibility is generally more successful but not always more efficient (given the high cost of personal selling) than advertising in changing attitudes and affecting behavior. But, in general, advertising and personal selling complement each other, with advertising developing a brand image as a basis for personal selling and salespeople securing dealer cooperation for advertising campaigns while, on occasions, being the key to success in implementing and monitoring sales promotions. For many companies, the sales force is the only revenue producing unit of the business and it is the sales force that wins and loses market share.

Many a company has failed because it has failed to appreciate that its product cannot be sold by catalogue or even through distributors but requires a specialist salesperson to do the job. But direct selling is not just adopted when the communications task demands it. Buyers like to "put a face to the company": to have someone to deal with; to complain to; to exchange information with; someone who knows them and their business to solve their problems and can be trusted to do the best for them; someone who will do the order writing chores and help them in their inventory control and other aspects of their business. These are some of the reasons for using a sales force to call on retailers or industrial buyers direct rather than leaving it to wholesalers. But not all firms employ a field sales force to call directly on consumers, industrial users or to sell through middlemen. Some firms sell over the telephone, or use manufacturing agents who are self-employed, working typically for several companies while others rely on, say, mail order because direct selling is considered too costly for the extra benefits received.

Under the title of salesperson comes a wide variety of jobs requiring very different skills. Thus the *sales engineer* selling complex technical equipment contrasts with sales-people calling on retail outlets, fighting for shelf space and better locations in the store. *Detail salespeople* do not actually sell the product but provide details as occurs with sales-people calling on doctors. *Development selling*, too, can be contrasted with *maintenance selling*. Development selling is concerned with opening the account for the first time; to "unfreeze" the buyer, to arouse latent wants, and activate passive wants by overcoming objections. With maintenance selling, on the other hand, the buyer/seller relationship is already in being with the buyer already aware of what is on offer or at least knowing enough to make the job of selling that much easier. Those undertaking maintenance selling are often called *account representatives*.

Missionary selling involves somewhat similar skills to development selling since, though a missionary sales force calls on the customers' customers to drum up business, they, too, have the job of evoking interest in the product often for the first time. There is also *systems selling*, where the salesperson tries to sell a combination of products to meet some overall function (for example, a communications system) rather than to sell just an individual item (for example, a telephone). On still other occasions, the salesperson will be concerned with *concept selling*, which consists of selling the basic concept of how the seller's product might fulfill some function or meet some application. Salespeople learn about their customer's business and identify applications which could be done better using their product. On other occasions, the salesperson may not try to sell at all but be concerned with *protecting* an order by ensuring it will not be canceled before delivery, or the salesperson may concentrate on *forearming*, which involves trying to find out the company's future plans that involve buying products the salesperson is trying to sell. Although only one salesperson typically calls on a customer, this need not be so. There can be *team selling* where several salespeople are involved in different aspects of the sale. There can also be *opposite number selling*, where people at different levels in the organization deal with their opposite number (whether engineer, production manager, accountant, etc.) in the customer organization with the salesperson not only selling but acting to coordinate the efforts of all those dealing with the customer.

There are two aspects of any sales manager's job—what Peter Drucker once called "doing the right things" and "doing things right."

- "doing the right things": this is the problem of achieving effectiveness and is the *strategic* aspect of the job
- "doing things right": this is the problem of doing what needs to be done in an efficient way and this is the *operational* aspect of the sales manager's job.

We deal first with the strategic aspect of the sales manager's job.

THE SALES STRATEGY

A sales strategy is a broad conception of how sales resources are to be deployed to achieve objectives: by contacting or calling on certain target customers; by promoting certain lines of products; by making certain types of sales appeals; by servicing, liaising, and collecting information; all within certain budget constraints.

The sales strategy and higher-level planning

The sales strategy is linked to higher-level planning like the other substrategies of the marketing strategy. Thus the investment objective for any product group (whether the objective is growth, hold/defend, or harvest) has a direct impact on the level of sales quotas, allocation of sales effort, and so on. This is so often forgotten. Thus it is not uncommon for a harvesting investment objective to be adopted by higher level management for some particular product without the sales force being aware of its implications; so they go on as before, putting all their efforts into pushing the product not only because they are not informed but because the financial incentive scheme has not been changed to take account of the change in policy. Similarly, the segmentation strategy and the advertising message strategy influence both the sales appeals made and the sales activities carried out, while both the segmentation and distribution strategies determine the target customers with whom the sales force must deal.

A first step in drawing up a sales strategy is to work out the implications of higher-level planning for sales force direction. The various profit objectives for the business are the basis for establishing revenue and cost goals for the sales force. The sales quotas for each sales region and each member of the sales force reflect the market share that is sought, while the allocation of sales effort must be in line with the investment objective for each product group. Figure 13.1 illustrates. Thus the investment objective of growth is associated with opening new accounts, providing a higher level of service, and so on. Similarly, the investment objective of hold/defend is concerned with retaining existing customers, while a harvest objective demands a cut back on service and a concentration on the most profitable accounts. All too frequently, coordination between sales force planning and higher-level plans is neglected, with the result that field selling policies are out of line with higher level business planning. As a consequence, top management intentions are nullified.

Sales strategy objectives

Mission and sales goals

The mission of any field sales force is to favorably dispose some target group of customers toward taking action that leads to buying the firm's product. The target group might include final customers like industrial buyers, consumers (in door-to-door selling), channel intermediaries like retail store buyers, or "gatekeepers" like doctors and architects. Some sales forces do not take orders directly as when they call on doctors and architects to persuade them to recommend the firm's product. When the sales force does

Higher-level plans	Sales force plans	Sales force functions (role)
Corporate profit goals ⟶	Revenue goals and cost goals	Communication Training
Market share goals ⟶	Sales quotas	Service
Investment objectives ⟶	Allocation of selling effort	Liaison Intelligence

Figure 13.1 Higher-level plans, sales force plans, and sales force functions

take orders, the revenue goals, cost goals and sales quotas reflect the goals agreed at the business-level planning stage.

Setting goals for the sales force in terms of sales seems to run counter to the argument that sales result from all elements of the marketing mix, not just from one element like personal selling. If we cannot normally evaluate advertising on the basis of sales, how can we justify using sales to evaluate the sales force? The main reason for setting goals for the sales force is to stimulate individual performance and to evaluate *relative* performance rather than the absolute level of performance. The ranking of salespeople on the basis of their performance on quota (standard) can give a fair measure of relative performance even if the level of quota, in absolute terms, is either too low or too high. Thus we may set some sales goals for a new product, but no sales force is likely to be held solely accountable for its failure. When we do hold the sales force responsible for the level of sales on established products, it is on the assumption that other things like advertising, buyer tastes and competitive activity have remained the same.

Revenue or sales goals constitute standards against which to assess performance but they provide little guidance for sales force direction. We need to think about goals for each of the functions to be carried out by the sales force, namely the sales force functions of communication (including promotion and the creation of trust); training; service; liaison and intelligence. These will be discussed in turn.

Communication goals

Personal selling, like advertising is concerned with persuasive communications. Sales force communication goals, however, vary with the marketing strategy's competitive objectives and the want-states of the target audience. Table 13.1 illustrates.

In consumer selling, persuasive communication involves not just making sales, but:

Table 13.1 Marketing's competitive objective and sales force communication goals

Marketing's competitive objective	Want-state of target audience	Sales force communication goals
Attract	Latent/passive	Attract X percent new customers by creating awareness of product's potential or overcoming inhibitions to purchase.
Increase	Latent	*Increase* level of business in Y% of outlets by showing suitability/profitability of such increases.
Convert	Habitual purchase of rival brand Picking from repertoire of brands, etc.	*Convert* Z percent of customers from rivals by demonstrating critical advantages of firm's offering.
Retain	Habit	*Retain* all current customers by reassurance and regular calling.

- getting brand display: this may require much skill in negotiation to get the right mix in the right store position; and
- influencing the price charged by the channel intermediary.

Where the focus in communication lies in attracting and retaining customers and not just with making the isolated sale, the key to success lies in building customer trust in the company. This is particularly true of service firms such as those selling financial services, like bonds to institutional investors. This is because buying securities is not like buying building materials whose qualities can be largely determined prior to buying. Where there is trust between seller and customer, regret over the individual transaction does not fatally damage the relationship. It is accepted that there may be a loss over the individual transaction but things will even out in the long run. In conditions of trust there is a sense that reciprocity will operate over the long term. Trust is the basis of customer loyalty whose generation must be a superordinate goal. Loyalty implies "sticking to someone through thick and thin," that is, continuing to deal with the company even when it is at a temporary disadvantage.

Training goals

Many forms of training are undertaken by salespeople—for example, training customers' salespeople to sell or use equipment. More and more large companies are starting programs designed to improve dealer efficiency: programs covering, say, inventory control, store layout, systems and procedures, accounting, and promotional methods. Salespeople may be involved in all such training, and goals can be set to measure their performances in that role.

Service goals

Salespeople are called upon to perform many service functions, from the design of some total system of which the firm's product is part, to the monitoring of some past installation, to solving customer problems associated with the firm's products. Service goals can be set and performance assessed by examining samples of service work. The service role can be vital in building relationships with customers and creating the goodwill that is basic to developing loyalty.

Liaison goals

Salespeople are engaged in communicating forward to the customer and backward to management. It is the job of salespeople to communicate back to management the opinions and sentiments of customers and to communicate to customers the company's policies. This liaison role is important in helping to enhance the credibility of the supplier. But much more can be involved in the liaison role in a company that believes in getting as many people (including the chief executive officer) as possible involved with customers. The liaison role can also be interpreted to cover concept selling, forearming, and systems selling. In certain industrial markets this liaison role is key. If some production modification is required, the salespeople may be obliged to liaise between the firm's production personnel and customers. If the product is to be individually designed to fit the buyer's application, salespeople may have to liaise with design personnel on behalf of the buyer. Finally, if extensive development work is required, salespeople may have to liaise between the firm's R&D and the customer's technical staff. Goals can be set to reflect the quality of that liaison.

Intelligence goals

Every salesperson is expected to report customer reaction to the firm's offering. But an important though neglected function in industrial markets is that of collecting market intelligence. Salespeople are close to the customer and can spot changing attitudes. Similarly, salespeople are the first to suffer from renewed competitive attack and the first to notice its significance. Of course, salespeople may be tempted to distort the "facts" (as all employees tend to do when their interests are involved) but ways can usually be found to reduce such bias. It is also true that, in consumer markets, there may be better ways of obtaining the information of interest, but this should not lead to the generalization that the sales force should not be used for intelligence work.[1,2]

Whichever of the above functions is relevant to a sales force, the setting of goals/standards starts off by asking: "What are the conditions that exist when the function is carried out satisfactorily?" A description of these conditions forms the basis for setting goals for the function. This topic is considered later in the text.

The strategic path

The development of the sales strategy follows steps already described in the chapter on strategy formulation (Chapter 3). There is a need for a historical review and situation analysis but also of importance is an analysis of territorial performance to identify the following typical weaknesses:

- spotty distribution of accounts around the country or the global market not justified by the regional patterning of sales, with active accounts (those accounts actually being serviced) being too small a percentage of potential accounts. This assumes we know the distribution of prospective accounts which may not be so. But, in any case, spotty distribution is a common problem with a firm's product being typically better distributed near its home base so that, when it comes to international markets, it becomes quite obvious the firm has still a long way to go. Distribution is very linked to market share in that if accounts are not customers, their business goes elsewhere;
- not selling over the range of products. Unbalanced selling is common as salespeople have favorite products and may neglect the rest. Usually this has something to do

with the salesperson's lack of early success in developing an appropriate sales appeal: one rebuff can be sufficiently emotional as to evoke a disposition to avoid trying again;

- not selling to all the accounts allocated to him or her to sell. Some neglected accounts may be considered too small to cultivate, but many are accounts which the salesperson just does not like calling upon: it is a common experience that when such accounts are given to newly trained salespeople they become active and profitable again;
- low account penetration. It is common to find low sales per account relative to competition. There is a need for salespeople to keep a customer record showing the competitive position of every product with every account. Allied to this low account penetration is a failure by the salesperson to obtain display and special feature spots.

There is no general agreement of the content of a sales strategy as sales forces can vary so widely. However, there will always be some statement of goals and some statement of how sales resources are to be distributed over customers, products, and appeals. An outline of a sales strategy along these lines is shown in Appendix 13.1. Typical elements of the sales strategy are customer targets, product focus, customer appeals, support activities, and a budget statement. We will discuss each of these.

Customer targets

In the absence of direct selling to the user, customers are channel intermediaries like wholesalers and retailers. In established businesses the target customer group is well established but for many new products and businesses, the customer group needs to be defined. "Suspects" are those who have a need of the product but such suspects have to be screened for likely "prospects." This is a matter of getting out a profile of the "ideal" customer to determine who among the suspects comes near enough to the ideal to justify contact by a salesperson. But all prospects are not equally worthwhile and the sales strategy may lay out general guidelines as to what type of call is to be made on what type of account and at what frequency.

Suspects can be located via:

- use of published records like directories of companies in the relevant businesses;
- unsolicited inquiries;
- observation by salespeople of likely outlets;
- advertising (direct mail or selected media);
- referrals from satisfied customers; and
- fact-finding interviews.

Product focus

In line with investment objectives and other relevant considerations, the sales strategy should give guidance to the sales force on which goods and/or services are to be given priority in the period covered by the strategic plan. When salespeople carry many different product lines, many of which are to be sold to the same buyer, such guidance is needed. It is not so much the salesperson's time but the buyer's time that is at a premium since every buyer sets limits on the time he or she will spend with a salesperson, so the best use should be made of that time with selling priorities in mind.

Customer appeals

There are at least three types of sales appeals:

- appeals based on product benefits;
- appeals based on the problems anticipated in adopting the product; and
- appeals based on the competitive objective adopted.

Appeals related to benefits. Every offering is a configuration of benefits. But customers seldom regard the various benefits of equal importance. Thus channel intermediaries will be concerned with receiving information that provides reassurance about the demand for the product; industrial buyers may focus on technical and economic criteria while Avon selling direct to the housewife might focus on intrinsic, integrative, and economic criteria. However, whatever the configuration of benefits, each benefit identified can typically be related to a number of corresponding sales appeals:

Benefit from purchase	*Appeals corresponding to benefits*
Less labor needed per unit of output	(a) saving in labor cost
	(b) less dependent on labor
	(c) fewer problems due to labor turnover
	(d) saving in recruitment and training

The appropriate appeal will vary. Thus while in the United States a dishwasher is primarily bought as a labor-saving device, in Brazil the major benefit lies in the sterilizing of dishes since most of the housewives who own a dishwasher do not wash the dishes themselves but have maids to do the work.

Appeals based on the problems anticipated in adopting the product. Customer appeals may take account not only of product benefits, but of the problems customers are likely to anticipate in buying the product.[3] *Procedural* problems occur in learning how to use or how to sell the product. A buyer intent on minimizing the difficulties associated with adopting procedural-problem products will favor the supplier who is perceived as likely to reduce to a minimum the time and difficulty in learning. Hence sales appeals offering technical service, training and showing the ease with which the product can be operated and used are those that will be most appropriate. If *performance* problems are anticipated, the buyer is likely to favor the supplier who can reduce doubts about whether the product will do the job. Sales appeals here should stress, say, free trial, sale or return, success in similar applications and the technical competence and flexibility of the supplier. Finally, some products give rise to *political* problems associated with reaching agreement when the product affects several departments of the buying firm. Where the product is a political-problem product, a buyer is likely to favor a supplier who possesses those attributes that must be good regardless of the application. Without such attributes, the product is a weak candidate when some participants to the buying decision seek to frustrate the purchase. Sales appeals here should stress the firm's reputation, known capability for service, delivery, and flexibility. Of course these three categories of problem are not mutually exclusive and a particular product may involve all three types of problem.

Appeals based on the competitive objective.   A *retention* (of customers) objective may be adopted if increasing sales with current customers is unlikely. The *increase* objective is appropriate if there are further applications for which the customer might use the product, or sales per current customer are below expectations. A *convert* objective is appropriate if the product is an innovative substitute for rival products. Finally, an *attract* objective is appropriate when a new set of prospective users is being sought or former objections to the use of the product have been overcome. Table 13.2 illustrates.

Industrial firms sometimes rank existing and prospective customers according to their likelihood of switching suppliers.[4] The key question is: What would it take or what additional inducements would be needed for some particular customer or prospect to incur the costs and risks attached to switching suppliers? The answer to this question will suggest whether more should be done to retain the customer, or if the firm is a prospect, whether some attempt at converting would be worthwhile.

Table 13.2 Competitive objectives and sales appeals

Competitive objective	Where appropriate	Sales appeals
Retain	For example, where supplier has high share of business.	Developing resistance to change, e.g. by joint projects, regular calling, joint promotions.
Increase	For example, where supplier's share is considered below standard.	Suggest profitable applications by concept selling.
Convert	For example, when need to get buyers to switch from competitive brands.	Demonstrate superiority of the offering—e.g. free trial—or show success in analogous application or outlets.
Attract	For example, new set of prospective users identified.	Solve application problems.

Support activities

Support activities are those activities that are designed to back up the sales force by the provision of promotional material, technical help, incentive plans or whatever is considered necessary to do a good job and have salespeople give of their best. Sales support can be particularly important in services like financial services where the provision of up-to-date information is a prerequisite to successful selling.

The sales budget

It is common to include a sales budget with the sales strategy, detailing the various cost constraints within which objectives are to be attained.

INDIVIDUAL ACCOUNT PLANNING

The more homogeneous the target group of customers in terms of what they seek and how they buy, the more detailed can be the sales strategy. The less homogeneous the customer group, the more general will be the sales strategy and the more the need to develop an individual strategy for each major account. Although *individual account strategies* are preeminently associated with industrial marketing, they are becoming more common in selling to central buyers in retailing and to any other organizations who buy on a large scale. What usually distinguishes the buying here is not so much the buying on a large scale but the buying decision being taken by a committee or decision-making unit (DMU) composed of a number of participants. Membership of a DMU varies depending on the product being bought and whether the purchase is routine or not. In any case, salespeople seek to identify each member of the DMU to induce a leaning toward their offering. This is done by asking who is or will be involved in the buying decision and continuing to ask each person mentioned until no new names are given. This procedure is called "snowballing" in the sociological literature from which marketing borrowed the term.

Typically, in industrial buying, the coordination of activities associated with the purchase is done by the purchasing department. In companies where the purchasing function is established on a professional basis, purchasing's responsibilities cover all the *commercial* aspects of the buy:

- the "careful" shopper role, ensuring delivery at the right time, right place, right amount, right quality, right price with the right level of service;
- search for suppliers;
- search for better/less expensive substitutes;
- translating the needs of various company personnel into product needs;
- selling suppliers on supplying (if need be) and other members of the DMU on "best buy" solutions;
- administration involving interviewing salespeople, analyzing bids, helping to select

vendors/suppliers, negotiation on contracts, issuing purchase orders, and, say, organizing buyer–seller symposiums; and
- building an organizational "memory" relevant to purchasing: recording items bought, analyzing markets and economic trends, identifying reliable sources of supply and evaluating current supplier performance.

In industrial buying, the specification of the offering sought can involve:

- description (e.g. market grades, commercial standards, chemical or physical specification, blueprints);
- a sample (e.g. for color);
- a brand-name specification though purchasing managers would prefer to insert the words "or equal"; and
- the function/application to be performed.

From purchasing's point of view, product specification should be in terms of description plus details of the function or application to be met. Purchasing also tends to favor standardization (where possible) as well as simplification of the product lines bought to reduce inventories and handling costs and to obtain better prices.

Organizational buying

Whatever the buying organization, all individual account strategies will be based on some model of the buying process. Models depicting the organizational buying process differ from consumer buying models in taking account of:

- organizational goals;
- how groups decide, since several people are typically involved; and
- choice criteria for selecting a *supplier*, since organizations are usually concerned with who is supplying the product, to ensure reliability of quality and supply.

A number of models have been developed for organizational buying, some suggesting the causal factors at work or the micro-level interactions likely to occur. Often these models are nothing more than a division of the causal universe, analogous to saying people's behavior is a result of hereditary and environment. For our purposes, Figure 13.2 is adequate. It depicts the *process* of organizational buying. Of course, all buying may not follow exactly this format while those involved in buying are less likely to view buying as a series of discrete decisions than to view themselves as being involved in an iterative process of defining organizational needs, identifying supply sources and choosing vendors.

Figure 13.2 looks complex but understanding just the initial stages is all that is required since the rest is somewhat repetitive. In Figure 13.2, the demand for industrial products is viewed as arising either to:

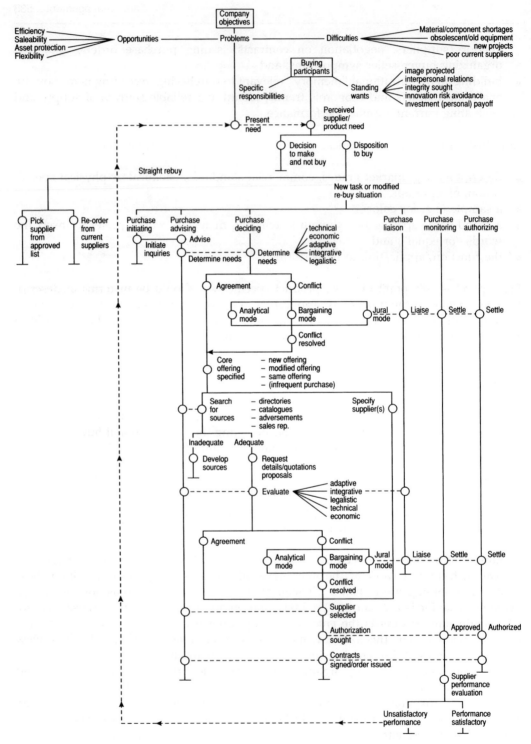

Figure 13.2 The process of industrial purchasing

- *exploit opportunities* for
  a) increasing efficiency;
  b) increasing salability of the firm's outputs;
  c) protecting its assets; and
  d) increasing flexibility in its operations; *or*
- overcome difficulties in achieving the firm's objectives such as
  a) material shortages;
  b) obsolescent equipment; and
  c) poor current suppliers.

If a seller's offering can contribute toward exploiting an opportunity or easing a difficulty, the organization with the opportunity or difficulty is a *suspect* for what the seller has to offer. Such suspects are screened for *prospects* though this does not mean that all such prospects are actively looking for what the seller has to offer: prospects are not always aware of opportunities or difficulties. Unless a proposed purchase is a *straight rebuy*, a major purchase is likely to involve several people who have differential self-interests, differential perceptions of reality, and possess differential knowledge and expertise. Thus the purchasing function will be concerned with the commercial aspects of the purchase such as price and life cycle costs, while the engineer is much more concerned with technical excellence, and production is concerned with ease of operation. In addition to various aspects of the offering, participants in a DMU have personal and professional goals. This needs to be said since the common view of industrial buying is as something uninfluenced by individual personality factors.

Personal and professional goals might be summed up as five I's:

- *Image projected*: each participant will wish to project a certain front or image (for example, of being efficient and a tough bargainer) and salespeople need to be supportive of that image;
- *Interpersonal relations*: participants to varying degrees are sensitive to what others think and anxious not to offend. Salespeople need to be sensitive, say, to the fact that the purchasing manager will wish to avoid any conflict with the engineers and so may be disposed to go along with key engineering values;
- *Integrity sought*: salespeople should not attempt to encourage behavior that is frowned upon by a participant who, for example, might be angered by attempts to elicit information on competitor bids;
- *Innovation risk avoidance*: participants are anxious to play safe and salespeople need to reassure such participants about the risks; and
- *Investment payoff to self*: participants are influenced by how a purchase will reflect on them personally (for example, making them look progressive) and salespeople should adapt their sales appeals accordingly.

Each participant's personal and professional goals (the five I's above) combine with organizational goals and job responsibilities to determine the particular buying criteria adopted. Thus the image, integrity, and interpersonal relations reflect themselves in integrative criteria; innovation risk avoidance emerges in adaptive criteria, while invest-ment payoffs are reflected in the technical and economic criteria that are chosen.

Where the decision is to buy rather than make (see Figure 13.2) the process will depend on whether the purchase is a straight rebuy, modified rebuy, or a new task.[5] (These cate-gories can be subcategorized still further by taking account of the degree of uncertainty encountered, range of choices and the relative power of buyer and seller, but more work is needed to demonstrate both the utility of this classification beyond what has so far been shown and its universality.[6]) How many participants and what part each partici-pant will play in these buys depends on such factors as the nature and value of the product, company size, and organization. But while the job titles of participants indi-cate broad functional responsibilities, they are not necessarily predictive of buying responsibilities. Thus the purchasing manager's influence can vary widely since the purchasing function itself may be little more than a clerical function or a distinct depart-ment or part of a wider materials management department. Trying to identify the *roles* played by participants in buying is likely to be more informative and useful than looking at their job titles.

The most frequently quoted classification of roles in buying is the five-category classification into

1   users,
2   influencers,
3   buyers,
4   deciders, and
5   gatekeepers.[7]

Users are those who will use the product; *influencers* are those who define the choice criteria, constrain choices or provide information on alternative offerings; *buyers* have the formal authority for choosing suppliers and dealing with the commercial aspects of the purchase; *deciders* are those who determine the ultimate supplier; and *gatekeepers* are those who control the flow of information to participants. But this is not a very operational criterion in that a user, for example, does not define any particular role in the decision process but a role after purchase, while every participant is there to be an influencer. An alternative set of categories used in consultancy is shown in Figure 13.2. These are:

- *Purchase initiating*: those who initiate the purchase. The formal initiator is often the unit needing the product but the real initiator might be the sales representative;
- *Purchase advising*: all purchase advisors need not necessarily be employees but can be "outsiders" like architects or consultants. Salespeople themselves can advise;
- *Purchase authorizing*: those authorizing a purchase may give automatic concurring approval to decisions made lower down the line. Because top management has the power to veto or authorize a purchase does not mean they are key participants. In many cases, by the time the decision reaches higher levels for approval, so many steps and actions have been taken, so many compromises made, that top manage-ment would hesitate before blocking lower-level choices;

- *Purchase monitoring*: some overall monitoring of what is going on is inevitable. Although there may be corresponding authority to veto a proposed decision, this probably seldom occurs if a decision process is in line with agreed procedure;
- *Purchase deciding*: the purchase deciders are the key people who determine
  a) the product specification,
  b) approve the list of acceptable vendors, and
  c) the actual vendor or vendors.

These are the three crucial decisions in industrial buying.

Participants in the DMU may weight the various choice criteria differently. The choice criteria are often not just concerned with buying the product but with engaging a supplier. The criteria thus apply to selecting the *supplier/offering*:

- *technical performance criteria*: this would cover not just the product's fit to functional requirements but the capabilities, experience, innovativeness, reliability, and accuracy of supply;
- *economic criteria*: total sacrifices that would be incurred in obtaining the product such as price, life cycle costs, operating costs, credit terms, etc;
- *adaptive criteria*: concern over supplier capabilities such as the financial stability of the supplier, experience in implementation, feasibility of the proposals, and so on;
- *integrative criteria*: the supplier's fit to the buying organization's culture. Overcoming procedural, performance and political problems; presale services, training, installation and monitoring promises to ensure post-sale satisfaction. The more the buying firm wants to consider the supplier like a division of its own organization, the more the supplier should appeal to integrative criteria;
- *legalistic*, or the need to conform to company or government policies: these may also include guarantees by the vendor that the product will adhere to legal specifications and company policies; and
- *intrinsic liking*: being favorably disposed not only to the style and so on of the product but the particular salesperson acting for the vendor.

Although the different participants to the buying decision may favor different choice criteria, this does not necessarily generate conflict or even debate among the participants. There can be agreement based on the explicit or implicit rules or norms laid down or emerge from past dealings among the participants: past practices and recognition of "territorial rights" set precedents and establish traditions for deciding future cases. However, although it is true that

- the more buys the same DMU makes,
- the smaller the number of participants in the DMU, and
- the more successful the group has been in the past,

then the more cohesive the group is likely to become, this does not automatically occur. Some participants will act against a background of intense attachment to their own functional department and this may make them see few buying commonalities with other members of the DMU.

Where conflict among DMU participants does develop, the conflict may be resolved in several different ways depending somewhat on the relative power of participants. This has led to studies seeking ways to identify the relative power of participants. Thus one study argues that participants derive power from the position they occupy within the buying system, with position being defined in terms of

- centrality or level of involvement in network relations;
- distance from the dominant reference group(s) such as higher management;
- formal rank or level in the hierarchy; and
- power of the departmental unit to which the participant is a member.[8]

These factors do influence the relative *potential* power of participants but some of the categories are likely to overlap giving rise to double counting, for example, formal rank and distance from dominant reference groups. In any case, *actual* power cannot be reduced to just position within the buying system since other factors such as personal performance and personality will inevitably have their impact.

Another study claims that those perceived by others in the DMU as being knowledgeable about relevant issues have *expert power* and these participants exert greater influence in DMUs that are large, viscid, and under time pressure, providing they do not try too hard to influence outcomes. In contrast, those within the DMU who primarily have *reinforcement power* (reward and coercive power) tend to exert greater influence in DMUs that are small, not very viscid, and under time pressure, providing they make strong influence attempts.[9] Although this contingency approach accepts that different conditions affect influence patterns, it seems nonetheless too simplistic since it ignores *position power* while both studies ignore the personal attractiveness of participants, interpersonal loyalties and the presence of *coalitions* or *cliques* within the DMU. But relative power is not the only way of settling differences.

There is still the opportunity for the *analytical* mode of conflict resolution whereby the conflict is settled amicably by appeal to reason, justice, fairness and precedent. There is also the *bargaining* mode where the conflict is resolved by compromises or an exchange of concessions. Bargaining among the participants leads naturally to the formation of coalitions and the very threat of coalitions forming can affect outcomes. Although much has been written about the formation of coalitions there is still little by way of robust, general findings. Finally, there is the *jural* mode of conflict resolution, whereby appeals are made up the line for higher management to settle. Where a salesperson gets round to each participant and persuades them into being even slightly more disposed toward his or her position, this can lead to more of a pro-consensus favoring his or her offering. In other words, if each member of the DMU can be induced to be even moderately in favor of the salesperson's offering, the tendency is to become more pro after discussion. This is known as *group polarization*. It is where members of the DMU stand initially in relation to the midpoint of the viewpoint continuum that predicts the direction of the polarizing shift. Thus, if members of the DMU are already leaning toward a supplier, the subsequent discussion will tend to become more extremely pro that particular supplier. Polarization is in conflict with the idea that groups converge and compromise on the average position of the group. Needless to say not all participants in a DMU will polarize when the group does: the phenomenon of polarization simply says what is likely to happen, not what will inevitably happen.

When agreement is reached or conflict resolved, the result is a *specification* of what is wanted. In any case, the specification may not actually specify the brand (and hence the vendor). Most do not, in which case the next step is to list what vendors are acceptable, perhaps by checking with salespeople, other firms, or by consulting directories of suppliers, catalogues on file, or advertisements in magazines. *Acceptable vendors* (sources) are approached for product details, quotations and/or proposals. The offerings of these vendors are then evaluated against the choice criteria while conflict among participants may occur once again to be resolved in the ways already discussed. In this way, a vendor or supplier(s) is finally selected by the DMU. However, even when there is unanimity over the choice of vendor, the selection may still be subject to contract and final approval from higher management. There may also be *negotiation* over level of quality, price, payment terms, and all aspects of service.

Suppliers entering into *negotiations* with buyers try to discover the importance of various components of the offering to the buyer, so as to concede something that is more important to the buyer than to the seller and obtain what is more important to the seller than to the buyer. It seems that successful negotiators:

- focus on the areas of conflict and establish what is common ground;
- try to anticipate the options open to both themselves and those with whom they are negotiating;
- avoid language designed to influence perspectives that just cannot be adopted such as "this offer is fair and reasonable";
- avoid advancing all the relevant reasons justifying their case since the other side is apt to focus on the weaker reasons to dilute the whole case; and
- do not accept that a proposal always requires a counter proposal since this can be distracting.

But buyers and sellers are not adversaries as if every buying encounter were a zero sum game where, if one gains, the other loses an equivalent sum. Many firms today prefer to deal with just one or two suppliers whom they can treat as if part of the company.

The question that naturally arises is: "How does a supplier/vendor identify the different roles participants might play?" One approach is to ask salespeople to construct a flow process chart of the buying process by getting them to inquire about participants and their roles. With a little more questioning, a chart can be drawn up similar to that shown in Figure 13.3. In this chart, five sets of people are involved in the purchase of capital equipment—namely, the future user, engineering, purchasing, top management, and finance. The roles played by the various participants can be inferred from the chart and these are shown in Table 13.3. But before turning to Table 13.3, the reader should try to infer the roles of the future user, engineering, purchasing, top management, and finance from studying Figure 13.3 and then check against Table 13.3.

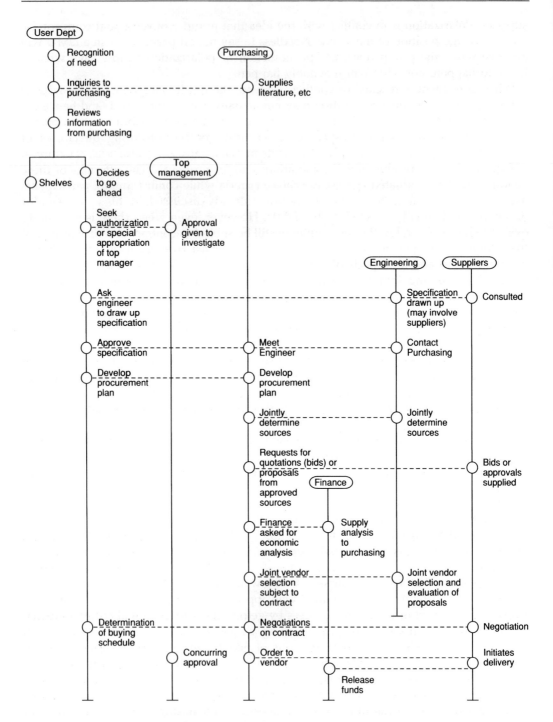

Figure 13.3 Purchase of capital equipment: process chart

Table 13.3 Participants in the purchase of capital equipment and their corresponding roles

Participant	Role(s)
User	Purchase initiator
	Purchase authorizer (approves engineering specifications)
Top management	Purchase authorizer (approves purchase)
Purchasing	Purchasing advisor (supplies literature, etc. to user)
	Purchase decider (sources and vendor)
	Purchase liaison
	Purchase monitoring
Engineering	Purchase decider (product specifications, sources and vendor specification)
Finance	Purchase advisor (supplies economic analysis)
	Purchase authorizing (releases funds)
Supplier	Advisor

Individual account planning and strategies

Planning for the individual account strategy

Figure 13.4 shows the information to be collected by a sales representative calling on hospitals as a basis for planning an individual account strategy. It draws on the theoretical insights discussed above. Within the hospital there are a number of buying centers, any of which might form a DMU. These centers are:

- *operating room*: this buying center consisted of the chief surgeon, various specialist doctors and the operating room supervisor;
- *central supply*: this buying center consisted of the central supply supervisor, the materials manager, and the engineer;
- *laboratory*: this buying center consisted of the pathologist, the laboratory supervisor, the materials manager, and the engineer;
- *labor delivery*: this buying center consisted of the chief of obstetrics, the obstetrics supervisor, the materials manager, and the engineer; and
- *nursing service*: this buying center consisted of the director of nursing, the materials manager, and the engineer.

Buying policies.   At the top of Figure 13.4, after the basic identification data are inserted, the sales representative attaches to the form the hospital's buying policies covering such policies as negotiation procedures, vendor selection procedures, gifts and so on. Buying policies may be explicit (for example, "If price is a matter of negotiation, suppliers must be prepared to disclose the cost makeup of the price quoted") or implicit (for instance, the buying firm's insistence on multiple sourcing). In either case there is a need to know and adhere to such policies.

Period ending ....
Date ....
Hospital ....

Buying center ....
Buying policies (Attach)

Part I

(1) Major equipment type	(2) Inventory			(3) Goals served*								(4) State of demand			
	Total	% share	% change during period	Opportunities				Difficulties				Active	Latent	Passive	Exclusionary reasons
				E	S	F	A	MS	OE	NP	PS				

Part II

(1) Job title	(2) Name	(3) Comment	(4) Role	(5) Buying criteria
1 Adm. or Asst.				
2 P.A.				
3 CS Supvr.				
4 OR Supvr.				
5 Surgeon				
6 Dir. Nursing				
7 Engineer				
8 Lab Supvr.				
9 Architect				
10 –				
11 OB Supvr.				
12 Contractor				
13 Infect. Control.				
14 Finance Off.				
15 Mat'l Mgr.				

Part III

Competition	Equipment type	Strengths	Weaknesses

*E = efficiency   MS = material shortages
S = saleability   OE = obsolescent equipment
F = flexibility   NP = new projects
A = asset protection   PS = poor current suppliers

Figure 13.4 Buying center account planning

Part I of Figure 13.4. This part is used to determine whether the buying center is a suspect purchaser for the up-coming period and, if so, whether the suspect is also a prospect. Column (1) lists the major pieces of equipment being sold. Column (2) obliges the hospital representative to undertake an inventory in the buying center by counting the number of pieces of equipment within each product category, calculating the percentage "market share" and whether the firm's competitive position has changed for the better or worse since the last audit. In column (3), the sales representative identifies the goals (opportunities/difficulties) to which the seller's product could contribute. Opportunities relate to increasing the buying firm's *efficiency* (E), increasing *salability* (S) of the buying firm's product, increasing the buying firm's *flexibility* (F), or ensuring *asset protection* (A). On the other hand, the difficulties that might be relieved by the seller's product relate to *material shortages* (MS), *obsolescent equipment* (OE), *new projects* (NP), and *poor current suppliers* (PS).

When a center has a need for the product it is a suspect, but not all suspects are prospects so the next step is to inquire whether a suspect is a prospect. This is done by the sales representative identifying the state of demand for each product category for which the buying center is a suspect (column 4). For example, suppose central supply could justify purchase on the basis of cost saving. Why has central supply held back from purchase? Answers fall into any of the following categories:

- *demand active*: the buying center is actively engaged in a search for such a product;
- *latent demand*: the buying center is not actively looking for such a product as it is not aware of the product's potential for the hospital;
- *passive demand*: the buying center is aware of the potential of the product for meeting goals but purchase is inhibited by, say, price; and
- *exclusionary reasons*: the buying center is excluded from the market at present due to, say, financial incapacity, policy, or obligations to current suppliers.

A suspect with an active demand for the product is a prospect, but a suspect with a passive demand is also a prospect if there is a belief that the buying center's objections can be overcome. Similarly, a suspect with a latent demand is a prospect if ignorance of the product's potential is the major stumbling block to purchase.

Parts II and III of Figure 13.4. These incorporate the rest of the information needed for developing an individual account strategy. In Part II:

- Column (1) gives the job title of the participant.
- Column (2) gives the name of the person holding the job.
- Column (3) gives space for the sales representative's comments on the personal goals etc. of the participant.
- Column (4) gives the role of the participant in the purchase decision as deduced from past history.
- Column (5) records buying criteria.

Part III directs attention to competition and to competitive strengths and weaknesses.

Date: ....   Period ending: ....

Hospital: ....   Buying center: ....   Revenue target: ....

Individual product target sales   1 ....   2 ....   3 ....   4 ....

Part II

1 Product ....   Goal(s) served ....   State of demand ....

Participant	Role(s)	Goals	Buying criteria	Action desired	Sales appeals and action to be taken
(i)					
(ii)					
(iii)					
(iv)					
(v)					

2 Product ....   Goal(s) served ....   State of demand ....

Figure 13.5 Individual account strategy

The account strategy

The information in Figure 13.4 is used to develop an individual account strategy along the lines shown in Figure 13.5. First, a revenue goal is established for the buying center for the period, whether the period is for a year or something less. This revenue goal is built up from the target goals for the individual products. The participants in the buying center (DMU) are listed together with their titles, personal goals, role, and buying criteria. The action desired of participants is agreed and the sales appeals to be used to bring about the action are outlined.

Selling overseas

Cultural and political/legal differences always complicate selling overseas since these determine what is socially or politically appropriate. We can illustrate this by using Japan and China. Thus the Japanese tend to be rather formal with a dislike of aggressive selling as being both ostentatious and confrontational. Sellers are customarily introduced by letter of introduction or some other communication from a third party. Those representing the supplier are expected to be "sincere," that is, people who act rationally in considering the consequences of all their actions and proposals and who will strive for a harmonious relationship. Reciprocal trust is expected as is loyalty, as used in this text to mean that a buyer will continue to do business with a supplier even when that supplier is at a temporary disadvantage.

In China, it is the Chinese state that does the buying since every major organization is likely to have both a professional management and government officials involved in buying. There are a number of ways to approach the Chinese market

- selling to or through a local enterprise;
- employing a local Chinese organization; or
- through a joint venture.[10]

The product can be introduced by offering a seminar to the relevant ministry who are supportive of anything that will educate China on the latest technology. But when it comes to buying the Chinese tend to be bureaucratically rule governed though as effective in negotiation as the best elsewhere. (It should be remembered that the Chinese developed government bureaucracy at least 200 years BC, long before Max Weber began to write on it.[11]) The chief government agency for the coordination of foreign trade is MOFERT (Ministry of Foreign Economic Relations and Trade) but there are also the foreign trade organizations (FTCs) under MOFERT, which liaise between central government and foreign firms and are often the first contact for foreign firms. There is also CCPIT (China Council for the Promotion of International Trade), which is tied to MOFERT and still other specialized trade offices. In selling, the first focus is on establishing rapport and trust as considerable trust is needed before the Chinese will take risks with a new vendor.[12]

THE SALES INTERVIEW

In development selling

Salespeople are probably engaged most of the time on maintenance selling, making regular calls on the same set of customers, obtaining repeat orders, or selling just minor new variations of their standard range of products. However, every salesperson on occasions will engage in development selling, opening up new accounts to sell a prospect for the first time. Prospective new accounts must belong to one of the firm's segments otherwise sellers are not starting from a position of strength in knowing their marketing is based on the relevant knowledge, skills, and competencies to successfully compete. Sometimes prospects need to be identified from the list of suspects but prospects for services often result from referrals. One reason for this is that the more direct approach, particularly for professional services, is considered socially inappropriate if not rather debasing.

In development selling the initial emphasis will be on *establishing rapport* with the buyer(s) to open up two-way communication so as to get the salesperson perceived as a source of help. In general, a salesperson might:

- seek some genuine common ground so that mutual interests are established. This may have nothing to do with business: buyers are just as interested in themselves e.g. likely reference groups such as family, or leisure activities;

- mention in favorable terms something the salesperson has noticed about the buyer's place of work or company reputation; or
- be supportive of the buyer by voicing agreement or giving praise.

Of course, each of the above could boomerang. The shrewd buyer can see through a pretense. Any communication carries not only a message but also a tone and a salesperson who overdoes any of the above may be dismissed as ingratiating or lacking in judgment. Yet there are always opportunities to use the above and there is no reason why such cannot be done genuinely. The essential point in establishing rapport is to discover *shared values* and experiences as a basis for mutual trust. Where salesperson and customer share the same values and already possess a close relationship, rapport has also been established so much of what the salesperson says in introductory sales talk may simply have the function of *solidarity building*. The problem arises when values and perspectives differ since these form the basis for understanding. One skill here lies in learning the language (the technical language if need be or the language of the subculture) of the prospect to create a language for communication and understanding.

The next stages deal with what Kurt Lewin in his model of attitude change refers to as:[13]

- unfreezing,
- moving, and
- refreezing.

These stages constitute a hierarchy of effects so we need to explain how the buyer is to be persuaded through the stages. The first stage of unfreezing consists of getting the buyer to perceive a performance gap that might be filled by the firm's product. Unfreezing has similarities to activating a latent want, in that the salesperson is trying to put across the potential of the offering for the buyer. In political marketing, the phase of unfreezing is called "consciousness raising." *Creative interrogation* is one way to bring this about. In creative interrogation the salesperson plays back what the buyer says, exposing assumptions so prospects face up to discrepancies between expressed beliefs and behavior so they say in effect: "This is what I believe and yet look at what I am doing." This is accompanied by highlighting the product's potential for the goals of the buyer by getting the buyer to *imagine* using the product. (Imagining using the product can be a form of self-persuasion.) But more is needed if a buyer's perspective needs changing. This is the problem of getting buyers on to the "right wavelength," discussed in the chapters on advertising.

The buyer is now aware of the product's potential but is held back by objections. Lewin's *moving* stage consists of activating the passive want by overcoming the objections to buying. In buying for the first time, buyers are typically inhibited by uncertainty. Thus in buying professional services, there is uncertainty over the likely quality of the service and costs since lawyers and so on may not be able to provide firm cost estimates. In getting the buyers to move, we are getting them to work through the implications of buying and confront the need for change. One way to encourage this, is for the salesperson to restate the buyer's objection or objections to show understanding and then seek to minimize the significance of the objections or offer compensating advantages. If the prospect is just generally uncertain, as is common in the buying of services (e.g. removal services), the focus should be on demonstrating expertise, experience, and a satisfied list of customers, together with successful case histories that parallel the prospect's own situation. But persuasion cannot just rely on words but needs to be reinforced by a professional manner, professional communications and a professional environment. Persuasion is further enhanced by *reference selling*. Reference selling occurs whenever some current customer agrees to talk to the prospect and recommend the seller, preferably by showing success with the product in an application similar to the prospect's. Evaluating a potential major supplier can involve plant visits, balance sheet analysis and an assessment of capabilities. In any case, there must at some time be an attempt to "close the sale" when intention movements (for example, praise of the product, rapt attention, buyer talks about delivery dates etc.) are manifested. The *refreezing* stage is post-sales reassurance about the wisdom of the purchase so as to overcome post-decision doubts or dissonance to secure a customer and not just an isolated sale.

After the exchange of contracts (if appropriate) and the delivery of the product, the buying organization may rate the vendor on both the quality of the product and the quality of the service. A vendor rating system can cover

- product quality,
- delivery to time and specification,
- post-sales service,
- technical emergency assistance,
- interpersonal relationships with the supplier, and
- inventory help and so on.

In any case, salespeople need to keep the customer sold by ensuring all goes well. Figure 13.6 is a model of the interview process as an interaction process between the salesperson and the buyer; it captures much of the communication process involved in the three stages.

Salesmanship

All sales managers need to know something about salesmanship. Salesmanship is not only involved in direct selling but in all activities that involve customer or prospective buyer contact. In service activities it should be part of the skills of everyone from waiters to doctors. Here we are more interested, but not entirely concerned, with salesmanship exercised in selling.

Personal selling is particularly important when the company markets throughout the world because of:

- the restrictions on advertising through the media or suitable media may not exist;
- the importance of personal contact in many countries; and
- the communications burden being higher when products well-established in the home market are new abroad.

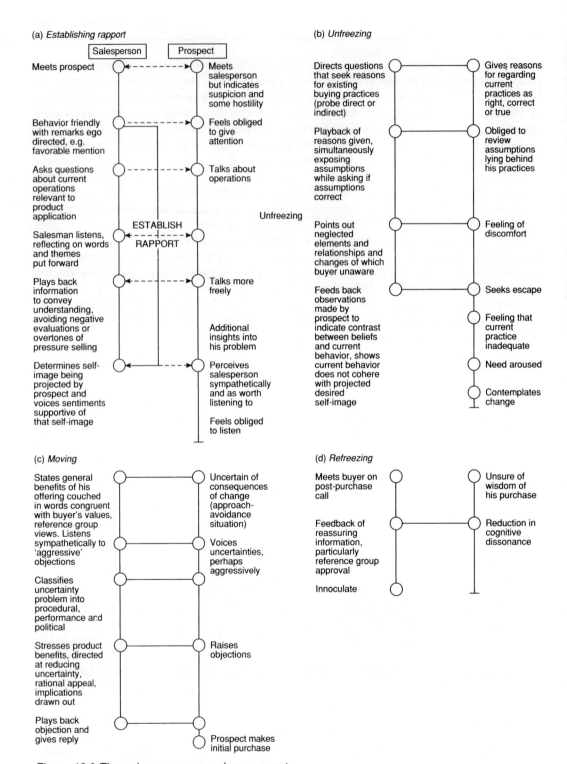

Figure 13.6 The salesperson as a change agent

Also for many industrial companies, advertising is virtually ruled out and a sales force is required to do the whole job of communicating about the product. There are traditional approaches to salesmanship, associated with selling a product for the first time or at least associated with arousing prospect interest in the product. These are:

- *The ring-a-bell technique.* This approach uses one dominant appeal and so assumes a homogeneous audience as to what appeal will motivate. Its theoretical underpinnings lie in behaviorism. It is the canned sales appeal, assuming a standard appeal ("ring-a-bell") will activate interest in the product. It is commonly used when the buying inducement is price. The approach fails to exploit the salesperson's potential for flexibility or adaptation to individual buyer peculiarities. It is not surprising that this approach has become common in TV shopping.
- *Barrier selling.* Here the salesperson is trained to guide the prospect into agreeing with each statement, starting with some socially endorsed statement ("Can I take it you are interested in education, Madam?"). If at the end of the presentation prospects fail to buy, they appear to be denying all their previous admissions. The theoretical underpinnings of the approach lie in consistency theory in that people seek consistency between their beliefs and their behavior. It is the most common approach to selling encyclopedias door-to-door. People are embarrassed by being inconsistent so the approach depends on pressuring people into buying and this has led to a lot of criticism about the ethics of so doing. It is not appropriate for most selling situations.
- *AIDA* (Attention, Interest, Desire, and Action). This is often considered the first of the *hierarchy of effects* models. The aim is to lead the buyer through each of these alleged mental stages on the way to buying. Thus the salesperson might seek to get *attention* by favorable mention, *create interest* by focusing on benefits, *activate desire* by showing the relevance of the product's benefits for the buyer's goals, and then getting *buying action* as a consequence. Although the approach was developed long before there was any talk about the information processing approach, the theoretical underpinnings lie in cognitive psychology, in viewing the decision-maker as an information processor who goes through some sequence of mental steps in arriving at the decision. However, none of these steps is sufficient to lead on to the next stage so courses in selling using this model focus on various "mechanisms" for moving the consumer from one stage to the next, much as in the Lewin model already discussed. But there is some arbitrariness in the stages which, together with the assumption of the process being a single unitary process and the target audience being uniform in terms of readiness to buy, has limited its application.
- *The need satisfaction approach.* Here the salesperson is taught to probe and diagnose customer wants to find as many needs as possible for which the seller's product is the answer. The next step is to show the match between the wants uncovered and what the seller has to offer. The theoretical underpinning of this approach is the rational model of decision-making. A variation of this approach is *consultative selling* whereby the sales representative helps the buyer define his or her problem and then shows how the firm's offering will solve the problem. Unlike previous approaches this approach acknowledges that selling should be two-way communication, a matter of talking with, not at.

- *The power model.* This approach focuses on how different influence sources can be used in activating wants. The sources are
  a) coercion with its appeal to fear e.g. "If you don't buy my product, we will not be buying yours";
  b) reward power with its appeal to material self-interest, e.g. use of gifts;
  c) attractiveness with its appeal to the self-image of the buyer, given that an attractive salesperson is one who is supportive of the buyer's self-image/self-esteem. Buyers are disposed to identify with someone supportive of them. Similarity of background, age and values facilitates mutual attractiveness though seller attractiveness also arises from supportive interaction through time ("He's not bad when you get to know him"). If there is one general characteristic in attractiveness it is probably the ability to come across as open (as if revealing all) so that people are reminded of some favorite uncle, friend etc; and
  d) credibility with its appeal to values. Credibility is particularly important in any major purchase. If buying is based on identification with the salesperson through that salesperson's attractiveness, buyers change their minds as the salesperson changes hers. This is not so when the basis of buying is credibility of the salesperson since the buyer internalizes the message. Credibility is tied to perceived trustworthiness and so to loyalty.

Credibility consists of trustworthiness and technical expertise. The perceived trustworthiness of a salesperson is a function of the sincerity and good intentions conveyed. This is a particular difficulty for car dealers, with their high power tactics and haggling over prices. As one commentator said: "how can a system create trust when a person who knows his way around can get a huge discount while the little old lady spending her savings on a car is likely to get no reduction?" Trustworthiness is important where the buyer cannot adequately evaluate what is said e.g. a delivery date or a promise. To create trustworthiness the salesperson may have to give up some short-term gain to build mutual trust. The technical expertise of a salesperson is established by his or her ability to field questions and the level of intelligence, education and experience conveyed. Technical expertise assumes the salesperson knows the product and its relevancy for the applications envisaged. Credible arguments are perceived as novel, valid and relevant. But as perceptions of novelty, validity and relevance are value judgments, credibility can be said to be an appeal to values. Consistency in an argument is also important since consistency is a sign of credibility: certainty and commitment to a viewpoint.

The power approach is rooted in exchange theory, particularly in Emerson's version.[14] Probably the essence of what we call salesmanship is the skilled use of attractiveness and credibility. While attractiveness is important to establishing rapport so that both parties feel at ease, credibility is key to both unfreezing and moving. But things are never quite so simple as high attractiveness can cast a halo over someone's credibility since it creates a wish to believe in the other. On the other hand, it is possible to view someone as a likable rogue!

Principles of automatic influence. Instead of focusing on the tactics of the salesperson we could focus on the buyer and the rules underlying persuasive messages.

Some of these are discussed under what Cialdini calls the principles of automatic influence:[15]

- *The consistency principle.* People like to be consistent and this is one reason used to explain why seeking a little favor facilitates asking for a big favor. Being consistent helps people maintain a positive view of themselves so that once people show some commitment, they are apt to go along with larger requests. Asking for small favors as a basis for getting people to agree to some big favor is known to salespeople as the "foot-in-the-door technique."
- *The reciprocity principle.* It is a social norm to reciprocate a favor and this is used to explain why "free" inspections, or giving small gifts tend to facilitate making a sale. It may explain on occasions why, when a brand has earned the buyer's trust, buyers reciprocate with loyalty. But it can also be used to explain what salespeople call the "door-in-the-face" technique, whereby some salesperson asks a very big favor which is refused. The salesperson then asks a much smaller favor which is accepted because the very act of making it a small favor is a sort of concession that brings into play the norm of reciprocity. Also at work here is the contrast effect between the original request and the final one.
- *The social validation principle.* People like their judgments to be socially validated and this explains the selling effectiveness of pointing out to the buyer that rivals have all bought the product or the buyer is the only one who has not yet recognized the superiority of the seller's offering.
- *The authority principle.* There are social rules as to what constitutes a credible authority and the quoting of such authorities (e.g. a doctor on medical matters) by the salesperson can be an effective tactic.
- *The scarcity principle.* Anything made to appear hard to get appears more desirable. This is what explains the frequent use of such appeals as "last few"; "last chance to buy"; "only one per customer." Owning something scarce and not generally available appeals to integrative criteria. The scarcity principle is used to explain why the banning of a film or a book, etc. makes the object that much more desirable.

A good deal of time in salesmanship courses is spent on how to overcome objections and how to close the sale. Salespeople are taught to view objections in the right way. From the buyer's point of view, it is a way of reducing the perceived risk of buying. From the salesperson's point of view, the prospects who raise an objection are getting involved and giving guidance as to what for them are the crucial issues. Every objection successfully surmounted is a step toward selling success. Some traditional ways of surmounting objections are:

- *boomerang*: this is converting the objection into a reason for buying, e.g. fewer sizes means less inventory;
- *compensation*: the objection is admitted but compensating benefits are demonstrated;
- deny the objection if based on untrue facts;
- dispel the objection by demonstration; and
- offer guarantee.

Where the sales situation is highly favorable, there is little need for lengthy product discussion. In any case, tentative trial closes need to be tried early in the interview as a test of how the sale is proceeding. Yet salespeople often hesitate to close the sale because of fear of failure. It is for this reason that courses in salesmanship stress tactics for closing a sale. If the salesperson fails to get an order, he or she should at least get some commitment, say, a future appointment. What is less stressed on salesmanship courses is the interpersonal skills which form the background for success in applying selling techniques. Typically such skills involve

- effective listening,
- interpreting nonverbal behavior,
- exhibiting the right degree of assertiveness, and
- skill in resolving conflicts.

A discussion of these topics is beyond the scope of this book but can be found elsewhere. However, a word can be said about nonverbal behavior.

People "give off" as well as give information about themselves. We may try to convey a certain impression of ourselves to others but the information we give off may make it impossible to sustain that impression. The information we give off mainly comes from our nonverbal behavior like the intonation (pitch and loudness, drawl, etc.) of our voice and the gestures we make. The "structural approach" to the study of nonverbal behavior focuses on the whole of a person's gestures on the ground that their meaning lies in the way they are combined. This contrasts with the "external variable approach" which relates particular gestures such as pupil size to external factors such as the time spent looking at an advertisement.

The study of nonverbal behavior now receives a good deal of prominence in textbooks on salesmanship. Such assumes there is a shared code among people within the culture for correctly interpreting nonverbal behavior. But many social scientists either deny the existence of such a code, or, more commonly, claim that the correct reading of the code is always situational. Thus gaze can express intimacy or be used when people want to be either persuasive or be deceptive. No single gesture can be regarded as "an isolated signal box." There is ambiguity in interpreting *all* behavior and such ambiguity is an inevitable part of social life. Courses in interpersonal skills, interpreting nonverbal behavior are in danger of denying such ambiguity if they assume that, regardless of context, there are fixed rules to be put across for ensuring success in interpersonal relations. Much, for example, depends on the initial expectations of the buyer and seller since these must be complementary if frustration is not to result. Nonetheless some attempt to develop interpersonal skills is needed wherever salesmanship is required. At the very least, it might help to do something about poor service: resentfulness, arrogance, peremptory, or condescending behavior or, the other extreme, of obsequiousness. Service people who do not like helping others; have a chip on their shoulder, believing themselves to be in a position of inferiority (and hence trying to redress the balance by acting superior); think customers are just an irritant and describe them as such in their language to each other (for example, in one hospital study, patients were negatively labeled "hits"), should not be employed in such work unless education, indoctrination and training are shown to be effective in changing attitudes. But to repeat, salesmanship cannot be reduced to some set of predetermined rules since rules cannot cover the impact of personality (e.g. personal charm) and of speech and other personal characteristics.

Telemarketing. Telemarketing is becoming more common in selling, covering applications such as:

- order processing,
- customer service,
- sales support, and
- account management.

As an aid to field selling, companies set up units devoted to writing orders, tracking the state of orders through production and ensuring orders go out to time and specification. The same unit is used to improve customer service by contacting customers about the state of their orders and bringing to their attention possible savings through increasing the size of their order, buying across the range or drawing to the attention of the customer likely shortages in their stocks of certain products.

Telemarketing has proved useful as a direct sales support by providing customer leads to field salespeople, arranging their calls and selling to marginal accounts which do not justify a direct call. But sometimes telemarketing is used to do the whole job of account management for all the firm's customers. Here all sales transactions are initiated and completed on the telephone. This is what commonly happens with salespeople selling various financial instruments, say, to those in charge of pension funds. This is not to suggest that such salespeople or brokers never meet their clients (they may meet them periodically for lunch to personalize the relationship) but that the actual selling is conducted over the telephone.

OPERATIONAL PROBLEMS OF SALES MANAGEMENT

We now consider the operational problems of sales management. The key leverage factors in "doing things right" are:

- *Salespeople*. The salespeople themselves need to have an aptitude for the job, which brings with it the problem of recruitment and selection. They also need to have knowledge and skills and this gives rise to the problem of how they should be trained. Finally, salespeople must be motivated, which encompasses the problems associated with supervision, compensation, evaluation of performance and the overall motivational climate in which they work, No *single* factor, whether individual aptitude, motivation, selling skill, organizational climate, or personal characteristics, has been found to be particularly predictive of high selling performance. It seems there are multiple determinants of performance and these tend to be job specific, so training is important.[16]
- *Work undertaken*. Just as on the shop floor and in the office, there is a need to examine

the activities carried out by salespeople to eliminate activities that cannot be justified and to simplify others.

- *Deployment.* The assignment of sales territories, the optimal allocation of effort among customers and products, the route plan and the call cycle are all problems for sales management.
- *Organization.* The organizational issues in field selling (for example, whether to organize on a product or regional basis and so on) are touched upon in the final chapter on the organization of marketing.

A single chapter on sales management cannot provide comprehensive discussion on all these problems. In any case, the above factors are simply those sales management find actionable. There are other factors, though, that influence field force effectiveness like the marketing support received by the sales force and competitive activity. There have been attempts to identify such factors and assess their significance but they will not be discussed here.

Recruitment and selection

The general objectives of any sales recruitment and selection program are to:

- define, locate, attract, and select qualifiable or qualified salespeople;
- raise the level of the human assets involved in selling. The sales function is only as good as the quality of the sales force. By controlling recruitment and selection a sales manager can change the whole orientation of the sales organization; and
- retain good salespeople. Although an extremely low labor turnover may suggest a too easy management (since however good the recruitment and selection process, some salespeople will be unsuited for the job), a high labor turnover adds to the cost of recruitment, selection, and training and results in revenue losses.

The recruitment and selection procedure adopted to accomplish these objectives involves

1 calculating the number of salespeople required;
2 specifying the abilities and traits demanded;
3 identifying sources of applicants; and finally
4 choosing a validated selection process.

Numbers required

Determining the numbers of salespeople required means estimating the number of retirements, promotions, resignations, and dismissals during the period and adjusting for growth or decline.

Specifying the abilities and traits needed

The specifying of the abilities and traits required is the function of the *job specification,* which stems from a *job analysis,* identifying the factors entering into the selling job. A job analysis is based on a combination of observational techniques and interviews. Thus selling manuals can be examined and an "activity log" kept of activities carried out by salespeople. Another technique is the "critical incident" method whereby sales supervision relate which incidents in their experience lead to outstanding success or failure. Thus in one study, the critical incident method led to specifying the following as critical functions:

- following up on complaints, requests, orders, and leads;
- planning ahead;
- communicating information to management;
- carrying out promises;
- persisting with difficult accounts;
- pointing to applications for other company products;
- knowing customer requirements;
- defending company policies to customers;
- calling on all accounts; and
- helping customers with displays.

From a job analysis comes the *job description,* describing the duties and behavior involved in selling, servicing and managing a group of accounts. Finally, there is the *job specification* which seeks to distinguish the sales job from other jobs and successful salespeople from the unsuccessful. This job specification sets out the abilities (cognitive aspects of the job) and the traits (noncognitive aspects of the job) needed for successful performance.

Sources of applicants

Potential sources of applicants are

- educational institutions,
- internal transfers,
- employee recommendations,
- employment agencies,
- advertisements,
- unsolicited applications, and
- other companies, whether rival firms or customer employees.

The recruitment process is important since without suitable applicants the firm is reduced to choosing the "best of a bad lot." Wide sources of recruitment are needed when the selection tools available are more effective than sources for predicting sales performance. In any case, judging the cost/effectiveness of various sources is recommended.

Selection process

The final step is the selection itself. A good selection system presupposes the firm knows the abilities and traits needed to do the job. As this is a choice situation, it is useful to set out the choice criteria formally, based on the job description. The choice criteria developed for buying apply here if suitably interpreted:

- *Economic criteria.* One reason for choosing one applicant over another is the lesser cost outlay associated with smaller salary, reduced training cost, and fewer removal expenses.
- *Technical criteria.* One reason for choosing one applicant over another is his or her motivation, education, experience, cognitive abilities, and aptitudes for performing the tasks called for by the job.
- *Integrative criteria.* One reason for choosing one candidate over another is the noncognitive aspects of personality: the applicant's style and appearance fit the company image and facilitate getting on with others in the organization; the applicant's goals fit the company's goals and the applicant's manner is suited to withstand the constraints imposed by the organizational structure, job assignments, and physical conditions.
- *Legalistic criteria.* One reason for choosing one candidate over another is his or her greater conformity to company policies regarding affirmative action, and the law over hiring practices.
- *Adaptive criteria.* In selecting candidates there is a need to adapt or come to terms with the risk that a candidate may not turn out as expected. In particular, there is the question of whether the person will stay with the company: evidence of constant job changes makes any company hesitate about employing that individual.
- *Intrinsic criteria.* Although the gut liking of an applicant can be very deceptive as to competence in the selling job, candidates found to be liked by every interviewer do have a positive plus for any selling job. The danger lies in attractiveness casting a halo over the applicant's other attributes so that he or she is credited with more abilities than warranted by the evidence objectively considered.

How the above criteria are weighted depends on what is suggested by the job description. The problem lies, however, in ranking applicants on the criteria. For factors entering the criteria that can be measured, the problem is illustrated in Figure 13.7. The aim is to achieve a high positive correlation between assessments (selection measures during the selection process) and subsequent performance. In Figure 13.7, obtaining an ellipse is the target; obtaining just a circle means that the selection predictor (the measure ranking the applicants) does not correlate with success in the job. The problem thus lies in finding measures of abilities and traits that do correlate with job performance.

The application blank.   A common error in all selection is to compare applicants with each other rather than against the job specification, leading to the selection of those considered the better candidates rather than being best for the job. In any case, there is a need for a quick screening of applicants to eliminate the unsuited so that adequate

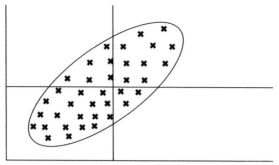

Actual performance (after selection)

Each ✶ represents a selected salesperson

Figure 13.7 Correlation between assessments and subsequent performance

time can be devoted to those remaining. This screening is usually based on the details obtained from the application form (the *application blank*) filled in by the applicant recording his or her experience and background. Sometimes the application blank is used as a predictor of job success. Thus, if one hundred salespeople have been recruited with a college degree and 50 percent have been successful, the possession of a college degree could be given a weighting of "50." All the scores awarded are summed to obtain a total numerical score for later correlation with performance. This type of approach has found favor with insurance companies. Care is needed to ensure the application blank contains only "relevant" scorable items, with a distinction being made between verifiable "hard" items and "soft" items that cannot be verified, such as subjects enjoyed at school.

Reference checks. References from those who know the applicant, at school, work, or socially are used to provide additional background, work success details and character of the applicant. In general, their usefulness can be increased if referees are contacted by phone since there is less likely to be bias and more specific questions can be asked. One way to reduce leniency in responses is to use a questionnaire where the referee chooses among several statements, to mark the one that comes closest to describing the applicant.

The interview. The interview is used almost universally as a selection device though assessments at interviews have not been particularly predictive of sales success. All too often interview appraisals are based on preconceived, untested assumptions. It is for this reason that attempts are made to tighten up the interview process through the use of structured forms to develop *quantitative* scores for correlating with success. Biases in interviewing include stereotyping, personality conflicts and failure in communication generally. Even where interviewers are given some framework with which to work to rate the applicant, biases occur, particularly the *halo effect*, which is the tendency to rate all characteristics high or low according to how the applicant is perceived on one particular dimension. However, the interview, as a behavior sample, allows the interviewer to assess motivational and social factors as well as communication skills. Will the applicant be dependable? Is he or she really interested in the work? Will the applicant be able to work with customers and others in the company? Is the manner and appearance of the applicant in line with job requirements? Are the aspirations of the applicant consistent with likely opportunities? It is advisable to ask interviewers to rate applicants as to likely success so these ratings can be related to subsequent job performance.

Work sampling and simulation.   In work sampling, applicants are given the opportunity to try and sell one of the firm's products and to perform other aspects of the job to help gauge their ability to do the whole job. This, of course, is not always possible so resort is made to some simulation of the activities involved in the job. For example, some member of management may take on the role of buyer and the applicant the role of sales representative. Such simulation differs from job sampling in that it uses a simulation of job content rather than using an actual sample of job content. The applicant performance is rated for effectiveness so that the scores can be later correlated to job performance.

Testing.   Testing consists of the pencil and paper tests for selecting salespeople. Thus to measure *abilities* we set tests consisting of problems to solve while to measure *traits* we use questionnaires, ratings, as well as tests. The abilities of interest are the cognitive skills required for territory management, acquiring product knowledge and solving customer problems. The traits of interest are those that capture the mix of attractiveness and other personality factors entering into credibility and motivation.

Tests of ability are varied. There are attainment tests to measure knowledge (e.g. of arithmetic) and skills (e.g. driving). But a commonly used test is still the I.Q. test used to measure scholastic aptitude. The items in a typical I.Q. test are intended to reflect experience common to all members of the population irrespective of schooling. Few believe this is possible. In any case, intelligence is no longer regarded as a single faculty but is modular and domain specific, that is, we have a specific intelligence for recognizing faces and another intelligence for languages and so on. For adults, I.Q. measures a person's relative position in the population in relation to his or her ability to solve certain problems. The average I.Q. is given the index of "100" with a standard deviation of "16" which implies that 95 percent of the population falls within the I.Q. range of 100 plus or minus 2×16, that is, from an I.Q. of 68 and up to an I.Q. of 132. Whether knowledge of an applicant's I.Q. adds anything to prediction over and above that provided by knowledge of an applicant's educational attainments can only be determined empirically. What, however, should be avoided is the error of believing that the I.Q. score is a good predictor of selling performance because it proves to be a good predictor of performance on a sales training course. All I.Q. tests stress speed of response and easy objective scoring but not complex problems requiring the subject to reach a decision in a realistic context or demonstrate moral reasoning—all of which may be required out in the field.

Tests of abilities tend to be standard tests as opposed to being specifically designed for selecting salespeople. The predictive validity of all such tests has shown little improvement in the last sixty years. At best, tests improve selection by 10–25 percent, and cannot be expected to do the whole job. Ideally, we need to isolate those cognitive aspects entering into perceived salesperson credibility and devise tests to measure them. Thus, for some sales forces, credibility might entail salespeople having to understand and solve complex application problems while, for other sales forces, credibility in selling might demand very few high cognitive skills.

The measurement of traits or personality factors has given rise to many problems. Although people probably do have enduring traits, leading to a certain consistency in behavior, the assessment of such traits ideally needs to be sampled over a long period of time. The problem with various personality questionnaires is also the possibility of faking. Yet many companies claim that specifically designed personality tests have proved extremely useful in the selection of salespeople.

Validating the process.   There is a need to relate the scores of applicants on the selection instrument (e.g. I.Q. test) to performance measures to check for reliability and validity. Reliability is defined as the consistency of measures of the ability or trait over time or across raters. Validity is concerned with establishing whether the inferences made from the scores are justified. One inference made is that, within limits, scores are positively correlated to performance on the job. Ideally, we should not initially use the selection scores for selection purposes but hire applicants covering a wide range of scores. We would then store the scores to calculate the correlation between performance on the job and the scores given by the selection instrument. The result is a test of predictive validity. However, a concurrent validity check is more common. In checking for concurrent validity, the selection tool is evaluated using the existing sales force. Members of the sales force are given the test and the scores on the test are plotted against measures of performance on the job. The correlation coefficient measures the concurrent validity of the selection tool. A predictive validity check is regarded as superior to a concurrent validity check since, in using the existing sales force, concurrent validity suffers from the danger that no current member of the sales force may have the crucial selling abilities or traits, or the resulting correlation may be heavily contaminated by training.

Whether we check for predictive or concurrent validity, there is the problem of cutoff points. If we insist on certain minimum scores, for any cutoff point we select, we can draw up a table showing which successful members of the sales force would have been rejected and which of the low-performing members would have been hired if such cutoff points had been in operation in the past. The particular cutoff points selected will depend somewhat on the possibility of recruiting sufficient numbers of people with the requisite level of test score.

Training salespeople

Selection and training are interrelated in that, to some extent, each can make up for the deficiencies of the other. Thus, a demanding selection procedure minimizes the need for training, while an inability to recruit sales trainees with the requisite skills may on occasions be rectified by training. The question of where the optimum balance lies is often determined not by any sort of cost/benefit analysis, but simply by the availability or otherwise of suitable candidates. Even if trained salespeople are hired (and small organizations typically do this), there is always some training to be done. This is because every sales job requires not just selling skills but knowledge of the company's products, company policies, and so on.

Objectives

The objectives of any sales training program are to increase selling effectiveness or decrease the cost of sales which, other things remaining equal, will increase efficiency. Thus training to increase sales effectiveness might include

- improving customer contact and sales effectiveness;
- enhancing the salesperson's motivation by developing selling confidence; and
- improving work habits.

Training aimed at reducing selling costs might aim at

- reducing labor turnover;
- reducing supervisory time spent in training; and
- reducing the time spent in acquiring product knowledge.

Although the training of salespeople is a never-ending process (since changes are constantly taking place in policies, products and markets), the major effort occurs on joining the company. This is because there is much to be learnt on taking on a new job and firms recognize the importance of first impressions and experiences. Early impressions of a company are an emotional experience that is not easily dislodged even though someone may spend most of his or her time on a territory away from the company itself. If new values are to be introduced, a training school is the place to do it; training can be a way of changing the whole orientation of field selling. The rituals, too, at the end of any formal course of training should not be slighted: they signify the importance attached to the course and are an opportunity to further identify the trainee with the organization.

What is taught?

The answer to this question concerns the content of the course. A *task analysis* is undertaken to establish what is needed, neatly summed up by the rule:

Training needs = Job needs less existing knowledge and skills.

Training is likely to cover:

- induction training;
- products and corresponding benefits offered by the firm;
- company history, management and sales policies, operations and procedures;
- markets and competitive offerings;
- customers' businesses and the relationship to the company's product line;
- selling techniques; and
- work organization.

Which of these topics are included depends substantially on whether the trainee is a new recruit or someone being retrained. Experienced salespeople require periodic retraining to deal with changing conditions, eliminate poor work habits and, most important, to improve their morale. Salespeople get discouraged and sometimes cease to sell in any meaningful sense, but depend for sales on inquiries or the replenishing of stocks. Some managements advocate changing around salespeople to prevent them from "getting into a rut" but this can be expensive and a more effective strategy might lie in retraining.

How is training carried out?

The answer to this question concerns choice of media. There is no one best way. Choice of media depends on what is to be taught and the background level of recruits. Thus, technical data can be learned from books and lectures, but selling skills need to be practiced by, say, role playing. Media in any case include

- lectures,
- readings,
- discussion of cases/incidents,
- programmed instruction,
- role-playing, and
- on-the-job training.

Many courses use all these methods. But all too often courses for industrial salespeople consist only of putting across product knowledge and company policies. There is a failure here to recognize the difference between "knowing that" and "knowing how" in that salespeople may know a good deal about the company's products but still not know how to use/apply such knowledge. Much product and other knowledge is easily forgotten unless it becomes internalized through training in applications.

Where to train?

The location of training is an important consideration. There are obvious advantages in centralized training in that each participant can be assured of receiving the same training, whereas training extensively on-the-job is often limited in scope to whatever problems actually occur. On the other hand, some on-the-job training is essential. In fact, the best training will consist of centralized training, some in-house or factory experience and field selling. For experienced salespeople, regional sales meetings and coaching on the job also provide a continuous source of learning.

When to train?

For the new recruit a major question lies in whether exposure to the selling situation should precede training in sales techniques. Many managers advocate previous exposure on the ground that it is much easier to "label" the trainee's experience rather than get the trainee to experience a label for some activity that is alien to him or her, as may happen if the trainee has had no prior exposure to the selling situation. For the experienced salesperson, the frequency of retraining depends on the rate of change in product and markets and considerations of preventing salespeople becoming "stale."

Who is to do the training?

The most important element in any course is the attractiveness and credibility of the instructor. In a formal centralized course of training, the instructor is the key to motivating the participant, just as out in the field the sales supervisor is the important determinant of the morale of the sales team. Probably professional instructors should be used, supplemented by outside help. Sometimes salespeople, being groomed for promotion, are also encouraged to spend time in sales training. Many of these are, or quickly become, highly competent instructors who bring with them the credibility of having successfully done the job.

Evaluation of sales training

Calculating or assessing the benefits of any training program is an important but neglected area of training. Sometimes, the assessment of saving is easy to calculate, as when it is possible to compare the time taken to learn using programmed learning versus some other method currently being used. More often, the benefits of training may have to be assessed through experiment. Thus controlled and experimental groups can be used to assess the effectiveness of training in selling techniques. However, it is the rare firm that seeks such evaluations and most companies, rightly or wrongly, are apt to rely on supervisory opinion, course reviews, observation, and customer feedback.

Deployment of salespeople

A major problem for any sales manager is the deployment of salespeople, that is, the allocation of manpower to territories, customers, products, and functions. Several approaches are available:

1 the so-called Semlow technique,
2 Callplan, and
3 the workload approach.

Each will be discussed in turn.

The Semlow technique

This approach uses the criteria of equal revenue potential as the basis for determining the size of territories. It originated with Heckert and Miner and particularly later with Semlow in the late 1950s.[17] A modified version of the so-called Semlow technique is illustrated in Table 13.4. Essentially this sales potential approach consists of:

1 The evolution of a curve relating sales volume to the number of salespeople employed. To take an example, if General Foods set up a separate sales force to sell a new product to the retail trade, we would expect, as the number of salespeople increased from zero, that sales would increase, steeply at first as the best retail outlets were covered, then more slowly as diminishing returns set in. Finally, saturation would be reached when all the outlets were covered.
2 The financial implications of the curve to determine the optimum number of sales-people to employ.

The problem is to construct a curve without the trial and error that would normally be needed. The solution (providing we already have a sales force) is illustrated in Table 13.4.

Table 13.4 Performance as a function of coverage

Sales territory	Sales revenue ($) (1)	Admissions ('000s) (2)	Revenue per 1,000 admissions [col. (1) ÷ col. (2)] ($) (3)	Salespersons per million admissions [col.1 ÷ col. (2) × 1,000] (4)
1 Jackson	77,132	5,174	14.9	0.19
2 Gibbens	108,956	13,646	8.0	0.07
3 Young	92,106	7,389	12.5	0.13
4 Moylan	57,120	3,015	19.0	0.33
5 Duncan	87,911	4,556	19.3	0.22
6 Robinson	127,099	9,788	13.0	0.10
7 West	92,250	5,181	17.8	0.19
Total	$642,574	48,749		

$$\text{Average relative territorial performance} = \frac{642,574}{48,749} = \$13.2$$

$$\text{Coverage or average salesperson mill. admissions} = \frac{7}{48,749} = 0.14$$

The table shows seven sales territories of a firm that manufactures and sells supplies to hospitals. Column (1) shows current sales revenue in each of the seven territories. Column (2) gives the number of hospital admissions in each of the seven territories on the assumption that sales vary directly with the number of hospital admissions in the territories. Column (2) can thus be viewed as measuring the relative market potential or relative demand. Column (3) shows revenue per thousand admissions which can be regarded as a measure of relative territorial performance, calculated by dividing the current sales revenue (Column (1)) by the number of admissions in the territory (Column (2)). Column (4) gives the salespersons per million admissions which is a measure of coverage, measuring how thinly the sales representative is spread over the number of admissions in the territory. Thus sales representative Jackson has 5,174,000 admissions in her territory. With just one salesperson spread over this number of admissions this means 0.19 salespersons per million admissions. If we plot Column (3) as the dependent variable and Column (4) as the independent variable, we get the curve as shown in Figure 13.8, which follows the shape of our General Foods example. The average relative territorial performance is $13.2 and the average coverage is $0.14. By increasing the size of the sales force, average coverage is increased and the average relative territorial performance is increased. On the other hand, by decreasing the size of the sales force, both coverage and the average relative territorial performance are decreased. Calculating the relevant field selling cost and revenues for different levels of coverage allows us to identify the optimum coverage and its corresponding relative territorial performance. In the Semlow approach, territories are designed to yield the same optimum sales level (relative territorial performance) with the same average coverage. The technique assumes that members of the sales force are of roughly equal ability and that we can identify the factor or factors with which sales will vary. But the major criticism of the approach is that, when territories are designed so that each territory has the same revenue potential, salespeople in geographically large territories may not be able to reap the potential when

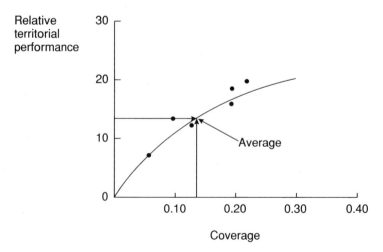

Figure 13.8 Relating sales performance to coverage

much of their time is spent in travel. It has also been claimed that the technique is based on a spurious relationship arising from dividing sales by relative market potential.[18]

Callplan

A number of management science models have been developed for dealing with deployment problems: allocating selling time across the range of products sold, locating base offices of salespeople, assigning them accounts and allocating time to the accounts. The most well-known of these approaches is "Callplan," which focuses on determining call frequencies and territory assignments.[19] Callplan uses the decision calculus method already discussed.

The objective of Callplan is "to determine call frequency norms for each client and prospect which maximizes total adjusted anticipated sales minus travel costs over a response period accepting the constraint that the salesman's time is limited." This is then used as a basis for determining the size of territories. The basis of the system is the salesperson's own estimates of the expected sales from present and prospective accounts, during some "response period" of (say) a year, given the following call frequencies per "effort period" of (say) one to three months:

- zero calls;
- call frequency at half the present rate;
- call frequency as at present;
- call frequency 50 percent higher than at present; and
- call frequency at the assumed saturation level.

The call frequencies and the corresponding salesperson estimates of sales are plotted and a curve through the plotted points fitted. This curve then becomes the basis for determining the optimum calling rate on each account after allowing for travel costs, adjustments for selling priorities and taking into account the salesperson's limited time. This is then extended to determining sales territories as well.

The assumptions of Callplan can be criticized. The first assumption is that salespeople are knowledgeable about the different levels of sales emanating from different call frequencies on accounts. No doubt if asked to construct such a graph showing calling rates and resulting sales for each account, the salesperson will oblige but may simply justify calling more frequently on favorite accounts, dispensing with the accounts whose buyers are disliked. There is no reason for assuming that salespeople know what will happen as a result of different rates of calling without direct experience of different calling rates. If salespeople already know there is profitable business to be had from doubling the calling rate why are they not already calling at that rate? More strangely, the approach ignores the time availability of the buyer, although it is the buyer's time that is at a premium. Buyers may be available for no more than, say, 20 hours per week in industrial markets and such a constraint cannot be ignored. The author of the approach claims an experiment designed to evaluate Callplan increased sales by around 8 percent but more evidence is needed to demonstrate the validity of the technique: an 8 percent increase is small enough to result simply from the "Hawthorne effect," that is, an increase in output resulting from monitoring sales performance and showing interest in the salespeople themselves.

The workload approach

Although Callplan does give consideration to the time needed to service an account, it is not the orthodox workload approach which is solidly based on industrial engineering (work study) methods except for the absence of any rating of salespeople for their pace of work.[20]

The sales potential approach of Semlow and the workload approach to determining sales territories are in conflict. Thus, 10 stores (say) in Manhattan may yield $200,000 of orders per annum for two days a week work. However, a territory in Arizona with a similar potential of $200,000 may consist of 200 stores that are widely scattered over the state. Unlike his Manhattan colleague, the salesperson in the Arizona territory may be unable to achieve that potential regardless of the number of hours he or she worked.

The workload problem in field selling is not immediately obvious. Yet, implicit in the decision to employ (say) 250 sales representatives to work around 40 hours per week is the assumption that 10,000 hours per week (250 × 40) are required. When salespeople are overloaded they adjust by "skimming the cream" of customers in their territories and/or reducing the frequency of their calls on their accounts. If salespeople are underloaded, they can fill in their work day by making uneconomic calls or just going home early. In either case, the company incurs a loss through inadequate customer servicing or excess costs on salaries and expenses.

To illustrate, let us consider an example, albeit an unrealistic one. Let us suppose:

- that customers are all lined up next door to each other;
- that making a call and moving on to the next customer takes 0.5 hours;
- that buyers are available for 40 hours per week; and
- that every buyer is called on once every four weeks.

Given the above assumptions, a sales representative could do 40/0.5 = 80 calls per week, and at a maximum could be allocated 4 × 80 = 350 accounts. In practice, buyers have different servicing requirements and so make different demands on the time of the sales representative. Buyers, too, are not always available, while sales calls, even on the same category of buyer, may not follow a set pattern. Also the sales representative spends time travelling from call to call and this reduces the time available to see buyers. There is also the problem of determining whether it pays to service a certain account or call on it often. In spite of these complications, it is possible (providing the past is a guide to the future) to have territories based on workload.

In any workload approach though, the first step is to consider the work itself. If we are not to fall into the trap of thinking of better ways of doing the unnecessary or cheaper ways of achieving unsatisfactory end results, we must first consider the current allocation of sales resources over the activities at present being carried out. Just as shop floor

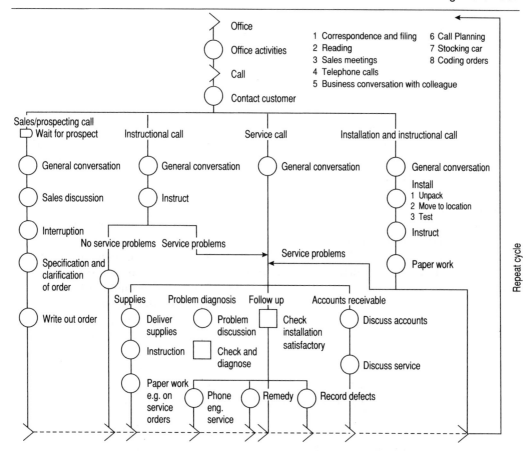

Figure 13.9 Flow chart of salesperson's work pattern

activities can be charted, so can the typical pattern of activities be recorded through accompanying a number of salespeople as shown in the flow chart in Figure 13.9. Each of the key activities as recorded in the chart can be examined as to purpose, person, place, means, and sequence.

Purpose.   What activity is carried out? Why is it carried out? What else might be done instead? Some activities have outlived their usefulness and should be eliminated or, at least, need to be reorganized if they are to justify their cost. The clerical work undertaken by salespeople tends to be a fertile field for eliminating useless chores.

Person.   Who carries out the activity? Who else might do the job better? Some activities, though necessary, could be done more efficiently by others such as suggested by the telemarketing example quoted earlier in the chapter.

Place.   Where is the activity carried out? Why there? Where else might the activity be carried out? There is often the implicit assumption that salespeople should always call on the customer at his or her location. But such selling can often be supplemented by getting the buyer to visit showrooms, or see applications at neighboring firms as a way of facilitating a sale.

Sequence.   When is the activity carried out? Why then? When else might the activity be carried out? If we change the sequence with which activities are carried out, we may eliminate delays or improve timing. Thus, consider waiting time. To utilize waiting time, salespeople may check stock, look through the visitor's book to check on competition, do administrative work, or visit the plant.

Means.   How is the activity carried out? Why that way? How else might the activity be carried out? There is great scope here for the use of laptop computers and the redesign of samples and sample cases to provide easier reference, transportation and storage. Many companies are also using portable disk players for their sales calls, for example, MCI Communications and Bell Atlantic. Computer software now exists to reveal every place of business in a salesperson's territory. In fact, computer technology has also had considerable impact in reducing the number of sales support staff needed.

Questioning existing practices in this way provides an opportunity to get salespeople involved in thinking about their jobs. In any case, there is a need to let the imagination run free: criticism applied too early can unduly inhibit the free flow of ideas. At a later stage, suggestions can be examined for good and bad consequences to determine which should be accepted. It is also at this stage that the activities being undertaken can be checked to ensure they do reflect the role allocated to field selling by the marketing strategy.

Only after examining current activities should attention be turned to measuring workload and basing territories on workload using the following criteria:

- Call time plus inter-call travel (i.e. the time spent in traveling from one call to the next) must not add up to more time than buyers are available. Thus, if buyers are available for about 40 hours per week, the time spent with buyers plus the time spent in traveling from one buyer to the next must not exceed this 40 hours since it would serve no purpose.
- Except for territories under development, the revenue yielded from a territory, customer or product group should provide an adequate surplus over cost.
- The total hours of work per week should be "reasonable" if personal efficiency is to be maintained. It is commonly forgotten that the mind adjusts to the length of the working day and long work days, sustained over a period of time, can considerably reduce average efficiency.
- Customer servicing should be "optimum" in terms of call frequency.

We will now briefly review one way of basing territories in *consumer* selling on workload.

All the basic data comes from the filling in (by a sample of sales representatives or someone accompanying them) of a *customer time study* sheet for each customer visited and a *daily study sheet* used to record daily travel time and clerical work. From the time data obtained in this way, the build-up to sales territories in the case of a *consumer* sales force is as follows:

Call time.   Customer study sheets are sorted into customer categories on the basis of likely differences in call times arising from differing service demands (e.g. differing activities carried out, typical size of order, etc.). Standard call times are established for each category of call. Thus, an analysis might establish four distinct buyer categories with call times as follows:

Buyer category	Standard Call time per occasion (hours)
A	0.5
B	1.0
C	1.5
D	2.0

Call time per town or location visited.   The amount of call time per town or location visited is calculated next. Because calls can be of different frequencies, there is a need to reduce the call time per town to some base period. In our example, call time per 4-week period is calculated as in Table 13.5 (a).

Column (1) lists the 4 distinct categories of customer in the town or location. Column (2) shows the estimated number of actual and prospective customers in each category. Column (3) records the call time that has been established for each of the categories. Column (4) gives the frequency of call per 4 weeks. Thus, a call frequency per 4 weeks of 1/2 means the call frequency is every eight weeks; a call frequency of 2 means the call is once every two weeks while a frequency of call of 1 means the call frequency is once per month. Column (5) is column (3) adjusted by column (4). Column (6) is column (2) multiplied by column (5) to give the total standard call time for that category of call per 4 weeks. The total of column (6) is the standard call time per 4 weeks for all categories of call in that town or location.

Call time per zone or unit area.   Towns or locations are grouped together into **unit areas** or zones for the calculation of call time per unit area or zone as shown in Table 13.5 (b). Each zone or unit area is numbered and later grouped to form sales territories. Unit areas are the stable building blocks for forming territories. They can also be used to record sales trends and other information about specific, defined and (in contrast to sales territories) fixed unit areas of the country. The design of zones or unit areas must take account not only of workload balance but also what constitutes "natural" groupings from the point of view of marketing. The aim is to have sufficient zones or unit areas to minimize the likelihood of needing to split them to form sales territories.

Grouping zones or unit areas to form sales territories.   Zones are grouped to form territories after taking into account travel time and the time spent on other than call time. There is usually no problem in calculating the time likely to be spent on clerical work. However estimating likely travel time can be more difficult as it must take into account the factors that give rise to differing amounts of travel time:

Table 13.5(a) Call time per four-week period. Town/location

Buyer category (1)	No. in town (2)	Std. call time per occasion (hrs) (3)	Frequency of call per 4 weeks (4)	Std call time per 4 weeks (5)	Total per 4 weeks (6)
A	4	0.5	½	0.25	1.00
B	10	1.0	1	1.00	10.00
C	20	1.5	1	1.50	30.00
D	8	2.0	2	4.00	32.00
				TOTAL	73.00

Std. call time per 4 weeks = 73 Hours.

Note: Town is Bedford.

Table 13.5(b) Call time per zone or unit area

Towns	Std. call time per town per 4 weeks
Y	73
X	60
Z	50
Total	183 Std. hrs. for Zone No. 1.

Note: Towns are grouped into unit or zones for the calculation of call time per unit area or zone.

Table 13.5(c) Call time and inter-call time against buyers' availability

Areas unit numbers (1)	Productive standard: hours per (lunar) month (2)	Travel: miles per (lunar) month (3)	Appropriate miles per hour (10 city, 20 Built-up, 25 country) (4)	Hours per months spent in travel (Col. 3 ÷ Col. 4) (5)	Intertown travel (Col. 5 minus 16) (6)	Productive standard hours + inter-town (Col. 2 + Col. 6) (7)	Total standard hours per month + 12 hours clerical work (8)
16	26	1108	25	44	28	159	171
17	35						
18	25						
20	45						
	131						

- One obvious factor is the size of the territory. Other things remaining equal, the larger the geographical size of the territory, the greater the number of miles that will be traveled.
- The distribution of business within the territory since a territory can be large but all the business may be concentrated at one or two locations.

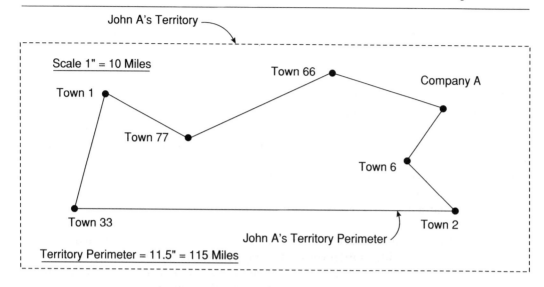

Figure 13.10 Linking towns and locations in a territory

- The time currently spent in travel for a particular size of territory may be excessive due to poor call planning.
- The home base of the salesperson. A salesperson who lives well off the territory adds to travel time. This is one reason for insisting or encouraging salespeople to live in a convenient location on the territory.

An estimation of travel time that takes account of the first two factors can be obtained from an analysis of current travel time. The procedure is to take existing territories and, for each territory, link the towns or locations visited, as shown in Figure 13.10. The perimeter of the line that links the towns or locations together, is plotted against the actual miles traveled to give the historical relationship between miles traveled per 4 weeks and the territory perimeter. If we then measure the perimeter of the new set of unit areas that links the locations to be visited, we can read off the graph the likely travel miles, with travel time then calculated by dividing through by the appropriate miles per hour. One broad classification of territories for m.p.h purposes is that of city, built up (suburban) and country areas but much finer distinctions can be made. The aim is to group zones or unit areas into territories in a way that ensures that call time plus inter-call travel amounts to no more time than buyers are available.

The appropriate calculations are shown in Table 13.5 (c). Column (1) lists the unit areas or zones being brought together to form a sales territory. Column (2) gives the call time per 4 weeks for each of the unit areas and totals them. Column (3) gives the likely travel miles for a territory of that perimeter size. Column (4) records the miles per hour for the territory. Column (5) is column (3) divided by Column (4) to give the estimated hours per 4 weeks likely to be spent in travel. Although inter-town travel can be estimated directly, little is lost by regarding all travel above (say) 4 hours per week as being inter-call travel. Hence 16 hours (4 hrs × 4) is deducted from column (5) to give the inter-call travel hours in column (6). The total of column (2) plus column (6) gives column (7) which is call time plus inter-call travel. The figure in column (7) should not be in excess of the time buyers are available. In this example, we assume buyers are available for 160 hours per 4 week period so that the figure of 159 hours in column (7) is acceptable. Time spent on other (e.g. clerical work) is added to column (7) to give column (8) which is the total workload. The hours recorded in column (8) must not be excessive if selling effort is not to be affected by a long working day. A question arises as to what unit areas to bring together in column (1), since what grouping is appropriate depends on likely travel, yet we cannot know travel hours until we have formed a tentative territory! In practice, this presents no problem as experience quickly indicates the mileage a particular territory is likely to require.

Industrial selling. For industrial selling the above (consumer) example may appear remote. In fact, no one illustration could possibly show how workload might be calculated for all industrial selling situations. Although industrial customers can be categorized on the basis of differences in workload, special problems arise. Thus, different types of call (e.g. prospecting call, service call etc.) give rise to different call times while, within each type of call, there are variations in call time depending on the class of product sold. Additionally, call times are apt to vary widely though this is less of a problem than appears since, providing the distribution of call times remains constant, we can estimate average call time and the corresponding range of likely error.

An example of an industrial sales force application is shown in Table 13.6. It shows the calculation of call time per town per year. Call time per year is usually more convenient in industrial selling than call time per 4 weeks. In Table 13.6, salespeople deal with two classes of customer: category "A" and category "B." For every sale, the salespeople have to make contact with the buyer, make a survey, discuss the survey and complete the sale by installing the equipment. Every contact does not result in a sale.

Table 13.6 Calculation of annual workload for Stanford Town

Customer	Number per year (1)	Contact hours (2)	Survey hours (3)	Discussion hours (4)	Completion hours (5)	Subtotal hours (6)	Total hours (7)	
Category A								
Set (i)	5	6	–	–	–	6	30	
Set (ii)	4	6	19	5	–	30	120	
Set (iii)	3	6	19	5	5	35	105	
								255
Category B								
Set (i)	10	5	–	–	–	5	50	
Set (ii)	10	5	25	5	–	35	350	
Set (iii)	10	5	25	5	5	40	400	
								800
								1,055 Hours

Even if salespeople are asked to do a survey, they may still not get an order. Thus every customer contacted during the year will receive one of the following *sets* of calls:

- *Set (i)*: sales representative makes contact only (fails to get permission to make a survey);
- *Set (ii)*: sales representative makes contact, does a survey and discusses the findings with the buyer;
- *Set (iii)*: sales representative makes contact, does a survey, discusses the survey findings, and completes the installation after receiving the order.

In Table 13.6, column (1) shows the number of customers likely to be visited within each set. This is a forecast based on trends and knowledge of local circumstances. Column (2) is simply the average time spent trying to make contact. Column (3) is the average time taken to do a survey. Column (4) is the time spent in discussion. Column (5) is the average time spent in completing the order during the pre and post-installation visit. Column (6) shows the sum of the time for the particular set. Column (7) shows the total time devoted to the category of customer (in that set) which is simply col. (1) × col. (6). The rest of Table 13.6 is self-explanatory. Overall it shows that in the town of Stanford, the two categories of customer provide 1,055 hours of call time per year. Once this call time per town per year has been calculated for every town or location to be visited, territories can be formed by grouping the towns. Thus, if:

- time spent per year on call = C,
- time spent per year on travel = T,
- time spent per year on other work = O, and
- time spent per year on inter-call travel = $T2$

Then

- $C + T + O$ = workload.

Travel time per year is calculated in the way already described. Inter-town travel is calculated directly or estimated as being total travel time less 4 hours per working week so $T2 = T - 200$ hours. We now simply add up town times to form a sales territory where

$C + T2 = $ *Annual buyer availability time.*

This is the figure to be approximated providing the addition of "other work" does not give too great a workload. In the examples above, no time has been allowed for seeking new business. Such can be taken into account, though it is a wise precaution to first establish that the new business is there to be had. When changes are proposed, the effect of the change (e.g. a new product introduction) on workload must be calculated. On the basis of such information, the sales manager judges whether corresponding territorial changes are justified.

The above merely sketches the essentials of the workload approach. There are problems unique to every sales force but none are insurmountable. But it is not enough that sales territories provide salespeople with a full work opportunity and be designed so that time spent with buyers plus time spent in inter-call travel does not exceed the time buyers are available. We must ensure that it is *worthwhile* to service a particular territory or a particular type of account or sell a particular product. We need to compare the actual costs of selling a product, servicing an account or a territory with the revenue derived in order to determine what is profitable. This means we must first work out the number of salespeople that are needed on the assumption that all potential accounts are serviced and all existing product lines are carried. Then the effect of cutting out marginal accounts, marginal product and marginal territories can be calculated to arrive at what is ideal.

Motivation of the sales force

Field salespeople cannot be directly supervised and they are subject to rebuffs and disappointments, so there is a special need for them to be self-motivated. We will not review the various theories of motivation and leadership but instead look at some of the policies that depress performance and others that can enhance it.

Disincentives

All too often sales management set "treadmill" quotas, where quotas are based on some percentage increase over the previous year's sales. Salespeople quickly learn to avoid such increases by keeping sales at a level that can be attained with ease. Quotas should be fixed, with changes in quotas being made only under agreed conditions such as a change in the size of territory, the addition of new product lines and so on. Another disincentive is the artificial blocking of career paths as occurs when all sales management positions are restricted to (say) those with an MBA. Salespeople are less likely to be management-oriented when their current position is known to be the end of the line for promotion.

Poor incentives

Whenever there is an absence of a clear link between performance and rewards, sales performance is diminished. This is the objection to the annual bonus given out by the sales manager, without salespeople being able to calculate what they will receive. Whatever payments are given they must not appear arbitrary or appear to reflect favoritism by the sales manager. Such payments are resented by those who receive little while they do little to stimulate those who benefit since the criteria by which they were allocated are unknown. Similarly, reward should follow on the heels of effort and not delayed until well after performance.

Table 13.7 Appropriate modes of influence can vary with goals

Mode of influence	Goals of management			
	Decrease labour turnover	Increase work effort	Improve morale	Rule compliance
Use of sanctions				x
Use of material rewards, e.g. prizes, money incentives		x		
Appeals to self-image, e.g. promotion, recognition, management praise, etc.			x	
Appeals to values, e.g. sense of achievement, worthwhile job, etc.	x		x	

Inadequate incentives

We should always ask: "What are the conditions that exist when the job is done well?" Salespeople are generally expected to do other than make sales, for example, open new accounts, nurse them, fight for shelf space, erect point-of-purchase material, provide information to management, do training and so on. Good performance in such tasks should not go unrecognized in the reward system. We need to list the modes of influencing behavior as in Table 13.7 and consider which mode is most appropriate for the various goals to be attained. For example, the use of sanctions is more likely to achieve compliance with rules but not likely to be effective if the goal is the reduction in labor turnover.

Sanctions. Some minimum level of performance is needed for salespeople to be retained. It is always an interesting exercise to calculate the effect on sales and profit if all those below standard performance reached that standard.

Material Rewards. Financial incentives need to be considered with earnings for high performance sufficient to retain the best salespeople.

Appeals to self-esteem. Appeals to self-esteem cover

- public acknowledgment of a job well done;
- reassurance of the importance of the selling function;
- feedback on performance to provide success experience; and
- distinguished selling awards.

Appeals to values.   Appeals to values cover

- ensuring salespeople have meaningful responsibilities and are treated with fairness and as responsible adults;
- setting challenging goals;
- providing feedback on performance;
- rewards geared directly to performance; and
- supervision that is seen to act decisively in the interests of the organization yet showing genuine consideration and understanding for the problems encountered by salespeople.

In constantly associating with customers, salespeople come to view the world through the customers' eyes. This is why salespeople are an important source of information on customer opinions and attitudes. But it can be carried too far and a salesperson, while adept at representing the customer's point of view to the company, may be incapable of representing the company's view to the customer. What may be needed is *group methods of supervision* to develop a team spirit by regular meetings structured to develop group feeling and a commitment to company goals. Salespeople at regional meetings report on their activities, discussing, say, the number and kinds of prospects obtained, calls made, presentations used etc. Every member of the sales team is encouraged to analyze, comment, and offer suggestions for improvement to develop a team spirit and further commitment.

Performance assessment

Performance assessment is tied to motivation and performance, as performance evaluation presupposes standards against which to compare actual performance and assumes the giving of feedback. There is a need for standards, however difficult the attempt to define them may be, since without standards there can be no guidance for improvement in performance. Similarly, regular feedback on performance is essential: the old adage "practice makes perfect" should be modified to "practice makes perfect providing we give feedback as to how well people are doing."

At the individual level, the purpose of performance assessment varies:

- *Comparison purposes.* High performance in the job must always be a factor in considering the salesperson's suitability for promotion, salary increase etc. For such purposes, the performance of the individual salesperson must be measured, not masked or blurred by measures that reflect the performance of the whole team.
- *Self-development and improvement.* Feedback or knowledge of results means salespeople are regularly informed as to their performance: when performance assessments are not fed back, there is little likelihood of improved performance.
- *Financial incentives.* The standards against which salespeople are assessed for payment purposes must be based on objective measures. Sometimes payment is unrelated to any objective standards as occurs when salespeople are given bonuses based on

ratings that merely reflect a supervisor's impression of selling performance. Such ratings can be arbitrary but foster the illusion of consistency in performance by being tied to assessments in previous years. If there is insufficient information to allow an objective assessment of performance, assessments should be delayed until the deficiency is remedied. Performance evaluations, if badly done, simply promote ill-feeling and a sense of grievance.

The first step is to consider the goals of the field sales force so as to set standards that relate to these goals. Such standards are in terms of the salesperson's outputs and inputs.:

- *Salesperson's outputs*: sales, mix of products, selling expenses, services performed, etc.
- *Salesperson's inputs*: number of calls, quality of calls, allocation of sales effort.

If the major goals of the sales force are volume and revenue quotas, each individual's performance should be measured in these terms. But performance on quota is seldom the only measure required. The idea that salespeople need only be assessed on final results presupposes that most of them will come up to standard, since, when many do not, there is a need for additional information as to what might have gone wrong. Hence performance may be assessed not just on achieving quota, as failure to achieve some position by a certain date may give advance warning that performance will fall short of standard. Measuring performance takes a number of forms:

- Actual sales results compared with goals set, for example, the percentage achievement of sales quota or the number of calls made as a percentage of the number of calls that should have been made.
- Observing and rating a sample of work, for example, rating the quality of the merchandising activity carried out by the salesperson in a sample of stores. This is the *scored job sample* approach and corresponds to what the instructor does in marking examination papers.
- Tests of knowledge, for example, multiple choice questionnaire on product knowledge to be completed by members of the sales force as a take-home test.
- Rating of recalled performance. This is particularly subject to bias. There is the so-called *halo effect*, or the tendency for raters to allow their assessment on one trait to influence their assessment of other traits. Other biases are the tendency to rate too tightly or too leniently or to rate everyone as average. Although various rating systems have been developed to avoid one or more of these biases, no rating system yet devised entirely eliminates bias.

For most sales forces, the sales quota is the most important goal to be achieved. But every sales quota is essentially a forecast since the basis of the sales quota is the sales forecast. The sales or budgeted forecast is broken down by sales territory to provide a sales quota or target for each and every sales territory. To do this, we need first to identify the factors with which sales vary over all territories. As an example, let us suppose that the sales of an individual product go to just three industries as follows:

Industry I   20 percent of sales
Industry II   25 percent of sales
Industry III   55 percent of sales

And sales within each industry vary with the number of workers employed. Thus if a certain territory Y has:

5 percent of all industry I's workers
10 percent of all industry II's workers
10 percent of all industry III's workers.

then the percentage of the budgeted sales that would constitute territory Y sales quota would *normally* be:

5 percent × 20 percent = 1.0 percent
10 percent × 25 percent = 2.5 percent
10 percent × 55 percent = 5.5 percent
Sales quota = *9.0* percent of budgeted sales.

"Normally", because such a method of calculating the sales quota (9 percent of budgeted sales in the above example) makes a number of assumptions such as all territories provide equal work opportunity and competition is evenly distributed. In practice, such problems cannot be ignored and adjustments must be made.

Remunerating the sales force and financial incentives

We have argued that there is a special need for salespeople to be self-motivated to maintain enthusiastic selling effort. Financial incentives are designed to reinforce the will to do the best job possible. But any financial incentive is but one component in what should be a system of incentives designed to stimulate maximum selling effort. A common error is to rely on the financial incentive to do the whole job when there is a need to look at the total motivational climate by examining other ways of influencing performance. The carrot tempts and the stick coerces but to use them as the sole motivators is dehumanizing. If other ways of influencing behavior are ignored, the organizational climate may be such as to work against any financial incentive having much effect.

Objectives sought

Since the aim of any financial incentive plan is to encourage behavior that enhances objectives, the first step is to set out objectives. These objectives are implicit in the role allocated to the sales force, for example, creating goodwill and trust; effectively liaising with customers; promoting knowledge about the firm's products; making sales; training future salespeople and providing intelligence. Objectives embrace more than sales revenue targets. To stress sales volume exclusively leads to the neglect of such activities as opening new accounts, nursing new accounts, pushing new products, training, post-sales service, and so on. An interesting exercise is to compare the performance factors in the job description with the factors on which payment is made. There should be considerable overlap, though this is not to suggest that payment should be tied to all performance factors as this leads to spreading the financial incentive over too many factors and dilutes the incentive to perform well in key areas.

Specific objectives for field selling are likely to combine several of the following:

- attract and retain good salespeople;
- increase/maintain market share;
- increase market penetration;
- retain existing customers;
- introduce new products quickly;
- reduce seasonality of sales;
- achieve balance in selling across the range;
- improve before and after sales service;
- provision of management information;
- keep product knowledge up-to-date;
- increase sales of profitable lines;
- reward teamwork; and
- develop new sales and product ideas.

The superordinate objective of creating goodwill, trust, and loyalty may make payment by commission dysfunctional. This may be the case with brokers who make their commissions from persuading customers to buy or sell. For some brokerage houses, there is a conflict of interest between brokers and clients when payment by commission is used. One solution is to pay a flat percentage of the assets managed so, as a client's net worth grows, so does broker compensation. Another dysfunctional financial incentive system is that common among insurance companies where the financial incentive is directly related to the percentage of claims rejected as if "rejection" or "acceptance" were simply a matter of infallible deduction from policy rules.

As sales objectives change with changes in markets and strategy, they need corresponding revision. However, an incentive scheme may not embrace all the objectives set out. Some objectives are better controlled by supervision so a decision needs to be made as to which objectives are to be promoted in the incentive plan. One consideration entering into this decision is the question of measurement. If payment is to relate to performance then the degree of attainment must be measurable.

Determine the average level of earnings sought

There are essentially three approaches to determining what the average earnings should be. The first is through undertaking a job evaluation where jobs are compared for relative skills, abilities etc. The second basis is through comparison with the average earnings paid by competitors. This can be decisive if the pool of potentially qualified salespeople is limited to those already in the industry. The third basis for determining average earnings is to consider the level that would be needed to attract and retain highly competent salespeople. Some combination of the three approaches is common.

Choose the appropriate payment system

No two sales forces are exactly alike so there is no one type of payment system which is best for all. In general a choice is made from the following options:

- salary only;
- commission only;
- salary plus commission:
  a) on all sales, or
  b) on all sales over some basic minimum level;
- a multi-factor incentive scheme (salary plus commission plus bonus for nonselling activities).

Salary only. In "salary only" earnings do not vary with performance. It is the form of payment most likely to be adopted when performance cannot be measured with the degree of accuracy needed to develop an equitable financial incentive. Thus the job of selling might consist primarily of account servicing, prospecting, advising rather than seeking orders or involves only products recently introduced into the market. If annual salary increases are related to merit and not just seniority, "salary only" does include a money incentive, but tends to have minimal impact for inducing extra effort. However, "salary only" may have advantages in terms of recruitment, in relieving financial anxieties, and in giving flexibility to management in redesigning territories, directing selling effort, and in ensuring nonselling activities are not neglected. Some firms, however, just reject the whole idea of financial incentives as being more trouble than they are worth. This raises the issue of the motivating power of money as an incentive. Financial incentives are neither a necessary nor sufficient condition for achieving a highly motivated selling effort. However, they can be a strong contributory factor. The whole weight of industrial consultancy experience and other evidence is on the side of money as a motivating force.[21] But behavioral scientists are often less enthusiastic. This is because there is a belief that management has put too much emphasis on money and neglected other forms of motivation such as the approval of colleagues and the intrinsic appeal of the work itself. In fact recent research has suggested that, when extrinsic rewards like money are given for performing an interesting job, the intrinsic appeal of the job diminishes, possibly because the individual experiences a sense of loss of control over his or her own behavior. However, the methodology of this research has been attacked together with the interpretation of the findings.[22] Individual financial incentives are also criticized for encouraging interpersonal competition at the expense of morale or team spirit and this criticism can on occasions be justified. Yet what hard evidence we have suggests money can be a powerful incentive. Another benefit of paying salespeople on the basis of their performance is that it obliges sales management to make a more serious attempt at evaluating performance and to consider selling objectives and priorities among objectives.

Commission only. "Commission only" has the distinct advantage of giving immediate feedback to salespeople as to their earnings while it protects the financially pressed firm from incurring compensation cost unrelated to performance. It is also perhaps the only acceptable way of paying agents. However, "commission only" can be a negative factor in recruitment, lead to high labor turnover in a recession, create financial insecurity and lead the sales force to neglect nonselling activities and to regard themselves as self-employed and not subject to management control. More important, the degree to which it pays an individual to cultivate a territory will not coincide with company interests. Thus a sales agent on 10 percent commission may neglect to call on an account for $1,000 order, as commission is just $100. On the other hand, the profit on an order for $1,000 might yield a net $500 to the firm. Finally, territories that give equal work opportunity only coincidentally provide equal sales potential so that "commission only" results in wide differences in pay for the same amount of selling skill and effort.

Salary plus commission on all sales. Salespeople can be given a guaranteed minimum salary with commission on all sales. Of course, if the average level of earnings is to remain the same, the commission rate will be lower than under "commission only" to cover this guaranteed minimum. With such a scheme, too, there is a danger of salespeople becoming prematurely self-satisfied as the concept of a financial incentive as a reward for additional effort is sacrificed.

Salary plus commission on all sales above some basic minimum level. This system while demanding some minimum level of sales before any commission is paid, nonetheless suffers by restricting the incentive to sales volume when performance on other factors may need to be encouraged.

Multi-factor incentive scheme. The payment system most generally applicable where multiple objectives are sought is the multi-factor incentive scheme. Such a scheme pays a basic salary, commission on all sales above some basic minimum, and a bonus for performance on nonselling activities. There is no need to pay the same rate of commission every time as the commission rate may be varied to direct selling effort:

- *new accounts*: a higher rate of commission can be paid to encourage the opening of new accounts by paying additionally for sales from such accounts during the first year of servicing;
- *hard-to-sell products*: some products (including newly introduced products) give a lower return per minute of selling time and it may be wise to recognize this in a higher commission rate;
- *seasonal swings*: a higher commission rate for out-of-season sales may help even out peaks in selling; and

- *profitability*: commission can be made to vary with unit profitability of the sales by paying commission on gross margin, or sales weighted for profit contribution and so on. Payment systems that take profitability into account are more rare than would seemingly be the case given management's concern with profit and not just revenue. But profit can vary with sales level while calculating profit contribution requires a sophisticated costing system. In any case, directing salespeople to focus on what is immediately profitable can lead to the neglect of currently small accounts or products that have high potential.

Bonus is paid for nonselling activities. Special difficulties arise in relating bonus to performance. There is first the problem of the split between bonus and commission. This will depend on priorities among objectives and on the degree to which objectives can be accurately measured. A high priority given to nonselling activities suggests a high bonus, while difficulties in measuring the attainment of the objective suggest earnings be made less dependent on that factor.

One method of calculating performance under conditions of fluctuating earnings is based on the use of the moving annual total (MAT): see Table 13.8. As an example let us assume an annual sales quota of $200,000 has been set and column (1) of the table shows this broken down into monthly quotas on the basis of seasonal pattern.

The moving annual total (MAT) is the successive sums of 12 months:

January:

         $200,000 Annual Sales Quota
Minus $10,000 Monthly Quota for January

         $190,000
Add $12,000 Actual Sales for January

MAT $202,000 MAT for January.

Table 13.8 Moving annual total (MAT) as a method of calculating performance

Month	Sales quota (1)	Actual sales (2)	MAT (3)
Jan	10,000	12,000	202,000
Feb	10,000	10,000	202,000
Mar	10,000	11,000	203,000
Apr	20,000	22,000	205,000
May	20,000	25,000	210,000
June	20,000	20,000	210,000
July	10,000	9,000	209,000
Aug	20,000	20,000	209,000
Sept	20,000	21,000	210,000
Oct	20,000	20,000	210,000
Nov	20,000	25,000	215,000
Dec	20,000	20,000	215,000
	$200,000		

February
$202,000 MAT for January
minus $10,000 Monthly Quota for February

$192,000
Add $10,000 Actual Sales for February

MAT $202,000

Commission could be paid on (say) each percentage the moving annual total (MAT) exceeds 75 percent of annual sales quota e.g.

MAT for Feb $202,000
Annual Sales Quota $200,000

Performance = 202,000/200,000 × 100 = "101" performance
Commission credits = 101 minus 75 = 26
Commission = 26 multiplied by the commission rate.

When sales fluctuate wildly and unpredictably, salespeople can be rewarded and penalized in a way unrelated to their efforts and abilities. In such circumstances, it may be advisable to pay commission not against a predetermined standard but against how well a salesperson performs in relation to others. This presupposes that we can set quotas that are relatively fair even if absolutely off target. This is commonly the case with the selling of new products. Suppose the average "quota" allocated is $1 million. If salesperson "A" is allocated a $1.5 million quota then all revenue from salesperson "A"'s territory is divided by 1.5 to give his or her adjusted revenue. Similarly, a salesperson allocated $0.5 million would have his or her actual sales divided by 0.5 to give the adjusted revenue figure. In this way salespeople can be *ranked* on the basis of their sales and some predetermined budgeted sum can then be divided up among them on the basis of their ranking.

Ideally, an incentive plan should be tested on a pilot basis. Both company and salespeople should benefit: if either loses, then the scheme will fail. If time pressure rules out a pretest, then the scheme should be tested by simulating how the scheme would have worked in the past. Of course, such testing is unable to show the motivating force of the incentive, but it can at least indicate the cost to the company, likely inequities, possible confusion over interpretation and factors ignored that should have been considered.

An incentive system also needs periodic revision, not only because familiarity may lessen its motivating force but because objectives change. For example, to quote an extreme case, an incentive scheme geared to the needs of a small sales force doing pioneer selling will not be appropriate when the sales force has grown and is doing mainly maintenance selling. However, any change in a scheme may be viewed by the sales force as an occasion for "rate cutting" and so viewed with suspicion. Salespeople need to be assured that it is not the intention to reduce average earnings, but only to redirect activity. An example of an incentive plan is shown in the Appendix 13.2.

ETHICAL ISSUES

As in advertising, we have simply put forward techniques and tactics that are employed in field selling. As a consumer we all need to be aware of those that are manipulative. But we also should recognize that many of the techniques of persuasion are ethically dubious. Yet payment systems can encourage unethical practices as can the absence of monitoring what actually occurs in field selling.

CONCLUSION

We have stressed the need to integrate strategic sales planning into business level planning and marketing strategy. Strategic planning in field selling is frequently subordinated to operational planning with the result that sales management carry on selling when they should be marketing. The job of the sales force is not to make sales regardless but to distribute their time to create goodwill and to sell in such a way as to secure a customer base for current and future operations.

For each and every product line, the role of the sales force in marketing strategy must be planned. Goals, tasks, and priorities among tasks must be carefully thought out as part of an overall strategy. Only when this is done can sales management confidently concentrate on operational issues without falling into the trap of thinking of better ways of solving the wrong problems. Of these operational issues, motivational issues and the deployment problem of allocating sales effort over territories, customers, and products remain of major concern. The difficulty, as with advertising, lies in measuring the customer sales response to different levels of resource allocation.

NOTES

1 Fouss, James F. and Soloman, Elaine (1980) "Salespeople as Researchers: Help or Hazard," *Journal of Marketing*, 44 (Summer).
2 Menzies, Hugh D. (1980) "The New Life of a Salesman," *Fortune* (August 11).
3 Lehman, Donald R. and O'Shaughnessy, John (1974) "Difference in Attribute Importance for Different Industrial Products," *Journal of Marketing*, 38 (April).
4 Jackson, Barbara Bund (1985) *Winning and Keeping Industrial Customers: The Dynamics of Customer Relations*, Lexington, MA: Lexington Books.
5 Robinson, Patrick J., Faris, Charles, and Wind, Yoram (1967) *Industrial Buying and Creative Marketing*, Boston: Allyn and Bacon.
6 Bunn, Michele D. (1993) "Taxonomy of Buying Decision Approaches," *Journal of Marketing*, 57 (Jan).
7 Webster, F. E. and Wind, Y. (1972) "A General Model for Understanding Organizational Buying Behavior," *Journal of Marketing*, 36 (April).
8 Ronchetto, John R., Hutt, Michael D., and Reingen, Peter H. (1989) "Embedded Influence Patterns in Organizational Buying Systems," *Journal of Marketing*, 53 (October).
9 Kohli, Ajay (1989) "Determinants of Influence in Organizational Buying: A Contingency Approach," *Journal of Marketing*, 53 (July).
10 Johnston, Wesley J. (1991) "Alternative Approach Strategies for Buyer-Seller Relations with the People's Republic of China," in Stanley J. Paliwoda (ed.) *New Perspectives on International Marketing*, London and New York: Routledge.

11 Lloyd, G. E. R. (1990) *Demystifying Mentalities*, Cambridge: Cambridge University Press.

12 Cronin, Aidan (1991) "Marketing to China: A Framework," in Stanley J. Paliwoda (ed.) *New Perspectives on International Marketing*, London and New York: Routledge.

13 Lewin, Kurt (1968) "Group Decision and Social Change," in Eleanor E. Maccoby, T. M. Newcomb, and E. E. Hartley (eds) *Readings in Social Psychology*, New York: Holt, Rinehart, and Winston.

14 Emerson, Richard M. (1976) "Social Exchange Theory," in Alex Inkeles and Neil J. Smelser (eds.) *Annual Review of Sociology*, Vol 2 Palo Alto, CA: Annual Reviews.

15 Cialdini, R. B. (1984) *Influence*, New York: William Morrow.

16 Churchill, Gilbert A., Ford, Neil M., Hartley, Steven W., and Walker, Orville C. (1985) "The Determinants of Salesperson Performance: a Meta-Analysis," *Journal of Marketing Research*, 22 (May).

17 Semlow, W. J. (1959) "How Many Salesmen Do You Need?" *Harvard Business Review*, 37 (June).

18 Weinberg, Charles B., Lucas, Henry C., and Clowes, Kenneth W. (1975) "Sales Response As a Function of Territorial Potential and Sales Representative Workload," *Journal of Marketing Research*, 12 (August).

19 Lodish, Leonard M. (1975) "Sales Territory Alignment to Maximize Profit," *Journal of Marketing Research*, 12 (February).

20 O'Shaughnessy, John (1971) *Evaluate Your Sales Force*, London: British Institute of Management.

21 Vroom, Victor (1964) "Some Psychological Aspects of Organizational Control," in W. W. Cooper, H. J. Leavitt, and M. W. Shelby (eds.) *New Perspectives in Organizational Control*, New York: John Wiley, p. 76

22 Boal, K. B. and Cummings, L. L. (1981) "Cognitive Evaluation Theory: An Experimental Test of Processes and Outcomes," *Organizational Behavior and Human Performance* (December), pp. 289–310.

APPENDIX 13.1   OUTLINE SPECIMEN SALES STRATEGY

1.   Objectives

(i)   *Mission*: to convert buyers and sales staff in selected outlets to promoting the company's product line in suits.

(ii)   *Goals*:

   a) revenue goal: to increase sales by 20 percent via segment penetration and development;

   b) convert 10 percent of the 150 department stores not at present buying the company's product line into exclusive dealerships;

   c) set up 10 regional training programs for our customers on the selling of quality suits;

   d) merchandising programs to be instituted in every territory;

   e) increase frequency of calls by 30 percent on all major accounts whose purchases are below the standards established by marketing research.

2.   Definition of customer targets

(i)   Description:

   a) buyers in outlets catering to patrons who seek advice and service in choosing a suit;

   b) sales staff in such stores.

(ii)   Both regular calling and development selling.

(iii) Exclusive distribution.

3.   Product focus
New style and in particular the new light-weight styles.

4.   Customer appeals
(i)   Benefits. Emphasis on profitable sales due to:
  a) high quality of product;
  b) patented features;
  c) high mark-up.
(ii)   Advice on how to sell the product, in store displays, training and cooperative advertising.
(iii)   Selling task:
  a) maintain—regular calling, joint promotions.
  b) increase—concept selling.
  c) convert—allow trial period; cash in on existing goodwill in trade.
  d) attract—show why profitable.

5.   Support services
(i)   Revised incentive plan.
(ii)   Advertising to supply promotional materials and cooperate on joint promotions.

6.   Sales budget (attached)

APPENDIX 13.2   XYZ PLASTICS REMUNERATION SCHEME

Introduction
This scheme of remuneration has been devised with the following objectives:
1. To ensure fair remuneration for XYZ sales representatives.
2. To encourage representatives to increase the level of business with existing outlets.
3. To encourage representatives to carry out merchandising in selected retail outlets.
4. To encourage representatives to call on potential retail stockists to obtain "transfer" orders for the wholesaler.

Each salesperson's remuneration will be made up of the following elements:
1. Salary.
2. Payment for sales volume.
3. Payment for satisfactorily carrying out merchandising and other nonselling tasks.
4. Payment for obtaining transfer orders.

Salary
A basic salary is guaranteed. This will vary with length of service: rising from a minimum of $— to $— at the normal rate of $— per year of service as an XYZ sales representative.

Commencing salary is subject to negotiation, but will be within the range of $— to $— depending on age, qualifications and experience.

Payment for sales volume

Considerable attention has been paid to designing sales territories to provide equal work opportunities for all representatives. Annual Sales Targets (A.S.T), expressed as a revenue turnover figure have been established for each territory.

These Sales Targets differ from territory to territory, even though work opportunities have been equalized. The guiding principles in setting a Sales Target will be to set a level which the average salesperson can attain if technically trained and strongly motivated to sell. Salespeople will be informed monthly as to how far they are likely to achieve the Annual Sales Target.

The A.S.T. for each territory will be reviewed annually by sales management in consultation with the sales representative. The final responsibility for each A.S.T. rests with Sales Managment.

The A.S.T. for a territory may be changed for the following reasons:
1. There is a change in the area comprising the sales territory.
2. There is a significant change in the present level of prices.
3. The range of products is substantially increased.
4. There is a significant change in selling conditions.
5. A demonstrable arithmetical or clerical error exists in the present Standard Sales Figure.
6. There is mutual agreement between the salesperson concerned and Management.

Basic volume

Your basic volume of sales is the point from which you begin to earn. This point has been fixed at a level corresponding to 30 percent of the Annual Sales Target. For example:

A.S.T.	$2,000,000
Basic volume	$600,000

In this case, no commission would be earned on sales below $600,000.

Moving annual total (MAT)

If your commission were paid strictly on monthly sales, your earnings may fluctuate due to the influence of holidays, seasonal buying, trade cycles, etc

For this reason, a Sales Target is given to you as an annual figure. Similarly, your actual sales are also expressed as the 12 months' total sales to date. To obtain this figure, the current month's sales is added to the preceding months MAT and the corresponding month's sales for the previous year taken away. Each month a new 12 months' figure is obtained, which is comprised of the current month and the preceding eleven months.

Performance

Your performance is obtained by comparing your present level of sales with your standard sales figure. In terms of performance your Sales Target is 100. Thus, if any month your MAT reaches three quarters of your Sales Target (is 75 percent), your performance for that month is 75. For example:

Sales Target	$2,000,000
Current MAT	$1,400,000
Performance	70.0

Commission will be paid at the rate $—for every performance point above 30, i.e. 30 percent of your A.S.T. In other words, the value of goods invoiced must be at least 30 percent of your A.S.T. before you begin to earn commission. For example:

A.S.T.	$600,000
MAT at 31.5	$580,800
Performance	$\frac{580,800}{600,000} \times 100 = 98$

Commission for May $(98 - 30) \times \$—$
$$= 68 \times \$—$$
$$= \$—$$

By reaching and maintaining your A.S.T., you can earn $—per annum for this part of the scheme. No upper limit is set to the earnings under this part of the scheme.

Merchandising bonus
Each representative will be given a list of retail outlets where he or she is to carry out merchandising. Points will be awarded by Sales Management every three months for the effectiveness with which this work is carried out.

Standard	Points awarded
1. Merchandising activity has been carried out in at least 75 percent of nominated outlets. Representative has achieved merchandising objectives given to him or her and has shown initiative and originality in display work.	15–20
2. Merchandising activity carried out is under 75 percent of nominated outlets but over 50 percent. Competent display work.	5–12
3. Merchandising carried out in less than 50 percent of nominated outlets.	0–5

For each point awarded to a representative $— will be awarded as bonus. The representative can add $— per annum to his earnings with this part of the scheme. This bonus will be paid at three months' intervals.

Payment for retail orders
Each representative will be paid 1 percent commission on retail orders. This commission will be paid at 3-monthly intervals. There is an annual upper limit of $— under this part of the scheme.

"Retail" includes orders taken by the representative from customers who are normally supplied by wholesalers. The customer may specify either direct delivery or delivery through a wholesaler. Such orders will be sent to Head Office by the representative.

Chapter 14

Pricing
Role, objectives, factors, strategies

Whether we are concerned with pricing a new offering or revising the price of current offerings, the pricing decision can be key to profitability since price, in influencing the quantity demanded, determines the surplus of revenue over the costs of doing business. Even modest price differences can have a dramatic effect on profit and a price at odds with the rest of the marketing mix (for example, the product's promoted image) can spell disaster. This is because price is information to the buyer; not just information about what money sum must be spent to complete the buying transaction but information that affects perceptions of the offering. For example, consumers on occasions will use the asking price as a guide to value so that the higher the price, the more valuable a consumer may estimate the product to be. Not every seller, though, is in a position to set prices which may be controlled by the government or some industry-sponsored, government-approved agency, board, or association. In this chapter we are assuming that the seller (including intermediaries) makes the pricing decision even if freedom to decide is highly circumscribed by forces other than those of the market place.

What is priced is not simply the product (the good or the service) but the bundle of benefits for the buyer. Take, for example, two brands of wristwatch, brand A and brand X, that are equally good for measuring time:

Brand A	**Brand X**
Highly attractive styling	Plain appearance (utilitarian looking)
Five-year guarantee	Six-month guarantee
A brand-name signifying quality	Unknown, unpromoted brand-name
Sold in the most reputable stores	Sold in variety chain stores only
Promoted by celebrities	Promoted only at the point of sale

Brand A and brand X may be equally good at keeping time but consumers will place a higher value on brand A than on brand X. Similarly, a computer sold by a firm of unimpeachable reputation backed by extensive service is going to be perceived as worth more than a computer without such support. Thus the Maytag washing machine commands a 15 percent premium over competitive makes, because of extra perceived value in Maytag's ten-year guarantee plus an image of product reliability. A firm that fails to recognize it is pricing an *offering* and not just a product can be stampeded into reducing price when buyers and salespeople complain about rival brands being cheaper. The opposite error lies in simply assuming that the consumer is prepared to pay in proportion to extra benefits provided. This depends on whether a segment of the market actually or potentially exists whose "want" embraces the demand for such extras. This is essentially a matter for empirical inquiry. Sometimes it is more profitable to "*unbundle*," taking away the extras to give the market an offering at a lower price and charging separately for everything else. It is not uncommon to add costly product differentiation beyond requirements and beyond what can be recouped in price. The seller needs to think and rethink about any augmentation of the basic product, about what it adds to customer value, and what it adds as a consequence to competitive advantage and incremental profits.

In addition to evaluating the value to the buyer of the total benefit being offered, the seller needs to calculate what he, the seller, is to receive in exchange. Received price is minus any giveaways. Thus there can be discounts, generous credit terms, cost guarantees, warranties, buyback agreements, allowances, deals, and price guarantees; all have to be taken into account in calculating likely net revenues.

In this chapter we consider:

- the role of price;
- the various objectives that guide pricing strategies and methods;
- the factors that enter into pricing decisions;
- pricing in microeconomic theory;
- cost-based pricing;
- pricing in marketing: determining *list* prices of new offerings and price revisions;
- price variations about list prices;
- pricing in specific marketing situations; and
- pricing in international markets.

THE ROLE(S) OF PRICE

As reflecting market valuation

In any market exchange, each party offers a benefit to induce a response. Exchange can be viewed as one way of controlling behavior. The seller controls behavior by making his offering as irresistible as possible, while customers control the firm's actions through the prices they are willing to pay.

The value put on the firm's offering by the market is indicated by buyers' responsiveness to changes in price and this in turn depends on the availability of acceptable substitutes. Buyers may have *conclusive reasons* for buying one brand rather than another but never *absolute reasons*, since there are always circumstances in which brand switching will occur, particularly circumstances involving price. For products perceived as commodity products, brand switching can follow the pattern of relative price changes. But this is not always true since there may be costs attached to switching brands as well as the propensity to switch being reduced by the habitual buying of a particular brand.

Consumers have a price range within which the product should fall for them to buy it. "Should fall" rather than "must fall" since the buyer's initial price range can change as more is learned about what is available and at what price. Even without such learning, a price range may not have rigid boundaries as consumers may be persuaded (say, at the point of purchase) to reassess spending priorities. Thus the bulk of buyers of consumer durables may desire the best technical performance possible whether the product is a stereo or a refrigerator. The fact that people do not buy what they regard as the best (given its availability) is because the best generally costs more. Nonetheless they can often be persuaded to see the long-term value of buying quality.

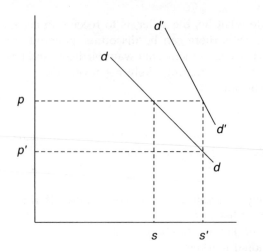

Figure 14.1 The relationship between price and demand

Role in the marketing mix

Price can be *the* major element in the marketing mix. Generally, though, pricing decisions have to be carefully coordinated with decisions on product, promotion and distribution. The framework for such coordination is the segmentation/positioning strategy, since this gives overall direction to determining the mix. Thus the luxury segments of consumer markets suggest a quality branded product, extra touches, high-class outlets, and advertising appeals and media that capture the luxury image—and a relatively high price to match.

In economic and marketing texts it is usual to regard price and promotion as to some extent substitutes. The position is illustrated in Figure 14.1. The demand curve *d-d* shows the relationship between price (along the vertical axis) and the quantity demanded (along the horizontal). At price *p* the quantity sold is *s*. A reduction in price to *p'* increases sales to *s'*. However, the same sales level might be obtained, without a price change, by advertising pushing *d–d* to the right, and perhaps making for the more inelastic demand curve illustrated by *d'–d'*. Where there are just a few rival brands, competitors are more likely to react to a lowering of price than to an increase in advertising expenditure as decreases in price are highly visible and are often associated with the onset of cut-throat competition.

PRICING OBJECTIVES

Although it could be argued that the superordinate goal of any pricing decision revolves round inducing the consumer to pay the price that is most profitable for the seller, any systematic approach to pricing will take account of several objectives relating to

- the seller's market/value orientation;
- the seller's earnings objectives; and
- the market situation or context.

As Figure 14.2 suggests, pricing objectives reflect the seller's values, the financial goals sought, and the market requirements as determined by competition. We will discuss each in turn.

Relating to market/value orientation

Although for the economist the goal of pricing is to maximize the rate of return on assets, such profit goals provide criteria rather than explicit precepts or guidance for

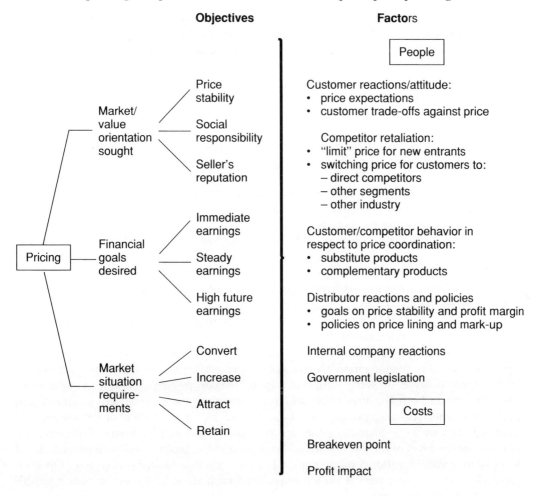

Figure 14.2 Objectives and factors in pricing

pricing. In any case, as Gabor points out, modern approaches to pricing recognize that top management is interested not only in profit but in factors such as price stability, generating trust, social responsibility, company reputation, and so on.[1] There may be good economic reasons for seeking price stability (e.g. to ward off government action) and there are long-term benefits from, say, not exploiting scarcity to increase prices or avoiding any damage to the firm's reputation by charging whatever the market can bear. Any set of operational objectives for pricing should take account of such factors. Additionally there should be objectives in terms of the earnings stream that is sought and objectives specific to the market situation (see Figure 14.2).

Financial goals relating to the earnings stream desired

Firms are concerned with achieving a certain level of earnings. Since pricing will influence differences in cash flows or earnings streams in the relevant time period, firms implicitly or explicitly set one of the following financial goals:

- a goal of *immediate* earnings;
- a goal of *steady* earnings; or
- a goal of high *future* earnings.

Earnings goals can seldom be pursued singlemindedly regardless of all else. Financial objectives operate within constraints, for example, constraints such as:

- perceptions of product quality must remain constant;
- dealers must receive their conventional mark-up;
- all distributors must receive equal terms; and
- prices must not fall more than, say, 10 percent below the brand leader's price and so on.

These constraints are imposed from considerations of what is required to evoke favorable reactions from the various groups affected by the pricing decision. When a price affects many stakeholder groups, the firm cannot just pursue the single goal of immediate profit maximization. It may postpone immediate profit in deference to those with whom it has long-term interlocking interests or whose retaliation it fears. As Gabor says, "no sensible businessman would knowingly endanger the long run profitability of his firm in favor of some temporary gain." Major pricing decisions vitally affect relationships in both the firm itself and with others in the external environment. For these and other reasons, pricing decisions require top management involvement and approval. In any case, financial goals are not simply dictated by financial preferences. Sometimes the level of output needed to keep production facilities fully employed, allied to customer considerations, may suggest just one feasible financial objective. On such grounds, some writers regard preferences about cash flows as being of minor significance in pricing decisions.

Relating to market situation requirements

Oxenfeldt lists what he terms "price-setting occasions."[2] These give rise to the need for specific situational objectives. Thus new rivals may enter the market, or current rivals reduce/increase prices, or costs unexpectedly increase or primary demand increases or declines, or a new product introduction may demand a pricing decision that affects the pricing of the firm's existing products. Although price-setting occasions are many and varied, they point to the adoption of one or more of the following *competitive goals*:

- *attracting* new buyers or users;
- *converting* existing users from other brands;
- *increasing* individual purchases from existing customers via heavier individual usage; and
- *retaining* customers by encouraging repeat purchase.

Each of these competitive goals is a way of meeting the competition. They are tied to *market share goals* as success in achieving these goals is a means to increasing or maintaining market share. However, if competitive goals are to provide maximum guidance to pricing they must be tied to the specific price-setting occasion, so that the particular problem to be overcome by pricing is kept in mind. For example:

- attracting new users *to gain rapid acceptance of the new product*;
- converting from rivals to *exploit an increase in a competitor's prices*;
- increasing individual usage to *exploit a fall in the cost of raw materials*;
- retaining customers patronage *with the entry of ABC into the market*.

FACTORS IN PRICING

There are two sets of factors in considering pricing: people (including competitors) and costs. Price generally needs to cover costs, while the firm chooses a price that will provide a coalition of support among stakeholder groups (see Figure 14.2). Price and price changes affect different stakeholder groups, not just those within the seller's organization and potential customers but also distributors, competitors, suppliers, and even the government. Each of these groups has different values, interests and beliefs about the "goodness" of the price in relation to its own goals. Such awareness gives rise to support, boycott, or overt opposition to whatever price is proposed.

No strong stakeholder group should be ignored in pricing decisions. There is a need for the "balancing of the interests of all parties" since, for example, "an excellent price for the ultimate customer may be a poor price if it left paltry margins for the retailer and thus elicited little sales support." The pricing decision involves trade-offs in support from various stakeholder groups to obtain a winning coalition. The seller is seldom able (if profit objectives are to be achieved) to dictate price, saying "take it or leave it" to everyone else. Even monopoly power is apt to erode long term, while past injuries through price changes give rise to future scores to be settled.

As with all social behavior, pricing decisions are influenced by norms or rules developed from past practices. Such norms are in the nature of reciprocal agreements about ways of stabilizing (if not resolving) conflict. For example, there may be an implicit agreement with customers to charge costs plus some percentage mark-up, or for prices to parallel some industry leader if price wars are to be avoided. Sellers feel obligated to justify price increases and may be required to cushion any loss on distributor inventories. For their part, distributors may be required to refrain from selling below suggested retail price and industrial purchasing agents to desist from disclosing bids to rivals. Where such practices represent the established ways of doing business, they become hallowed by tradition and appear fair. As an example, take the fixed commission system that operated on Wall Street until 1975. Brokers argued that the umbrella of fixed rates was vital to the health of the securities industry. It was predicted that leaving rates to be determined by competition would have the perverse effect of destroying the nation's stock exchanges, creating chaos in the stock markets, and (for those under any delusion that price competition and free enterprise were associated) even burying the free enterprise system!

Customer considerations

In any pricing decision, we start with the market segment and the price expectations of customers. If a product is developed to fit the market segment, it will be produced with some price in mind as there are few (if any) market segments where customers buy regardless of price. This is not to suggest that prices must never exceed customer expectations or that segment members have firm expectations of the price they will have to pay. Neither would be true. Buyers often pay more than they expected or more than they consider reasonable simply because of an absence of acceptable substitutes. Other customers, with limited experience in the market, may have no idea about prices except within a very wide price range. Nonetheless, buyer price expectations are important since a price in excess of the top end of the range may exceed the buyer's maximum (*reservation*) price or, if buying does occur, it is more likely to give rise to dissatisfaction. The reservation price depends on

- the centrality of the product for the function for which it is being bought;
- the uniqueness of the product to the seller;
- the social perceptions of the wisdom of purchase at that price (including perceptions of fairness);
- the outlet where the product is being bought; and
- the salience of the product in the life of the buyer.

The idea that buyers have a reservation price may lead a firm to seek ways to absorb a cost increase other than by raising price (for example, a reduction in package size or contents). But reservation prices like price expectations, do change as a result of experience. However, if prices are increased dramatically to adjust, say, for several years of inflation, demand can drop off disproportionately, picking up again if price is later lowered. This is the so-called *MW process*, the *M* representing the up and down of the manufacturer's prices and *W* representing the down and up in buyer response. It is for this reason that firms may adjust for inflation as it occurs so that the impact of the individual increase is less dramatic.

The question arises: "If price expectations can influence reservation price, what factors influence these expectations besides the prices of competitive offerings?" The major factors relate to buyer perceptions of a fair/just price, past prices and perceptions of quality and value for money.

Fair/just price.   The medieval concept of the *"just price"* is still with us and is a factor in forming expectations of price. Perceptions of the cost of producing a product or knowledge of the prices of related products influence views about the fair price to pay. Although a price need not appear fair to be effective, "the price below which a purchase would be considered a bargain is identical with the individual's subjective idea of the just price." There are occasions when buyers reject what they consider an unfair price and refuse to buy, even though price is actually below their reservation price. Many vacation resorts refrain from charging higher prices in peak periods so as not to appear to be price gouging, fearing that this will affect goodwill, trust, and loyalty on which sales long term depend. Buyers resist transactions which they perceive to be unfair and may resist price increases not justified by cost increases.

Past prices.   Buyers hesitate to pay much beyond what they have been paying in the past without first shopping around. But the influence of price-last-paid varies with different products. In fact the consumer's ability to recall past prices varies from product to product in a way that does not appear related to the frequency of purchase. Many consumers do not know the exact price of the brands they frequently buy. However, this can be misleading if it is concluded that the consumer is insensitive to price. Consumers often have trust in the supermarket they patronize, in assuming prices will be competitive and major changes will be noticed. Gabor's work suggests that the price-last-paid has little influence in the purchase of consumer durables but he regards the price of the last purchase *as remembered* to be of great importance "since this will indicate how the market will respond to a price adjustment."

Quality and value perceptions.   The consumer's perception of quality is his or her evaluation of the brand's overall superiority relative to other known brands.[3] Perceptions of quality are inferred from various surrogate indicators, one of which can be price. Even if a high price is not perceived as an indicator of quality, a low price might suggest low quality. While for the whole population of products there may be no general relationship between perceived quality and price, there *can* be a positive relationship between price and perceptions of quality. There is, for example, a very positive correlation between the price of potato chips and perceptions of quality. The evidence would suggest that a positive association is likely to be strongest under one or more of the following conditions:

- in the absence of other clues as to quality like brand-name;

- if there is a wide range of prices within the product category;
- where there is an absence of cues for judging quality objectively, e.g. physical inspection not revealing;
- if the purchase is infrequent;
- if quality does in fact vary widely within the product class;
- when the purchase is relatively cheap in relation to the importance of its function or in relation to the cost of the other products with which it will be used;
- brands are unfamiliar;
- high fear of making an error because of the risk involved in the purchase;
- if the buying occasion puts the emphasis on adaptive criteria;
- with certain products like consumer durables; and
- the particular situation suggests such a relationship can be expected e.g. the store image/reputation.

The relationship between price and "objective" quality as assessed by consumer reports is generally low.[4] This is not surprising since consumer reports do not necessarily take account of the same factors as the consumer. As one journalist points out, she takes for granted that the thing will work and if it doesn't she can take it back and get a replacement pronto. She claims that consumer reports are out of touch with the psychology of shopping, which is far more about style, image, design, and ambience than working out which washing machine runs more efficiently or whose electric kettle boils fastest.[5] Thus one consumer organization evaluates panty hose on the basis of

- median life in hours,
- comfort,
- fit,
- reinforced toes, and
- wideness of waistband

while ignoring style, color, fineness of knit, and brand-name which may be important for the buyer. In any case, quality is always relative to the market segment. A high price can be very much part of a brand's image, suggesting the brand is exclusive and so distinguishing the owner or user. If a firm's product is of high quality, then a high price reinforces the quality image.

Perceptions of *consumer value* can be distinguished from perceptions of quality since perceptions of consumer value relate to how well the offering meets the buyer's choice criteria. Such choice criteria, covering technical, economic, legalistic, integrative, adaptive, and intrinsic criteria, will include social, ethical, and aesthetic value. After all, not every buyer is interested in the highest quality, however measured. Brand loyalty is more likely to be tied to perceptions of value than to perceptions of quality. Perceptions of value, though, can be influenced by the way the deal is presented. For example, selling something 2 for a $1 rather than 50 cents each can enhance perceptions of value. In the same way, consumer evaluations of value were enhanced when beef was labeled "75 percent" fat-free instead of being labeled "only 25 percent fat".

If we look at an offering as a bundle of benefits, a seller would like to know the consumer's trade-offs between extra benefits and lower price. Extra benefits can be in the form of additional attributes (for example, leather car seats) or in the level of some attribute (for example, size of car engine). There is increasing interest in using conjoint analysis to calculate what money equivalents the consumer attaches to each change in the bundle of benefits, whether the change involves adding or subtracting a benefit. The technique is also used to estimate the percentage change in market share likely to result from a price change. Such trade-offs do occur suggesting consumer loyalty can often be traded at a price. Moreover, the level at which the trade-offs are made changes with the times, for example, when income falls, more attention is paid to price.

Competition

One reason for identifying consumer perceptions of value is to compare such perceptions with the perceptions of rival offerings since consumers expect brands falling within the same value range to be roughly the same price. Whenever a firm charges more than its competitors, it needs to signal value differences equivalent to the price difference. In any case, the price setter should gauge the effect of price on the behavior of competition. At some price level, new entrants are tempted into the market and customers are tempted to switch. The *limit price* is the highest price that can be set without attracting such entry. Where the price setter is concerned about possible market entry, some attempt must be made to assess the limit price.

The *switching price* is the highest price that can be set without customers being tempted to switch to:

- direct competitors,
- other (lower-price) segments of the market, or
- substitutes from other industries.

The extent to which customers will switch to rival brands depends on the extent to which the two offerings appeal to the same choice criteria. The more they were alike before the price change, the more customers will switch brands to the lower-priced offering. The less alike the two offerings, the less likely is brand switching, but the more we need to know what the differential between the two offerings is worth to our customers. Consumers do not expect brands to be equal in price but expect differences in price to be justified in terms of differences in the offering. In discussing brand switching, some authors refer to the concept of the *net value of the brand*, which is the overall perception of gross benefits minus all perceived costs. It is argued consumers compare net values of brands in deciding whether to switch. However, net values differ among members of the target market while the perceived net value before purchase can vary from the perceived net value after buying.

Henderson, the originator of the experience curve concept, claims the basic objective in pricing a new product should be to prevent competitors from gaining experience and market share before the product has achieved high volume.[6] He claims that there are two principal reasons for a shift in market share between competitors. The more common reason is a lack of capacity and the other is the willingness to lose market share to maintain price. The weakness of this claim is that it assumes that the rival brands are perceived as alike, which may not be so. What commonly happens in maturing markets is a decline in price variation among different competitors, with competition occurring more in promotion.

Firms may cut prices to gain market share. Whether the competition follows or not depends on the cost structures of competitors, the importance of the segment to them and their manufacturing capacity utilization. In any case, response to price cuts can be selective. Thus the airlines learned they need not reduce prices across the board in responding to the low price airlines but need only cut prices on routes that were crucial to their overall strategy. As one analyst commented (*Fortune*, October 29, 1984): "the trick is not so much being competitive as being perceived as competitive." In segments of the computer market subject to stiff price competition, IBM has traditionally reacted with competitive prices, compensating by charging "inflated" prices to customers in the less competitive segments. But the old tactic of eliminating competition through price wars is not as easy as it once was as the defeated do not just exit but get taken over by other firms with deeper pockets.

Competition in many consumer goods markets comes from *private label* (the retailers' own brands). Thus private label has increased significantly in market share even in such markets as that for diapers, which means the firms manufacturing diapers have failed to convince the consumer that their brands are worth a premium price.

Coordinated prices and customer/competitor behavior

A problem occurs in coordinating the prices of a firm's products if they are substitutes or complementary. Two products are *substitutes* if the sales of one product fall when the price of the other is reduced. The products are *complementary* if sales of both products increase when the price of one of them is reduced. The pricing of such products needs to be coordinated since they have *cross-elasticities*, that is, as price changes for one, sales change for the other; substitution implies positive cross-elasticity and complementarity implies negative cross-elasticity.

Complementary products

It may be more profitable to price, say, equipment (e.g. the razor) at below a competitor's prices to increase sales on the complementary product (e.g. the razor blades). For example, Polaroid prices its cameras low compared to its rival Nikon. However, its films are high-priced and, since Nikon does not make film, Nikon is at a disadvantage. *Cross-subsidization* of one product by another is not uncommon when the demand for the lower priced product is very price sensitive but not so price sensitive for the higher priced product. However, there is a danger of buyers "cherry picking" the bargains, and unless there are barriers to entry, there is a danger of competitors entering the more profitable market.

Substitute products

An example illustrating the importance of coordinated pricing in substitute products concerns IBM, as reported in *Fortune* (May 19, 1980), the IBM 4300 series of medium-scale computers was so popular on introduction that delivery schedules were stretched into 1983. This was because the new machines were low priced in terms of their use-value. The users of large computers believed IBM would soon be in a position to offer a similar bargain to them, "so droves of them scrapped plans to buy IBM's existing big computers and turned instead to leases." The result was that IBM "got caught in a financial squeeze." IBM later raised prices on the 4300 series.

The constraints imposed by the need for coordinated prices can produce a price structure rigidity that may be exploited by competition. Thus a competitor might reduce the price of his single market entry. The big firm, with its set of related products, may find it difficult to respond with a price cut as the prices of the whole set of products may have to be reduced to maintain established differentials.

Distributors

When the firm sells through intermediaries, the effect of the pricing decision on the distributor should be anticipated. The price setter seeks to avoid alienating the distributor while at the same time preventing intermediaries from adopting policies that could frustrate pricing intentions.

Goals on price stability and profit margins

A distributor is alienated by constant price changes. On the surface it is not clear that frequent price changes would annoy distributors, since price reductions (if passed along) please their customers while price increases enhance the value of their inventory. On the other hand, price increases (if passed along) irritate their customers and price reductions reduce the value of inventory. Constant price changes add considerably to ticketing and record keeping and reduce the likelihood of staff knowing prices, while customer routines are upset by having to guess future prices. On these grounds, distributors generally favor price stability in *list* prices while encouraging discounts. Where the manufacturer's recommended price tends to be followed, distributors are concerned with margin. Selling price is margin plus cost. If the recommended selling price is $1 and the cost is 60 cents, then margin tends to be calculated by the distributor not on cost but on selling price, that is, 40 percent.

Policies on price lining and mark-up

If a manufacturer's marketing strategy depends on strong support from intermediaries, this makes the manufacturer very sensitive to distributor reactions to prices. There are a number of policies adopted by distributors to which a price setter might have to adapt:

- *Price lining* occurs when the retailer selects certain prices, quality levels, or price zones as appropriate for his market segment and carries merchandise only at these levels. If the manufacturer wishes to retain the patronage of such stores, their price-lining policy should be kept in mind.
- *Mark-up policy*: A manufacturer cannot always guarantee that distributors will adhere to recommended prices, and therefore cannot always guarantee the price to the final customer. Yet, with a "push" distribution strategy in particular, price maintenance is important so there may be a need to select retailers who will maintain prices. In practice, as Gabor says, price variations that are actually *feasible* are not likely to allow distributors to cross price-segment boundaries. What is apt to be more important is for the seller to help the distributor to be consistent in the mark-up to avoid, say, customers finding large sizes cost more per unit.

Internal company functions

Many different people in different departments of an organization are affected by pricing decisions and will want to have their say. As their interests differ, so will demands conflict. The director of finance may seek a growth in earnings and a higher rate of return on equity and wants higher prices to accomplish this. The production department may seek full plant utilization and believes price stability would help. The sales manager argues for lowering prices, and so on. These varying viewpoints cannot be ignored but must be reconciled if intergroup relations are to be preserved.

Government

Whether manufacturers can insist on distributors adhering to recommended prices and whether they can discriminate on price are often matters for government legislation. Some governments even dictate how prices are to be determined. Generally, governments ban collusion on prices among competitors but, in some countries, cartels, combines and trade associations that openly practice price-fixing are encouraged. In exporting abroad, *intra-corporate* pricing practices seek to minimize the effect of tariffs, taxes and control over dividend repatriation but governments are concerned to see that such practices are not ways of avoiding taxes. Of general concern to exporters has been the antidumping legislation, which prohibits selling at prices believed to be below cost or below domestic prices. Why foreign governments should insist on their citizens paying more than need be is explained by the lobbying efforts of local producers, the need to support local industry, and the general fear of increasing unemployment.

Costs and breakeven analysis

In practice, cost factors are usually given more consideration than any other factor. Although relentlessly criticized as a general method of pricing, pricing purely on the basis of costs is still probably the most common method used. We shall postpone discussion of this method until later in the chapter and confine our attention to the *role* of costs.

Any proposal to *lower* prices raises a number of questions:

- How many more units must be sold to achieve the previous profit level with the former price?
- What is the lowest price that can be charged (say, to meet competition) without making a loss?
- If a product cannot be sold at a profitable price, what is the loss that must be carried if the product is marketed just to fill out a line?

Any proposal to *increase* prices raises questions such as:

- What fall-off in the amount demanded must occur before profit drops below the previous profit level?
- At different prices, what is the rate of return on assets invested?

A useful technique to answer some of these questions is *breakeven analysis*. The breakeven point occurs at the level of operations where:

Total revenue = total cost

i.e. where no losses or profits are being made.

The breakeven point expressed in terms of units of output is:

Total fixed cost
_____
Price less variable cost per unit (if costs are linear)

Price less variable cost per unit is unit *contribution*, and is calculated as follows:

		$
Price to the customer		100
Minus variable costs per unit:		
manufacturing	30	
shipping	3	
commission	5	38
Unit contribution		$62

If fixed costs are $100,000, the breakeven point would be 100,000/62 = 1,613 units. In

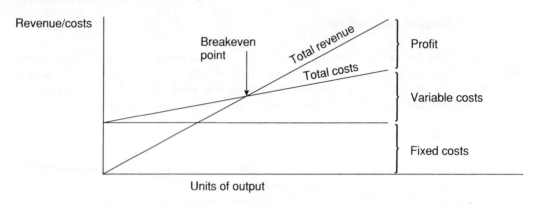

Figure 14.3 Graphical representation of breakeven analysis

other words, each unit sold contributes $62 to fixed costs or overhead, so that 1,613 units must be sold to cover the $100,000 fixed costs.

Breakeven analysis assumes that costs can be divided into fixed costs (costs that remain constant regardless of the level of output) and variable costs (costs that vary directly with the level of output). This assumption can be maintained only for short-term planning. In the long term, all costs become variable. Also the costs per unit today may not be the costs tomorrow as future costs may be higher or lower. Interests must focus on costs in the future though these can be difficult to anticipate. The other questionable assumptions in traditional expositions of breakeven analysis is that costs are linear, that is, if the variable cost per unit is $2, then the total variable cost of 1,000 units is $2,000 and the total variable costs of 1,000,000 units will be $2,000,000 and that fixed costs remain fixed. More sophisticated breakeven analyses deal with the lifting of these various assumptions.

A graphical illustration of the breakeven technique is shown in Figure 14.3. Such graphs are easy to draw if, as is assumed, costs and revenues vary proportionately to output. There are many uses of breakeven analysis. We can, for example, calculate the breakeven point at different prices. Thus, given the assumption that fixed costs are $125,000 and the proposed prices and corresponding variable costs per unit are:

Price	$10	$11	$12
Variable cost per unit	$8	$8	$8

then the contribution to fixed costs and the corresponding volume breakeven points are as follows:

Contribution	$2	$3	$4
Volume breakeven	62,500	41,667	31,250

Another use of breakeven analysis lies in calculating the change in breakeven point as a result of an increase in fixed costs or overheads. For example, suppose the firm proposed to increase advertising expenditure by $25,000, which increases fixed costs from $125,000 to $150,000. If price-minus-variable-cost is $2, the breakeven point would be raised from 125,000/2 = 62,500 units to 150,000/2 = 75,000 units. If the aim is to make a profit of $50,000, then 25,000 units ($50,000/2) would have to be sold over and above the breakeven point of 75,000 units to reach a target sales figure of (75,000 + 25,000) = 100,000 units.

Once having established objectives and obtained basic information on costs and an understanding of the likely behavior of those affected by the pricing decision, we are in a position to determine the pricing strategy. This section of the chapter sets out two approaches to pricing that have wide currency but are rejected by marketers as universal solutions to pricing problems. These are:

1 pricing in microeconomic theory, and
2 cost-based pricing.

The first approach is regarded as conceptually elegant but inadequate and impractical, while the second approach is considered feasible and convenient but generally misleading and wrong theoretically. These criticisms should not be taken to imply that the two approaches have nothing to recommend them. Microeconomic theory embraces useful concepts, while the cost approach to pricing may on occasions be necessary. The final part of the chapter deals with strategic approaches and methods for determining:

- the declared list price of new offerings and price revisions on existing products;
- price variations (for example, discounts) and methods of payment (for example, credit terms) to achieve the firm's competitive goals;
- prices in specific situations encountered in organizational buying; and
- pricing in international markets.

Strategic pricing should be proactive rather than reactive so that the firm retains the initiative rather than merely following competition. In this way, pricing decisions help to maintain a consistent value image for the brand in the eyes of customers.

PRICING IN MICROECONOMIC THEORY

Economists' pricing models are not designed to describe realistically the way people make pricing decisions or the way consumers respond to these decisions.[7] Nonetheless, these models provide useful heuristics for understanding pricing consequences while explaining certain principles to which successful pricing strategies should conform. But Gabor and perhaps most marketers, regard "the abstractions on which the traditional theory of price is based [as] far too restrictive to justify its applications, except in some rather special cases." Some of these *limitations* are:

Narrow focus. Traditional economic theory takes as given that product, promotion and distribution strategies have already been developed. As a consequence it focuses exclusively on the remaining strategic decision of price and corresponding output level. In contrast to this, the marketing executive must consider all the individual strategies as one coordinated system geared to influencing demand. Also no consideration is given to the need to elicit support except from customers.

Consumer preferences known and ordered. In economic theory, consumers do not indulge in complex deliberation when buying. Their preferences are known and ordered as if they know immediately what they prefer.

Cost and demand functions known. The business executive is assumed to know costs at each level of output and to know how much he can sell at each price.

Consumer as utility maximizing and all knowledgeable. Traditionally, economic theory has assumed that consumers know all about alternative products and distribute their purchases so as to maximize utility.

The demand curve

The pricing recommendations of economists stem from the assumption of a U-shaped average cost curve in relation to a demand curve whose shape differs under the different market structures of pure competition, oligopoly, monopolistic competition, and monopoly. The categories are based on the number of sellers in the market and the extent to which competitive offerings are differentiated. Figure 14.4 illustrates.

- *monopoly*: there is a single seller of a product with no close substitutes;
- *homogeneous oligopoly*: there are just a few firms with similar offerings;
- *differentiated oligopoly*: there are also just a few firms, but their offerings are differentiated. (Differentiated oligopoly is the dominant mode. We need only to look at the small number of firms in cars, cigarettes, detergents, analgesics, razors, cereals, toothpaste, pens, deodorants, and so on. If we think in terms of market segments, the oligopolist nature of much of competition becomes even more apparent);
- *pure competition*: a situation in which a large number of firms sell identical offerings; and

| | | Number of sellers | | |
		One	A few	Many
Product/ offering	Homogeneous		Homogeneous oligopoly	Pure competition
	Differentiated	Pure monopoly	Differentiated oligopoly	Monopolistic competition

Figure 14.4 Market structures

- *monopolistic competition*: in this situation, there are also many firms but their offerings are differentiated and so not perfect substitutes for each other

These market structures are essentially ideal types or abstractions that may only approximate reality. The *demand curve* is an estimate of the quantity that is likely to be sold over a whole range of prices, that is, an estimate of the buyer's reaction to different prices, other things remaining equal. All firms, other than those in purely competitive markets, are assumed to face a demand curve that slopes from left to right (see Figure 14.5), which indicates that a reduction in price leads to an increase in sales and an increase in price leads to a fall-off in the amount demanded. "Demand" can refer to the demand of the individual consumer, the total demand for the firm's product or the total demand for all the products competing in the market. The exact slope of the demand curve shows the responsiveness of demand to a change in price and relates to the *elasticity of demand*. More specifically, the elasticity of demand refers to some part of a demand curve. If the price is lowered from one point to another and

- total revenue increases, then demand is elastic between these points;
- total revenue decreases, then demand is inelastic; or
- total revenue remains the same, then the elasticity of demand is unity.

Critique

A demand curve that slopes sharply downward (inelastic demand) generally indicates a lack of acceptable substitutes, so that a big change in price must occur before major changes in the amount demanded occur. On the other hand, where the demand is fairly flat (elastic demand), this indicates an availability of substitutes, so that a small change in price brings about a big change in amount demanded (see Figure 14.5).

Although the amount demanded will vary with price, a lowering of price will not win back old customers if tastes have changed or better substitutes have come along.

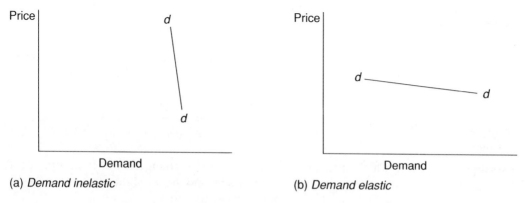

(a) *Demand inelastic*

(b) *Demand elastic*

Figure 14.5 Demand elasticity

A substantial reduction in the price of the horse and buggy would not have prevented its being superseded by the automobile. An important change in any significant factor, for example, taste and income, means the movement of the whole of the demand curve to the left or to the right. A change in taste or income must thus be distinguished from the effect of a price change, which is measured and reflected by the *slope* of the demand curve.

As any slope of demand curve is possible, the idea of a demand curve is not something that can be falsified: it is a truism. However, if a demand curve is meant to represent more than the state of demand at a particular moment, it assumes that consumers have a relatively stable and comprehensive preference system. Such an assumption lacks realism, as preferences change with experience. Could a company lower price and later raise the price back to the previous level and find demand as before? One reason for temporary price offers is to attract new users, some of whom are retained on return to the earlier (higher) price.

If for every marketing strategy envisaged, a button could be pressed to show on a screen a corresponding demand curve that was reasonably stable, there would be few product failures. Unfortunately, the stability of the demand curve cannot be taken for granted, and determining the likely amount demanded at different price levels is a process of guess-estimating. As to the belief in a demand curve sloping down from left to right, Table 14.1 shows price changes and changes in the volume sales of instant and ground coffee in Sweden in 1975–1977:

Table 14.1 Changes in price and volume sales for instant and ground coffee

Instant coffee		Ground coffee	
% price increase	% change in volume	% price increase	% change in volume
87	143	150	−20

Source: Harold Lind (1978) "Beverages: The Demand Curve that Soured," *Financial Times*, September 28

How are to we to account for the 143 percent increase in sales of instant coffee given that the price of instant coffee had increased 87 percent? The answer lies in remembering that consumer reaction to price changes depends vitally on the price of *perceived* substitutes and anticipated prices. Though the price increase of 87 percent was high in absolute terms, it was small compared to the price increase of 150 percent for ground coffee.

Gauging reaction to price changes

Every price setter would like to know reaction to price changes both long and short term. What conditions make for demand elasticity and how might elasticity be estimated? The conditions favoring high demand elasticity are:

- the product can be shown to have high potential for cost saving (likely latent demand);
- the product before the price reduction was considered too costly in relation to the customer's budget (passive demand activated);
- habit and picking behavior common (price (economic) incentive likely to undermine both);
- intrinsic preferences for rival products not strong;
- the product has low value-in-use;
- highest market shares going to the lowest price offering (economic criteria paramount);
- the product has no premium price image nor is it regarded as a social "must" (integrative factors not important);
- little uncertainty in product evaluation (adaptive criteria absent); and
- buyers have the facility, business system, transportation or whatever to accommodate buying on a larger scale.

Estimates of demand at different prices can be made by:

- *surveys* to estimate price awareness and the price that buyers are prepared to pay, together with brand switching intentions in the event of a price change;
- *executive judgment;*
- *statistical analysis* relating demand and past price changes; and
- *experimentation.*

Gabor's *buy-response* (survey) method is an established way to gauge consumers' reactions to contemplated prices. Buyers of a brand are asked to say if they would buy at each of the prices called out. About ten different prices are called out in random order starting with the prevailing price or one near it. The percentage of the buy-responses (that is, the affirmative answers to the question "would you buy brand X at price Y?") gives the buy-response curve. The general shape of the buy-response curve and the relationship with the "price-last-paid" curve is shown in Figure 14.6. The shape of the curve suggests that low prices engender suspicion for many consumers, leading to an actual fall-off in demand. *Buy-response curves* should not be confused with *demand curves* in that they simply indicate the proportion of sampled consumers who would be willing to buy at a given price but do not indicate the quantity that would be demanded at each price.

Pricing recommendations in economics

We will briefly review the economists' traditional pricing recommendations within each of the market structures.

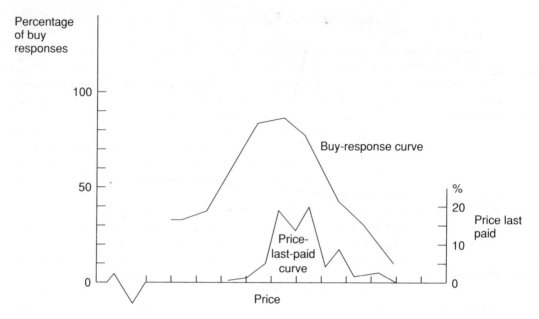

Figure 14.6 Buy-response and price-last-paid curves

Source: After Gabor, 1977

Pure competition

In pure competition all firms sell the same (totally undifferentiated) product. Each seller has such a small market share that no one firm can influence market price by its output decisions. Given that the buyer is interested in getting the lowest price possible and has perfect knowledge of the market, prices are not within the individual firm's control. There is no question of any individual firm having a pricing strategy. It must accept the going price, as the demand curve of the individual firm is parallel to the horizontal axis. If a firm raises its price above the ruling market price, no sales will be made. On the other hand, there is no point in lowering price since the firm can sell all it can produce at the market price.

Markets in commodities are quoted as the best approximation to pure competition. Marketers typically recommend branding or value added to create new segments as one way out of the commodity trap. A brand-name can suggest some guarantee for which some consumers are willing to pay more. We see this in the drug markets where generics may be equal in all respects to the same drug sold at a premium price by the big-name pharmaceutical companies. The familiar name, backed by advertising, allows the companies to command higher prices. Interestingly, the big drug makers like Warner–Lambert, Ciba–Geigy, and American Cyanamid's Lederle Laboratories also produce generics "seeking to be the leader in generics against their own brands." One reason for this is the insistence by governments funding healthcare that, where possible, generics should be substituted for branded drugs.

Monopoly

In a monopoly there is a single seller of a product for which there are no close substitutes. Of course, alternatives almost always exist, since "substitution among products from different industries always keeps competition alive." But, by definition, the monopolist's demand curve is the industry demand curve. It will be fairly inelastic (i.e. fairly unresponsive to price), depending on the extent of near substitutes. Given knowledge of costs at different levels of output and knowledge of the demand curve, the firm can choose the output that maximizes profit. Patents can give companies a temporary monopoly while in many countries the government may create a monopoly, for example, in the postal service.

Monopolistic competition

In monopolistic competition many firms sell differentiated versions of the same basic product but there are so many firms that no single firm has an appreciable effect on the decisions of other firms. The demand curve for the firm is more elastic than under monopoly and the monopolistic competitor can raise prices relative to competition without losing all its customers. This is because the offering presumably contains elements critical to some consumers. On the other hand, because competitors have differentiated their products, a firm may lower prices without converting all the customers of competitors. Again, the output that maximizes profit can be determined, given the simplifying assumptions. Something approximating monopolistic competition is common in fragmented industries.

Oligopoly

Most manufacturers probably operate in oligopolistic market segments. In oligopoly there are so few firms that the pricing decisions of any single firm have an appreciable effect on competitors. Each oligopolist must, therefore, consider possible competitor reactions to changes in price. Different predictions lead to different strategies being adopted. For the economist this means that there is no unique answer to the question, "what price will maximize profit?" It depends on the anticipated reaction. Of course, there is always the possibility of collusion (as in the case of OPEC), but such collusion presupposes agreement on production quotas and is generally illegal.

The various "theories" traditionally put forward by economists on *optimal* pricing strategies in oligopoly are:

- game theory,
- kinked demand curve assumptions, and
- price leadership.

Game theory. John Von Neumann and Oskar Morgenstern promoted a new way of thinking about the oligopoly problem in viewing it as a game.[8] Game theory sets out to identify the most advantageous strategies for rational participants in situations in which participants compete or cooperate. But the approach has a number of simplistic assumptions, viz:

- in assuming that neither the performance characteristics of the players nor the rules of the game will change over time, it ignores the possibility of the players learning from experience; and
- it fails to take into account the time and cost of acquiring information, while expecting the players to know all the options that relate to a particular "game."

The kinked demand curve. A common observation is that firms in oligopoly eschew price cutting except

- in response to cost pressures,
- in response to price cutting by competition, or
- when a product is newly launched.

Economists quote the hypothesis of a "kinked" demand curve to explain this behavior. The hypothesis regards the oligopolist as acting as if he visualized two demand curves for his product (see Figure 14.7). One curve depicts likely sales at various prices on the assumption that rivals will maintain their prices. This is *d–d'* in Figure 14.7. Curve *D–D'* depicts sales if rivals match every price change. The elasticity of *D–D'* follows the overall demand curve for the industry.

   The current price level is at the point where the two curves intersect. The oligopolist expects his rivals to retaliate to a price cut so as not to lose market share, but that rivals will not match a price rise. The oligopolist thus sees his demand curve as comprising the more elastic segment *d–P'* (which assumes no rival price reaction) and the less elastic segment *P'–D'* (which assumes price reductions will be matched by rivals). The solid line, curve *d–D'*, shows what is likely to happen in oligopoly if price is changed: price increases are not followed by rivals, so demand falls off drastically; but price decreases are matched by rivals, so sales do not show a dramatic increase. The conclusion is that

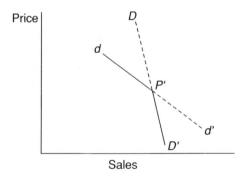

Figure 14.7 The kinked demand curve

oligopolists facing an inelastic demand (with similar costs and market shares) will hesitate to reduce or increase prices.

The kinked demand curve suggests what rationally is likely to happen but it does not always happen this way. Thus Pet Foods (part of Mars) in Britain once actually reduced its price when its rival in the canned dog food oligopoly raised its price. By so doing Pet Foods considerably increased its market share. The assumption of a kinked demand curve is more explanatory than the mere assertion that oligopolists fear price wars. Its major limitation lies in its failure to explain how the existing price level came into being in the first place or how prices do in fact change with costs and demand conditions.

Price leadership.   One of the oligopolists may be the price leader whom the rest follow. Such firms are often dominant in terms of market share or, say, technical competence. However, if the price leader wishes to continue exercising leadership, the firm must conform to the behavior expected of a company intent on promoting common industry interests. Competitors are only likely to follow when the leader seems to be doing what is in the interests of the industry. For example, price changes must be perceived by competitors as justified. Zenith, a one-time price leader for the TV industry, raised its prices in 1977 but had to change back when others did not follow its lead. The price leader often has the most to lose in the event of market collapse.

The danger in exercising price leadership is that followers may not recognize the move as in the interests of all concerned (e.g. a price rise in line with inflation). Where the price is raised, and a competitor's costs are lower than the price leader's, there is an opportunity, with an elastic demand curve, to increase market share by not following the price rise or even actually lowering price. If the price leader lowers price with an inelastic demand curve, all could lose. However, the more distinct the segments of competitor firms, the less they will see the need to reduce prices in line with the market leader. In other words, the more the products of the oligopolists are differentiated, the less the scope for price leadership. Price leadership will also be more difficult in a depression when orders are scarce and infrequent or where the situation approaches monopolistic competition with a large number of firms in the market.

COST-BASED PRICING

Prices are often set on the basis of cost, either total costs or direct costs.

Total cost pricing

In the full cost, cost-plus, or absorption costing method, prices are set to cover all costs (including overheads) plus a reasonable profit margin. A variation of this cost-plus pricing is *pricing for a targeted rate of return*. Typically, a sales forecast is made and an estimate of the corresponding plant utilization. For example, the sales forecast may estimate sales at 100,000 units, which achieves a 75 percent plant utilization. Given that the total cost of producing 100,000 units at 75 percent capacity is $200,000 and that the targeted rate of return is 20 percent of this cost, the price per unit would be calculated as follows:

Sales forecast	100,000
Total cost of producing 100,000 units	$200,000
Target rate of return at 20 percent of total cost	$40,000
Therefore price per unit	($200,000 + $40,000)/100,000
	= $2.4

General Motors has used this approach, calculating cost per unit on the assumption of an 80 percent utilization of production capacity. To the cost per unit is added a profit margin to yield a 15 percent return on capital employed after payment of taxes. In practice, the prices, as calculated by this procedure, are adjusted to take account of competitive pressure.

Cost-plus pricing may be the only way of charging for a custom-built product. But elsewhere it makes the uneasy assumption that the firm can in fact charge the price that yields the target profit. Competitive activity, and competitive prices cannot usually be dismissed so easily. Cost-plus pricing ignores the fact that the amount demanded will itself vary with price: the amount sold affects cost, but the amount sold is also affected by price. Sometimes contracts are made on a cost-plus basis, in which cases no fallacious reasoning is involved. However, costs can still be misleading since the rules for the allocation of overheads are essentially arbitrary.

In practice, simple cost-plus pricing is probably seldom followed. If the estimated price based on cost is too high relative to rival products, a company will seek to bring costs down. If demand slumps, or alternatively is extremely high, cost-plus pricing seems less relevant. *Costs determine what must be recovered in the price and the value to the customer determines the upper ceiling on price: competition determines where, within that range, price can be set.*

Sometimes the calculation of cost-plus prices is complicated by "givebacks." A classical example is the fashion industry. A dress manufacturer may sell a hundred dresses at $100 each with price being based on cost plus a generous mark-up. The store expects to sell them at $200 each to make $10,000 gross profit. Unfortunately, fifty have to be marked down to $125 to clear them at the end of the season. This means that gross profit is $3,750 less than anticipated. When the store reorders, the manufacturer is asked for the $3,750 in discounts as a condition for buying again. In this way store buyers meet their budget but at a cost to the manufacturer. The manufacturer, as a consequence, builds this extra cost into the prices of the next collection. But consumers may refuse to pay the higher prices, leading to a still higher proportion of the next collection being marked down by the store and so it goes on!

Some nonprofit organizations such as universities base their tuition fees on costs but actually sell below costs and rely on grants, endowment, and fund-raising to make up the difference. This policy of offering subsidized tuition fees to *all* students is being more and more questioned when many can afford to pay the full fees.

Direct cost pricing

Sometimes prices are based not on full costs but on direct cost. The method (sometimes known as the *incremental cost approach*) is usually used as a criterion for the acceptance or rejection of orders. When the firm has to choose among incoming orders it chooses on the basis of contribution, that is, those orders are chosen whose contribution (the difference between price and direct cost) to overheads and profit is the highest. Gabor regards the method as ideal for jobbing firms subsisting on large numbers of relatively small orders.

Henderson when at BCG claimed that, in a high-growth market, the initial price should be set even below cost if necessary, until approximately 50 percent or more of the total market has been obtained. He argues that, over time, prices must inevitably parallel costs. If the market leader does not set his prices in parallel with ever-declining costs, market shares change and the leaders replaced. Henderson's argument follows from the logic of the experience curve. Sometimes the argument holds, often it does not. What must be emphasized is that knowledge of costs is vital in pricing to ensure profitability. In service industries, the cost structures are usually heavy with fixed costs (variable costs being minor in comparison) and such costs need to be recovered. Without a firm knowledge of costs we are unsure of what is being exchanged. But except for those instances where the sale agreement specifies cost-plus, knowledge of costs alone, without a consideration of demand, must lead to a sacrifice of opportunities to do better.

PRICING NEW OFFERINGS AND PRICE REVISIONS IN MARKETING

Figure 14.8 sets out a basis for the pricing of new offerings and price revisions on existing products. The first step is to think in terms of pricing objectives and constraints, particularly those regarding people to influence:

- customers,
- distributors,
- competitors, and
- internal functions

and the need to coordinate prices with

- costs,
- the existing product line, and
- government legislation.

All this was discussed earlier in the chapter. The next step is to recognize that pricing strategies differ depending on whether the price setter is pricing a new offering or merely revising prices of existing products.

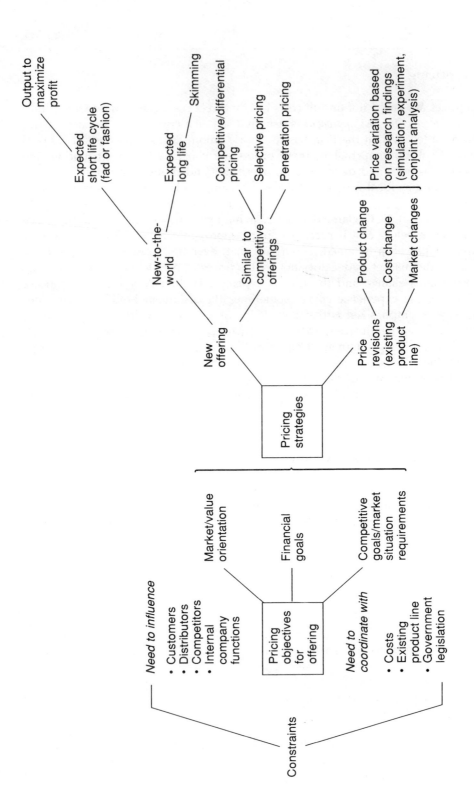

Figure 14.8 Pricing new products and price revisions

New offerings

New-to-the-world

An offering that is new-to-the-world has no close rivals. Other products may perform the same *general* use-function, but these substitutes are not close substitutes, no more than the slide rule was a close substitute for the hand calculator.

Expected short life.   Where the new-to-the-world product is expected to have a short life (a fad or fashion product, for example), the pricing strategy is likely to be to *maximize immediate earnings*. The price setter follows the economist in considering the costs of the various outputs that might be produced during the short life of the product, in relation to likely sales at different prices, as a basis for determining the output that maximizes profit. An early market test should give some idea of the price/demand relationship. Price sensitivity can perhaps best be estimated by setting the highest price in one test market and the lowest in another on the ground that extreme high and low prices will provide the best information on what price is optimal. The maximum price that can be obtained by the seller depends on the customer's dependency on the brand. If the buyer believes that what the brand has to offer is of central importance to the function for which the product is being purchased, and yet is unique to the brand, the customer is highly dependent on the seller and the seller is in a position to charge a premium price.

In recent years the goal of maximizing immediate earnings has come under attack, particularly in the marketing of drugs. When drug companies are granted a monopoly via a patent to sell their new drugs at any price they wish, they are tempted to charge whatever the market will bear. But, if a drug can save lives, is it ethical to charge a price which limits its use to the few who can afford it? Many drug firms claim that they need to recover the costs of development while critics argue that factoring total research costs into the price is not only unethical but, in paying for the unsuccessful products, encourages mediocre research. A company, too, must ask about the impact on customer goodwill and trust of a strategy that exploits a situation to maximize immediate earnings.

Expected long life.   Gabor refers to new-to-the-world offerings that are not ephemeral as pioneering products. In general, he recommends a *skimming price* for such offerings. A skimming price is sometimes described as "sliding down the demand curve" as it seeks to capture buyers at the top of the demand curve before reducing price to attract the other price segments of the market. In effect, a skimming price strategy discriminates between initial and future buyers and is appropriate to the goal of *steady earnings* and a build-up to maximum distribution. Thus distribution may initially be confined to certain high-class outlets to reinforce the unique image and later to select outlets before (if appropriate) intensive distribution. In certain cases, where the new product results in improved efficiency and measurable cost saving, the initial price can be based on *value-in-use* to those who would benefit most. In other words, the saving to the customer provides a basis for considering initial prices.

A skimming price strategy assumes that the market can be broken down into segments that differ in sensitivity to price and that demand, at least initially, is fairly inelastic. Hence skimming is not always possible unless the product, at the start of its life cycle, is perceived as having critical core benefits by enough buyers in the segment for skimming to be profitable. It is argued that a skimming price policy should be adopted only during the innovating firm's monopoly of the new-to-the-world product, providing the demand curve is fairly stable and experience curve effects occur.[9]

On the surface, a skimming price strategy is similar to experience curve pricing associated with the BCG system. But purposes differ. A skimming price strategy sets out to exploit different segments of the market while experience curve pricing simply lowers price in line with the lowering of costs (following the experience curve) in order to hang onto market share. Thus experience curve pricing has much in common with cost-plus pricing in that prices are related directly to costs. However, experience curve pricing is primarily used as a competitive weapon rather than just emphasizing cost recovery.

Gabor argues that the role of costs in new-to-the-world products is not so much to price the product as to decide whether the product should be produced at all or to check the acceptability of a price. He argues that the proper procedure with new products is to choose the price first and "derive from it the appropriate limit for the cost of production."

Similar to competitive offerings

New products to the firm that are not new to the market are similar to competitive offerings. Hence in pricing such products, a price setter must take account of the prices of competitive offerings. In general there are three strategies that may be open to the price setter:

- competitive pricing,
- penetration pricing, and
- selective pricing.

Competitive pricing. In competitive pricing the firm sets the same prices as competition or, more appropriately, sets a price above or below competitors to establish a price that reflects the differential benefits between the firm's and competitive offerings. Gabor claims that the shape of the buy-response curve and its relationship to the price-last-paid curve will suggest the most appropriate price point. He recommends setting the price just off the peak of the buy-response curve. This argument is similar to that made in Chapter 10 when considering positioning within a segment.

The concept of competitive pricing presupposes some way of measuring the relative value of rival offerings to the typical buyer. Table 14.2 illustrates one way of trying to estimate relative values of rival offerings for some industrial market. Column 1 lists the choice criteria and column 2 the weighting of the various criteria as expressed in surveys. In column 3 the three competitors are rated on each set of criteria; the highest rating being 3 and the lowest being 1. Column 4 gives weight multiplied by rating and the

Table 14.2 Industrial pricing: estimating relative value of rival offerings

Choice criteria (1)	Weight (2)	Competitive rating A	Competitive rating B (3)	Competitive rating C	Rating X weight A	Rating X weight B (4)	Rating X weight C
Economic criteria Price, delivered cost, total life costs, credit terms, operating costs, warranties, maintenance costs, etc.	30	1	2	3	30	60	90
Technical performance criteria Performance characteristics (quality and reliability), core-use function, ancillary and convenience-in-use functions, design characteristics, quality of materials, etc.	40	3	1	2	120	40	80
Integrative criteria Technical services, sales support, personal relations, etc.	20	3	2	1	60	40	20
Adaptive criteria Firm's image and reputation, perceived capabilities in post-sales service, local repair services, time guarantees, production capability, etc.	10	3	2	1	30	20	10
	100				240	160	200

Estimate of Competitor A advantage in segment:

(i)   over B $= \dfrac{240}{160} = 1.5$ (50 percent advantage)

(ii) over C $= \dfrac{240}{200} = 1.2$ (20 percent advantage)

overall sums estimate the relative values. Thus the advantage of competitor A over competitor B in the market segment is estimated to be 50 percent and over competitor C, 20 percent. Value pricing is commonly recommended in industrial marketing but no method of setting price differentials has met with universal agreement.[10]

Another way of looking at competitive pricing is to consider the position of the firm in the market as the dominant firm in the market may have the opportunity to be the price leader. But in addition to what was said earlier about price leadership, there is the danger of new market entrants if prices are raised too high. Where several firms share the leadership, competitors may seek some uniform price or prices justifying differential pricing, without any open collusion. This strategy may be adopted when competitors feel price changes only lead to a loss in market share and higher unit costs resulting from lower output. Those competitors who are neither leaders nor in a position to share leadership may be obliged to follow the prices of the leaders or seek a segment niche where they can charge a premium price. In any case, competitors will seek to avoid a price war as "there are often no winners but all losers." If a firm is going to enter into price competition, however, it needs to know about

- competitor intentions,
- competitor costs,
- likely subsidies by the parent company, and
- how crucial the market is to each competitor.

A question that needs to be addressed is whether lowering price in line with the dominant competition is always required. In one case, where a firm was considering lowering the price of its soap in line with competition, a consultant suggested showing a display of soaps at various prices to a sample of the target segment, who were then asked to choose the one they preferred. Prices were then changed with the sample members being asked to choose again taking the new prices into account. In this way it was possible to estimate the brand's value which told the marketer how high the price could go before customers switch to other brands. In this case, brand loyalty was shown to be high, so high that the firm actually increased the price and made more profitable sales!

Penetration pricing.   In general, for most functionally similar and identical products, Gabor suggests that, where possible, a penetration price strategy is likely to be most appropriate. This strategy involves the adoption of both low prices and perhaps heavy promotion to penetrate mass markets and gain market share. Penetration pricing assumes substantial experience curve/economies of scale with competitive offerings perceived as alike by the consumer. Penetration pricing can also convey the image of a tough, mean (and likely to get meaner) competitor to frighten off rivals.

   If a firm needs immediate cash or there are barriers to market entry, penetration pricing may be less attractive. In fact, the more the market is differentiated into distinct offerings, each with central and unique product benefits for its buyers, the less important is price generally. But, if pricing is an issue, penetration pricing can be an entry-deterring strategy provided

- production capacity is available to meet demand;
- the product is of an acceptable quality; and
- the distribution channels are there to make the product available.

Whatever the market structure, lower prices will have little effect when a product is in the obsolescent stage of its life and former customers are moving on to better substitutes. But this is not always so. Low prices may attract new uses for the product, while customers remaining loyal may be prepared to pay higher prices when former competitors have all left the field.

Selective pricing.   A good illustration of selective pricing occurs in the airline industry. Under the concept of "yield or revenue management," airlines have learnt to obtain the maximum revenue out of each flight. The airlines look at the history of flights and many other factors to predict future demand from the different segments of the market. This enables an airline to determine the number of seats to sell (well in advance) to the vacationer for, say, a $100 for the trip and how many to hold back for the last-minute business traveler to be charged $400 for the same flight. The result is a wide range of prices to keep flights full by mixing business and leisure travelers. But it is a contro-versial strategy since it most likely penalizes the regular, and perhaps, loyal customer. It was selective pricing that undermined People Express, built on offering low prices. Competitors matched the People Express fares on just enough seats to offer effective price competition yet could still show a profit on the other routes not covered by People Express. In this way, competitors could offer a whole range of fares and still make money while appearing to be a "low fare airline without really being one."

If the law allows and they see a profitable opportunity, companies will practice price discrimination. For example, Schering-Plough Corp., charges hospitals $2.03 for 100 tablets of its potassium supplement, K-DUR, while retail pharmacies pay $27.31. This is because hospitals have the knowledge and the bargaining power while retail pharmacies are obliged to stock all the popular drugs or face losing customers (*Business Week*, November 1, 1993). This type of price discrimination differs in social appropriateness from the theater that charges different prices for different times of the day or charges less to senior citizens.

Price revisions

Price revisions or adjustments occur through changes in cost or in the product or in market conditions. The key issue in all cases lies in knowing the effect, short term and long term, of a price change on sales. We are once again trying to gauge the consequences of the price change on the actions of those affected by the decision.

Product change

Where the suggested price change results from some proposed product change, we need to establish that the trade-offs we are proposing are in line with target segment prefer-ences. The technique of *conjoint analysis* may prove useful for this purpose.

Cost change

Where costs rise in line with inflation, prices will generally need to be increased incre-mentally with inflation rather than adopting the strategy of large increases at long time intervals. But, on occasions, prices in a growth business may have to go up faster than inflation to meet financial goals. Some companies try to get round having to increase prices by, say, keeping the old price but reducing the amount in the package. Others take account of buyer behavior. Thus Wrigley views most of its chewing gum sales as impulse purchases with consumers easily discouraged from buying by price increases. It was the last of the major gum makers to raise the suggested price of its seven-stick packs from 30 cents to 35 cents but, to get round the price barrier, it introduced a five-stick pack at 25 cents per pack. Even though the price was also 5 cents per stick, sales well exceeded all expectations.

Market changes

Studies show that the elasticity of demand for any brand is apt to change over the life of a brand.[11] Where market conditions change, for example, through competitor price cutting or a decline in market sales, there is a need to *experiment* to gauge likely reaction to a price change. Gabor refers to the hypothetical shop situation survey where, for example, members of the target segment are asked which of several brands they would buy at the stated prices if they met the same situation in a store. The problem lies, of course, in judging the realism of such a simulation.

It is commonly claimed that consumers in a recession become more value-conscious and less brand conscious. This was presumably why Philip Morris reduced in 1993 the price of its Marlboro cigarette, whose sales had been in decline due to competition from much lower-priced brands. Philip Morris extracted a lower premium from the brand, no doubt hoping that the lower price would lead to higher sales volume, sufficient to stem the decline in profit and recover market share.

PRICE INCENTIVES

List or declared prices may be held constant, while actual prices are varied. Deviations from the list price are common to meet the competitive goals of:

- attracting new users;
- converting customers from rivals;
- increasing the level of business with existing individual customers; and
- retaining the patronage of existing buyers.

The particular form of price variation adopted to attract, convert, increase or retain will also depend on the particular financial goals that have been chosen (see Figure 14.9. The relationship between competitive goals/tasks and specific price incentives is shown in Figure 14.10.

Attract

Price incentives can be used to attract new users of the product. This use of price incentives presupposes that a passive want exists, that the prospective customer is uncertain

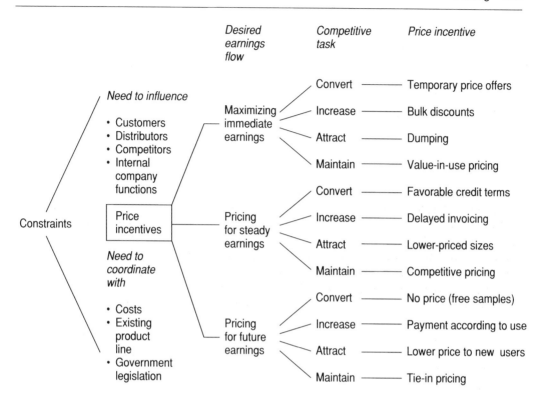

Figure 14.9 Price incentives

whether the benefits derived from the purchase justify the price being demanded but that, once the product is tried, repeat purchases will be made at normal prices. A price incentive to attract new users is common during the growth stage. It generally assumes a low level of market penetration. Where market penetration is high, price incentives to attract may be too costly unless price discrimination can be exercised to insure that only new users receive the price reduction. But price discrimination assumes firms are able to separate the target audience into groups with different price elasticities of demand and are able to prevent arbitrage, that is, resale to those paying the higher price. A typical example of price discrimination to new users occurs in magazine subscription rates.

If *immediate earnings* are sought, *dumping* abroad, say, at low prices is a way of attracting new (foreign) users. If *steady earnings* are sought, new users may be attracted by *lower-priced sizes*. Finally, if the emphasis is on *future earnings*, the product may be offered almost at cost to new users (for example, cable TV subscribers), provided such price discrimination is legal and feasible. *Leasing* is another way. Around 20 percent of all capital expenditures in the United States in recent years have been financed by leases. This attracts new users who wish to conserve working capital.

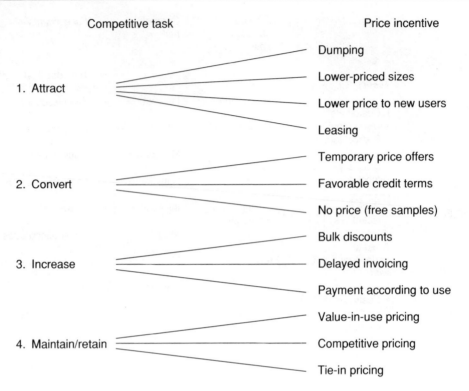

Figure 14.10 Price incentives and the competitive task

Convert

If the aim is to create a customer and not just make an isolated sale, price incentives presuppose that the offering embodies some set of advantages over rival offerings. If an offering is new, with advantages that need to be experienced to be appreciated, price incentives to convert from rivals may be appropriate. This is not to suggest that these are the only occasions when such a price incentive may be adopted. For example, where the incentive lies in the offer of credit terms or more favorable credit terms, it may secure long-term allegiance if financial considerations are crucial to the buyer.

Temporary price offers can both convert and yield *immediate cash*, perhaps at a cost below the borrowing rate. However, the constant use of temporary price reductions can dilute a product's image, become increasingly ineffective and are unlikely to reverse the fortunes of a product on the decline. If *future earnings* are sought and the product is new with a critical advantage, *free samples* (a no-charge price incentive) as a way of converting are recommended. Where the need for *steady earnings* rules out converting via free samples or large temporary price offers, then more *favorable credit terms* might be appealing.

The basic question to be answered is whether true converting is possible. Does the firm's offering have that extra something to induce a conversion and not just temporarily buy allegiance? Much brand switching reflects the chase after price deals that have no effect on long-term buying. A change will not persist unless the consumer comes to prefer the new brand.

Increase

A price incentive to increase the level of usage by current customers presupposes either that new applications for the product become acceptable at a lower price or that the current level of usage of the product for existing purposes is inhibited by price. Many products do not fall into this category (for example, spark plugs).

If the aim is to increase sales for *immediate earnings*, discounts might be considered, viz:

- *volume or quantity discounts*. Price per unit is reduced for volume orders either for some specific order size (noncumulative discount) or the quantity ordered within some period (cumulative discount). Cumulative discounts have the advantage of rewarding buyer "loyalty";
- *seasonal discounts* to encourage increasing the level of business in off-peak periods; and
- *Competitively more attractive trade and cash discounts.* Trade discounts are discounts off list price that differ on the basis of customer classification, for example, a lower discount to the wholesaler than to the retailer. But competitively higher discounts are unlikely to get distributors to increase their order level unless they believe that the increase can be sold. Cash discounts are given for prompt payment. Thus "3/14 net 28" means that the buyer will be given a 3 percent discount if payment is made within 14 days but the whole payment must otherwise be made within 28 days. The period for qualifying for the cash discount can be extended to encourage early buying as well as increased buying. If steady earnings are emphasized, an increase in sales per customer might be stimulated by favorable credit terms such as delayed invoicing. If the focus is on future earnings, payment according to use (as in the case of Xerox copiers) might be appropriate to increase business per customer.

Maintain/retain

A firm with a high market share will be interested in maintaining that share and retaining the patronage of current customers. Its strategy is to build up resistance to change.

If *immediate earnings* are the goal, *value-in-use pricing* (that is, ensuring price is in line with benefits) could be one way to keep customers when a product is built to customer specification. If the goal is *future earnings*, prices can be varied to tie-in the customer to the supplier (for example, by supplying the basic equipment at a low cost but making up for this on the price of supplies). If *steady earnings* are sought, *long-term competitive prices* can be agreed with the customer, providing such price discrimination is legally permitted (for example, in the selling of professional services). Tie-in pricing ties the buyer to the seller by, say, offering the use of free facilities like a refrigerator in the store.

Competitive pricing to retain customers, particularly in consumer package goods, has increasingly come to mean in Europe and the United States offering constant price-cutting promotions. Such price promotions signal the consumer to be price conscious rather than brand conscious, thus eroding brand equity. The more that is spent on such promotions, the less is spent on advertising to build and sustain brand equity so leading to further erosion in equity. The problem lies in knowing what to do since manufacturers feel trapped into adopting a policy that long term can be destructive to brand equity. The problem is exacerbated by the supermarket chains demanding such promotions as the price for adequate stocking. P&G has complained that only around 30 percent of trade promotion money goes to the consumer in the form of lower prices; 35 percent goes straight into the retailer's pocket and the rest is lost in inefficiencies. P&G's answer for many of its products is to reduce its discounts on wholesale prices and at the same time reduce its wholesale list prices, for example, 25 percent on Oxydol in the United States. P&G expects lower list prices will reduce handling inefficiencies resulting from deal buying and lead to lower regular prices for the consumer. Such constant, "fair" prices are expected to provide a stabilizing element that adds to the integrity of the brand image, leading to more brand loyalty. But the big chains are unhappy since their warehousing, marketing and administration are designed to handle such deals which are important to profitability.

PRICING PROCEDURES IN SPECIFIC SITUATIONS

Industrial pricing practices

The pricing of industrial products often involves special practices such as bidding, negotiation and contracts.

Bidding

For nonstandard products there is no established market price. As a consequence, buyers may ask for competitive bids from suitable suppliers. In government buying, a bid system is often mandatory to help prevent corruption. Suppliers are asked to submit sealed bids by a specific day, together, perhaps, with a performance bond guaranteeing the level of quality and service. For a bidding system to work, the product specification must be airtight; adequate time must be allowed for drawing up of bids; the amount involved must justify the cost; finally there must be enough qualified suppliers for the bidding to have some realism. Buying policies may insist on the lowest bid being accepted, but this is not always so. Bidding may simply narrow the field for negotiation.

The decision on whether to bid will depend on the value of the order; the likelihood of being successful, time pressures and whether the specification is clear enough to proceed. Determining the price at which to bid can be difficult for a supplier and several mathematical models have been developed to help. As a simple example, for each bid, the bidder multiplies the estimated profit by the probability of success to give expected profit. The bid price yielding the highest expected profit is the bid price submitted. Much of the input to such a procedure rests on management judgment.

Negotiation

Negotiation is widespread in buying and is not just confined to negotiating over price. It is particularly appropriate where unique equipment is being purchased and the number of potential suppliers is strictly limited. Where industrial prices are negotiated, price differentiation among customers or customer groups could be the key to profitability. But both suppliers and purchasing managers generally dislike a bidding system that gives no weight to past performance and the services that can be provided by suppliers. When bidding simply narrows the field for negotiation it allows buyers to consider factors other than price in the course of negotiation. Thus the specification may be modified to take advantage of some offer that could not be considered in a pure bidding system.

Where the supplier is in a strong position, negotiation will include bargaining, with both sides seeking to get acceptance of their "norms" for deciding a "fair" price. The buyer's idea of a fair price is often based on manufacturing costs. Industrial purchasing departments often contain price analysts to estimate material, labor, overhead and administrative costs, and requests for proposals (RFPs) may demand that quotations include an analysis of the supplier's costs. If the goals of the other side are known, concessions of least value to oneself but of most value to the other side can be given, while concessions can be sought that are of most value to oneself and of least value to the other side. Ideally, negotiation is the nature of a joint inquiry to see how both sides can achieve their goals. Negotiation occurs not only over the product itself but also over other benefits like discounts, terms of payment, delivery charges and so on.

In respect of *transport charges*, we have:

- *FOB (free on board)*: the buyer himself selects the method of transport and takes title to the goods immediately after they are loaded;
- *basing-point pricing*: certain geographical locations are designed as basing points and freight is charged as if the goods were being delivered from the nearest basing-point; and
- *zone pricing*: the country is divided into zones and all buyers within a zone pay the same freight charge per ton regardless of distance.

Contracts

Successful negotiation results in a contract. Such contracts might be *fixed price* or *cost type*.

Fixed price contracts.   These include:

- *firm fixed price*: this type is most preferred by the buyer, although it exposes the seller to most risk;
- *fixed price with escalation*: this provides for an upward or downward price change as a result of any changes in materials or labor costs;
- *fixed price with redetermination*: a temporary price is agreed until the amount of material and labor to be used has been estimated; and
- *fixed price incentive*: any cost saving over some target price is shared between the seller and the buying organization.

Cost type contracts.   Under this type of contract the vendor receives back his *cost plus some specific fee*:

- cost plus a percentage of the cost;
- cost plus a fixed fee;
- cost plus some incentive fee for any reduction in costs;
- cost sharing (if the seller views the development of the product as a possible basis for future sales).

Cost type contracts tend to be disliked by buyers since the buyer assumes most of the financial risk.

Licensing.   Instead of selling a technology, a firm may license it. One reason for licensing is the belief that other firms would get round any patents to develop their own version. Porter is uneasy about licensing, arguing that licensing should only be adopted if:[12]

- there is an inability to exploit the technology;
- licensing is needed to tap certain markets;
- licensing helps in the standardizing of the technology;
- licensing creates "good" competitors in the sense that such competitors help increase primary demand; share in the cost of development; help legitimize the technology or act as a standard that puts the licensing firm in a favorable light.

Leasing.   Firms often offer the opportunity to lease or buy. The leasing of equipment is essentially a payment for the services provided by the product. Although it has always been a common practice to lease machinery (including computers) and buildings, it is not confined to industrial markets as witness the growth in the leasing of automobiles to the general public. Leasing can expand the market to those who otherwise would not be able to buy or would not want to take on the risks of ownership. For the supplier, leasing provides an opportunity for establishing a close relationship with the lessee. But the leasing price must take account of the capital tied up and the risks involved since, unless inflation is taken into account, leasers may find they are subsidizing the leasee in the later portion of the lease. For the lessee, there may be tax advantages while it allows use of the product for the short periods for which it is needed. But leasing also appeals to adaptive criteria in that it lessens risks associated with technological obsolescence and being "stuck" with a product found later to be unsuitable or for which there is no longer a need. The financing of short-term leases may be undertaken by the firm itself with long-term leasing being taken over by the financial institutions that have units of their organization that specialize in leasing. In some contracts, lease payments can be set against price if at any time the lessee wants to buy.

Services

Many providers of services avoid the word "price" with its overtones of a purely commercial transaction and prefer words like "fee," "tuition," "service charge," and so on. For many services, the market is less price sensitive than value sensitive. Nonethless, clients or customers for pure services, like using an accountant, are apt to think in terms of a "reasonable" hourly rate. Not surprisingly many of the methods for determining the prices of services are cost-based, for example, fixed fees and contract fees are usually cost-based. Other methods are based on the "going rate" or what competition is charging or some contingency fee such as in the selling of a house. But those who recognize their scarcity may charge what the market will bear or ration by price. But service providers often have to be particularly sensitive to the symbolism of their charges, whether a high price will suggest quality or price gouging. But all the methods of pricing services tend to be driven by a formula approach, though much of what we have said about pricing in general has applicability also to the pricing of services. What can be distinctive in the pricing of services, however, is the recognition that, adding the marginal customer, may add nothing to costs (e.g. air travel, movie theaters, hotels, sporting events, and so on). This fact underlies the extensive price discrimination that is practiced in service indus- tries like the airline industry. A related factor in the pricing of services is the frequent need to influence the pattern of sales whose uncontrolled fluctuations puts a great strain on resources and capacities during peak periods.

PRICING IN INTERNATIONAL MARKETS

Pricing in international markets covers:

- pricing of exports,
- intra-company transfer prices, and
- pricing by overseas divisions.

Export pricing

Export prices may be higher or lower than those in the domestic markets. However, selling at lower prices than those prevailing in the domestic market can give rise to accusations of dumping. Yet prices may be justifiably lower in that the product may be sold without incurring the promotional and other marketing costs associated with selling it in the domestic market. Also prices may need to be lower because of competitive conditions and the general level of income in the foreign market. On the other hand, higher prices may be charged because of the image of the exporting country for that type of product and the individual reputation of the brand. In any case, prices are apt to vary with competitive conditions. Thus traditionally, American software companies in Europe charged much higher prices. Thus Borland Paradox sold in France in 1992 at 152 percent over the price in the United States and Microsoft Windows at 101 percent. Such increases could hardly be justified by claims of higher costs for language translation and other factors since, for example, the Borland Paradox was sold in Germany at only 29 percent above the US price. More recently, with the increase in competition, prices are falling. Also corporate buyers are demanding big discounts so Microsoft is allowing such buyers to pool orders throughout the EC to receive volume discounts of around 60 percent.

Pricing can be key to breaking into foreign markets. A good example here is the Japanese market for desktop computers. This had traditionally been just a market for Japanese manufacturers because of the seeming difficulty of producing software in the Japanese language. Compaq and Dell are changing all this. Dell has introduced a low-priced desktop computer while Compaq has introduced a computer at about half the price of comparable Japanese-made PCs. Both firms regard this price strategy as the most effective way to gain market share. But Japanese firms like NEC are unlikely to just sit back and see their market taken away but have already responded with price cuts of their own—and no doubt will be insisting that the remaining price differences are reflected in quality. And the local firms still have one big advantage in having an established distribution network of specialist dealers.

Although conventional economic wisdom argues that lowering the value of a currency makes imports more expensive, exporters know they need to pay attention to what that price increase will do to their market share. Thus a recent devaluation of the dollar did not lead to the automatic increase in the price of cars from abroad. As the president of BMW of North America was reported as saying: "If you base your prices here only on exchange rates, you will be out of the market immediately. You have to look at currency movements as a long-term factor and figure your costs and prices from there." On the other hand, floor prices will depend on the incremental costs of producing for export in relation to *incremental* sales revenue. Nonetheless, as Gabor says, pricing for export should start, where possible, from the price the final buyer is willing to pay.

Although we have said that export prices can be lower or higher than the home market, prices for exports to overseas markets do generally have to cover additional costs, viz:

- transport costs,
- tariff charges,
- customs duties, and
- adaptation costs.

On occasions, "counter-trade" rather than money prices may be the basis of exchange in international markets. There are essentially four types of *counter-trade*:

- *barter*: vodka for Pepsi Cola!
- *compensation deals*: part in goods, part in acceptable currency;
- *counter-purchase*: money payment on condition that the money is spent on purchasing goods in the buying country; and
- *product buyback*: seller agrees to accept as partial payment a percentage of the output of the product sold (for example, a tractor plant).

Barter and counter-trade are not uncommon where the overseas buyer is short of foreign exchange. Thus Ford of Britain bartered cars for coffee in Colombia while General Motors bartered $100 million of earthmoving equipment for Russian timber. But there is the possibility of a low return on the barter deal; difficulties in negotiating a deal; selling unfamiliar goods and waiting for payment. But specialist third parties may buy the goods offered to the exporter at a discount because they have the knowledge and organization to sell them elsewhere for hard currency.

Intra-company transfer pricing

Where there is the sale of goods to overseas subsidiaries or foreign partners, there is the problem of transfer pricing. A company may set

- minimum transfer prices to minimize ad valorem duties when the goods cross borders; or
- maximum prices to minimize taxes, get around restrictions on dividend repatriation or to extract the most from the foreign partner.

Although it is common to sell at minimum transfer prices to those overseas markets where there are lower corporate tax rates, tax authorities are monitoring such practices throughout the world.

Pricing by overseas divisions

In certain countries, the overseas division or subsidiary may have little discretion over price. The government, for social purposes, may legislate margins or maximum prices, or the division may belong to some association that regulates prices. If a company or company division operates through a region such as the EC, it has to consider prices in the various countries to eliminate arbitrage: buyers buying the product in the low price country and selling it in the high price country.

A policy of uniform prices throughout the world or a region is generally neither feasible nor desirable. Subsidiaries in the various countries will have different objectives; face different competitive pressures; encounter different legal constraints and different levels of service being demanded. Even distributor mark-ups vary with, for example, a 30 percent dealer margin on cars in the UK but only a 10 percent mark-up in Belgium. In the EC, there is pressure on firms for uniform prices, more particularly to lowering prices to the lowest national level. These pressures do not just come from EC bureaucrats but by parallel importers and strong retailer chains. Since most profit comes from sales in the big (country) markets, companies resist reducing their prices to the levels set in small countries. Also price elasticity for a brand varies from one country to another and to ignore this is to fail to exploit profit opportunities. One solution is to raise prices in the cheapest markets or withdraw from such markets altogether. Thus Johnny Walker Red Label Whisky sold at a higher price on the continent of Europe than in the UK. When pressure for uniform prices was exerted, Johnny Walker withdrew from the UK market instead! But many believe that fear about pressures for uniform pricing are exaggerated since cross-border retailers are still few while products tend not to be identical for the various countries: some modification is usually demanded even if it is just in the packaging. Nonetheless, the problem of uniform pricing is leading many companies to centralize pricing decisions, to determine a *price corridor* within which prices in each national market will be determined.

ETHICAL ASPECTS OF PRICING

Governments typically seek to prevent any form of collusion on prices by outright price fixing or the exchange of information about prices in order to "coordinate" prices or to encourage uniform pricing among rival firms. But equally of concern is deceptive pricing. This can take many forms from deceptive packaging to the high-low pricing of retailers who set an abnormally high price initially so as to offer some tempting "bargain" a couple of weeks later through a high percentage discount. A more subtle practice is to declare all competitors prices will be matched, knowing that the particular model of TV or other piece of electronic equipment is exclusive to the seller, a practice facilitated by manufacturers giving distinct numbers to insignificant variations in the product.

CONCLUSION

This chapter has provided a guide as to how a firm might systematically proceed to set prices and price variations. It should be used only as a guide. There are no algorithms for pricing that, if followed, lead to the right answer. If economic theory seems to offer answers it is because of the simplifying nature of the assumptions being made; it achieves rigor at the expense of realism. The cost-plus approach, on the other hand, offers convenience at the expense of effectiveness. What complicates advice on pricing is the recognition that the requirements (objectives and constraints) to be met by the pricing decision can be so varied. If we specify the wrong requirements, we solve the wrong pricing problem, which can be more ineffective than meeting the right set of requirements in a less than optimum way. Even if we lay down the correct requirements, given the situational factors at work, we still have to contend with the major problem of predicting the effect of the price options considered.

An outline of a pricing strategy is shown in Appendix 14.1.

NOTES

1 Gabor, André (1977) *Pricing: Principles and Practice*, London: Heinemann Educational Books.
2 Oxenfeldt, Alfred R. (1983) "A General Price Setting Procedure," unpublished manuscript, New York: Graduate Schools of Business, Columbia University.
3 Zeithaml, Valerie A. (1988) "Consumer Perceptions of Price, Quality and Value: A Means-End Model and Synthesis of Evidence," *Journal of Marketing*, 52 (July).
4 Lichtenstein, Donald R. and Burton, Scott (1989) "The Relationship Between Perceived Quality and Objective Price-Quality," *Journal of Marketing Research*, XXVI (November).
5 Drummond, Maggie (1994) "Now We Shop in a Different Way," 14 June, London: *The Daily Telegraph*.
6 Henderson, B. D. (1979) *Henderson on Corporate Strategy*, Cambridge, MA: Abt Books.
7 Nagle, Thomas (1982) "Economic Foundations for Pricing," Working Paper, Chicago: Graduate School of Business, University of Chicago (August).
8 Von Neumann, J. and Morgenstern, O. (1947) *Theory of Games and Economic Behavior*, Princeton: Princeton University Press.
9 Dolan, Robert J. and Jeuland, Abel P. (1981) "Experience Curves and Dynamic Demand Models: Implications for Optimal Pricing Strategies," *Journal of Marketing*, 45 (Winter).
10 Shapiro, Benson P. and Jackson, Barbara B. (1978) "Industrial Pricing to Meet Customer Needs," *Harvard Business Review* (November–December).
11 Simon, Hermann (1979) "Dynamics of Price Elasticity and Brand Life Cycles: An Empirical Study," *Journal of Marketing Research*, 16 (November).
12 Porter, Michael E. (1985) *Competitive Advantage*, New York: The Free Press.

APPENDIX 14.1   PRICING STRATEGY EXHIBIT

Memo (Extract) on
Pricing Strategy for Product X

A. Background

The introduction of Product X into the market currently dominated by company ABC requires careful consideration of our pricing policy. Company ABC has in effect had a monopoly in selling the product though, for reasons unexplained, has confined its sales to the biggest customers.

B. Price level: considerations

(i) *Semi-constraints*

   a) *Customers*

   Existing users of the product buying from Company ABC, though probably welcoming a second source of supply, will expect to pay no more than they are at present paying, namely, 76 cents a gallon. Prospective users, on the other hand, are in the main unaware of the product, but will not pay more than the value-in-use of the product. Thus the upper limit to the price that can be charged is determined by the cost savings to such customers, i.e. 86 cents per gallon.

   b) *Competition*

To seek to convert via pricing below competition will invite a price war as this is competitor ABC's major market and source of profit.

c) *Distribution*

This will be a push selling situation, so there is a need for a high distribution margin.

d) *Finance*

Finance agrees to a goal of steady earnings or future growth providing costs are covered.

(ii) *Current sales of Company ABC*

Six million gallons for revenue of $4,500,000. Research estimates potential is double this, i.e. 12 million gallons.

(iii) *Breakeven for Product X*

Breakeven analysis

Variable cost		$0.45	
Fixed costs			
General administration	$40,000		
General factory	20,000		
Salaries	89,000		
Depreciation on extension and new machinery	50.000		
		$199,000	

Price	60 cents	76 cents	85 cents
Variable cost	45	45	45
Contribution	15	31	40
B/E point (199,000 fixed)	1,326,666	641,935	497,500
Market share (market 10 million)	13 percent	6.4 percent	5 percent

If, as we believe, our Product X has a cost advantage due to its being made from brewer's waste, penetration pricing might be adopted to drive competitor ABC out of the market.

C.   Earnings goal

All agree that the company should concentrate on future earnings rather than immediate cash flow.

D.   Price variation

Bulk discounts might be offered to existing users as a market entry strategy but charging the same basic price as competition.

Prospective users are unlikely to avail themselves, because of their small size, of such quantity discounts.

E.   Suggested strategy

The aim should be to insure fast market penetration before Company ABC can respond. Given the considerations outlined above, we suggest the following:

(i)   *Existing users*

Convert by having same basic price as rival but offering bulk discounts to heavy users. (Competition will have difficulty meeting the prices.)

(ii)   *Prospective users*

Attract by demonstrating saving (bulk discounts not likely to apply) and efficiency to stationary engineers.

Chapter 15

Distribution strategy and channel management

A distribution system is a network of people, institutions or agencies involved in the flow of a product to the customer, together with the informational, financial, promotional and other services associated with making a product convenient and attractive to buy and rebuy. A major problem for many firms lies in securing wide distribution. Yet for those firms selling consumer products through retail outlets, market penetration and store distribution are equivalent. Even if the firm's offering vis-à-vis competition is "right" for the segment in terms of product, proposed advertising and price, no sales occur unless arrangements are made that allow the customer to purchase and receive the product when needed and ordered. But insuring that a product is made conveniently available for purchase may not be enough. If customers are to be retained and sales to be high, certain pre- and post-sale services as well as promotional activities may need to be provided by the channel.

The selection of a distribution system is key as it usually binds the firm long term, involves heavy investment and can be the deciding factor in determining the success or failure of a marketing strategy. In fact, it is not uncommon for a firm's marketing thrust to lie with its distribution system and, in certain cases (for example, General Motors Corporation in the 1950s), for this distribution system to be so superior vis-à-vis competition's that it constitutes a competitive advantage. Where this is so, a firm might add new products not because they are superior to competitive brands but to exploit the firm's distribution system. On the other hand, a firm may add a new product just to strengthen its distribution system if, say, channel intermediaries demand a wider range of products as a price for cooperation.

Distribution channels, once selected, are not easily changed, not just because of the expense involved but because of the risks that accompany making such change. Thus when Jhirmack tried to augment the distribution of its shampoo to hairdressing salons by selling through mass-market outlets, its salon business disappeared. There is a long history of once famous brands being destroyed by ill-considered changes in distribution. An early well-known example is Mazawattee tea. This was the most popular brand of tea in England during Victorian and Edwardian times. At that time it was distributed to retailers through wholesalers. Then Mazawattee decided to set up its own chain of stores. But this assumed consumers would be prepared to seek out such stores rather than choose a rival brand more conveniently at their regular store. This assumption proved to be erroneous and Mazawattee found their wholesale and retail customers were no longer willing to sell the product. Mazawattee never regained its former market position and disappeared into history. Even changing from retail *back* to wholesale can cause friction. When Heinz did this, many retailers demanded to deal direct with the firm's own sales force. When Heinz obliged, wholesalers in turn complained bitterly!

Sometimes a firm may select the conventional distribution channel for its product and find the channel unwilling to stock the product. Thus Timex found that jewelry stores in the United States would not handle its watches because of the larger dollar margin (mark-up) offered by more expensive watches. It was for this reason that Timex chose to sell through drugstores in the United States. Sometimes, too, the services provided by the conventional channel are no longer needed and alternative channels are sought that allow the product to be sold at a lower price. This was the case with cheap quartz watches since service/repair was no longer needed, allowing them to be sold through many other outlets. Other products, like ski equipment and hi-fi equipment, that were initially sold in specialist stores so advice could be given, were later sold in, say, department stores when such advice was no longer needed for the bulk of buyers.

On occasions, market success comes about by recognizing the channel intermediary as the "key" customer. Thus Citicorp owes its success in home mortgage lending in the United States to recognizing the importance of the realtors or real estate agents, since they refer customers to the lender. Citicorp has won over realtors by offering a fast loan-approval service. The top eight major airlines similarly recognize the importance of the travel agent, establishing computerized reservation systems which makes it difficult for the smaller airlines with flights less prominently displayed in the systems.

This chapter covers:

- a brief review of *the role of distribution*;
- *channel distribution strategy*, which is concerned with the selection of the distribution channel and individual channel members;
- *channel management and policies*, where the focus lies on managing channel relationships to influence channel members into support of the seller's policies; and
- *physical distribution*, where discussion is centered on the role of physical distribution in marketing with a brief review of the problems associated with achieving and maintaining an effective and efficient system.

ROLE(S) OF DISTRIBUTION CHANNELS

Creating purchase opportunity

We will first discuss the role of distribution in creating *purchase opportunity*; in promoting the product; in servicing the product; while, in addition, the overall social role of distribution will be described.

If a product is to sell, it must be made readily available to the target segment. "Place utility" is the function most commonly associated with distribution channels. Although shopping can be fun for many consumers, shopping often requires effort and takes away from more desirable pursuits, which are costs to be subtracted from the benefits associated with buying, consuming or using the product. The greater the perceived cost of shopping in terms of effort, time and expense, the fewer will buy, even if the price and the product are "right." On the other hand, the easier and more pleasant it is to buy a product, the less the cost, and the more who buy. Convenience in buying (for example, Avon cosmetics) can be the buying inducement, as can be the general availability of the product (for example, Coca-Cola). If segment penetration is the path to growth, extensive distribution is required to reach as many in the segment as possible. Restricted geographical distribution means that the product is bought by fewer and probably less often as most products cannot depend on customers undertaking long journeys or extensive search: the product must be available where and when needed.

The degree of purchase opportunity is a major factor, whether the competitive objective is to convert, increase, attract or retain present customers. Even if we cannot convince people to buy only our brand, distribution can affect whether our brand belongs to the repertoire from which the consumer picks. Similarly, the degree of purchase opportunity can affect both the frequency of use and the number of different uses to which a product is put. Finally, the availability associated with product exposure may be necessary to attract customers in the first place, as well as necessary to retain their patronage.

Promotional role

A channel cannot always just confine its role to making the product available; it may have to be active in promotion. When RCA first marketed its videocassette in the United States, it estimated that there were around 20,000 stores that could handle the product but that only about 8,000 could do the selling job required. Where there is doubt about a channel's ability to undertake the requisite promotion, the manufacturer may have to help. For example, fragrance firms put their own salespeople into stores and manufacturers of consumer durables frequently provide demonstrators for periods of the year. In addition there is *cooperative advertising* whereby the seller helps to pay for ads that promote the seller's brand under the retailer's name.

The promotional role of distributors is always important. Promotion at the point-of-sale can activate latent or passive demand, while both habit and picking behavior can be affected by novel distributor promotions or salesmanship. Point-of-sale demonstrations and salesmanship at the point-of-sale can be instrumental in changing buying criteria. This is so because buyers are seldom experts on the product class and usually seek just enough information to determine a brand preference: salespeople may provide the information that just swings the sale.

Service role

There are certain services, which are frequently an integral and necessary part of a firm's product offering that are best provided by the channel, for example:

- advice on the suitability of the product for some application;
- advice on storing, using, maintaining or selling the product;
- provision for speedy servicing and repair; and
- provision of credit and other financial assistance to purchase the product.

The relative capability of various channels for carrying out such services can be the major criterion in evaluating alternative distribution systems. Manufacturers of top brand TV sets would hesitate to sell through variety chain stores like Woolworth's, when Woolworth's itself sells its sets at a lower price to compensate for lack of services. However, as a market matures and product knowledge broadens the need for service tends to decline and additional, less service-oriented, channels become acceptable.

Another reason why fewer services are being demanded is the growth of products that can be replaced more cheaply than they can repaired, or are made up of components easily replaced without specialist attention or advice. Nonetheless, for many manufacturers there is a problem in finding enough outlets to provide the level of service required. Sometimes the manufacturer can help. Thus Apple Computer Inc. some years ago eliminated around 600 of its dealers to increase the quality of service and provide additional support (for example, sales training, seminars for customers) for the dealers remaining.

Social role

Although the most direct method of distribution is from manufacturer to consumer/user, only a small percentage of products are sold door-to-door to the consumer or direct to the industrial user. Most products are sold through "middlemen" because it pays the manufacturer to do so. If the manufacturer believes he can perform the middleman's functions more efficiently, he does so. However, the fact that "middlemen" survive suggests that they reduce the cost of distribution with benefits for society. How a wholesaler increases the efficiency of purchase availability is perceptively illustrated by Alderson and Halbert:[1]

> If, in a given industry with 100 manufacturers supplying 100 retailers with their products, each manufacturer must deal directly with each individual retailer, then the number of contacts involved equals the product of these two numbers, that is, 10,000 different contacts are necessary. If, however, just one intermediary buys all the products from all of the manufacturers and sells them to all the retailers, then the number of necessary contacts is reduced to the sum of the two numbers, or 200 contacts.

Similar savings result from the interjection of retailers. From the society's viewpoint, the major function of distributors is to bring into a convenient location the variety and assortment of benefits that buyers seek, so that each consumer does not have to deal directly with numerous individual manufacturers.

CHANNEL DISTRIBUTION STRATEGY

The channel distribution strategy is a broad conception of how resources are to be deployed to build a channel (or channels) linking the producer to the consumer/user to insure that the product and associated services are made available to the target segment. The distribution strategy (see Figure 15.1) involves:

1 determining the objectives to be achieved by the channel system;
2 selecting the type of channel system, whether, for example, to sell direct or through intermediaries;

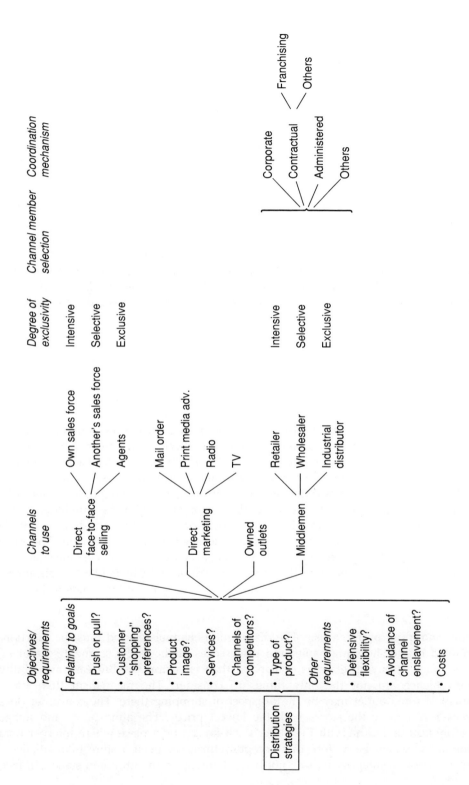

Figure 15.1 Distribution strategy

3 determining whether a policy should be followed of selling to all outlets within a channel or to a few; and
4 selecting the individual channel member.

Objectives to be achieved by the distribution strategy

Mission and goals

A strategy geared to the wrong objectives solves the wrong problem, since what is considered a problem depends on what we are trying to achieve. The manufacturer's *mission* in designing a channel strategy is to choose the most efficient system possible. If an alternative channel increases sales but not costs, or decreases costs without reducing sales to offset the saving in costs, the alternative system is, by definition, more efficient. A manufacturer's *goals* for a distribution system seek to ensure that, within some overall cost constraint, the channel performs the functions implicitly assigned to it by the segmentation strategy.

Functions assigned to channels

The functions assigned to a channel should take account of several considerations:

Push or pull system.   The most basic consideration in choosing a channel is whether the firm needs a mainly *push* or a *pull* system of distribution, or a balance between the two. In a push system, the manufacturer relies more on the reseller (wholesaler and retailer) to "push" the product toward the consumer/user, while a pull system seeks to "pull" the consumer/user toward the product by creating, via promotion, customer insistence for the product. The more involved the customer is with the purchase, or the greater the education and communications burden, or the more that adaptive criteria enter into the buying decision, then the more the need for a push system. The most extreme form of push is direct selling. On the other hand, where the customer has low involvement with the purchase, or the product is standard with standard applications, or the product is low cost and frequently bought, then a pull system tends to be more appropriate.

Customer shopping preferences.   The distribution channel selected must be functionally adapted to the shopping habits and preferences of the target segment so that no more shopping or buying effort is demanded than is customary. But easy availability and convenience are not the only things to consider. The magnetism that draws consumers to some outlet may be the prospect of shopping there. The consumer does not necessarily choose the stores with the lowest prices. The atmosphere and image of the store *may* be in line with the buyer's self-image; be a place where interpersonal relations are pleasant; be a store that accepts returns, or even a store that satisfies a consumer's sense of integrity in, say, not being known for an anti-union stance. In fact, consumers may choose where to shop on the same basis they choose their brands, namely habit, picking, intrinsic liking or choice criteria covering technical, economic, legalistic, integrative or adaptive criteria.

Image.   The distribution channel must be consistent with the image projected by the rest of the marketing offering. An image of elegance must be supported by elegant shops. Dispoz-a-lite, whose target segment is all who want a lighter that is easy to carry, disposable, etc., distributes in drugstores and grocery outlets, but Dunhill needs a more exclusive channel system for its high-priced, luxury lighters.

Services offered.   The buying inducement may include certain promises regarding services (for example, financing) that have to be provided by the channel. The problem is to ensure that a channel can provide such services with the efficiency expected.

Competition.   If the competitive task is to convert customers from rivals, then using the same distribution channels as competition may be a sound strategy. On the other hand, if the competitive task is to attract new users, the firm may find it more effective to seek novel distribution channels.

The type of product.   The type of product, whether a convenience, shopping or specialty product, influences choice of channel. *Convenience* goods (for example, groceries) are those that are customarily purchased and bought when wanted at the nearest convenient outlet. *Shopping* goods (for example, many household durables) are those for which the buyer is prepared to shop around before choosing, so as to compare prices, features, quality and style. *Specialty* goods are those for which buyers will, within broad limits, accept no substitute, so they are prepared to go to some lengths to secure them. In general, convenience goods need to be widely distributed through multiple channel systems. This is not the case with shopping or specialty goods. However, not everyone views the same product in the same way, so what may be a convenience product to one person may be a specialty product to another. This limits the usefulness of the categories. Some writers argue for a fourth category they call *preference* goods where there is low shopping effort, low ego involvement but high brand preference while others regard this preference goods category as a subcategory of convenience goods, arguing that all four categories are a classification based on "costs" to the consumer split into effort costs (price and energy expended) and risk costs (psychological, financial, social, and physical).[2,3]

Constraints

The choice of a distribution system will take account of certain constraints that exclude certain channels from being considered.

Defensive flexibility.   If a manufacturer is to have influence in a channel, the channel must value the business. On these grounds, an industrial firm may avoid the large industrial distributor in favor of a smaller one. Similarly, it may be unwise to deal with only one big chain, since dependence on that one chain may result in being "out of business" if their custom is lost. In any case, sellers try to avoid being dependent on just a few customers or just one industry as this reduces their *defensive flexibility*.

Channel enslavement.   Far from playing a passive role, channel members may make demands on suppliers. Thus, a channel may require the manufacturer to offer bulk discounts, to carry a "comprehensive line" or even to modify the product line to fit the channel. Such requirements may present no problems when both manufacturer and channel intermediary benefit. However, some demands may be so extreme that, if accepted, they would enslave the manufacturer to the channel. A retail chain, for example, may like to regard its suppliers as an extension of its own organization to be ordered at will. The large manufacturer, on the other hand, would similarly like to regard the channel intermediary as part of its vertically integrated system and to act accordingly. Such differential self-interests lead to the need for competent channel management if destructive conflict is to be avoided.

Costs.   Calculating the profitability of the various alternative channels presents difficulty, since estimating alternative costs and corresponding revenues is never exact. However, estimates need to be made if channel alternatives are to be ranked

Selecting the type of channel system

With a completely new product there is *usually* the problem of selecting appropriate channels or the best combination of direct selling, owned outlets, and resellers. "Usually," because, on occasion, a new product may be marketed simply to exploit the firm's distribution channel. Thus one ski manufacturer added ski clothes. Of course, it is not within the firm's control to choose just any channel, and failure to obtain appropriate channels has led to market failure as the inability to win over distributors leads to a drastic reduction of the target segment's opportunity to purchase.

Direct face-to-face selling

In direct face-to-face selling a sales representative sells the product direct to the consumer or industrial user. The conditions favoring the adoption of direct face-to-face selling are:

- *high level of pre- and post-sales service* needed;
- *complex product*, where the education and communications burden is high, for example, as occurs when applications advice is sought; and
- *large order size*, as is common in industrial buying.

But direct face-to-face selling is often adopted when these conditions are not present (if, for example, channel intermediaries refuse to accept or promote the product) and may not be adopted even when these conditions are present because of costs. But if doubts about the product can be removed and the product has the potential for frequent repeat sales, direct selling to the consumer (for example, Avon) may be one way of securing distribution and customer acceptance quickly while avoiding vast promotional expenditure. Direct face-to face selling, though, is a high-cost operation that has to be covered by resulting sales. Its expected benefits may not be forthcoming when buyers order in small quantities or are widely spread. Alternatively, the firm's line of products may be too narrow to justify a direct selling operation. A company that finds it too costly to sell using its own sales force may use a firm with excess selling capacity that is prepared to sell a noncompetitive product. Thus Alpen and Wilkinson's Sword Blades were both once distributed by Palmolive, while Kraft Foods distributed Pillsbury's refrigerated dough and Xerox the Magnavox Telecopier. Nestlé in Europe distributes and stocks Mars ice cream in the 20,000 cabinets it owns in stores, but, given the competitive relationship between the two companies, this is unlikely to be a stable arrangement. Most unusual of all, the driver salespeople for Ever Ready batteries in India are commissioned by the Indian government to distribute birth control aids!

Manufacturer's agents act as independent sales representatives who sell both the firm's product and carry noncompeting lines of other manufacturers. They can supplement the firm's own sales force in marginal territories or constitute the major distribution channel. They are frequently used when starting off in business because they usually work purely on commission (so costs are incurred only if a sale is made and paid for) and have established contacts in the market. Typically, the arrangement with an agent is covered by contract covering commission rate, territorial boundaries, pricing, and order procedures. It is unusual for an agent to carry inventory, and working on commission makes them reluctant to do any job not directly tied to making a sale. Whether to use one's own sales force or manufacturing agents is somewhat analogous, as a problem, to the make or buy decision.[4] In any case, there is a reluctance to use manufacturing agents when the product is complex; the product is very easy to sell; there is difficulty in measuring performance, or confidential information is involved.

Direct marketing

Selling direct to the customer through the mail, telephone, television, magazines or newspapers is big business in most of the industrialized countries of the world. We have already discussed direct marketing in Chapter 12 but a little more about direct response marketing, particularly mail order. Purchases by *mail order* in the United States now account for around 3 percent of all retail sales. Some estimates put the figure as high as 17 percent of all retail sales but such a figure includes such things as cruises and insurance and so deviates from common usage. The advantage of mail order to the manufacturer or seller relates to the speed with which the market can be entered at relatively little cost, with the likelihood of being able to use highly segmented mailing lists targeting those predisposed to buy. Lists now being sold classify prospective customers on thousands of characteristics. From the point of view of the buyer, there is the comfort and convenience of home shopping and the pleasure of receiving goods by mail. Of particular importance has been the convenience of the credit card and toll-free numbers. As people place their orders, their purchases can also be recorded by the supplier for developing more finely tuned mailing lists.

American Express sells around 7 percent of all the luggage bought in the United States by sending mailings describing the luggage to its cardholders. Over 20 percent of all personal computers (PCs) in the United States are bought by customers who read a catalogue or magazine and order by calling a toll-free number. The appeal of such direct computer marketing surprised the big companies like IBM who were slow to copy. They assumed people would not be prepared to buy an expensive, complex piece of equipment without physically seeing and handling the product. In other words, they assumed that adaptive criteria would dominate, ruling out such a risky buy. This was a reasonable assumption. But what had not been anticipated was the growing sophistication of the PC customers who were used to buying large items from reputable mail order firms and encouraged to buy PCs that way by the deceptive practices and poor service of computer retailers. Dell Computer Corporation, the major seller of mail order PCs, with an enviable reputation for service, is now selling in Europe with sales over $240 million per annum in 1992, 95 percent of the sales going to business customers.

Whether the organization contacting people by mail is a fund-raising firm or a seller of goods or services, a good deal of attention is paid to persuasion in the mailing. The large official-looking envelope to arouse interest; long messages to suggest message importance and credibility; the small gift such as personal address labels to evoke the norm of reciprocity; the questionnaire with questions to evoke certain predispositions toward the "cause" being advocated; request for donations asking the recipient to tick off some donation figure that starts low and rises quickly to exploit the contrast effect so that at the least the lowest sum is given—and more gimmicks to distract the recipient from counterarguments against going along with the message!

The problems associated with mail order are the handling costs, the difficulties of communicating about complex products and the fear of buyers that the unseen product may never arrive or be below advertised expectations. But none of these problems has been insurmountable. In the United States in particular, certain mail order houses have acquired outstanding reputations. Supplementary support activities are to open offices where ranges of catalog merchandise can be ordered, or alternatively to place catalogs in shops selling noncompetitive merchandise. But catalog showrooms have suffered from being unable to match the prices of the discounters.

Selling direct through *television* (usually classified as a category of telemarketing) differs from normal television advertising in providing the opportunity to buy immediately by calling a toll-free number. This system known as *home shopping* was the first advent in telemarketing and its origins go back to the 1940s and 1950s in the United States. It is now a $2 billion industry in the United States. There are also the *infomercials*, which are program-length advertisements, currently focusing on selling such durables as gym equipment and cookware. There is also the *video mall* with some particular retailer selling its wares. Thus R. H. Macy announced it plans to launch a 24-hour channel called "TV Macy's" in the fall of 1994 (*Business Week*, July 26, 1993). Finally, there is *interactive* telemarketing (e.g. Prodigy) where the use of digital technology allows viewers to request information on their TV screens and place orders. At least one grocery chain (Kroger Co.) is now offering an interactive service that allows customers to choose from around 10,000 items, including packaged foods, health and beauty aids, laundry and cleaning products and so on. Interactive TV for grocery and drugstore shopping is now being tested by Time Warner and Shopping Vision.

From the consumer's point of view, home shopping etc. saves time and the chores and hassle of much shopping as well as giving value for money. From the retailer's point of view, the three largest cost items in retailing (excluding the cost of goods and transportation), namely, labor, rent, and promotion, are all considerably reduced. *Telemarketing*, too, puts less of a burden on advertising since advertising has the job of creating images that have to endure until the viewer goes shopping. But telemarketing has its problems. Since few prospective customers want to sit through lots of advertisements waiting for a product to be displayed that interests them, the future would seem to be with those shows that are best able to tell the viewer when to tune in to view the merchandise of interest.

Using the *computer* to order services can also be classified under (interactive) telemarketing in that the system uses the telephone lines. One successful such on-line computer system is Minitel in France. This is a computer service consisting of a computer screen and keyboard that links 6.5 million French homes and offices to 20,000 different services from airline bookings, to bank transactions and the home delivery of products. The system costs about $4 per month to rent from France Telecom, the state telephone company, and can be attached to any telephone in France. A number is typed together with the service code number. Thus calling "3615 arts" provides details about theaters, movies, festivals, and exhibitions throughout France. Those looking for a job can call "3615 Ulysse." After that it is just a matter of following the instructions that appear on the screen. The cost of using the telephone to reach the service appears on the screen and is added to the caller's monthly telephone bill. Companies offer their services through Minitel by simply creating the relevant computer program and getting it approved by France Telecom. If approved, they pay a fee to France Telecom who also receive a commission on all calls made. Many firms in France are using Minitel to both advertise their products and to take orders, with payment being made by credit card.

In the United States, Prodigy, a joint venture by IBM and Sears, is another computer shop-at-home system. Here the PC has to be equipped with a modem but it allows the user to shop at, say, Kmart; buy stocks; make airline reservations; check movie listings; review Consumer Reports and use many other services. In fact it offers products from 125 merchants. Prodigy in the United States costs $9.95 per month for unlimited usage. CompuServe and America On-line similarly offer a wide range of services. CompuServe has launched a CD-Rom catalog as a supplement to its on-line shopping service. The global network Internet links about 20 million computer users. The Internet Shopping Network puts on offer an electronics superstore offering more than 15,000 electronic products including computers and software. The low cost of selling on-line is attractive for merchants while the main attraction for consumers is the convenience of computer shopping. Another joint venture of interest is that proposed between Microsoft, Time Warner, and Tele-Communications Inc to develop interactive software for cable television. Microsoft is to develop the software to provide cable subscribers with access to a wide range of interactive information and services, allowing subscribers to shop by television; view individually selected films, video games, news, and statistics from an electronic library.

Owned outlets

A firm may sell through its own intermediaries, so that the intermediaries must stock the manufacturer's product while maximum control is exercised to achieve better coordination between the firm and its distribution channel. The manufacturer formulates channel objectives to reap synergistic benefits (for example, in inventory control, order handling, sales promotion, etc.), and insists that activities be carried out in the most appropriate location and sequence. In this way, the distribution functions of buying, reselling, transportation, storage, service, finance, and so on are guided and controlled by an overall plan. In the absence of ownership, the possibilities for tight control are limited, particularly when the field is dominated by one or two large retail chains. (A compromise solution is for a company to "lease" facilities in department stores.) But the changeover to owned outlets is never easy, often generating ill-feeling and a transitionary loss of sales. Existing distributors are likely to be alienated by the move; company departments might find difficulty in adjusting to unexpected channel needs; while learning to manage and finance a more vertically integrated firm can represent a formidable challenge.

Middlemen

Most products are not sold direct. Middlemen are likely to be used when: a firm's product line is narrow; the product is standard and well known; orders are small; the market is geographically wide; the firm's products are jointly demanded with other products not produced by the firm; or where there is a need for extensive distribution or for fast servicing at the local level.

Consumer marketing.   The typical channel for consumer goods includes the retailer, who sells to the consumer, and the wholesaler, who sells to retailers, to institutions or to industry. These middlemen not only buy and resell but may also provide services like credit, repair, and maintenance and are involved in various logistical functions such as storage and transportation. In consumer marketing, middlemen are classified in a number of ways including:

- *stage in distribution*, for example, whether wholesaler or retailer;
- *goods and services offered*, for example, department store, supermarket, variety store;
- *ownership*, for example, independent, multiple chain, cooperative; and
- *method of operation*, for example, discount house.

There are many categories of wholesaler, depending on the services they provide: the merchant wholesaler both buys and resells the product; the "cash and carry" wholesaler gives no credit; while the "drop shipper" does not keep stock but has the supplier ship direct. There are wholesalers and retailers that manufacture. There are even wholesalers that retail and retailers that wholesale. Although circumvention of wholesalers may occur when the product is highly perishable and large-scale orders from geographically concentrated retailers can be expected, the survival of the wholesaler results from the service provided in terms of specialist local market knowledge, inventory holding and so on.

Manufacturers find many problems in using distributors since distributors often carry competing products and distributor salespeople often lack the knowledge, skills or motivation to push the products of any one manufacturer. It is to get round such problems that manufacturers offer to train their distributor's sales force and offer sales aids and support services.

Industrial marketing. In industrial marketing there are industrial distributors, jobbers, agents and brokers. Some of the distributors are general distributors, handling a wide range of products selling to a variety of buyers while others are limited line distributors like jobbers. The typical industrial distributor carries inventory, usually offering credit and technical services to a large number of customers. The *jobber* also buys ("takes title"), but sells a limited line and often has the manufacturer "drop ship" to his customers. The *agent* and *broker* sell on commission, but, whereas the agent has his regular set of customers, a broker typically has a varying set from one time to the next.

International marketing. In international marketing, distribution channels can be much more complex. Where a firm simply exports abroad it can export via domestic resellers who may or may not take title to the goods, or the firm may use middlemen in the country to which it wishes to export. Sometimes manufacturers cooperate in selling through a common sales organization to markets overseas. Thus Finnpap is the sales and exporting organization of eleven paper mills in Finland.

The distribution channel options are shown in Table 15.1.

Considering channel evolution and trends

The *wheel of retailing* was an early explanation of evolutionary change in distribution channels.[5] This refers to the observed tendency for new types of retailer to break into retailing as low-price operators. On finding profits decreasing over time through others copying them, they trade up to higher price levels by offering services, etc. and so join the ranks of higher-margin retailers. Hollander reviews the possible causal mechanisms involved in such a process, although he points out the exceptions to the process, e.g. in suburban branches of department stores as well as the concomitant rise of planned shopping centers have been neither low status nor low priced.[6] Hollander argues for what he calls an *accordion view* that, in the United States at least, distribution has tended to swing from general line retailers with wide assortments to the highly specialized retailer with a narrow line and back again, because excesses create their own set of reactions.[7] Another view is the *vacuum view*, which simply regards channel changes as a response to an opportunity to fill a vacuum in the market. Finally the *crisis view* regards threats

Table 15.1 Distribution channels for exporting

---

1 Exporting via domestic middlemen (i.e. situated in exporter's own country):
   - Combination export manager (CEM), authorized to undertake all marketing abroad under manufacturer's name.
   - Manufacturer's export agent (MEA). Exporter may employ many such agents.
   - Broker who merely acts as liaison between manufacturer and buyer.
   - Selling group that is set up to act on behalf of several manufacturers who sell abroad.

2 Exporting via domestic merchant middlemen *who take title to the goods*:
   - Export merchants operating in foreign markets.
   - Export buyers and importers on the look out for "good buys."
   - Trading companies that buy and distribute in many countries.

3 Marketing in foreign countries through foreign middlemen:
   - Agents.
   - Brokers (commodities mainly).
   - Manufacturing representatives.
   - Factors who distribute and also cover credit risk.
   - Managing agent who has an exclusive contract to market the product in the foreign country.

4 Marketing through *merchants* in foreign country *who take title to the goods*:
   - Import jobbers who sell to wholesalers and retailers.
   - Wholesalers and retailers.
   - Dealers who represent the last step in a distribution chain selling direct.

5 Additionally a manufacturer might consider licensing or entering into some joint venture, as well as manufacturing abroad.

---

to the external environment as the major factors triggering change. Firms are first shocked on becoming aware of the threat and respond initially by *defensive threat* rather than directly meeting the threat through institutional change. When firms finally acknowledge the true nature of the threat, they take more aggressive action necessitating adaptation and change.

In this review of the factors (all of which may play a part) claimed by writers to be instrumental in bringing about changes in channels, others rightly point out that change is not automatic but "involves strategic managerial decisions, not merely tactical reaction."[8] But there can be strong pressures for change. What may be significant from the point of view of selecting distribution channels is the likelihood of consumers first deciding on the shopping center to patronize before considering which particular stores.

The different types of consumer middlemen are constantly changing. In the United States *traditional department stores* continue to lose ground relative to others (e.g. discount department stores) perhaps because of their high cost structures. There is also (as in retailing generally) the move toward more concentration so that the top 10 department stores in the United States account for something like 70 percent of category sales. As a result they are dropping many low-margin products in favor of high-margin goods such as fashion apparel though there are exceptions such as low-margin computers. Department stores are also cutting costs, which has led to a reduction in customer service and more pressure on suppliers to maintain inventory. None of these policies is likely to substantially increase customer patronage. Yet department stores are unlikely to disappear. Even in the United States, several department store chains like Nordstrom's are highly profitable (largely because Nordstrom understands the concept of customer service), while the "discount" department stores are increasing their share of the market in the United States. While needing to adapt, the department store still has attractions for the consumer. Thus in Bangkok, the number of department stores is expected to increase from 86 in 1993 to 115 by 1996. But national chains of department stores, with centralized buying and administrative control are seen by many commentators to lack staying power though currently some, like Sears, are doing well. Given regional differences and the need to wield power with suppliers, the return to regional chains seems more likely.

Even *discount stores* are having to change as they are under attack from new outlets such as *warehouse clubs* (see below). The pressure is on for them to broaden their range of goods to maintain their market position. While those sellers with a pull strategy are keen to sell to outlets like Wal–Mart, manufacturers of branded goods with a push strategy remain shy of discounters. The placing of a high-quality branded good (e.g. designer jeans) with discounters, while initially increasing sales, can tarnish a brand's image and lead the high-quality stores to cease taking the brand which, in turn, leads the discounters to reject it on the ground that it is only attractive to them when consumers can do comparative shopping.

There is considerable growth in the United States of small, highly focused, specialty stores and food emporiums. Many of these are branded apparel newcomers who have opted to go vertical, either through owned stores or via franchising. To some extent "going vertical" is a reaction to recent department store policies. Bennetton, for example, believes it can give better service, better preserve its image and add that excitement to shopping that may be disappearing from department stores. Many of these specialty stores set out to cater to some specific segment of the market based on data on tastes and lifestyle. But while one trend is toward the highly specialist shop (e.g. selling just cookies, ties or socks), another trend lies in the opposite direction toward offering wider and wider selections of goods.

In consumer marketing, manufacturers have to deal with the growth of *hypermarkets* (around 200,000 square feet), *warehouse clubs* (around 100,000 square feet), and bigger *discount stores* (around 65,000 square feet), each of which can be contrasted with the typical supermarket of around 40,000 square feet.

Hypermarkets and warehouse clubs focus on price in the belief that "a poor man needs a bargain, and a rich man loves one." The first hypermarket was started in the 1960s at an intersection near Annecy, France and named Carrefour, meaning "crossroads." The basic assumption was to sell everything the consumer wanted at the lowest price. Typically about 40 percent of hypermarket sales are nonfoods. They can also offer inducements to the consumer other than price such as child care and aisle telephones to provide information and directions. While hypermarkets are designed for convenience, they are frequently criticized for being anything but that. They often fail to appeal to the busy consumer, who in surveys and focus groups, complain that hypermarkets are tiring (as people lose their way in finding what they seek) and less satisfying than shopping at a conventional supermarket. Carrefour has 115 hypermarkets in Europe and South America and one in the United States in Philadelphia which is 330,000 square feet; the size of about six football fields. While a big supermarket may stock around 30,000 items, a hypermarket may have 50,000 items, representing about 8 percent of a consumer's regular buys.

Doubts have been raised about the future of the hypermarket in the United States, where only Biggs in Cincinnati seems to be prospering. One reason is the large volume of business needed to cover the huge amount of fixed costs. Customers also complain that the price deals are not sufficient and selections not broad enough to compensate for the fatigue of shopping there. Other commentators, however, claim that hypermarkets will adapt and grow.

In contrast to hypermarkets, warehouse clubs are in general doing well in the United States. Warehouse clubs are "no-frills" businesses conducted in warehouses on the outskirts of towns, limiting access to members only. Around 60 to 70 percent of the membership consists of small business owners. Business and individual members pay an annual fee of around $30 for membership. Membership induces the feeling of exclusivity in being offered a deal that is not available to everyone. Besides selling food, they sell office supplies and other necessities to businesses at prices typically around 8 percent above the cost from the manufacturer. Whereas the shelves of hypermarkets do not rise beyond eight feet so buyers can see the goods, this is not so with warehouse clubs, where goods are stacked to the ceiling. Typically, however, warehouse clubs stock only around 3,500 items of frequently demanded goods. In the United States, the home of the warehouse club, four companies have had around 85 percent of the business: Sam's (belonging to Wal-Mart), Price Club, Costco Wholesale Club, and the Kmart Corporation's PACE Membership Warehouses. But Price and Costco have become Price-Costco and Kmart has mainly sold out its PACE Membership Warehouses to Wal-Mart so, in the United States, the industry now has just two major players: Sam's Wholesale Club warehouses and Price-Costco Inc., with its Price and Costco warehouses. The success of warehouse clubs has led to the setting up of smaller warehouse-type companies that specialize in certain categories of goods like office supplies. In areas where land prices are high, where traffic is heavy and homes have little storage space, warehouse clubs are unlikely to take root. In fact, many commentators on the distribution scene believe that consumers will in the long run tire of warehouse clubs.

Whereas the hypermarket caters more to the middle income family, *discount stores* cater more to the lower income as the focus is even more on price. In the United States, Wal-Mart, a discount department store, is generally considered the most efficient discounter, trading largely in small towns often ignored by the big retail chains. In Europe Netto is the major food discounter. While the large chain European supermarkets may offer a premium service at a premium price, the food discount stores in Europe will rent small, cheap sites on street corners near where their customers live. With few staff or overheads, they concentrate on the fastest moving consumer goods, selling from the boxes in which the goods were delivered so as to undercut supermarket prices by up to 40 percent. Carrefour has responded by setting up its own discount subsidiary, Erteco, which now has 400 stores. The spread of such discounting is transforming food retailing in Europe with cross-border alliances, mergers and acquisitions.

One development in the United States deserves mention and that is the *discount-outlet center*. These centers are essentially regional malls occupied solely by stores offering goods at discount prices. The average size of a discount-outlet center in the United States is around 250,000 square feet. The Franklin Mills center near Philadelphia is one discount-outlet center that occupies 1.8 million square feet. At a cost of $300 million it is one of the costliest shopping malls of any kind in the world.

Technology has had a major impact on retailing. Computers are already being used extensively among retail chains to keep track of stock and to identify winners and losers. *Direct-product-profitability* (DPP) computer programs have been adapted to calculate the profit on each product, taking into account shelf space plus the time on the shelf. Such data can be persuasive in rejecting "third division" brands. Current interest lies with using the computer to link up with suppliers. Thus, for example, the retail chain Designs Inc. in Brookline, Mass. is linked directly with Levi Strauss Company. As a consequence, Levi Strauss can identify which of its product lines are selling, with the relevant data being sent directly from the point-of-sale to the Levi Strauss computer network. Levi Strauss can thus keep Designs Inc. with the right amount of inventory. Wal-Mart supplies 5000 vendors with point-of-sale data. At Kmart around 3000 suppliers have some sort of electronic linkup. Manufacturers need such sales information quickly, particularly in the early stages of the life of the brand. In Europe there is the same trend to "paper-less trading" or electronic commerce as it has been called. In the UK, orders from Tesco's computer go straight, say, to the order processing system on Colgate's computer. From Colgate's point of view, there is a closer relationship with the retailer with no rekeying of the order data while Colgate reverses the process by sending its invoices to Tesco down the telephone line.

Within the chains themselves, it is possible to make price changes in all stores simultaneously, with the head office sending the instruction by satellite to change the price display above the particular product on the shelves while updating the store computers. There is also sophisticated software for space management to determine, say, how shelf space is to be allocated among products and what brands are most profitable to stock. There is even the technology to dispense with those manning cash registers. In the system being suggested, the shopper runs a hand-held wand scanner over the bar code on goods. At the check-out, the scanning wand slots into a payment console which displays the total bill. The shopper's credit card is put through a machine where the till used to be. The shopper then verifies her identify by placing a finger or palm on the scanner and leaves the store through a security arch which sounds an alarm if goods that have not been scanned are included.

Degree of exclusivity/number of outlets

A firm must decide on whether to have an intensive, selective or exclusive system of distribution.

Intensive distribution

An intensive distribution system seeks maximum market penetration as an aid to customer attraction and retention. Intensive distribution is adopted for most nationally distributed brands that are of low unit value and purchased frequently as convenience goods. Intensive distribution is most likely to be adopted for convenience goods. It is less appropriate when the customer shops around before choosing. The adoption of an intensive distribution system reduces the incentive for a retailer to push the product and perhaps even to stock it. For example, department stores are loath to stock intensively distributed perfumes. If the product is bought for its status appeal, an intensive distribution system may be incompatible with the product's desired image, which is why Michelob beer is not distributed to every retailer that is willing to buy but distributed only to high-class retailers and restaurants.

Selective distribution

A selective distribution system selects only those outlets that are likely to perform well in promoting and selling the product. If the buyer is prepared to shop around before choosing, a selective distribution system with broad geographical coverage is not likely to lead to reduced segment penetration. Hence selective distribution is associated with high priced shopping goods.

Exclusive distribution

A selective distribution system may not reinforce an image of exclusivity or induce the most sought-after retailers to push the product or even to stock it. Exclusive distribution, whereby the firm selects one or two outlets per defined geographical area, is adopted when exclusivity characterizes the product or when dealer cooperation is sought to provide aggressive promotion and technical services.

Channel members may demand exclusivity as an incentive to stock the product. In an exclusive system, detailed agreements may be drawn up covering, say, the level of inventories to be carried, territorial sales boundaries, sales quotas, joint promotions and similar matters. When distribution is selective or exclusive, channel members may be unhappy if the additional "selected" outlets are of a lower standing. Thus Levi Strauss in 1982 agreed to sell its jeans through Sears, Roebuck and J. C. Penney. This type of expansion into low-priced outlets angered the department stores and other traditional outlets and their business with Levi Strauss dropped off. Levi Strauss has been winning back its traditional outlets with promises of improved service and (most important) promises of merchandise different from that offered by them elsewhere.

Sometimes when referring to exclusive outlets we mean that an outlet only stocks that particular brand. This is common in the selling of cars. From the point of view of the car manufacturer, the setting up of an exclusive dealer network makes sense as the dealer concentrates on just the one brand while potential buyers are exposed to just that brand at the dealership without the distractions of competing makes in the car lot. But this means dealers are tying their business future to just one brand rather than a wide selection of makes. If the car is a new entry into the market, dealers recognize that it may take time to get the requisite level of business (if any) while there are no used cars to sell or cars coming in for repair. As a consequence, there is a reluctance of dealers to accept a contract that binds them to selling just the one make.

Choosing individual channel members

Where a selective or exclusive distribution system is adopted, criteria must be developed for choosing individual channel members. If the target set of customers patronize a particular outlet or outlets, which can or could provide the functions sought, then such outlets would generally be selected. However, the target group of customers may not patronize, say, just one department store, jeweler, etc., in a town, nor will industrial users necessarily deal with only one distributor. Hence more elaborate criteria are needed. In selecting the best of the outlets that have the necessary qualifications for performing the functions required, we would list the relevant factors on which the prospective outlets differ: relevant, that is, to high achievement of our goals. Table 15.2 illustrates. The items relevant to distributor efficiency are shown in the first column. The second column shows a series of weights (adding up to 10) that reflect the relative importance of each of the differential consequences for achieving efficiency. Each of the five distributors is rated on a scale 0 to 3, depending on the likely contribution to the differential consequences. A rating of "3" gives the highest score. The weights are multiplied by the rating and summed to give the distributor's overall score. In Table 15.2, "Jones" has the highest score. If there is agreement on weights and rating, "Jones" may be selected. But the result of such a procedure (as we have previously argued) normally forms only a basis for discussion, as the method, with its assumption of interval scaling and its linear weighting system, does have limitations. An alternative system (as with consumer decision-making) might set minimum standards of attainment for each of the relevant factors. Each outlet is evaluated against the highest ranked factor, then the next leading factor, and so on, with any outlet failing to reach the minimum standard being eliminated from consideration. This procedure also has weaknesses as it, too, makes no estimates of relevant costs and revenues. Some writers advocate remedying this by the use of simulation techniques to estimate the payoffs.

In selecting among outlets for consumer products, a major consideration in the future might be the shopping center. If the customer first decides on which center to patronize, this influences the store frequented and the product bought. Hence selection of the "right" shopping center might be the first consideration for the manufacturer.

Not-for-profit channels

The not-for-profit organization typically deals with its patrons direct so public libraries, museums, symphony orchestras and universities deal directly with the public.

Table 15.2 Selection of individual channel members

Differential consequences	Weight[a]	Lee[b]	Smith[b]	B&G[b]	R&R[b]	Jones[b]	Sitwell[b]
			Industrial Components, Inc.				
Coverage including frequency of reminder calls	4	$(4 \times 2)8$	$(4 \times 1)4$	$(4 \times 3)12$	$(4 \times 1)4$	$(4 \times 2)8$	$(4 \times 1)4$
Inventory and efficiency in order handling	3	$(3 \times 1)3$	$(3 \times 2)6$	$(3 \times 2)6$	$(3 \times 2)6$	$(3 \times 3)9$	$(3 \times 2)6$
Credit facilities	1	$(1 \times 3)3$	$(1 \times 2)2$	$(1 \times 3)3$	$(1 \times 2)2$	$(1 \times 2)2$	$(1 \times 2)2$
Actual or potential value of abrasives to distributor	1	$(1 \times 1)1$	$(1 \times 1)1$	$(1 \times 1)1$	$(1 \times 2)2$	$(1 \times 3)3$	$(1 \times 2)2$
Actual or potential value of Industrial Components, Inc. to distributor	1	$(1 \times 1)1$	$(1 \times 1)1$	$(1 \times 1)1$	$(1 \times 2)2$	$(1 \times 3)3$	$(1 \times 2)2$
		16	14	23	16	25	16

a Sum of weights = 10.
b Rating of 1, 2, or 3.
Note: Vary figures for sensitivity analysis.

Nonetheless, intermediaries are sometimes used such as intermediaries selling tickets or those raising funds.

CHANNEL MANAGEMENT AND POLICIES

This section deals with the problems of channel management and associated policies under the following headings:

- sources of conflict between channel members and the manufacturer;
- vertical integrated channel systems; and
- bases of relative power or dominance.

Sources of conflict

Conflict is the experience of tension that arises from inter-dependent groups striving for incompatible goals. A conflict is zero-sum if one party's gain is another's loss. But many conflicts are not zero-sum even though there may be no solution that leaves either party feeling happy.

Conflict occurs between retailer and manufacturer whenever the actions of one of them frustrates the achievement of the other's goals. Such conflict is not necessarily all bad since some conflict is constructive as it may lead to improvements that make the manufacturer more efficient and result in a better deal for the consumer. How much conflict is constructive or destructive in terms of channel efficiency is not known. In the past, writers have argued that destructive conflict should not occur if sellers followed the marketing concept since, in serving the interests of resellers, firms are serving their own interests. On this view, adherence to the superordinate goal of customer orientation would dissolve differences while benefiting both parties. Even if this were believed, the manufacturer and channel intermediary may still not see eye-to-eye on how such an orientation is to be applied. A mass retailer might legitimately believe he is serving his customers best by pushing his own private label and restricting the manufacturer's in-store merchandising. Also the individual channel member could benefit by deviating from what would best meet both producer's and customer's interests in the long term. Thus, to quote just one example, the individual mass retailer might benefit from selling well below the suggested resale price, claiming customer orientation, while the result might be a fall-off in image and sales for the individual brand. More generally, conflict between manufacturer and reseller can arise over the "equitable" distribution of benefits, perceptions of relative functional and transactional efficiencies, lack or otherwise of innovativeness and other performance criteria.

A manufacturer does not and cannot just blindly adjust policies to serve the "best" interest of distributors on the assumption that such action always serves his own interest long term. However, although channel enslavement is to be avoided, it is true that the manufacturers and channel intermediaries often assume an adversary relationship when cooperation could lead to increased benefits all round. In general, integrative relationships are to be encouraged by following what is termed the "dual concern model" where each opposing group comes to see that the best overall outcome will be reached when each party feels some concern for the other's needs and not just his own or her own needs.

When one party to an exchange becomes more powerful, it would be unusual if that party did not seek better terms from the exchange. The growth of the supermarket chains has shifted the balance of power toward the retailer. An article in the *Financial Times* (July 18, 1992) expresses the manufacturer's frustration with this development. In the article, the chief marketing strategist of Nestlé and head of its food products division, expresses skepticism about relying on mass-media advertising as the main method of trying to counterbalance the increasing power of the retail chains. The Nestlé executive talks of its brands finding themselves "imprisoned in a ghetto from which advertising provides no escape." He argued that three developments had brought this about:

- The consolidation of food retailing into fewer, bigger supermarket chains, many of which actively promote their own "private label." Such chains are in a strong position to dictate to even their biggest suppliers.
- The growth of new media such as satellite television which splinters the mass audience, while consumers are in any case becoming more resistant to advertisers' messages.

- Food manufacturers have sent the wrong signals by basing their marketing and brand strategies too narrowly on product and process technologies, such as frozen food. "But people today do not think in terms of frozen foods, they think in terms of concepts like Lean Cuisine, Weight Watchers and Healthy Options—consumers are no longer interested in how food is processed but chiefly in taste, aroma, texture and convenience."

The problem, the article goes on to say, is to find more effective ways of forging relationships with consumers and building up brand loyalty. He recommends the focus be on designing credible communication links with consumers to establish the right brand image; show the product as part of the lifestyle or consumption system of the consumer; associating the brand with the interests of the target group; experimenting with new channels like vending machines and stressing more point-of-sale promotion. The trend indeed in the retailing of packet goods is toward large chains with central buying. This is particularly so in Europe where, in each EC country, five to ten buying points are likely to control over 80 percent of food distribution. This means that the relative importance of such retail chains as Aldi and Tegelmann in Germany and Tesco and Sainsbury in the UK has grown enormously in recent years. Also much of the buying is coming to resemble industrial buying in that buying is done by a team of specialists, constituting the decision-making unit (DMU), which immediately suggests the need to develop individual account strategies. The proliferation of brands, exacerbated by the international nature of competition, means retailers have to be more selective so many brands will disappear.

There are many sources of conflict. One which has already been mentioned is the pressure put on manufacturers for constant price promotions which are often perceived as not being in the interests of the brand being discounted. Also supermarkets are apt to stock up on a promotion to sell later at the regular price, reducing the manufacturer's subsequent sales. Such actions have costs, too, for the supermarket chains in the need for warehouses to store the "surplus" bought; the need for transportation to move it around and additional administrative staff to keep a check on it. In packaged goods, manufacturers may object to the retailer's demand for "slotting allowances" as the price to be paid for accepting a new product or the clothing manufacturer may resist paying "markdown allowances" by which the manufacturer contributes to the "loss" in profit to the retailer arising from the retailer having to reduce the price of goods that cannot be sold at the original mark-up price. But the major source of conflict today lies in *private label*. The term "private label" is used not only to cover brands identified with the name of the store like Pathmark in the United States but also brand-names that are exclusive to a retailer such as the name St. Michael (which is exclusive to Marks & Spencer in the UK), or the designer labels exclusive to the retailer or the name of some well-known personality, licensed to cover a product range that is exclusive to the store. Private label is growing as a percentage of supermarket business. Supermarket chains view their private label brands as a way of building loyalty to the chain as well as offering keener prices to the consumer and higher margins to the retailer. Successful private label brands enhance the image of the store rather than the manufacturer and the supermarket's aim is to make the consumer more loyal to the store rather than to manufacturers of national brands. The retailer has an advantage in being there to serve, to complain to, and to rectify any errors or deficiencies. Thus naturally, as with manufacturers, retailers try to build brand loyalty and one way of doing this is by offering extra value to customers through brands that can only be purchased at their stores. Retailers seek a competitive advantage beyond just the location of the store and price can be a major competitive advantage. Indeed some of the major supermarket chains like Wal-Mart make price *the* competitive weapon. But all supermarkets must be interested in price, as a reputation for low prices will always be a major attraction for their customers. After all, retailers cannot use the stocking of national brands as a competitive weapon when these are extensively distributed.

Private label has led to a shift in power toward the store chains when dealing with national brand manufacturers. The store chains have a price advantage as they typically do not spend anything on R&D; have no problem in obtaining distribution; need little or no advertising and can decide which national brand winners to copy. Manufacturers are particularly incensed when such copying takes place. When the copying is too blatant, manufacturers feel obliged to protest as it is an invasion of valuable property rights. But many store brands are no longer just cheap imitations of national brands. Some chain stores have brought out innovative new products and it has not been unknown for manufacturers to copy such innovations!

Manufacturers of packaged products have long had to cope with chains adopting private label or store brands. The first own-label appeared in 1880 in Manhattan for baking soda for the Great Atlantic & Pacific Tea Company. But the growth of private label in recent years is what disturbs manufacturers. While in 1992, 18.2 percent of supermarket sales in the United States were private label, it is estimated that this will be 25 percent to 30 percent by the year 2000. The recent increasing success of private label is attributed to growing consumer sophistication and skepticism about competing advertising claims as well as the belief fostered by price discounting (where brands are "bargained, belittled, bartered, and battered") that price should be the key choice criterion. If brands are not proclaiming and demonstrating a significant competitive advantage, it appears foolish to pay more. The prices of store brands are about 25 percent less, on average, than those for national brands. But there has also been increasing sophistication on the part of the retail chains. Thus, at the end of the 1970s "generic brands" were promoted purely on price. The store chains simply bought from the cheapest source. But there was no consistency in the quality which reflected badly on the store with the result that generics never amounted to anything more than 2 percent of the market.

The next step was to create store brands (private label) which were competitive in quality with the national brands. In fact, in the UK, Sweden, Germany and Switzerland store brands have long been important and a major worry for manufacturers. Long ago J. Sainsbury and Tesco upgraded their own store brands to the quality of the national brands. The next step for the chains is already underway; identifying gaps in the market and asking suppliers to develop products to fit neglected segments. The retail chains see less need to go through the same product development cycle as manufacturers (often taking up to three years) as less is at stake in demand failure. Just as generics originated in Europe (France), the idea of developing *premium* private label brands was inspired by the big marketing chains in Europe (Britain in particular), helped somewhat by the invasion of such chains into the United States. Thus Tengelmann, a German firm, now owns the A&P chain in the United States and Sainsbury, a British firm, owns Shaw's Supermarkets in the Boston area.

The problem of private label for branded goods manufacturers is common throughout the developed, industrialized world. Thus in Japan, Daiei, the biggest supermarket chain, has been the catalyst of a recent boom in private label there. Other big supermarket chains in Japan like Jusco and Ito-Yokado are also experiencing increasing private label sales. Daiei's private label videotapes (source Korea) have forced TDK, the leading video-tape maker, to abandon the low priced segment of the domestic market. Manufacturers of store brands are frequently the same companies selling some national brand. They may, for example, sell their "overproduction" as a store brand or make for private label to keep at full production. But when manufacturers really have something extra to offer, they are unlikely to offer it as private label. For many manufacturers, there is little security in just catering to private label while some manufacturers identify the success of private label as indicating an opportunity to bring out another brand at a price compet-itive with private label. Thus Kodak sells its own cut-price film known as Fun Time, which costs 25 percent less than Kodak's Gold brand. In any case, private label is affecting brand pricing policies. Even Philip Morris felt obliged to reduce the price of its Marlboro cigarette brand because it was losing out to cheaper brands. This sent a frightening signal to the stock market because many of the takeovers in the 1980s were premised on the belief that famous brand-names could be further exploited in brand and line extensions. If this assumption was unwarranted then so was the price paid for the company with famous brand-names.

Many consumers perceive rivals' brands as having no relevant or discernible differ-ences in many product categories. But the question arises as to whether promotional image building and lifestyle repositioning alone, as speculated by the Nestlé spokes-person above, can reverse the decline in brand equity and stem the trend to private label. Consumers are educated to be suspicious of claims to differences among super-market products that cannot be demonstrated in some tangible way while, as the Nestlé spokesperson says, TV advertising no longer has the wide reach it once had with the proliferation of channels and the fragmentation generally of the media. Last, but not least, there is the proliferation of brands, all seeking to get attention. What is likely to happen is the death of the second division brands. Manufacturers cannot give them visibility and the supermarket chains will not stock them for long when they discover their true profitability. This is leading some manufacturers to eliminate the weakest brands to concentrate on the strong brands that can take on private label.

What can be said is that there is a limit at present to stores just using private label. National brands are essential to the store since, without them, consumers have no basis for comparison and are not persuaded to buy on price alone. The magic figure quoted as the upper limit is around 35 percent private label. But some chains like Marks & Spencer in the UK have got away with higher percentages as have many clothing store chains. Sears in the United States is 60 percent private and 40 percent national though it is now aiming at a 50/50 split. Consumers want to be reassured that own-label and the national brand are equal in quality. When experience with a brand is ambiguous, the national well-advertised brand usually has the advantage. Thus private label washing powders have not been successful since ambiguity about differences remains. Also where the difference in price between private label and the nationally advertised brand is marginal, the national brand is likely to be preferred. In any case national brands with a strong brand image still dominate. But the development of such images is not all done with mirrors since product benefits are important. Perhaps our spokesman from Nestlé should think more in terms of product improvement than just in product promotion.

Just as stocking up on price promotions has a cost for the retailer so does private label. When retailers become too involved in private label, it can distract from the marketing side of retailing. It is claimed this occurred in the case of A&P in the 1970s when it had over 35 percent of its sales in private label but consumers sought a wider choice and looked elsewhere. Consumers like to feel they do have a wide choice even if they habitually buy private label. A&P now limits private label to about 25 percent of its sales.

What should manufacturers do about differences with distributors? The first step is to recognize that the retailer is the immediate customer and that many brands live or die by their supermarket listings. There is no way to win the trust and loyalty of middlemen by adopting an adversarial stance or suggesting that the relationship will be other than long term. If, as we have argued, names influence perceptions, the term *immediate* customer is much preferred to using terms like distributor, retailer, wholesaler or stores as such terms affect attitudes. The manufacturer must think in terms of trying to meet the expectations of immediate customers and seek to build loyalty, recognizing that it is now more difficult and more expensive to get the advertising message across. This means knowing something about immediate customers and researching them, and talking to them about their merchandising policies instead of confining market research to just the final consumer. Since around 50 percent of US companies reach their customers through distributors and middlemen, they have a strong incentive to be cooperative with their distributors. Du Pont, the chemical company, keeps contact with its distributors through a committee composed of thirty-five distributors which meets regularly to discuss common problems, markets and customers' needs. Additionally, Du Pont sends out a newsletter about its new products and the intended markets and organizes training programs for distributors.

Vertical marketing systems

Where the power in a distribution system is aligned in a way that gives rise to a centrally coordinated system, the result has come to be known as a *vertical integrated channel* or *a vertical marketing system*. Vertical marketing systems imply the "existence of a power locus in the system that provides for channel leadership, role specification, coordination, conflict management, and control."[9] Vertical marketing systems can be classified into corporate, contractual and administered.

Corporate marketing systems

In a *corporate system*, successive stages of production and distribution come under a single ownership. With every link in the distribution chain owned and operated by the owner (as is common, say, in the shoe industry), the total system can be run as an integrated whole and the behavior of individual channel members becomes more controllable and predictable. Many economies are possible under corporate marketing systems, for example, field selling eliminated, ordering, financing and billing drastically reduced, and so on.

Contractual marketing systems

Contractual systems are based on the ethical and/or legal obligation to comply with freely entered into agreements. Many firms at different levels in the manufacturing and distribution system coordinate their activities on a contractual basis. Typical contractual systems are the various *wholesaler-sponsored voluntary groups* that agree to reduce their own individual freedom in decision-making in return for the benefits of economies of scale from large-scale production, better coordination and so on.

A contractual system of particular interest is *franchising*, which is generally defined as a "contractual agreement under which a person, partnership or corporation (the 'franchiser') sells to other persons (the 'franchisees') certain goods or services." But this definition (like others that have been proposed) does not embrace all arrangements which are included under the term franchising. Franchising is one way of achieving leadership and coordinated decision-making between supplier and distributor. Typically, the franchisee is allowed to use the name and products of the franchiser and, most important, follow a successful formula in exchange for an initial and continuing fee, like a royalty on gross sales. The franchiser in turn typically provides marketing back-up, though he may oblige the franchisee to buy supplies (for example, hamburger buns) from the franchiser. There are *manufacturer-sponsored franchises* (for example, car firms licensing dealers), *manufacturer-sponsored wholesale franchisers* (for example, Coca-Cola licensing its bottlers) and *service-sponsored retail franchisers* (for example, McDonald's). A franchise can cover an entire outlet, a department within a particular outlet or a brand within the outlet. A firm may adopt a franchise system because it lacks the capital for the rapid expansion sought; because it believes that the franchise system with its appeal to individual entrepreneurship will attract more dedicated managers or can save on taxes and attract less government regulation. In the United States around 2,000 companies are franchising their products to some extent, and about 9 percent of the country's working population either own a franchise or work for one. The failure rate of franchised operations is lower than that of regular business.

Franchising continues to grow. It has been estimated that there are now over 500,000 franchise outlets in the United States doing at least $250 billion (some estimates put the figure at $640 billion) in sales. With growth has come franchisee associations to represent their interests vis-à-vis the franchiser and to lobby for legal reform. Franchisees no longer just acquiesce to whatever is proposed by the franchiser, as witness how the Burger King franchisees blocked Pillsbury from spinning off the fast-food subsidiary as a defense against Grand Metropolitan PLC's takeover bid. Franchisees complain of broken promises and being obliged to buy supplies from the franchiser at a higher price than can be obtained elsewhere. But with many franchisees now owning multiple units, organizing with others and employing lobbyists, they are getting more power. Franchisers in several states in the United States are being legally obliged to follow strict rules in

- disclosure,
- franchise terminations,
- renewals,
- transfers, and
- protecting franchisees from competition from company-owned outlets.

If the franchiser has a fully integrated relationship with the franchisee, then the product, service, trademark, marketing strategy, operating manuals, and such like are standard. In such an arrangement the franchiser may be tempted to abuse his position by obliging, say, franchisees to buy centrally at higher than competitive prices.

Not all franchises are built on a solid business foundation and deceptive practices are still all too common. Some features of successful franchises are:

- the "product" has proved itself before franchising gets under way;
- franchisees have the capital to get the operation off the ground;
- the system is properly supervised by the franchiser to ensure that standards are maintained (even though the individual franchisees may resent such supervision); and
- the franchiser has a continuing interest in the franchisee's success otherwise franchisees are particularly open to deception about the potential of a franchise when franchisers have little after-sale involvement.

Administered marketing systems

In an administered vertical marketing system, coordination is achieved by getting agreement to a plan. For example, a manufacturer may draw up a plan for the marketing of his products by the other channel members, specifying the role to be played by each member. But conflicts can occur. A reseller may perceive his interests as different from the manufacturer over, say, stock levels, full line stocking, display efforts, joint promotions, adequacy of servicing, suggested resale prices and the provision of information. Alternatively, the manufacturer may reject demands for exclusive territorial rights, higher call frequency, better delivery, or payment for shelf-position.

Systems for achieving channel coordination often only approximate to the three systems described (corporate, contractual, and administered). For example, ownership may not be extended throughout the whole system, while contractual systems are seldom comprehensive. In any case, directive leadership may not be forthcoming or accepted by all parties, so coordination becomes piecemeal and unstable.

Bases of relative power

Conflict inevitably does occur on occasion between manufacturer and channel. How does the manufacturer handle conflict? Whatever actions the manufacturer adopts, the actions can be categorized as one or more of the following:

- *Competition*. For example, the manufacturer can produce a line extension that competes directly with the retailer's private label brand.
- *Analytic problem solving*. Thus the manufacturer can try to solve by rational discussion, say, the dispute over the retail chain too closely copying the firm's brand. The aim of the manufacturer here would be to persuade the chain that such action is neither desirable in terms of establishing good relations with suppliers nor ethically defensible nor, if exposed, would be socially endorsed.
- *Withdrawing*. The manufacturer can withdraw from dealing with the retail chain. This is usually a last resort since the manufacturer typically needs the chain more than the chain needs the manufacturer's products. With retailer chains so dominant in Europe, each is too important to lose. Even in the United States around one hundred chains account for 80 percent of P&G's grocery business.
- *Accommodation*. The manufacturer may decide to produce private label for the retail chain. In fact the manufacturer may have little choice if the firm's brands are becoming "de-listed" by the retailer as no longer worthy of stocking.
- *Bargaining/compromise*. The manufacturer may negotiate with the retailer over price discounting or whatever.
- *Jural*. The manufacturer may sue the retailer for violation of agreements. However, legal fights strain future relations, so arbitration is common.

Conflict is encouraged when there is an atmosphere of mutual mistrust. Mistrust can develop quickly as a result of one act of deception or whatever and may not be easy to erase. It sometime helps to dispel the mistrust by admitting the error or the wrongdoing.

What action to take depends somewhat on the relative power of the manufacturer. Power is the basis of influence and influence the actual exercise of power. Power in the context refers to the potential ability of the manufacturer to influence the behavior of the retailer to do something the retailer would not otherwise do. It is *potential* ability since that potential might not be exercised. The exercise of power assumes some relationship exists between the parties, with the more powerful party in the relationship being, as a matter of definition, less dependent on the other.

The aim of manufacturers is to increase their power vis-à-vis the retailer. The major source of manufacturers' power is their brands as these make profit for the retailer. Supermarket chains will buy major national brands and the other brands that dominate specialty segments of the market but, with brand proliferation and the desire for private label brands, retailers are de-listing weak brands. Manufacturers need to prune their ranges of these weaker brands and focus on those that do have sufficient of a following to justify stocking by the retailer.

In perceiving the retailer as the immediate customer, there is a need to think, plan and act on the basis of retailer expectations:

- The big supermarket chain wants, for example, low prices. Thus there is a need to cut costs and pass on the saving to the supermarket consumer in the form of lower prices for standard products or the chains will find some supplier who will.
- The retailer wants brands that differentiate his store from the competition. Modern computerized production methods allow production variation or the mass production of parts with variety in assembly. This should lead to providing something distinctive for each chain without the sacrifice of margins.
- It may even be possible to work with a chain on the development of new products for that chain.
- With regard to the independent retailers, suppliers might offer support in their fight for survival as such support is usually reciprocated with more loyalty. If a manufacturer is to give a lead in coordinating channel members, the manufacturer must possess and exercise the requisite amount of power bearing in mind that the superordinate goal is to inspire trust and loyalty not fear.

For a manufacturer to have power over channel members means manufacturers have a general ability for getting their way in *relationships* with channel members. The essence of power is having access to the resources needed by others and this leads one writer to argue that leadership in a channel relates to which institution can command the loyalty of the target body of customers.[10] The term "channel captain" is used for the institution that provides such channel leadership, whether the institution is the manufacturer, wholesaler-retailer, or whatever. Power over customers is the way to channel leadership, that is, the way to become channel captain. Before endorsing this position we might first consider the bases of power. The best-known classification of the bases of social power is the original five category classification by French and Raven.[11] By the basis of power they mean the relationship between groups or individuals, O and P.

> These five bases of O's power are: (1) based on P's perception that O has the ability to mediate rewards for him; (2) coercive power, based on P's perception that O has the ability to mediate punishments for him; (3) legitimate power, based on the perception by P that O has a legitimate right to prescribe behavior for him; (4) referent power, based on P's identification with O; (5) expert power, based on the perception that O has some special knowledge or expertness.

We shall build on this classification, drawing on the work of others to form the following categories of power.

Coercive power

Coercive power refers to the ability to harm the interests of the other party in the relationship. For example, an automobile manufacturer can slow down deliveries to dealers of cars in short supply and high demand. Major brand manufacturers can threaten to close a retailer account. Even the most private label oriented retailer chain recognizes the need to stock major brands because their customers will go elsewhere if such brands are not available while they are needed to show the price advantage of private label. But coercive power used alone leads to minimal compliance. There is public acquiescent but private resentment so that while the retailer chain might feel compelled to stock a brand, the chain will see no need to give it high visibility either through store promotion or position on the shelves.

Reward power

Reward power is the ability to withhold or to bestow some material reward on the other party in the relationship. A manufacturer can offer all sorts of rewards to channel intermediaries such as price discounts, inventory and layout advice, salespeople as demonstrators, etc. On the other hand, the retailer's major reward is shelf-space and customers who are store loyal. Reward power is flexible, understandable and consistent with business norms.

The adoption of an adversarial relationship suggests the perception of *a zero-sum game* where one of the parties can only gain at the expense of the other. In general, it is better for both parties to view the relationship as potentially a *variable-sum game* so as to focus on exchanges that are mutually beneficial. What is needed here is information on the retailer as the immediate customer and an understanding of the retailer's operations including current methods of space management, inventory control and calculations of the profit on the different brands. This is more feasible and more needed in dealing with supermarket chains as, with fewer but much larger scale buying centers, fewer but better salespeople are required: salespeople who are more knowledgeable in supermarket operations and skilled in negotiations.

Reward power is the major means of influencing the retailer by making it worthwhile to cooperate. One way is through constant innovation to update the product line so the firm's brands continue to have that fresh new look to convey an element of novelty. Another way is to bring out variations of a brand for different retailers so what is being sold is exclusive to them. There is also cooperative advertising, where the retailer advertises the manufacturer's brands and the manufacturer pays. This can be cost effective in that the news media costs less for the retailer than for the national advertiser while the retailer is making a public endorsement of the manufacturer's brands.

There is a movement toward establishing cooperative relationships with distributors because of the recognition that there is much that can be done that will benefit both parties. For example, department stores may find it to their advantage to allocate specific areas of the store for, say, distinct brands of clothing (e.g. Ralph Lauren's) on the ground that the boutique enhances the store image while at the same time giving the brand increased visibility. Allocating space in this way is something distinct from leasing a department, like a perfume counter, where the manufacturer rents the counter space, runs it and pays for all outgoings. Another example of cooperation is P&G's special teams to help its big customers like Wal–Mart to improve inventory control, promotion and distribution. P&G receives, in return via satellite, daily data on Wal–Mart actual sales and forecasts and, on this basis, sends replacement sales on a "just-in-time" system to cut down Wal-Mart inventories. A just-in-time system like this saves retailers a great deal of money. P&G has teams drawn from finance, marketing, distribution, manufacturing and other functions just to cover the big retailers. Another example of using reward power is the installation by P&G of Visions, a state-of-the-art checkout system in Dahl's supermarket in Iowa. The customer at the checkout inserts a card that calls up her account. As the customer's purchases are scanned, a color monitor on the counter may announce a discount. Visions automatically tallies points for the buying of certain products. With enough points the customer gets a prize. This attracts customers to Dahl while providing P&G with marketing information. As in industrial buying, the major chain retailers in both Europe and the United States are seeking cooperative alliances with a select few suppliers.

Legitimized power

The perceptions by retailers and manufacturers of the policies and actions of the other are influenced by whether these policies and actions are considered *legitimate* or not. Retailers and manufacturers comply with what is considered legitimate because they feel a duty to comply with the law, past agreements or norms established by precedent as to each other's role. Thus manufacturers will regard private label brands that are copies of national brands as not legitimate even if within the law. It is this sense of illegitimacy that so sours relationships over private label brands. But what might be considered legitimate based on precedent can come into conflict with new conceptions of what is fair: legitimacy must be grounded in current industry norms, practices and shared meanings that always govern the exercise of legitimate power. The extent of legitimate power depends on the extent it conforms with established rules whether legal or otherwise; whether the legitimacy is justified by beliefs shared by both retailers and manufacturers and there is evidence of consent as to what the legitimate rules imply.

Credibility and attractiveness power

A source of high credibility convinces (the message is internalized), while a source of high attractiveness persuades (the subject identifies with the communication source and so wants to comply). A manufacturer's requests, depending on how they are put forward, can on occasions have high credibility (for example, by showing how cooperative advertising pays) and attractiveness (for example, a personal flattering visit from the marketing director).

A reliance on coercive power alienates the party coerced while a reliance on reward power simply rents allegiance for as long as the material rewards are being given. While many marketers believe that "renting the allegiance" of the retailer is all that a manufacturer can expect to do, there are others who recognize the importance of the attractiveness and credibility of the supplier in building up a relationship of liking and trust so leading to goodwill and, within limits, to loyalty. Thus there has been the growth of *opposite number selling*, whereby teams from the different functional areas of the manufacturing company meet their opposite number in the retail organization to discuss how the seller can help the retailer toward greater profitability and convenience in buying. Trust is easily broken whenever some action, that adversely affects the other is taken unilaterally. Thus steep price reductions, not accompanied by the granting of credit for stock on hand, are likely to be regarded as a violation of trust.

Good service helps build up the manufacturer's image of being an attractive and credible supplier. Although multiple sourcing in industrial buying is still considered important, lists of approved suppliers are tending to be narrowed. The major retailers and industrial firms in both Europe and the United States are seeking cooperative alliances with a select few suppliers. Thus, Hughes Aircraft, a subsidiary of General Motors, reduced its list of suppliers from twenty-two to just seven. This was accompanied by a demand for much better service including just-in-time delivery and the acceptance of performance evaluation reports being sent to the supplier.

The key to knowing which power base to use lies in knowing how *critical* to the other party is (that is, how dependent is the other party on) the coercion, the reward, the legitimized obligation or the attractiveness and credibility effects. A manufacturer closing a retailer's account may not be critical to the retailer when other manufacturers continue to offer a similar product. On the other hand, the threat to withdraw supplies could be perceived as critical to survival. Compliance with legitimized power depends on the particular principle of legitimacy involved (for example, whether law, custom, industry practice, etc.). Compliance with contractual agreements, for example, might be perceived as critical to the reputation of the organization, while compliance to a suggested price list might not be regarded as critical at all. Power based on credibility depends on the extent to which those exercising such power can turn their expertise to showing their proposals are advantageous to all. Power based on attractiveness depends on the extent to which compliance enhances personal satisfaction without detracting from other goals.

As yet, there is no generally accepted theory of how power operates in marketing channels. However, we do know a good deal about the likely consequences of focusing exclusively on coercion, reward power, legitimized power or manipulative power. In general, coercion achieves only minimal compliance. Procter and Gamble can force retailers to stock its Tide, Crest, Pampers, and Crisco oil and "pull" customers into the store, but a retailer forced to stock some product will not push it. Effecting only minimal compliance becomes insufficient when the firm seeks a "push" strategy. With a push strategy there is a need to keep distributors happy.

Reward power gets results in the line with the magnitude of the reward, but results can slump when the reward is withdrawn. In 1981, Pan Am (no longer in business) suspended commission overrides for surpassing quota and withdrew such bonuses as free travel for those who arrange convention business. The business dropped off by 40 percent. A push strategy requires considerable and continuous use of material rewards at a level geared to the degree of distributor push and the volume of business that is sought. Legitimized power is exercised to achieve compliance with rules and agreements. As with coercive power, there is apt to be no higher performance beyond that formally needed to signify compliance.

The use of credibility and attractiveness is the essence of salesmanship. Where suppliers are otherwise equal in what they have to offer, the credibility and attractiveness of salespeople can swing the sale. It may be that reward power is generally the most important source of power but it is also true that few manufacturers have thought out a comprehensive approach for seeking reseller support that contains a strategy for enhancing the firm's attractiveness and credibility.

Of course, manufacturers are not likely to use just one source of power but several in combination. Sellers, however, will wish to avoid any suggestions of coercion. In general, the focus will be on reward power with attractiveness and credibility being used in the management of conflict. The greater the amount of supportive interaction between seller and dealer through, say, dealer councils, joint seminars, liaison personnel, the more the likelihood of enhancing each other's goals. The fact is that cooperation between retailer and manufacturer is most likely when neither feels more powerful than the other: power equalization makes people more inclined to settle differences in an amicable manner.

One final note on power. In the above discussion, power is treated as the basis of influence and influence as the actual exercise of power. A view that is emerging is to treat influence and power as alternative processes: the exercise of power being equated with the demand for compliance through the use of coercion and reward while influence is equated with trying to get subjective acceptance through the change agent's appeal to legitimacy, attractiveness and credibility. This is still very much a minority view but the distinction makes a good deal of sense for it seems to capture more the layperson's view while seeming to offer more scope for development of the power concept.

INTERNATIONAL ASPECTS

International retailers

As home markets mature, firms turn to international expansion. Retail chains are no exception in seeking cross-border expansion though with uneven success. Makro, a Dutch wholesaler, is pioneering discount bulk buying in South-East Asia. Yet UK's Marks & Spencer failed in Canada and France's Printemps failed in Japan. The major error made by retailers crossing borders is in believing that there are few differences between the home market and that across the border, whereas, with different cultures and climates, customer demands can vary widely. Luxury goods retailers, often tied to one manufacturer, seemed to have fared best with firms like Gucci, Ferragamo, Burberry's, Hermes, Escada, Louis Vuitton, Tiffany's, Cartier, and Zara having retail establishments in many different cities of the world. Zara even quotes its prices in Spanish, Portuguese, Mexican, Greek, French, and US currencies. The challenge lies in knowing what regions go together in that, even in Switzerland, there are acknowledged to be at least three separate cultures. On the other hand, Germany's Aldi, a discount grocer, has more than 500 stores outside Germany; Carrefour and Marks & Spencer are developing in Spain and Portugal while Italy with its plethora of independent, family-run stores seems ripe for entry by the big chains of Germany and the UK.

One way of expanding is by acquisition. UK's Tesco in December 1992 bought Catteau, a 92-store French supermarket chain and early in 1993, Kingfisher of the UK bought

Darty, which is France's largest electrical retailer. Migros of Switzerland, the most successful cooperative society in Europe, is currently building supermarkets in France and Germany. It manufactures about a third of what it sells in its own factories.

A development to watch is the growth of *buying consortia* composed of several retail chains for buying in bulk. One such consortium was the European Retail Alliance, composed of Ahold, the Dutch food retailer, Argyll, which operates the Safeway supermarket chain in the UK and Casino, a French hypermarket chain. It has now expanded to become the core of Associated Marketing Services which includes an additional six grocery chains. The nine chains between them include 11,000 stores with combined sales of $43 billion. What is worrying here for manufacturers of branded supermarket products is not the bulk buying but the plan to develop own-brand goods and to share the advertising of these brands while at the same time keeping costs even more low by sharing distribution networks and technology.

Price-Costco Inc. has expanded from the United States into the UK in spite of intense opposition from the major supermarket chains Sainsbury, Tesco, and Safeway, whose litigation held up Costco's opening for six months. But it was worth it to Costco since the resulting publicity about its low prices established its position without further promotion! The US home shopping channel of QVC now operates in Europe, Mexico, Spain, Portugal, and Latin America.

Seeking distribution abroad

Root views the selecting of a foreign distributor as involving four stages.[12] The first step is to draw up a profile of the distributor being sought. The second stage is to locate distributor prospects on the basis of the profile. The third step is to evaluate each of the prospects with the fourth step being concerned with actually choosing the distributor. Root suggests interviewing prospects to establish their interest in being distributors for the company and insisting on a written contract covering

- exclusive rights,
- competitive lines being handled, and
- termination and cancellation of the contract.

But contracts must be in line with the law as many countries have laws making it very costly to terminate agreements with distributors (and agents). If licensing is adopted then the contract should cover

- royalties,
- performance demands (including use conditions),
- territorial rights,
- technology transfer conditions, and
- settlement of disputes.

Franchising, too, may be considered as it allows rapid expansion into foreign markets with low investment. Franchisers enter foreign markets in several ways including franchising directly to individuals, operating company-owned units, joint ventures or selling a master franchise. It is not uncommon to find government restrictions on franchising while the lack of control over the franchisee and the possibility of the franchisee abandoning the franchise once having learned the business are dangers inherent in franchising abroad.

Distribution systems can vary widely throughout the world. Japan can be used to illustrate the difficulties. Japan is commonly regarded as having an inefficient distribution system. Thus it has 13 retailers for every 1,000 inhabitants. This contrasts with 6 per 1,000 in the United States and Europe. Many of these outlets are committed to just one supplier. Thus the cosmetic firm of Shiseido has around 25,000 outlets that sell no rival firm's cosmetics while Matsushita similarly has around 19,000 outlets that almost exclusively sell its brands. One reason for so many retailers was the Daitenho or Large Store Retail Law which was designed to protect the small retailer from competition from big firms. Big retailers must apply to the government for permission to build any store more than 5,382 square feet. However since 1990, with the reform of the law, it has become harder for small shops to prevent the opening of big stores.

Many foreign firms have resorted to some partnership with Japanese firms to distribute their goods. There is the assumption, often well grounded, that selling through too many different distributors can mean none is sufficiently committed. Thus Allied–Lyons, the UK drinks and food conglomerate, has an arrangement with the Japanese firm of Suntory, the country's largest distiller of whisky, whereby Suntory will sell its Scotch. What frequently happens in a case like this is that the foreign partner ensures that the product it has agreed to distribute never reaches adulthood so as to become a real rival. Allied–Lyons, aware of this danger, has tried to win more cooperation by distributing Suntory's drinks outside Japan and taken a share in Suntory's business. Foreign companies dealing with Japanese industrial buyers will need to have inventory at hand to service on a just-in-time basis. The adoption of domestication (more or less all of employees of the firm in Japan to be Japanese) plus some Japanese identification in the company title (e.g. IBM-Japan) seem almost obligatory and are likely to be important elsewhere.

PHYSICAL DISTRIBUTION

Logistics management seeks to minimize the total cost from reception of raw materials to the delivery of the finished product to the customer. It embraces both physical distribution (order processing, transportation from producer to purchaser, production control, materials handling and customer service) and materials management. Where the claims for logistics management predominate, *physical distribution* will be separate from marketing on the ground that to study a narrower system leads to sectional efficiency at the expense of the total system of distribution. The opposing view claims that the difficulty and cost of dealing with a total system, as embraced by logistics management, inevitably makes for the acceptance of something less than ideal, whereas placing physical distribution under marketing facilitates coordination of all those activities that have an impact on the customer.

The study of physical distribution has become a fertile field for management science in the use of simulation, linear programming and heuristic model-building to minimize costs of distribution. In general, the sources of cost saving arise from:

- *reduction in inventories*: consolidating inventories at fewer locations; centralizing slow-moving items; shortening the replacement time for stock in field warehouses;
- *more efficient methods*: improved materials handling; better warehouse layout; simplification of order processing and redesigned packaging to permit greater efficiency in warehousing; and
- *more efficient service*: minimizing out-of-stock occurrences; reducing the customer's own inventory requirements; integrating the supplier's delivery facilities with the customer's receiving facilities; enabling expanded market coverage by reduced freight costs.

In recent years there has been a growth in automatic order assembly and one-storey warehousing for ease in handling. This has led some writers to make a sharp distinction between a warehouse and a *distribution center*, with a distribution center being specifically designed to reduce and speed the flow of goods. In industrial purchasing in particular, an efficient physical distribution system can be the key criterion in selecting a supplier when the product being bought is standard with standard applications. Indeed the core competence of some firms lies in the service provided by their physical distribution system. The segments they serve are those whose "want" is distinguished by the relative importance they attach to the service component emanating from the supplier's systems of:

- production planning and control,
- warehousing,
- transportation,
- materials handling,
- inventory control,
- order processing,
- packing,
- accounting, and
- technical and other customer services.

The marketing approach to physical distribution consists of two stages:

First, *identifying the level of service demanded by the customer and that given by immediate rivals catering to the same segment*. Once a level of service is laid down, the aim would be to minimize the cost of delivering the service to the customer. Unfortunately, service standards cannot be decided regardless of likely costs (even if minimized). There is a need (for example, via conjoint analysis) to understand the customer's trade-offs. For example, the customer might be consulted about the relative importance of delivery time, errors in invoicing, and out-of-stock positions.

Second, *designing several physical distribution "service packages" and interrogating the customer as to likely purchases for each particular service package*. Given estimates of costs and sales for each package, management is in a position to select one for market testing. What all this means is that the level of service adopted must be based on cost considerations and on likely customer sales response to different service packages. Such likely response is tied to what competitors are doing.

ETHICAL ISSUES

There are a number of ethical issues raised in distribution. In direct marketing, many query the collecting of detailed information on consumers as an invasion of privacy while the sale of such information to all and every organization willing to buy it is considered ethically dubious. Customer retail practices are also criticized such as the demand for slotting allowances which are regarded as a sort of ransom, discouraging small manufacturers from innovation and new product introductions.

CONCLUSION

Because building up a system of distribution is always difficult and tends to bind the firm long term, there is a tendency to neglect the dynamic aspects of reformulating a distribution strategy. One writer speaks of the constant need to re-shape channels as a market matures or changes by:[13]

- filling in holes, for example, use of mail order;
- revitalizing a distribution network by offering financial help, cooperative advertising, and sales support;
- developing a multi-channel system as a result of recognizing that existing outlets do not command the exclusive patronage of the target segment;
- dropping channels and adopting new ones: channels suited to a product early in its life cycle may become inappropriate at the maturity phase; and
- creating a new channel as with magazines sold in supermarkets and Scholl shoes in pharmaceutical outlets.

It is because channel changes affect relationships with members of the existing channel network that channel management is such a delicate and potentially explosive operation. A successful pull strategy with the consumer might tempt the manufacturer to dismiss the reseller but resellers may retaliate by withdrawing trade support from companies whose behavior suggests that they regard resellers as no more than a necessary evil.

Reward power is likely to remain key: competition for shelf space is as keen as competition for the consumer. Bali, for example, offers sales assistants incentives, including trips abroad. Additionally, the retailer's margin is one of the highest in the industry, and in-store promotions and cooperative advertising are developed round the new styles and store image. Similarly, Konica gives retailers camera accessories to encourage them to stock more than just their cameras, while the L'Eggs brand of hosiery established its distribution network by not requiring any financial investment by the retailer.

NOTES

1 Alderson, Wroe and Halbert, Michael H. (1968) *Men, Motives and Markets*, Englewood Cliffs, NJ: Prentice Hall, p. 17.
2 Holbrook, Morris B. and Howard John A. (1977) "Frequently Purchased Nondurable Goods and Services," in Robert Ferber (ed.) *Selected Aspects of Consumer Behavior*, Washington DC: National Science Foundation.
3 Murphy, Patrick E. and Enis, Ben M. (1986) "Classifying Products Strategically," *Journal of Marketing*, 50 (July).
4 Anderson, E. (1985) "The Salesperson as Outside Agent or Employee: A Transaction Cost Analysis," *Marketing Science*, 4(3) (Summer).
5 McNair, Malcolm (1958) "Significant Trends and Developments in the Postwar Period," in A. B. Smith (ed.) *Competitive Distribution in a Free, High Level Economy and its Implications for the University*, Pittsburg: University of Pittsburg Press.
6 Hollander, Stanley C. (1960) "The Wheel of Retailing," *Journal of Marketing*, 25 (July).
7 Hollander, Stanley C. (1966) "Notes on the Retail Accordion," *Journal of Retailing* (Summer).
8 Guiltinan, Joseph P. (1974) "Planned and Evolutionary Changes in Distribution Channels," *Journal of Retailing*, 50(2) (Summer).
9 Stern, L. W. and El-Ansary, A. L. (1977) *Marketing Channels*, Englewood Cliffs, NJ: Prentice Hall.
10 Little, Robert W. (1970) "The Marketing Channel: Who Should Lead this Extracorporate Organization?" *Journal of Marketing*, 49(2) (January).
11 French, J. R. P. and Raven, B. (1959) "The Bases of Social Power," in D. Cartwright (ed.) *Studies in Social Power*, Ann Arbor, Mich: University of Michigan, Institute for Social Research, p. 324.
12 Root, Franklin R. (1987) *Entry Strategies for International Markets*, Lexington, MA: Lexington Books.
13 McDonald, A. L. (1964) "Do Your Distribution Channels Need Reshaping?," *Business Horizons*, (Summer).

Part V

Implementation and organization

Chapter 16

Strategies for change

Formulating a strategy is one thing but getting it agreed and implemented is another. This is why formulating strategy and thinking about likely problems in its implementation go hand-in-hand.[1] However, before a marketing strategy can be implemented it must receive the approval of top management and, before this can happen, it must get onto the agenda of top management. This chapter considers the three areas of

1 getting the proposed strategy onto the agenda of top management for review;
2 generating support for the proposed changes; and
3 actually implementing the strategy.

STRATEGIC AGENDA-BUILDING

The academic study of group decision-making focuses on how decisions are made and the power plays of participants. But equally as important is the *nondecision* (inaction) that arises when proposals for a change in strategy never reach the agenda of top management for discussion. Marketing directors are not chief executives. They are not in overall control but operate under constraints like resource allocations or they cannot change technological investments that reduce flexibility or organizational subcultures that may be in conflict with whatever is proposed. Hence, how does a need for a change in strategy come to command a position on the agenda of top management? The traditional answer is that top management comes to recognize a performance gap between expectations and current performance. But while a gap usually initiates discussion, it does not necessarily invite action to reassess strategy.

In a sense, all current strategies fall short of what the situation demands, owing to the lag in planning. But the greater the disparity between the firm's current marketing strategies and the ideal, the greater the danger of competitive inroads into the market becoming irreversible. Such can occur, accompanied by strategic inertia on the part of the company losing market share, because the basic questions raised by poor performance:

- how has the situation come about?
- what does the situation suggest in terms of threats or opportunities? and
- what actions must be taken to meet the demands of the situation?

are questions that different groups answer differently. A performance gap is simply an undesirable condition. Whether management regards that condition as an actionable problem depends on how top management defines the problem. Management may define the problem in a way that the burden of solving it falls on someone else. Thus the problem of a loss of market share may be attributed to unfair competition from foreign imports with the government being asked to take action. Sometimes there is the belief that the problem will simply go away with the passage of time. For example, in the 1970s, the sales of Swiss watches declined dramatically, but the Swiss interpreted the advent of quartz slivers and electronic digital movements as "specialties" offering no long-term threat. How managers categorize a problem structures their perceptions of the problem and guides their thinking on what should be done about it.

Surface similarities with events in the past lead management into false historical analogies. As a result they react to the past rather than to the situation facing them. Also managers hold images, models, or systems of beliefs about their markets, that can be erroneous in terms of causes and effects and this can rule out in advance certain courses of action. Thus a top management, if wedded to the belief that the firm's product is "the best" in the market, and believing passionately that falling market share is caused by sales force incompetence, will change the sales management before making changes to the product. Managers commonly ignore evidence that fails to fit preconceptions and interpret "facts" in a way that is consistent with predispositions. In moments of crisis and time pressure, people are apt to fall back on unspoken assumptions and old beliefs that offer reassurance. Past success with a strategy gives rise to the belief that all the situation demands is a more intensive application of the strategy. The Roman legions lost to the "cavalry" of invading barbarians but the significance of the cavalry remained unrecognized with simply more intense attention being given to improving existing strategies and tactics. In the nineteenth century, in spite of the fact that guns had made cavalry largely obsolescent, many armies focused on improving the cavalry instead of changing to artillery. The self-aggrandizement of a corporate culture reinforces similar errors. Companies are reluctant to acknowledge that they are no longer capable of competing with the giants in the high-volume segments of a market and need to find some "niche" more suited to their resources and thrust. One interesting historical example is the American Motors Corporation (AMC). Only slowly and too late did AMC come to recognize that it could no longer compete "head-on" with General Motors, Ford, and Chrysler. While Romney, on taking over AMC in 1954, realized that competing with the "big three" was the road to disaster, others at AMC believed the "big car" strategy was the only sensible way to proceed and opposed any idea of catering to an "alleged" compact segment of the car market. Strong culturally shared values and beliefs can impede or facilitate change as they act as a framework for all decision-making. When proposals support core values (e.g. in respect to remaining independent) they are likely to win support and proposals that violate core values are likely to be denied support. Corporate cultures, while influenced by societal values and those prevailing in the industry, are influenced most of all by the founder and other dominant company leaders.

Those advocating a change in strategy have many battles to win

1 getting their change position recognized as a legitimate topic for discussion;
2 getting agreement on a new strategy and the requisite funds allocated; and
3 winning commitment on implementation.

Defenders of the current position need only succeed in preventing the suggested change from coming up on the agenda, for example, by dismissing it for "more relevant issues," or by arguing it would be too disruptive, or simply by making the suggested change sound unintelligible or absurd. This does occur. Self-imposed constraints and biases often rule out innovative, new strategies. This is not surprising as the status quo has a certain legitimacy while it is supported by all sorts of vested interests.

Companies usually have regular scheduled meetings to discuss market performance.

If performance is below expectations within a reasonable period, the rule should be to include on the agenda "Evaluation of current market strategies." This is not to imply that radically new strategies are necessarily demanded, but that suggestions for changes should be sought. In this way, the meetings become a legitimate arena for the airing of views about change and managers are provoked into reflecting on possible improvements.

Another suggestion is institutionalizing the role of *devil's advocate* so those questioning basic assumptions can let it be known that they are assuming this role to allow them to disagree without being perceived as disagreeable. They should be encouraged to dramatize the possibilities and consequences of inaction. However, if encouraging discussion is to be anything more than lip service to notions of democracy, openness of discussion must command the support of top management. It should be accepted that military historians can criticize generals and lower levels can criticize strategies without the implication that the critic could have done better or that the generals and top management are incompetent.[2]

Although the need for change must be recognized, the rate of change should not be elevated into a policy. At present, some pragmatists have elevated a "piecemeal" approach to change into a sort of cult though major crises can demand radical change. There are also those who advocate "permanent revolution" or constant change so change becomes a way of life. But constant change can be highly destructive since it undermines the understandings that are needed for coordination. With constant change there are no rules of the game, no stability in relationships and a lack of shared rules to allow people to predict the actions and reactions of others.

STRATEGY CONSENSUS-BUILDING

Assessing likely opposition

Consensus-building involves getting commitment to the proposed changes. Getting commitment is basic to cooperation and cooperation is needed if changes are to be successfully implemented. The fact that top management supports change does not ensure the cooperation of all those involved in implementation. They can drag their feet or even sabotage the program. It is not enough for the problem to be recognized and a workable solution be available as an organization needs a motivational climate that is supportive of whatever has to be done. If *politics* means articulating and aggregating interests to resolve actual or potential conflicts so as to create some coalition of support, then politics is inevitable in strategy and strategy implementation. It is useful to look at the firm as a political arena comprised of different groups with differential self-interests, with each group using whatever power it possesses to pursue its own goals at the expense of others. Hence designing a potentially effective innovative strategy is not enough. It is necessary to carry other groups along if they have the right to veto proposals or their support is needed for successful implementation. Unlike medieval monarchies, even the most totalitarian regimes today go to extreme lengths to win public support: otherwise, at every stage in execution, orders can be diluted (*authority leakage*).

Calculating the probability of acceptance

Every step to successful implementation should be listed or at least each step that is a *clearance step*, or a hurdle to be surmounted. Any clearance step that involves veto authority or concurring authority is a *decision point*. Assuming each decision point is independent of the others, and there are four decision points with the following probabilities of getting agreement at each decision point:

	Decision point 1	Decision point 2	Decision point 3	Decision point 4
Probability:	0.80	0.75	0.85	0.80

then the overall probability of getting acceptance is

$$0.80 \times 0.75 \times 0.85 \times 0.80 = 0.41$$

Hence the probability of getting overall agreement is 41 percent. Fortunately, not all decision points will be independent of each other. Often the support of just two key decision-makers may ensure approval at other decision points. Nonetheless, the above example illustrates the difficulties of making substantial changes if too many people have the right of veto and there is insistence on unanimity of support.

Assessing the basis of opposition

At each decision point we need to assess the basis of likely opposition (see Figure 16.1), since knowing the reason for opposition is a guide to its likely intensity and what might be done to mute it.

Agree with merits but still reject.   As Figure 16.1 indicates, there can be opposition to a strategy even when the merits of the strategy are fully understood and appreciated. In fact, opposition may be defensible. The strategy may be incompatible with projects already adopted or other strategies are considered to have more merit. Others may be in opposition because they believe existing commitments leave them no time for fulfilling the role visualized for them if the strategy were adopted.

Disagree with merits and reject.   The second category in Figure 16.1 comprises those who reject the merits of the proposed strategy. They question its effectiveness for achieving objectives or likely achievement in relation to cost. There can be genuine differences of opinion given the evidence. In respect to effectiveness, it may even be claimed that the proposals will make things worse or will fail altogether because they run up against overwhelming contrary forces such as those operating at the life cycle stage. On the question of efficiency, it may be argued that the cost of the proposed change is too high, not because of the money expenditure involved, but because it endangers present achievements such as its threat of cannibalism. What must be recognized

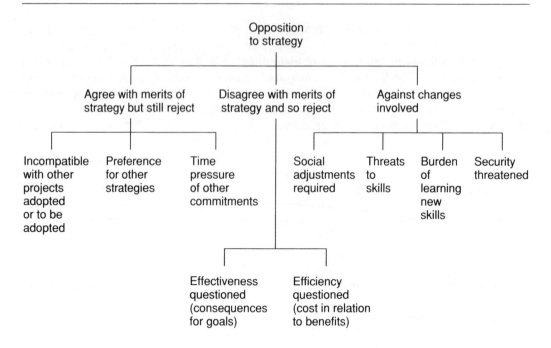

Figure 16.1 Reasons for opposition to proposed strategy

is that "proof beyond reasonable doubt" (to satisfy a criminal court of law) is not a feasible goal in amassing evidence to justify the adoption of a strategy. The "balance of evidence" (as in a civil legal case) is the best that can be sought. As the philosopher A. J. Ayer once said: "It is in demanding impossible standards of perfection that the skeptic feels secure."

Against change involved.   The third category in Figure 16.1 comprises those reasons most mentioned in the literature on resistance to change. Proposals are seldom evaluated purely on their merits for promoting corporate goals. The first reaction of managers and other employees to a suggested change is to think about how it will affect them personally. Unless the change is perceived as making them better off than before, they may believe, rightly or wrongly, that they will be worse off. The change may suggest that old work groups will be broken up and new relationships have to be formed. Alternatively, old skills may be made obsolete and new skills have to be acquired, with the threat to the ego of not being able to cope. But worst of all, there is perhaps a danger to job security and the possibility of redundancy. The perceptions of those affected by a possible change are always important. Most managers acknowledge this but, with so much to do, it is easy to postpone any consideration of others until active opposition arises. With a little empathy it is often not too difficult to anticipate the perceptions and attitudes of others toward the change and to take appropriate action.

Those who oppose change will, as an emotional persuasive ploy, tend to stress the "harm" to the organization that could result from change; focusing perhaps on the inherent dangers of what is proposed but dangers that objectively are unlikely to manifest themselves. On the other hand, those advocating change tend to be excessively confident that everything proposed is simply a recipe for success; is coherent and supportive of the organization's true goals as well as of the best aspects of the organization.

There are, needless to say, dangers of both action and inaction. The risks of both need to be identified and assessed and thought given to whether negative consequences can be guarded against before a final decision is made. The fact is, of course, that the full set of negative and positive consequences of any proposed action or inaction can never be known with certainty but this should not rule out judgment as to probabilities. What must be stressed from the top is that all are expected to engage in meaningful discussion in the sense that each person should be ready to modify and change initially held opinions in the light of new information or arguments that arise during the debate.

Gaining acceptance of change

Generating support

When the same strategy is pursued over many years, there will be a coalition of support for it. Sometimes the leaders of such coalitions come to question the strategy and this may lead the coalition itself to adopt suggested changes. But frequently change is less than unanimously endorsed and, for the reasons already given, there are likely to be some who are opposed. In such circumstances, coalitions supportive of the current position may have to be weakened and another coalition developed that is supportive of change.

Active support for any strategy is generated by:

- education,
- incentives,
- participation, and
- indoctrination.

Education is used to clear up misunderstandings about job security and other false but perceived threats to interests. Similarly, education is used to convince others of the superiority of what is proposed over alternative options.

Incentives are used to compensate for losses and encourage commitment. Opposition to suggested change is usually conditional: compromises can be reached, accommodations made, bargains struck and resistance weakened, providing sufficient incentive is offered. *Participation* in decision-making by all those involved in the implementation of the strategy might be considered under the category of incentives but its distinctive nature justifies giving it separate treatment. Active support for a change in strategy is generated by letting those who are affected by the change have a say in what happens. Although there is no guarantee that participation (with its promise of enhancing individual self-esteem, sense of accomplishment, and the satisfaction stemming from group cohesiveness) will lead to commitment to change, it does help, particularly where resistance is more emotional than rational. Participation is likely to highlight the implications of the strategy for other areas (for example, the compensation system) and the corresponding need for coordination and adjustments. However, participation cannot be equated with either achieving unanimous endorsement of whatever is proposed or counting heads to determine what the majority wants. Although management may be obliged to make compromises, they retain the right of veto on proposals and will control the time spent in discussion. Finally, *indoctrination* of values is needed to stimulate commitment and active support. This does not mean that the strategy being proposed must become everyone's preference. All that is required is sufficient agreement to proceed in a coordinated way.

The setting up of a committee to consider proposals legitimizes the open discussion of strategies and their shortcomings and creates a recognized arena for working out bargains and compromises. Additionally, the composition of the committee can bring together relevant expertise and key decision-makers at each level in the hierarchy. A proposed strategy must receive support at each level affected by it. There is no simple, mechanical way of gaining such support. Much depends on the credibility of the proposals themselves and on the way it is intended to deal with the fears and anxieties of those who see a loss for themselves. The perceived credibility of proposals relates not just to their intrinsic merit but whether they cohere with the way others view the problem; the perceptions others have of the author; the seeming thoroughness with which the study has been carried out; and whether the study solves their own particular headaches. Major changes are bound to upset someone, so there is no question of trying to please everyone. However, each aspect of a strategy should be questioned and weighed against the evidence of likely damaging effects on motivation and morale. Management should try to anticipate losses of power, money, prestige, social contacts and convenience both to gauge the strength of likely opposition and for developing compensation packages.

Resolution of conflict

Conflict is endemic when major changes are suggested as people compete over scarce resources, scarce positions, or symbols of power. Figure 16.2 shows the various methods used to resolve conflict within an organization and the primary source of influence lying behind each method.

Jural method.   Here, higher management intervene and adjudicate. The power underlying the jural method is the possibility of coercion if higher management's decision is ignored.

Any conflict has a number of dimensions:

- *scope*, i.e. the number of people involved;
- *intensity*, i.e. the degree to which preferences are held; and

Method of conflict resolution

Source of influence used		Jural	Bargaining/ negotiation	Analytic
	Force	✖		
	Material reward		✖	
	Attractiveness and credibility			✖

✖ = major relationships

Figure 16.2 Methods of conflict resolution and major underlying influences

- *visibility*, i.e. the extent to which the conflict is known to others.

The wider the scope, intensity and visibility of the conflict, the more higher management is likely to get involved. There are also occasions when management direction is required. But coercive power is counter-productive unless its use is perceived as suited to the situation and not employed to humiliate or stress differences in rank. The jural method of resolving conflict carries a high probability of achieving *minimal* compliance as private commitment is unlikely to be forthcoming.

Bargaining/negotiation. In bargaining, an attempt is made to build up a coalition of support through mutual exchanges of concessions. However, with each bargain struck, more constraints are introduced on freedom of action and this can seriously dilute the original strategy. Hence there should only be enough bargaining to form a winning coalition. A coalition of support based on extensive bargaining among many groups, is unlikely to command enthusiasm from anyone.

Analytic mode. The analytic mode of resolving conflict is essentially a problem-solving approach. Where "making changes" becomes part of the organization's way of life, ways of dealing with conflict develop. These ways, governed by rules, become institutionalized and routinized to avoid heated argument and debate. The more changes instituted over a period of time, the more an analytic mode becomes the dominant method of settling conflict. An analytic mode of settling differences is facilitated when proposals themselves can be shown to cohere with company culture and values, are shown to be technically feasible, and are tailored to anticipated resource constraints.

Destructive conflict is less common in business than Hollywood would have us believe. When it does occur it is most likely to be the result of people being given incompatible responsibilities. In practice, overlapping and multiple group membership in an organization can dampen the intensity of any group conflict, while organizational norms are likely to reinforce the desire not to engage in overt in-fighting.

STRATEGY IMPLEMENTATION

As we have seen, a proposed strategy may never reach the stage of implementation unless we seek to

- minimize the number of clearance steps and decision points; and
- develop a satisfactory mode of resolving conflict.

But once a strategy has been chosen and approved, the implementation becomes analogous to a scientific hypothesis that is put out for testing:

> *Assuming strategy ABC is implemented, we predict the result will be an increase in market share of X percent, providing no major unforeseen events or upsetting influences occur to affect the strategy once implemented.*

An implementation is successful if it achieves the predicted consequences, within acceptable limits, with no major side effects occurring to diminish the achievement. But the unexpected does occur so there is a need for flexibility or, if alternative futures can be set out, contingency plans should be drawn up. A strategy may appear to fail when it is the implementation or execution that is at fault. In fact, it is not easy to attribute failure as arising from deficiencies in the strategy when there is the alternative hypothesis of poor strategy execution. The strategy, as a paper document, is a thin conceptual creation. The implementation and execution of a strategy involves fleshing out this conceptual creation into detailed systems, programs, action steps and actions that constitute the strategy in being. A strategy on paper is like a story or a script for a movie. However good the original script, the skills of the actors, producers, and directors, etc. are essential to success. We are all aware of how different movies of the same book can vary from outstanding success to dismal failure. Similarly, just as a substandard plot (*Casablanca*?) can be a successful movie through brilliant execution, so a suboptimal strategy may be successful through skillful execution. There is truth in the observation that, though a strategy is understood through conceptual schema, it is always lived in the details. The details count. For example, in one case a firm's strategic success was very tied to selling its mail order dresses in the color preferences shown to hold in tests around the country. This did not occur, not because the color preferences were different from those forecast, but because the mail order catalogue showed the dresses in black and white, simply listing the colors available. In another case, a belief among the sales force that the sales of a new product would be much less than the strategy forecast became a self-fulfilling prophecy as the sales force unenthusiastically "pushed" the product.

Paths to strategy implementation

How the strategy is implemented—the enthusiasm, the dragging of feet, the conflicts, the delays and distortions—that can attend the implementation, can ruin or reshape the

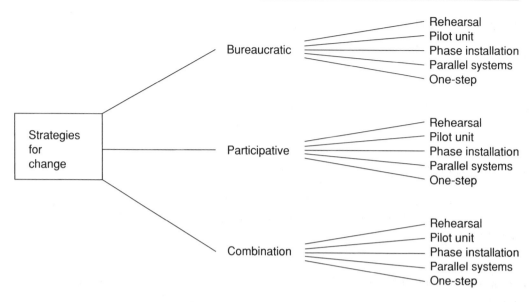

Figure 16.3 Strategic and tactical methods of implementation

strategy's intended effects. There are three strategic approaches (see Figure 16.3) to implementation, based on the degree to which participation is adopted:

1 a central planning or bureaucratic approach;
2 a participative approach; and
3 a combination of central planning and participation.

Bureaucratic approach

In the central planning or bureaucratic approach, experts conceive and formulate strategy
and management approve and authorize implementation. The experts are assumed to
have all the expertise, and gaining support is of secondary concern. This approach is
often adopted and justified in a crisis when speed is required.

Participative approach

In the participative approach, the aim is to generate a broad commitment to implementation. All those affected by the strategy and involved in its implementation are
given the opportunity to help shape its final form. The technical aspects of strategy may
not be important, while enthusiastic support might be vital to success. Thus a strategy
of market penetration, which often requires high sales force commitment, may be left
to those lower down the line to implement. While consultation should be carried out as

far as it will go, full participation with all its discussion groups, is perhaps most effective when neither the quality of the decision nor the speed of the decision is absolutely paramount but broad-based support for the proposals is a necessity.

Combination approach

The third approach combines elements of the other two approaches. Experts are used to study the situation and draw up a recommended strategy but there is participation and discussion of proposals at every level. Under the combination approach, plans move up and down the various levels with committees and liaison managers acting as coordinators. All those affected by the strategy have an opportunity to participate, so the final implementation strategy will emerge much more as a joint effort. This is a favored approach in implementing strategy, where there is no time constraint.

Tactics of conversion to the new system

It may not be possible to implement all programs simultaneously as this may outstrip the resources. Hence it is necessary to resort to other tactics:

1 test rehearsal,
2 pilot scheme,
3 phase installation,
4 parallel systems, or
5 full one-step implementation.

Test rehearsal

In a test rehearsal, parts of the strategy are tested before full implementation. Thus selling and service routines can be tested and internal office procedures tried out, for example, for order handling. Testing should be undertaken whenever there is time so as to spread the learning burden and eliminate any loose ends.

Pilot scheme

A strategy can be implemented one unit at a time. A "roll out" approach in launching a new product, starting in one area of the country then extending to the rest of the country, captures the idea of a pilot scheme. There will always need to be revisions and improvisations to meet unanticipated problems and a pilot scheme makes it easier to make the necessary adjustments. This is not to suggest that what is accomplished on a pilot basis can be done when extended to a full launch, unless the attention and resources, if lavished on the pilot scheme, are generally available.

Phase installation

Where training and supervisory problems are likely to outstrip resources, a phase installation is appropriate. Under this approach the strategy is installed by stages. Thus a new product may at first be sold only to key accounts, or additional services may be offered initially only on the more expensive items in the line.

Parallel systems

Where parallel systems are adopted, work is duplicated. Some part of the old system is continued and run side by side with its eventual replacement to check that the new system is satisfactory. For example, the old system of distribution via mail order might be continued side by side with the new system of door-to-door selling, or the old clerical system of order handling might be continued until the computer system is satisfactory. Parallel systems are common in changeovers to computer systems but a high price can be paid in terms of duplicated work.

Each of these strategies and tactics is worthy of consideration, even for changes other than major strategic ones, for example, in changing the sales compensation plan. In respect of tactics, a compensation scheme can be test rehearsed via simulation, or a pilot scheme instituted in just one region. Alternatively, a phase installation approach might be adopted: first the data-gathering phase, then the measuring of performance, leaving the implementation of the actual payment system to the last. Even parallel systems can be appropriate on occasions. If the new system pays less than the old for existing performance levels but more at higher levels, the sales force can be given the choice of being paid on either system until most are doing better on the new scheme.

Operational problems

If implementation is to go smoothly, then each participant must:

- know what relates to his or her responsibilities;
- have the ability and resources to act; and
- be present to act on events when they occur.

If these conditions are to be fulfilled, there is a need to develop the bureaucratic side to implementation. This is done by drawing up a *campaign*. A campaign translates the strategy from a statement of intent into who does what, where, when, and how and with what resources. It consists of:

1 policy statements translating the strategy into corresponding directives;
2 programs made up of systems and procedures;
3 schedules relating the sequence of activities to a calendar;
4 schedules of responsibility for implementation; and

5 budgets relating the sequence of activities to the resources allocated to support the campaign.

Standard operating procedures, schedules of responsibility, etc. are often perceived as "bureaucratic" and restrictive, but, in implementing strategies, they serve to increase the ability of everyone to predict the behavior of others. If time was no problem, and resources were unlimited, such rules would be unnecessary, but this is seldom the case and efficiency demands operational planning. How detailed the plans will be must depend on the discretion thought to be necessary given the degree of uncertainty faced. *Network analysis* or *critical path analysis* is a simple but major tool for planning and scheduling an implementation and should be considered.

In every campaign, operational problems arise. These can be technical, administrative or human relations.

Administrative problems

Administrative problems are common. Some are avoidable by careful planning. For example, the starting date for the implementation of proposals must be far enough ahead to allow for the completion of all preparatory work and training. Where crises arise, those in charge should be on the scene to maintain a mood of urgency.

Technical problems

Technical problems occur that are either procedural (for example, over learning new routines) or performance (for example, sales targets not being met). The first problem calls for additional resources to be committed to training, while the second problem depends on identifying the reason for poor performance.

Human relations

The major operational problems are generally those of morale. If morale or team spirit can be kept high, all administrative and technical problems seem more solvable. Frequent meetings at every level help. In a change situation, where people are still trying to find their feet, interpersonal conflict is inevitable. If disputes are over technical and administrative issues, they are best hammered out in open discussion. Where the conflict threatens to be destructive, higher management must insist on a compromise or throw its weight behind some solution. While there is always a need to inspire cooperation and a climate of enthusiasm based on an expectation of success and better times to come, there is also a need to act decisively in the interests of the organization which may require taking drastic action rather than tolerating any "dragging of feet."

NOTES

1 Piercy, Nigel (1991) *Market-led Strategic Change*, London: HarperCollins.
2 Cohen, Eliot, A. and Gooch, John (1990) *Military Misfortunes: the Anatomy of Failure in War*, New York: The Free Press.

Chapter 17

Organization, strategy, and marketing

An effective organization is needed to support a strategy when implemented. Yet organizations can be very ineffective. While every firm is an organization, not every firm is well organized. The extent to which a firm is well organized is the extent to which the structure and functioning of the organization support the firm's objectives and strategies, namely:

- the investment objective, whether growth, hold/defend or turnabout;
- the management strategy, the key competencies and thrusts to be exploited; and
- the implementation strategies, like the marketing strategy to ensure that organizations serve markets.

The functioning of organizations depends on other factors besides structure. Galbraith and Nathanson claim that major changes in strategy should be accompanied by changes not only in organization structure but in processes, reward systems and people.[1] The writers go on to say:

> Our basic premise is that effective financial performance is obtained by the achievement of congruence between strategy, structure, processes, rewards and people.

In a sense this statement is a truism, in that all parts of a system must work together if the system's performance is not to be weakened. But strictly speaking the statement is untrue, as merely achieving congruence among the components of a system is not sufficient to ensure effectiveness. Effective financial performance depends substantially on *what* strategies are adopted.

In this chapter we review:

1   the problems of organization;
2   the criteria used in organization design; and
3   the implications of these criteria for marketing.

THE PROBLEMS OF ORGANIZATION

From the overall company point of view, organization is an implementation strategy since it is chosen to support the objectives and strategies of the business. Figure 17.1 shows the organization structure and its functioning as supporting investment objectives, management strategies and implementation strategies. In Figure 17.1, the marketing strategy is also shown as an implementation strategy as it constitutes one of the strategies that implement corporate strategy. Although it is not uncommon to assert that there is just one best way to organize, this is to substitute formula for thought. There is no theory so compelling or empirical evidence so overwhelming as to justify the universal adoption of one organizational form or one approach to organizing.

Just as some of the most fundamental marketing decisions are made at the business level, so the major organizational issues affecting marketing are dealt with by top management with marketing's participation. Thus it is a top-level decision to have

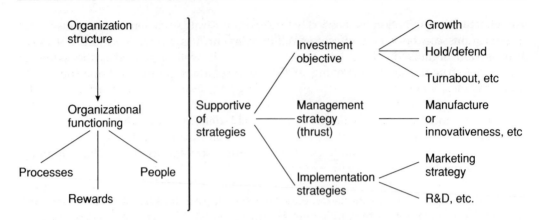

Figure 17.1 Organization and strategy

separate marketing departments in each division or to have a central marketing head-quarters catering to all divisions.

It was Chandler who first demonstrated that organization structure follows the growth strategy of the business (see Figure 17.2).[2] As a firm grows from a "one-man-band" with a single product line, it adopts a functional organization. At some stage in growth via market penetration, specialist functional departments such as marketing, production, finance and so on are set up to achieve uniform administration of these functions company-wide, and to reap economies of scale by grouping like work together. At some point, growth comes from adding products. As such growth occurs via market development, product development, vertical integration or diversification, firms tend to divisionalize. A major factor in determining how far the multidivisional company should remain centralized depends on the extent to which the different products or businesses are related in manufacturing or marketing.

Much work has been done subsequently to Chandler, relating strategy to organization structure. One study, for example, showed a strong association between diversification and the subsequent adoption of a multi-divisional structure.[3] But diversification

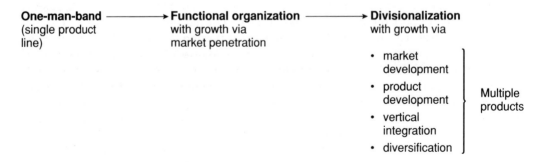

Figure 17.2 Organization/growth strategy

is not a sufficient condition to bring about the adoption of a multidivisional structure. There are several reasons for this. First, organizational change redistributes power and, as a consequence, is often resisted. Second, any organization, operating in a lucrative market, may tolerate the cost of an ill-functioning organization to avoid the trauma of change. Third, those with an entrepreneurial flair, who lead the firm into new growth paths, are not necessarily sensitive to the need for organizational change so organizational issues may be shelved until administrative problems, attendant on growth, plus declining performance, force a review of organization.

It is not uncommon to blame the organization structure for every type of company failure and new management often equates major reorganization with reform and reform with progress. But nothing is this simple. There is something in what the satirist, Caius Petronius of ancient Rome, once said: "I was to learn later in life that we tend to meet any situation by reorganizing, and a wonderful method it can be for creating the illusion of progress, while producing confusion, inefficiency, and demoralization." A firm often builds up an immunity to organizational deficiencies that allows it to function fairly well in carrying out its day-to-day activities. On the other hand, it may have nothing to protect itself from the ills accompanying the dysfunctional consequences of a major reorganization.

Recognizable failures in organization

The effects on costs of a poor organization structure are difficult to isolate. In spite of one controversial study, which claims to have established a positive relationship between organizational structure and economic performance, the evidence is still being collected.[4] Historians, however, increasingly produce evidence linking failures in mission and goals to deficiencies in organization. Thus, historians Cohen and Gooch argue that "it is in the efficiency of organizations that the embryo of misfortune develops" as the organization can be very instrumental in failures to anticipate, to learn or to adapt. For example, to quote just one of their case studies, the "unparalleled massacre of American shipping" that took place in 1942, within a few miles off the American coast. America failed to learn from the British and adapt an organizational structure that enabled the Royal Navy and the RAF to "make use of all the intelligence at their disposal, to analyze it swiftly and disseminate it immediately to those who needed it."[5] At a more general level, Lazonick, a historian, claims that Britain's early economic success was associated with its small, vertically integrated, family-owned firms that later proved to be inferior to the large, professionally, multi-divisional corporations that developed in the United States.[6] Later still the Japanese success was related to the ability to organize cooperative investment strategies across firms through the *keiretsu* system and improve coordination within firms by organizational arrangements that got everyone involved in the decision-making process.

Another study claims that the organization of global corporations around a home base, with all top management being from the home country, hinders efforts to become truly global.[7] It is expected that today's global firm will be superseded by what is termed a *relationship-enterprise* or a network of strategic alliances among firms which span many different industries and countries, held together by common goals. While emphasizing the trends in joint ventures, licensing, franchising and different forms of alliances between firms, Webster, in marketing, argues for a network or wheel (in contrast to the pyramid organization structure) where the spokes are the knowledge links between the core organization at the hub and its strategic partners around the rim. Such an organization has the capacity "to respond quickly and flexibly to accelerating change in technology, competition and customer preferences."[8]

Other writers speak of the *virtual corporation*, which focuses on the function it does best while forging temporary links with other organizations that similarly concentrate to bring the "best of everything" organization to the market.[9]

The recognizable but not necessarily measurable costs of a poor organization are:

- failure to coordinate inter-unit activities because of a lack of consistency in goals, poor specification of duties, and so on;
- functions not administered on a uniform basis, giving rise to anomalies and grievances;
- decisions made too late or poor in quality; and
- sluggishness in response to the need for change.

Each of these is a possible symptom of some organizational deficiency.

Issues in organization

We have said that organization structure should follow strategy. However, in certain cases, a firm's organization may be regarded as so efficient at carrying out the firm's business that it is the firm's competitive advantage. The firm may, as consequence, seek new products and missions that exploit the organization. In such a situation, strategy would seemingly follow structure. But only "seemingly" in that the firm's organization structure in the first place would be designed to support the firm's strategies. Although organization structure is important, organizational issues also embrace functioning and performance. More specifically, organization covers:

1   *the structure of the organization, viz:*
   - grouping tasks to form individual jobs;
   - grouping jobs into sections, process teams, departments and higher administrative units such as divisions;
   - delegating authority, allocating responsibility and determining the number of levels in the managerial hierarchy; and
   - the systems and procedures used in communication and control;
2   *the functioning and performance of the organization, viz:*
   - providing an organizational climate that motivates people to give of their best;
   - designing communication and information systems for effective decision-making, control, and coordination; and
   - building an overall organization that is innovative, responsive and adaptive to technological and environmental change.

ORGANIZATIONAL CRITERIA

In evaluating an organization, criteria can be classified into:

- *economic criteria*, such as grouping like work together to achieve economies of scale;
- *technical criteria*, such as ensuring an optimal workload for management and supervision;
- *quasi-legalistic criteria* in developing rules, say, to avoid jurisdictional conflict;
- *integrative criteria*, where the emphasis is on creating a motivational climate so people give of their best to achieve an integrated effort;
- *adaptive criteria*, where the focus is on coping with environmental uncertainty and information for decision-making; and
- *intrinsic liking* as represented in preferences for simplicity and consistency in organizational design.

Early *"classical"* writers on organization focused almost exclusively on "economic", "technical" and "legalistic" criteria. But an exclusive concern with economic and technical criteria alienates people, while too much "legalism" or regulation can result in inflexibility and slowness of response. The so-called *human relations* movement was associated with "integration" to achieve a motivated, cooperative, and unified effort. But an overemphasis on the need for integration can lead to "groupthink". The *organizational behavior* movement which followed sought simply to understand and explain behavior within organizations without adopting an ideological stance. Later developments such as the *contingency approach* and the *systems approach* were to place emphasis on "adaptive" criteria in coping with uncertainty and information overload, with the organization being designed to facilitate decision-making. Carried too far, adaptive criteria can lead to the neglect of economies of scale and other economic criteria. However, all the criteria listed above are relevant for evaluating and building an organization. It is a mistake to believe that moving from the classical criteria (economic, technical, and legalistic) to human relations criteria (integrative) and on to contingency criteria (adaptive) is a movement from error to truth: that past writers got it wrong but today at last we have the truth! Each set of criteria is simply an additional window from which to view an organization with some windows, for some problems, being clearer than others.

Economic and technical criteria

Economic and technical criteria are commonly used to group activities into teams, sections, departments and higher administrative units. In operational terms such criteria come down to considerations of:

- workload,
- economies of scale,
- coordination, and
- nature of activity.

Workload

Workload sets a limit to what can be grouped under one supervisor or manager. If there were no problems of workload, there would be no problems of organization, since one person could do all the work. The optimal workload on managers and supervisors is not fully measured by the number of subordinates under them (the so-called "span of control"). Optimal workloads must also take account of individual capacities and the nature of the supervisory task. For example, the workload of a sales supervisor depends on the extent to which

- subordinate salespeople are given decision-making authority, are trained, and policies laid down for them to follow;
- work is routine and repetitive, since this affects the amount of guidance that needs to be given;
- salespeople are satisfied with their jobs and are cooperative, since their willingness to get on with the job affects the amount of supervision that is necessary;
- control information is available so that management time is saved by being able to focus on deviations from the standards laid down; and
- supervisors are obliged to do work other than that concerned with subordinates

Economies of scale

Economies of scale refer to size. Economies of scale arise from grouping like work together so the scale of operations becomes larger. For example, putting all marketing research together reaps technical economies (for example, arising from increased specialization or the use of machines), managerial economies (for example, a large section can better afford a first-class head), and so on. Economies of scale are distinguished from *economies of scope*, which are the economies arising from using the same resources to make a variety of products. Chandler argues that successful pioneer firms make all the investments that are needed to reap both economies of scale and scope.[10] The basic question is how big does a firm have to be to reap the maximum economies of scale? This is important since there are disadvantages to bigness as well as advantages. The disadvantages relate to the inflexibility and lack of adaptability associated with big, bureaucratic companies. Thus small companies often find it easier to tailor their products to foreign markets. But the use of computers seems to be narrowing economies of scale in both manufacturing and distribution, with factory automation making it easier to produce cheaply in small volumes. Nonetheless, grouping to achieve economies of scale is a factor to consider.

There is still, however, a good deal of debate over the relative advantages of large firms versus small firms of around 50 to 100 employees. Since big firms dominate and their strengths are so well documented, it is not surprising that the tide turned to the claim that the balance of advantage had shifted from the large to the small firm. This claim has not gone unchallenged. It is argued that big firms are not inefficient because they are big but because they are often too diverse in being conglomerates. Perhaps a more defensible position is to argue that the distinction between bigness and smallness is becoming less and less relevant. Today large firms try to achieve the flexibility of the small firm by, say, organizing themselves into semi-autonomous teams or dividing themselves into independent companies and so on. On the other hand, small firms seek the advantages of size by, say, seeking alliances with other companies. Bennetton may not be very large if judged by its core of workers but, when contract workers are added and its associated outlets, it is very large indeed.

Coordination

One thing that unites both past and current writers on organization is the importance of organization for securing coordination. Crusoe alone needs only to organize himself but when Man Friday arrives, reciprocal obligations begin and activities need to be coordinated. Activities are grouped to achieve greater coordination and worry over coordination can lead management to doubt what otherwise seems like a good idea. Take the subject of "outsourcing" whereby an organization defines its core business and outsources much of the rest to both save money and allow more focused management. But with outsourcing, problems of coordination (and control) arise between the company and those who now supply it with what it once produced. In fact backward integration is often undertaken to achieve more backward coordination and control.

The greater the degree of coordination, the more individual efforts are integrated during performance rather than reconciled afterwards. Inter-unit coordination, though, can have as its aim the achievement of economies of scale and not just integrated action. Thus there is coordination between divisions to share activities arising from having common technologies or customers as well as coordination for the exchange of know-how. Also, where there is multipoint competition (rival firms competing with each other in several distinct businesses) there is a need to coordinate actions taken against the multipoint competitor in one market with the actions taken against the multipoint competitor in other markets, since actions toward a competitor in one market have implications in another.

A business organization that is *functionally organized* is divided into the functions of marketing, production, finance, and so on. A functional organization reaps economies of scale by putting all like work together as well as achieving the uniform administration of the function company-wide. However, in conditions where a firm has different products catering to distinct markets, each with its own requirements for success, and demanding separate strategies and programs, a functional organization has drawbacks. As the number of management levels increases to cope with the volume and diversity, marketing management becomes less sensitive to individual market needs. Equally as important, as the marketing departmental hierarchy grows, top managers can become more administrative than innovative. They become physically and psychologically separated from those down the line, unable to evaluate proposals or monitor performance, while relying on financial reports to give them the whole picture.

At some stage it becomes far more important to coordinate activities associated with a customer group, a product group, a geographical region, or a process than to coordinate activities common to *all* product groups. These various positions are illustrated in Figure 17.3. Of particular current interest is grouping by process. Thus in issuing

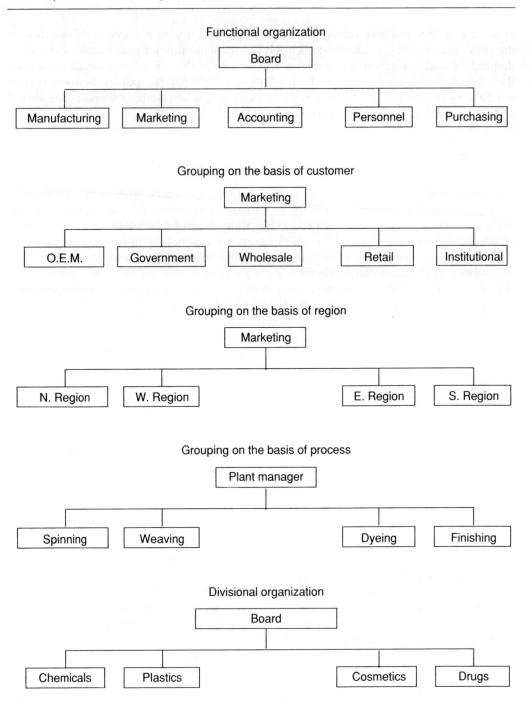

Figure 17.3 Organizational groupings

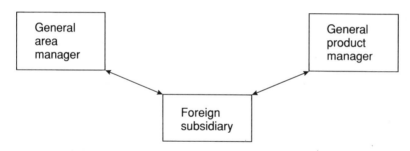

Figure 17.4 The grid structure of organization

an insurance policy, many specialists might be involved from different departments when, given that 95 percent of the forms are straightforward, the whole process could be done in just one unit. Organizing around a process is the major tool in what is called "re-engineering" to both achieve cost economies and better coordination. Re-engineering is discussed later in the chapter.

One radical solution to the problem of achieving better coordination of activities associated with a product group or market is *divisionalization*, that is, splitting up the firm into distinct divisions, each responsible for its own manufacturing and selling. Each division (for example, Cereals Division, Coffee Division, etc.) resembles the functional organization, except that certain functions like finance may be centralized. But divisions can take many different forms. Thus IBM has nine distinct product divisions catering to four regional marketing and service divisions. Yet within a division there is still likely to be a problem of *cross-functional coordination*. Where the focus is on the customer, managing across functional boundaries in multiproduct companies has become much more important than managing up and down the chain of command.

Multinational firms may initially adopt an international marketing division, later developing worldwide product divisions, or regional marketing divisions, or some combination of product and area as occurs in the grid structure of organization (see Figure 17.4). In the grid structure, the subsidiary overseas is subject to both a regional coordinator and a product coordinator, on the ground that both regional and product coordination are of equal importance. There is a need to work out, on a business-by-business basis, the right balance between the regional emphasis and the global product emphasis, rather than adopt one general solution for all the firm's businesses.

Some writers regard the organizational evolution of the multinational (or at least the multinational pharmaceutical firm) as the movement of the nature and locus of control from the overseas market back to corporate level.[11] When knowledge and understanding of worldwide markets is absorbed, the final phase locates the control of marketing, etc. at corporate HQ. This is termed a *global structure* and is viewed by Galbraith and Nathanson as a distinct stage in evolutionary development on the ground that categories of distinct organizational forms should be based on distinct "ways of life:"[12]

There are changes in the financial control system designed to handle such factors as national variations, profits by product and region, and transfer pricing. Different

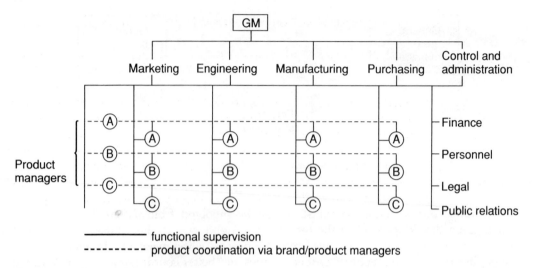

Figure 17.5 The matrix organization

and multiple standards of evaluation appear; careers and compensation practices are changed; new committees and staffs evolve. Most important, an international mentality gets created to various degrees. All together, we feel these changes constitute a different 'way of life' and therefore a different form.

This quotation hardly qualifies as an operational definition of a distinct new way of life. Many of us have made changes such as those described, even in a functional organization, without believing we have created a new organizational form!

Another traditional solution to the problem of coordination in conditions of product diversity lies in the *matrix organization* (see Figure 17.5). In this form of organization, someone is appointed to coordinate across departmental lines. This matrix leader cannot usually give orders to any functional head but is obliged to rely on consultation, cooperation, compromise and bargaining. The functional departments remain to achieve economies of scale and coordination of the *function* company-wide, while, say, the brand or product managers as matrix leaders, located in marketing, are responsible for coordinating the activities associated with the product or brand across all the functional boundaries. Usually they are involved in the whole of the marketing of a product, as well as concerned with market analysis and research. However, they are also responsible and accountable for profitability, even though they may be denied corresponding authority over production costs, prices and advertising budgets. This is because, while the matrix organization crosses departmental lines, authority remains with the functional departmental heads.

The matrix organization is also reflected in the grid structure in international marketing (see Figure 17.4). It attempts to get the best of all possible worlds, but has limitations:

- the coordinator or matrix leader (brand manager) must rely on consultation, cooperation, compromise and bargaining in dealing with the functional heads;

- employees within the departments often feel they have two bosses and resent the fact; and
- it is not always clear who settles conflicts between the functional manager and the coordinator or product manager.

Because of such limitations and to achieve greater coordination, *project management* may be adopted. In project management, the activities associated with some project or product are brought together under a project leader to achieve coordination and a strong customer orientation. Whereas under a functional organization, each functional manager is responsible for the function's work on a project, under project management, projects are more or less self-contained, with project leaders and the teams falling under them being responsible for completing the project according to specification. But project management, too, has limitations:

- loss of economies of scale;
- dilution of the technical skills of "experts" separated from their professional colleagues; and
- problems associated with the reintroduction of members of the project back into their former departments after the project is completed.

Recently more drastic solutions to the coordination problem and the drawbacks of the functional organization have been proposed. One is the *horizontal corporation*. It is a corporation that has a flat organization structure, with just a skeleton group of senior executives at the top carrying out traditional support services such as finance. The horizontal corporation seeks to eliminate the boundaries between functional areas. The focus is on the organization as a system in which "the functions are seamless." In its major development, the horizontal organization is composed of self-managing teams which become the building blocks of the organization where performance objectives stress customer satisfaction. Budgets are based on processes not departments. Instead of organizing around functional departments, the company *or* the company division is structured around 6–10 market-driven processes. Yet no major company has completely eliminated functional departments.

A more recent focus among corporations is *vertical coordination*. It relates to what was said early about outsourcing as the stress on vertical coordination arises from the recognition that, creating value for the customer, involves a whole chain of independent organizations, starting with suppliers. It is this recent stress on vertical organization that has led to the breaking down of the barriers/boundaries between manufacturers and their suppliers. The manufacturer ideally would like to so integrate major suppliers that they could be treated like subsidiaries. But such "partnerships" are not easy to manage while there is the constant danger of one of the "partners" being too dependent on the other.

Talk about the removing of "boundaries" and the "boundaryless" corporation are common today with the realization that company boundaries, departmental boundaries and so on can be an impediment to coordination. Thus Jack Welch of GE in the United States, speaks of running the business on just three principles.[13] The first principle is *boundaryless behavior* on the ground that "walls" cramp people, inhibit creativity, waste time, restrict vision, smother dreams, and generally slow things down. The second principle is *speed*, on the ground that the faster the pace of change, the bigger the advantage. It is boundaries, management layers, bureaucracy and formality that is viewed as being a drag on achieving speed. Finally, the third principle is *stretch*, which is establishing targets without knowing initially how they might be achieved. The stretch principle is similar in concept to the idea of the vision statement.

Nature of activity

The nature of the activity itself may determine its grouping:

- *key activities*: for example, activities that are associated with key issues for the company at the time, are grouped higher in the hierarchy;
- *goal conflict*: some activity (for example, determining sales quota) may be separated from the unit to which it would normally belong (for example, district manager-level) to achieve more objectivity; and
- *coordinating nature of activity*: some activities come directly under the coordinator to help him or her do a better job of coordination. For this reason sales administration may come directly under the sales manager.

Technical and economic criteria often conflict as grouping to achieve economies of scale may conflict with grouping to achieve coordination. For example, grouping sales training under the personnel department to achieve economies of scale weakens coordination between sales training and the realities of field selling. As with all decision-making, there are trade-offs to be made and decisions about the organization are no exception. It is because all organizations result from trade-offs, leaving corresponding deficiencies, that leads to constant tinkering with the organization in the implicit belief that trade-offs can be avoided. They cannot.

Legalistic criteria

Every organization's structure is affected by rules. The age of the organization, its size and formalization, all go together. This is not surprising since, as an organization grows older, managers develop standard answers to standard problems and these become policies and instructions with more and more policies and instructions building up the bureaucracy. Similarly, with size come rules to help run the organization as more control systems are developed. The result may be a centralized and rigid organization.

Government legislation affects both the structure and functioning of an organization. New functions and bureaucracy are added to the organization to insure that the law is obeyed. Indeed, lawyers are not unknown in marketing departments to cope with patent law, advertising and anti-trust legislation. Most rules affecting organization, though, are imposed by management. In particular, rules are introduced that schedule responsibility and authority to lessen jurisdictional disputes and ensure accountability. What authority is actually delegated depends on circumstances, but holding back authority should be justified. Such justification is typically associated with the technical and economic reasons just discussed. Thus authority may be held back from some manager because:

- there may be a need to centralize a function to achieve uniformity, for example, sales salaries and commissions;
- there may be a need to coordinate inter-unit activities, for example, technical service and sales; and
- there may be economies of scale to be reaped by doing a job centrally, for example, marketing research; and
- the activity is "key," justifying the manager's personal attention, for example, selling to major accounts.

Decentralization is the systematic delegation of authority to all organization units and centralization is the tendency to withhold authority. Computers can make for either centralization or decentralization. Extensive computer-based information systems give top management an unprecedented ability to centralize decision-making. On the other hand, the same information, packaged differently, can also empower lower levels and promote decentralization. Divisionalization facilitates decentralization. What inhibits decentralization is doubts about the competence of those to whom authority is to be delegated: delegation presupposes there is professionalism at lower levels. Early writers on organization put great emphasis on scheduling responsibilities, that is, scheduling obligations to carry out certain work with accountability for performance. It was argued that vagueness in assigning responsibility leads to confusion and jurisdictional conflict.

The extent to which a firm should be formally structured or be bureaucratic is a major topic of discussion. At first, interest lay in gauging the effect of bureaucracy on individual motivation but later the interest shifted to considering how environmental uncertainty limits the desirability of too much formalism. High uncertainty indicates the need for flexibility: too many rules implies an absence of uncertainty and a definiteness as to what needs to be done. Some rules are necessary to regulate and control any complex organization. The aim of rules is to achieve greater *definiteness* (for example, in uniformity, justice, stability, etc.). Without some rules employees cannot be protected from arbitrariness and the company from chaos. The aim of fewer rules, on the other hand, is to achieve greater *flexibility*. Since both these goals are desirable, there is always a problem in balancing off one against the other. Flexibility contrasts with rigidity where every choice situation is listed and categorized and choice is determined by some predetermined rule laid down for the category. Where there is flexibility there is no one-to-one relationship between choice situation and solution but a decision is made which takes account of goals and the unique set of circumstances. Where rigidity makes for definiteness, flexibility avoids standard solutions when standard conditions do not exist.

The *contingency approach* to organization claims that environmental uncertainty necessitates a balance in favor of flexibility. An organization facing many uncertainties should be loosely structured rather than highly structured or bureaucratic so as to be flexible enough to adapt to changed or changing conditions. This is not easy to do as bureaucracy tends to come with growth and age. Thus it is not surprising to find writers arguing that "small is beautiful" or trying to build "smallness within bigness" to create market responsive units within a framework of shared resources.

Integrative criteria

A high degree *of integration* within an organization means there is a strong sense of common interests and a willingness to collaborate in furthering the organization's goals. A high degree of integration is associated with a high degree of coordination, since coordination presupposes:

- a sense of common purpose or a mutual understanding and acceptance of common goals;
- ease of communication among those whose efforts need to be coordinated; and
- a desire to eschew destructive conflict.

Competition has forced many companies to stretch toward levels of quality and efficiency that are achievable only by near perfect integration of all efforts involved in meeting customer requirements. A focus on integrative criteria studies individual motivation, group behavior, leadership, organizational culture, and politics as a basis for suggesting how the individual's goals and group goals might be influenced to cohere with the organization's goals. Participation by employees in the decisions that affect them has been the major mechanism suggested. But the evidence in support of participation, as a mechanism for enhancing individual productivity, is weak. The effect of participation on productivity *can be* effective, but only under certain conditions, which cannot as yet be fully specified. But the focus on participation and its relationship to individual productivity is too narrow. No one has a monopoly on rationality or all the considerations that can legitimately to entertained when considering strategies, policies and tactics. Participation helps tap ideas from everyone.

   Motivation is the process of providing others with a motive for doing something but, since motives alone do not direct *specific* action (beliefs do this), it is less misleading (and more understandable to managers) to talk about providing employees with reasons for doing something. *Leadership* is related to motivating subordinates in that it is concerned with exerting influence within some group. The organizational behavior literature on leadership generally focuses on supervisory leadership, in general stressing (in one form or another) the two supervisory functions first identified by Bales: the *task function* performed by giving a definite lead ("initiating structure") in relation to the task to be done and the *socio-emotional* function carried out being "relationship-oriented."[14] Studies since Bales have focused on determining the right emphasis between these two factors, though many terms have been used, such as autocratic/democratic, authoritative/participative, task-centered/relationship-oriented or other related concepts. While these are ingredients of leadership style, these two functions do not capture the whole concept of top management leadership since being successful and acting decisively in the interests of the organization also enter into leadership.

We have commented on the behavior of people in groups: the concept of group norms, reference groups, and groupthink. All have relevance to the functioning of an organization. Of particular interest, is the concept of task *teams*, formed to deal with new-product development, new marketing programs, new business ventures and quality. In fact, the term *organizational architecture* is used to describe new forms of organization that revolve round the idea of semi-autonomous work teams. Self-managing teams have become an article of faith in many companies. Each team has a designated leader and may have representatives from several functional areas. Interest in teams has arisen because of

1 the belief that teams generate commitment;
2 the "quality movement" in business where teams play the key role; and
3 "re-engineering" with its focus on interdisciplinary teams concerned with some process/outcome.

US car makers have been converted to cross-functional teamworking. But success is not guaranteed. Advice on forming and using teams suggests several rules.[15]

- there must be top management and company-wide support for the concept;
- they should be led by someone of substance within the organization to give a team credibility;
- each team must have a clear mission/goal;
- teams would preferably have fewer than ten members; and
- the mix of people on the team should have complementary skills.

There can be problems with teams depending on how members are related for the job to be done. Thus *additive* tasks require all members of the team to work individually and then pool their efforts to meet team goals. Such additive tasks are vulnerable to social loafing. In the case of *conjunctive* tasks, team members perform separate but interdependent tasks in turn so that conjunctive tasks are only as good as their weakest members.

The influence of *culture* can be a weakness or a strength. The core of a company's culture is shared values. Sometimes a company will try to propagate the values it believes should be the shared values. Thus Kodak proclaimed that the firm's culture should be built around the values of trust, integrity, credibility, continuous improvement and respect for the individual. Company values, if internalized, can lead employees to care about customers, innovation or just with getting by. Within an organization, the culture influences

- the degree of cooperation encountered;
- tolerance for risk;
- degree of autonomy granted;
- recruitment criteria; and
- how employees conduct themselves and so on.

A strong culture can substitute for formal rules and regulations. Thus a culture where each person is expected to know his or her role and place, is one that will place a high value on formal behavior.

As part of the culture, company myths and stories both propagate the organization's values and legitimize current practices. Myths in a culture tend to reflect, define, defend, and reinforce the status quo and the value system that lies behind it. For example, take the myth associated with Seymour Cray, who built up Cray Research. It promotes the firm's philosophy of radical innovation. Cray is said to burn his sailboats at the end of each season so as not to be bound by that year's mistakes when he sets about designing a better craft for the following year. When running EDS, Ross Perot established a strong culture, helped by stories about his rescuing employees from prison in Iran and many stories about his other "caring" actions. Myths (as in the Greek myths) often reinforce traditional values by telling what disasters are apt to occur when traditional values are lost. Thus in many companies today there are myths (with some basis in fact) of the disasters that beset the company's fortunes as a result of deviating from core competencies. Myths in any culture can bring about changes in behavior: they have a redemptive function.

Rituals are also part of company culture. It is unfortunate that the term "rituals," as popularly used, has come to suggest empty conformity to rules. For rituals (as defined by anthropologists) are actions performed in a symbolic way that define the participating group as one that is distinct from other groups, while, within the group, rituals are apt to delineate the role and status of members. Rituals can be important in developing group solidarity, as witness the rituals that start the day in Japanese corporations. The very performance of distinctive rituals reinforces group cohesiveness, binding the employees together as if holders of life's secrets.

At least one book argues that superior company performance is heavily dependent on having a company culture which helps the organization to anticipate, learn, and adapt to changes in the business environment.[16] The authors argue that successful companies with strong cultures seem to have in common one key value: their managers do not let the short-term interests of shareholders override everything else or other stakeholders. But strong-culture firms seem as likely to perform poorly as their weak-cultured rivals, since too strong a culture can lead to corporate arrogance and insularity, a charge frequently leveled at General Motors and IBM. Finally, the authors claim that it can take decades to change a culture, even when helped by an unconventional CEO or a nonconformist outsider.

Major strategic change may necessitate a corresponding change in performance measures and the reward system. All too often reward systems are inconsistent with strategy. Yet, as far as people within the organization are concerned, the firm expresses its strategy not through its declared strategy but on the basis of what it rewards and penalizes. But what it rewards and penalizes reflects the firm's culture so changes can signal management's desire to change the culture.

Those emphasizing integrative criteria favor a "flat" rather than a "tall" organization structure. A tall structure has a high number of levels in relation to the number of people employed, while a flat structure has relatively few levels. The flat structure is favored on the ground that more authority is likely to be pushed downwards and, with less of a need to communicate up and down the chain of command, there are fewer delays in decision-making, less distortion in the flow of information and less authority leakage (that is, dilution of commands). Sales departments are notorious for having tall structures, with national, regional, district, and area managers. The number of levels can often be reduced through simplifying decision-making, accompanied by further delegation of authority. The basic question is whether the requisite degree of coordination and control can be achieved by a more flat structure. This depends on:

- the extent to which the work of subordinates is interdependent, since the greater the interdependence, the greater the coordination required and the taller the structure needed; and
- the complexity of subordinate jobs, since task complexity affects the amount of supervisory guidance that is required, and this in turn affects the number of levels.

There are many management writers arguing that "flatter" organizations will be the trend, with one view of the future organization predicting it will be like a "doughnut," consisting of just an essential core staff, around which will be resources to be called on at will. Companies on this view will expand as project needs require and shrink back again when the project is complete. This is tied to the concept of outsourcing mentioned earlier and was basic to Bennetton's early success. But it assumes that the labor resources are there to be recruited and let go according to company needs and that labor skills will remain as sharp as ever when reemployed. The problem with some turnabouts has been the release of skilled workers who constituted the basis of the firm's core competencies and who were then not available when later needed or, alternatively, could not recapture the former skill level. It seems reasonable to assume that the constant recruitment and laying off of workers would lead to labor alienation and would be a move away from encouraging labor loyalty as a basis for stimulating people to contribute to customer satisfaction.

Adaptive criteria

An organization must adapt to informational overload and environmental uncertainty. High environmental uncertainty brings with it high uncertainty in making strategic decisions. In many instances, uncertainty rules out *coordination through planning* well ahead, and instead favors *coordination through feedback* as the activity progresses.

In the *systems approach* to the design of an organization, the organization is regarded as a decision-making/information processing system that should be designed to facilitate decision-making. This is done by:

- specifying the outputs (objectives/strategies) sought;
- identifying the subsystems or main decision areas in the company;
- determining and providing the information needs for each decision area; and
- grouping decision areas together to facilitate decision-making and minimize the communications burden.

Some writers claim that a systems approach generally leads to the design of a flat organization composed of semi-autonomous units or, alternatively, a network of specialized companies, held together and coordinated by a market-driven company at the center.[17] If this is so it is a return to some nineteenth-century organizations such as those in textiles. In the last century in the UK, textile merchants were the center of a network of specialized independent organizations as they coordinated the production and marketing of textile products. This arrangement gave the merchant a great deal of flexibility. The vertically organized textile ·company came later when markets were more established and the vertical organization offered the prospect of economies of scale.

The need for information often results in the setting up of a specialist department (for example, a marketing research department) while information processing requirements necessitate that the corresponding information processing capacity be available. The level to which decisions are delegated depends not just on the availability of professional management but on the feasibility of information systems to monitor and control performance so that delegation does not become the abrogation of responsibility. Since information has to be communicated, the flow of information through communication channels can be hampered or facilitated by the organization structure. A common error is to ignore the implications of a change in organization structure or strategy for the redesign of information systems, whether these are:

- *execution systems* concerned with conducting the firm's business such as the order handling system;
- *monitoring systems* concerned with recording the state of processes or activities being undertaken; or
- *control systems* such as budgetary controls concerned with ensuring systems or processes meet the standards laid down.

The systems approach is concerned with adaptive criteria since it is concerned with information to reduce the risk in decision-making. However, the approach that is most focused on adaptive criteria is the *contingency approach*. It is the contingency approach that places most emphasis on coping with uncertainty. The word "contingency" is used to suggest the rejection of organizational solutions that claim universal applicability. But unlike situational management, which also rejects the idea of universal solutions, contingency approaches seek to specify under what conditions a particular solution is justified. The variables that have received most attention by contingency writers are changes in:

- the external environment;
- the company's core technology; and
- the size of the organization.

In general terms, those researching the relationships among changes in the firm's environment, its core technology, company size, and organization structure, claim that such changes generate uncertainty about how to cope with them. The more the uncertainty generated, the less appropriate is a *mechanistic* (bureaucratic) organization and the more the need for an *organismic* (loosely structured) organization. The mechanistic organization is one of high formalization (rule-bound), limited information networks (mainly down from upper management) and little participation by lower levels in the decision-making process. It is more suited to stable environments where changes take place slowly over time. The organismic organization is characterized by low formalization and utilizes a wide information network (downward, upward, and lateral). Where there is

- high environmental uncertainty,
- ever-present change, and
- elements in the environment increasingly interrelated,

the organization needs an organismic structure. Although early researchers saw their findings as applicable to the firm as a whole, more recent work recognizes that what may apply to the organization as a *whole* may not apply to some individual department or unit within the firm.

Contingency approaches raise the question of how far the firm should *formally* organize ("formally" because any company will at least be informally organized). An early pioneering study was that of Burns and Stalker who postulated a continuum from mechanistic to organic (later changed to organismic) organization.[18] A mechanistic organization follows bureaucratic lines with jobs and responsibilities rigidly defined. The organismic system, on the other hand, is loosely structured, with jobs defined loosely in terms of methods, duties and powers (authority), and redefined continuously as the need arises. Burns and Stalker argue that a highly mechanistic/bureaucratic system presupposes stable, predictable future environments for which rules can be formulated to guide action. Where such stability does not exist, bureaucracy becomes dysfunctional. Organismic systems are needed to cope with variable environments, for example, unstable markets. Thus it is argued that General Motor's (GM's) centralized, highly bureaucratic structure resulted in its being too inflexible for a market where the Japanese could design and produce new models every three years and reprogram their manufacture quickly to respond to changes in demand. This contrasted with GM's committee-designed models that seemed out-of-date by the time they reached the showroom. Similarly, it is claimed that IBM became too bureaucratic for an industry where changes in markets and technology were constant.

Innovators need the flexibility of an organismic organization. On the other hand, cost minimizers in a stable environment may seek the efficiency of a mechanistic structure. Also a marketing department, faced with a market where wants are changing and competitive actions are becoming unpredictable, should avoid rigid policies, tightly defined responsibilities and any other rules that constrain speed of response. The problem, though, with any organismic organization is determining the extent to which there can be a lack of formal rules governing relationships since some sort of structured order is needed to allow people to predict the behavior of others. It is simplistic to believe that the abandoning of all formal organization and emphasizing fellowship and goodwill is all that is needed. As Mary Douglas, the anthropologist, says, it constitutes an unrealistic idea of human nature.[19]

The work of Lawrence and Lorsch suggests the need for *both high integration* (high collaboration, social cohesion) and *high differentiation* (different ideologies or points of view) among the functional departments of the firm in conditions of environmental uncertainty.[20] In stable environments, however, where decision-making is more certain, a more highly structured, more bureaucratic organization is preferred. With environmental uncertainty comes uncertainty in decision-making, which is highest in the R&D function, followed by marketing and then production. Lawrence and Lorsch claim that, the more these three functions differ in terms of certainty in decision-making, the more they should be differentiated in terms of:

- *informality*: (R&D should be the most informal);
- *interpersonal orientation*: where decision-making is either highly certain or uncertain, the more a task orientation should be adopted in contrast to an interpersonal orientation;
- *time orientation*: the more the uncertainty, the longer the time orientation. As a consequence, R&D should have the longest time orientation; and
- *goals*: the more uncertainty differs among the three functions, the more departmental goals should be *specific* to the function.

On this basis, in times of high market uncertainty, the marketing department's organization should be neither too formal nor too informal; should avoid too long or too short a time orientation and should have goals that can be seen to reflect corporate goals. In times of high market stability, a more mechanistic approach is appropriate but *high integration is always sought*. To Lawrence and Lorsch, a factor in whether to locate the function of new product development outside marketing is the extent to which it needs to be differentiated from the rest of marketing. Where there is a constant need to innovate, there may be a need for high differentiation, with new product development being placed outside marketing. There may also be other reasons for the separation of new product development from the rest of marketing:

- to get undiluted advocacy for the function;
- a suspicion that marketing is dominated by current products and would neglect new product development; and
- where there is reason to believe that new product development may be starved of funds if placed in marketing because marketing has other priorities for its limited resources.

There are, however, dangers in separation. New product development, until it has established its potential, is in danger from functional rivals who believe its resources could more usefully be spent on their own function. Also those in marketing may be the only supporters of new product development. Equally as important is that new product development may require constant interaction with the expertise that is available in marketing.

Perrow classifies organizations into four *information technology* types based on:[21]

- the extent to which novel cases (problems) arise that require individual consideration as exceptions to the general pattern; and

- the extent to which these exceptional cases are amenable to solution by analysis as opposed to some form of institution guesswork.

These four types are shown in Figure 17.6. Boundaries are necessarily somewhat vague because the factors form continuous and not discrete attributes as suggested by the matrix. Although the cells classify firms, they could also categorize sections or departments. On this basis we might classify sections in *marketing* as follows:

- Cell 4 might embrace the typical *sales* organization, order handling and distribution. In sales, novel cases are few and generally analyzable, providing "analyzable" involves no suggestion of deriving an optimal solution.
- Cell 2 might include *new product development*. The very nature of new product development brings with it many exceptional cases and most of the problems that arise are not amenable to techniques that have a high probability of success.
- Cell 3 might include *marketing research*, with its many new problems but with a developed set of techniques for analyzing a large proportion of them.
- Cell 1 might include *advertising* with few cases that are exceptional, which, when they occur, are often solved more on a hit-or-miss basis.

Perrow argues that, if unnecessary stress and conflict are to be avoided, an organization must fit its underlying information technology. Cell 4, for example, should have a mechanistic system. Thus, if (as we suggest) most sales organizations fall into cell 4, then such organizations should be fairly mechanistically run, for example, central coordination and control, well-defined responsibilities and goals that emphasize stability and high performance. Cell 2 suggests an organismic management system. If new product development falls into cell 2, a highly decentralized, loosely structured organization is

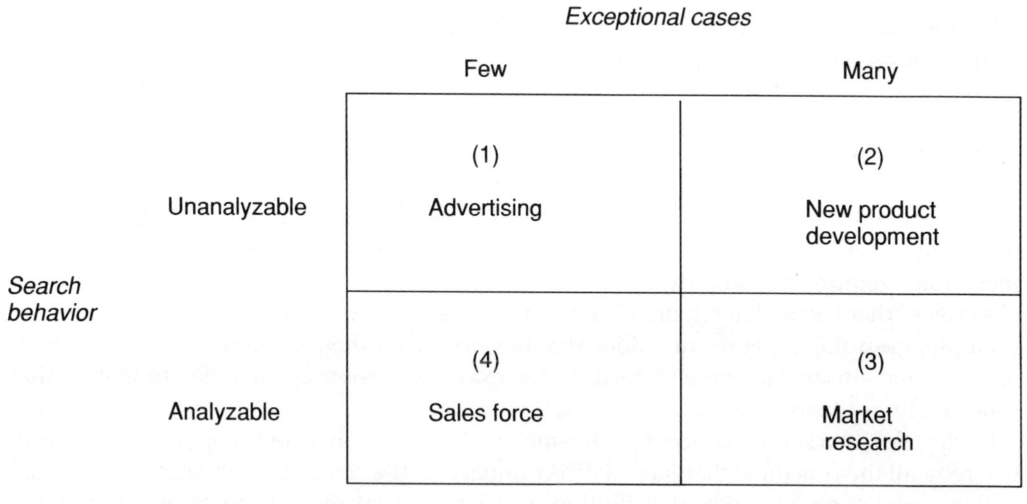

Exceptional cases

		Few	Many
	Unanalyzable	(1) Advertising	(2) New product development
Search behavior			
	Analyzable	(4) Sales force	(3) Market research

Figure 17.6 Perrow's matrix classification: organizations into four information technology types

recommended. With uncertainty, there comes doubt about what needs to be coordinated. High interaction is needed to achieve coordination by feedback while the inability to forecast problems militates against coordination by planned program. For cell 3 (for example, marketing research), the organization should be more decentralized than for cell 4, but more formally structured than for cell 2. Perrow argues that goals in cell 3 should emphasize both stability and quality of output. Recommendations for cell 3 are an attempt to balance the need for quick, adaptive action on exceptional cases against the need for formal coordination and control mechanisms. Coordination and control are easier than for cell 2 because the techniques for analyzing the problems are known. Finally, for cell 1 (for example, advertising), the organization should be more decentralized than in cell 4, but goals should, as in cell 2, emphasize risk and innovation with the need to meet deadlines.

Contingency theories take account of changes in the environment, and technology. But size also has its effects. Child's research found:[22]

- in stable environments, as firms grow, the better-performing firms tended to develop more formalized structures at a faster rate than did poor performers; and
- in variable/unstable environments, the rate of increase in formalization (bureaucracy) accompanying growth, was high for the good performers *but* the absolute level was less than in stable environments.

But no contingency approach is supported completely by the evidence, and we still do not know how important it is to match organizational design to the contingencies so far identified.

SOME IMPLICATIONS FOR MARKETING ORGANIZATION

Although in the above there has been constant citing of marketing examples, it is useful to think more about the implications for marketing of what has been said.

Objectives and marketing organization

Objectives and strategies determine what marketing activities are required. A mail order distribution system needs no sales force, while an industrial firm selling to the government may require no advertising or marketing research. Without a consideration of objectives, there is a danger of thinking of better ways of doing the unnecessary (for example, grouping together functions that have outlived their usefulness) or better ways of achieving unsatisfactory end results (for example, grouping together functions that collectively are inadequate to do the job).

Under the marketing concept, a business adopts a policy of integrated marketing whereby all the functions that have a direct impact on the customer (advertising, personal selling, marketing research, distribution and product planning) are grouped into the marketing department to ensure coordination. Figure 17.7 illustrates this concept. But for many companies it is not intuitively obvious that all the functions shown in Figure 17.7 should come under marketing. It is not uncommon to find advertising, field selling, product planning or distribution separated both physically and in the management hierarchy from the rest of marketing. For example, warehousing and the rest of distribution may be grouped into a separate department on the ground that the whole flow from suppliers to customers constitutes an integrated system that needs to be coordinated by experts in materials management. In other words, there may be more compelling reasons for *not* grouping some function in with marketing.

What can be said is that one person must be ultimately responsible for developing the marketing strategy and that this job is made more difficult if the functions of advertising, sales, etc., do not come directly under one person. In the absence of a common head, there are problems in reaching agreement, since what may be best for marketing as a whole may not appear best for field selling or advertising, and so on. There must be some way to settle disputes over the integration of strategies and a common superior is the best way. On the other hand, as we have seen, the horizontal corporation would eliminate altogether boundaries between functional areas.

In general, the functions coming under the head of marketing have grown since the 1950s. Some of these functions, like physical distribution, involve skills and technical

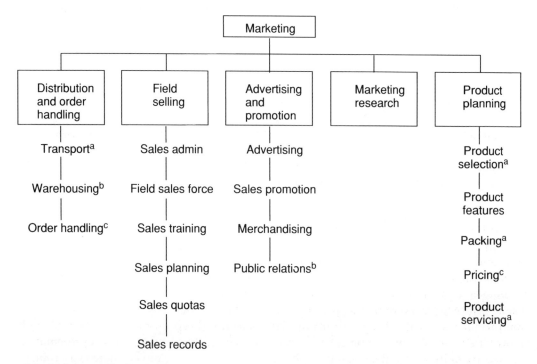

a Sometimes under Production
b Sometimes under Personnel
c Sometimes under Accounts

Figure 17.7 Marketing under the marketing concept

expertise not commonly acquired by those trained in marketing *per se*. What seems on occasions to be needed is some sort of management services unit embracing management scientists, systems experts, and so on, to insure that marketing runs an efficient operation.

Strategies and marketing organization

Overall organization

A growth strategy, if successful, gives rise to a need for organizational change. Market penetration via segment enlargement may lead to geographical divisionalization or international divisions. On the other hand, market development, product development, vertical integration and diversification (providing sales warrant this) may lead to product/market divisionalization, project or matrix management, with the degree of bureaucracy being determined by the degree of uncertainty faced.

The particular strategies adopted to turnaround a business depend on the extent to which the business needs to be turned around. Where a turnabout can be accomplished by just cutting costs, this may lead to few organizational changes beyond some regrouping. Where a turnabout demands the selling of assets, product eliminations, or line reductions, the impact on the organization might even lead to a return to a functional organization from a divisionalized structure. However, where a turnabout involves simply market repositioning and market development, the implications for organization might be no more than an extension of the product manager system.

A marketing organization or division can be organized on a product, process, regional, channel or customer basis. Each has advantages and disadvantages in terms of economies of scale and coordination. Only the facts of the case can determine which is the best, although most of those in marketing have a predisposition to favor organization around markets.

Field selling organization

A field sales force can be organized on a product, regional, channel, or customer basis, or some combination of these. The organization of a field sales force on the basis of product sold is common when products are very different and sold to different buyers. Having a separate sales force for each product group may occur even if one and the same buyer purchases all the firm's products. Where the length and complexity of the product line make it difficult for the salesperson to keep up to date, it may be both more effective and more efficient to specialize than to train every sales representative on every product. Also if several products are sold to the same buyer, there is a problem in getting enough of the buyer's time. Buyers' time is at a premium and they are apt to ration time among salespeople. Using just the one salesperson may get an average of, say, one hour per call, while two salespeople calling on different occasions may get a total of one and a half hours: the additional revenue brought in from the extra half hour of selling might more than compensate for the additional selling costs. But this can be overdone: retailers once complained bitterly about the numerous P&G salespeople calling on them until the system was changed.

Organizing the sales force on a customer basis is also common so salespeople become more knowledgeable about the problems of a certain type of customer. IBM's sales force, within each country, was organized by product but this meant it could be difficult to bring together a package of products from different product groups. Now IBM has organized its sales force by customer, with the salesperson assigned to that customer being responsible for all that customer's IBM needs. In the marketing of supermarket products, the big advent is the growth of the chains so that 80 percent of P&G's US grocery business is done by just one hundred chains. This has led P&G to use teams, which could be composed of people from marketing, finance, manufacturing and other functions, to cover some big account. For example, a team of a dozen is assigned solely to looking after the Wal-Mart account.

Which specialization is best can be decided only by empirical inquiry and not on the basis of logic alone. Nonetheless, distinct sets of customers or markets, demanding distinct sales strategies, are generally better served by distinct sales forces. The disadvantage is cost, since several salespeople may be traveling the same area.

Centralization/decentralization

Problems arise when a company becomes divisionalized. Should advertising and/or marketing research be centralized, decentralized or situated at both corporate and divisional level? *Centralized advertising* achieves economies of scale and a uniform administration of advertising on a company-wide basis. Against this is the difficulty of coordinating advertising and marketing at divisional level The more distinct the divisions in terms of marketing, the stronger the case for *decentralized advertising*. The chief disadvantages are losses in economies of scale and the possibility of neglect of inter-divisional advertising coordination. There are arguments, of course, for having *advertising at both corporate and divisional level*. Corporate advertising would undertake institutional advertising, coordinate inter-divisional advertising and determine advertising policy, budgets, and evaluate criteria.

Similar arguments apply to marketing research. Centralized marketing research achieves economies, but can be cut off from the day-to-day marketing in the divisions. Decentralized marketing research achieves better coordination with marketing but may be less useful if it ignores long-term issues. Where marketing research is at *both* corporate *and* divisional level, central research generally carries out research that has company-wide implications and coordinates, guides and helps the divisional marketing research units.

A flat structure puts pressure on top management to decentralize. It is common to find a tall structure in field selling and introducing a flat structure should be considered. For example, in one sales force with regional, and district sales managers as well as area supervisors, it was found that much of the work of the district sales supervisors could be done just as well by clerks at head office and the rest passed on to the area supervisors and (when policy was more explicitly stated) to salespeople themselves.

The product/brand manager

Product or brand managers are employed to coordinate the actions of other departments in planning the marketing of some specific product. This improves coordination of all the activities associated with that particular product and makes for flexibility and specialized attention to the product. It is not uncommon for product managers to be part of a team that includes sales, marketing research and manufacture who collectively become responsible for championing the product. The brand manager is a type of matrix organization and so has the problems inherent in that arrangement. But additionally, there is the danger of brand managers being so focused on just the one product that the company view is ignored, with a failure of brand managers to coordinate, say, over cannibalization and multipoint competition. The problem is exacerbated when there are so many brand managers that access to common bosses becomes difficult or at least a very slow process. Because of such problems, P&G created in 1987 the *category management system*, where P&G is broken into thirty-nine product categories under twenty-six category managers. The category manager has total profit-and-loss responsibility (that is, each is a profit center) for an entire product line which includes any competing brands. Brand managers come under some category manager whose job it is to sort out the coordination problems and respond quickly to requests for a decision. Reporting also to the category manager is what is known as a "product supply manager." When a new product is ready to be launched or an old product repositioned, the category manager assembles a team that includes the product supply manager who is responsible for all aspects of purchasing, manufacturing, engineering, and physical distribution in respect to that product. Product supply managers at P&G have been credited with doing much to speed up P&G's innovations and response to changes.

Organization of new product development

The development of new products requires the coordination of a number of functions, for example, R&D, finance, marketing, engineering, and purchasing. The degree of coordination needed depends on whether new product development is concerned with

- developing new models of established products;
- developing new products for existing markets;
- developing new products for existing markets not previously exploited by the firm; or
- developing new products for entirely new markets.

Obviously, developing new models of established products is likely to be easier organizationally than developing entirely new products for new markets. The traditional organizational arrangements are:

1 group with R&D;
2 locate under a product manager;

3 set up a project group;
4 set up a venture group;
5 set up a new products committee;
6 set up a new product department; and
7 joint ventures.

Group with R&D. The uncertainty in new product development may be technical rather than commercial. If a product is highly technical and likely to take years to develop and if close liaison with marketing can be planned, then new product development may legitimately be placed in R&D. Even within R&D, a decision might have to be made whether to organize around a science group or a project group.

Product manager. Where the major decisions require marketing expertise and the physical aspects of the product present no problems, product managers may oversee the whole of the development process. They coordinate all activities to do with the development of the product and remain as overall coordinators throughout the life of the product. The activities themselves usually remain under the various functional heads to insure uniform administration of the function company-wide and to reap economies of scale arising from doing work on a larger scale. The product manager concept, however, may not work:

- if the product development period is likely to be protracted;
- if conflict develops between the product manager and the various functional heads over priorities; or
- if the product manager lacks the breadth of knowledge required for the job.

Project group. A project group is brought together under a project manager who is responsible for developing the new product through to the commercialization phase. The project manager is generally outside the marketing department. The use of a project manager, like the use of a product manager, gives better control and coordination of development work. However, unlike the product manager, a project group avoids the possibility of conflicts over priorities with the functional heads as the project manager is in complete control of most, if not all, the activities associated with new product development. But this self-sufficiency can also be a source of inefficiency: losses in economies of scale, remoteness from marketing, and so on.

Venture group. A venture group, unlike a project group, is a company in miniature: an independent, new business. The venture group develops the product to a level where one of the divisions finds it attractive to take over, or the venture group itself continues the business. A venture manager is selected for entrepreneurial skill, drive and experience and is given the resources to develop a self-sufficient organization.

New product committee. Committees are often given the job of searching and screening new product ideas. On occasions, committees also carry out new product development, particularly where the development process is short and uncomplicated. However, committees can generate problems, reflected in:

- a lack of any central authority to give overall direction;
- no one person responsible for cost, time and sales estimates; or
- a lack of continuity of committee members.

New product department.   A new product department may be set up either within or outside the marketing department. If concerned only with developing new models of existing products, a new products unit can appropriately be grouped with marketing. Otherwise, grouping with marketing may lead to a short-term emphasis unless precautions are taken.

Joint ventures.   Another development is the growth of alliances or joint ventures in the development of products. Thus P&G has worked with Upjohn, Syntex, Gist–Brocades, Alcide, and so on to extend its product range into other markets than its present ones. Joint ventures with other independent organizations are becoming more common both for getting into a market and for developing new products. Some of the questions to ask in considering the wisdom of a joint venture are shown in Appendix 17.1.

In practice, there are solutions based on a combination of the above, for example, there may be what has been called a *growth and development department*, which is composed of a small staff that is supplemented, as the need arises, with venture teams for specific projects drawn from the various functional areas.

Proactive/reactive orientation

A firm adopting a proactive, highly innovative orientation toward the market will in general need:

- a loosely structured (organismic) organization, rather than a bureaucratic one, to give the flexibility needed to cope with the uncertainty attendant on the innovative process;
- slack resources (that is, uncommitted resources) to support the innovative activity; and
- the use of task groups or teams to generate the variety of ideas that are needed and the innovative climate that is sought.

The nonpioneer, "follow-the-leader" firm, in contrast, must be geared to efficiency and low costs. An example is the BIC Pen Company, when it entered the ball-point market. It captured market share by low pricing, mass advertising and mass distribution. However, a firm entering a mature (no-growth) market may need an even greater competitive advantage to unseat well-entrenched market leaders than a slight price edge. Thus BIC was less successful as a late entry into the fine-line porous point pen market. As always, things are never this simple. There is only a slight tendency for the same firms to be consistent innovators; the leaders in one innovation are often the followers of another. The most common occurrence is for major product innovators to come from outside the industry, as newcomers seek market entry with a product breakthrough. The established firms in the market typically respond by process innovation with the earlier innovators moving from radical product innovation to product improvement.

International arrangements

International marketing can be organized on the basis of function, product, market, region, or some grid (which is essentially a matrix) structure could be introduced. No arrangement is perfect. The *product* organization may result in neglecting inter-product coordination and regional differences; a *market* grouping may fail to exploit the knowledge gained in other markets; *regional* organization is in danger of treating the whole region as one homogeneous market while the *grid* solution may not get the right balance as promised. However, whatever the basis selected there is the problem of what authority to delegate since firms might centralize all market planning in home headquarters or give broad directives and manage by results or set up subsidiaries around the world, with the firm run like a conglomerate.

One of the most interesting organizational developments has been the use of a network of suppliers around the world, just as Nike, the sports-shoe firm, has developed a closely knit network of subcontractors in Taiwan, South Korea, and China with the result that Nike can respond immediately to changes in fashion by its knowledge of what each supplier is capable of doing. This can be good for Nike but a danger for the supplier who may become too dependent on the buying firm at the center of the network.

Interdepartmental coordination

Marketing management must coordinate its activities and decisions with other departments. There is the coordination required to insure that the marketing strategy and corporate strategy are mutually reinforcing. But there is also the lateral coordination needed to integrate the efforts of manufacturing, design, R&D, finance, and marketing. Coordination mechanisms are often needed (see Figure 17.8). Inter-unit coordination between R&D and marketing is particularly important for innovative firms. The evidence suggests that successful innovative companies are those whose technical and marketing departments work closely together, with top management taking a close interest in the progress of each project.

It is the problem of achieving interdepartmental coordination that commonly lies behind the "killing off" of the marketing department. Thus at Pillsbury in the United States, multidisciplinary teams have replaced the marketing department. Each team revolves around a specific product group and includes not just marketing people but managers from production and other areas of the business. The aim is to achieve better coordination of the product group and to make all team members "the champion of the brand." But there will inevitably be the sacrifice of some economies of scale and in

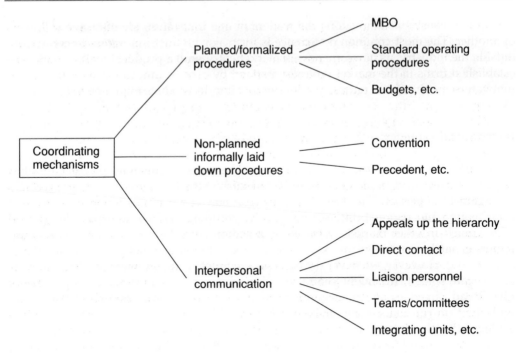

Figure 17.8 Inter-unit coordination mechanisms

the coordination of functions company-wide. With the shift of power from consumer products manufacturers to retailers, flexibility and speed have increased their importance—as indeed has the importance of understanding the consumer! No one is suggesting that marketing is losing its importance. On the contrary, it is being argued that everyone should recognize its importance and be involved with making every activity of the company customer oriented.

RE-ENGINEERING: A CURRENT VIEW

Although few organizational theorists would support any suggestion of a "one best way" to organize, in *Re-engineering the Corporation*, Hammer and Champy suggest that organizing by process *is* the one best way for the large company to organize if it wants to be "lean, nimble, flexible, responsive, competitive, innovative, efficient, customer-focused, and profitable" in today's world.[23] The authors define a *process* as "a collection of activities that takes one or more kinds of input and creates an output that is of value to the customer." The word "collection" seems unfortunate as it does not take account of what will be a systemic relationship among the activities while, under this definition, every single job with an input and an output that directly or indirectly can be shown to have value for the customer, is a process. *Re-engineering views companies as performing just a few core processes and recommends starting from scratch in the redesign of these processes and organizing around these redesigned processes.* Organizing around processes facilitates self-management while allowing management to dismantle its hierarchical structures. Re-engineering aims at changing functional, vertical organizations into process managed, horizontal ones as a basis for improving performance.

The systems approach, with its focus on grouping decision areas to facilitate decision-making and minimize the communications burden, can lead to a grouping by process with the re-engineered core process having an organismic structure. But re-engineering generally advocates radical change as opposed to incremental improvements, focusing on redesigning core business processes, not on reorganizing departments or other organizational units of the business. The authors claim that re-engineering cannot be carried out in small and cautious steps as it is "an all-or-nothing proposition that produces dramatically impressive results." This runs contrary to the advice of those who advocate an incrementalist approach to change, except in a turnaround crisis, on the ground that managers cannot be sure of the consequences of their actions sufficient to warrant radical change.

With re-engineering, as with other fashionable theories on management, there is always a danger of committing the *genetic* fallacy which consists in justifying a theory simply on the ground that it is the most recent or of reinventing the wheel born of an ignorance of the history of management ideas. The core of re-engineering revolves around ideas that have been in vogue for many years, namely, putting customers first, tearing down boundaries, empowering employees, rewarding performance and using teams. Re-engineering, as a doctrine, has had little impact on academics in organizational theory, not just because they reject any "one best way" approach but because its advocates ignore or seem completely ignorant of the last 40 years of organizational studies. Hammer and Champy give the impression that, until re-engineering, the stress was on bureaucratic structures and the sort of specialization advocated by Adam Smith. This, of course, is just nonsense. In fact, although the particular *combination* of concepts and techniques coming under the rubric of re-engineering is novel and useful, there is not one single concept or technique that cannot be found in the management literature before the term "re-engineering" came into being. The approach borrows heavily from industrial engineering/work study and ideas drawn from the organizational behavior literature. Even the belief that processes must be created from scratch and not from any analysis of existing systems, was a big debate in systems and procedures work in the 1960s (Figure 10.9 in Chapter 10 was part of a contribution by the author to the debate at that time.) However, just because the ideas are not new, does not mean that the whole set of concepts and techniques constituting re-engineering does not have something unique to offer.

Re-engineering appeals to many marketers because of its focus on the customer and the use of the computer in providing a better service. Thus Xerox took two weeks to approve credit but now one person at a computer performs the functions that used to require the approval of several departments, with the result that credit approval takes around two hours. Re-engineering is given separate treatment in this chapter not just because of its wide current appeal but because it does have something important to say as well as being an example of how ideas are marketed to management!

It can always be assumed that managers have a latent want for new ideas to better help them solve their problems. Hence in selling "new" ideas or techniques to management, the *first* task is to dramatize the potential of the ideas or techniques to solve important problems. Hammer and Champy do this by claiming that the "conceptually new business model" of re-engineering and its associated techniques will *have to be* used by mangers to "reinvent their companies for competition in the new world." "America's largest corporations—even the most successful and promising among them—must embrace and apply the principles of business re-engineering, or they will be eclipsed by the greater success of those companies that do."[24] The potential is thus to save the company from oblivion, which is quite a promise! No evidence is quoted for this claim beyond the authors' experience, observation and the logic of their argument which can be persuasive.

As the latent want is activated, it can move into a passive want so the *second* step is to overcome inhibitions to change. The authors' strategy here is to remove doubts by arguing that:

1 The old ideas about organization suited conditions of the past. In the past, the chief operational concern of company executives was capacity, that is, being able to keep up with ever-increasing demand in a high growth environment. For example, for thirty years after World War II, consumer goods were in "chronically short supply." The authors claim that a high degree of specialization and the standard, bureaucratic, pyramidal organizational structure of most companies was well suited to a high growth environment since, when a company needed to grow, it could simply add workers as needed "at the bottom of the chart and then fill in the management layers above."

   This claim about consumer goods being in chronically short supply so manufacturers could sell all they could produce is the distortion of history mentioned in Chapter 1. The marketing literature, however, is at last no longer subscribing to this myth.[25] It is true that competition is much more intense today but this does not mean that in the past manufacturers could just sell whatever they produced. Even in one of the longest upswings in American history between 1934 and 1937, the unemployed by the latter year still numbered around eight million.[26] It is also not the case that mechanistic structures were always appropriate before the 1980s. Contingency theories go back to the 1960s. Also writers on management and organization have criticized highly specialized jobs since the 1950s, advocating job enlargement and job enrichment as alternatives, while the dysfunctional consequences of highly bureaucratic structures were well documented by Merton in the 1930s[27] and Downs in the 1960s.[28]

2 Times have changed making obsolete all previous ideas about how business should be organized and run. The authors argue, as did the early contingency writers in the 1960s, that today's environment is characterized by
   a) more and more advanced technologies;
   b) the disappearance of boundaries between national markets; and
   c) the altered expectations of customers who now have more choices than ever before.
   (It might be pointed out that these factors were also noted at the end of the nineteenth century—with justice!). The three forces at work are customers, competition

and change. The mass market has broken into pieces with some segments as small as a single customer. As regards competition, niche competitors have dramatically affected practically every market. Changes in market growth rates, customer demand, product life cycles, and technology have come to characterize the environment. Hence companies built to thrive on mass production, stability and growth cannot be just modified to succeed in a world where customers, competition and change demand flexibility and quick response. The authors further claim that complex processes involving many people working across departmental lines cannot be made flexible enough to deal with special requests or to respond to inquiries so companies must organize work around processes while companies that fragment processes stifle innovation and creativity.

3 Rival ideas of current interest can be dismissed as fads. The authors argue that such "fads" as management by objectives (MBO), diversification, Theory Z, zero-based budgeting, Michael Porter's value chain analysis, decentralization, quality circles, the precepts of Thomas Peters and Robert Waterman in their *In Search of Excellence* (1982), restructuring, portfolio management, intra-entrepreneuring have all failed to reverse the deterioration of America's corporate performance.[29] In other words, there is no viable alternative to what the authors propose as only they have the secret of success.

Except for its puffery of their own case, this is an odd statement to make since it suggests that

a) these "fads" have all been tried throughout corporate America;
b) were promoted as sufficient for reversing corporate performance; and
c) were tried and then abandoned ("fads") as making insufficient contribution to justify their cost.

The authors offer no hard evidence to support their dismissal of rival proposals or for the superiority of what they themselves propose.

"Re-engineering is the *fundamental* rethinking and *radical design* of business processes to achieve *dramatic improvements* in critical contemporary measures of performance, such as cost, quality, service, and speed."[30] In this definition, the authors use the term "fundamental" to mean questioning the very existence of the activity. As in methods study on the shop floor, the first question asked is: Why do we do what we do? "Radical design" means disregarding all existing structures and procedures and inventing completely new ways of accomplishing work. (Whether to just start from scratch or start with a detailed analysis of the existing system, reflects an old debate in the systems literature. There is a very real danger, in reinventing from scratch, of devising cheaper ways of achieving an incomplete set of objectives and dreaming up solutions that take no account of current resources and skills.) "Dramatic improvements" through major change are recommended rather than minor improvements through incrementalism. The way to eliminate bureaucracy and flatten the organization is by "re-engineering the processes so they are no longer fragmented through functional departmentalization."

Grouping by processes in this way has many of the advantages of project management—but also the disadvantages such as dilution of skills, lack of functional and inter-process coordination, and losses in economies of scale which are too easily dismissed by the authors. Many of the benefits claimed for re-engineered processes are those associated with a flat structure (decision-making pushed downward, more flexibility, and better customer response), job enlargement (several jobs combined into one), checks and controls reduced and one person (the "case" manager) providing a single point of contact for the customer. Other benefits claimed, such as a change in values from "protective" to "productive," cannot be so easily demonstrated. In any case, flat structures are not always the answer even if viable. Although flat structures are regarded as supportive of good human relations, this may not always be the case. Thus in one study, a flat structure adopted by a research department led to those within the department wasting time fighting each other: a return to a hierarchy led to a smoother running department.[31]

The process teams that replace the functional departments can be permanent teams or temporary ones (called "virtual" teams by the authors) which stay together (as with project management!) to complete the task assigned to them. Pay, recognition, job enrichment, and promotion are all team-based. In fact, performance appraisals are made by peers, subordinates and outsiders like customers. It is claimed that all members of the team will have a basic familiarity with the whole process and will share responsibility for performing the whole process. It is not clear, however, how the whole team can be made responsible for process success and, even if it is declared responsible, whether a team can be meaningfully held responsible with individual members likely to resent being made responsible for something over which they do not have complete control.

The authors later in the text introduce another necessary condition for success in re-engineering. They claim that a company intent on re-engineering *must* make information technology one of its core competencies since information technology developments such as shared databases, expert systems, telecommunications networks, decision support tools, interactive videodisks, high performance computing, automatic identification and tracking technology, allow companies to break many of the former rules in respect to how they carry out their work.

In doing re-engineering, the authors focus first on identifying core processes of the business or division. The authors recommend getting a handle on the core businesses by expressing the beginning and end states such as "concept to prototype" for new product development; "order to payment" for order fulfillment and so on. Instead of the usual organization chart, there are process maps that show the process flows through the company. Few company divisions will have more than ten principal processes. Thus at TI's semiconductor division, the main processes are strategy development; product development; customer design and support; manufacturing capability development; customer communications; and order fulfillment. But to many managers, it will not be clear as to how core processes are identified and measured. The Network Services Division of AT&T, with around 16,000 employees, initially identified 130 processes but later brought the number down to just thirteen but it is not clear on what basis since criteria can differ and difficulties can be encountered in getting agreement on core processes and their design. These problems are not discussed by the authors.

Organizing around processes suggests such processes are self-contained with little need for inter-process coordination and little scope for economies of scale. In any case, a company must know first what it will take to create and maintain customers *before* attempting to define core processes. In other words, re-engineering should not be undertaken without being linked up to company objectives and strategies.

It is recognized that all processes cannot be designed simultaneously so some criteria are needed to select the order of redesign. The criteria suggested are

1 dysfunction of the process most in trouble;
2 the most important process in terms of impact on customers; and
3 feasibility or the process most susceptible to redesign.

Once a process is selected, the team leader (called the "owner") is designated, the team convened, and the existing system studied just enough to understand (no deep analysis) the process, starting from the customer end to determine the customers' real requirements, that is, their underlying goals and problems. Re-engineering's stress is on seeing things from the point of view of the customer and using teams in redesigning processes.

Hammer and Champy acknowledge that 50–75 percent of the organizations that undertake re-engineering effort do not achieve the dramatic results they sought. The authors list nineteen common errors, which, if avoided, "you almost can't help but get it right." But the errors listed are too vague to qualify as operationally watertight and *any* failure to achieve results can be attributed to one of these errors, without the need to question the appropriateness of re-engineering itself. There is evidence to suggest that re-engineering works best in small, self-contained divisions of large corporations.

As is often the case, there is some gold among the dross of rhetoric regarding re-engineering. The useful concept of the *horizontal corporation* (a term coined by two McKinsey consultants) is the outgrowth of re-engineering thinking. *Business Week* (December 20, 1993) neatly identifies the seven key elements in developing the horizontal corporation:

1 Build the company around its core processes with specific performance goals. Assign an "owner" to each process.
2 Cut the activities within each process to a minimum; eliminate work that fails to add customer value; combine fragmented tasks and use as few teams as possible to perform the entire process.
3 Make teams the building blocks of the organization; let them be largely self-managing and self-policing while holding them accountable for measurable performance goals.
4 *Make customer satisfaction—not stock appreciation or profitability—the primary driver and measure of performance.* Stock appreciation and profits will come with satisfied customers.
5 Reward team results and not just individual performance. Encourage team members to acquire multiple skills and have them develop an overall understanding of the process. *Explain* processes so employees are not just trained but educated in the process.
6 Ensure that as many employees as possible come into direct contact with customers and suppliers. Add customer and supplier representatives as full working members of in-house teams to advise and consult.

7 Provide information to employees and train them to perform their own analysis and make decisions based on that analysis.

The horizontal corporation, like any other organizational solution, is a trade-off so there is always a need to check what will be lost. It may be that losses in economies of scale are of no consequence, that workload problems are minor while coordination among core processes can be done by planning well ahead, but these are matters for empirical inquiry not dogmatism. In any case, coordination within a core process and with the rest of the company is likely to require appropriate computer information systems for collecting, analyzing, and redistributing information to organizational units.

CONCLUSION

It is not possible to do justice to organization issues in a short review. But even an extensive review would leave many questions unanswered since organization theory is still developing. But many so-called developments are "reinventions of the wheel," born of a failure to attend to history because of a belief that the modern corporation has nothing to learn from past thinkers on organization. But, in organizational studies, it is not the problems that change but their relative importance and with this comes different weighting of the organizational criteria. Every age and every organization will operate in unique circumstances that give rise to special problems, demanding nonstandard solutions. But nonstandard solutions do not necessarily entail entirely new concepts but simply new combinations of ideas already born. If a company wants simply to be fashionable, it may end up simply being sold on inappropriate but "glitzy" solutions.

NOTES

1 Galbraith, Jay. R. and Nathanson, Daniel A. (1978) *Strategy Implementation: the role of structure and process*, St. Paul, MN: West, preface.
2 Chandler, Alfred (1962) *Strategy and Structure*, Cambridge, MA: MIT Press.
3 Rumelt, Richard (1974) *Strategy, Structure and Economic Performance*, Boston: Harvard Business School, Division of Research.
4 Cable, John and Steer, Peter (1977) *On the Industrial Organization and Profitability of Large UK Companies*, unpublished working paper: Liverpool Polytechnic, February.
5 Cohen, Eliot, A. and Gooch, John (1990) *Military Misfortunes: The Anatomy of Failure in War*, New York: The Free Press.
6 Lazonick, William (1992) *Business Organizations and the Myth of the Market Economy*, Cambridge: Cambridge University Press.
7 Friedham, Cyrus (1993) "The Global Corporation—Obsolete too Soon?" *The Economist* February 6.
8 Webster, Frederick E. (1992) "The Changing Role of Marketing in the Corporation," *Journal of Marketing*, 56 (Oct).
9 *Business Week* (1993) February 8, page 134.
10 Chandler, Alfred D. (1990) "The Enduring Logic of Industrial Success," *Harvard Business Review*, March–April.
11 Smith, William and Charmoz, R. (1975) "Coordinate Line Management," Working paper, Chicago: Searle International (February).

12 Galbraith and Nathanson, *op. cit*, p. 110.
13 Welch, Jack (1993) in the GE Annual Report to share owners.
14 Bales, R. F. (1950) "The Analysis of Small Group Interaction," *American Sociological Review*, 15.
15 Katzenback Jon R. and Smith, Douglas K. (1993) *The Wisdom of Teams: Creating the High Performance organization*.
16 Kotter, John P. and Heskett, James L. (1992) *Corporate Culture and Performance*, New York: The Free Press.
17 Miles, Raymond E. and Snow, Charles C. (1984) "Fit, Failure and the Hall of Fame," *California Management Review*, 26 (Spring).
18 Burns, T. and Stalker, G. M. (1966) *The Management of Innovation*, London: Tavistock Press.
19 Douglas, Mary (1982) *Natural Symbols*, New York: Pantheon Books.
20 Lawrence, P. R. and Lorsch, J. W. (1969) *Organization and Environment: Managing Differentiation and Integration*, Homewood IL: Richard D. Irwin.
21 Perrow, C. (1970) *Organizational Analysis*, New York: Wadsworth.
22 Child, John (1977) *Organization: A guide to problems and practice*, New York: Harper & Row.
23 Hammer, Michael and Champy, James (1993) *Re-engineering the Corporation*, New York: Harper Business, p. 35.
24 Ibid, p. 2.
25 Fullerton, Ronald A. (1988) "How Modern is Modern Marketing? Marketing's Evolution and the Myth of the Production Era," *Journal of Marketing*, 52 (January).
26 Cochran Thomas C. and Miller, William (1961) *The Age of Enterprise: A Social History of Industrial America*, New York: Harper Torchbooks, p. 357.
27 Merton R. K. (1940) "Bureaucratic Structure and Personality," *Social Forces*, 18.
28 Downs, A. (1967) *Inside Bureaucracy*, Boston: Little Brown and Co.
29 Hammer and Champy, *op. cit*, p. 25.
30 Ibid, p. 32.
31 Werth, Barry (1993) *The Billion Dollar Molecule*, New York: Simon & Schuster.

APPENDIX 17.1 JOINT VENTURES: SOME CONSIDERATIONS

1. Technical

(i) Is the joint venture a good way to grow via market development, diversification or integration?

(ii) Is the joint venture needed to hold/defend market share by expanding competitive capabilities or acquiring up-to-date technologies?

(iii) Will the joint venture be a way of keeping informed about the next generation of technologies?

(iv) Is the joint venture a way of ensuring survival in conditions of shortening techno-logical life cycles?

2. Legalistic

(i) Is a joint venture being demanded by the foreign government as a condition of entry?

(ii) Is the joint venture the best way of adjusting to the culture of the foreign country?

3. Integrative

(i) Will the partners have complementary objectives and resources to offer?

(ii) Will the joint partners be able to cooperate without creating conflicts of interests?

(iii) Is the relative bargaining power of the partners evenly matched?

(iv) Is the "chemistry" among partners such that there will be cooperation and smooth coordination in respect to how the venture will be managed?

(v) Does each of the partners have an open society where there will be no resentment of ideas from outside?

(vi) Will all the managers from top to bottom cooperate?

4. Economic

(i) Are the partners in the venture likely to make exchanges that are economically worthwhile?

(ii) Is the firm unable to afford to go at it alone?

(iii) Will costs be shared on an equitable basis?

(iv) Is "bleedthrough" possible, that is, firm's team learns much from just working with other teams?

5. Adaptive

(i) Will joining the venture allow the firm to respond faster to competitive challenges?

(ii) Will the joint venture avoid creating competitors?

(iii) Will the joint venture avoid any threat to diluting the firm's thrust and core competencies?

(iv) Is there enough certainty about what needs to be done to allow coordination by mutual planning agreements?

(v) Will the joint venture compensate for weaknesses and achieve synergy?

(vi) Will the projects adopted be geared to the firm's needs?

(vii) Will the joint venture avoid weakening the firm's relative technological edge?

Source: *Managing for Joint Venture Success*, Kathryn Rudie Harrigan, Lexington, MA: Lexington Books (1986)

Postscript

The reader of this book has been made aware of the complexities of marketing. Success in a market is not easily attained and there is no simple formula saying how it can be done. Those who claim otherwise go beyond what a knowledge of marketing can deliver. This is because marketing first and foremost is concerned with behavior and human behavior is like a good detective story; it makes sense when understood but prediction of outcomes is never certain. The social science approaches and other techniques discussed here can reduce risk but do not ensure success. What the best in marketing bring to the study of their markets, over and above concepts and techniques, are insight, creativity, and experience: insight to target what is key; creativity in finding solutions that are sought; and experience to make it all happen ... hopefully at a profit.

Author index

Subject index

References in **bold face** denote chapters concerned with a subject throughout. *Italics* indicate a reference to a figure or table.